ENCYCLOPEDIA OF

PLAY

in Today's Society

ENCYCLOPEDIA OF

PLAY

in Today's Society

Rodney P. Carlisle
Rutgers University
GENERAL EDITOR

Volume 1

Los Angeles | London | New Delhi
Singapore | Washington DC

A SAGE Reference Publication

For information

SAGE Publications, Inc.
2455 Teller Road
Thousand Oaks, California 91320
E-mail: order@sagepub.com

SAGE Publications Ltd.
1 Oliver's Yard
55 City Road
London EC1Y 1SP
United Kingdom

SAGE Publications India Pvt. Ltd.
B 1/ I 1 Mohan Cooperative Industrial Area
Mathura Road, New Delhi 110 044
India

SAGE Publications Asia-Pacific Pte. Ltd.
33 Pekin Street #02-01
Far East Square
Singapore 048763

Library of Congress Cataloging-in-Publication Data

Encyclopedia of play in today's society / Rodney P. Carlisle, general editor.
p. cm.
Includes bibliographical references and index.
ISBN 978-1-4129-6670-2 (cloth)
1. Recreation--Encyclopedias. 2. Leisure--Encyclopedias. I. Carlisle, Rodney P.
GV11.E555 2009
790.1--dc22 2008054639

09 10 11 12 13 10 9 8 7 6 5 4 3 2 1

GOLSON MEDIA
President and Editor J. Geoffrey Golson
Director, Author Management Susan Moskowitz
Layout Editors Mary Jo Scibetta
Oona Patrick
Copyeditor Kenneth W. Heller
Proofreader Anne L. Hicks
Indexer J S Editorial

SAGE REFERENCE
Vice President and Publisher Rolf A. Janke
Senior Editor Jim Brace-Thompson
Project Editor Tracy Buyan
Cover Production Gail Buschman
Marketing Manager Amberlyn McKay
Editorial Assistant Michele Thompson
Reference Systems Manager Leticia Gutierrez
Reference Systems Coordinator Laura Notton

Photo credits are on page 980.

Contents

Volume 1

Volume 2

About the General Editor

Rodney P. Carlisle, Ph.D.

An expert in social history and prolific game player, Rodney P. Carlisle earned an A.B. in history at Harvard College, and a Ph.D. in history at the University of California at Berkeley. He taught for more than 30 years at Rutgers University, Camden, New Jersey, and is the cofounder of History Associates Incorporated. He is the author or editor of more than 35 books, including works in military history, maritime history, technology, and social history. Among the works he has authored are the *Encyclopedia of Invention and Discovery*, *Eyewitness History to World War I*, and the forthcoming *Sovereignty at Sea*. Among the encyclopedias and series that he has edited are the *Encyclopedia of the Atomic Age*, *Encyclopedia of Intelligence and Counterintelligence*, *One Day in History*, *The Twenties*, *The Thirties*, *Encyclopedia of Politics: The Left and Right*, and the forthcoming *Handbooks to Life in America.*

Editorial Advisory Board

Playing With *Play*

We have created a word puzzle with the *Encyclopedia of Play in Today's Society*. The clues below are straightforward: You need to discern what P and W refer to and how the puzzle comes together. The solution is a quote from a leading scholar on the concepts of play, taken from a seminal work on the subject. Note: hyphenated words are counted as one word. We have added a few hints at the end of the clues.

Girls' Play P7W83
Academic Learning and Play P1W7
Inter-Gender Play P4W93
Egypt P1W4
Chess and Variations of P16W36
Play and Literacy P1W4
Assyrian/Babylonian Culture P5W38
Dice P10W11
Europe 1960 to Present P5W54
Casino P3W22
Fantasy Play P2W2
Hockey (Amateur) P10W17
History of Playing Cards P10W10
Stilts P8W45
Dolls, Barbie and Others P16W7
Cricket (Amateur) P5W13
Faro P6W49
Bridge and Variations of P2W6
Inter-Gender Play P7W4
Europe, 1960 to Present P6W10
Games of Deception P15W34
I Spy P1W3
Inter-Gender Play P20W61
Bullying P7W11
Memory and Play P1W2
Play as Mock War, Psychology of P3W38
Games of Deception P1W13
Europe, 1900 to 1940 P2W3
Risk, the Game P2W12
Cuba P1W1
Montessori P34W19
Galoob P1W3
Hungary P1W5
Athletics (Amateur) P5W12
Human Relationships in Play P7W5
Role-Playing P1W4
India P11W63
Crosswords P3W5
Freud and Play P5W3
Europe, 1800 to 1900 P4W84
"Bad Play" P4W4

Golf (Amateur) P1W27
Wargames P3W64
Kenner P10W94
Israel P1W2
Europe, 1960 to Present P8W37
Croquet P5W4
Skat P8W35
Finger Games P4W71
Hornby P6W9
Gamesmanship P2W16
Australian Aborigines P5W5
Slapjack P1W6
Iraq P2W1
Common Adventure Concept P4W2
Soccer (Amateur) Worldwide P2W10
Games of Deception P13W13
Monopoly and Variations of P2W20
Car and Travel Games P8W25
Racing Demon P1W40
Adlerian Play Therapy P3W136

Hint 1: There are 3 words in the solution not included in the clues above. You need to place them correctly: spoils, robs, creates.

Hint 2: The following are the punctuation marks in the solution:
5 periods
1 colon
1 set of quotes
4 commas

Hint 3: The quote solution author's initials are J.H. and an acronym for the seminal work is HLASOTPEIC. An anagram for the short title is: SHOLOM DUNE.
Last hint: page 10.

Preface

Brian Sutton-Smith, Ph.D.

Frankly, I was in shock when I suddenly received so much new information on play when I received the editor's proofs for the *Encyclopedia of Play in Today's Society*. For example, there are approximately 450 articles written by 130 authors from 22 countries. I had the excited feeling that the whole story of play that has baffled us all for so long might be finally solved.

The encyclopedia articles in alphabetical order begin with Volume 1 "Academic Learning and Play" and end with Volume 2 "Ziginette," which is a gambling card game. Clearly it was going to be hard to find anything missing in such a cauldron of multiplicitous ambiguity. But more importantly, it looks as if these volumes might now bring an ending to the old-fashioned view that play is not really very important. That is, we say conventionally that play might be fun but unlike religion, the arts, science, and politics, it is not really very serious for the human condition or even worthwhile for academic studies.

Against this, I have been telling myself that, on the contrary, play is important because it heralds the beginning of civilization by imposing routines, rituals, and rules upon the expression of the universal primary and relentless adaptive emotions (loneliness, anger, fear, shock, disgust, and apathy). These emotions are basic in their raw character within the evolutionary struggles for survival.

For example, without play you might have murder—with play, you have multiple, unique forms of bonding within which the violence is expressed within the rules. Imagine my excitement on reading on page 484 the article "Play Among Animals," in which the author discusses various signals that animals make in pursuit of a morality that bonds them together, rather than driving them apart. And then, in an article on page 489 "Play and Evolution," the author says: "it is sobering to realize that since both vertebrate and invertebrate animals engage to some extent in play, the potential for play goes back as far as 1.2 billion years."

Given the increasing number of toy museums around the world (including the Strong National Museum of Play in Rochester, New York), the development of university degrees (such as in the United Kingdom), and with play as a major topic for those who will be in charge of child play in the streets, we are perhaps beginning to give the topic of play the seriousness of a major cultural form that it deserves, which is testified to so remarkably by these two volumes.

Introduction

Children and adults spend a great deal of time in activities we think of as "play," including games, sports, and hobbies. Without thinking about it very deeply, almost everyone would agree that such activities are fun, relaxing, and entertaining. However, as anthropologists, philosophers, psychologists, and other social thinkers have studied the role and function of play in different societies, and among different age groups, they have developed a wide range of theoretical explanations for why human beings and many animals engage in playful activities. The theoretic questions they raise suggest that simply to regard play as fun and entertainment misses the central role that play has in our lives. For a subject that we mostly consider a lighthearted one, the topic of play as a research topic has generated an extensive and sophisticated literature, exploring a range of penetrating questions.

Play has many functions that run much deeper than simply "entertainment." For children and many young animals, such as kittens and bear cubs, play clearly is part of the preparation for adult roles, including the manipulation of nature, hunting for food, peaceful interaction with others of the same species, or combat with those who are hostile. In humans, childhood play has many other functions as well. Among those are aspects of human interaction such as competition, following rules, accepting defeat, choosing leaders, exercising leadership, practicing adult roles, taking risks in order to reap rewards, and many others. Clearly, many childhood games and toys also assist in the learning of intellectual skills such as reading, arithmetic, and even gaining knowledge of such subjects as physics, geography, and history.

Adults engage in play and games for many other reasons besides learning. Many games and sports serve as harmless releases of feelings of aggression, competition, and intergroup hostility. Many team sports and board games such as chess, as well as many contemporary computer games, have a basis in warfare. Other games represent forms of harmlessly experiencing risk-taking, while still others, such as gambling at Poker or Blackjack and active sports such as skiing and parachuting, can involve actual risks to fortune, life, or limb. Many games and toys represent forms of mastery over nature itself, and their ancient origins suggest ties to religion or to cycles of nature, such as planting and harvesting. The keeping of pets and playing with them can be seen as aspects of mastering nature.

When such aspects of why we play are considered, the topic takes on a new light, going to questions about the very nature of the human condition. Do we play in order to avoid danger, or to experience it? Do we play as an escape from work, or do we work to engage in another form of play? Some people seem to be employed only in order to earn enough money to be able to enjoy their play activities, such as surfing, skiing, bowling, skydiving, or mountain climbing. Others indulge in a few sports and games only as a momentary escape from their workaday lives. Still others derive most or all of their income from an activity that for others would seem a form of play, such as artists, musicians, and athletes.

Looked at as something common to the whole of humankind, play takes still greater significance. Every culture, it seems, has some unique forms of play, and most cultures seem to share some fundamental types of games and play. Such children's games as Leapfrog, and Rock Paper Scissors (or "Rochambeau") are found all over the world. Are such worldwide forms of play a reflection of the spread of cultural artifacts from one society to another, or are the similarities in games, sports, and toys the result of varied reflections of the same underlying human nature expressed in similar ways in diverse cultures? Perhaps such common games represent both dispersion of culture and the underlying structure of human nature. What are the precise reasons why some games, toys, and sports have flourished and survived, while others appear to have died away with the passage of time?

Some games, such as Chess and Backgammon, appear so perfectly conceived and developed that they have been played for centuries, while others, such as the gambling game of Faro, have had much shorter lives and have been largely supplanted by others. The historic origin of many games is known, while others remain shrouded in mystery. For example, we know that playing cards appeared rather suddenly in Europe around 1380 C.E., but whether the idea of cards had been introduced from Asia, or whether they grew from fortune-telling decks, or whether fortune-telling tarot decks were a later development, is the subject of historical inquiry.

One of the earliest theoretical treatments of play is that of the Dutch cultural historian Johan Huizinga (1872–1945), in his 1938 work *Homo Ludens*. In that study, Huizinga suggested that play as a form of contest involves both cooperation (in agreeing to rules) and competition (in leading to winners and losers). Play becomes a surrogate or harmless expression of the exercise of power. Another early writer who thought deeply about play was the Russian Lev Vygotsky (1896–1934). Among his contributions was his view that play represented ways of internalizing and understanding the world, and as such, play was an essential element in learning. Vygotsky's work underwent a revival in the West, with translations published in the 1960s and 1970s. Many modern educational psychologists have expanded on, or criticized, some of the perceptions and concepts brought up by Vygotsky. Jean Piaget's (1896–1980) monumental work, *Play, Dreams, and Imitation* provided structural criteria for evaluating play's development and the useful idea that play often consolidates new learning, even though play is not the domain where children actually learn.

Using a different lens, Vygotsky gave to play a more important role, namely, the role of leading edge of development because play helps young children go beyond thinking solely in terms of what they can perceive directly in front of them and to think in terms of what they can imagine.

The New Zealand–born educational theorist Brian Sutton-Smith (b. 1924) has studied play, using many ideas and concepts derived from the study of rhetoric. During an extensive academic career at Columbia University and the University of Pennsylvania, he produced numerous works on the subject of play, including *The Ambiguity of Play* (1997). Sutton-Smith sees seven different kinds of rhetoric at work in the "discourse" of play. Some rhetorics hold that play is a kind of adaptation, teaching skills or easing the passage or induction into different communities.

Another view of play is that it is an expression of power, pursued in contests of prowess. Still another view holds that play is an expression of the working of fate or "Lady Luck," as expressed in games of chance like Bingo, Poker, and Blackjack. Under another rhetoric, play is an extension of daydreaming, enacted in art. For some, play is just frivolity. In our modern society, adults tend to define play as a rhetoric of progress toward adulthood, whereas children have an entirely different rhetoric of play as a highly prized frivolous activity.

Those ambivalent aspects of play often come into conflict in our times, but they need not. Sutton-Smith, now retired, has served as a consultant to television shows such as Captain Kangaroo and Nickelodeon, as well as to the Philadelphia "Please Touch" Museum.

Educators have struggled with these underlying issues of the function of play as they attempt to capture the magic of play and harness it effectively in learning situations. Sometimes those efforts succeed, but the fact that children seek out and play games that are not always approved by adults, such as "playing doctor," or engaging in dangerous activities such as climbing trees or clandestine swimming parties outside of adult supervision, suggests the underlying truth of Sutton-Smith's view of the ambiguities of play. Clearly, playing with an educational puzzle and roughhousing on the playground represent two entirely different "rhetorics" of play.

In this encyclopedia, we have gathered together an international group of scholars and writers to provide access to the fascinating literature that has explored such questions of psychology, learning theory, game theory, and history in depth. In addition, we have provided entries that describe both adult and childhood play and games in dozens of cultures around the world and throughout history. Through articles about cultures as diverse as the ancient Middle East and modern Russia and China, and in nations as far-flung as India, Argentina, and France, the reader will find a guide to the common childhood and adult games and toys.

As one might expect, many countries and cultures have adopted similar games. In many countries, for example, one can find variations on the famous American game Monopoly, with street names from diverse cities substituting for the familiar street names of Atlantic City, such as Boardwalk and Park Place. Games such as soccer have spread almost all over the world, while others, such as American baseball, have penetrated only a few societies.

With its diversity of approximately 450 entries, this unique encyclopedia provides access not only to the sophisticated analyses of social thinkers like Huizinga, Vygotsky, and Sutton-Smith but to the wide variety of games, toys, sports, and entertainments found around the world.

We have not attempted to include coverage of "professional" sports and sport teams but, instead, have included the hundreds of games played not to earn a living but to exercise all the aspects of play as an informal activity—from learning, through competition, mastery of nature, socialization, and cooperation. And simply enough, this encyclopedia explores play played for the fun of it.

One caveat: There are thousands of games around the world, and no encyclopedia can include them all. We have made an earnest effort to include the most popular and widespread games—hundreds of them—in an attempt to provide a good representation.

Rodney P. Carlisle
General Editor

Reader's Guide

Children's Games

History of Play

Central Asia, Ancient
Europe, 1200 to 1600
Europe, 1600 to 1800
Europe, 1800 to 1900
Europe, 1900 to 1940
Europe, 1940 to 1960
Europe, 1960 to Present
History of Playing Cards
Mesoamerican Cultures
Native Americans
New Zealand Maori
South Americans, Traditional Cultures
Spanish America
United States, 1783 to 1860
United States, 1860 to 1876
United States, 1876 to 1900
United States, 1900 to 1930
United States, 1930 to 1960
United States, 1960 to Present
United States, Colonial Period
Vikings

Outdoor Games and Amateur Sports

Athletics (Amateur)
Ballooning
Baseball (Amateur)
Basketball (Amateur)
Bicycles
Bocce
Boules
Bungee Jumping
Cracking the Whip
Cricket (Amateur)
Croquet
Curling (Scottish)
Dodgeball
Fishing
Folk Dancing
Football (Amateur)
Highland Games
Golf (Amateur)
Hockey (Amateur)
Horse Racing (Amateur)
Kayaking and Canoeing
Kite Flying
Maypole Dancing
Morris Dancing
Music, Playing
Netball
Paintball
Ping Pong
Rodeos
Roller Coasters
Rugby (Amateur)
Sailing
Skateboarding
Skating
Skiing
Snail Racing
Snowboarding
Soccer (Amateur) Worldwide
Stilts
Surfing
Swimming (Amateur)
Tennis (Amateur) and Variations of
Volleyball (Amateur)

Play and Education

Academic Learning and Play
Models
Montessori
Mother-Child Play
Play and Evolution
Play and Literacy
Play in the Classroom
Recess
Teacher-Child Co-Play
Toys and Child Development

Play Around the World

Afghanistan
Albania
Algeria
Arctic Play (First Nations)
Argentina
Armenia
Australia
Austria
Azerbaijan
Bahamas and Caribbean
Belarus
Belgium
Bolivia
Bosnia and Herzegovina
Brazil
Bulgaria

Psychology of Play

Video and Online Games

List of Articles

List of Contributors

Adams, Jeffery
Massey University

Adams, Lynette
Sport Waitakere

Adams, Suellen
University of Rhode Island

Adler, Jennifer
City University of New York

Apter, Michael John
Independent Scholar

Baghurst, Timothy
University of Arkansas

Barnhill, John
Independent Scholar

Basha, Selma
University of Virginia, Wise

Baron, Cynthia L.
Northeastern University

Barron, Carol M.
Dublin City University

Beck, Jack
Independent Scholar

Behrenshausen, Bryan G.
Kutztown University of Pennsylvania

Bekoff, Marc
University of Colorado, Boulder

Bell, Robert J.
Ball State University

Beresin, Anna
University of the Arts, London

Biron, Dean
University of New England, Australia

Bittarello, Maria Beatrice
Independent Scholar

Bonura, Kimberlee
Walden University

Breedlove, Marci M.
University of Tennessee

Brown, Fraser
Leeds Metropolitan University

Brown, Harko
Kerikeri High School

Burger, Jean E.
New York University

Burghardt, Gordon M.
University of Tennessee

Buttery, David
Independent Scholar

Calleja, Gordon
IT-University of Copenhagen
Denmark

Caponegro, Ramona Anne
University of Florida

Carr, Neil
University of Otago

Carr, Sarah
University of Otago

Cemore, Joanna J.
Missouri State University

Clements, Rhonda
Manhattanville College

Cohen, Allison T.
New York University

Collins, Mary C.
Clemson University

Cook, Daniel Thomas
Rutgers University

Cooper, Abby
Australian National University

Corfield, Justin
Geelong Grammar School

Cossu, Andrea
Università di Trento
Italy

Cranwell, Keith A.
University of Greenwich

Crawford, Thomas
Claremont Graduate University

Daw, Jessie
Northern State University

Degroult, Nathalie
Siena College

Dénes, Ilona
Central European University

Deutsch, James I.
Smithsonian Institution

Dickman, Nathan Eric
University of Iowa

Dubbels, Brock
University of Minnesota

Dufer, Miriam D.
Old Dominion University

Dunkin, Jessica
Carleton University

Dusenberry, Lisa
University of Florida

Eckhoff, Angela
Clemson University

Eliassen, Meredith
San Francisco State University

Eversole, Theodore W.
Independent Scholar

Factor, June
University of Melbourne

Farr, Daniel
Randolph College

Fehrle, Johannes
Albert-Ludwigs-Universität

Flannery Quinn, Suzanne M.
University of South Florida

Fleming, Dan
University of Waikato

Fogel, Curtis
University of Calgary

Gallo, Ernesto
University of Turin
University of Birmingham

Galofaro, Francesco
Bologna University

Garrison, Joshua
University of Wisconsin, Oshkosh

Gemeinhardt, Melissa
New Orleans University

Gentner, Noah
Ithaca College

Golinkoff, Roberta Michnick
University of Delaware

Gomez-Galisteo, M. Carmen
Universidad de Alcala

Grieve, Owen
Brunel University

Groth, Miles
Wagner College

Han, Myae
University of Delaware

Hansen, Gregory A.
Arkansas State University

Harbour, Vanessa
University of Winchester

Hartle, Lynn
University of Central Florida

Harvey, Jessamy
University of London

Hemphill, Joyce
University of Wisconsin, Madison

Henry, Gage
University of Georgia

Hirsh-Pasek, Kathryn
Temple University

Hutira, A. A.
Youngstown State University

Janssen, Diederik Floris
Independent Scholar

Jewkes, Abigail M.
Hunter College
City University of New York

Jones, Janice Kathleen
University of Southern Queensland

Josephson, Bruce
Baekseok Cultural College

Judge, Larry
Ball State University

Kindler, Vardit
Independent Scholar

Kiuchi, Yuya
Michigan State University

Kling, Helena
Educational Centre for Games in Israel

Kozma, LuAnne
Michigan State University Museum

Kte'pi, Bill
Independent Scholar

Kücklich, Julian
University of the Arts
London

Kullman, Kim
University of Helsinki

Laird, Jay
Northeastern University

Lang, Diane E.
Manhattanville College

Laukaitis, John J.
Loyola University Chicago

Leandro, Mauricio
City University of New York

Lee, Joon Sun
City University of New York

Lester, Stuart
University of Gloucestershire

Levi, Amiya Waldman
Hebrew University, Jerusalem

Lobera, Ana Luisa Baca
University of Puerto Rico

Lowe, Virginia
Independent Scholar

MacCallum-Stewart, Esther
University of East London

Maksudyan, Nazan
Bogazici University

Martin, Cathlena
University of Florida

Martinez, Michelle
Sam Houston State University

Matthews, Elizabeth
City University of New York

McDonnell, Wayne G.
New York University

McKinty, Judy
Independent Scholar

McNamee, Gillian Dowley
Erikson Institute

Medellin-Paz, Cristina M.
City University of New York

Medler, Ben
Georgia Institute of Technology

Michalski, David
University of California, Davis

Michon, Heather K.
Independent Scholar

Millbank, Anna-Marie
Independent Scholar

Moore, Mary Ruth
University of the Incarnate Word

Morris, Avigail
Ben Gurion University

Morrison, Heidi
University of California, Santa Barbara

Navidi, Ute
London Play
International Play Association

Norman, Jason
Old Dominion University

Nwokah, Eva E.
University of North Carolina, Greensboro

O'Donnell, Casey
University of Georgia

Osgerby, Bill
London Metropolitan University

O'Shea, Gerad F.
New York University

Overholser, Lisa M.
Indiana University

Padula, Alessandra
Università degli Studi di L'Aquila
Italy

Palmer, Sue
Leeds Metropolitan University

Parsler, Justin
Brunel University

Patel, Ashwin
Western State College of Colorado

Patrouch, Joseph F.
Florida International University

Pope, Clive C.
University of Waikato

Pratt, Anastasia L.
State University of New York

Pringle, Richard George
University of Waikato

Puente, Rogelio
Independent Scholar

Ramšak, Mojca
Center for Biographic Research

Reid, Jason
Ryerson University

Reynolds, Daniel
University of California, Santa Barbara

Ríos Orlandi, Yma N.
Independent Scholar

Roberts, Frank W.
University of Texas, Austin

Ryan, John S.
University of New England
Australia

Sayer, Karen Anne
Leeds Trinity and All Saints

Scheinholtz, Laura
University of Wisconsin, Madison

Schneider, Sharon
Hofstra University

Schott, Gareth
University of Waikato

Shuffelton, Amy
University of Wisconsin, Whitewater

Siedentop, Daryl
Ohio State University

Sluss, Dorothy Justus
James Madison University

Smith, Dorsia
University of Puerto Rico, Río Piedras

Sobe, Noah W.
Loyola University

Stacy, Robert
Independent Scholar

Stanley, Christopher
Winston-Salem State University

Stanzak, Steve
Indiana University

Sterling, Linda K.
Northwest Missouri State University

Sutterby, John A.
University of Texas, Brownsville

Tanta, Kari J.
Independent Scholar

Terry, Jennifer
California State University, Sacramento

Thorpe, Holly
University of Waikato

Tobin, Samuel F.
New School for Social Research

Tredinnick, Luke
London Metropolitan University

Trotti, Patrick
Independent Scholar

Tsipursky, Gleb
University of North Carolina Chapel Hill

Tucker, Elizabeth
Binghamton University

Unger, Dallace W.
Independent Scholar

Valentin, Andrea
University of Otago

Valentine, Deborah S.
Rutgers University

Vaughn, Brandon K.
University of Texas, Austin

Walker, Christine M.
University of Michigan

Watrall, Ethan
Michigan State University

Weintraub, Naomi
Hebrew University

Welch, Wendy
University of Virginia, Wise

Westgate, Christopher Joseph
Texas A&M University

Willans, Becky
Thurrock and Basildon College

Wong, Wilkey
University of Delaware

Woodford, Darryl
IT-University of Copenhagen Denmark

Wragg, Mike
Leeds Metropolitan University

Chronology of Play

30,000 to 10,000 B.C.E.—A period of cave art traditions in Europe where cave paintings, primitive writing, and signs at Lascaux, France, reflect a fascination with hunting and interaction between man and nature and recognition of passing seasons. Play becomes a natural part of survival training. For instance, aboriginal Australians develop an ancient game of keep-away called *Mungan-mungan* that pits young athletes against their elders.

10,000 to 8000 B.C.E.—Sedentary hunter-gatherer Natufian culture and rituals form in the Levent region, and permanent farming villages develop. Throw sticks in Egypt, South India, North Africa, and the Americas are used during this period, possibly indicating that play is associated with hunting. In Australia, the oldest existing boomerangs date to this period.

5500 to 4000 B.C.E.—The indigenous Badarian culture in Egypt trades in copper, ivory, shells, and turquoise. The sail, plough, and potter's wheel are developed in Mesopotamia. Contests of traveling through snow country occur in central Asia,

3650 to 3200 B.C.E.—Wheeled vehicles are invented. Permanent fishing villages emerge along the Pacific coast of South America. Skiing in Scandinavia becomes a more efficient means for crossing snow-encrusted terrain than snowshoeing.

3000 to 1500 B.C.E.—Survival training transforms into combat sports including boxing, wrestling, gladiator contests, and bull jumping in Sumaria. Backgammon boards inlaid with mother-of-pearl, tortoiseshell, and ivory, along with dice, are found in southeastern Iran. A Minoan palace civilization on Crete draws craftsmen who manufacture goods for a wide-ranging maritime trade network. Pearls used in religious healing and magic inspire commerce. Trade, more than any other factor, shapes the history and movement of play. For instance, the pearl trade reaches across Asia, the Middle East, North Africa, and Europe, and much later into the Americas.

2600 to 2100 B.C.E.—Excavations of the royal tombs of Ur reveal that board games like Senet originated in Egypt and nearby. Construction of the Stonehenge megalithic stone circle in southern England indicates a ritualistic culture aware of seasons and astronomy. A version of Go, a tabletop game, is invented in China. Children in various regions play with wooden tip cats.

2000 to 1700 B.C.E.—A Hockey-type game played with two men squaring off using curved sticks and a small hoop occurs in the Nile Valley. Throwing and catching games are depicted symbolically on the walls and stone spheres in Egyptian tombs. An Egyptian wall painting in the 15th Beni Hassan tomb of an unknown prince contains depictions of female dancers and acrobats juggling. Girls in Nilotic communities play change-hand clapping games. Small clay balls (marbles) become popular in Crete.

1700 to 1200 B.C.E.—The two-wheeled horse-drawn chariot is developed in the Middle East. Chinese and Mongolian societies practice archery as a pastime. Hebrew patriarch Abraham leaves Ur and establishes a new nation, Canaan, between Syria and Egypt. Canaanites invent an alphabet with 28 letters, and Egyptians develop geometry. Greeks and Egyptians play Knucklebones. The earliest record of a fierce hurling game in Ireland appears in a description of the Battle of Moytura in 1272 B.C.E., when invaders defeated the residents in a hurling game and then replicated the victory on the battlefield.

1250 to 400 B.C.E.—The Mesoamerican fast-paced ballgame, utilizing a rubber ball played on a court enclosed with stone walls in the shape of an "I," becomes important in Central American Olmec culture.

1200 to 200 B.C.E.—The game *T'ou hu*, an early version of darts, where an arrow is thrown from a fixed distance into a small receptacle positioned on the ground, is played. Phoenicians become leading maritime traders in the Mediterranean region, and their jewelry and beads depict doll-like faces. The skilled breeding of the Arabian horse, so influential in combat from 2000 B.C.E. until 500 C.E., coincides with development of horse sports like Polo and *Buzkashi*. Amrit, an ancient city located in Syria, contains a stadium with a racetrack.

1122 to 256 B.C.E.—Chinese first practice martial arts blending self-defense and religious and spiritual growth. Kites, first used in China, are later adopted for military signaling during the sixth century C.E. and migrate to Japan, Korea, Malaysia, Burma, India, the Middle East, and North Africa.

850 B.C.E.—Homer's *Odyssey* depicts how a lost ball roused the shipwrecked Odysseus from his sleep and led to his discovery by Nausicaa. Homer also describes a game of Hide-and-Seek that was thought to have originated in Ethiopia, called *cock-a-loo*.

776 B.C.E.—The first Olympic games are held every four years in Olympia, Greece, until 393 C.E., when the Roman emperor abolishes them. Meanwhile, less proficient athletes play an early version of Chuckie at the Hole, by bouncing a ball on the ground and then catching it on the rebound, with the player catching the most rebounds winning. Clay tops appear in Greece in about 750 B.C.E. Later, an early form of the yo-yo arrives in Greece, possibly originating in China.

387 B.C.E.—The Greek philosopher Plato establishes the Academy to train a class of rulers through a process of the dialectic, using logic, ethics, and reasoning to reach solutions. Plato describes maze patterns to illustrate the study of true realities, but labyrinths date back to the ancient religions of Judaism, Brahmanism, Sufism, Jainism, Buddhism, Christianity, and Taoism.

333 to 146 B.C.E.—Athletic play related to the pentathlon events are recorded in art during the Hellenistic Period. Athletes use jumping weights like modern dumbbells when training for races and gymnastics. Javelin throwing is considered to be part of military training. Indigenous cultures including Hohokam, Anasazi, and Mogollon tribes in North America use play to foster running, hunting, and gathering skills.

52 to 43 B.C.E. —Roman children play Castles, or Pyramids, with nuts.

6 or 7 C.E.—Mancala, a strategic counting game, is played in Africa, Asia, and the Caribbean.

125 to 170—Puppetry becomes popular in Greece and Rome. Lucius Apuleius chronicles how Roman marionettes have rolling eyes.

300—Roman emperor Diocletian opens public baths in Rome as a place for socializing, though the pattern for the Roman baths as public places for socializing and exercise had already been well established for at least two centuries. Germanic peoples begin bowling with variations traced to Finland, Egypt, and Yemen.

600—*Shatranj*, an early version of Chess, is invented during the later years of the Persian Empire.

711—Berbers from western Africa invade Spain and establish a distinctive civilization that lasts almost 800 years until Grenada is recaptured by Spanish Christians in 1492. The Moors introduce technology, design, and foods like sugar, rice, and saffron to the Iberian Peninsula. The Middle Eastern game of choice, *Astraglis*, becomes popular, and the pitch-and-toss game of *Abbia* from western and central Africa migrates northward.

768 to 814—Charlemagne, king of the Franks, attacks the pagan Avars from eastern Europe. Popular romantic tales including *Valentin and Orson*—and later, during the 1340s, *The Tale of Gamelyn*, which chronicles a peddler named Gamble Gold, or Gamewell, one of Robin Hood's Merry Men—are passed on by generations of storytellers who inspire play.

800—*Patolli*, a board game of chance popular with Mayas, and later the Aztecs, is played on woven mats, similar to *pachisi*, which is played in India.

995 to 1005—*Aelfric's Colloquy*, the first English book of instruction for children, written in dialog format, provides vivid details of Anglo-Saxon daily life and play. Scottish King Malcolm III organizes footraces and athletic contests, including the caber toss, stone put, hammer throw, and sheaf toss, as an entertaining means for developing warfare and survival skills.

1120—Dominoes are developed in China.

1133—St. Bartholomew's Fair is established in London's Smithfield.

1147—Woodcuts are first used to illustrate manuscripts at the monastery in Engelberg, Switzerland. Playing cards appear in Europe after woodblock printing facilitates mass production.

1274 to 1594—Venetian explorer Marco Polo travels throughout Asia. His account, *The Description of the World*, which includes descriptions of daily life and pastimes, serves as the chief source of European intelligence on China for centuries.

1300—Jacques de Cessoles, a French Dominican friar, writes a treatise on Chess as it relates to human affairs. It is written in Latin and published in Genoa, Italy.

1314—English King Edward II issues a royal decree prohibiting "the hustling over large balls" in mob Football because games negatively impact local merchants.

1325 to 1335—The illuminated manuscript *Luttrell Psalter* depicts men chucking and pitching small objects into a hole for entertainment in a game of Chuckie.

1377—Giovanni di Juzzo da Covelluzzo, a chronicler of Viterbo, records the introduction of playing cards in that city. Arabs later introduce the game of *Taracco* from the Far East to Europe.

1385—The Bishop of London declaims against ball-play around St. Paul's Cathedral.

1390s—During the late 1390s, the Great Plague kills an estimated 30 to 60 percent of Europe's population, irrevocably altering its social structure. Meanwhile, in China a yo-yo is invented as a precursor to the modern *Diabolo,* a game of skill where a spool is tossed on a string suspended between two sticks.

1410s—Doll manufacturing starts in Germany.

1440s—The English develop the Morris Dance, often incorporating swords, hobbyhorses, sticks, and handkerchiefs in performances.

1496—Upon his return from a second voyage to the New World, Christopher Columbus reports that indigenous people have developed a ball made from gum of a tree that while heavy, flew and bounced better than leather air-filled balls used in Europe. Columbus describes games including *Bamboula*, *Tlatlico*, and *Tlachtli*.

1500 to 1525—During the High Renaissance, ABC hornbooks, battledores, and primers are used. The sturdy construction and design of hornbooks and battledores allows them to be used in physical games. Niccoli Machiavelli's *The Prince* (1513) offers advice on how the ruler of a small state might strategically preserve power with judicious use of force, inspiring some leaders to seed sources for developing continuous wealth. By the 15th century, card games emerged in other parts of Europe. *Pochspiel*, a German game involving bluffing and strategy, similar to the Persian game of *Nas*, appeared. This became the game of Poker, where the object is to take the pot by holding the best combination of cards or by bluffing the other players into withdrawing.

1533—France establishes a lottery to raise revenues for the state. The first English lottery is held in 1569; tickets are sold at St. Paul's Cathedral in London to raise money to repair British harbors.

1539—Peiter Bruegel's famous painting "Children's Games" depicts 80 games played by Dutch (and other European) children, many of which require special apparatus.

1543—English King Henry VIII commissions a hunting lodge known as Great Standing to be built in Epping Forest, one of the last stands of great oak forests that had surrounded London since medieval times, to provide panoramic views of hunting expeditions.

1550—Water power, using water and air pressure to drive machinery, allows for automation of certain manufacturing, including paper production, that leads to an increase in printing books. Five years later, Olaus Magnus's *Historia de Gentibus Septentrionalibus* depicts young people jumping through hoops decorated with bells alongside a band of sword dancers.

1585—An English expedition lands on North Carolina's Roanoke Island carrying dolls as gifts for indigenous people.

1595—William Shakespeare's *A Midsummer Night's Dream* inspires the children's singing game "Old Roger."

1600s—The Dutch, English, and French arrive in West Africa, heralding cultural exchanges that continue until the 1800s. *Mu torere*, a wood board game created in New Zealand, is played with a Tic-Tac-Toe philosophy prior to British rule in 1840. Meanwhile, a new design for a yo-yo utilizing a looped slip string emerges in the Philippines; it allows for the yo-yo to move back and forth more easily.

1601—Professional actress and poet Isabella Andreini's *Rime d'Isabella Andreini Padovana: comica gelosa* presents outlandish metaphors. Andreini becomes the model for the character of Isabella in *Commedia dell'arte,* derived from classical Roman and Greek comedy. *Commedia dell'arte* fosters improvisational motifs that spread throughout Europe during the 17th century, inspiring the creation of trickster characters like Punch, Kasperl, and Petrushka.

1618—The Dutch poet Jacob Cats's *Emblemata* includes verses of "Kinder-spel," describing children's jump rope games.

1621—English settlers traveling on board the *Fortune* bring a game popular with women called Stoolball to Plymouth, Massachusetts—Puritan leaders are not amused.

1631—John Amos Comenius's *School of Infancy* states that children use natural materials for building and learning. This later inspires toy manufacturers to produce building toys and model kits.

1633 to 1639—Duke Frederick of Holstein compiles reports of travels of ambassadors to Russia, Asia, Iran, the East Indies, and the South Pacific, describing social life and customs of those regions that are later published in London in English. In 1628 the *Casino di Venezia* becomes the first casino in Italy.

1653—Laws forbid work, travel, and other activities like play on Sundays in Boston, Massachusetts, to maintain the Sabbath.

1657—Jacques Stella's *Les Jeux et Plaisirs de l'enfance* depicts cherubs playing Hopscotch.

1693—English philosopher John Locke's *Some Thoughts Concerning Education* promotes the idea that a toy is a plaything for the exclusive use of children and as an educational device.

1694—The English government Stamp Office imposes "duties on vellum, parchment, and paper," to raise revenues to finance a war against France, creating the first tax on playing cards.

1698—D'Urfrey's comedy *The Campaigners* includes the children's finger game "Pat-a-cake, pat-a-cake, baker's man."

1700—Rebuses, or hieroglyphic puzzles, become popular novelty items. The rebus presents a message in a semipictorial form, using images of objects in place of selected words or syllables.

1720s to 1740s—Chapbooks feature adventure stories and romances that introduce English translations of the *Arabian Nights* (1704–1708) and Daniel Defoe's *Robinson Crusoe* (1719) into children's play.

1740—Irish tinsmith Edward Patterson settles in Berlin, Connecticut, producing some of the first American-made toys that are sold door-to-door.

1744—John Newbery's *A Little Pretty Pocket-Book* contains a description and illustration of boys playing baseball.

1750s—Boys' street games begin to have specific seasons. Colonial merchants who want to cultivate growing consumerism in North America import toys from England and the Netherlands, including dollhouses, furnishings, and commercially produced children's board games.

1759—John Jefferey's *Journey Through Europe, or, The Play of Geography*, includes a linen-mounted hand-colored folding map game depicting a seventy-seven-stop trip through Europe.

1763—British soldiers observe indigenous people in North America playing lacrosse and indigenous women play physically demanding team sports like double-ball and shinny.

1767—London engraver and mapmaker John Spilsbury invents the jigsaw puzzle.

1768—British horse trainer Philip Astley erects an arena in London. Astley, known as the father of the modern circus, hires novelty acts including professional equestrians, musicians, tightrope walkers, tumblers, and dancing dogs to entertain audiences.

1770—The Industrial Revolution begins in Great Britain. The British children's novel *Little Goody Two-Shoes* (1765) depicts a heroine introducing an educational game utilizing letter pieces (like Scrabble) to teach reading. This game becomes a model for enlightened parents who want to prepare their children for success in an increasingly industrial world.

1777—At a party at Chateau de Bagatelle, French King Louis XIV and his wife enjoy playing with a new table game featuring a narrowed billiard table, where players use cue sticks to shoot ivory balls through an inclined playfield. The game, called *Bagatelle*, spreads throughout France and evolves into the game of pinball.

1777 to 1778—Captain James Cook reports observing surfing in Tahiti and on Oahu in Hawaii.

1783—French architect Richard Mique creates the *petit hameau*, a forerunner to modern theme parks consisting of a farmhouse, dairy, and mill as an extension of the Petit Trianon for Marie Antoinette. At this rustic retreat, Marie Antoinette and her attendants play out roles of dairymaids and shepherdesses. Elsewhere in France, Brothers Joseph and Etienne Montgolfier introduce hot air ballooning using a balloon made with paper and linen.

1798 to 1826—Alois Senefelder's invention of lithography in 1798 inspires the first coloring book published with uncolored images in Germany. Toy theaters, or juvenile dramas, are introduced in London for young people to produce popular plays of the day with miniature stages, backcloths, prosceniums, and characters, along with scripts printed on paper that can be cut out and assembled. Paper dolls first appear in the marketplace to provide consumers with previews of garment designs that can be commissioned. The scrapbook-compiling craze starts with publication of John Poole's *Manuscript Gleanings and Literary Scrap Book* (1826) containing a one-page introduction explaining the concept of a commonplace journal as a tool for collecting and arranging materials.

1804—Jane and Ann Taylor's *Original Poems for Infant Minds* contains a poem, "Twinkle, twinkle little star," that becomes a popular singing rhyme.

1806—William Roscoe's poem "The Butterfly's Ball and the Grasshopper's Feast" appears in *Gentlemen's Magazine*. Thomas Jefferson clips this early nonsense rhyme for his granddaughter Cornelia.

1808—French Empress Josephine travels to Bayonne, France, to join Napoleon, and the municipality sends young Landes stilt-walkers to greet her. Although stilts were invented in the early 1600s for practical purposes of walking elevated above normal height, court jesters adopt them to entertain audiences.

1817—Englishman David Brewster reintroduces the kaleidoscope (known to the ancient Greeks) as a toy.

1818—German Baron Karl Drais von Sauerbronn develops the *Laufmaschine*, or "Running Machine," a prebicycle consisting a wooden frame supported by two in-line wheels.

1824—Dr. P.M. Roget systematically analyzes the principle of moving images. His findings are later adapted into optical toys including the Pheniksticope, Praxinoscope, Thaumatrope, and Zeotrope.

1826—German educator Friedrich Froebel's *The Education of Man* encourages parents to install mobiles in cradles to ensure "occupation for the senses and the mind" to foster early child development.

1827—Catherine Beecher requires students at her Hartford Female Seminary to do calisthenics.

1830s to 1850s—Carpenter William S. Tower, from Massachusetts, manufactures wooden toys in his leisure hours. Tower establishes a cooperative guild consisting of 20 members, coinciding with a golden age of folk art. Parents make whirligigs in human forms with arms that spin and Noah's Ark sets, which become popular Sunday toys. Scrimshaw acrobatic toys emerge at the height of the whaling industry.

1837—The accession of Queen Victoria to the English throne brings a tremendous period of sentimentality when nursery play is spotlighted. The continuing Industrial Revolution brings a migration of families from rural settings into urban areas. Children lose play time as they are employed in hazardous jobs in factories and mines, and as chimney sweeps, inspiring several Factory Acts in Great Britain.

1838—The American company Francis, Field, and Francis, also known as Philadelphia Tin Toy Manufactory, produces and sells lacquered (or japanned) tin toys along with dollhouse furnishings.

1840s—Amusement sheets containing puzzles, games, enigmas, and jokes for family entertainment are sold in bookstores and given as free advertisements. In England, students at Rugby School begin playing a team game where players can pick up a ball and run with it. The game is called called Rugby Football. In Germany, Frederick Froebel opens the first kindergarten, stressing the importance of environment, self-directed activity, physical training, and play in the early development of children in 1841.

1843—English entrepreneur Alexander Dabell establishes the Blackgang Chine amusement park on the Isle of Wight, combining unusual and whimsical walk-through attractions, exhibits, and rides. Massachusetts firm W. & S.B. Ives publishes a board game called The Mansion of Happiness: An Instructive, Moral, and Entertaining Amusement.

1845—Alexander Cartwright leads an effort to delineate rules for a bat and ball game in the United States and comes up with the Knickerbocker Rules that evolve into the modern sport of baseball.

1849—Charles Goodyear invents and patents "vulcanizing" rubber, using chemicals to create elasticity and stability. Goodyear's invention, known as India rubber, is used in air balls, ball rattles, rattleboxes, doll heads, and a variety of animal toys.

1853—French spiritualist M. Planchette develops the Ouija Board, consisting of a large piece of paper, a heart-shaped wedge with two wheels on each end, and with a pencil. In this game the players' fingers move the wedge to draw pictures and form words and messages. The name "Ouija" is supposedly derived from the French and German words for "yes"—*oui* and *ja*.

1855—At the women's rights convention at Seneca Falls, New York, some women wear bloomers to draw attention to artificial distinctions created by restrictive clothing that limit daily physical activities for women.

1856—George W. Brown & Co. toymakers introduces the tin clockwork toy in the United States.

1859—*Godey's Lady's Book* is the first publication to feature paper dolls.

1860—Milton Bradley invents The Checkered Game of Life and establishes his eponymous American game company. He is also the inventor of the paper cutter.

1861—Charles Dickens's *Great Expectations* describes Beggar-My-Neighbor as the only card game that the novel's protagonist Pip knows how to play as a child.

1861 to 1865—In Philadelphia in 1862, a flurry of children's fairs raise cash and supplies for a local companies and Army hospitals during the American Civil War. Schools gather wagons of food and linens. Stephen Foster's popular song "Don't Bet Money on the Shanghai" draws upon the music of European settlers and African slaves and captures the love of cockfighting in the American South.

1869—Completion of the transcontinental railroad in the United States makes rapid distribution of manufactured goods possible on a national scale. J.W. Hyatt invents plastic celluloid in New Jersey. Meanwhile, William H.H. Murray's *Adventures in the Wilderness; or Camp-Life in the Adirondacks* starts an outdoors movement. The term "Murray's Fools," in popular culture, referred to city folk who packed specially outfitted railroad trains each weekend to pour into resorts.

1870—The United States establishes Christmas as a national holiday. Americans begin the practice of exchanging handmade or inexpensive toys and gifts among a wide circle of acquaintances and charities.

1870s—Milton Bradley takes Dr. P.M. Roget's discoveries about optical theory and comes out with the Zoetrope, an illusion-motion toy.

1871—British inventor Montague Redgrave patents his "improvements in Bagatelle," resulting in the birth of the modern pinball game. In the United States, the Frisbie Baking Company inadvertently starts a new craze when their pies are distributed to colleges in New England. Students discover that pie tins can be tossed and caught for sport and entertainment. Later, Walter Frederic Morrison and Warren Franscioni devise a plastic version that can fly a greater distance with more accuracy in 1948.

1872—The United States establishes the National Park system when an act of Congress creates Yellowstone National Park. American James A. Bailey develops the concept of a three-ring circus. P.T. Barnum produces "The Greatest Show on Earth." Later Barnum and Bailey merge enterprises and tour the United States.

1873—Mary Mapes Dodge becomes editor of *St. Nicholas Magazine*.

1874—W.E. Crandall designs and patents Toy Building Blocks, the precursors for plastic LEGO units. In 1932 Danish carpenter Ole Kirk Christiansen starts producing wooden toys and soon calls them LEGO before expanding to plastics. LEGO manufactures interlocking bricks called "Automatic Binding Bricks" in 1949, and in 1974, LEGO introduces Minifigs.

1870s and 1880s—American kindergarten pioneer Elizabeth Peabody inspires Milton Bradley to manufacture Froebelian "occupations" for young children. The toy steam engine is developed. In England, fireworks governed by safety regulations became available for home use. Embossed tin rattles and whistles are manufactured. Advances in printing technology create new levels of play and home hobbies. In the United States, acquaintance cards were novelty items used in courting rituals. Flirtatious and fun, these visiting cards became tokens of subsequent friendships. The invention of gum coating fosters the manufacturing of stickers.

1881—Thomas Edison invents the carbon filament electric lamp and later the phonograph. He later designed a power supply system that enables lamps and other electrical equipment to be powered by the same generator but can be switched on and off individually. Italian writer Carlo Collodi's *Pinocchio* writes the popular fantasy about a puppet that is transformed into a boy.

1883—W.W. Newell's *Games and Songs of American Children* describes Jack-stones as little double tripods of iron and the game of Jacky-Five-Stones as an 18th century Irish game. George S. Parker establishes a toy and game manufacturing company called Parker Brothers and publishes his first game, called Banking, at the age of 16 years.

1884—The National Society for the Prevention of Cruelty to Children is established in the United Kingdom.

1891—Dr. James Naismith develops the sport of basketball. Although basketball is immediately popular at women's and men's colleges in the United States, four years later, Clara Gregory Baer invents a noncontact sport derived from basketball called netball. Netball, primarily played by women, becomes popular in Australia, New Zealand, the West Indies, Sri Lanka, and Great Britain.

1893—*Stern-Halma*, known in the United States as Chinese Checkers, is invented in Germany. Meanwhile, brothers Frederick and Louis Rueckham mass produce Cracker Jack, a mixture of popcorn, molasses and peanuts called "Candied Popcorn and Peanuts," and sell it at the Chicago World's Fair. Cracker Jack becomes a popular treat at baseball games and is mentioned in the 1908 baseball song, "Take Me Out to the Ball Game." In 1912, Cracker Jack boxes come with prizes.

1895—Paul Boyton establishes Sea Lion Island on Coney Island, the first permanent amusement park in North America to charge admission fees. By the 1920s and 1930s, midway arcade games, including shooting galleries and coin-operated machines where a mechanical genie reveals a fortune, appear in amusement parks.

1896—Baron Peirre de Coubertin initiates the modern summer Olympics in Athens, Greece.

1900—L. Frank Baum's fantasy *The Wonderful Wizard of Oz* becomes popular, spawning games, toys, and dreams. A year later, psychologist Karl Groos's *The Play of Man* introduces concepts of fantasy play.

1901—British businessman Frank Hornby invents reusable strips, plates, wheels, and other parts for working mechanical construction kits known as Meccano that can be assembled at home.

1904—While G. Stanley Hall had earlier argued that infancy should be prolonged until the age of 14 years, F.A. Verplanek in his article "Shortening the Period of Infancy," in *Education Review*, volume 27 (April 1904), pages 406 to 409, asserts that adolescence is the transitional period of development between puberty and adulthood, extending mainly through the teen years, and legally terminating when the age of majority is reached.

1906—The Wallie Door Company patents and first manufactures a specialty automotive card game called Tour. Later, Frenchman Edmond Dujardin creates another automotive card game called Mille Borne. Meanwhile, Will Keith McVicar establishes the Battle Creek Toasted Corn Flake Company, which becomes cereal giant Kellogg's. The company ambitiously markets Corn Flakes with celebrities and cartoon characters, and to increase sales, they offer a special toy and movable book called *Funny Jungleland Moving Pictures Booklet* with any purchase of two boxes of cereal in 1909.

1907—Italian educator Maria Montessori establishes her first *casa dei bambini* in Rome, a school where children can develop creatively and intellectually, utilizing practical life exercises and sense-training materials.

1911—Caroline Pratt develops Do With Toys, pretending toys designed around specific themes with figures representing aspects of real life. Meanwhile, the Camp Fire Girls is established to offer outdoor recreational activities to girls in urban areas. The Boy Scouts is also established. A.C. Gilbert invents the Erector Set, a toy construction kit made famous by the first national advertising campaign in the United States.

1913—Liverpool journalist Arthur Wynne invents the word-cross puzzle for the *New York World*, and crossword puzzles become a craze in the United States.

1915—Artist and political cartoonist Johnny Gruelle gives his daughter Marcella an adapted rag doll with red yarn as hair. Marcella tragically dies after being vaccinated for smallpox without her parents' consent, and the Raggedy Ann doll becomes a symbol for the antivaccination movement. In 1918, Gruelle's *Raggedy Ann Stories* introduces the doll to the public. Later, some sororities adopt Raggedy Ann as a mascot.

1917—Helen Kinne and Anna Cobley's *The House and Family* encourages parents to think about child safety when selecting toys. The book asserts, "Baby will put everything into his mouth. Toys made of wool and hair are bad. Those which can be washed are best."

1920—Milton Bradley purchases McLoughlin Brothers, a leading manufacturer of washable durable linen books, paper cut-out figures, and games for children. The A.C. Gilbert Company manufactures home chemistry sets.

1923—Henry and Helal Hassenfeld establish the textile remnant company Hassenfeld Brothers, which grows into the toy-making giant Hasbro.

1927—Alfred Adler's *Practice and Theory of Individual Psychology* promotes a psychodynamic approach to individual self-image that inspires play therapy.

1930—Fisher-Price manufactures sturdy toys for preschool children using lithographed paper on wood.

1931—The Starex Novelty Company produces the guessing board game called Battleship.

1932—Maurice Greenburg establishes Coleco (Connecticut Leather Company), which later experiences phenomenal success with Cabbage Patch Dolls during the 1980s.

1933—As part of his New Deal, President Franklin D. Roosevelt launches the Civilian Conservation Corps to relieve the Great Depression by employing thousands of men in a wide range of conservation and construction projects for state parks and recreational areas.

1935—Although Quaker Elizabeth Magie had developed The Landlord's Game to explain political economist Henry George's land value tax and to illustrate the "evils of land monopolization" in 1904, Parker Brothers produces the popular board game Monopoly during the Great Depression, which captures the public attention.

1938—The Fair Labor Standards Act establishes severe restrictions on child labor in the United States. Architect Alfred Mosher Butts creates a variation of a word game he invented called Lexiko. Utilizing frequency analysis to determine the distribution and value of letter tiles from various sources, including the *New York Times*, he calls the game Scrabble.

1940—The plastics toy industry emerges.

1943—Milton Bradley introduces the Indian morality game known as *Moksha Patamu* in the United States as Chutes and Ladders.

1945—Harold "Matt" Matson and Elliot Handler establish Mattel, Inc., which becomes the world's largest toy importing company.

1950s—Architects begin integrating hobby-oriented spaces into homes. Sewing rooms, workshops, darkrooms, and recreation rooms are added to houses.

1952—Alexander S. Douglas develops OXO, a Tic-Tac-Toe computer game also known as Noughts and Crosses. Mr. Potato Head is first sold.

1954—Barbara Frankel and Louis Galoob establish Galoob Toys, which manufactures Micro Machines in south San Francisco, California.

1955—Disneyland amusement park opens in Anaheim, California.

1956—Yahtzee is patented. Noah and Joseph McVicker invent the nontoxic clay modeling compound Play-Doh and sell it as a children's toy.

1957—Freeman Tilden's *Interpreting Our Heritage* sets forth guiding principles for how the National Park Service in the United States shapes visitor experiences.

1958—Charles S. Roberts establishes Avalon Hill, a company specializing in wargames.

1959—Mattel, Inc., launches a new adult figure doll called Barbie. The Ken doll is introduced in 1961.

1961—Bob Stewart's *Password*, an American television game produced for Goodson-Todman Productions, first airs on October 2, 1961.

1963—In one of the oldest forms of fantasy sports, Strat-o-Matic, players manage imaginary baseball teams based upon the performances of real-life players.

1964—During the Vietnam War, Hasbro launches G.I. Joe, a line with a World War II theme inspired by the 1945 war film *The Story of G.I. Joe*.

1966—Charles F. Foley and Neil Rabens patent the game Twister. Milton Bradley launches Twister, and Eva Gabor and Johnny Carson turn it into a craze when they play it on *The Tonight Show*.

1969—Imperial Toys manufactures Bubbles and other novelty toys.

1970—Parker Brothers introduces the NERF ball made of polyurethane foam, invented by Rene Guyer, as the "first official indoor ball." NERF balls and darts bring traditionally outdoor play into the workplace.

1971—The earliest known coin-operated arcade video game, Galaxy Game, debuts at Stanford University in California. The following year Atari Inc. launches Pong, achieving great commercial success.

1972—Michael Bond's *A Bear Called Paddington* (1958) inspires the first stuffed Paddington Bear, created by Gabrielle Designs.

1974—Hungarian sculptor and professor of architecture Ernö Rubik invents a mechanical puzzle that he calls the Magic Cube. Ideal Toys renames it as Rubik's Cube. Tactical Studies Rules, Inc., publishes a fantasy role-playing game, originally designed by E. Gary Gygax and Dave Arneson, called *Dungeons and Dragons*.

1975—Advertising executive Gary Dahl successfully markets the Pet Rock, an ordinary rock sold as if it was a live pet with instructions for care and feeding.

1979—Members of the Dangerous Sports Club execute bungee jumps from the Clifton Suspension Bridge, spanning Avon Gorge in North Somerset, England. Commercial bungee jumping starts in 1986.

1980—Namco launches the popular game Pac-Man. In 1981, Donkey Kong becomes a pioneering platform game. After a group of hunters including Bob Guernsey, Hayes Noel, Mark Chapin, and Alex Reiger discuss the adrenaline rush gained from sport hunting, Guernsey establishes the National Survival Game and then contracts with the Nelson Paint Company to be sole distributor for paintball equipment used in the game Survival.

1984—In an industry acquisition, Hasbro, Inc., purchases the Milton Bradley company.

1991—MicroProse publishes Civilization, a turn-based strategy computer game produced by Sid Meier.

1994—Canadian cartoon artist Todd McFarlane establishes McFarlane Toys to manufacture detailed models of comic book and video characters, musicians, athletes, and figures from popular culture.

1996—Satoshi Tajiri develops a role-playing game called Pokémon.

1997—The Scottish company Rockstar North launches the popular game Grand Theft Auto as a sandbox-style video game for the tabletop computer console Sony PlayStation.

1999—The Stadium Giveaway Company revamps the German *Nodder* doll by creating a novelty poly-resin bobble-head doll, and the San Francisco Giants make Willie Mayes bobble-head dolls popular as a home game give-away for fans.

2001—Roger Caillois's *Man, Play and Games* investigates the phenomenon of play as "an occasion of pure waste: waste of time, energy, ingenuity, skill, and often money."

2008—Will Wright designs a single-player online game called Spore that allows a player to control the evolution of a species.

Meredith Eliassen
San Francisco State University

A

Academic Learning and Play

Play has an important place in the classroom and is a critical element of the learning process, particularly for younger children. For preschool-aged children, play is a key learning experience that teaches social skills and self-regulation and fosters cognitive capabilities, such as creativity and working memory. For older children, play continues to support learning objectives by increasing literacy, strengthening writing skills, and enhancing self-regulation skills. When play is used in the academic environment, children may enjoy the learning process more, which helps children to become self-directed and self-motivated learners. Overall, play is a critical component of the learning process, and an understanding of the role of play in academic learning is necessary for parents and educators.

Defining Play

According to Victoria Dimidjian, editor of a volume on play in public education, play is best understood as one end of a work-play continuum. To define play by these terms, where play is internally motivated, controlled, and valued, work is externally motivated, controlled, and evaluated. Play is both self-initiated and self-ended, while work starts and stops according to a set schedule. Play is open-ended while work is done to achieve a specific goal. Dimidjian writes, "Traditionally during much of this century, play has been defined as the activity children do until they are 'ready to begin real work' or after they have successfully completed schoolwork tasks." Children may understand that play is what they do for fun—on weekends, after school, during recess with friends—whereas work is what teachers force them to do in the classroom.

However, for very young children, these boundaries between work and play are less clear. The *preoperational stage* is a learning stage identified in Piaget's *Theory of Cognitive Development*. Preoperational stage is observed in children between the ages of 2 and 6 to 7 years old and is marked by the beginning of cognitive schemes and symbolic thinking, although these children have not yet developed adult reasoning. Children in the preoperational stage may still enjoy "chores" and "work" and view them as fun—and therefore, play. Parents or teachers who use a fun manner and excited demeanor to present tasks such as cleaning up, reading, and other learning activities will encourage children to see these activities as play rather than work.

As children move into the "concrete operations stage" (ages 6 or 7 through 11 or 12 in Piaget's theory, marked by the development of reasoning about concrete reality), they are more likely to clearly distinguish between play—what they want to do—and work—what others want them to do. The task-focused nature of contemporary education reinforces this categorization, and elementary-age children come to see work as what they do during school and play as what they do on their own time.

Learning Through Play

A body of research suggests that the separation of work and play is counterproductive. Prominent psychologists support the idea that play is important throughout childhood, into adolescence, and even into adulthood. Play provides stress relief, supports creative engagement, and fosters specific types of learning.

Fantasy play is particularly important for learning in early childhood. Fantasy play involves various forms of make-believe, including decontextualized behaviors (for instance, eating behaviors without food, such as in the tea party) and substitute objects (for instance, using a toy bottle to feed a toy doll). Fantasy play is most common during the preoperational stage and makes up about 17 percent of preschool play and 33 percent of kindergarten play. Psychologist Lev Semyonovich Vygotsky suggested that pretend play is a spontaneous childhood activity in which children function at their highest level of competence—at the top of what Vygotsky termed the *zone of proximal development.* Key skills that are strengthened through fantasy play include working memory (when children pretend with other children, they have to remember their role to stay in character), cognitive flexibility (they have to adjust to the decisions other children make in the fantasy), and creativity.

Research has identified several academic benefits of fantasy play. One study found that quality of fantasy play predicted early writing abilities—theoretically, fantasy play is a form of symbolic media just as writing is, and children who learn to convey thoughts and feelings in fantasy may be better able to convey thoughts and feelings in writing. Likewise, children who understand storylines from a fantasy play perspective will be more apt to comprehend and follow story lines when they begin reading.

Fantasy play also helps children to identify with other people and learn about other people's points of view. This helps children work through a classic characteristic of the preoperational stage, *preoperational egocentricism* (the idea that children are unable to see any viewpoint other than their own). Through fantasy play, a child imagines that he or she is a parent, a worker, or a nonhuman animal, and therefore imagines the point-of-view of this other. In the preoperational stage, the child is only capable of seeing others' perspectives in pretend play, but this work-in-play builds the foundation for the child to understand others and develop characteristics such as empathy. By the time the child reaches the concrete operational stage, he or she will be able to think about and discuss other people's points of view.

Literacy Education and Play

While a traditional perspective viewed literacy as a linear process based on the development of specific, sequential skills, a more holistic perspective now supports the idea that reading is a holistic and interactive process which involves meaning making and pattern recognition. Likewise, writing skill development is a holistic process which is built simultaneously to reading ability. Skills involved in both reading and writing include risk-taking, the negotiation of roles, problem solving, understanding meaning and giving meaning to experience, active questioning, decontextualization of experience, awareness of subtleties, and symbolic representation. All of these skills are implemented in play—particularly in fantasy play—so the child involved in play and storytelling is building skills that will be utilized in learning to read and write.

When children understand that blocks can symbolize buildings, that crayons can be used on paper to symbolize flowers, and that stuffed animals can symbolize comfort and support, they are understanding symbols in the same way they will learn to understand words as symbols representing tangible objects. Thus play is an important prerequisite for literacy. Likewise, for older children who are learning to read or to improve their reading skills, playful reading can increase motivation for reading tasks. Humorous readings can be used to increase the playfulness of reading tasks and therefore support intrinsic motivation for reading.

Mathematics Education and Play

Jean Piaget's theory of *constructivism* proposes that children learn by building knowledge through experience—rather than adopting the cognitive schemes presented by teachers and parents, they must rebuild those schemes from scratch. Constructivism is particularly relevant in mathematics education—children acquire knowledge and understanding of mathematics through their interaction with math in their environment. For instance, children learn about numbers through objects rather than through vague concepts on paper. Children

Play can be integrated into the academic curriculum through playful activities such as the use of stories (telling, reading, and writing), art (drawing, painting, and sculpture), and drama (putting on plays and perhaps learning set design).

learn about addition and subtraction by manipulating physical objects, removing five buttons from a stack of 10 and counting how many remain. Games are particularly appropriate for teaching primary mathematics and for providing children with tangible mathematics experiences that they then use to construct their understanding of mathematical concepts. The use of games in mathematics has several benefits. As in other forms of play-based learning, games-based mathematics can create greater internal motivation for the learning process. Children are internally motivated to do what is fun, so when learning is presented in a fun context, they are more likely to choose participation. Self-motivated learning fosters an intrinsic love of learning that will enhance future academic experiences. Math-based games provide students opportunities to experiment with multiple methods of solution, to develop social interaction skills, and to observe (and correct, as needed) others.

Social Development Through Play

Another important benefit of early childhood play is the acquisition of social skills. When children play with other children, they learn to negotiate with and relate to others. Play with other children affords the opportunity to interact on equal footing with peers (in contrast, play with teachers and parents, while valuable, always occurs in a context of unequal status). Play with other children is important, as it helps children to learn appropriate methods for dealing with conflict and appropriate forms for expressing frustration and aggression and to develop skills and tactics for self-protection. Communications inherent in the play environment continually develop language skills.

Self-Regulation Through Play

One key cognitive skill that play helps to develop is executive function. Executive function includes several elements, including working memory, cognitive flexibility, and self-regulation. Self-regulation is the ability for an individual to control his or her emotions and behaviors—children with strong self-regulation make good decisions and resist temptation, while children with poor self-regulation are more likely to get in trouble and later in life get addicted to substances or involved in crime. Self-regulation has been associated with both school completion (students with low levels of self-regulation are more likely to drop out of school) and school success (some research shows that self-regulation is more important than intelligence in determining school performance). Because play promotes self-regulation, play is useful in helping children develop skills that lead to success, both in school and later in work.

Some psychologists worry, however, that children who are predominantly involved in adult-regulated forms of play (for instance, sports leagues, music and dance lessons, youth center activities) will not have the opportunity to benefit from the self-regulation-promoting aspects of play—precisely because they are playing but not self-regulating when their playtime is structured by adults. For the same reason, television and video/computer games, while fun, do not promote self-regulation in the same way that free-play does because television and video/computer games are outside of the player's control.

Likewise, task-specific toys (for instance, fireman and princess costumes instead of a box of old clothes, plastic swords and guns instead of sticks) can limit creativity and self-regulation in play, because the toys define the form of the play. Research shows that the introduction of more regulated forms of play in the late 20th century (toys, video games, and parent/teacher-regulated activities) has actually changed how children develop. In a study of self-regulation in the 1940s, children ages 3, 5, and 7 years were ask to stand still without moving. The 3-year-olds could not stand still, 5-year-olds could stand for three minutes, and 7-year-olds could stand still for as long as instructed. The study was replicated in 2001; contemporary 5-year-olds could not stand still, and contemporary 7-year-olds could only stand still for three minutes.

For this reason, early child psychologists suggest that the best kind of play requires no equipment and should focus on the child using his or her imagination. When children learn to rely on themselves for play, their playtime builds self-regulatory skills. This does not mean that children should play by themselves, or that adults should not be involved in playtime. Adults can effectively play with children in fantasy play, and adults should supervise playtime for safety and to quickly stop any inappropriate behaviors. However, adult participation and adult supervision should be distinguished from adult regulation of play.

Integrating Play Into the Context of Academic Learning

Play versus work need not be mutually exclusive alternatives. Play can be integrated into the academic curriculum through playful activities such as the use of stories (telling, reading, and writing), art (drawing, painting, and sculpture), and drama (putting on plays, including set design). Math and science as play can involve a focus on hands-on experiments and activities instead of problem sets worked out on paper. Music can be playful and creative if students feel they have some say in the matter—for instance, picking the song to learn out of a selection provided by the teacher. Even physical fitness can be fun when children are provided with physical activity options that involve social interaction with friends and creative engagement.

Complex imaginative play can be particularly useful in the academic context, as it requires a child to think creatively, interact socially, and engage working memory. Complex imaginative play should last a minimum of 30 minutes to challenge self-regulation and working memory, with elaborate sustained play over several hours being even more beneficial. Also, while realistic props (premade costumes and devices) may be useful for very small children, older children should make their own props or use symbolic representations to further challenge their creative development.

Planning-based activities can also be useful learning play experiences, as they allow creative expression to be expressed in a context of self-regulation. Patterns for drawing, construction, and sewing; games and sports with directions; recipes for cooking; and instructions for scientific experiments all provide the opportunity for fun and self-discipline.

Overall, when the learning environment is built in a context that allows learning to be enjoyable and provides children with an opportunity to feel in control of the learning process, it becomes possible for work to feel like play and for play to lead to productive outcomes in the classroom.

See Also: Cooperative Play; Memory and Play; Organized or Sanctioned Play; Piaget and Play; Play and Learning Theory; Play and Literacy; Play as Learning, Psychology of; Play as Learning, Sociology of; Play in the Classroom; Psychological Benefits of Play; Psychology of Play (Vygotsky); Recess; Sociological Benefits of Play; Speech Play; Teacher-Child Co-Play.

Bibliography. Victoria Dimidjian, *Play's Place in Public Education for Young Children* (National Education Association of the United States, 1992); Roberta Golinkoff, Kathy Hirsh-

Pasek, and Diane Eyer, *Einstein Never Used Flashcards: How our Children Really Learn—and Why They Need to Play More and Memorize Less* (Rodale Books, 2004); Robin Henig, "Taking Play Seriously," *The New York Times* (February 17, 2008); Dorothy Singer, Roberta Golinkoff, and Kathy Hirsh-Pasek, *Play = Learning: How Play Motivates and Enhances Children's Cognitive and Social-Emotional Growth* (Oxford University Press, 2006); Alix Spiegel, "Creative Play Makes for Kids in Control," *NPR* (February 21, 2008); Alix Spiegel, "Old-Fashioned Play Builds Serious Skills," *NPR* (February 27, 2008); Vikki Valentine, "Q&A: The Best Kind of Play for Kids," *NPR* (February 27, 2008); Elizabeth Wood and Jane Attfield, *Play, Learning, and the Early Childhood Curriculum,* 2nd Edition (Paul Chapman Educational Publishing, 2005).

Kimberlee Bonura
Walden University

Ace-Deuce-Jack

Ace-Deuce-Jack is a simple game where bets are placed on whether one of three cards will not be turned over. If one of the three cards is turned over, then the bank wins, otherwise the player wins. Bets are paid at one for one. The game is heavily weighted in the favor of the banker. The game became popular among hustlers during World War II.

Game play is straightforward. The banker shuffles, or he can let one of the players do it since the shuffle is not important to the game. There is no manipulation of the cards during the shuffle or for that matter at any time during the game. Thus it is unimportant to the banker who shuffles or turns the cards over. After the shuffle, players can place their bets. Each player is betting that none of the three cards—ace, two (also called the deuce) or jack—will be turned over when three cards are turned over. The trick is that the game sounds like it is unbalanced in the player's favor, since the bank can only win if one of three (out of possibility of 13 different cards) is turned up. What most players miss is that only one of the turned up cards has to be one of the three. Statistically this means that out of 22,100 possible combinations of three cards in a deck of 52 cards, of those, 12,220 win for the bank. Which means the bank wins just over 55 percent of the time while the players win just under 45 percent of the time.

Since the banker is strictly playing the odds, he can make a number of changes in the game if the players think he is cheating. These include allowing one of the players to shuffle the cards or allowing the players to cut the deck. The top three cards can be used, or the deck can be divided into three stacks and one card is taken from each stack, which could be the top card, the bottom, or cut from the middle. The banker can even have the players pick the three cards he wins on.

What the banker is counting on is that most people will not do the math to figure out the actual odds of winning. He relies on most players assuming that he has less than a 25 percent chance of winning, based on the fact that he is only picking three out of 13 cards as winners. What they miss is that he needs only one of those cards out of the three draws to win.

See Also: Gambling; Play and Power, Psychology of; Play as Competition, Psychology of.

Bibliography. Diagram Group, *The Little Giant Encyclopedia of Card Games* (Sterling Publishing Company, 1995); John Scarne, *Scarne on Cards* (Crown Publishers, 1973); Brian Sutton-Smith, *The Ambiguity of Play* (Harvard University Press, 2001).

Dallace W. Unger, Jr.
Independent Scholar

Action Figures

Although action figures are an integral part of a boy's upbringing in the United States, this was not always the case. At one point in our history action figures were simply unheard of. This changed in 1964 with the introduction of G.I. Joe, considered to be the first action figure. The aim of Hasbro, its producer, was to create the toughest and most masculine doll ever made. These characteristics clearly delineated it from the dolls on the market at that time, and thus the action figure was born. Typically, an action figure must possess these characteristics: the figure is usually made of plastic, designed as a superhero, can be articulated, is intended to be able to stand on its own, and is designed specifically for males. These specifics help to distinguish the action figure from other male figures such as Ken, the accoutrement to Barbie.

Although G.I. Joe sales have risen and fallen as a reflection of societal opinions and trends, he has stayed the course and remains one of the most prominent toys within the boyhood market. Indeed, Hasbro estimates G.I. Joe sales alone to be a staggering 375 million units worldwide. The success of G.I. Joe is largely because of the social environment in which it was created. In 1964, the United States was still reeling from the assassination of John F. Kennedy and found itself embroiled in the Vietnam War. During this early period of the war in particular, the military male was honored and his courage promoted by the media. There was no better time to release a military toy figure.

G.I. Joe was released in appropriate Army, Navy, Marine, and Air Force attire. Sales were impressive, with Hasbro generating nearly $17 million in its first year. Hasbro released an African American version the following year. Sales plummeted, however, following the Tet Offensive in 1968, suggesting that the action figure was indeed tied to societal trends. Hasbro responded by altering G.I. Joe's identity from a member of a team to a solitary warrior, followed soon after as a team member of an elite independent fighting unit. Sales climbed once again, and G.I. Joe's physique and appearance began to diversify, especially as new equipment and technology were developed.

With increasing production costs in the mid-1970s, sales once again began to fall, and Hasbro was forced to release a smaller but more muscular G.I. Joe. However, production was halted in 1978 in part because of cost, but also because of competitors such as Star Wars figures beginning to compete for the market. By this time, other companies had taken an interest in the action figure market, and soon other well-known characters, particularly from comic books and movies, began to emerge. Indeed, the development of action figures during the 1960s and 1970s created a transformation in the toy industry that continues today. The sales statistics alone are impressive, with wholesale action figure sales generating approximately $1 billion annually.

Action Figures and Education

Regardless of whether a toy is specifically designed to educate, every toy educates. They are designed to portray information and to raise questions concerning its type, how it is played with, and the modes of self-expression it can provide. They can also teach adult-appropriate roles and communicate messages about gender.

Action figures have roles, friends, characters, enemies, missions, weapons, equipment, struggles between good and evil, and violent confrontations. According to Wendy Varney, boys in particular like action figures because they demonstrate masculinity, strength, and invincibility. She also suggests that toys establish worldviews and explain to children why things are the way they are largely because they are accepted by their parents or those whose opinions they value. Toys can teach boys that being male means being competitive, strong, aggressive, inexpressive, and courageous.

We know that toys and thus action figures influence behavior. Some question the violent mechanisms behind action figures such as G.I. Joe, suggesting that these physically violent toys could encourage the actual use of violence. Interestingly, researcher Stephen Kline found that the role imparted on an action figure is dependent on the role presented by outside influences such as the media and parents. Therefore, a figure such as a firefighter can either use his accoutrements as tools of the trade for good or as weapons of destruction. The key is how boys are taught to interpret the figure they are playing with.

The physiques and physical dimensions of action figures have grown larger and more muscular over the last few decades, which some male body image experts believe could be related to male body image dissatisfaction in later life. Although it has long been recognized that Barbie's dimensions may encourage body image disturbances in females, disproportionate action figure physiques may also create similar occurrences in males.

For example, Timothy Baghurst and colleagues presented a group of elementary schoolboys with current action figures and their original counterparts. Even though the figures were the same height, the boys preferred the current action figure, citing the primary reason for their preference to be the muscularity and physique of the figure. We know that society promotes a muscular, lean physique for men, and now this ideal image is reflected in the design of these action figures. From these action figures, males are taught from preadolescence that their heroes are large and muscular. However, there is no empirical evidence, one way or another, that action figures do indeed influence body image later on in childhood and adolescence.

Where do action figures go from here? Throughout their history, action figures have followed societal trends. Traditionally, action figures were created from comic book characters, movie characters, and even real-life heroes such as professional wrestlers. However, with the dawn of a new computer gaming generation, expect to see more and more action figures appearing on store shelves based on this booming industry. According to the market research company NPD Group, $9.5 billion were generated from computer and video game sales in 2007, an increase of 6 percent from the previous year. In fact, the gaming industry surpassed both the U.S. movie and music industries in 2005 and 2007, respectively. As computer games and their characters begin making their way more frequently to the big screen (e.g., Doom, Resident Evil, Tomb Raider), expect action figures to follow the scent of success.

See Also: Dolls, Barbie and Others; Fantasy Play; G.I. Joe; Play and Learning Theory; Play as Rehearsal of Reality; Psychological Benefits of Play.

Bibliography. T. Baghurst, D. Carlston, J. Wood, and F. Wyatt, "Preadolescent Male Perceptions of Action Figure Physiques," *Journal of Adolescent Health* (v.41, 2007); S. Kline, "The Role of Communication in Supporting Pro-Social 'Play Scripts' in Young Boys' Imaginative Play With Action Hero Toys: A Pilot Study of Rescue Heroes," http://www2.sfu.ca/media-lab/research/rhreport.html (cited June 2008); C. Sartori, "Jump into Action," *Playthings* (2004); W. Varney, "Of Men and Machines: Images of Masculinity in Boys' Toys," *Feminist Studies* (v.28, 2002).

Timothy Baghurst
University of Arkansas

Adaptive Play

Adaptive play refers to play that has been altered in form, complexity, or intent to serve the needs of children with disabilities. This can range from developing new play materials or altering the form of traditional play materials for children with severe physical disabilities to modifying the rules of play or setting up situations to promote play opportunities for children who are cognitively impaired, as described by Musselwhite. Adaptive play through the use of assistive technology can offer a wide range of opportunities for children with developmental delays.

Play is a way for children to explore, adapt, and develop. It is an activity that is engaged in for its own sake and that entails a freedom of choice in the activity as well as a sense of enjoyment. Children play because it is fun and because they have a desire to play. Although play differs among individual children and different cultures, it is their primary occupation. Research shows a strong connection between play experiences and the development of motor, cognitive, emotional, and language skills. All children, regardless of their age or ability, need opportunities to play.

Developmental Delays

For children with developmental delays, the experience of play is different and sometimes even nonexistent. Because of lack of appropriate play materials and opportunities, these children are at an increased risk for additional secondary delays. Adaptive play serves as the window that enables children with developmental delays to have greater independence and more active involvement in play. Within adaptive play, various types of assistive devices permit these children to move in their environments, speak and communicate with others, and participate in developmentally appropriate activities that otherwise might not be possible.

The play characteristics of children with developmental delays vary and depend on their specific physical, sensory, or cognitive condition. Depending on the disability, some children may not have the same access to play as children without disabilities; therefore, their play may be more contrived and have less inner direction than the play of other children. Children with more severe disabilities may have increased limitations, resulting in less access to play and less ability to play. For example, the play characteristics of children with physical limitations may include fear of movement, decreased active play, and preference for sedentary activities. These children may also have problems with manipulating toys and show decreased exploration.

Children with cognitive impairment often show delayed or uneven skills, difficulty in structuring their own behavior, or lack of sustained attention. They may have a preference for structured play materials, limited or inflexible play repertoires, decreased curiosity, destructive or inappropriate use of objects, decreased imagination and symbolic play, and decreased social interactive communication.

The play of children with autism is characterized by the lack of inner expressive language, stereotyped movements and/or types of play, decreased imitation and imagination, lack of variety in play repertoires, and decreased play organization, manipulation of toys, and social play. The child with a visual impairment may be not only delayed in exploratory and sensory motor play but also more delayed in imaginative and symbolic play. All these limitations affect skill acquisition and potential for developing play skills through experience and interaction with other children. They result in frustration, unsuccessful experiences, and ultimately, learned helplessness. It is important to be aware of the problems that certain conditions impose on the child, and yet in actual practice, each child must always be considered individually.

In addition, as in typically developing children, the importance of environmental variables such as physical settings and available play material, cannot be underestimated. The restraints imposed by the surrounding environment have to be taken into account in order to provide empowering settings that will enable these children to engage in developmentally appropriate occupations in general and play activities in particular. By adapting the child's play environment and/or play materials, he or she can overcome great obstacles and thus engage and participate in play.

Assistive Technology

Assistive technology is any item, piece of equipment, or product system, whether acquired commercially off the shelf, modified, or customized, that is used to increase, maintain, or improve functional capabilities of individuals with disabilities.

Technology for children with disabilities enables participation in play and leisure activities, both alone and with others, and provides opportunities to socialize in the same settings as their peers without developmental delays. As assistive technology becomes more complex, it is considered high technology. This typically includes computers, electronic augmentative communication devices, environmental control units, powered mobility devices, and virtual reality systems. Low assistive technology includes nonelectronic communication aids, switch-adapted battery-operated toys, etcetera.

To enable play for children with developmental delays, toys with universal design features are selected and simple toy and environmental adaptations are made. This ensures that these children are exposed to a range of interactive and reactive experiences through fuller participation than would otherwise be possible. In addition, toys are being developed that are switch operated, brightly colored, and noise producing, features that make them usable and appealing to children with different abilities.

When adapting play materials the following strategies are considered: stabilizing the play material by attaching it to a steady surface, enlarging materials to enhance visual perception, enlarging parts to allow access for the physically disabled, keeping play materials within physical range, making play more concrete, removing extraneous cues, removing distracting stimuli, increasing tactile and visual stimuli, and improving safety and durability.

Simple modifications can be achieved by adding an element to the toy, stabilizing it, modifying the response mode, and unconventionally positioning the toy. For example, attaching plastic rings to a small and light toy can facilitate the child's grasp, wooden knobs can be glued to wooden puzzle pieces to make them easier to manipulate, foam pieces or hot glue can be added to page corners to make it easier to turn the pages, and Velcro can be applied to sweatbands to make it easier to pick up and hold a toy. Suggestions for stabilizing toys include using suction cups, clamps, Dycem matting, and Velcro. Toys with on and off switches can be modified by adding larger or pressure-sensitive electronic switches that can be accessed by any body part. Adaptive switches can be activated by a touch of the hand/head etcetera, by blowing on them, by raising an eyebrow, or even by blinking one's eye.

When communication is compromised by impairments, the use of augmentative systems is considered. Carefully selected augmentative or communication systems can make it possible for children with communication impairments to take part in a variety of play activities, such as participating in a game of Simon Says with other children, engaging in playing a board game, sharing stories, or singing with peers.

The computer, combined with specific access systems and software, can enhance play experiences by providing simulations of experiences that would be difficult, if not impossible, for the child to engage in without the computer, and with related software, which provides play opportunities (interactive stories, adventure challenges, problem-solving games, etc.).

Play can also be facilitated by making adjustments to the play environment. These environments are carefully arranged to reduce distractions and promote engagement in play with people and with objects. When adapting the play environment, the following strategies are possible: arranging the physical environment to promote play, engagement, and learning; selecting toys that encourage social exchanges and turn taking with peers (balls, bubbles); arranging the social environment to include play partners and responsive adults (exposing the child to competent play partners); and using children's preferences for toys and activities. (By observing the child's preference, one can determine if the child is interested in toys that elicit particular types of play behaviors.)

It is important to recognize the influence of cultural values and beliefs on young children's toy preferences and play behaviors. To some extent, the way young children approach and interact with toys reflects their diverse experiences, cultural backgrounds, and beliefs, structuring daily routines and play activities; using differential reinforcement (reinforcing under defined conditions); responding to child-initiated play, play coaching, or the use of direct instructions (when needed may emphasize imitation skills and presymbolic forms of play); and using stimulus modifications (i.e., changing the materials that elicit responses from the child).

The primary goal of adaptive play is to enable appropriate and enjoyable play skills for children with developmental delays. It is done through altering the form, complexity, and intent of play materials and the play itself. Assistive technology enables accessing all forms of play, altering the form of traditional play materials, and developing new play materials.

Children are probably the best teachers of play. Not only are they good at it, they are genuinely excited about sharing play experiences with others. Children with developmental delays are no different. In fact it may be even more exciting for these children to demonstrate and teach their play skills with the use of assistive technology because with assistive technology they can lead the activity and provide the expertise. It is what enables them to be a child.

See Also: Idealization of Play; Play and Learning Theory; Psychological Benefits of Play.

Bibliography. J. Hackette, "Perceptions of Play and Leisure in Junior School Aged Children With Juvenile Idiopathic Arthritis: What are the Implications for Occupational Therapy?" *British Journal of Occupational Therapy* (v.66, 2003); L. Harkness and A. C. Bundy, "The Test of Playfulness and Children With Physical Disabilities," *Occupational Therapy Journal of Research* (v.21, 2001); H.R. Rep. No. 100–819, 100th Congress, 2nd Session, "In Virtual Reality, Tools for the Disabled," *New York Times* (April 13, 1994); A.J. Luebben and P. Kramer, "Legitimate Tools of Pediatric Occupational Therapy," *Frames of Reference for Pediatric Occupational Therapy* (Lippincott, Williams & Wilkins, 1999); C.R. Musselwhite, *Adaptive Play for Special Needs Children* (College-Hill Press, 1986); L.D. Parham and L.S. Fazio, *Play in Occupational Therapy for Children* (Mosby Elsevier, 2008).

Vardit Kindler
Independent Scholar

Adlerian Play Therapy

Adlerian Play Therapy, founded and developed by Terry Kottman, Ph.D., is a psychotherapeutic intervention for children that combines the practical elements of play therapy with the philosophical tenets of Individual Psychology. Individual Psychology is based on the works of Alfred Adler, who began his career in the psychoanalytic tradition but broke from this modality to define a more holistic, socially grounded theoretical framework.

Individual Psychology

According to Carlson, Watts, and Maniacci, Individual Psychology holds that people develop interpersonal approaches to living, called *life-styles*, which subsequently inform the feelings, behaviors, and thoughts they experience. Life-styles are mental and emotional "maps" that are shaped by past experiences, provide explanations and motives for behaviors of the self and of others, and determine how individuals respond to certain situations in life. Adler asserted that individuals possess a pervasive need to belong to a social system, and it is within this social system that the individual enacts his or her experientially derived life-style. Life-styles are said to stem from the individual's experience within his or her first social group, the family. The family is thought to be a system that encourages or discourages the individual's development of *social interest*, or the quality of being connected with and concerned for others.

The extent to which an individual possesses social interest purportedly affects his or her satisfaction and functioning in daily life. Inevitably, people are believed to be socially embedded, and according to Adler, they cannot be understood or analyzed independent of their social roles, purposes, and perceived worth. Through the family, and in relating to members therein, people acquire a self-concept, such as "I am intelligent and competent," "I am lazy," or "I am successful if I impress others," which flavors their expectations of the world and of the self. These self-concepts provide the basis for the development of one's *private logic,* or the global belief system that individuals form and employ to make sense of the world. Examples of private logic include "it is better to control than to be controlled" and "people will think you are worthless if you don't win." Life-styles may be adaptive or maladaptive and are malleable if the individual becomes aware of them and chooses them to be so.

The Process and Purpose

Adlerian play therapists use the framework of Individual Psychology to help children and parents understand the child's pertinent life-styles that are propelled by their private logic and, subsequently, decide when and how to use, discard, or modify them to create positive change in their lives. The therapeutic process, following this modality, involves four predominant phases: rapport or relationship building, exploring the child's life-style, helping the child gain insight, and reorientation or redirection. In her book titled *Partners in Play: An Adlerian Approach to Play Therapy*, Terry Kottman describes these phases and their purposes.

During the initial phase, *building the relationship*, the therapist approaches the child in a way that is nonthreatening, egalitarian, and respectful of the child's feelings and interpersonal stance. Trust and mutual power and respect between child and therapist are integral to the effectiveness of therapy. A therapist attempting to build a therapeutic relationship may meet the child with the parent present, introduce him or herself to the child using first names, spend a few moments relating to the child, and with the child's readiness, invite the child into the playroom. The therapist works to maintain this therapeutic alliance with the child throughout each phase of therapy.

In the second phase of therapy, *exploring the child's life-style,* the therapist collects information to ascertain what social and familial forces influence the child's ways of relating to the world. This may be done by asking the child questions (e.g., "Who are all the people in your family? Describe ____ and what he or she does best."), observing the child's play and artwork, and collaborating with parents and other significant figures, such as teachers. Life-styles may become illuminated through the child's early recollections and roles the child appears to play according to his or her position within the family constellation (e.g., second-born children are often said to feel inferior to firstborns, since they reportedly often feel a need to compete with and "measure up" to firstborn children).

The third phase of therapy, *helping the child gain insight,* is a process of helping the child become aware of his or her perceptions of the self, others, and the world, and how these concepts define how the child relates and behaves. During this process, the child begins to understand his or her private logic in a manner that is commensurate with his or her age and developmental level. To facilitate this course, the therapist may engage the child in symbolic role-play, providing reflective statements about the child's style of play. For example, if a tentative and compliant child consistently seeks the therapist's approval or advice on what to do next, the therapist may reflect, "It seems like you want to make sure what you're doing is O.K. with me. I wonder if you're concerned that I won't like you if you make a mistake." Other techniques, such as mutual storytelling, may assist the child in becoming aware of the particular goals stemming from his or her self-concept and private logic.

During phase four, *reorienting or re-educating,* the child learns new perspectives by which to see the self and others. Upon acknowledging and modifying his or her prevalent social and interpersonal goals, he or she may also learn and practice new and more adaptive ways of behaving and relating to others. The therapist may, at this time, begin to "teach" specific skills and ways the child may reconstruct his or her thinking, feeling, and responding to situations and to people. The child may choose a new self-concept, private logic, and life-style that is more adaptive and likely to produce satisfying relationships and experiences for the child.

Critical Opinion

Adlerian Play Therapy is reported to be appropriate for most children, with the general exceptions of children who are psychotic (i.e., experiencing delusions, hallucinations, and/or other marked distortions of reality) and children with severe forms of autism. Its proponents and those of play therapy in general contend that since children lack the cognitive and emotional development to adequately verbalize their abstract experiences, they do so symbolically through play. Accordingly, advocates of this modality prefer it to traditional "talk therapy."

It is deemed to be especially helpful for children who have experienced trauma, poor self-esteem, impaired social functioning, and discord within the family. Critics of Adlerian Play Therapy have cited its directive and didactic nature as compromising the child's right to autonomy in the therapeutic process. Others disapprove of its reputed focus on the past; however, some argue that its emphasis on the child's power to choose new perspectives and behaviors denotes an inherently present- and future-orientated approach.

See Also: International Play Association; Play Therapy; Psychoanalytic Theory and Play; Psychological Benefits of Play; Psychology of Play (Vygotsky).

Bibliography. Jon Carlson, Richard E. Watts, and Michael Maniacci, *Adlerian Therapy: Theory and Practice* (American Psychological Association, 2006); Terry Kottman, "Integrating the Crucial Cs into Adlerian Play Therapy," *Journal of Individual Psychology,* (v.55/3, Fall 1999); Terry Kottman, *Partners in Play: An Adlerian Approach to Play Therapy* (American Counseling Association, 1995).

Marci M. Breedlove
University of Tennessee

Adventure Playgrounds

An adventure playground is a nonasphalted, fenced-off area containing a play hut for indoor recreation and natural areas for the construction of play structures, which might include rope swings, slides, water play, and dens. The requirements for an adventure playground include provision of tools (e.g., hammers, spades, saws, chisels, screwdrivers, and axes) and materials (wood, nails, rope, bricks, and other building material) children can use to explore new play opportunities or change their activities. Two features distinguish the adventure playground from other types of playgrounds. First, adventure playgrounds employ paid, trained play workers who facilitate children's free play. Second, the workers are instrumental in guiding the construction of self-build playground structures in consultation with children rather than buying-in manufactured fixed play equipment.

The adventure playground was described as a location where children could experiment in their play through being free to dig in the earth, build dens from wood and other waste materials, make fires to cook outside, garden, engage in arts and craft activities, or participate in other freely chosen creative or recreational activities. The age range of children and young people who may use the playground varies according to local agreements established by the managing agency and the level of facilities available on-site. The widest documented age range of children who could access the provision was from 2 to 18 years. However, the generally accepted age range today is from 5 to 15 years.

There is no agreement on the size of an adventure playground site. Many of the early playgrounds used space left over after planning or sites awaiting development. Shier suggested that, bearing in mind issues of safety and the nature of the site, a playground could vary from 0.2 to 0.8 acres. The size, situation, and terrain of the site will dictate the types of activities that can take place. For example, some playgrounds might accommodate "kickabout" areas for team games, whereas others in built-up areas may not have sufficient space to include such a resource. An adventure playground's opening hours vary according to the season. In general, in the United Kingdom (UK), these playgrounds function as after-school provision (3:00 P.M.–8:00 P.M. in the summer or 3:00 P.M.–6:00 P.M. in the winter) and are open all day Saturday.

During school vacations, they may operate between 10:00 A.M. and 6:00 P.M. Adventure playgrounds may also run a regulated after-school care facility, but usually children are free to come and go as they wish. The atmosphere of the playground should be a "pro-child" and nonrestrictive one where children are not forced to participate in structured play activities.

The adventure playground has largely thrived in Western European countries, although there is a burgeoning movement in this type of play in Japan.

Origins

In 1931, the Danish architect C.T. Sorenson first coined the term *junk playground,* from which evolved the now-accepted title of adventure playground. Sorenson observed that children naturally played with materials on building sites or found objects on wasteland. In 1943, John Bertelson developed the first adventure playground, based on Sorenson's idea, in Emdrup, a suburb of Copenhagen, Denmark. In 1948, Lady Allen of Hurtwood introduced the idea into the UK as way to bring the country in to an urban setting to encourage children's creative play.

In the UK over the next 10 years, there was a slow growth in the number of playgrounds.

In the UK, the National Playing Fields Association (NPFA) recognized that the adventure playground met several play needs of city children and supported the promotion of adventure playgrounds. The NPFA's advocacy for the adventure playgrounds was based on the fact that they provided a cost-effective solution to meet the lack of natural play areas in urban settings. The NPFA gave support to the permissive play philosophy developed by Bertelson, believing it would be attractive to young people whose needs were not met through structured youth provision and to provide diversionary activities to deter juvenile delinquency. In the 1960s, growth of interest in adventure play was helped as ideas of progressive education entered the mainstream. The adventure playground attracted the attention of architects like Nicholson, who developed a theory of "loose parts" that recognized the potential of the space for experiential learning that might assist "under-achieving" working-class children to access education.

In 1972, Lady Allen of Hurtwood set up the first adventure playground for children with special needs that offered respite to families and an environment for them to express their ability to play. This type of adventure playground remains an important part of local play provision today.

Adventure Playgrounds Today

The high costs of building materials and concerns about litigation over health and safety of children have today curtailed some of the bigger construction projects undertaken by children on playgrounds. Engaging children in the design of playground structures has, in part at least, replaced this element in the activities offered.

Through model building, drawings, and discussion with specialist play structure engineers, children have taken an active role in the design of play equipment. In the UK, adventure playgrounds are recognized as being part of national youth work strategies for the prevention of antisocial behavior, as they provide diversionary activities for children who experience social exclusion. Adventure playgrounds represent a form of play provision that has proved capable of evolving to meet the recreational needs of children, as the philosophy, which drives the work, allows them to explore a space creatively. Also, the strong community identity adventure playgrounds appear to enjoy enables them to provide a communal space for activities that is accessible to the whole neighborhood.

See Also: Play and Learning Theory; Playground as Politics; Playground Movement, U.S.

Bibliography. Lady Allen of Hurtwood, *New Playgrounds* (The Housing Centre, 1964); A. Bengtsson, *Adventure Playgrounds* (Crosby Lockwood, 1972); K. Cranwell, "Adventure Playground and the Community in London," in W. Russell, B. Handscomb, and J. Fitzpatrick, *Playwork Voices* (The London Centre for Playwork Education and Training, 2007); K. Cranwell, "Towards a History of Adventure Playgrounds (1931–2000)," in Nils Norman, *Architecture of Play: A Survey of London's Adventure Playgrounds* (Four Corners Books, 2003); A. Holmes and P. Massie, *Children's Play* (Michael Joseph, 1970); M. Nicolson, *What is an Adventure Playground?* (National Playing Fields Association, 1976); S. Nicolson, "How NOT to Cheat Children: The Theory of Loose Parts," *Landscape Architecture* (1971); H. Shier, *Adventure Playgrounds. An Introduction* (National Playing Fields Association, 1984).

Keith A. Cranwell
University of Greenwich

Afghanistan

Afghanistan is a landlocked country in Central Asia. Since Medieval times, much of the country has been poor, and as a result, the games played in villages have tended to be relatively simple. A game called *Buzel-Bazi*, similar to Marbles but using the knucklebone of a sheep, is common. The making of models by and for children, including carved dolls for girls, is also common. There is a game in which boys play with a hard-boiled egg clenched in their hands. While each participant tries to crack their opponent's egg, each player tries to keep theirs undamaged.

For boys and young men, many of the games involve some test of strength or prowess. Boys practice with a slingshot, with teenagers and men involved in *Pahlwani*, or wrestling, whereby two adversaries have to topple each other by grabbing the arms or clothes of their opponent but must not touch their legs. *Buzkashi*, played on horseback, in which people vie for the carcass of a calf or goat, is also very popular, with dozens, and sometimes hundreds, of players on each side.

One of the most popular pastimes is the making of kites and kite flying, known as *Gudiparan Bazi*. Boys and men make "fighter kites" out of a bamboo frame with tissue paper, varying in size from one to five feet across. A line is attached to the kite and is coated with ground glass, the aim being to cut the line of another person's kite. Children are allowed to keep all kites that they find at the end of these competitions.

In the 1910s, there was an effort by Habibullah, Emir of Afghanistan from 1901 until 1919, to introduce European sports such as golfing, tennis, and cricket. It only had limited success, with traditional pursuits remaining the most popular. In 1933 the Football Federation of Afghanistan was established, and many boys and young men started playing soccer. There is also a game similar to stickball called *topay-danda* that is pursued in some parts of the country, and cockfighting and fighting between other animals also takes place. In 1979 Dutch child psychologist Nico van Oudenhoven was able to write an extensive survey of 146 games commonly played by the children of Afghanistan.

During the rule of pro-Soviet governments from 1979 until 1997, playing card games and Chess became popular in the cities. When the Taliban took over most of the country in 1997, they started introducing strict laws that banned many games such as those involving cards (they were opposed to gambling), Chess (because of connotations of gambling and because they were a distraction from prayers, and also because the figures were representations of people), and puppet shows (which had been popular in the early 1970s when the Australian Peter Scriven took *The Tintookies* to Afghanistan). They also banned non-religious music and all forms of dancing. The end of Taliban rule in 2001 led to return of many games banned under the Taliban.

In his book *The Kite Runner* (2003), later turned into a film, Khaled Hosseni tells the story of a boy in Kabul who enjoyed kitefighting. Since 1979, many toys have also been fashioned out of war "junk" such as discarded artillery shells and shell casings. In February 2002, some 138 players turned up for a Chess competition in Kabul. In January 2007 Oliver Percovich and some other Australians managed to locate some secondhand skateboards that they took to Afghanistan, starting a rapid interest in skateboarding in Kabul, in a project to help the youth later known as *Skateistan*.

Mention should also be made of the Wargaming set in Afghanistan. Wargames set during the First and Second Afghan Wars were popular with British players for many years, but most of these have now been replaced by games involving the war against the Soviet Union and the War on Terror. Foreign servicemen in Afghanistan, as well as Afghan exiles who have returned to their country, have been involved in playing these games, but given the poverty of so many people in the country, they are unlikely to be played by anybody outside the foreign community and the small elite.

See Also Boys' Play; Chess and Variations of; Cricket (Amateur); Croquet; Kite Flying; Marbles; Wargames.

Bibliography. G. Whitney Azoy, *Buzkashi: Game and Power in Afghanistan* (University of Pennsylvania Press, 1982); Sharifah Enayat Ali, *Afghanistan* (Marshall Cavendish, 1995); Khaled Hosseni, *The Kite Runner* (Riverhead Books, 2003); Halima Kazem, *Afghanistan* (Times Editions, 2003); Lucie Street, *The Tent Pegs of Heaven* (Robert Hale, 1967); Anthony Tucker-Jones, "Afghanistan 1979–89," *Miniature Wargames* (v.239, April 2003); Nico J. van Oudenhoven, *Common Afghan Street Games* (Swets & Zeitlinger, 1979); Declan Walsh, "Skateistan Gives Kabul's Kids Reason to go Overboard," *The Sunday Age*, Melbourne, Australia (June 29, 2008).

Justin Corfield
Geelong Grammar School

Africa, Traditional Play in

In 1974, the Association for the Anthropological Study of Play began. In 1977, they published a book of articles: *The Study of Play: Problems and Prospects*, with David F. Lancey and B. Allan Tindall acting as editors. It contains an article by Helen B. Schwartzman and Linda Barbera, which presents an overview of what scholars, and particularly anthropologists, wrote about traditional play among children in Africa. They stated that anthropologists of Africa wrote about play in four ways: play as imitation or preparation for adult life, play as a game or sports activity, play as projection or expressive activity, and play as unimportant or as a miscellaneous pastime.

It is said that these models are western models of play, not African ones. In the same book, two articles dealt with play, one describing religion as play, the other referring to playing and an African kingdom. Both examples are of the Hausa of Nigeria. The first shows how a "witchdoctor" uses "frivolity" to make "serious" points, acting as a trickster figure. The witchdoctor also refers to the spirits he talks to as being more playful than Allah, whom he does not address.

The other follows the "play as imitation model" in some ways, since playing at being a king helps prepare people for adult social roles, but it also says that rivalry is an element of play. Since the publication of this book, there has been an increase in the study of play in Africa. Three of the most important theorists in anthropology who also have written about Africa have made significant contributions to the anthropology of play: Victor Turner, James Fernandez, and Pierre Bourdieu.

Victor Turner

Turner helped develop symbolic anthropology and the dramaturgical approach in anthropology. In *The Ritual Process*, Turner talks about how people resolve conflicts in society in many ways, including play, in order to both express and eliminate conflict. He illustrates this with the Ndembu, the people of central Africa he lived among when he conducted field research. From his Ndembu research, he developed the notions of liminality and communitas. He writes about how in the Ndembu rite of installation of the highest Ndembu chief, the chief is in a "betwixt and between state," out of ordinary time and space.

The chief is leaving his former status but has not yet moved into his new status. During this liminal period, commoners are revealed to have authority over the highest chief, and the highest chief is portrayed as a slave. The chief and his wife are dressed in ragged waistcoats. Turner says features like sexlessness, anonymity, submissiveness, silence, and sexual continence characterize liminality, both among the Ndembu and worldwide. He calls liminality the cultural manifestation of communitas, where people feel intensely intimate and experience equality with each other, creating an intense social bonding. He says we can see these elements among other African people: the Tallensi, the Nuer, and the Ashanti. He continues this approach in many works that also talk about his dramaturgical approach.

Using the dramaturgical approach, he writes about social drama among the Ndembu and others that he says plays a part in both ordinary life and large-scale events of life. He says that analyzing the stages of breach, crisis, redress, and reintegration allows one to understand Ndembu social organization and values. For Turner, examining drama allows him to understand traditional society.

James Fernandez

Fernandez has written a lot about the "play of tropes." Fernandez did research in West Africa between 1958 and 1961, focusing on a minority religion among the Fang called Bwiti. His description of Bwiti focuses on metaphors and tropes. The Fang live in northern Gabon and the Spanish African territory of Rio Muni. Fernandez states that about 10 percent of the Fang belong to Bwiti. He refers to tropes as an assertion people make about themselves or others. He calls tropes bridges between metaphor and action. He writes about this in his analysis of Bwiti, a Fang revitalization movement that developed after World War I.

Fernandez calls Bwiti traditional play because this revitalization movement developed as a reaction to French colonialism and Protestant missionaries to protect and revitalize old ways. He says Bwiti meets many local and individual needs and cannot be said to have one solitary purpose or explanation. Bwiti has an all-night ceremony with two phases. In the first phase, from 6 P.M. to midnight, the dancing people do concerns creation and life. In the second phase, after midnight, the dancing they do concerns death and destruction and a reunion with the ancestral spirits.

This allows the cult members to become of one heart. Fernandez says people engage in these playful activities to persuade people to come to a feeling of being one heart. He writes that while the purpose of the ritual is clear, people interpret the various symbols used in the ritual differently. He says that the members of Bwiti make little effort to unite people in their meanings, since the members of Bwiti feel that social cohesion is more important than cultural agreement. For Fernandez play brings about cultural cohesion.

Pierre Bourdieu

Pierre Bourdieu took a different approach to play when he wrote about the Kabyles people of Algeria in North Africa, a people he calls traditional because most of them cannot write. Bourdieu looks at human relationships in terms of games and developed the notion of strategies to help him understand how people were acting. A key concept in this approach is habitus, which has the play characteristic of being "regulated improvisations." Jim Wolfreys writes this about this strategies approach: "Individuals are ... as free and as limited as when they engage in any kind of game ... Although the player does what the game demands of him, this does not mean that individuals are slaves to rules, since these can be manipulated to the player's advantage, bent and subverted to suit his needs. The player's freedom to invent and to improvise allows for the production of an infinite number of moves made possible by the game, and is subject to the same limits as the game." Bourdieu says people try to use the game for their own advantage. Bourdieu also developed the concept of field.

A field is a form of social organization where human action takes place. Bourdieu conceives of a field as an arena where agents both distinguish themselves from each other and try to gain different types of capital. Bourdieu compares a field to a game. He sees it as a language game where someone strives for something within the limits of rules—it is the assumptions of the game, and the stakes that can be won or lost in the game. Bourdieu describes the Kabyles in relation to his theoretical approach, which focuses on the use of proverbs among them. Bourdieu says that Kabyles describe themselves according to the rules of their society. However, he says they also have a "practical knowledge," which characterizes habitus. He says that you can uncover practices by looking at proverbs and other types of oral lore among them. For Bourdieu, looking at proverbs allows him to understand habitas.

See Also: Algeria; Congo; Ethiopia; Ghana; Kenya; Liberia; Nigeria; Play and Evolution; Play as Learning, Anthropology of; Play Fighting; South Africa; Sudan; Tanzania.

Bibliography. Pierre Bourdieu, *Outline of a Theory of Practice* (Cambridge University Press, 1977); James Fernandez, "Symbolic Consensus in a Fang Reformation Cult," *American Anthropologist* (August, 1965); David F. Lancey and Tindall B. Allan, eds., *The Study of Play: Problems and Prospects* (Leisure Press, 1977); Victor Turner, *The Ritual Process* (Aldine, 1969); Jim Wolfreys, "In Perspective: Pierre Bourdieu," *International Socialism Journal* (Summer, 2000).

Bruce Josephson
Baekseok Cultural College

Age of Empires

Age of Empires is a real-time strategy (RTS) computer game set in a real-world historical context. This historical content can be used for pedagogical purposes in the classroom. However, some critics have stated that its pedagogical benefits are inefficient given that the game is built for entertainment purposes and is focused on war.

In Age of Empires, players gather resources, construct buildings, and produce fighting units that will be used strategically to destroy other players in the game. Each player's buildings and units are determined by which culture or civilization they choose to represent. Every game in the Age of Empires series focuses on a different era of human history, and the civilizations that players may choose reflect those time periods. The first Age of Empires time period included civilizations from the stone to the iron age (e.g., Egyptian, Greek). The second Age of Empire title, The Age of Kings, was set in the middle ages (e.g., Celts, Vikings). Finally, the third installment, Age of Empires 3, takes places from the 14th to the 18th centuries (e.g., British, Spanish). While these are the three main titles in the series, many other expansions and spin-off games have been produced covering historical content such as the Roman Empire and Native American societies.

The Age of Empires series may not adhere to the history books exactly, but the designers have drawn upon historical facts when producing the series (which has increased as the series has continued). This means that although each Age of Empires game is for entertainment purposes, players can learn about history through playing the game. James Gee comments on this phenomenon by saying "designers face and largely solve an intriguing educational dilemma, one also faced by schools and workplaces: how to get people, often young people, to learn and master something that is long and challenging and enjoy it, to boot."

For instance, studies have shown that novice RTS players will use visual cues of the game's buildings and units to learn how to play the game. Since Age of Empires is set in a historical context, this means new players can draw upon their knowledge of history in order to appropriately function within the game. This has a cascading effect, because once a player applies their current historical knowledge to the game's context, they will then begin to learn other historical facts, in connection with their previous knowledge, that were not known to them prior to their experience with the game.

Besides being utilized for its historical content, Age of Empires can also be used for other pedagogical purposes. For one thing, players learn a number of skills from playing RTS games. This includes learning to problem solve, plan strategies, and think abstractly about how to achieve goals. Beyond this, players also learn to cooperate by teaming up with other players or learning to be competitive when facing opposition. Yet, some critics have stated that these skills being taught are linked to an environment surrounded by war and conflict. Since the game does not show the proper consequences of war, it has a negative social framing and imparts a moral impurity on any teachings the game provides to players. However, others have stated that Age of Empires, as well as other games, should not be the sole tool used for teaching pupils in a classroom. Instead, games such as Age of Empires allow teachers to get students engaged in a topic that can then be discussed in a greater scope, filling in any areas that the game was not built to address or where the game is not as accurate.

See Also: Cooperative Play; Play as Mock War, Psychology of; Play as Mock War, Sociology of; Play in the Classroom.

Bibliography. James Gee, *What Video Games Have to Teach Us About Learning and Literacy* (Palgrave Macmillan, 2003); John Graham, et al., "A Cognitive Approach to Game Usability and Design: Mental Model Development in Novice Real-Time Strategy Gamers," *CyberPsychology & Behavior* (v.9/3, June 2006); David Shaffer, *How Computer Games Help Children Learn* (Palgrave Macmillan, 2006).

Ben Medler
Georgia Institute of Technology

Airfix

Airfix is the United Kingdom's longest established manufacturer of scale plastic model kits. The hobby of building plastic models developed after World War II, with Airfix releasing many different kits. The range has included aircraft, ships, cars, and products licensed from film and television series. The models have been

1957 Airfix models included the Model T Ford and a scale model of the Tiger Moth II, *a British Air Ministry basic trainer.*

largely aimed at children but have also proved to be popular among adults.

Airfix was founded in 1939 by Nicholas Kove, a Hungarian refugee, who originally manufactured inflatable rubber toys. Kove chose the name "Airfix" partly because the manufacturing process involved fixing air into the products and partly because he wanted the company to appear at the beginning of toy catalogues. In 1947 Airfix switched to producing plastic combs and was the first manufacturer to introduce an injection moulding machine. In 1949 the company was commissioned by Harry Ferguson, a tractor manufacturer, to produce a cheap model of one of his vehicles for use as a promotional tool by his sales representatives. Initially, the model was molded in cellulose acetate plastic and was hand assembled for the Ferguson sales team. To increase sales and lower productions costs, however, the model was also sold in kit form by F.W. Woolworth's retail stores.

In 1952, a Woolworth's buyer suggested that Airfix should produce a model kit of Sir Francis Drake's ship, *The Golden Hind*. The kit was made in polystyrene, a more stable plastic, and to meet Woolworth's suggested retail price of two shillings, the packaging was changed from a cardboard box to a plastic bag with a paper header which also included the kit's instructions. The model ship was a huge success and prompted Woolworth's to request additional kits.

Released in 1955, the first Airfix model aircraft kit was a 1/72 scale version of the *Spitfire*. During the 1960s and 1970s, the company's range grew to include a wide variety of cars, motorcycles, historical figures, trains, military vehicles, classic ships, and spaceships, as well as a huge number of aircraft. The 1/72 scale was generally used for the aircraft and smaller kits, with the 1/144 scale used for bigger rockets and airliners. During the 1970s, Airfix introduced larger scale kits, including 1/24 scale models of aircraft such as the *Spitfire*. Airfix kits were categorized into series from 1 to 20, depending on their size and complexity, and were priced accordingly. Airfix also launched a monthly modeling magazine, *Airfix Magazine*, which appeared from 1960 to 1993. After acquiring the toy companies Meccano and Dinky in 1971, Airfix also produced a wide range of toys and craft products.

The 1980s saw a big decline in the popularity of plastic kit modeling. This was because of increasing competition from computer games and diecast metal models. Rising oil prices also increased the cost of plastic, while decreasing birth rates brought a market decline. Slumping sales forced Airfix to declare bankruptcy in 1981. The firm was subsequently bought by the company General Mills (owner of the American kit maker MPC), and the Airfix kit molds were shipped to a factory in France.

In 1986 Airfix was sold to the Hobby Products Group of Borden, Inc., the owner of model brands such as Heller and Humbrol. The Hobby Products Group was sold to an Irish investment company, Allen McGuire, in 1994 and continued under the Humbrol name. In 2006, however, Humbrol, Ltd., went into administration. The Airfix and Humbrol brands were bought by Hornby Hobbies, Ltd., and both were relaunched in 2007. Airfix remains synonymous with the hobby of building plastic model kits, and in Britain a model is often termed simply "an Airfix kit"—even if made by another manufacturer.

See Also: Boys' Play; Hobbies; Meccano; Models; Revell.

Bibliography. Arthur Ward, *Airfix: Celebrating 50 Years of the Greatest Modeling Kits Ever Made* (Collins, 1999); Arthur Ward, *The Boys' Book of Airfix* (Ebury Press, 2009); Arthur Ward, *Classic Kits: Collecting the Greatest Kits in the World from Airfix to Tamiya* (Collins, 2004).

Bill Osgerby
London Metropolitan University

Albania

One of the poorest countries in Europe, Albania is located in the Balkans, sharing borders with Greece, Macedonia (Former Yugoslav Republic of Macedonia), Montenegro, and Serbia. It gained its independence from the Ottoman Empire in 1913, and until the Communists took control in 1944, Albania was the only majority Muslim country in Europe. With many of its people living in desperate poverty, most of the games in the country, especially in villages, involved crudely fashioned dolls for girls, while boys practiced hunting with slingshots. Teenagers and men were involved in wrestling and also archery.

Albania had been a part of the Roman Empire, and Cicero held estates there. It was said to have been a source for wild animals killed for entertainment either locally or in Rome itself. In Medieval times, while the hinterland was a part of the Byzantine Empire, some of the coastal parts of the country came under the control of Venice. This led to a continued Italian influence in Albania that would continue up to the present day—Italy annexed Albania in 1939 and only gave it up when the Communists took Tirana, the country's capital, five years later.

This has meant that Italian games, such as Bocce, are common among the older generation. Soccer was first played in the country in Shkodra in 1913 and has been popular since the 1920s, and there are few villages that do not have their own improvised (or actual) soccer fields. Soccer in Albania is now coordinated by the Albania Football Association. During the 1960s, Albania had a close alliance with China, and this led to an interest in Ping-Pong throughout the country. Chess has also continued to be popular, with Aldo Zadrima (b. 1948) being the country's Chess champion, and it is coordinated by the Federata Shqiptare e Shahut. The Young Pioneers youth groups during the Communist period involved many boys and girls in camping expeditions and hiking in rural and remote parts of the country.

Since the end of Communist rule, many Albanian exiles have returned to the country, and although much of Albania remains poor, many of the cities such as Tirana, Durrës, and Shkodra have sufficiently large middle classes to generate interest in wargaming, particularly the Romans, and during the Byzantine period, the Crusades, and also World War II. The making of wargame dioramas is also becoming more common, as is the fashioning of model boats and aircraft. In Tirana there are amusement arcades, places for playing computer games, and bowling alleys, with boys involved in skateboarding and roller blading. Hiking and rambling have also recently gained many new local adherents as well as being popular with tourists visiting the country.

See Also: Boys' Play; Europe, 1200 to 1600; Play Fighting; Wargames.

Bibliography. Glenn Kirchner, *Children's Games Around the World* (Benjamin Cummings, 2000); Nina Millen, *Children's Games from Many Lands* (Friendship Press, 1943); Norman Rimmell, "Walking in Albania," *Albanian Life* (v.53, 1992); Serge van Hoof, *Football in Albania* (privately published, 1988); Jim Walkeley, "World War One in the Adriatic," *Miniature Wargames* (October, 1984).

Justin Corfield
Geelong Grammar School

Algeria

Located in North Africa, Algeria was a part of the Ottoman Empire until 1830, when the French took Algiers, and gradually occupied the rest of the country, with many migrants from France, Italy, Spain, and Germany settling in northern Algeria, which became a part of France. In 1954 war broke out, as Algerian nationalists wanted independence, and France finally granted independence in 1962. Oil revenue made the country prosperous, but in January 1992 the military took control to prevent Islamic fundamentalists from winning the elections, and there was mass violence, which continued until about 2003.

The Ottoman influence on the country has resulted in the playing of the Turkish form of Backgammon, called *Tavla*, and also Dominoes and cards in coffee shops in the cities and towns around the country. Under the French, many new sports were introduced such as boules and later soccer, with the writer Albert Camus playing in some teams as a young man. Indeed soccer rapidly became the most popular recreational sport in the country, with boys and young men playing it in school groups, in local community and social clubs, and in an ad hoc fashion against others in courtyards and patches of flat ground in every city and most towns. For the poor, universal games such as Hide-and-Seek and Hopscotch remained popular. The rebirth of conservative Islamic ideas from the late 1980s led to many changes including sermons against the playing of cards, as it would encourage gambling, and against puppetry.

The fighting in the country from 1992 led to many people staying at home, worried about the killings, and this in itself led to a revival of many indoor pursuits, such as Chess, and playing card games. Prior to that, and indeed after the end of the fighting, attending bodybuilding shows and wrestling were popular forms of entertainment; and Algerian Olympic athletes did much to encourage jogging for the young—although many conservative Muslims disliked the idea of women participating. Fencing started to attract many young people especially, after Waqssilia Redouane Said-Guerni participated at both the 2000 and the 2004 Olympics, as did tennis from 2004, when Lamine Ouahab made it into the Barcelona Olympics. For younger children, the Libyan version of Hopscotch, known as *Negeza*, is often played at primary schools.

Although some well-to-do Algerians have been involved in Wargaming, this has generally proven more popular with French Algerians and French from Algeria, who have recreated many of the battles from the 1830s, the rise of the French Foreign Legion, and also the war of independence from 1954 until 1962. Many of the rules for fighting Wargames on the French Foreign Legion, and indeed most of the makers of figurines connected with them, are from Britain or the United States, where people have long been fascinated by the conflict through the film *Beau Geste*. For Americans, the Barbary War of 1815 has also led to the making of several games, but these generally have not proven popular in Algeria itself.

See Also: Africa, Traditional Play in; Backgammon; Dominoes and Variations of; Soccer (Amateur) Worldwide; Wargames.

Bibliography. Edgar Barclay, *Mountain Life in Algeria* (Kessinger Publishing, 2007); François Maspero, *Les Enfants d'Algérie* [Children of Algeria] (Imprimerie Clerc, 1962); Jeff Taylor, "The U.S. Navy & The Corsairs," *Miniature Wargames* (no.222, 2001).

Justin Corfield
Geelong Grammar School

All Fives

All Fives can refer to both a card game played with a standard deck and a Dominoes game played with a double six set.

Card Game

The card game is part of the All Fours family, descended from the English card game All Fours and played in most former English colonies, especially the West Indies. It is the legacy of All Fours that gives us the name "Jack" for the card previously known as the Knave, and other members of the family include Auction Pitch, California Jack, and Cinch. Spoil Five is a close relation, with similarly unusual rules.

The name All Fours comes from the scoring system, which awards points in four categories: the highest trump in play, the lowest trump in play, the Jack (given to the player who takes the Jack in a trump), and the Game (given to the player who takes the highest value of tricks). An amalgam of point-trick games and shorthand games like Euchre, All Fours dates from about the middle of the 17th century, and may have been adapted by the English from a Dutch game. Typically a low-class gambling game for most of its history, it was introduced to the United States in the 18th century and became the most popular card game by the 1800s.

It was in the United States that All Fives was introduced, in the middle of the 19th century, when variants of All Fours developed in order to compete with Poker, which was beginning its steady rise in popularity. All Fives is fundamentally the same as All Fours—its direct descendant, not an odd cousin like some of the other variants—but with a fifth category of points, for the player who takes the five in a trump. The trump five in All Fives is usually called the Pedro, and variants of All Fives soon developed in California—the Pedro Sancho, where the trump nine took points, the Double Pedro or High Five, in which both the trump five and the five of the opposite color take points (borrowed from Euchre), and Dom Pedro, in which the Joker (the Dom) counts 15 and takes points.

Dominoes Game

The All Fives Dominoes game is part of the Fives Family. The games in the Fives Family all base scoring on the total of the exposed ends of the tableau in multiples of five; in other words, if the pips total 15, the player gets three points. The Fives Family is widespread and old, and so a great many variations exist that are difficult to properly catalogue—Dominoes are such a community-based game that it is not uncommon to find variant rules that have been played for decades or generations, but only in one town. The basic areas of variation are in the number of tiles drawn per player's hand (and, accordingly, whether or not the game has a boneyard), the number of spinners, and the scoring of spinners.

Five Up—using all doubles as spinners—is the Fives Family variant most common in Spanish-speaking parts of the world. In Europe, Sniff is more common, which uses the first double as a spinner. All Fives is used to refer to two different members of the Fives Family, the first of which is also known as Muggins. Muggins is a fast-paced two-player game with no spinner that is popular in Europe. The other All Fives uses a single spinner, and up to four players. Another variant is All Fives and Threes, which changes one aspect of the Fives Family rules, giving players a score for every multiple of five and every multiple of three, a variant useful when using sets larger than the standard double six is All Odd Primes, which is just what it sounds like—points accrued for every multiple of odd prime numbers (3, 5, 7, 13, 17, etc.).

See Also: Auction Pitch; Dominoes and Variations of; History of Playing Cards; Spoil Five.

Bibliography. Elliott Avedon, *The Study of Games* (Krieger Pub., 1979); Roger Caillois, *Man, Play, and Games* (University of Illinois Press, 2001); Johan Huizinga, *Homo Ludens* (Beacon Press, 1971); David Parlett, *The Oxford Guide to Card Games* (Oxford University Press, USA, 1990); Brian Sutton-Smith, *The Ambiguity of Play* (Harvard University Press, 2001).

Bill Kte'pi
Independent Scholar

Amiga

Amiga is the name for a family of computers originally developed as a video games machine but launched as a general-purpose personal computer for the home market by Commodore International in 1985. The name *Amiga* was chosen both because of its meaning in Spanish and Portuguese and because it preceded Atari and

Apple alphabetically. Like its main competitors, the Atari ST and Apple Mac, the Amiga was built around the Motorola 68000 processor chip, which, although incorporating 32-bit architecture, featured a 16-bit external bus. The generation of computers therefore became generally known as 16-bit machines. The Amiga incorporated a custom chipset with advanced audio and graphical capabilities and an operating system featuring a graphical user interface (GUI), and was capable of pre-emptive multitasking, allowing two or more programs to run simultaneously. It was the first computer targeted at the home market to support multi-tasking. Production of the Amiga ceased in 1994 when Commodore International went bankrupt.

The development of the Amiga is entangled with that of its main rival the Atari ST. The Amiga was originally designed in the early 1980s by the Amiga Corporation, a small company that had received development funding from Atari Inc. in return for some rights over the design. In 1984 Atari was acquired by Jack Tramiel, the founder of Commodore International, who had departed from Commodore in the same year after a dispute with its chairman. At about the same time, Commodore entered into negotiations to buy the Amiga Corporation outright. Commodore settled (in its own terms) the outstanding contract with Atari by reimbursing the $500,000 funding provided to the Amiga Corporation. However, Atari Corporation subsequently sued Commodore International, delaying the release of the Amiga by long enough to allow it to develop and release a direct competitor, the Atari ST. The ST was released to market in 1985 several months ahead of the Amiga and the two machines became the subject of an ongoing rivalry. The case was eventually settled in 1987 with an undisclosed out-of-court settlement, with both parties claiming victory.

The Amiga represented a considerable advance in performance and power over the previous generation of home computers, and this led to its adoption as a gaming platform. However, although generally considered more powerful than the Atari ST, their similar architecture meant that most games were produced simultaneously for the two machines. Notable games released for the Amiga during the late 1980s and early 1990s include Dungeon Master, an early fully immersive first-person perspective fantasy adventure game; Sid Meier's Civilization, a turn-based strategy/simulation game; Lemmings, a real-time puzzle game in which the player leads groups of lemming across innumerable obstacles to safety; Stunt Car Racer, a three-dimensional driving simulator; and Populous, an isometric strategy/simulation "God" game. The release of AMOS Basic in 1990, a high-level programming language geared toward game development, allowed hobbyist computer users to easily create their own games, distributed through bulletin boards and public domain software libraries.

Although architecturally similar, the Amiga, Apple Mac, and Atari ST carved out very different niches in the productivity sector. Apple's computer became synonymous with design and desktop publishing. The ST was widely adopted within the music recording industry, largely because of its inbuilt MIDI ports. The Amiga became widely used within the film and television industries not only because of its advanced graphical capabilities but also because of its ability to genlock—adapt its own screen output timing to that of a television signal. Notable uses of the Amiga within television production include the series *Max Headroom*, ITV's *The Chart Show*, and early episodes of the science fiction series *Babylon 5*.

See Also: Civilization (I, II, III, IV); Coleco; Hobbies.

Bibliography. Brian Bagnall, *On the Edge: The Spectacular Rise and Fall of Commodore* (Variant Press, 2006); Winnie Forster, *The Encyclopedia of Game Machines: Consoles, Handhelds and Home Computers 1972–2005* (Gameplan, 2007); Gareth Knight, *The Amiga History Guide*, www.amigahistory.co.uk (cited July 2008).

Luke Tredinnick
London Metropolitan University

Amusement Parks

Amusement parks are a place where entertainment and fun are offered to visitors in a variety of forms: shows, prepared activities, places to shop and eat, games of various types, and rides. Amusement parks, whatever their differences—and there are many—do have several elements in common. First, they are consciously designed and constructed to provide a concentrated experience and have the stated objective of providing enjoyment. There is nothing incidental about people visiting to have a good time; that is the stated purpose of the amusement park. How parks do that in their various forms, now and in the past, provides an interesting picture of what people in different time periods and locations have thought of as fun and what has constituted play. Second, and most important to the majority of visitors, amusement parks have rides. These rides can vary from a fairly sedate small auto traveling in a circle or a carousel to thrill rides such as roller coasters. Third, even though there are cultural differences, amusement parks in the United States, Europe, Middle East, and Asia are remarkably similar in that they all have rides, games, and food; often have themes; and are dedicated to fun and play. Fourth, they are a place for children, adolescents, and young adults. Everything is aimed at fulfilling the desires of that demographic group. Generally, an adult going to an amusement park is usually accompanying younger family members.

Amusement parks are generally permanent establishments, although the term can be stretched to include the amusement section that can be found at state, country, or regional fairs. Not only are amusement parks usually permanent, but they are carefully designed to channel traffic, leading visitors to one high point after another. There is often a theme, whether it based on a general concept (such as Europe or Africa at Busch Gardens), on a form of entertainment (such as the Universal and other film theme parks), or on a particular identity (such as Disney and all its characters or the Warner Brothers cartoon characters at Six Flags).

The Earliest Amusement Parks

Our idea of what makes an amusement park is informed largely by current amusement parks, with their large collections of rides, state-of-the-art electronics and mechanical engineering, and often nonstop entertainment found throughout the park. Amusement parks have not always been like that, however, and have undergone a dramatic change, especially since the 1890s. Further, although it may surprise many Americans, amusement parks are not an American invention but are originally from Europe.

The world's first amusement park appeared in Denmark in 1583 and still exists. Known as Bakken, it has, of course undergone substantial changes over the past centuries. Bakken has evolved from something like a medieval fairground into a modern amusement park. Today it is visited by over 3 million people in its yearly March through August season. While it has new rides and other changes each year, there are still some elements of continuity. The organization that manages the park has existed since the mid-1880s and combines an old-style management of small operations with modern machinery. Bakken is home to a clown representing the 18th-century character, Pierrot, and while many of the rides are new, Bakken has retained its 1932 roller coaster, which is one of the oldest in Europe.

Amusement parks did not spread through Europe until the 18th century, with the opening of parks in Vienna, Austria, and in Britain. This progression then came to a halt until the middle of the 19th century, when parks in Britain, Denmark (the famous Tivoli), and elsewhere also came into existence.

The Growth of Amusement Parks

The real boom in amusement parks would not occur until the last quarter of the 19th century. A major impetus for the appearance of amusement parks was that with the development of the industrial revolution, there was some increase in disposable income for families to spend on amusements. Transportation networks, such as railroads, began to develop, allowing people to travel to where a park might open. The relative ease of movement encouraged Sunday trips to amusement parks.

Another factor encouraging the appearance of amusement parks was the appearance of international expositions and world's fairs. In addition to their mission of "improvement" and education, these fairs provided opportunities for visitors to eat and be entertained. As the century progressed, the fairs, which brought together large crowds of people also grew more frequent and increasingly became more sophisticated in their amusements. By the time of the Chicago Exposition of 1893 (World's Columbian Exposition), visitors could see the wonders of industry, or go to another part of the fair and see "Little Egypt" dance, or take a ride on the world's first Ferris wheel. At the Saint Louis Exposition of 1904, visitors could not only take rides but also visit replicas of Pacific, Asian, and North African villages with real natives or eat what some claim were the world's first hot dogs. As each year progressed, the range of amusements increased. Unlike today's amusement parks, fun was not the objective, but its various venues provided many of the basics we see in amusement parks today: shows and other entertainment, rides, and food.

Inspired by the success of the amusement venues of the fairs and expositions, amusement parks began to appear in cities in both America and Europe. In many locations, amusement parks with some rides and other entertainment were opened by trolley companies. The idea was that trolley companies had little business on the weekends. By starting amusement parks, the trolley companies would then also provide the transportation for visitors. The concept worked very well and trolley parks opened throughout the country, particularly in the northeastern United States. One of these was Whalom Park, which was opened in Lunenburg, Massachusetts, in 1893 by the Fitchburg and Leominster Street Railway Company. The park was a success and remained open until 2000.

A little to the south, another trolley park named White City opened near Worcester, Massachusetts, with local trolleys carrying visitors to and from the park. That particular amusement park opened in 1905 and stayed in existence until 1960. The name "White City" had first been used for the Chicago Exposition of 1893 and became a fairly common name for amusement parks by the end of the 19th century in places such as Atlanta; Cleveland, Ohio; New Orleans; and New Haven, Connecticut. "White City" came from the large number of electric lights at the parks. In a time where electricity was a novelty, the use of lighting added what was a festive tone to a place dedicated to amusement and fun. A trolley park in western Pennsylvania known as Kennywood opened in 1898, and would later develop into a major entertainment corporation with international affiliations.

In the following years there were many other amusement parks that came into existence. Euclid Beach Park operated near Cleveland, Ohio, from 1895 to 1969. Riverview Park in Chicago, best known, perhaps, for the Bobs roller coaster, ran from 1904 to 1967. Another was New Jersey's Palisades Amusement Park (often advertised in issues of *Superman Comics* in the 1950s), which operated from 1898 to 1971.

Similar parks also began to appear throughout Europe and Asia, and those that existed began to expand. Vienna's Prater amusement park, which had been in existence since the 18th century, became the first amusement park in Europe to have a Ferris wheel.

Coney Island, perhaps the most famous collection of amusement parks in America before World War II, began its operations in the second half of the 19th century. By the 1860s, visitors were coming to this location on Long Island (where some claim that the hot dog was first sold in 1867, predating the Saint Louis item). Here several amusement parks operated side by side through the years. The first of these was the Sea Lion Park, which opened in 1895, to be followed that same year by Steeplechase Park. In the next decade other amusement parks would open, such as Luna Park and Dreamland. By 1920, Coney Island would boast a Ferris wheel, and in the same year a subway line ran from Manhattan to Coney Island. In 1927, a major roller coaster, the Cyclone, would open. Coney Island's time as a center for amusement parks would slow by the time of World War II.

Amusement parks themselves did not all go the way of the parks at Coney Island with the end of World War II. In 1945, new amusement parks were beginning to open. With the increased availability of the automobile, theme parks, often with a Christmas or other theme, opened, principally in the northeast. These parks, whether they were known as "North Pole," "Santa's Village," "Frontier Town," "Six-Gun City," or "Storyland," were family destinations. They had rides that would seem tame compared with later parks, some games, and food, and were very popular. These were small-scale operations, often family owned and operated, and from the end of World War II until the mid-1950s, they were a common form of amusement park.

Modern Amusement Parks

In the mid-1950s, however, there appeared an amusement park that not only would become popular in its own right but would influence the expectations of visitors and the design and appearance of amusement parks throughout the world. In 1955 Walt Disney opened Disneyland. Disney's amusement park marked a radical departure and eventually served as a model for amusement parks in the future. It was not a family or small-scale business but was the project of a corporate entity with substantial financial assistance from the American Broadcasting Corporation (ABC), another corporate entity. It was a large park that was based on themes such as Frontierland, Fantasyland, or Adventureland. In each instance, rides and other attractions were combined into a specially created environment. From the beginning, Disneyland was a success, with new features such as a recreation of the Matterhorn and a monorail being introduced before the 1950s were over.

In the 1960s, the larger theme parks became more prominent as many of the smaller operations either made changes and expanded, or went out of business altogether. In the early 1960s, Six Flags Over Texas opened, beginning a franchise of 21 amusement parks that would establish a presence throughout North America.

Just as Disney had begun amusement parks based on films and television, the entertainment business, specifically film studios, would begin to develop their own amusement parks with tie-ins to their films. The Universal Studios theme park evolved from back lot tours for tourists in Hollywood to entertainment complexes there and in Orlando, Florida. The Orlando complex began as a movie-inspired theme park with rides based on popular films. Since that time, it has expanded with hotels, restaurants, and the Universal Islands of Adventure. The Islands of Adventure is another theme park, based on the premise of different islands, each with their own theme. Even though the park is very sophisticated technically, it still employs some of the basic concepts first developed by Disney. Not only is there the idea of themed rides and other amusements, but just as Snow White and other characters greeted Disneyland visitors in the 1950s, tourists at the Universal Studios complex can see and spend time with Spiderman or the Cat in the Hat.

A typical modern roller coaster. Today, they are designed on a computer and built out of steel instead of wood.

Amusement Parks Worldwide

Theme parks are also common throughout Europe and in many ways, with their advanced technology behind a great deal of the entertainment, are similar to American parks. They are, however, related to European culture. Asterix Park in France is based on the French cartoon character Asterix. Disneyland Paris (formerly known as Euro Disney) opened in 1992 and hastily made concessions to European expectations; it has since become very successful. In Germany, there has been a fascination with the American West and Native Americans, and that motif shows up in several theme parks either as the main theme or as a theme area within a larger park. LEGOLAND, based on the LEGO toys, first opened in 1968 in Denmark and has expanded into Germany, the United States, and the United Kingdom. There are plans to open a LEGOLAND in Dubai. The LEGOLAND parks are targeted toward younger children, with themes based on LEGO toys and rides that are generally less extreme than those found at other parks.

Amusement parks are prominent in Asia. There are two Asian Disneylands, one in Hong Kong and one in Tokyo. Japan also has a Universal Studios theme park, and Korea has several amusement parks located near the capital, Seoul. Australia has a Sea World, a Warner Brothers Movie theme park, and Dreamland, which claims to have some of the fastest thrill rides in the world.

In the Middel East, the most prominent center for amusement parks is Dubai, where a collection of theme parks known as Dubailand is constantly undergoing expansion. Universal Studios, Six Flags, Dreamworks, and other franchises have all announced plans to develop new parks there.

See Also: Arcades; Play as Catharsis; Play as Entertainment, Psychology of; Play as Entertainment, Sociology of; Roller Coasters.

Bibliography. Judith A. Adams, *The American Amusement Park Industry: A History of Technology and Thrills* (Twayne Publishers, 1991); Salvador Anton Clavé, *The Global Theme Park Industry* (CABI, 2007); Michael DeAngelis, "Roller

Coasters, Theme Parks, and Postmodernism," *Cultural Critique* (no.37, Autumn, 1997); Carl Hiaasen, *Team Rodent: How Disney Devours the World* (Ballantine Publishing Group, 1998); Institute for Theme Park Studies, www.themeparkcity.com/itps/index.htm (cited November 2008); John F. Kasson, *Amusing the Million: Coney Island at the Turn of the Century* (Hill & Wang, 1978); Andrew Lainsbury, *Once Upon an American Dream: The Story of Euro Disneyland* (University of Kansas Press, 2001); Scott A. Lukas, ed., *The Themed Space: Locating Culture, Nation, and Self* (Lexington Books, 2007); Edo McCullough, *World's Fair Midways; An Affectionate Account of American Amusement Areas from the Crystal Palace to the Crystal Ball* (Exposition Press, 1966); Alexander Moore, "Walt Disney World: Bounded Ritual Space and the Playful Pilgrimage," *Anthropological Quarterly* (v.53, 1980); Tim O'Brien, *The Amusement Park Guide: Coast to Coast Thrills* (Globe Pequot Press, 2001); Woody Register, *The Kid of Coney Island: Fred Thompson and the Rise of American Amusements* (Oxford University Press, 2001).

Robert Stacy
Independent Scholar

Ancient China

Because of the survival of so many written records from ancient China, much is known about the daily life of the people, supplementing the discoveries of archaeologists. Throughout most of the dynasties of ancient China—the Shang dynasty from 1166 until 1122 B.C.E.; the Zhou (Chou) dynasty from 1122 to 255 B.C.E.; the Qin (Chin) dynasty from 255 to 206 B.C.E.; the Han dynasty from 206 B.C.E. until 220 C.E., the period of the Warring States; the Jin (Tsin) dynasty from 265 to 420; the Sui dynasty from 581 until 618, and the Tang dynasty from 618 to 907—the life of the vast majority of the people in China, the peasantry, did not change markedly.

As a result, many of the games they played were also similar to those of their ancestors. Children played Hide-and-Seek, used spinning tops and marbles, played with hoops, and were involved in running and skipping. Other children and also adults would play with darts or in ball games. Kite flying was also popular, as were embroidery, spinning, weaving, making brocade and tapestry, basket weaving, and making hats—all pastimes for girls—and making pots, porcelain, toy soldiers, and woodcuts, as well as bronze work and leather work, for boys and young men. Both boys and girls were also involved in making toys from corn stalks and in fashioning scarecrows and the like.

Adults, in what little time many of the peasants had for relaxation, were involved in playing simple musical instruments such as flutes. Storytellers and theatrical groups would also visit villages, and in some of their performances, some locals would participate as well as watch. Many villagers kept pets, and children played with cats and dogs and also with birds. In the cities, it was popular to keep caged songbirds, and these were often taken around to local parks for them to interact with other birds, which still happens today. One particularly Chinese pet was the cricket, and even relatively poor people would keep a pet cricket, carving elaborate cages to protect them and prevent them from flying away. Tribal people from northern and western China, such as the Hsiung-nu, the Mongols, and the Uighurs, were involved in training birds of prey for falconry. Because of their heavy use of horses, many people were occupied with the making of elaborate bridles, and for the Chinese, stirrups.

Arts and Entertainment

Music was very much a part of Chinese culture, and this varied from simple bamboo flutes, to more advanced pan-pipes, to far more complicated and costly instruments such as the half-tube zither, with these used in eastern China from at least the late Han period. So important was music to the Chinese that in 243 C.E., when a mission came to China from the southeast Asian "empire" of Funan, the precursor to medieval Cambodia, and brought with them new musical instruments, they were invited to stay for many months until many Chinese had, no doubt, picked up the method of playing them.

Chinese theater in cities, and for the emperors, was highly developed and stylized and utilized many aspects of acting and singing, as well as acrobatics and juggling from street artists, with some people in ancient China involved in working as acrobats and jugglers for the entertainment of other people. Performances could be conducted from elaborate pavilions, or from makeshift stages. In many cases, whole families were involved in these acts, with a frieze from a tomb in eastern China dated to just after the Han dynasty showing an acrobat balancing what would appear to be a wooden cross on his head, with two child acrobats on the horizontal arms of the cross and a third child balancing on a wheel at the top of the cross.

For recreational sports, some people, especially soldiers, were involved in running, horseriding, chariot-racing, archery, wrestling and boxing, most of which were used as training in times of war, or in preparation for war. Since ancient times, martial arts have also been an important part of Chinese recreation, with various types of unarmed combat such as kung fu, karate, and taekwondo (originating in Korea) being practiced, as well as the use of defense with sickles, thrashing flails, and knives. Tai chi and meditation have also been popular as a form of morning exercise for adults and children.

Among the scholar class, there was a much greater interest in calligraphy, painting, and writing poetry. There were also a number of board games, the most important being Chinese Chess, sometimes called the Chinese River Game, on account of the river down the middle of the chess board, and played with elephants instead of bishops, and chariots. The game in ancient times was possibly developed from *Chaturanga*, the Persian game that has some similarities, which in turn might have originated from the "original" Chess game, although it is equally likely that *Chaturanga* developed from Chinese Chess. Obviously the cannon in Chinese Chess was not introduced until the 13th century C.E.

Ancient Games

Backgammon seems to have been introduced to China in the 3rd century C.E., with the local variation known as "double-six." Its popularity, however, was largely from the Song (Sung) dynasty (960–1279), when it was played by gamblers, some of whom were known to lose large sums of money after being paid for their harvest. Another game that may date from ancient China that remains popular today, and also involves heavy gambling, is Mahjong. By tradition this game has its origin in Confucius (551–479 B.C.E.), but others say that it is a far more recent game with claims that it developed from Dominoes as late as 1850. "Money cards" were used in ancient China, and these had four "suits" like Mahjong sets and modern packs of cards, although there are suggestions that these were actually paper money used in normal transactions as well as in gambling and other games of chance.

Mention should also be made of the game Go, which, according to legend, was played from the reign of the Emperor Yao (reigned, according to legend, 2337–2258 B.C.E.), who devised it to help teach his son about concentration and balance, with the earliest surviving written reference to the game being from the 4th century B.C.E. Some scholars have suggested that it could have been used by generals planning their military campaigns. Certainly it was being played by the 6th century B.C.E., and was enjoyed by the scholar class, being described in the Analects by Confucius, and also books by Mencius. The oldest surviving board is one made from porcelain, which was located in the ruins of a watchtower at the tombs of the Emperor Jingdi (188–141 B.C.E.) from the Western Han Dynasty. It was probably a floor tile and was likely to have been played by guards at the tomb to occupy their time.

See Also: Backgammon; China; Chess and Variations of; Go; Kite Flying; Mahjong; Play as Mock War, Sociology of; Wargames.

Bibliography. Jacques Gernet, *Daily Life in China on the Eve of the Mongol Invasion* (George Allen & Unwin, 1962); Harry Golombek, *Chess: A History* (G.P. Putnam's Sons, 1976); Anders Hansson, Bonnie S. McDougall, and Frances Weightman, *The Chinese at Play* (Kegan Paul, 2002); Michael Loewe, *Everyday Life in Early Imperial China* (Batsford Books, 1968); W.H. Wilkinson, "Chinese Origin of Playing Cards," *The American Anthropologist* (v.8, 1895).

Justin Corfield
Geelong Grammar School

Ancient Egypt

To contemporary ears, the notion of "play in ancient Egypt" sounds contradictory. The nearly ubiquitous image of ancient stonemasons slavishly constructing pyramids without the use of modern tools while at the behest of whip-wielding overlords appears incommensurable with concepts such as amusement or recreation. Nevertheless, ancient Egyptians enjoyed a variety of leisure activities including games, sports, songs, and dance. Evidence culled from archaeological remains, reliefs, and papyri attest to the importance of "play" in everyday Egyptian life.

Play is a culturally conditioned phenomenon that denotes a variety of activities pursued recreationally for amusement. To write about play in ancient Egypt requires one to import modern concepts into antiquity and extrapolate from static evidence. Such a process potentially distorts the data by forcing it to conform to one's own expectations, but that is all that a scholar can do. Ancient Egypt is a distant and foreign past, and one must keep in mind that much of its cultural interworkings have been lost in the Egyptian sands of time.

Regarding social class, play appears to be a predominantly elite activity; ancient Egypt was no exception. Only those with excess time had the means and liberty to pursue activities of leisure. Within the highly stratified Egyptian society, lower classes worked longer hours, had access to very limited resources, and were expected to conform to the regnant status quo. Life in Egypt (especially during the early periods) was highly structured; craftsmen and their families lived in enclosed communities near their work sites, worked tediously long hours, and had little time for recreation. This is not to say that farmers and laborers did not play. To the contrary, evidence suggests that the lower classes' play probably consisted of less formal activities, used fewer and simpler props, and probably occurred with less frequency than did the play of those with means. Of course the upper divisions of Egyptian society—the pharaohs, courtiers, and other high-ranking officials—enjoyed ornate games in a variety of venues.

Perhaps the most famous example of Egyptian play is *Senet*. Omnipresent in reliefs, papyri, and etchings, this board game played a central role in royal life. The game consisted of a board divided into a gridlike pattern of square spaces. A player moved his or her game pieces along the board in an attempt to reach the finish before his or her opponent. No intact rule books survive, however, so scholarly speculation accounts for most reconstructions of *Senet*'s rules and procedure. Excavators found numerous *Senet* boards in King Tut's tomb and in the tombs of most of Egypt's other wealthy kings.

Most of what is known of Egyptian play and sports is from the information found in tombs, like wall reliefs and papyri.

Likewise, cruder examples survive where stones function as game pieces and a hand-scratched piece of flat wood or rock serves as the board. Such evidence suggests that lower classes probably enjoyed *Senet* as well. Other Egyptian board games survive, but even less is known about them than about *Senet*. *Taw*, an imported amusement during the late Middle Kingdom era, as well as the six-person game *Mehen*, both use elaborately crafted animal-shaped game pieces on boards, variously arranged in rows and columns of squares. In short, ancient Egyptians enjoyed board games in much the same way today's society does.

Much ancient play included public displays and/or competitions of sporting capabilities and dexterity, although such activities functioned to keep warriors fit and prepared when at peace. Target shooting with bow and arrow (sometimes atop a moving horse) provides an ancient parallel to darts or archery. Players accrued points according to their accuracy, and presumably a winner emerged. Wrestling too was evidently popular, and surprisingly little has changed between the ancient sport and its modern practice. Many paintings and papyri depict holds and tactics analogous to the headlocks and half-nelsons of today's sport; one mural—the Ben Hasan paintings—even depicts an ancient Egyptian "trash talking" to his opponent.

Children too played sports—from wrestling to a variety of ball-type games to piggyback riding—and groups of children all playing together frequently appear on Egyptian wall reliefs. Archaeological digs uncover toys shaped like dolls, animals, etcetera, and children probably played with them in a similar manner as do today's youth. Tomb paintings show children juggling, dancing, and playing with balls in a variety of group and solitary ways. Ancient Egyptian children played a version of Tug-of-War, ran, jumped, played Catch, and put one another on their shoulders. Static paintings make it difficult to decipher the exact nature of the games played. Still, what the scholar can reconstruct of children's games in ancient Egypt appears similar to the variety and whimsicality of children's play today. Multiple children communed together, and whether such activities involved a ball (as often they did) or not, one can discern looks of amusement on the painted figures' faces.

Water played a crucial role in Egyptian life; Egypt's population hinged upon the ability to procure water, and thus the Nile River, Red and Mediterranean Seas, and numerous irrigation channels were central to Egypt's way of life. It should come as no surprise, therefore, that water games also figured prominently in ancient Egyptian recreational life. Egyptians devoted both a special hieroglyph and a unique goddess (*Wadjet*) to swimming. Depictions of young and mature swimmers decorate art works and assorted artifacts.

Egyptians of means enjoyed "Water Jousting," a game where crews of rowers maneuvered a stick-carrying combatant around a body of water on a pontoon-like boat. The fighter attempted to knock others off their boats. The last boat with a standing fighter won the game. River rafting too provided amusement for the prosperous. Seneca the Younger's fascination with adventurous Egyptians "shooting" the Nile's rapids attests to its uniqueness in the ancient world. From simple and common to elaborate and dangerous, water games were popular diversions for the ancient Egyptians.

In sum, the evidence for play in ancient Egypt is largely inferential—one must cull from the paintings, artifacts, and literary remains to construct a portrait of games and recreation in antiquity. Still, from such evidence one can infer that Egyptians of all ages, social classes, and occupations enjoyed playing as much as we do today.

See Also: Ancient Greece; Ancient Rome; Egypt; Play as Competition, Psychology of; Play as Competition, Sociology of; Water Play.

Bibliography. Lionel Casson, *Everyday Life of the Ancient Egyptians* (Johns Hopkins University Press, 2001); Manfred Decker, *Sports and Games in Ancient Egypt* (Yale University Press, 1992); Vera Olivova, *Sports and Games in the Ancient World* (St. Martin's, 1984); Ian Shaw and Paul Nicholson, eds., *Dictionary of Ancient Egypt* (Harry N. Abrams, 1995); Eugen Strouhal, *Life of the Ancient Egyptians* (University of Oklahoma Press, 1992).

Thomas Crawford
Claremont Graduate University

Ancient Greece

Many of the recreational activities found in ancient Greece contain elements easily recognizable as sport or entertainment today. The holding of games every four years in Olympia, Greece, has its equivalent in the modern Olympic Movement, which has been part of world sports since the formation of the International Olympic Committee in 1894 and the beginning of the new Olympics in 1896.

The Greek Olympics

The ancient Greek Olympics date from 776 B.C.E., when the first winner can be confirmed. These games have also contributed to our understanding of ancient Greek values and culture. The Greeks established sport and games as a way to honor their gods and therefore made sport a central feature of religious observation. The ancient Olympics were played over five days, however, the athletes and their trainers decamped in preparation for 30 days before the competitions began. In addition, standards of play were formalized that allowed competitors and spectators to share common approaches to known spectacles.

Sports such as boxing, weight lifting, and the pentathlon gained great popularity in the ancient Greek world. The pentathlon was composed of five sports including discus and javelin throwing, wrestling, running, and long jumping. The events tested a range of sporting skills. Victors in these competitions were recognized with a wreath of laurel or olive leaves and were further celebrated when crowds shouted their name and that of their families and their city. Given the importance of the city-state in ancient Greece, such tributes were of great significance.

Boxing was also part of the Olympic competitions and was seen as one of the significant heavy events, held on the fourth day of the meeting. Boxers' hands and wrists were wrapped in leather strips and their bodies were oiled. Since there were no judges, the fights were hard affairs with few rules and no time frame. Damage came through blows to the head and neck and ended only when a boxer collapsed from total exhaustion, was knocked out, or lifted his right hand in defeat.

Greek wrestling was another key Olympic sport and was geared to throwing the opponent to the ground without the necessity of pinning him. The fighters fought in the nude and oiled their bodies, making modern-style gripping holds difficult. Nudity was seen as a means of separating the Greeks from barbarians, who in Greek eyes always covered themselves in animal skins. Sweat was removed by scraping with *stirgils*, implements that removed excess oil and perspiration. As with boxing, there were no time limits, set ring, or even weight limits. When three falls were achieved, victory was declared.

Sporting success also became a source of inspiration for poets and artists who admired the athletes' bodies as representations of masculine beauty. Competitions featured both men (*andres*) and boys (*paides*), but the actual age classifications remain hard to determine conclusively. Yet there appeared to be a minimum age, as well as an upper division for boys of 17, after which they had to compete as men. Older athletes were welcome to compete as long as they could avoid embarrassment. There was also evidence indicating that as athletes aged, horse racing became an alternative activity.

Other Greek Games

The Olympics was but one part of a multitude of similar festival games that spread throughout Greece in celebration of different gods. The Pythian Games held every four years at Delphi in honor of Apollo; the Isthmian Games, played at Corinth every two years in honor of Poseidon; and the Nemean Games held on alternate years in celebration of Zeus were all popular events. Over time, festival games spread throughout Greece, so that by the 2nd century C.E., over 300 different games were held in the Greek world. By the time of the Roman conquest the Olympic games had lost their appeal, and by the end of the 4th century C.E. they had disappeared into obscurity and were replaced by the more brutal gladiatorial contests that the Romans preferred.

Horse racing was also a sport that attracted many spectators, and different city-states did mount competitive teams. The sport required considerable wealth for participation. There were two basic races: those where the horse pulled a chariot, and those where the horse had a jockey. The owners in most cases did not ride the horses but provided riders. They did, though, receive the awards that came with victory. Chariots races usually had chariots pulled by four or two horse teams. In these times, the horse-drawn chariot was not of great military or economic importance. Without stirrups, saddles, or horseshoes, a horse's value in warfare was limited. In ancient Greece, the horse was primarily a transport device that took men into battle, and the chariot itself became largely obsolete in warfare by the 4th century B.C.E.

The evidence for playing ball games in Greece is harder to document. However, there were a variety of ball-type games played that used several different types of balls: the *harpastum*, which was small, hard, and made of hair; the *follis*, a bladder filled with air; and the *pila*, a larger ball packed with feathers. Since our evidence remains limited, it is difficult to explain in detail how these balls were actually used. What we do understand stems largely from the writings of Galen during the 2nd century C.E.

One ball game played by the Greeks was *episkyros*, which was a team game where the ball had to be moved across a boundary by throwing. Ball games, though, were not seen as serious games for real athletes but were useful for building team play, which appealed especially to the Spartans. A much later ball game that was popular after the Roman conquest was *harpastum*, meaning snatch. A small group of players, possibly as few as five, moved the ball by throwing it. Some scholars have interpreted this activity to be a game similar to keep-away. Without having clear and specific applications in the established sports arena, these games were viewed as less important and essentially forms of personal exercise and team activities.

Surviving vase illustrations showed that there were still other unknown games on offer. One such game had players riding on the shoulders of others, where they moved a ball-like object. Other artifact representations showed players dribbling a ball as well as players using a ball and a stick. Besides ball-type games, other activities such as Knucklebones were played with bones, and these had several different variations in the ancient Greek world. In terms of actual rules and objectives, there is little surviving hard evidence, although some scholars have described the game as one similar to Jacks, where the bones were thrown in the air and the players tried to catch them on the backs of their hands. It was reported that it was a common sight in Greece for children to play this game. There also were suggestions that a game similar to Knucklebones amused Greek soldiers before battle during the Trojan War.

In regard to the participation of girls and women in Greek sports the evidence is elusive. There were, however, many mythological celebrations of women hunters and runners. Further, there were competitions held at Heraea, where unmarried girls ran foot races in celebration of the goddess Hera. Winners received a crown of olive leaves and a cow was sacrificed to the goddess.

Given the antiquity of the subject, it is astonishing that we know as much as we do about Greek games and sport, even though exact details are often vague. Nevertheless, sport was essential to Greek living. The gymnasium and various forms of exercise formed central features in Greek culture and architecture. Wrestlers trained in the gymnasium's *palestra* section, and there were as many as 140 such sites spread throughout Greece. These sites functioned as modern-day sports centers do. Sport, competition, and victory shaped ancient Greek attitudes toward games. Games built the necessary attributes for survival in a hostile and warlike world.

See Also: Ancient Rome; Athletics (Amateur); Greece; Horse Racing (Amateur); Jacks; Play as Competition, Psychology of; Play as Competition, Sociology of; Play as Entertainment, Psychology of; Play as Entertainment, Sociology of.

Bibliography. Mark Golden, *Sport and Society in Ancient Greece* (Cambridge University Press, 1998); Donald G. Kyle, "Winning and Watching the Greek Pentathlon," *Journal of Sports History* (v.17/3, 1990); Stephen G. Miller, *Ancient Greek Athletics* (Yale University Press, 2004); Stephen G. Miller, *Arete: Greek Sports From Ancient Sources* (University of California Press, 1991); Vera Olivova, *Sports and Games in the Ancient World* (Bloomsbury, 1986).

Theodore W. Eversole
Independent Scholar

Ancient India

In ancient India, there were a number of civilizations that, because of their locations, developed different forms of recreation. The oldest was in the Indus Valley, which flourished from 3000 until 1500 B.C.E., largely in modern-day Pakistan and northwestern India, where some ideas appear to have originated from Sumer and other Mesopotamian civilizations. Elsewhere on the Indian Subcontinent, there were numbers of different centers of the ancient world, including that on the Ganges, where Asoka (d. 232 B.C.E.) reigned in the city of Patna, which at one time was credited with being one of the largest cities in the ancient world.

In all of these areas, many people were involved in the making of pottery and in fashioning models of the Hindu deities, large numbers of which survive. Some of the smaller figures from the Indus Valley might also have been made as toy soldiers and the like for boys, and from the many seals that have been found by archaeologists and the size of houses, it seems likely that there would have been toys, possibly made from wood or from clay. Indeed, as many of the houses themselves were made from clay, the making of miniature versions of them, which could then be baked in the sun, was not only a common pastime but also a useful one, as many people were involved in building or enlarging their own homes.

There is also evidence of people in Ancient India having pets including songbirds and dogs. Probably because of the dusty location, as well as the heat, many of the cultural activities of the Indus Valley Civilization likely took place around public bath-houses, where many of the games were played. In the Indus Valley, and indeed throughout ancient India, there were many martial arts and also recreational sports that involved a show of strength, such as racing, archery, chariot racing, horse racing, sailing, and in the areas where there were elephants and camels, riding these animals.

While some games tested dexterity and skill, many existed to test strength. One of the celebrated tests of strength can be found early in the great Hindu epic, the *Ramayana*, which forms a major part of Hindu mythology. It involves the stringing of the famous "Great" or "Wondrous" bow by Rama at the court of King Janaka. It is while hunting a deer that Rama and his brother are drawn deeper and deeper into the woods. In Hindu India, the mythological tales such as the *Ramayana* and the *Mahabharata* led to much storytelling and also dance and theatrical performances, whereby the stories were elaborated on, and some aspects became morality tales for the young, as did the later tales of the life of the Lord Buddha.

Throughout Indian society, however, the caste system very much restricted activities and hence modes of play. There were also taboos connected with gender. For girls and women, the fashioning of brightly colored textiles was important, with spinning, weaving, sewing, and embroidery all skills that were learned at home, as well as, for those from higher castes, the making of parasols. Boys and men were also involved in some craft work, including woodwork, the making of fly whisks, and also

There were many different civilizations throughout ancient India. Some of the children's toys that were common to many of them were kites, spinning tops, hoops, chess, and the game Snakes and Ladders.

cane balls, which were used in games that children and young men played. While girls learned to skip from a young age to teach them coordination, boys enjoyed playing with rope. Spinning tops and hoops made from cane were used by both genders, but playing with kites was primarily undertaken by boys.

Music featured heavily in ancient India, and there are many references to it in the Ramayana. Stone carvings also show people playing the *vina*, a wooden instrument with strings, as well as flutes, often played by girls, and harps and a variety of drums. Dancing by girls was also common throughout India, where girls and young women would show their dexterity and charm. The dance occasionally became heavily ritualized, and these are not only described in ancient texts but also shown on stone carvings in temples.

In the early life of the Lord Buddha, folk stories relate to Prince Gautama Siddhartha being involved in many games in the royal palace where he grew up, and some storytellers have added elements into the story, with other children coming to the palace and playing with him, and the prince being presented with many toys—although he was not allowed to leave the palace and did not do so until he was 29 years old. Indian stone carvings, and later manuscripts, showing the period of Prince Gautama Siddhartha's early years show people playing musical instruments, juggling, or playing various ball games as a way of contrasting this life of "play" with his later one of a search for spiritual enlightenment.

About 150 years after Buddha reached enlightenment, Alexander the Great arrived at the borders of India, and his soldiers came across the game *Chaturanga,* which had been played in Persia, but was now closer to the present game of Chess, which therefore probably originated in its present form in ancient India. In the *Mahabharata*, there is a part of this great epic when two sets of warring cousins play the game. The old boards for playing *Chaturanga* look similar to those used for playing the Checkers version of Solitaire. The Indians had added the King (or Raja) and the Adviser (or Bishop), with the rooks being represented by elephants, their *howdahs* becoming, in Europe, the "castle." There was also the use of monkeys for the pawns of one side to represent the struggle against Ravana in the *Ramayana*.

Some games are believed to have originated in ancient India, the most famous being Snakes and Ladders, as well as *Ludo*—the former is definitely known to have been played by the Jains in India in the 16th century and had its origins in the ancient Indian game of *Moksha Patamu*.

Mention should also be made of the early playing cards, which are also thought to have their origins in ancient India, where the game known as *Kridapatram* was well-known, as was a game that featured a number of elephants including *Gajapati*, the "Lord of the Elephants." Other designs involved characters from the *Ramayana*, although it is likely that the old card games used bamboo or domino-like tiles, with the designs being transferred to cardboard or tough card in medieval times.

See Also: Chess and Variations of; Dominoes; History of Playing Cards; India; Kite Flying; Pakistan, Snakes and Ladders.

Bibliography. N. Bland, "On the Persian Game of Chess," *Journal of the Royal Asiatic Society* (v.13, 1852); Haran Chandra Chakladar, *Social Life in Ancient India: Study in Vatsyayana's Kamasutra* (Cosmo, 1984); Irina Glushkova and Anne Feldhaus, *House and Home in Maharashtra* (Oxford University Press, 1998); P.T. Srinivas Iyengar, *Life in Ancient India in the Age of Mantras* (Asian Educational Services, 1982); Gustave Le Bon, *The World of Indian Civilization* (Minerva, 1974); H.J.R. Murray, *A Short History of Chess* (Oxford University Press, 1963); Marie Neurath and John Ellis, *They Lived Like This in Ancient India* (Max Parrish, 1967); Jogesh Chandra Ray, *Ancient Indian Life* (P.R. Sen, 1948).

Justin Corfield
Geelong Grammar School

Ancient Rome

Ancient Rome presented a model for how affluence affected play communally and individually over time. Play—sedentary and active, indoor and outdoor, solitary and social—was woven throughout life in ancient Rome. Country homes had porticos for playing ball or exercising. Young men and boys sometimes amused themselves by whirling along metal hoops. Parents in ancient Rome hand manufactured or supplied toys for their children, but adult play dominated recreational time in this sophisticated agricultural region, where work, and not leisure, was emphasized. Young men were encouraged to become physically strong and agile by mastering jumping, throwing, hunting, wrestling, boxing, racing, swimming, and playing handball. A "sound mind in a strong body," *mens sana in corpore sano*, was culturally significant in this society that spawned great wealth and unprecedented empire building. Rome's first gymnasium, Campus Martius, was built beside the Tiber so that men could exercise for recreation and military training.

Etruscan Culture

The Etruscan culture emerged at the beginning of the Iron Age in the area of Italy today known as Tuscany. Etruscans shared cultural traits with Greece, so Greek advances and influences were absorbed into Italy—young Etruscans played a form of piggyback ride called *Ephedrismos*. The Etruscans reached their peak from the 7th to the 5th century B.C.E., when they were first to exploit the mineral potential of Italy to develop a bronze industry that fueled continuing prosperity. The Etruscans extended their power over most of Italy, achieving one of the most affluent civilizations in the western Mediterranean. Markets and fairs held every ninth day became hubs for socializing and established patterns for play that Romans later expanded.

When riches were introduced by the extension of conquest, the manners of the people changed when the pursuit of luxury seized all ranks. Captives and slaves of war provided labor and were exploited for entertainment, luxury, and vice.

Etruscan women experienced more autonomy than did other women in the ancient Mediterranean world. Etruscan mothers reared their own children, whereas in Greece, fathers legally "raised up" the children. Dolls made of wax or terracotta were first used as adult religious articles and then were adopted by children when the rites ended. Bows and arrows, rattles, and small dishes to use for playing with dolls were popular.

The Etruscans ruled Rome, building it into a city that boasted of great engineering and architecture. Public art chronicled a great abundance of natural and enjoyment of the good life. Greek-style athletic festivals never achieved the popularity, but chariot races, *ludi circenses*, held in conjunction with annual festivals and holidays occurred in Rome's great hippodrome racecourse Circus Maximus, situated between the Aventine and Palatine hills.

This was the first location used for public games and entertainment, where people of all ages viewed equestrian and other athletic events, which were held as early as the 6th century B.C.E. Circus Maximus became the venue for wild animal shows, *venations*, and massive hunts of leopards, bears, and elephants. Romans kept lapdogs, monkeys, nonvenomous snakes, and trained songbirds as hobbies. Small numbers of animals were kept for sport, including hounds for hunting and cocks for fighting. Romans also raised pigeons and doves on rooftop aviaries in order to carry messages.

Roman Culture

The Romans expelled the Etruscans from Rome in 510 B.C.E. Gladiatorial shows, *menera*, were established in 264 B.C.E. Once betting was introduced, racing rules and arena designs were developed to ensure fairness. When Circus Maximus was not operating, it served as an open space for entertainment including jugglers, bawdy performing artists, prostitutes, and fortunetellers. Puppetry was a popular form of entertainment in Greece and Rome. Lucius Apuleius (125–170 C.E.) chronicled that Roman marionettes could even roll their eyes.

Ancient Rome held games in the Colosseum, but children played with marbles, hobby horses, hoops, tops, and dolls.

Public games required immense planning and expense in order to make their visual and sensory impact: They were designed to awe the crowd and shape public memory. During the Roman republic, seven festivals or staged games, *ludi*, were organized at public expense at regular intervals throughout the year to honor Roman gods: *Ludi Megalenses*, for the Great Mother of the Gods (April 4–9); *Ludi Cereales*, for Ceres (April 12–18); *Ludi Florales*, for Flora (April 28–May 2); *Ludi Apollinares*, for Apollo (July 6–12); *Ludi Romani*, for Jupiter (September 4–12); *Ludi Victoriae*, for Victory (October 26–31); and *Ludi Plebeii*, for Jupiter (November 4–12), held in Circus Flaminius. Staged games, *ludi scaenici*, were occasions for dramatic performances where Romans came together in temporary theaters to strengthen and sustain community identity. *Lude Magni* and *Ludi Romani*, similar to Greek Olympic games, were annual celebrations that preceded circus games, *ludi circenses*, comprising chariot races and hunts.

Public games were celebrated 66 days out of the year, and diagrams found in the Roman Forum suggest the presence of adult board games and gambling.

Children built small playhouses with bricks and enjoyed games known throughout the ancient world. They played with clay marbles, bones, dice, hobbyhorses, hoops, tops, dolls, and nuts in neighborhoods. Castles or Pyramids was played when nuts were arranged in "castles" of four, three, and one on top. Boys would toss clay marbles in order to knock down the castles or pyramids in order to win the nuts. Early versions of Backgammon, Checkers and Chess were known. Children also played Hide-and-Seek just as it is played today. Heads-or-Ships was a game like Heads-or-Tails, in which children tossed coins, shouting to guess which side would come up.

Adults enjoyed drinking, gambling, and playing games of chance. *Alea* was played with dice: *tesserae*, that had six sides like modern dice, and *tali*, which had four elongated sides that were numbered. To play, three *tesserae* or four *tali* were placed into a box made in a form of a small tower called *frittillus*; the dice were shaken and thrown upon a gaming board or table, and the count was tallied in the form of odds and evens. In Knucklebone, or *Astragulus*, the anklebone of a cloven-hoofed animal served as a naturally good item to play with like dice. A game called *Pentalitha*, or Fivestones, was played as a divination (by women) or to gamble (by men). The ancient game with five knucklebones was a popular pastime for women and men. The knucklebones were tossed up simultaneously, so that the thrower, turning his hand over, would receive them on his forehand; if they did not all land properly on his hand, while he kept those that did land in place, he had to pick up the rest. *Sortes* was a diversion similar to the lottery, in which sealed tablets were sold at equal price.

Opened *sortes* revealed prizes of unequal value; for instance, one reward might be 100 gold pieces, and another might be a toothpick. *Morra* was a finger game of chance played by two people. Players simultaneously raised or compressed their fingers, and each guessed at the number of fingers raised in the opponent's hand.

See Also: Checkers and Variations of; Chess and Variations of; Gambling; Hobbies; Jacks; Play Among Animals.

Bibliography. Roland Auguet, *Cruelty and Civilization: The Roman Games* (Routledge, 1994); J.P.V.D. Balsdon, *Life and Leisure in Ancient Rome* (MaGraw-Hill, 1969); John H. Humphrey, *Roman Circuses: Arenas for Chariot Racing* (B.T. Batsford, Ltd., 1986); George Jennison, *Animals for Show and Pleasure in Ancient Rome* (Manchester University Press, 1937); David Matz, *Daily Life of the Ancient Romans (The Daily Life Through History Series)* (Hackett Pub., 2008).

Meredith Eliassen
San Francisco State University

Anti-Competition Play

Throughout history, play has been considered an important element in the development of children. Play serves to help children develop cognitively, emotionally, and socially, as well as serving as an expressive activity done for its own sake. Play isn't just for children, however, as adolescents and adults may play in their leisure time as well. While the meanings and outcomes attached to the play of children and adults are different, they are nonetheless compelling. This entry will examine these different aspects of anti-competition play in our society.

Play of Children

The play of children in their formative years is crucial to their ongoing development. While theorists have struggled to comprehensively define play and its impact, to children, the activity of play is simply fun and enjoyable and serves as an end to itself. Through study, it is known that play is very important for youth developmentally, as well as for the historical, psychological, cultural, and sociological meanings it represents. When watching children play, there appears to be no obvious goal or end conclusion, although it is easy to observe the amount of joy and satisfaction that comes from their play. Their play is also spontaneous, free, uncertain, and unplanned, as children exhibit a variety of play types, ranging from explorative and manipulative play to imitative play to play involving rules.

Playing games with rules starts for children around the age of 4 years, but even though rules exist, these games are still often noncompetitive, as until about the age of 8–10 years, children cannot fully understand the concept of competition. So, for youth, their play is often characterized by a lack of competition. Although this is not a conscious choice, it is inherent in their ability to play, as evidenced by their level of cognitive development.

Adolescent and Adult Play

When adolescents and adults engage in noncompetitive play, it is often much more of a deliberate choice than is the play of children. The orientations, meanings, and organization of noncompetitive play activities are vastly different from those of competitive play. While the goals of competitive play include overcoming opponents, winning, and demonstrating superior ability compared with others, the goals of noncompetitive play often center on fun, mastery, escape, and cooperation. When adolescents and adults participate in noncompetitive play, they often (although not always) play in a way where there is less structure and organization.

Play opportunities tend not to be formally organized in ways that competitive activities are. Similarly, the orientations of those who play noncompetitively tend to focus on the process of involvement. The end results, particularly in comparison to others, tend not to be salient; instead, becoming engrossed in the activity, creating something beautiful, and/or experiencing significant interactions with other participants tends to be most important. This also impacts the meanings of these activities for participants, as participants find the most satisfaction in these activities when they have met their goal(s). In sum, the most important aspect for many is the process or means, rather than the product or the end.

Anit-Competitive Play Patterns

While anti-competitive play can take many forms and functions for adolescents and adults, two specific areas are explored further here.

First, some adolescents, in a conscious attempt to subvert authority, choose to engage in noncompetitive alternative sports like skateboarding, snowboarding, and hacky sac. Much of the focus of these play activities is on excellence in performance, but not at the expense of competing with others.

The meanings attached to these activities for the participants often center around displaying individuality, avoiding the authority inherent in many organized competitive activities, and becoming proficient in the activity. Over the past 10–20 years, as commercialization and competition have entered some of these activities, participants at times have resisted these intrusions to turn their activity into competitive sport. Efforts are made on the part of participants to maintain the definition and meaning of the activity as a noncompetitive activity, hoping to avoid the authority and restrictions that are brought into their activities by organizing agencies.

Second, technology increasingly has a greater role in play patterns of children, adolescents, and adults. Over the past decade or two, the availability and prevalence of technological games has grown dramatically. The full effect of this growth is not yet known, but it is clear that when children, adolescents, and adults choose to play, they now have a much greater range of possibilities given the recent developments of electronically based activities. While it is true that many of these activities are competitive in nature, other noncompetitive activities are proving to be popular, as well. Recently, virtual reality games, in which users live a corresponding life in a cyberworld, have become popular, as well as learning activities for children.

While anticompetitive play has been around as long as play itself, its purposes vary depending on the age of the participant. Further, while adolescent and adult noncompetitive play is often a conscious decision, the types of noncompetitive play available change with the times, as is apparent with the rise of alternative sports as well as technology.

See Also: Cooperative Play; Fantasy Play; Hobbies; Play as Competition, Psychology of; Skateboarding; Skiing; Snowboarding; Unstructured Play.

Bibliography. Jay Coakley, *Sports in Society* (McGraw-Hill, 2007); D. Stanley Eitzen and George H. Sage, *Sociology of North American Sport* (McGraw-Hill, 2003); Mary D. Sheridan, Jackie Harding, and Liz Meldon-Smith, *Play in Early Childhood: From Birth to Six Years* (Routledge Press, 2002); Daryl Siedentop, *Introduction to Physical Education, Fitness, and Sport* (McGraw-Hill, 2004); Dorothy G. Singer and Jerome L. Singer, *Imagination and Play in the Electronic Age* (Harvard University Press, 2005).

Jessie Daw
Northern State University

Arcades

Arcades offer consumers the opportunity to play various mechanical games and machines for the purpose of entertainment. Game play is facilitated by depositing money, which results in a predetermined game play or action. Arcades may take the form of a distinct business locale constructed around these games, such as a video arcade that caterers to video game play offering a variety of game options. Alternately, quasi-arcades are common in public venues, such as in restaurants, malls, truck stops, bars, bowling alleys, and lobbies of movie theaters, where the games and entertainment machines are secondary entertainment used to bolster revenue from patrons. One is particularly likely to find these machines in areas where people are found unoccupied or waiting.

Early Arcades

Early "penny" arcades emerged in the late 1800s. These arcades may have been stable businesses set up in urban or tourist settings, but they also travelled with amusement parks and circuses. Within these arcades they had shooting galleries, various ball games, picture and peepshow machines, and the earliest coin-operated machines. Moral crusaders often critiqued the immoral nature of the arcade, particularly peepshow machines that would show brief erotic or nude "films" or picture stories. Arcades of this era drew audiences from youth and young adults primarily—persisting patrons over the course of the last century.

By the 1930s pinball machines had entered the arcade scene. During the following decades, arcades remained relatively limited in many parts of the nation, with most

Many people enjoy Skee-Ball, a physical arcade game of skill. The game is similar to bowling in concept; however, the ball must hit a ramp and soar into a hoop for a point score. The center hoop at the top generally has the highest score.

arcade games appearing in limited numbers at public locations catering to youth and families.

Growth of Arcade Games

During the 1970s and 1980s, the video arcade emerged as video games such as Pac-Man and Space Invaders became available. These coin-operated video games often cost a quarter per play. The length of play was determined in part by time limits, but also in part by successful play. The more skilled a player became at a game, the longer game play would continue. During this era, multiple-player video games also entered the scene, in which two players could compete with each other in the video game. During this era, corner video arcades and arcade centers appeared throughout the United States, catering to adolescent and teen youth, particularly boys. Teens could go to the video arcade not only to play video games and perhaps consume minor refreshments such as soda, candy, and popcorn but also to socialize. Indeed, the video arcade became a central location of teen socialization during the 1980s and as such was portrayed in various teen films of the era. Additionally, entertainment centers catering to children emerged, such as the restaurant Chuck E. Cheese. Based on the arcade theme, these centers integrated food and iconographic characters, fostering the socialization of ever-younger populations into arcade culture. Meanwhile, adult-oriented entertainment centers, such as Dave & Busters, also emerged, engaging adults with game play and food and alcohol consumption.

In the late 1980s, the video arcade declined in popularity. This decline was fostered by increasingly affordable personal video consoles for the home as well as social concern about the safety of the arcade. The image of the arcade had begun to transition from a teen safe space to a space embedded with drugs and teen angst and perhaps violence.

During the 1990s, the arcade decline persisted, yet the game technology continued to evolve. Video games that had already begun to integrate gun-like controllers, which the player would point at the screen to shoot, were expanding to include enclosed game booths. Games with more sensory experiences began to emerge as players began to physically ride mechanical motorcycles and jet skis that would allow the player to feel the virtue bumps and turns of the game. New video games such as Dance Dance Revolution engaged the player in dance moves. This video game is played upon a game pad with sensors to indicate player foot movement and has been noted as a positive shift in video technology, encouraging physical activity.

Today, the video arcade is dominated by technology that is too large or costly for home consumption. Yet various fighter games that do not require specialized controllers or technology persist, allowing for individual play and competition for high scores and establishing skill status among peers.

See Also: Amusement Parks; Pinball; Play as Catharsis; Play as Entertainment, Sociology of.

Bibliography. Christopher Barlett, Richard Harris, and Ross Baldassaro, "Longer You Play, The More Hostile You Feel: Examination of First Person Shooter Video Games and Aggression During Video Game Play," *Aggressive Behavior* (v.33/6, 2007); Joanna Demers "Dance Dance Revolution, Cybernetic Dance, and Musical Taste," *Popular Music* (v.25/3, 2006); Robert Fox "Socializing Around Arcade Technology," *Communications of the ACM* (v.40/8, 1997); Jeroen Jansz and Raynel Martis, "The Lara Phenomenon: Powerful Female Characters in Video Games," *Sex Roles* (v.56/3–4, 2007).

Daniel Farr
Randolph College

Arctic Play (First Nations)

Play is a central component of cultural vitality. Nowhere is this clearer than in the example of arctic games, a designation applied to a range of traditional activities carried out by indigenous groups in the circumpolar regions of the globe. Within a historical context, these games served to reproduce sociocultural values, develop physical capabilities necessary to surviving the harsh climate of the north, and promote the acquisition of subsistence skills. Today, attempts to maintain traditional cultures and values have resulted in a renewed interest in play in the north.

Unlike contemporary sports and games that strongly emphasize asymmetrical outcomes (i.e., winning and losing) to the exclusion of other recreational or athletic values, traditional arctic games seek to balance the needs of the community, the survival of which depends on an ethic of cooperation and sharing, with the development of individual self-reliance, an equally important communal skill. As such, traditional games encourage competitive engagement; that is, participation with an intent to compete, to do well, and to emerge as the winner, all the while promoting the success of your opponents.

Games were also used in traditional northern society as a means of maintaining the skills and physical capability necessary for life in the north through play, which mimicked subsistence activities such as harpoon throwing and archery, as well as through games whose outcomes promoted the development of strength, endurance and resistance to pain. Arm Pull, for example, is a game of strength in which two participants sit on the floor facing each other with their legs straight and their feet placed against their opponent's feet. The objective is to pull the opponent off the ground. The Knuckle Hop, on the other hand, which is intended to develop the ability to resist pain, sees participants "hop" along the floor on only their toes and knuckles until they collapse. The longest distance wins.

Arctic games reflect traditional northern Aboriginal life in other ways as well. For example, while the objectives and form of play represented by these games vary widely, they all have simple rules and little if any equipment, which suits the historically nomadic lifestyles of their creators. Furthermore, the majority of these games were/are the exclusive terrain of men. This gendered access to participation is a reflection of the strict division of labor characteristic of northern indigenous communities.

In contemporary northern Aboriginal society, the playing of traditional games represents one aspect of cultural preservation. In the case of Canada, for example, the reorganization and centralization of Inuit life that accompanied the federal government's colonization of the north in the mid-20th century precipitated a decline in participation in traditional play because of the enforced break with "the land" as well as the introduction of "southern sports."

Despite these incursions, Aboriginal communities in the north have made a concerted effort to maintain this particular aspect of their culture with varying degrees of success. Most commonly, this act of preservation has been carried out at the community level through the playing of traditional games at village celebrations. However, with the establishment of the Arctic Winter Games in 1970, this particular component of indigenous culture was also ensured a place in the larger social sphere of northern life.

See Also: Australian Aborigines; Canada; Native Americans; Play as Learning, Anthropology of.

Bibliography. R.G. Glassford, *Application of a Theory of Games to the Transitional Eskimo Culture* (Arno Press, 1976); Michael Heine, "'It's a Competition, Not a Show!' Traditional Games at the Arctic Winter Games," *Stadion* (v.31/1, 2005); Elliott Avedon Museum and Archive of Games, "Inuit (Eskimo) Games," www.gamesmuseum.uwaterloo.ca /VirtualExhibits/Inuit/english/index.html (cited July 2008).

Jessica Dunkin
Carleton University

Argentina

Argentina is the second largest country in South America, and one with a wide range of temperatures, from the hot and arid subtropical lands along the border with Paraguay to the cold and damp regions of southern Patagonia. The vast expanses of countryside and the fact that the country has welcomed a wide range of migrants have led to many different pursuits taking place throughout the country, with a detailed study of them undertaken by Jorge Páez in 1971.

Buenos Aires, with a population of 12 million (2007), has long attracted Spanish and Italian migrants, but there are also substantial British, German, Greek, Eastern European, and Chinese communities. The early Spanish settlers enjoyed riding horses—the great Pampas being the perfect venue for horse riding and rodeos, leading to the emergence of the *gaucho* culture. The earliest reference to bullfighting in Argentina was in 1609, but it was banned in Argentina in 1856, although it did take place illegally as recently as 1950. Girls from wealthy families learned sewing and embroidery. Many also were involved in playing music, listening to it, and dancing. It was from the African slave community in Buenos Aires, and also from nearby Montevideo, in Uruguay, that the hard rhythm of tango music originated.

Most children in Argentina were involved in playing games such as Hide-and-Seek, playing with marbles, and girls playing with dolls. However soccer—both recreational and professional—is one of the most popular pastimes in the entire country; their national team won the World Cup in 1978 and 1986, and only losing in the final in 1990. Boys can be found playing soccer, often with improvised goal posts, all around the country. Most other games are also played, with the British community, through St. George's College and St. Andrew's Scots School, as well as the Hurlingham Club and the Belgrano Club, being centers for cricket and rugby.

Recreational Activities

Indeed, the British community in Argentina are responsible for introducing many of the nation's recreational sports, such as cricket in 1806, athletics in the following year, horse racing in 1826 (with the establishment of the Buenos Aires Racing Club), rowing in 1857, swimming in 1863, rugby in 1873, polo in 1874, and lawn tennis in 1880. At both the Hurlingham and the Belgrano clubs, as well as others in the country, billiards is played, and in many nightspots around Buenos Aires and other large cities, there are regular darts competitions. The Hurlingham Club also has one of the only two Eton Fives courts in the Southern Hemisphere. The French and Catalan communities in Argentina play boule, and some older Italian migrants play bocce, in places such as San Telmo in Buenos Aires. Card games—especially Bridge and Poker—and Backgammon are also common throughout the country.

Many Argentines enjoy "outdoor" pursuits, including hiking, cycling, and going to adventure playgrounds, with some traveling to Patagonia, where many youth groups organize excursions with skiing, sailing, windsurfing, ballooning, bungee jumping, and whitewater rafting. Although indoor ice-skating rinks can be found in all the large cities in Argentina, many Argentines prefer to go to the south of their country in winter for skiing, skating, snowboarding, and tobogganing. At Ushuaia, there are many opportunities for cross-country skiing. At Lake Lenas, near the inland city of Mendoza, downhill ski racing has started to attract visitors not only from Argentina, but also from overseas. In other areas, teenage boys can be found involved in skateboarding and rollerblading.

In August-September 1939, Buenos Aires hosted the 8th Chess Olympiad, and this had dramatic effects on Argentine Chess for decades. The competition coincided with the start of World War II, with the German invasion of Poland; the games in which Polish and French players were to compete against Germans were cancelled, and the Germans managed to get the Czechoslovakian team excluded. Argentina came in fifth overall, and of the competitors, some 23, including the famous Polish player Mikhail Najdorf, decided to stay in Argentina, with Miguel Najdorf (as he became) remaining one of the top players in the world, with the result that many Argentines became interested in Chess.

In primary schools, swings and slides, as well as sandpits, are used by children. Wargaming and model-making have also been of great interest to Argentine youths and men, with Revell and Airfix models being available in shops around Avenida Corrientes in Buenos Aires, and in shops throughout the country. Although Wargaming for the Ancient World and the Napoleonic Wars remain the most popular, the recent availability of metal figurines for armies (including Argentine) who fought in the War of the Triple Alliance from 1864 until 1870, when Argentine, Brazilian, and Uruguayan soldiers defeated Paraguay. The battle over the Falklands/Malvinas has also grown in popularity in recent years. At a number of schools there are model-making and Wargaming clubs, and for adult participants, there are also regular meetings and fairs.

As well as European migrants, there have also been many Chinese who have settled in Argentina, and Mahjong and Ping Pong groups are not unknown, especially in Buenos Aires. Indigenous groups are also still involved in playing games such as *Pelota,* originally a Basque or Catalan game. Bowling alleys and amusement arcades are popular, especially for boys and young men, with younger children still enjoying LEGOs. Computer games are overtaking board games, such as Monopoly, in popularity, although there is a version of the game set in Argentina with the properties being the names of *estancias* in different provinces of the country, and the train stations being those in Buenos Aires. Hand-drawn games of *Dungeons & Dragons* are now largely played on computers.

See Also: Arcades; Brazil; Chess and Variations of; Cricket (Amateur); *Dungeons & Dragons;* Skiing; Snowboarding; Soccer (Amateur) Worldwide; Wargames.

Bibliography. Emilio Alberto Breda, *Juegos y Deportes Entre los Indios del Río de la Plata* [Games and Sports of the Indians of the River Plate Region] (Ediciones Theoria, Buenos Aires, 1962); Christopher Chilcott, "Falklands 2003," *Miniature Wargames* (August 2003); Gustavo Levene, "Hoofbeats From the Pampas," *Américas* (v.40/6, 1988); Jorge Páez, *Del Truquiflor a la Rayuela: Panorama de los Juegos y Entreteniemientos Argentines* [From Brag to Hopscotch: A Panorama of Games and Amusements in Argentina] (Centro Editor de América Latina, 1971).

Justin Corfield
Geelong Grammar School

Armenia

The Republic of Armenia is a young, independent political entity, yet the geographical area and Armenian culture and heritage are quite old. Thus, this entry presents an overview of the culture of play in the historical Armenian lands, the traditions that were developed during the Ottoman era, the altered meanings of play during the Soviet Armenia, and the revival of older traditions in modern Armenia based on ethnographic studies conducted in the 19th and 20th centuries.

Dikran Chituni was among the first to research children's play during the first decade of the 20th century. His study, titled "The World of Play in the East or the National Games," was published in 1906 as an article and became a book in 1919 with the title *The World of Play in the East.* Inspired by a French book, *200 Jeux d'Enfants* by Harquevaux and Pelletier, Chituni unearths and describes 256 Armenian children's games with their variants and gives detailed information on the nature of the playground, the number of players, and their approximate ages. His detailed descriptions add an ethnographic dimension to the study.

Emphasizing the antiquity of the games, Chituni argues that play is a primary quality of human beings from childhood to old age—as Huizinga's *Homo Ludens*. Mottos such as "the child grows up by playing," "play is both living and self-development for the child," or *mens sana in corpore sana* are repeated in Chituni's book. Play was defined as an activity giving meaning to idle time, and such habits as the use of a rosary were analyzed for their playlike functions. Admitting that closely living communities have similar traditions of play, Chituni argues that play still carries the "cultural marks of a people" and conveys their "moral conceptions." Therefore, the compilation of children's games was like an archaeological excavation, the findings of which should be professionally conserved.

Decimation and deportation of the Armenians of Anatolia in 1915, their diasporic existence all around the world, the sudden and austere changes in the lives of Caucasian Armenians under the Soviet rule, and modernization in general interrupted the investigations on play. New interest only appeared in the 1950s, when Vard H. Bdoyan undertook a survey in the whole "historic Armenia" in 1951 and classified the games under 11 categories: babies' games, delineating the relations between adults and infants; games developing creativity and manual skills in 5- and 6-year-olds; sportive games for the preservation of the "memory of Armenian traditions"; movement games, sports; games situated between play and dance; dramatic games projecting the "image of society"; games for cultural education; games played with animals (bull fights, various races); games commemorating myths; competitive games, played during feasts; and games commemorating struggles against invaders.

Normative, repetitive, and restrictive characteristics of the classification were related to the ideological pressures of the Soviet regime on ethnographic studies. The inventory was compiled 1952–57, and the geographical dimensions of the study included Ararat plain, Lori, Zangezur Mountains, Georgia, Azerbaijan, and eastern Anatolia. Bdoyan's masterpiece, *Armenian Folk Games*, compiled a list of 200 games and remains a reference source.

Under Soviet rule, an artificial folk culture was created and authenticity was reduced to a standardized set of celebrations, monuments, and artistic performances. Though historically it was the Armenian custom to celebrate many festivals, in the Soviet and post-Soviet periods, only remnants of a once-vibrant festive life have been in evidence. Yet, in modern-day Armenia, there are efforts being made to recover and revive ancient cultural artifacts. Both religious and historical events are commemorated with celebrations, during which traditional circle dances are performed with folkloric music and historic games are played. For example, there are a number of games associated with the return of spring and the Paregentan festival—the equivalent of the European carnival, seven weeks before Easter. One is a game played with children called *Karpetalakhi*. In the game, two teams of men use their belts to lash at each other, with one group guarding children hidden under a carpet and the other trying to release them; when the children are finally released, they appear to be magically revived. Other games played in Paregentan include a shadow-puppet theater, spoon puppet plays, a theatrical farce called Khan Pasha, and a tightrope act with acrobats dancing above the crowd, mimicked by clowns. Further anthropological studies are needed to comment more extensively on the meaning of play in modern Armenia.

See Also: Georgia; *Homo Ludens* (Huizinga); Memory and Play; Turkey.

Bibliography. Levon Abrahamian and Nancy Sweezy, eds., *Armenian Folk Arts, Culture, and Identity* (Indiana University Press, 2001); Vard H. Bdoyan, *Hay Joghovrtagan Khagher* [Armenian Folk Games] (Armenian SSR Academy of Sciences Press, 1963); Dikran Chituni, *Arevelian Khaghashkharh* [The World of Play in the East], (Arzuman, 1919); Anahide Ter Minassian, "Les Jeux des Adolescents Arméniens dans L'Empire Ottoman," in François Georgeon, Paul Dumont, ed., *Vivre dans L'Empire Ottoman, Sociabilités et Relations Intercommunautaires, XVIIIe-XXe Siécles* (L'Harmattan, 1997).

Nazan Maksudyan
Bogazici University

Assyrian/Babylonian Culture

The Assyrians are perhaps best known today as disciplined warriors and skilled technicians and engineers; the Babylonians are still associated with the Hanging Gardens of Babylon mentioned in the Bible. However, the culture created by these two peoples was complex and sophisticated. They enjoyed literary word games as much as practicing hunting or gardening and were probably the inventors of games still played today such as Backgammon and Chess.

The Assyrians were a people speaking a Semitic language who inhabited the northern part of Mesopotamia (modern Iraq); they conquered most of Mesopotamia, Syria, and Anatolia, thus dominating an area including modern Syria, Iraq, and Turkey, between the 13th and 7th centuries B.C.E. The Babylonians, who also spoke a Semitic language, created an empire that had, as its center, the metropolis of Babylon. The Assyrian and Babylonians worshipped the same gods and goddesses (though under slightly different names) and spoke closely related languages, so that these two cultures are often examined together. In turn, all aspects of their culture were heavily indebted to previous civilizations, such as the Sumerian and the Akkadian.

Language Games

Assyrians and Babylonians were particularly well-versed in language games. Scholars have found several examples of puns in grammar, religious, and even official texts. In particular, the myths narrating the stories of the gods and goddesses of the Mesopotamian pantheon offer several examples of word games that become central for the development, or the resolution, of the story, as Jean Bottéro has highlighted. One interesting text tells the story of the god Nergal and of his wife-to-be, Ereshkigal, the powerful and independent Queen of the Underworld. Ea, the king of the gods, manages to combine the wedding by using a language game: the goddess wanted Nergal to put him to death (*ana muti*), but she is given him as consort (*ana muti*). Another fascinating story tells how Ea played a trick on human beings. Following the tricky suggestions of Ea, Adapa, the first human being, misses the chance to gain immortality for humankind by refusing the foods that will grant him immortality. The ancient Mesopotamian cultures have also left examples of verbal duels or challenges; in a poem written in Sumerian, a language that Assyrian erudites knew and used, the goddess Ninmah challenges her husband Enki, the god who creates the humankind from clay, to find a use for the men and women he has badly crafted.

Board Games

Archaeological findings have shown that the early Mesopotamian cultures, and later the Assyrians and Babylonians, knew a variety of board games, whose structure and rules may have had a religious content and most probably had their origins in divination practices (such as rolling the bones of animals to predict the future), as Nigel Pennick has illustrated. The so-called Royal Game of Ur, which the archaeologist Leonard Wolley found in a royal tomb in the Sumerian city of Ur, is probably the ancestor of the various board games known to the Assyrians, who used board games with 12 or 20 squares and a set of dice and small signposts to play a game possibly rather similar to Backgammon.

The archaeologist C.J. Gadd was the first to suggest, instead, that the Babylonians may have been the inventors of a form of Chess. He interpreted a passage in a Babylonian augural text as a reference to a peculiar board game resembling to Chess. This is not surprising, since the Babylonians were expert mathematicians, and were interested in astronomy, the science that studies the movements of celestial objects, which was then not yet separated from astrology, which is interested in the study of the possible effects of such movements on human lives and events. There are some specific clues that suggest a Babylonian origin for Chess; for example the presence, as an element of the game, of the river (this is later found in Chinese chessboards), and the possibility that rooks were originally chariots. The chariot was a key element in the Assyrian and Babylonian war strategies and armies, so it may be possible that one of the many ancestors of modern Chess, as C.J. Gadd cautiously suggested, could be found in Babylon.

Recreational Activities

The recreational activities of the Assyrian and Babylonian upper classes were not limited to games of chance; the Assyrians were especially fond of hunting, and used to keep lions and other wild animals in their urban gardens. The walls of the Assyrian royal palaces are covered in bas-reliefs and sculptures representing Assyrian kings hunting lions. According to Maureen Carroll, the Assyrian kings used their royal gardens as a symbol of power, displaying their victories abroad, since the gardens hosted seeds unknown to the regions where they were located. Archaeologists have not yet located the famous hanging gardens of Babylon, which were probably built on architectural supports and formed artificial forests perhaps resembling a stepped pyramid (*ziggurat*) covered in trees, as ancient Greek and Roman descriptions seem to suggest.

Religious festivals in honor of the gods and goddesses of the Mesopotamian pantheon were probably an occasion for playful activities, since rituals involved solemn processions, dances, and playing music. Some have thought that the Akitu festival, which was the New Year festival in Babylon, was a carnivalesque festival, during which a temporary reversal of roles took place, but Benjamin Sommer has pointed out that the reversal of roles concerned only the king, who was temporarily deprived of his dignity and resumed kingship shortly after, thus enacting the renewal of the Cosmos.

Assyrian and Babylonian children used to play not very differently from children today, and their toys seem to have reflected gender differences typical of patriarchal societies. For example, young boys played with miniature weapons (such as bow and arrows), and young girls had dolls or other toys made of clay or wood.

See Also: Backgammon; Chess and Variations of; Dolls, Barbie and Others; Word Games (Other Than Crosswords).

Bibliography. Enrico Ascalone, *Mesopotamia: Assyrians, Sumerians, Babylonians* (University of California Press, 2007); Stephen Bertman, *Handbook to Life in Ancient Mesopotamia* (Oxford University Press, 2005); Jean Bottéro, *Religion in Ancient Mesopotamia* (University of Chicago Press, 2002); Maureen Carroll, *Earthly Paradises: Ancient Gardens in History and Archaeology* (British Museum, 2003); C.J. Gadd "Babylonian Chess?" *Iraq* (v.8, 1944); Oswald Jacoby and John R. Crawford, *The Backgammon Book* (Penguin Books, 1970); Nigel Pennick, *Games of the Gods. The Origin of Board Games in Magic and Divination* (Century Hutchinson Ltd., 1988); Benjamin D. Sommer, "The Babylonian Akitu Festival: Rectifying the King or Renewing the Cosmos?" *Journal of the Ancient Near Eastern Society* (v.27, 2000).

Maria Beatrice Bittarello
Independent Scholar

Athletics (Amateur)

Athletics consists of an immense variety of related sporting events. These events, referred to as track and field in the United States, fall into the categories of track, field, road racing, multisport, cross country, mountain running, and race-walking events, each of which will be discussed in some detail below. The discussion here begins with the official national and international types and distances of events, but also considers events now popular or gaining popularity with a broader cross section of amateur athletes. Also considered here are some of the historical, sociological, and philosophical concepts relating to amateurism itself, particularly as it relates to athletics.

Track, race walking, and other racing events fall into the broad range of running events, whether run on the 400-meter track, as most formal competitions are, or on a road as is the case in longer races, such as the marathon, or in other venues. Field consists of the jumping and throwing competitions, which include the throwing of differing objects, some intended to go further than others. The jumping competitions also break into categories of height and distance.

Multisport events in athletics include the decathlon, heptathlon, and pentathlon, which include 10, seven, and five different events, respectively, and are rarely seen in competitions outside of Olympic, collegiate or other national or international contests.

Also included in this category is the triathlon, a three-sport event, which has gained a great deal of popularity among amateurs at all levels. Other multisport events that have gained a measure of popularity among amateur racers are such events as the duathlon and aquathlon.

Amateurism

Amateurism as a concept likely originated in England, where, in essence, it prevented the working classes from competing against the aristocratic elite. Englishmen used the concept to help define their social status since, as Eric Howbsbawm asserts, an important aspect of amateur sport was the self-selection of worthy opponents. Upper-class and middle-class sport with its systematic emphasis on amateurism as a criterion was a spontaneous attempt to draw class lines against the masses.

Under this system, leisure time was required to pursue sport, which was to be an avocation entirely independent of work. The idea among the early proponents of amateur sports was that participation for money was disdainful and did not correspond to the gentlemanly spirit of competition. The amateur athlete was considered to be untainted and morally superior.

The sports clubs formed in the latter third of the 19th century were the domain of wealthy, white men in positions of power. In the United States, for instance, during the last third of the 19th and early part of the 20th century, the driving force in amateur athletics were the urban athletic clubs, which at the outset at were primarily interested in track and field.

In the 1870s the New York Athletic Club (NYAC) promoted competitions including only amateurs, defined by the NYAC as "any person who has never competed in an open competition for public or admission money, or with professionals for a prize, nor has at any period in his life taught or assisted in the pursuit of athletic exercises as a means of livelihood," were allowed to participate. This was the definition later adopted by the National Association of Amateur Athletes of America, and the games of any athletic club were restricted to those who met the club's definition of an amateur and a gentleman. In the intervening years the notion of amateur has taken on a far more populist, if somewhat less clear, definition.

Early History

Athletics may arguably have grown out of the ancient past, when it was prosurvival to run and throw things well. It is also arguable that the wish to prove one's superior ability may have led to competitions against one another. In fact, even now, in terms of amateur athletics, it is a case of rivalry hinging on a qualities such as speed, endurance, strength, and skill. While the need for such attributes may have changed and any rules may have been formalized, the essence of many of the abilities required remains.

The first track and field events on record appear to be the ancient Olympics circa 776 B.C.E. Foot races, as well as other events, were held as athletes represented their various city states. The first Olympic athletes, however, could not have been considered amateurs under the amateur ideal of the 19th century or even today. These ancient athletes had much more in common with professional athletes, as they were well paid both financially and in terms of prestige. It was only in the "modern" Olympic games, founded in 1896, that amateurism as an ideal for Olympic competition emerged. By 1974, the rules regarding amateurism in the Olympics had changed, thus changing the concerns about amateurism in other venues.

Amateur athletics remain popular, with a great number of track and field, running, and multisport clubs available internationally to people of all ages. Today, all of the events discussed here are practiced at the amateur level in school and collegiate programs, and most are also available through other amateur associations. There are training programs and clinics to teach children and adults alike the fundamentals of a variety of athletic events. Such clubs often put on what some call open or all-comers track meets, in which anyone—regardless of training or level of ability—can take part.

Running Events

Standard on-track running events usually take place on a 400-meter track and consist of four categories of events; sprints, middle distance, hurdles, and relays. There is an indoor season for athletic events as well, but because of limits of space, the concentration here will be on outdoor events. In the sprint category of athletic running are the 100 meters, 200 meters, and 400 meters. The 400-meter race is also known as the quarter mile, although, since English measures are no longer used, the tracks having been converted metric lengths, it is not precisely a quarter mile.

These distances, particularly the 100 meter, are the purest expression of all out human speed. The basis in tradition of the 200 meter is the ancient Greek sprint event the "stadion" (literally, length of the stadium), however, it actually is based on a furlong, or one-eighth mile.

Typical middle distances are the 800 meter (or half mile), first run by professionals in the 1830s and presumably run by amateurs before this time; 1500 meter (or metric mile); and 1600 meter (or mile). In some instances the 3000 meter (roughly two miles) is considered a middle-distance run. However, most include it in the long distance category, along with 5K and 10K track runs.

There are a variety of road races. These races are run on the open road, although they sometimes end on a track. Events in this category include 5K, 10K, half marathon (21.0975K), and marathon (42.195K). Other less common distances include 15K, 20K, 10-mile and 20-mile races. Road races are run by a variety of amateurs and are often less formal than school- or college-related events. The movement toward this type of road racing is considered here under the subheading of road racing and multisport.

Hurdles and relays are variations on running races. In hurdles, athletes add the element of jumping to running by clearing evenly spaced barriers or hurdles on the track. Distances range from 100 meters to Steeplechase, which is a 3000-meter race. The modern events in hurdling began in England in the 1830s

Amateur Steeplechase, born out of a wager among Oxford students in 1850, was initially an imitation of horse racing. The first two-mile events included hurdles, streams, and obstacles in open country. Just like the jockeys in horseracing, the runners were given weight handicaps. Steeplechasing came to the track in Britain in 1879 and entered the Olympics in 1900. Relay adds the element of team competition, in that four athletes pass a metal baton between them, usually at evenly spaced intervals. Common distances are 400 meters (4 x 100), 800 meters, mile, and two-mile relays. Relay medleys with uneven distances are more rarely seen.

Jumping Events

Jumping events fall into categories of height and length. Height events are the high jump and the pole vault. The two most common length events are the long jump and the triple jump. The high jump was practiced commonly by the Celts. The first formal competition was organized in England in 1840. By 1865 the rules that remain in force today were systematized. Pole vaulting has a longer history, as it was known to the Ancient Greeks. The Celts, too, used poles for jumping, but for length rather than height. The Germans adapted the event to a vertical jump in 1775. In 1850, the first competitions of "running pole leaping" with heavy, stiff poles occurred. Bamboo was introduced for poles in 1900 and fiberglass in 1956, both of which changed the nature of the sport by allowing flexibility in the pole.

Vertical or long jumping is equally important in athletics. The long jump was known in ancient times and was used as part of the pentathlon as early as 708 B.C.E. The Greeks practiced the triple jump as three consecutive long jumps. The Celts invented a style of three jumps in a continuous action that was later regulated, first by the Irish and then by the Americans. After 1900 the form of hop-step-jump became the three movements of the triple jump.

Throwing Events

All of the events that are included in this category have ancient origins. The ancient Greek poet Homer tells

When we think of amateur athletics, track and field events may come to mind first, then perhaps baseball and other ball games. Fencing is an amateur status sport, unless one is a paid instructor.

of rock-throwing contests at the siege of Troy. In the 16th century, King Henry VIII was known for his skill in court competitions of weight and hammer throwing. Seventeenth-century soldiers organized cannon ball–throwing contests. All of these activities evolved into modern-day shot put. The hammer toss, too, has ancient origins. It was originally a freestyle run with the toss of a rigid hammer consisting of a wooden handle with a cast iron head. The hammer has now been transformed into a grip with a connection to a ball (the head of the hammer), looking somewhat like a mace.

Hercules was reputed to be one of the first javelin throwers. By 708 B.C.E. the sport included throwing for distance and throwing at a target. The javelin is now thrown for distance. In 1780 Scandinavians, particularly the Finns, adopted javelin as their own and popularized the sport. Discus too has ancient origins, going back at least as far as 708 B.C.E., when the discus was made of bronze or stone. The sport was included in the first modern Olympics in 1896.

Multisport Events

Because they are much more rarely seen in amateur sport outside of collegiate competition, little time will be devoted here to three types of multisport: decathlon, heptathlon, and pentathlon. These events consist of combinations of 10, seven, and five sports, respectively. Each event is a combination of track and field events.

Other multisport events, however, are increasing in popularity at all levels. While some might not include this event in the purview of athletics, the road running component places them among the range of athletic activities. The most popular, and most well-known, of these is the triathlon. Duathlon and aquathlon will also be discussed briefly.

Triathlon, which consists of swimming, cycling, and running consecutively, has a relatively short history. In 1974 in Mission Bay, California, several friends began to work out together. Some were swimmers, some cyclists, and some runners. Friendly competition between them emerged and eventually led to impromptu competitions. In the fall of 1974 the first triathlon attracted 46 participants.

Like track and road races, there are various distances involved in triathlon, including the minisprint, sprint, Olympic, Half Iron, and Ironman. The Ironman distance is the mostly closely regulated, and courses must be certified. The same is true for the Half Iron, or 70.3 distance. The most famous Ironman race, the Hawaii Ironman, began in 1978 with the combination of three previously existing stand-alone races: the Waikiki rough water swim of 2.4 miles, the Oahu bike race of 112 miles, and the Honolulu marathon consisting of 26.2 miles.

Duathlon is also a three-leg event but includes only two sports, running and cycling. The participants in this instance run, cycle, and then run a second time. There are a variety of distances in this sport as well. This sport has repeatedly waxed and waned over the last 20 years but continues to have some measure of popularity among those who do not have a swimming background. Anyone who can run and cycle can participate.

Aquathlon, consisting of running and swimming, is probably the least well known of these multisports. It is gaining in popularity, however, because of the fact that less expensive equipment is required and the distances are smaller, making training time more manageable for amateur athletes and space management easier for race directors. The format for an aquathlon is either run, swim, run, or simply swim and run.

Other Athletic Competitions

Included under the umbrella of athletics are three other sports that attract amateur participants: cross country or trail running, race walking, and mountain running. Each of these will be briefly considered here.

Cross country, or the related racing that is called trail running, requires a different kind of technical skill than road or track racing. Cross country is, in many instances, a winter event, but it can be a summer event. The International Association of Athletics Federations (IAAF) describes these runners as the "four-wheel drive vehicles of athletics," as they face not only their competition, but also the vagaries of nature. Many amateur athletes who participate in this type of race do double duty, running trails or cross country, but returning or alternating with road or track racing.

Mountain running is based on a human instinct to survive and the need to run both short and long distances on hillsides to do so. Mountain running is related to cross country in that it is a run through a predetermined course in natural surroundings. The philosophy of athletic mountain running is based on time, rather than survival or orienteering. The goal is to compete with other runners to reach the finish on a defined path as quickly as possible. Courses are designed to eliminate danger. No equipment is needed.

The history of race walking goes back at least to the English footmen of the 12th and 13th centuries, who alternated running and walking in accompanying their masters' coaches. The competitions began in the last quarter of the 18th century and entered the Olympics early in the 20th century. Visual race walking may look unusual, but the difficulty of walking as fast as possible and in a particular form without breaking into a jog or run is challenging.

History of Governing Bodies

The history of governance of amateur athletics, including event certification and sanctioning as well as considerations regarding the amateur status of athletes as it pertains to the United States, is considered here. While the history and rules in other countries are different, there seem to be similar governing bodies in other nations.

In America, a "win at all costs" mentality overcame the English gentlemanly ideal. This drive to win caused an early corruption of amateur tradition in which organizers of amateur athletic events began to seek surreptitious ways of compensating and subsidizing star athletes. The rampancy of this type of behavior, among other issues, led eventually to the formation of governing bodies for amateur athletics.

Need of administrative help with the 1876 national championships caused the NYAC to send a call to other clubs to form an association to take up the burden of the games. The result was the formation of the National Association of Amateur Athletes of America (N4A).

This association was the first viable governing body and claimed to be the national governing body for amateur sport, but within 10 years the organization lost power. It never really reached national prominence, nor did it succeed in controlling the rise in corruption that was taking place throughout the 1880s. Increasingly, clubs were offering more and better perquisites to the fastest and strongest athletes in order to lure them away from rival clubs, a matter that defied the amateur ideal of the sport.

The NYAC was also fundamental in the foundation of the Amateur Athletic Union (AAU), a more truly national organization. Under the influence of the AAU there was a reduction of gambling and professionalism by the mid 1890s. The AAU heralded a return to the purist interpretation of amateurism; that is, the true amateur competed merely out of the love of the sport and not for any monetary gain. While this stance may no longer seem applicable, it did a great deal to promote the growth of amateur athletics.

In fact, the whole movement toward rooting out corruption made athletics more acceptable. When upper–middle class professionals of all kinds dedicated significant time and effort to competing in and promoting amateur athletics, it reduced the image of such pastimes as frivolous and useless. This allowed amateur athletics to take root in schools and colleges, as well as society in general.

By the end of the 1890s the AAU had begun to seek broader control over amateur athletics by involvement with college athletics. By the turn of the century, there was a fight for influence over amateur sports of all types between the AAU, the colleges, and the American Olympic Committee, each with its own stake in its athletes and activities.

Early in the 20th century, the two developing sports movements, the modern Olympic Games (beginning in 1896) and the American intercollegiate athletic system, had both adopted the concept of amateurism, believing that it developed morally superior competitors, though there were lingering questions about amateurism.

Colleges are allowed to pay all the educational expenses of their athletes, and while athletic scholarships are the norm, the current governing body for college sports in the United States, the National Collegiate Athletic Association (NCAA), provides and enforces strict eligibility rules for athletes in all sports. These rules preclude a student athlete from accepting a patronage job or taking part in product endorsement, for instance.

Early on, representatives of the International Olympic Committee and other associations struggled to determine the definition of amateur. The discussions often revolved around minute points, such as whether someone who had coached or taught athletics could also participate as an amateur. The objective of these talks was to preserve the character of sport as play and not business. The debate has continued through the years until the concept has become more a technical than a moral distinction.

While the AAU continues to exist, the Amateur Sports Act of 1978 changed its role in amateur sport. Previous to 1978 the AAU governed all aspects of international amateur competition and regulated amateur athletics in the United States. With the passage of the act, the AAU became a volunteer organization whose role was the continued promotion of amateur athletics for children and adults. The act established a new U.S. Olympic Committee to oversee amateur sports. This committee then chartered a national governing body for each Olympic sport, such as the U.S. Track and Field (USATF), for athletic events at all levels. The national governing bodies set the rules for selection of the Olympic team in each sport and promote amateur competition in that sport, including the sanctioning and certification of smaller athletic events.

The line between professionalism and amateurism has become further blurred as small local races have begun to award cash and merchandise prizes. By accepting such a prize, a young collegiate or college-bound athlete can still endanger his or her amateur status for college sports in the United States

Road Racing and Multisport

In the late 1970s, there was a rise in the popularity of jogging as a fitness exercise. Thereafter, road racing was established as a populist athletic activity. Now, road racing ranges from fun runs held in towns and cities small and large, to competitive races of all lengths, to the elite marathon events in large cities worldwide.

Many amateur and recreational running clubs and other groups hold these fun run/walks and races. Usually participants pay to participate in such events, as they are held to raise money for a program or charity. One notable example of a fundraising effort of this type is the Susan G. Komen race series, a series of 5K events for runners and walkers intended to raise breast cancer awareness and funding for research.

While 5K is arguably the most popular distance for these road races, at least in the United States, there are many longer-distance races available, including 4-mile, 5-mile, 8K, 10K, 20K, 10-mile, and 20-mile races, as well as half marathons and full marathons. Many, though not all, of these races identify themselves as sanctioned or certified. In the United States even small road races can be certified by the USATF.

The popularity of the marathon can be traced to the success of the first modern Olympic marathon in 1896. The beginnings of both the New York and Boston Marathons can be attributed to that race. The length of the race was not standardized until 1924 at 26.22 miles, or 42.195K. The first marathon of this particular length was run in 1908 in London, but contrary to popular belief, the distance had more to do with logistical issues than the direct influence of the British royal family.

With the increasing popularity of multisport, a large number of triathlon clubs, some of them with duathlon and aquathlon divisions, have appeared as well. These clubs also sponsor races, either to support themselves or for charitable causes.

The popularity of all of these athletic endeavors, among members of the general public and elite athletes alike, has given rise to paid training programs for amateurs, whether experienced, beginner, or recreational athletes. Some of these coaching programs are internet based, but others take place in face-to-face groups. In many of these groups the athletes simply pay for coaching, but in others, notably Team in Training, group membership depends upon raising money for a specific charitable cause.

See Also: Ancient Greece; Organized or Sanctioned Play; Play as Competition, Psychology of; Play as Competition, Sociology of.

Bibliography. Amateur Sport, *American Eras,* www.encyclopedia.com (cited July 2008); Eric Habsbawn, "Mass-Producing Traditions: Europe, 1870–1914," in Eric Howsbawm and Terence Ranger, eds., *The Invention of Tradition* (Cambridge University Press, 1983); International Association of Athletics Federations, *IAAF,* www.iaaf.org/community/athletics/index.html (cited August 2008); United States Olympic Committee (2008), USA Triathlon, usatriathlon.org (cited August 2008); United States Track and Field (USATF), www.usatf.org (cited July 2008).

Suellen Adams
University of Rhode Island

Auction Pitch

Auction Pitch is a card game played with a standard deck and is a member of the All Fours family that descended from the English card game All Fours, played in most former English colonies, especially the West Indies. It is the legacy of All Fours that gives us the name "jack" for the card previously known as the knave, and other members of the family include All

Fives, California Jack, and Cinch. Spoil Five is a close relation, with similarly unusual rules.

The name All Fours comes from the scoring system, which awards points in four categories: the highest trump in play, the lowest trump in play, the Jack (given to the player who takes the Jack in a trump), and the Game (given to the player who takes the highest value of tricks). An amalgam of point-trick games and shorthand games like Euchre, All Fours dates from about the middle of the 17th century and may have been adapted by the English from a Dutch game. Typically a low-class gambling game for most of its history, it was introduced to the United States in the 18th century and became the most popular card game by the 1800s.

In the middle of the 19th century, the rapid ascendancy of Poker threatened All Fours' dominance of American card playing, and variants of the game developed quickly in response. Auction Pitch was originally called Commercial Pitch and is sometimes known as Sell-Out, and differed from All Fours in that there is no turn-up phase. Instead, the first card played—pitched—determines the trump suit and is sold to the highest bidder for points. The game is usually played by four, but it can accommodate two to seven players.

See Also: All Fives; Euchre; Gambling; History of Playing Cards; Spoil Five.

Bibliography. Elliott Avedon, *The Study of Games* (Krieger Pub., 1979); Roger Caillois, *Man, Play, and Games* (University of Illinois Press, 2001); Johan Huizinga, *Homo Ludens* (Beacon Press, 1971); David Parlett, *The Oxford Guide to Card Games* (Oxford University Press, 1990); Brian Sutton-Smith, *The Ambiguity of Play* (Harvard University Press, 2001).

Bill Kte'pi
Independent Scholar

Australia

Play appears to be a universal characteristic of childhood throughout history. Children, compared with mature adults, are small, weak, have less mental capacity, and are largely powerless. They are also intensely curious, imaginative, physically active, and, past infancy, passionately attached to the company of other children. They inhabit a play culture shaped and patterned by the particular adult world in which they are reared, and this world determines whether the children play with sticks and stones or miniature battery-operated cars and talking dolls. It is also from the adult world that children receive the songs, rhymes, and stories (oral, written, and electronic) that provide both models for their own verbal lore and subject matter for exploration and parody.

Connected and yet separate from the play activities and traditions provided by adults lies the playlore of childhood, with features remarkably common across place and time. A continuing children's play subculture exists in communities where children are kept apart from much of adults' daily life and sent to special institutions for learning called schools, just as it does in hunter-gather and agrarian communities, where children are closely integrated into the family's daily activities. Australian children, both before and after European settlement in 1788, exhibit a range of playways familiar to children anywhere in the world, though everywhere marked and modified by the particular circumstances in which the children live and by the ingenuity and imagination of the players.

The children of Aborigines, whose many tribes and clans have inhabited this ancient continent for at least 40,000 years, are known to have had—and continue to have—a rich variety of playlore. There is a smattering of evidence that some children from the British Isles who came to Australia after 1788, as well as some Australian-born children of immigrant families, especially those who lived outside cities (in what Australians call the bush, or outback), learned games and songs from Aboriginal playmates. There was certainly a mingling of play practices, such as marbles—whether the clay and glass European-imported variety or the local small shells and stones—and string games—the latter a popular and widespread tool for story-telling in many Aboriginal communities.

Postsettlement Australia

Ever since its European settlement, Australia has been a predominantly urban society, with the majority of its children having had little ongoing contact with the indigenous Australians. The waves of immigrants, which for the first 150 years were largely Anglo-Celtic, and then post–World War II, increasingly from many parts of the world, brought with them playthings and the traditions associated with play, such as dolls, balls, go-carts, and board games. (As always and everywhere, poor children, lacking expensive toys, made do with homemade and self-made toys: footballs constructed of tightly wrapped newspaper, dolls made from clothes-pegs, dressed colorfully in scraps of material.) The invisible luggage of the immigrant children included the playlore—games, rituals, and so on—of their pre-Australian lives. Now we have children playing marbles using an Asian method of projecting the marble, labelled the Chinese Flick; and the game of Elastics can be seen with the usual long piece of white elastic replaced by colored elastic bands joined together, an alternative technique learned from immigrant Vietnamese children.

Cultural exchange in play is an everyday practice in many school playgrounds. That does not mean that there is no evidence of racial, national, and religious antipathies: adult prejudices seep into children's lives. These same prejudices also disappear, particularly when the adult culture changes. The once ubiquitous sectarian chants of "Catholic dogs" and "Proddie frogs" have vanished in recent decades, thanks to the ecumenical movement among Christian churches.

Intergender Play

Small rural schools have always permitted girls and boys to play together, while many city and town schools separated the sexes in the playground until the 1960s. This effort at social engineering may be a partial explanation for the existence of a number of boys' games and girls' games, although historical and cross-cultural evidence suggests that there are probably deeper developmental reasons for this phenomenon in middle childhood. Even where such gender divisions were enforced (and reinforced by adult-encouraged sporting activities), children continued to draw the bulk of their play from the same reservoir of tradition and invention.

An example of the commonality of children's play interests emerged from two studies of youngsters' collecting habits, the first in 1910 in Sydney, replicated in 1987 in Melbourne. Children's passion for acquiring, organizing, displaying, and swapping objects, from birds' feathers to football cards, is well known. These two studies showed that the majority of favored objects were common to both boys and girls—although girls' collections were somewhat more diverse.

Skateboarding, roller-skating, and kick-to-kick football are still visible in some suburban streets, while urban life, with its ever-increasing road traffic, and the moral panic of "stranger danger," has greatly diminished the street play, once a feature of Australian children's lives. Many youngsters are also kept busy with extracurricular activities in the hours once spent in street play, such as sport teams and violin lessons.

Now the school playground is the major arena for children's voluntary play. Games known to the ancient Romans—Knucklebones, Hand-Clapping, Chasing and Hiding—co-exist with Spider Man, Batman, and singing and clapping games incorporating advertising slogans, movie stars, and failed politicians. Most of the games portrayed in Pieter Breughel's 1560 Flemish painting *Children's Games* are still performed in Australia.

Imaginative Play

The extensive play repertoire includes imaginative and fantasy games—little girls building "houses" from sticks, stones, and leaves among tree roots; boys and girls playing Martians and using a fallen tree-trunk as an imaginary spaceship; vigorous, noisy games involving much running, shouting, and negotiation; games of competition and skill—Skipping, Hoppy, Marbles, Knucklebones (called Jacks in Australia), elastics, rubber bands; and a vast quantity of verbal play—rhymes, riddles, jokes, secret languages, insults, chants. It is all entirely self-regulated, collaborative, and flexible. Children will adapt an old game or rhyme to a changed environment, invent new rules when desired, and utilize any material at hand. The aim, above all, is the continuity of their play. The school playground is criss-crossed by invisible lines of play—a complex map of tradition and invention created and respected by the children.

Modern Issues

Unfortunately, a lack of understanding of the central importance of play to children, together with a fear of litigation if a child is hurt, are resulting in more and more schools limiting recess and restricting children's freedom to play. The effort to prevent children from engaging in their own play traditions may be futile; it is also damaging and counterproductive, educationally and socially.

The first nationwide study of Australian children's playlore was undertaken by an American scholar, Dorothy Howard, in the mid-1950s. Her extensive collection and analysis is now part of the Australian Children's Folklore Collection, housed in Museum Victoria; the collection was recently listed on UNESCO's Australian Memory of the World Register. The Oral History and Folklore section of the National Library of Australia also holds substantial audiotapes of children's verbal lore. The first significant publication in this field was Ian Turner's 1969 uncensored collection of children's rhymes, *Cinderella Dressed in Yella*, later expanded in a second edition. There are now a number of books of and about children's lore and language, for both children and adults, and a developing academic interest in playlore research.

See Also: Australian Aborigines; Boys' Play; Cooperative Play; Dolls, Barbie and Others; Fantasy Play; Girls' Play; Jacks; Marbles; Pretending; Recess; Role-Playing; Tag.

Bibliogrpahy. Kate Darian-Smith and June Factor, eds., *Child's Play: Dorothy Howard and the Folklore of Australian Children* (Museum Victoria, 2005); Gwenda Davey, *Snug as a Bug!* (Brolly Books, 2005); Gwyn Dow and June Factor, eds., *Australian Childhood: An Anthology* (McPhee Gribble, 1991); June Factor, *Captain Cook Chased a Chook: Children's Folklore in Australia* (Penguin, 1988); June Factor, *Far Out Brussel Sprout!* (Brolly Books, 2004); June Factor, *Kidspeak: A Dictionary of Australian Children's Words, Expressions and Games* (Melbourne University Press, 2000); P.L. Lindsay and D. Palmer, *Playground Game Characteristics of Brisbane Primary School Children* (Australian Government Publishing Service, 1981); Wendy Lowenstein, *Shocking, Shocking, Shocking: Improper Play Rhymes of Australian Children* (The Rams Skull Press, 1988); Ian Turner, June Factor, and Wendy Lowenstein, *Cinderella Dressed in Yella* (Heinemann Educational, 1978).

June Factor
University of Melbourne

Australian Aborigines

Australian Aboriginal and Torres Strait Islander (TSI) people have been playing a rich diversity of games in organized forms for tens of thousands of years. Many traditional games were recorded by early settlers, government officials, scientists, and missionaries who travelled throughout Australia during the 19th century. Aboriginal games can be viewed in relation to their direct and indirect association to daily activities, whether economic, political, or domestic in nature, including the formation of group identity and social interaction. Sadly, after colonization, many traditional games were lost because of factors such as loss of land, loss of tradition, and fragmentation of Aboriginal communities.

Author Ken Edwards explains that "one of the first activities to be suspended when a society comes under threat is games." Most games are played for fun and enjoyment; therefore, they are largely abandoned in the face of an imminent threat to the survival of their people. Today, very few traditional games exist even in areas that have retained a semitraditional lifestyle. As a result, there is little literature on the topic of traditional Aboriginal games.

Gendered Roles

Nineteenth-century anthropologists observed that imitation games were one of the largest categories of games among Aboriginal children, as play was used in preparation for later life. Imitating elders' camps was a common pastime for Aboriginal children across Australia. Pastimes associated with domestic aspects included caring for dolls fashioned from sticks or pieces of bark and gathering and preparing food. Noisy, fast, and potentially dangerous games, such as sham fights and battles, were acted out by boys using sharp blades of grass as spears and wooden shields to protect them from the enemies' attack. Role-play, as in many cultures, provided Aboriginal children with an opportunity to test their understanding of traditional roles and relationships.

Education

Aboriginal games were also intricately linked to instruction of roles. While traditional games were often played for pleasure, most required skills that helped prepare children for the daily tasks of life by promoting mental and physical capabilities. Many games resembled hunting situations and were designed to prepare youths for warfare occasions, placing an emphasis on protection, precision, and agility—all vital for survival in a threatening situation. For example, in North Queensland young men played a game called *Kalq*, where they threw spears at each other and deflected them with wooden shields. *Wana*, a traditional game known in Western Australia, was only played by girls. It taught them to defend their young by warding off attacks from other girls with large sticks.

Memory games, played by the Walbiri tribe of the Northern Territory, helped children to remember and identify the surrounding landscape. A large circle was

Australian Aborigines preparing a meal in a lithograph from 1895. Games gave adults and children an opportunity to take a break from the daily survival tasks, such as hunting, gathering, and preparing food.

drawn on the ground that contained a variety of sticks and stones, each representing a prominent landmark in the area. Each player turned their back on the circle and named the objects in order until they made a mistake. Memory games were an essential tool in the education of children's spatial awareness.

Seasons and Resources

Games played depended on the natural resources the seasons made available. For example, some Torres Strait Islander groups used beans from trees and balls made of fruit to play games on nearby beaches. On the mainland, other groups collected seed heads of spinifex, a native rolling grass, and threw them in the air, chasing and catching them. In South Australia and Victoria, games such as Keepings Off, handball, and football games were played using opossum or kangaroo skin balls filled with grass or charcoal. While different in nature and the materials used, almost all traditional games required high levels of agility, precision, coordination, and physical fitness.

Social Interaction

Played solely for pleasure, games enabled both adults and children to escape the daily tasks necessary for survival, such as hunting and gathering food and setting up camp. The majority of group pastimes involved people of both sexes, young and old. Fair play was always encouraged, and the emphasis of games was not winning but, rather, promoting goodwill and interpersonal relationships. Group pastimes included swinging, skipping, and water games. Team games included *Marn Grook*, which means Game Ball, a traditional game played by the Djab Wurrung people in western Victoria. Each team had a leader, like a captain, and the object of the game was to keep the ball (made from opossum skin filled with charcoal) from the other side for as long as possible by throwing and kicking it to one another. Teams would have up to 100 or so men, and the games would go for days and even weeks on end. *Marn Grook* is said to be the Aboriginal game that provided the foundations for Australian Rules football. There are also accounts of instances in which Aboriginal play was adapted to or imitated European play with bats and balls.

While some traditional games were common to all Australian Aboriginal and TSI groups, others were limited to a small group or region. Games were often learned by watching and not by instruction, thus encouraging the development of skills such as memorizing, sequencing, spatial awareness, and language. Although providing food, water, and shelter for Aboriginal and TSI people, the landscape also afforded them the opportunity to transform their surroundings into a playground for recreational pursuit.

See Also: Australia; Play as Learning, Anthropology of; Play as Learning, Psychology of; Play as Learning, Sociology of.

Bibliography. Ken Edwards, *Choopardoo: Games from the Dreamtime* (QUT Publications, 1999); Claudia Haagen, *Bush Toys: Aboriginal Children at Play* (Aboriginal Studies Press, 1994); Michael Albert Salter, *Games and Pastimes of the Australian Aboriginal* (Unpublished M.A. Thesis, University of Alberta, 1967).

Abby Cooper
Australian National University

Austria

The physical characteristics of Austria have influenced the leisure activities and games in which women and men there have participated. Mountainous and largely rural, much of Austria is also marked by relatively long winters. These facts helped structure how Austrians play and played. Winter activities such as sledding, ice-skating, and *Eisstockschiessen* (a target game played on ice or snow and similar to lawn bowling) continue to be popular, and skiing has developed over the last century or so as one of the the national pastimes. The often scattered nature of settlement patterns with individual peasant and later farmhouses resulted in the centrality of the tavern or inn (*Gasthaus*) for social life.

The relatively modest economic position of the numerous domestic servants or resident farmhands required them to board in their employers' homes, making the tavern even more attractive as the place for whatever limited free time these laborers may have had. In some areas, the rural landlords who owned the properties and leased them to subject peasants (until peasant emancipation in the 19th century) mandated the use of particular licensed inns or taverns for social activities. In these locales activities such as candlepins and card playing were popular, as were contests of strength such as arm wrestling and weight lifting. A well-known Austrian card game, *Schnapsen*, served and serves as an important pastime. It is recognized often as a particularly Austrian game. Playing cards were introduced early into this area. Examples from the early days of printing in the 15th century have been found. (Printing was invented and initially developed in southwestern Germany, not far from Austria.)

As a predominantly Christian country and one heavily influenced by the Counter-Reformation of the 16th and 17th centuries, traditional Roman Catholic practices and customs have also influenced patterns of play in Austria. Religious festivals such as church dedication anniversaries and saints' festivals have served as opportunities for celebrations that include parades, music, and games of luck. Advent is marked still in many places by collective singing, processions with candles or lanterns, and sometimes costumed young men who play the role of mountain spirits. The longest period of festivities is associated with Carnaval (*Fasching*). During these weeks preceding Lent, musical performances—particularly operas, balls, and costumed galas—mark a playful period in the year. Children often dress up and are rewarded with candy. As in many places in the Roman Catholic world, the festivities culminate on the Tuesday before Ash Wednesday: *Fasching Dienstag*. Parades and parties mark the end of the holiday season.

Austria was for many years an aristocratic society. A relatively small number of nobles controlled much of the government, especially in the countryside. These nobles' tastes influenced the pastimes and games they and their subjects enjoyed. One of the most significant of these pastimes was hunting. A legal prerogative reserved to the nobles, hunting involved many people, not just the hunters. Huge tracts of land in Austria were reserved for game and its pursuit. These tracts included a large amount of land immediately outside of Vienna, the capital city. They became known as the Prater and were opened to the public in 1766. Part of these one-time hunting grounds developed into a popular entertainment district complete with burlesque shows, rides, penny arcades, and more. Another aristocratic pastime that could turn into a public spectacle was jousting. Throughout the later Middle Ages and into the Early Modern period, noblemen competed in public contests, both on horseback and on foot. This form of male athletic competition later influenced the development of formal sports in Austria. The Austrian military supported the training and participation of its officers in equestrian and fencing competitions into the early 20th century.

Athletics were increasingly politicized in Austria in the 19th and 20th centuries. Workers' advocates strongly supported open-air activities that would attract men (and to some extent women), getting them out of the taverns and into the fresh air. Large numbers of clubs were founded to organize various activities, from bicycling to soccer. Some disagreements arose over the role of physical activity: Should it be organized around the English model of sport, with competitions, referees, and records, or should it be collective and concentrate on general physical fitness through group gymnastics and similar activities? The question remains to some extent unanswered.

An urban counterpart to the tavern developed over the course of the 19th century: the coffee house. There, middle-class urbanites could partake in colonial wares, read the latest news, play board games such as chess, or shoot billiards, another popular English import. To some extent, these public places of socialization and play compensated for the limitations in private spaces available to many people in Austria at the time, particularly in rapidly growing and hugely overpopulated Vienna. The tenements, which were hastily constructed for the migrants to the city, were more reasons for alternative play areas to develop. For many, games and play could not be enjoyed anywhere else but in the public spaces of taverns, coffee houses, or sports clubhouses.

The Austro-Hungarian Empire was dismantled in 1919 after the end of World War I, and suddenly Austria was without its geographic contexts. Some effort was made to reconcile the impoverished population with the new state of affairs. The old aristocratic world and its pastimes such as horseback riding and hunting were now devalued. Working-class clubs, mass gymnastics, and even paramilitary training replaced them as the political scene degenerated into civil war and then fascist takeover in the 1930s. One symbol of the attempt to cultivate a new national identity in the Austria of this first republic was the development of the board game Speculation. Based largely on the U.S. game Monopoly, this version was squarely based in Austria. Players bought property not in one oceanside resort town such as in the U.S. example but in cities across the new republic. Later this game was renamed DKT (Das kaufmännische Talent: The Skill of a Salesman.) It remains one of the most popular Austrian board games.

After the annexation of Austria by the German Reich in 1938, the horrors of the Holocaust, and World War II, the Allies reestablished the Austrian republic in 1945. Units of their armies remained there until a decade later, when an international peace treaty was signed, giving the second Austrian republic independence.

Two themes would mark the institutional histories of play and sport in the new Austria: desires to reconnect with the sporting and political landscapes of the pre-German period, and desires to create a sense of Austrian national identity. Sports would play a significant role in the latter undertaking, particularly Alpine skiing and soccer.

The country cohosted the men's European soccer championships in 2008, giving Austrians the chance to communally celebrate, reinforcing their experience of belonging to one political unit through the playful use of flags, pennants, hats, scarfs, and bodypaint in the national colors of red and white. The unprecedented economic prosperity of Austria in the late 20th century provided the opportunity for play and leisure activities on an unprecedented scale. These provided avenues for the development of a national identity.

See Also: Amusement Parks; Billiards; Bocce; Chess and Variations of; Cityscapes as Play Sites; Europe, 1200 to 1600; Europe, 1600 to 1800; Europe, 1800 to 1900; Europe, 1900 to 1940; Europe, 1940 to 1960; Europe, 1960 to Present; History of Playing Cards; Monopoly and Variations of; Skiing.

Bibliography. Roman Horak and Georg Spitaler, "Sport Space and National Identity. Soccer and Skiing as Formative Forces: On the Austrian Example," *American Behavioral Scientist* (v.46/11, July 2003); Gilbert Norden, "Sport in Österreich: Entstehung, Verbreitung und Differenzierung (19. und frühes 20. Jahrhundert)," *Historicum* (Winter, 1998–99); "Zwanzig Jahre Spielforschung," www.spielforschung.at (cited June 2008).

Joseph F. Patrouch
Florida International University

Avalon Hill

Avalon Hill, now owned by Hasbro and operating as a division of Wizards of the Coast, was a tabletop game company specializing in Wargames and strategic boardgames. They were not only responsible for pioneering many of the key concepts of modern tabletop Wargaming, such as the hex grid and zones of control, but were also responsible for publishing some of the most recognizable titles in the board game industry such as Civilization, Axis and Allies, Runequest, and Dune.

In 1958, Charles Roberts founded Avalon Hill in order to capitalize on the success of his game Tactics. Self-published in 1952, Tactics was particularly noteworthy because it was based on actual war tactics and scenarios. As such, Tactics is considered to be the first modern tabletop war game. Shortly after the company was founded, it released Tactics II, the sequel to Roberts' original game. The game, which was an improvement on the original design, featured a series of concepts that have long since become ubiquitous in modern tabletop Wargames.

One might argue that many of these concepts have become pivotal mechanics in many other types of tabletop games beyond the wargaming genre. Chief among these newly introduced mechanics was the Combat Results Table (CRT), a tool to determine in-game combat success or failure. Shortly after the release of Tactics II, Avalon Hill published Gettysburg, which is widely considered to be the first tabletop Wargame based upon an actual historical battle.

By the end of 1962, Avalon Hill had fallen on difficult economic times. Roberts was forced to sell the company to Monarch Printing, Avalon Hill's printer, as a way of paying back his debt to them. Upon the sale of Avalon Hill, Roberts left the company and founded Barnard, Roberts, and Co., a small press. Monarch Printing, who changed their name to Monarch Avalon after they acquired the company, continued to run Avalon Hill as a subsidiary for 36 years until its sale to Hasbro in 1998.

Throughout the 1970s, Avalon Hill continued to publish tabletop Wargames, including such noteworthy titles as Midway, Afrika Korps, The Battle of the Bulge, and Blitzkrieg. However, in addition to its tabletop Wargame products, Avalon Hill continued to publish tabletop games in other genres, a strategy pioneered by Charles Roberts before he was forced to sell the company to Monarch Printing. Among these games were Acquire, an economic game of acquisitions and mergers, and Twixt, an abstract strategy game, the rights to both of which had been acquired by Avalon Hill when they purchased the products from 3M's Bookshelf Game series.

During this period, Avalon not only published original titles, but also purchased the rights to republish games that had been previously published by smaller companies. Included in these republished games were Battleline Publications' Wooden Ships and Iron Men, Jedko Games' The Russian Campaign and War at Sea, and Hartland Trefoil's Civilization. In response to the enormous popularity TSR was experiencing with *Dungeons & Dragons*, Avalon Hill also published several traditional pen and paper role-playing games (RPG), including Lords of Creation and Powers and Perils. Through a complicated agreement with the publisher Chaosium, Avalon Hill was about to secure the rights to release RuneCraft, an RPG that had established itself as the second most popular fantasy role-playing game after *Dungeons & Dragons*.

At the beginning of the 1980s, Avalon Hill began developing numerous computer games based on their various boardgames. Platforms for these new computer games included the VIC 20, Commodore 64, and Apple II. Unfortunately, Avalon Hill saw little success with their computer games.

Avalon Hill enjoyed moderate growth through the 1980s and early 1990s. However, during the mid 1990s, the boardgame industry as a whole began suffering a downturn in sales. Not only had overall sales of their board games decreased, but the company had also lost the rights to two of their most popular games, Civilization and 1830, in a legal battle with the computer game publisher MicroProse.

In 1997 and 1998 Avalon Hill lost significant money in both its computer division and its boardgame division. In the summer of 1998, Eric Dott, president of Monarch Avalon, Inc. (the parent company of Avalon Hill), sold the rights to all Avalon Hill titles, all back stock, and the company name itself to Hasbro, Inc. Hasbro continued to publish games under the Avalon Hill name. In addition, they sold the rights to several games, such as Advanced Squad Leader, to other publishers. In late 1999, Avalon Hill was made a division of Wizards of the Coast, who had been purchased by Hasbro earlier that year. Wizards of the Coast continues to release games under the Avalon Hill name, including Axis & Allies, Betrayal at House on the Hill, RoboRally, and Risk 2210 A.D.

See Also: *Dungeons & Dragons*; Hasbro; Role-Playing; TSR; Wargames Research Group; Warhammer.

Bibliography. Avalon Hill Official Home Page, www.wizards.com/default.asp?x=ah/welcome (cited November 2008); Brad King and John Borland, *Dungeons and Dreamers: The Rise of Computer Game Culture from Geek to Chic* (McGraw-Hill Osborne Media, 2003); J. Patrick Williams et al., eds., *Gaming as Culture: Essays on Reality, Identity And Experience in Fantasy Games* (McFarland, 2006).

Ethan Watrall
Michigan State University

Azerbaijan

Located in the Caucasus, Azerbaijan was a part of the Soviet Union until it gained independence in 1991. It shares borders with the Russian Federation, Georgia, Armenia, and Iran, with its capital, the city of Baku being one of the major ports on the Caspian Sea. The Azeri people, who make up 89 percent of the population, have an extensive culture that can be traced back to medieval times.

The Azeris developed many of their cultural pursuits from their position along some of the trade routes between Turkey and China, and Turkish games such as Backgammon became popular, as did later card games, which probably came from Persia (modern-day Iran). Storytellers used to take up positions in the cities of Baku, Ganja (formerly Kirovabad), and Sumgait and other places, imparting great heroic stories of Azeri history, such as *Nizam ul-Mulk*, as social entertainment. Music was heavily drawn on in the Persian Asiq Bard tradition with famous bards such as Dede Korkut in the 11th century, Shah Ismail and Asiq Qurbani in the 16th century, and Asiq Alaskar in the 19th century, well-known bards who are all themselves now the subjects of stories for later bards. Nowadays, the Mayzana Wedding Rap is probably the best-known Azeri music in the country.

There were also many sports involving shows of prowess, strength, and skill, such as wrestling, and also horse riding and archery. There was much emphasis on horse riding and leatherware, as well as the making of saddles and bridles that were important in the lives of many Azeris. The wealthier Azeris were and are involved in falconry both as a hunting sport and an entertainment, and often as a competition, something which was probably introduced in its present form from the Mongols. Women were involved in embroidery and sewing, including with silk, which forms such an important part of the current national dress of the country's women. The region has also been known for carpet weaving, although this is now undertaken in Baku and other places as a home-based industry.

The oil wealth of Baku, which back in 1901 accounted for half of the world's petroleum, attracted many people from around the world, and sporting and recreational clubs were established. Many of these were destroyed in the Russian Civil War. The oil industry is still important in Baku, even though it was quickly outpaced by other oil-producing nations. During the period of the Soviet Union, sports in general became important in the everyday life of all school children, and later to the people throughout the country. This influence has created the popularity of certain sports and led to many Azeris of all ages being involved in playing soccer, as well as netball, volleyball, and gymnastics.

The Russian influence led to the avid playing of Chess. Chess still remains very popular, with Azerbaijan being so close to the Republic of Kalmykia, the current center of world Chess, which has remained in the Russian Federation.

From the 1950s on, many toys made in European Russia also became available in Azerbaijan. Wargaming also attracted a sizeable following, although much of it during the period of the Soviet Union was concerned with Russian military successes such as during the Great Patriotic War (World War II). Since this country's independence there has been greater interest in events in Azeri history.

See Also: Armenia; Backgammon; Chess and Variations of; Hobbies; Iran; Russia; Soccer (Amateur) Worldwide.

Bibliography. Michael Axworthy, "The Persian Army of Nadir Shah," *Miniature Wargames* (no.226–28, 2002); Glenn Kirchner, *Children's Games Around the World* (Benjamin Cummings, 2000); Razia Sultanova and Simon Broughton, "Azerbaijan," in Simon Broughton et al., eds., *The Rough Guide to World Music: Africa & Middle East* (Rough Guide, 2006).

Justin Corfield
Geelong Grammar School

B

Baccarat

The casino card game Baccarat has its origins in late Medieval Italy. Legend has it that it was invented by an Italian gambler named Felix Falguierein, who used a deck of Tarot cards and claimed that the game was based on an Etruscan mythical ritual involving a virgin throwing a nine-sided dice. It was introduced to France by the Italians during the reign of King Charles VIII (r.1483–98), and was known as *Chemin de Fer*. After it was introduced to England, it became known as European Baccarat. It debuted in the Dunes Casino in Las Vegas in the late 1950s, by which time it was available in many other casinos around the world.

In history and literature, baccarat was seen as a way of either making a large fortune or losing it. The French writer Alphonse Daudet, in *The Nabob* (1878), makes reference to people progressing from the Stock Exchange to the Baccarat table. French short story writer Guy de Maupassant refers in his writing to men losing all their money at Baccarat, and Sir Max Beerbohm mentioned in *James Pethel* that he "supposed baccarat to be as good a way of wasting time as another." Baccarat is also played in Robert Louis Stevenson's *Merry Men* (1887) and John Galsworthy's *The Forsyte Saga* (1906–21); Arnold Bennett in *Clayhanger* (1910) noted the "terrible baccarat scandals."

In World War I, one of the British lines was known as Baccarat, but Margot Asquith, the wife of Herbert Asquith, the British Prime Minister at the start of that war, never played Baccarat, nor Bridge, and wrote that she did not believe that it was an intellectual or literary way of spending an evening. However, many wealthy people of the period did enjoy the game. Theodore Dreiser in *The Titan* (1946) refers to Mrs. Cowperwood winning $25,000 playing Baccarat all night and the following day, and then losing it in the next sitting; and the fictional British spy James Bond often plays Baccarat, such as in Ian Fleming's *Casino Royale* (1953), but he more often plays *Chemin de Fer*, a version of Baccarat where players compete against each other, rather than traditional Baccarat, where a player competes against the house.

Because the odds are almost even—the casino takes a small fee—Baccarat rapidly became the chosen game of many professional gamblers, because winning involved more skill and less chance than most other games. It was also the reason why many European casinos do not offer Baccarat—the Monte Carlo Casino being one of the leading ones—and instead offer *Chemin de Fer*.

In February 1990, Akio Kashiwagi, a Japanese billionaire property developer, went to the Trump Plaza in Atlantic City—in the United States Baccarat is common—bet $200,000 a hand, and won $6 million in 25 minutes. The character K.K. Ichikawa in the film *Casino* (1995) is modelled on him, but Kashiwagi was murdered in 1992, at which time he had debts to various casinos estimated at $9 million. Baccarat was also the favorite casino game of the Australian billionaire and avid gambler Kerry Packer, who on April 30, 1992, went to Caesar's Palace in Las Vegas and played baccarat all night, betting over $100,000 on each game, with some bets as high as $250,000. By midnight Packer had won $9 million, and the chairman of Caesar's Palace, Henry Gluck, later stated that Packer had single-handedly wiped out most of the profit from that quarter of gaming. Many gamblers, however, do not have the luck or skill of Packer, nor the deep pockets to continue playing for such a long time.

See Also: Dice; Gambling; History of Playing Cards.

Bibliography. Paul Barry, *The Rise and Rise of Kerry Packer* (Bantam, 1993); Jean-Louis Curtis, *Baccarat* (H.N. Abrams, 1992); Mario Puzo, *Inside Las Vegas* (Grosset & Dunlap, 1977); Ralph Tegtmeier, *Casinos* (Vendome Press, 1989).

Justin Corfield
Geelong Grammar School

Backgammon

Backgammon is a two-player racing game of luck and strategy, a descendant of one of the oldest lineages of board games—the table game. The earliest examples of the table game, found in the royal tombs at Ur (Mesopotamia), date back to around 3000 B.C.E. Although Backgammon is now primarily played as a recreational board game, its origins as a form of gambling are still evident in the modern game's scoring system for tournament play. Various countries and churches have at times banned Backgammon because of its connection to gambling.

Basic Table Game Mechanics

In Backgammon, players roll two dice to determine movement of their pieces. The value of each die represents the number of spaces (or points) that a piece may move. A player may elect to apply both die values to a single piece's move, but each die's worth of movement is counted as a single move; a twice-moved piece must land on a legal space after the first move, before the second half of the move is executed. Movement is always in a forward direction from the player's start area to the player's home area. Once the player has moved all of his or her pieces to the home area, he or she then bears off the pieces by moving them off the board. The player who first bears off all their pieces wins the game. In tournament play, the player earns one point if the opponent has also borne off pieces, two points if the opponent has not yet borne off any pieces, and three points if the opponent still has any pieces in his or her start area or captured (on the bar).

The mechanics for Backgammon are roughly the same as for all other table games. The table game family refers to games that involve players racing multiple pieces across a board based on dice throws. Although the die rolls bring an element of luck to the games, the number of options that a player has in applying those die rolls provides the opportunity for deep strategy. Players must consider not only the tradeoffs between rushing forward toward the win versus taking a more defensive position but also the odds of various die throws occurring. For example, in most table games, a lone piece may be captured, while more than one piece forms a defensive unit. Therefore, each player must decide whether his opponent is likely to roll the number required to exactly land on any of his unprotected pieces. In Backgammon, for example, a player who realizes that a piece is vulnerable to capture from seven spaces away should act to protect it much more than a piece that is 12 spaces away, since a roll of seven on two dice is 10 times more likely than roll of 12.

Evolution of the Table Game

Although a possibly older version of the game was recently found in Shahr-i Sokhta, Iran, and close variations have been found in other parts of the ancient world, the game found in Ur, Mesopotamia, is commonly known today as The Royal Game of Ur. The variety of gaming boards found at ancient sites suggests that the game was played by a wide cross-section of the population, and not just by royalty. Some of the boards have intricate shell, red limestone, and lapis lazuli inlay work, while others are simple works of clay with colored squares. The exact rules of this game are unknown, but dice and tokens found inside the boards (which doubled as the game's box), as well as later documented games, have given researchers clues about the original game's rules. Like Backgammon, the player has a choice of

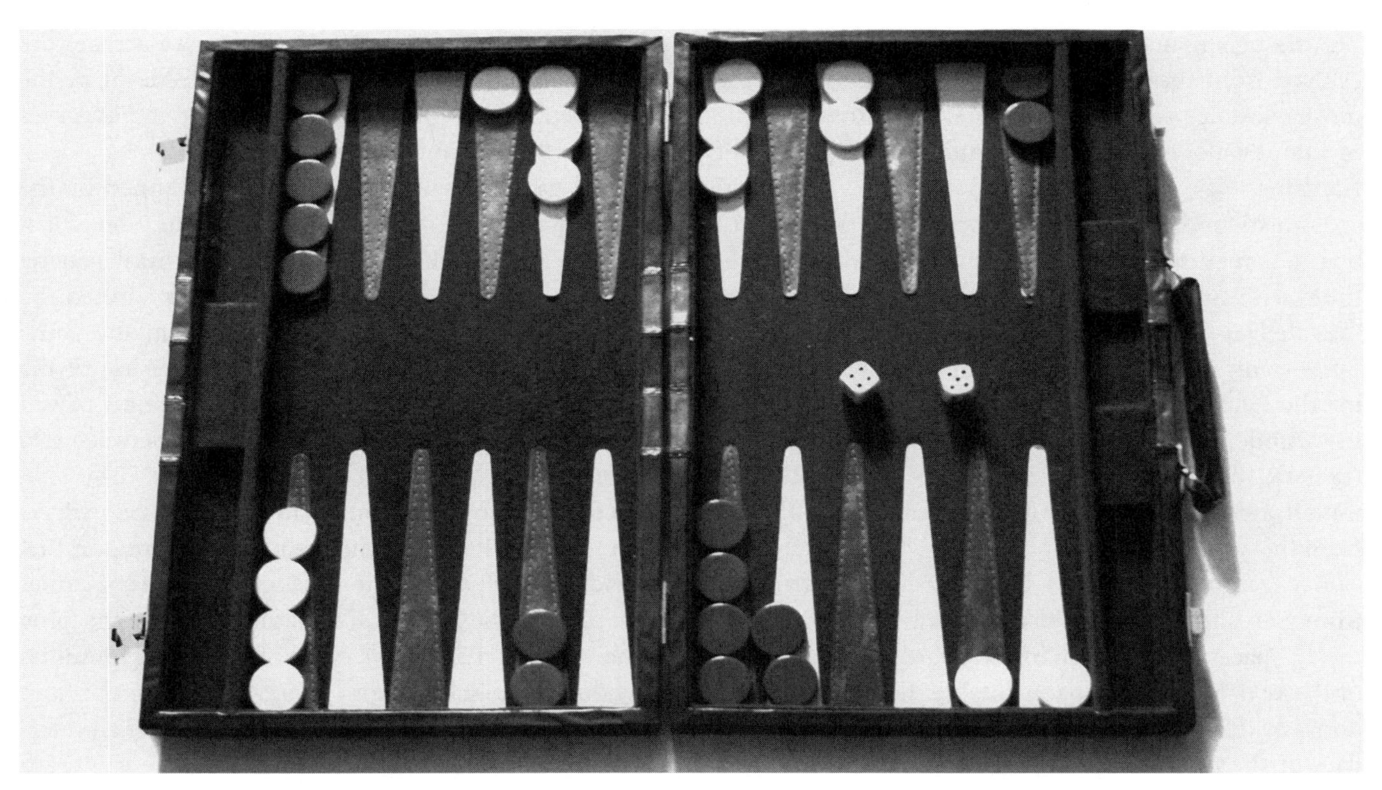

A Backgammon set consists of a board, two sets of 15 checkers, two pairs of dice, a doubling cube, and dice cups. The objective is to be the first player to remove all of your checkers from the board.

which piece or pieces to move each turn, with the goal being to take every piece across the board to the end space. In addition, like Backgammon, players may land on an opponent's piece to send it back to the start position. Unlike Backgammon, only one piece is allowed to occupy a space at a time, and each player has special safe spaces that the other player may not enter.

The Royal Game of Ur is also one of the earliest known gambling games. Players start the game by each placing a small wager in the pot, but the amount of the pot increases during play. Whenever a player lands on one of five squares marked with a rosette, his opponent must place an additional point (the smallest agreed-upon wagering unit for that game) into the pot. This means that a player who is winning will spend as much time trying to land on rosettes as moving pieces across the board.

The first descendent of Ur is the game of *Senet,* first found in the Tomb of Hesey (2686–2613 B.C.E.). Four game boards were subsequently discovered in Tutankhamen's tomb; many fragments thought to be clay game boards created by the laborers who build the pyramids have also been found. Senet games often were played on one side of the game box, with a slightly simplified variation of the Ur game board on the other side.

Swiss archaeologist Gustave Jéquier is credited with reconstructing the game's rules, which are similar to other table games. The two major exceptions: both player's pieces share the same path and direction across the board, and captures involve swapping places with the captured piece rather than sending the captured piece back to the start. Determining the rules to Senet proved an archaeological challenge because of the Egyptian style of drawing figures only in profile and with no perspective. With this drawing style, only one row of pieces ever appears in pictures documenting the game, but the game is played on a board of three rows and 10 columns.

Well before the game rules were recreated, the sculptural art of the pieces and the artwork on the boards of the royal Senet games made the game's theme clear. The game is a journey through the land of the dead. The competing playing pieces are jackals and lions. Hieroglyphics and illustrations on the board denote each square as the house of a different Egyptian god.

Although many other variations of the table game evolved from these roots, the other two that have the most relevance to Backgammon are the Roman game of Ludus Duodeci Scriptorium and the Arab game of Nardshir.

Ludus Duodeci Scriptorium was played on a 3 x 12 board, sometimes populated with symbols and sometimes with six six-letter words, two in each row, such as "Levate:Dalocu / Ludere:Nescis / Idiota:Recede" ("jump up:push off / you can:not win / get out:baboon"). During the 1st century B.C.E., the board was reduced to two rows and became more popularly known as *Tabula* (tables), and sometimes as *Alea* (gambling). Backgammon draws its movement rules and its bearing-off rules from this game.

Backgammon draws its board and piece structure from Nardshir's symbolic use of numbers. In Nardshir, the 12 spaces on each side of the board are the months of the year, and the 24 spaces total on the board are the hours of the day. The 30 pieces used in the game are the days of the month, and the dice used (like all modern dice) have opposing sides that add up to seven, the number of days in a week. Although the symbolic meanings did not carry over into Backgammon, the board layout and piece count did. The most unique aspect of Nardshir is its capture system: a captured piece does not get sent back to start on the board, as in Backgammon and most other table games, but is instead held in place until the capturer moves his piece.

Although many variations of Backgammon continued to flourish under different names, the game's rules did not change from 1743 until the 1920s. In 1743, Edmund Hoyle, who wrote the authoritative reference for many games, authored the modern rules for Backgammon. In the 1920s Americans added the doubling cube to the game. The doubling cube adds another element of betting to backgammon: a player may, at the start of his turn, double the point value of the game, if he was not the last one to do so; the other player is then given the option to resign instead of accepting the double. Players track the point value of the game (not counting the bonus for a gammon or backgammon) by which side of the cube is face-up: the six sides contain the powers of two between two and 64.

Table Games and Society

A cartoon in found in the ancient Roman city of Pompeii depicts two men fighting over a move in a game of Ludus Duodecim Scriptorum. One man accuses the other of cheating, and they are both kicked out by the innkeeper. This is the earliest known anti–table games document, but many more followed.

Table games played for money were banned by the church in Spain c. 305 C.E. In 520 C.E., the *Codex Justinianius* forbade all men of the church from playing the game at all. The Russian church later banned the game, and in 1561, Tsar Ivan IV declared the game illegal throughout Russia. The Japanese version of the game, known as *Sunokoro*, was popular, but only played in secret during the ban by emperor Jito between 690 and 697 C.E.

References to table games and Backgammon have been found in literature throughout the Common Era, providing much of the information on how early games were played. The *Hun Tsun Sii*, written during the Sung Dynasty (960–1279 C.E.), documents Backgammon's introduction to China from India. A poem in the English anthology *The Codex Exoniensis* (c.1025 C.E.) refers to the game. Charles Cotton's *Compleat Gamester* (1726) documents several variations on Backgammon, noting that there existed many "ridiculous" variations of the game at the time.

Perhaps the most bizarre documentation of the game comes from Iceland in the form of magical formulae. Players of *Kotra*, the Icelandic variation of Backgammon, treated the game with the same reverence as Chess and viewed victory as an important show of strength. Achieving good die rolls was considered a sign of favor from the gods rather than mere luck, bringing a completely different kind of strategy to *Kotra*. Some players would go so far as to pay witches for recipes for good luck charms specific to the game. One such charm calls for a dried raven's heart to be crushed and rubbed on the dice before play in order to ensure a win.

See Also: Ancient Egypt; Ancient Rome; Dice; Gambling; Luck and Skill in Play.

Bibliography. R.C. Bell, *Board and Table Games from Many Civilizations*, Volumes 1 and 2 (Oxford University Press, 1969); Jack Botermans, *The Book of Games: Strategy, Tactics, & History* (Sterling Publishing, 2008); Charles Cotton, *The Compleat Gamester* (Imprint Society, 1970).

Jay Laird
Northeastern University

"Bad" Play

A teenager plays a first-person shooter video game. A young girl plays with her Barbie and Ken dolls and has them go on a date that finishes with a sexualized kissing game. A preschooler watches a combat-based television program then starts running around the house kicking and punching. A group of adolescent girls and boys secretly play a Spin-the-Bottle-type kissing game. All of these play activities have been critiqued by social commentators, educators, and researchers interested in children's play because they are seen as examples of "bad" play. "Bad" play is generally seen as play that some adults consider to be harmful to children in one way or another. Generally "good" play is play that adults consider educational or therapeutic and that represents positive social values. On the other hand, "bad" play is play that is seen as encouraging negative social values like violence, consumerism, and sexuality, or play that puts people at physical risk of harm. Adults signal their disapproval of this play by encouraging parents and teachers to ban certain activities or to intervene to change to play that is seen as representing more positive social values. There is some debate as to whether adults should intervene too much in children's play even if it touches on topics that adults are uncomfortable with.

What is often called bad play (especially play that does not do children physical harm) has yet to be linked empirically to a child's developing problems later on. A useful discussion of this observation is play researcher Brian Sutton-Smith's article "Does Play Prepare the Future?" in which he argues against seeing play as directly causing problems in the future but indirectly supporting a child's developing for the future by helping a child thrive in the present. Sutton-Smith calls "bad" play that makes adults uncomfortable phantasmagorical play, in that it includes elements from children's fantasy worlds that are often violent or obscene. Consensus is that banning the play does not make it go away.

One of the most criticized aspects of play is media-based play, most commonly for excessive violence. Violent television programs and movies often become the source of content for children's play. Nancy Carlson-Paige and Diane Levin have written about how war play based on media is often imitative and excessively violent. They argue that although war play is common, today's play is different because of this influence. Based on this belief they feel that play should be mediated by adults to challenge the content of the media. Violent video games have also been criticized as leading to desensitizing children to violence. When it was discovered that the two shooters at Columbine High School were fans of these games, an effort was made to have them more carefully regulated. On the other hand, Vivian Paley and others have argued that children's media-based violent play is not only not bad, but actually beneficial for children in that they can take on the role of powerful superheroes. And defenders of video games point out that despite the proliferation of these games, crime rates have actually been going down.

One aspect of play that can make play "bad" is if the play activity puts the child at risk for physical harm. Physical risk taking is a large part of children's play. Taking risks can lead to injury or even death. Children leap from swings or climb high up in trees. As children get older they begin to use wheeled toys like bicycles, skateboards, and scooters, which can lead to a risk of serious injury, and are even part of an extreme culture of risk taking. Older teens and young adults engage in risky activities like drag racing or binge drinking games. Adults worry about the physical risks of play and take precautions to keep children safe including using rules and even laws to limit risks. Adults try to find a balance between letting children take risks that are seen as important for development and taking a risk that leads to a serious injury.

Finally, the element of play that has drawn a lot of recent interest is the idea of how popular culture impacts play in what some would say are positive and negative ways. Manufactured toys are an important part of play and are also regularly critiqued for their cultural importance and the impact they might have on developing social values. Candy cigarettes, for example, were common play materials for decades, but now have been relegated to novelty status, and most would see giving them as playthings to young children as negative. The figure most emblematic of these debates is Barbie. Barbie is an icon in the toy industry but has been critiqued for encouraging consumerism and unrealistic body ideals and encouraging sexuality outside of marriage. The concern is that allowing girls to play with Barbie encourages these negative social values when they become adults. Defenders of Barbie say that Barbie follows popular culture rather than leads it and that girls' doll play allows them to take on powerful roles as independent women.

"Bad" play is difficult to define. That is, if play has positive benefits for children, then how can it be bad? At the same time, as adults we try to shape play by the toys we purchase and the supervision and guidance we provide. This is a constant reminder to children that some of the play activities they enjoy are disapproved of by adults.

See Also: Anti-Competition Play; Dolls, Barbie and Others; Idealization of Play; Rhetorics of Play (Sutton-Smith).

Bibliography. Nancy Carlson-Paige and Diane Levin, *Who's Calling the Shots: How to Respond Effectively to Children's Fascination with War Play and War Toys* (New Society Publishers, 1990); Gerard Jones, *Killing Monsters: Why Children Need Fantasy, Superheroes, and Make-Believe Violence* (Basic Books, 2002); Stephen Kline, *Out of the Garden: Toys and Children's Culture in the Age of TV Marketing* (Verso, 1993); Vivian Gussin Paley, *Boys and Girls: Superheros in the Doll Corner* (University of Chicago Press, 1984); Shirley Steinberg and Joe Kincheloe, eds., *Kinderculture: The Corporate Construction of Childhood* (Westview, 1997); Brian Sutton-Smith, *The Ambiguity of Play* (Harvard University Press, 1997).

John A. Sutterby
University of Texas, Brownsville

Bahamas and Caribbean

The Caribbean is the inhabited region of the Caribbean Sea, consisting of some 7,000 islands north of South America and east of Central America. Over the decades of European colonization of the Americas, various Caribbean islands were controlled or settled by the Dutch, Danish, Swedish, Portuguese, Spanish, French, and English, and all of their influences persist in one Caribbean nation or another, along with that of the Africans who were brought to the islands as slaves. The French and British influences are especially strong, and each retain some territories in the area (as do the United States and the Netherlands).

Throughout the Caribbean, sports and athletics are highly popular not only as spectator activities but especially (thanks to the climate and the isolation of islands) as participatory activities.

Cricket

Though soccer and basketball have recently risen in prominence, cricket is the traditional main sport of the West Indies (Anguilla, Antigua and Barbuda, Barbados, British Virgin Islands, Dominica, Grenada, Guyana, Jamaica, Montserrat, St. Kitts and Nevis, St. Lucia, St. Maarten, St. Vincent & the Grenadines, Trinidad & Tobago, and the United States Virgin Islands) and enjoys popularity throughout the rest of the Caribbean as well. The West Indies Cricket Board (WICB), a member of the International Cricket Council, oversees amateur cricket in addition to governing professional cricket in the region. The amateur cricket component of WICB's mandate consists of promoting and developing cricket throughout the area by organizing domestic tournaments, amateur leagues, and youth leagues. Like baseball in the United States—especially baseball a few decades ago—cricket is the premier sport in the West Indies not only for spectators but also for organized and informal participants, and especially in the public imagination.

Soccer

The colonial age was largely over by the time the sport of soccer was organized, and the sport was introduced to the Caribbean through European tourists and workers, as well as through the sport's popularity in South America. It's a distant second to cricket in most Caribbean nations, but as a youth and recreational sport soccer is growing in popularity thanks to the media attention on professional soccer and players like David Beckham.

Karting

In the Bahamas, karting is increasingly popular. While in most countries, racing is a sport left to professionals—or pursued illegally—karting licenses are available for anyone over the age of 8 years, and the fee is cheap enough that it is a popular amateur sport, with classes for children and tracks open to the public for a small fee. Karting uses four-wheel vehicles called karts, go-karts, shifter carts, or superkarts, depending on the region and the model. Childrens' carts typically reach no more than 15 miles per hour (mph), like American amusement park go-karts; other models can reach 85 mph, and superkarts can exceed 150 mph. In some cases—like amusement parks and on tracks for childrens' karts—there are external controls that let the attendant slow or stop the karts remotely.

Carnival

Throughout the Caribbean, Carnival is a popular festival, similar in some respects to Mardi Gras—though unlike Mardi Gras or Brazil's Carnaval, the festival is often not celebrated the season before Lent and is more likely to be derived from a harvest calendar than a liturgical one. This varies wildly: on the island of Jost Van Dyke, Carnival is a New Year's celebration, while Guadeloupe celebrates it on Mardi Gras, Curacao the week after Mardi Gras, Anguilla months later in August, and so on. Caribbean Carnival is traditionally populated by costumed characters similar to those of the commedia dell'arte, and crowns a king like various krewes do for Mardi Gras in New Orleans. The celebration is more music-driven than Mardi Gras, featuring native dance and steel band music. In Barbados, Carnival's popularity is usurped by Crop Over, a 12-week festival from May to August (when Carnival itself is held), celebrating the end of the sugar cane harvest. Crop Over is very similar to Carnival, especially as celebrated in Trinidad, birthplace of calypso music and calypso tents—significant parts of Crop Over.

The game of cricket was exported from England to all of its colonies in the 19th century and remains popular.

Baseball

Baseball is the official sport of Cuba, where it has a long history: the Spanish outlawed baseball in the 19th century when its popularity overtook bullfights at a time when Cubans were chomping at the bit for independence, as part of a widescale attempt to "make Cubans more Spanish." This in fact only made baseball more popular, as the sport came to symbolize Cuban independence, and later, Cuban national identity—much as the sport is associated with national identity in the United States. Professional baseball has a long history in the country, but amateur baseball continues to hold the popularity enjoyed by soccer in other Spanish-speaking countries. Boxing is popular too, and since the beginning of Fidel Castro's socialist reign, athletics have been especially emphasized as recreation and in the schools.

Baseball was introduced to Puerto Rico at the end of the 19th century by Puerto Ricans and Cubans who had played the sport in the United States, but it was not a popular sport for a long time—one familiar by name, but considered arcane in its rules, much the way cricket is to the average American. Only in the 20th century, well after Puerto Rico becoming an American territory, did the sport enjoy mainstream success, following in the footsteps of the professional leagues on the mainland. Since then, Puerto Rico has become an active part of the baseball community, integral in the so-called Latinization of the sport—Roberto Clemente, the first Latin player elected to Major League Baseball's Hall of Fame, was Puerto Rican and first attracted attention as a high school player.

Basketball, popularized by the Young Men's Christian Association (YMCA)'s presence on the island, grew in popularity after cockfighting and bullfights were banned at the turn of the 20th century. Street basketball is extremely popular among young Puerto Ricans, offering the same benefits it does on the mainland—minimal space requirement to play, flexibility in number of players, and inexpensive equipment costs. The cockfighting ban has subsequently been lifted, and Puerto Rico has become the largest center of the sport; because of the gambling that surrounds it, it remains almost entirely an adult activity, even for spectators.

On the Virgin Islands—both American and British—baseball and basketball tend to be more popular than in the rest of the Caribbean, while cricket is significantly less popular, reflecting the U.S. influence.

Dominoes

Dominoes are a popular game in the Caribbean, often played among the family or groups of friends; even before the egalitarian present, it was a game played between men and women, children and adults, and yet at the same time tied to family traditions, as the game was often taught to children by their grandparents. Like other sedentary games, Dominoes is often a social occasion, something to keep the hands and mind occupied while socializing, gossiping, or mingling in the community. At the same time, it is an emotional game, with players known to chip or break dominoes when slamming them down on the table. Throughout the Caribbean, play usually passes to the right (counterclockwise) instead of the left.

In Jamaica, two Domino games dominate play: Partner and Cutthroat. Partner is a double-six game played by two pairs of partners; Cutthroat is essentially an "every player for himself" variant for two to four players. A four-player Cutthroat variant called French begins play with the holder of the double-zero domino instead of the double-six and then continues counterclockwise. Four zero tiles are played against the sides of the double-zero, creating a four-armed layout; the matching double must be played on each arm for play to continue on that arm, at which point normal matching rules apply.

In Puerto Rico, the Dominoes game Chiva is essentially the same as Partner or Cutthroat, but other Domino games are more popular. The standard double six set is usually used; in the Bayamon opening variation, the players draw one bone each, with the highest value going first instead of opening with the double six. A blocked game is called *trancado*, the double-zero is the *chucha*. Puerto Rican variants include *Quinientos*, played to 500 points; *Doscientos*, played to 200 points; and Doubles in the Boneyard, a three-player game in which the doubles all remain in the boneyard and are not drawn for play.

In Cuba, Dominoes are played with a double nine set, and the standard game is played by two pairs of partners, each player drawing 10 tiles (leaving 15 unused).

See Also: Baseball (Amateur); Basketball (Amateur); Central American Nations; Cricket (Amateur); Dominoes and Variations of; Organized or Sanctioned Play; Soccer (Amateur) Worldwide.

Bibliography. Arnold Arnold, *World Book of Children's Games* (Fawcett, 1973); Elliott Avedon, *The Study of Games* (Krieger Pub., 1979); Jesse Hubbell Bancroft, *Games* (Macmillan, 1937); Roger Caillois, *Man, Play, and Games* (University of Illinois Press, 2001); Patricia Evans, *Rimbles: A Book of Children's Classic Games, Rhymes, Songs, and Sayings* (Doubleday, 1961); E.O. Harbin, *Games of Many Nations* (Abingdon Press, 1954); Sarah Ethridge Hunt, *Games and Sports the World Around* (Ronald Press Company, 1964); Glenn Kirchner, *Children's Games Around the World* (Benjamin Cummings, 2000); Nina Millen, *Children's Games from Many Lands* (Friendship Press, 1943); Brian Sutton-Smith, *The Ambiguity of Play* (Harvard University Press, 2001).

Bill Kte'pi
Independent Scholar

Ballooning

Ballooning began in France, and has been around for over 200 years. The first balloon was successfully launched on September 19, 1783, by the scientist Pilatre De Rozier. His balloon, called the *Aerostat Reveillon*, lasted only 15 minutes in flight but ushered in a new era in flight travel. Onboard for this historic flight were a sheep, a duck, and a rooster. The very first manned attempt at balloon flight came on November 21 of the same year, when brothers Joseph and Etienne Montgolfier flew their balloon for a period of 20 minutes in Paris.

Just two years later another landmark achievement took place when Jean Pierre Blanchard and John Jeffries, his American copilot, became the first balloonists to fly across the English Channel. That same year, de Rozier died while trying to duplicate the flight across the channel. On January 7, 1793, George Washington was in attendance to witness Jean Pierre Blanchard become the first person to fly a balloon in North America.

During much of the 19th century, the sport of hot air ballooning reached new heights as it became an increasingly safer mode for space exploration and travel. By August 1932, Swiss scientist Auguste Piccard became the first person to fly to the Stratosphere. His height of 52,498 feet set a new altitude record and was broken several times over the ensuing couple of years. By 1960, Captain Joe Kittinger set two world records when he successfully manned his balloon to a height of 102,000 feet, then jumped from the balloon with a parachute.

Much of the second half of the 20th century saw balloonists attempting to take the sport to a new level as people tried to cross the Atlantic and Pacific Oceans. In 1978, the Double Eagle II became the first balloon to cross the Atlantic. The three-person flight took 137

Hot air balloons are inflated at dawn, as it is easier to control the balloon during the cooler parts of the day.

hours to complete. Three years later the first balloon crossed the Pacific Ocean. The Double Eagle V, which had four passengers, took 84 hours to successfully travel from Japan to California. Both of these trips were done with helium/gas-filled balloons, and in 1987 Richard Branson and Per Lindstrand became the first to cross the Atlantic in a hot air balloon. Four years later the duo became the first to cross the Pacific in a hot air balloon as well. In 1999 Bertrand Piccard and Brian Jones became the first balloonists to fly around the world, as they departed from Switzerland and landed in Africa, after almost 20 days of flying.

With the invention of gas/helium-filled balloons, the hot air method became almost obsolete for a while, before it came back into popularity within the last half century. The actual balloon is made up of three main parts. The basket is where the passengers and pilot stand, the burner is the unit, which propels the heat up into the envelope, and the envelope is the fabric balloon, which holds the air.

Hot air balloons are used for a variety of reasons today. The most popular use is for commercial leisure flights. This is a flight in which members of the public take a ride in the balloon with the help of a pilot. These flights range from three to four passengers to as many as 20 passengers. Balloons have recently been used for corporate events as well as for promotion and advertising purposes. A growing trend is that of hot air balloon weddings, in which the couples can combine their love for each other with their love of flight. Another popular use for balloons is for sporting purposes, in which professionals from around the world compete against one another to see who can travel the furthest distance or reach the highest altitude.

Ballooning has come a long way since the early days of the sport over 200 years ago. In recent years, the popularity of the sport has increased tremendously and shows no signs of letting up.

See Also: Europe, 1600 to 1800; France; Hobbies.

Bibliography. eBaloon.org, www.ebaloon.org (cited September, 2008); Christine Costanzo, *Hot Air Ballooning* (Coughlan Publishing, 2000); Andrew Nahum, *Flying Machine* (DK Publishing, 2004).

Patrick Trotti
Independent Scholar

Bandai

Bandai is a pioneering Japanese company in toy and brand development and deployment. Best known throughout the world for its Power Rangers, Tamagotchi, and Gundam properties, Bandai has been active in almost every aspect of children's toys and play, from producing model kits to running amusement parks.

An early example of Bandai's importance to the toy business was its Toyopet toy car (a small-scale model of an early Toyota sedan), which it first produced in 1950, the year the company was founded. With the Toyopet, Bandai established the company's model of combining advanced production and distribution of licensed products. The story of the Toyopet toy car can be thought of as the Bandai story in miniature, as it is an early product of a distinctly Japanese version of the toy business that links physical and intellectual properties through the integration of production, branding, and licensing. While this practice is now the norm in the toy industry, Bandai's effort represents an early and dynamic example of branded toys.

Among Bandai's most important toys and products have been its Power Rangers (Super Sentai) and Gundam lines. Both brands are tied to successful television shows as well as to videogames and other products. Gundam is based primarily on scale-model kits of giant robots. Power Rangers, known originally as Super Sentai in Japan, is meant in general for younger children and is centered around action figures and robot toys.

After merging with the Japanese videogame company Namco in 1995, the Bandai Namco Group expanded on Bandai's branding and toy strategy to create ever more sophisticatedly integrated brands, characters, games, and toys combining multiple media and markets. Namco is best known for its videogame titles, such as Tekken, as well as for amusement parks and arcades. The merger reflects the importance of companies building connections between electronic toys and videogames.

Bandai has had a long, if mixed, relationship to video and computer games. While it has produced game titles for nearly every home console system, it has had less success on the hardware side. Bandai attempted—by partnering with Apple (then Apple Computers)—to introduce a crossover between a videogame console and a personal computer—the Pippin—which did not sell well. Bandai was more successful, if mainly domestically, with its hand-held Wonderswan series of game consoles. The company has since stopped producing its own hardware, focusing on licensing and software development through its Namco division. Many of its titles are based on popular Bandai characters from the worlds of Dragon Ball Z, Tamagotchi, and Gundam.

In 1996, Bandai released a range of electronic portable toys, or digital pets, called Tamagotchi. Based on simple programs with liquid crystal display screens, Tamagotchi were virtual pets that owners took care of by pressing buttons to attend to the needs of the pet. Over the years there have been increasingly technologically advanced variants of Tamagotchi and, as with other Bandai lines, many tie-in products.

Bandai has had a long history as both a Japanese and international company. It is associated with both the "made in Japan" explosion in the United States in the 1950s and a strong domestic orientation. More recently it has suffered losses in the U.S. market, seeing better results in Europe. Domestically, Bandai has recently had to deal with a shrinking pool of clients, as Japan ages and fewer and fewer children are born there. In response Bandai has attempted to produce more toys for young adults as well as trying to further penetrate other Asian countries, North America, and the European markets.

See Also: Amusement Parks; Arcades; Japan; Models; TOMY.

Bibliography. Anne Allison, *Millennial Monsters: Japanese Toys and the Global Imagination* (University of California Press, 2006); Carol Lawson, "Love it, Feed it, Mourn it," *New York Times* (May 27, 1997); Todd Zuan, "Power Rangers Meet Pac-Man in $1.7 Billion Deal," *New York Times* (May 3, 2005).

Samuel F. Tobin
New School for Social Research

Baseball (Amateur)

The "national pastime" in the United States, evoked alongside such icons of Americana as hot dogs and apple pie (and the only major league sport conducted in July, concurrent with Independence Day), baseball has a long history and strong association with America, in addition to its popularity elsewhere. The odd man out of the major American sports, it lacks a goal and a definite endpoint—a game of potentially infinite length (there are no ties) played in finite innings in which the teams take turns playing offense and defense.

The origins of baseball are unclear. There are half a dozen competing origin stories, at least one of which—the 1839 invention of baseball by Abner Doubleday in Cooperstown, New York—is known to be false, though it continues to be repeated because of the association of the name with the sport and the location of the Hall of Fame in Cooperstown. In the end, this much is clear: There have been many bat and ball games, dating back to ancient eras, and they were especially popular in England, where cricket is the best-known example. The sport of baseball shares aspects with English bat-and-ball games, as well as with tag games. Though possibly invented in England, baseball first became popular in New England in the 18th century—a 1791 Pittsfield (Massachusetts) bylaw forbids playing the game within 80 yards of the town meeting house, presumably for the sake of the windows.

The sport spread as the country did, across the continent and soon beyond, taking advantage of the many available empty fields. One of the hallmarks of the sport is the unique character of each park, whether at the major league level or in amateur play. Though the infield conforms to specific dimensions, there is significant leeway in the configuration of the outfield and the park as a whole, making some parks better for hitters, worse for left-handed pitchers, etcetera. Even the amount of foul territory, which in some sense affects every at-bat, varies. Most parks, for the sake of convenience, are oriented to keep the sun out of pitchers' eyes—though professional baseball is often played at night for the sake of ticket sales and television ratings, the sport is traditionally a day game.

To a greater degree than the America's other major team sports—football, basketball, hockey, soccer—baseball is both a team sport and an individual sport. A far greater number of individual statistics are tallied, some of them position-specific and many of them not, than in other sports. Team-driven plays do not exist to the same degree, in the same sense, as in other team sports. Though there may be runners on base, and fielders ready to catch fly balls or chase down grounders, the discrete unit of baseball play is a confrontation between two players: the pitcher and the hitter.

This is also what has changed the most since the earliest days of the game, when a hitter had an unlimited number of strikes and could call for a specific pitch; the pitcher then was an enabler of the game more than the hitter's obstacle. But now, with the pitcher doing his best to keep the batter from making a hit without throwing a ball (a pitch outside the designated zone), the fundamental act of baseball—hitting a 90-mile-per-hour ball with a stick—is widely considered the most difficult act performed as part of the ordinary activity of a sport. The fact that hitting the ball two times out of five is an almost unattainable feat, achieved only by a small handful of professional players, attests to this.

The time element distinguishes baseball as well. There is no clock. Though umpires encourage batters to prepare quickly without dallying, there is technically no time limit enforced on them, nor on the pitcher; in the 2008 season, a minor league game was delayed for minutes when a switch-hitting batter and ambidextrous pitcher kept switching back and forth between right- and left-handed stances, each in response to the other. The game ends when it ends: when the third out of the second half of the last inning has been made. A tie-breaking run in the first half of an inning does not end the game, and many extra-innings games are played precisely because the other team is given a chance to catch back up.

Organized baseball is played at many levels: Little League (childrens' competitive league), scholastic and college leagues, and the various professional leagues. Companies often field baseball or softball teams to compete after-hours with other companies; other amateur leagues exist for teams without business-specific affiliation. But the sport is especially revered for its informal games, in which a group of young players head to an empty lot or town field, pick teams—often lacking a few positions—and play until dark. There is rarely an umpire, and house rules may develop in order to prevent arguments about certain calls, especially relating to home runs and foul balls.

Farmers play baseball in Arkansas in the late 1930s. The origins of American baseball are disputed.

Whether baseball originated in the United States or not, it was from the United States that it spread to the rest of the world, primarily in the late 19th century (when Americans overseas introduced it to other countries, particularly throughout Latin America and in Japan) and the early 20th century, when it was the principal team sport in the country when modern media developed and turned athletes like Babe Ruth into celebrities. The popularity of youth baseball in other countries has gradually changed the character of professional baseball in the United States, as more and more of its players grew up in other countries.

Baseball also has different meanings depending on culture. In some countries, baseball is used as a means to socializing the young into central ways of defining the self. In Japan, for example, the emphasis is on players coming to see themselves as responsible to their teammates, their school, and even their country—interdependence and being responsible is what matters, not independence and individual stardom.

Baseball Superstitions

A game so tied up in tradition naturally develops superstitious practices, observed by players at every level. "Lucky" pieces of equipment or clothing (which are not washed as long as their luck holds out) are common, as are "playoff beards"—grown when players stop shaving after the team's first win in the playoffs. The foul line is sometimes considered unlucky, and players will avoid touching it, whether there is a game in progress or not. Midgets, albinos, and other people with unusual congenital conditions are sometimes considered "lucky" to touch—this is an especially old tradition, which would be considered insensitive to act on now.

Above all else, situations in progress are not to be discussed in certain circumstances. It is the worst breach of decorum to comment on a no-hitter (or, by extension, a perfect game) in progress, and even sportscasters will usually abide by this. But it is also inappropriate to talk about a player's statistical performance when that situation is at hand, and is seen as a jinx.

Baseball and Statistics

More than any other sport, the statistics generated by baseball games have long been an object of fascination among spectators. Scorecards have been provided at baseball games since the early days of organization, to give spectators something to do during the natural breaks in action—when a new batter comes to the plate, when a pitcher warms up, when a half-inning ends and the teams switch places. Basic statistics have been maintained since before the inception of Major League Baseball; historical baseball statistics have been available to fans since the 1950s, when baseball encyclopedias were published for the first time. Computers have revolutionized statistics, allowing for the computation of highly specific information such as the performance of a particular batter against a particular hitter every time they have faced each other in tie games.

One of the uses of statistics is in fantasy or rotisserie baseball, in which the real-world statistical performance of players on a fantasy manager's team affects the success of his team in the ongoing game.

Baseball and Language

That common denominator has affected American speech, as well, in the form of an extraordinary number of baseball-related idioms that have made their way into everyday vocabulary, even among people who have never watched a baseball game in their lives. Something that's close enough to a particular goal or category is "in the right ballpark." Advancing to a certain station in one's field is to arrive "in the big leagues," but acting unprofessional is "bush league." Rather than crossing your Ts and dotting your Is, you might "cover your bases," particularly so that you are prepared if someone surprises you by "throwing you a curveball" that may be so unexpected it is as if it "came out of left field" and could "catch you off base." If you rise to the occasion you will "knock it out of the park."

In particular, there is the use of baseball as a metaphor for sex. Just as a runner advances around the bases, so too does an ambitious young man advance through stages of intimacy. The specifics can vary from cohort to cohort, but are generally agreed on. "First base" is kissing. "Second base" is genital contact—masturbation or fondling through clothes. "Third base" has shifted in meaning as sexual mores have shifted. A "home run" is sexual intercourse. And "striking out" means to be rejected entirely—in sex or any other arena.

See Also: Athletics (Amateur; Basketball (Amateur); Football (Amateur); Play and Sports Education; Team Play.

Bibliography. Jim Albert and Jay M. Bennett, *Curve Ball: Baseball, Statistics, and the Role of Chance in the Game*

(Copernicus Books, 2001); Bob Elliott, *The Northern Game: Baseball the Canadian Way* (Sport Classic, 2005); Alvin L. Hall and Thomas L. Altherr, "Eros at the Bat," The Cooperstown Symposium on Baseball and American Culture (McFarland & Company, 2002); Lawrence Ritter, *The Glory of their Times* (Macmillan, 1966); Alan Schwarz, *The Numbers Game: Baseball's Lifelong Fascination with Statistics* (St. Martin's, 2005).

Bill Kte'pi
Independent Scholar

Basketball (Amateur)

A Canadian Young Men's Christian Association (YMCA) instructor in the state of Massachusetts named Dr. James Naismith developed the sport of basketball in 1891. Naismith created the game to allow for competitive sport to take place indoors during harsh winter months—it began as a game to keep young athletes in shape during the winter when they were unable to perform outdoor sports. The original ball used was a soccer ball, and the original hoops were peach baskets attached to gymnasium walls. The use of these baskets gave rise to the name basketball. Peach baskets continued to be used until 1906, when they were replaced by metal-rimmed hoops attached to a wooden backboard. From these early beginnings, basketball has turned into a global sport played around the world by men and women, both young and old.

Unlike many other activities that were seen as unwomanly in the late 1800s, basketball was quickly adopted as a game that women could play as well. In 1892 a physical education teacher named Sendra Berenson modified Naismith's rules to form a women's game of basketball. While the first official men's game took place in 1892, the first collegiate women's basketball game commenced shortly thereafter, in 1893.

In the 1890s basketball spread to YMCAs around the country, as well as to Canada. It became popular in high schools and universities, as it required little equipment and personnel. As the game continued to grow in Canada and the United States, American soldiers then spread the game to countries around the world to locations they were stationed in. Basketball is now played at most high schools, colleges, and universities in Canada and the United States and has become one of the most popular international sports.

By 1932, basketball had risen to international prominence with the development of the Federation Internationale Basketball Amateur (FIBA), which still governs international basketball. The founding countries included Argentina, Czechoslovakia, Greece, Italy, Latvia, Portugal, Romania, and Switzerland. The amateur component of FIBA has since been dropped, as professional basketball players now compete in FIBA-sanctioned tournaments such as the Summer Olympic Games, but the acronym FIBA still remains, with the "BA" now denoting the first two letters of basketball. FIBA has grown immensely in size since its inauguration and now includes over 200 member countries.

Olympic Basketball

While a basketball demonstration tournament was held at the 1904 Olympics, the first time it became an official Olympic event was during the 1936 Olympic Summer Games in Berlin, Germany. Twenty-three countries competed in the Olympic basketball tournament, making it the largest team event held at the Olympic Games that year.

The U.S. men's team was victorious in winning the first-ever Olympic gold medal, while Canada won the silver. The United States has gone on to dominate international basketball in both the women's and men's games, winning more international events than any other country. It was not until 1976, however, that women's basketball was added to the Olympic program.

The U.S. men's basketball team won every Olympic gold medal until 1972, when they were defeated by the Soviet Union. The men's team has only failed to win the gold medal three times since, with the latest coming in 2004 with a disappointing bronze medal finish. The U.S. women's basketball team did not have the early dominance of the men's team, as the Soviet Union won the first two Olympic events. The U.S. women have, however, gone on to win five out of the last six Olympic basketball events.

FIBA dropped the amateur status of its organization in 1989, which allowed National Basketball Association (NBA) players the opportunity to compete in international basketball tournaments including the Olympics. The first year that professional basketball players played in the Olympics was 1992, leading to the introduction of the U.S. "dream team," with NBA greats like Earvin

Women have been playing collegiate basketball since 1893. The game was played with modified rules for women.

"Magic" Johnson, Larry Bird, and Michael Jordan on the roster. While the original dream team was able to coast to an Olympic gold medal, the standard of play that other countries have been able to achieve since these games has been steadily rising. For example, in the 2002 World Championships, the U.S. men's basketball team, a team comprising NBA players, finished sixth behind Yugoslavia, Argentina, Germany, New Zealand, and Spain. Then in the 2004 Olympics, the United States men's team failed to win the gold medal, which they had done in each previous year since professional players were granted the right to play.

College Basketball

While college basketball competitions began emerging shortly after the formation of the sport, the game did not rise to national prominence until the development of the National Invitation Tournament (NIT) in 1938. At the time, this was the most prestigious college basketball tournament that a team could play in at the end of the season after winning their respective division. However, a few years later, another national championship tournament emerged that would far surpass the prestige of the NIT. This tournament was held by the National Collegiate Athletic Association (NCAA), gained immense popularity in the 1960s, and has since become a premier sporting event held in the United States each year. The tournament, held in March of each year, is also commonly referred to "March Madness."

The rise of the NCAA tournament has led to the downfall of the NIT tournament. While the NIT tournament was once the premier college basketball event in the United States, it is now reserved for teams that were unable to qualify or not selected for the NCAA tournament. As such, it is now sometimes referred to humorously as the "Not-Invited Tournament" instead of the National Invitation Tournament. Likewise, when teams are losing important qualifying games for the NCAA tournament, it is common for the crowd to taunt the team with N-I-T chants.

The NCAA tournament—March Madness, or simply "the tournament" to college basketball fans—is a national tournament comprising 65 invited NCAA Division 1 basketball teams. The "Big Dance" is another common term to refer to the NCAA tournament to distinguish it from other national championships, such as the NIT. The tournament is made up of Division 1 conference champions who receive automatic bids, as well as teams chosen by an NCAA selection committee. A tournament bracket is established based on team rankings, with teams being knocked out after a single loss. When 16 teams are left, it is often refereed to as the "Sweet 16," the last eight teams are the "Elite Eight," and the last four are termed the "Final Four." Apart from possibly the Superbowl in American gridiron football, the Final Four of college basketball is among the biggest sporting events in the United States each year.

The NIT and NCAA tournament for both men and women are not the only national college basketball championships in the United States. The NCAA is divided into three divisions, based on size and resources, and a national champion is determined in each of these divisions. There is also the National Association of Intercollegiate Athletics (NAIA), which is divided into two divisions with a national champion in each. A National Junior College Athletics Association (NJCAA) also exists with three separate divisions, with a national champion in each determined as well.

Wheelchair Basketball

New versions of basketball have been developed since its formation, with one popular form being termed wheelchair basketball. Wheelchair basketball was developed in the years following World War II for men who had experienced wartime injuries that limited their ability to play sports. It was developed to allow these men to experience the exhilaration and excitement of competitive sport, even though their bodies were no longer able to play the original version of the game. The game has similar rules to those of basketball, with some adaptations to allow for the use of wheelchairs and the various disabilities of the athletes that participate in the sport. For example, the hoop in wheelchair basketball still stands at 10 feet, but instead of a travel denoting more than two steps with the ball, it denotes touching the wheelchair wheels more than twice after receiving or dribbling the ball.

Wheelchair basketball became part of the original Paralympics held in Rome in 1960. The Paralympic Games is an international event for athletes with physical disabilities and is held two weeks after the Olympic Games in the same host city. Wheelchair basketball has grown immensely since this time, with over 80 countries belonging to the International Wheelchair Basketball Association (IWBA), the official governing body of international wheelchair basketball.

Street Ball

Another common version of the original game of basketball is referred to as "street ball." Street ball is a less-formal, urban version of basketball that is played around the world on outdoor and indoor courts. The rules of street ball are typically similar to those of the regular game, although it can be adapted to be played by as few as two players and is often played on only one hoop instead of two. The most apparent difference of street ball from ordinary basketball is the hip-hop undertones, which are often characterized by baggy clothing and flashy moves. The primary objective in street ball is still to score more baskets than an opposing team, but there is more at stake such as spectacular dunks, impressive ball handling, and demeaning trash talk.

See Also: Baseball (Amateur); Athletics (Amateur); Play and Sports Education; Team Play.

Bibliography. Peter J. Bjarkman, *Hoopla: A Century of College Basketball* (McGraw-Hill, 1998); James Naismith, *Basketball: Its Origins and Development* (University of Nebraska Press, 1996); Alexander Wolff, *Big Game, Small World: A Basketball Adventure* (Grand Central Publishing, 2003).

Curtis Fogel
University of Calgary

Battlefield 1942

Battlefield 1942 is a three-dimensional, first-person shooter (FPS) computer game developed by Digital Illusions CE and published by Electronic Arts for Microsoft Windows (2002) and the Apple Macintosh (2004). The game can be played in single-player mode against the computer or in multiplayer mode against players on the Internet, although the latter is the more popular option. As the title suggests, the game is set during World War II. Battlefield 1942 is popular not only with players, but also with the large-scale community of modders (modifiers) who write new content, levels, and simulations for the game. In this way, the game follows the tradition of games such as Half-Life and its sequel, Counter-Strike (which, in itself, is a mod), as a game that allows the source code to be freely used, adapted, and sometimes even improved by its own users. The game won various rewards on its release in 2002 but is in fact a uniformly average example of the FPS genre.

In Battlefield 1942, players take the role of one of five different types of solider, each with different attributes. In this respect, the game contains a clear carryover from roleplaying games (RPGs), in which character classes often dictate a vital part of each avatar's ability and relative strengths. Like many RPGs, this means that the emphasis of the game is shifted toward cooperative play, with each character class providing its own benefits in a group situation. Online group play involves large groups of players in opposing teams who try to either kill their way to victory or secure/successfully defend key points on each map by gaining or losing "tickets." The game ends when either one side has lost all of their tickets or certain objectives are fulfilled. This type of PvP (Player versus Player) scenario deliberately means that players have various gameplay options, although usually, strategic group play is the more successful route.

In the online incarnation of the game, these missions are repeatedly carried out by players on opposing teams. Battlefield 1942 was one of the first games to seriously consider its online persona as a multiplayer PvP event within the game design. For this reason, the cooperative elements were heightened in the game; an aspect which, ironically, caused a great deal of difficulty during the early months of the game for players used to solo play in online FPS games (even in what might have appeared at first to be group situations). Early bugs in the game such as unstable spawning points, coupled with some obvious exploits and the high level of PvP grief play meant that, initially, this aspect of the game was even harder to achieve. However, these elements were gradually tweaked or removed.

Battlefield 1942 demands that players form swift trust groups who need to work collectively and cohesively together in order to succeed; however, the transitory nature of these groups, as well as their unpredictability, means that the social processes needed within the game are as important to success as good gameplay. It is this latter aspect that has become a core part of PvP gaming over recent years, and as the understanding of it grows, designers often seek to introduce conflict through different goals and objectives in order to make the game both more complex and more rewarding when a win is achieved. Overall, it is also this human aspect—the fact that players are fighting against and with other people—that has led to the ongoing success of PvP online gaming.

See Also: Counter Strike; Play as Mock War, Sociology of; War; Warhammer; World of Warcraft.

Bibliography. Esther MacCallum-Stewart, "From Catch the Flag to Shock and Awe: How World of Warcraft Negotiates Battle" (DiGRA Conference, 2007); Battlefield 1942, www.ea.com/official/battlefield/1942/us (cited July 2008).

Esther MacCallum-Stewart
University of East London

Battleship

Battleship is a two-player game of luck and logic. The game has been popular since its development by Russian soldiers during World War I. Although it has been published in many variations, the best known is the 1967 Milton Bradley version, which remains popular today.

The game's initial popularity came from the ability to play it anywhere with any writing implement and on any writing surface. Soldiers often improvised naval battles on scraps of paper while waiting for orders on the battlefield. According to historian John Toland, by the 1920s, the game had become a popular way of passing the time in prisons as well as on the battlefield, with prisoners drawing play grids on their cell floors and calling moves to each other between cells.

In 1931, the Starex Novelty Company published the game as a pad of preprinted grids, calling it Salvo. Soon after Salvo was published, imitators appeared, including pad-and-paper variations called Broadsides and Combat. The convenience of printed grids and rules guides on each page of the game pads helped to further popularize the game.

Players begin by marking a grid with the position of their ships, each of which are one grid square wide. The number and length of ships varies across rule sets, but in the popular Milton Bradley (now Hasbro) version of the game, each player has six ships, ranging in length from one square (the submarine) to five squares (the aircraft carrier), with an additional two-square ship (the cruiser). Generally, the game grid is labeled on one axis with letters and the other with numbers. Players use one grid to record their ships' positions, and a second identical grid to record the results of their attacks.

The two players alternate turns, calling out "shots" in the form of grid positions: "A-1" for the upper-left square, for example. In early versions of the game, each player called out six shots at a time, which increased the chances of hitting something, but which made deducing the position of ships more difficult, since the player being fired upon did not have to specify which squares were the successful hits. In an effort to market the game to children, Milton Bradley simplified the rules for its 1967 version, requiring players to only call out one shot per turn.

In all versions of the game, when all parts of a ship have been hit, the player is required to let his opponent

The Milton Bradley version of Battleship has toy ships and red and white markers, allowing players to keep score.

know which ship was sunk. This aids the attacker in deducing the position of other ships through the process of elimination, an idea inspired by the use of sonar to detect positions in naval warfare. The cry "You sank my battleship!"—which originated in Milton Bradley's 1970s ads—has become a part of the American pop cultural landscape.

Milton Bradley also introduced plastic ships, red "hit" and white "miss" markers, and a briefcase-like set of two plastic grids for each player. The lid of the briefcase provided the "sonar" record of each player's attempted strikes against his opponent, as well as obscuring the view of his opponents' ship placement on the second grid. In 1983, Milton Bradley released Electronic Battleship, which took care of the details of hits and misses with lights and sound. Since then, many computer versions of Battleship have appeared, some offering enhanced game play, but all using variations of the Milton Bradley rules.

See Also: Hasbro; Luck and Skill in Play; Play as Mock War, Sociology of; War.

Bibliography. Jim Gladstone, *Gladstone's Games To Go* (Quirk Books, 2004); Andrew McClary, *Toys With Nine Lives: A Social History of American Toys* (Linnet Books, 1997); Merilyn Simonds Mohr, *The New Games Treasury* (Houghton Mifflin, 1997).

Jay Laird
Northeastern University

Beggar My Neighbor

Beggar My Neighbor is a British card game that may date back to a late-16th-century card game known as Knave Out of Doors, which was mentioned in a 1604 play, *A Woman Killed with Kindness,* by John Haywood. Regardless of when it originated, it was a very popular game by the 19th century. It has also been known as Strip Jack Naked, Beat Your Neighbor Out of Doors, Corsican Battle, Egyptian War, and Egyptian Ratkiller. The "Egyptian" versions have added rules allowing slapping the stack when certain combinations show up, allowing the "slapping" player to gather up the stack. There is also a variation played in the Caribbean known as Suck the Well Dry. The main difference in this variation is that when there are more than two players, the sequence of play is counterclockwise, as opposed to the clockwise sequence played in the United States and Great Britain.

As can be inferred from the different names, this game has been given, it is a zero-sum, or constant-sum, game in which winning depends on defeating the opponent and taking everything they have.

The game is usually played by two players, although sometimes there are more. The deck is divided evenly between the players who keep the cards in face-down piles. Aces, kings, queens, and jacks are known as "pay cards." The other cards are considered "ordinary cards." The players take turns placing the top card from their stack face up in the center of the table. When they place an ordinary card, face up, on the stack, nothing happens. When a player places a pay card, the other player must pay a number of cards out, the number depending on the pay card. The rate is four cards for an ace, three for a king, two for a queen, and one for a jack. The player who played the pay card then takes all of these, as well as all of the cards in the stack. If, however, the paying player plays a pay card, then the player who originally played the pay card must pay cards, and the stack reverts to the player who played the second pay card. The game continues in this fashion until one player completely runs out of cards.

The game most famously appears in Charles Dickens's *Great Expectations,* when Pip plays and loses a game of Beggar My Neighbor to Estrella while Miss Havisham looks on, encouraging Estrella to "Beggar him!" In the novel, it is used as more than a card game, as it shows a great deal about the characters. Further, it also provides an analogy for Miss Havisham's past, with its financial and personal failures and total loss. Literary critics have also discussed it as a further analogy for the difficulties and failures of financial enterprises in Victorian England.

Beggar My Neighbor is a game of pure chance, with no element of skill involved. Theoretically, it is possible that a game of Beggar My Neighbor could be played forever without a player winning, a subject that has been written about in mathematical journals.

See Also: Play as Competition, Sociology of; United Kingdom; War.

Bibliography. *Beggar My Neighbor Rules*, www.pagat.com/war/beggar_my_neighbour.html (cited October 2008); John Haywood et al., *A Woman Killed with Kindness and Other*

Domestic Plays (Oxford University Press, 2008); Marc M. Paulhus, "Beggar My Neighbor," *The American Mathematical Monthly* (v.106/2, February 1999); Daniel Pool, *What Jane Austen Ate and Charles Dickens Knew: From Fox Hunting to Whist–the Facts of Daily Life in Nineteenth-Century England* (Simon and Schuster, 1994); Susan Walsh, "Bodies of Capital: Great Expectations and the Climacteric Economy," *Victorian Studies* (v.37/1, 1993).

Robert Stacy
Independent Scholar

Belarus

Belarus was, until recently, a constituent region of the Soviet Union, and an earlier part of the Russian empire.

Echoing the behavior of rural children everywhere, Belarusian children played games such as Hide-and-Seek and Catch—made unique by their cooptation of characters from Slavic folk tales, like the witch Baba Yaga. Games, especially for older children, were often gendered: boys tested strength and skill in games such as *Lapta*, similar to baseball, where players used a bat to hit a small, heavy stick; for girls, games of skill included rope-skipping, or *Skakalochka*. Rural kids moving to the city adapted traditional games to the urban context and developed new forms of play, such as riding on tram couplings or card-playing; they experienced less social control and had more access to tobacco and alcohol. Adult peasants traditionally spent their leisure time visiting friends, promenading in the village streets, singing songs, drinking in taverns, going to village fairs, and celebrating the many Orthodox religious festivals.

Urbanization saw the persistence of such forms, but also new modes of leisure characterized by increasingly wide class divisions. The presence of masses of young working-class males in the cities encouraged the "rough" leisure of hooliganism. For the middle class, the late 19th to early 20th century witnessed the growth of restaurants, plays, "gypsy" songs, the new movie theaters, and *estrada*, the name for varied performance art.

While earlier forms of play remained popular after the revolution, the Party founded new institutions meant to socialize youth into communist ideology and furnished "appropriate" leisure spaces, such as playgrounds, youth clubs, and sport complexes, especially after the economy's recovery from World War II. For example, the Minsk youth club *Minskaia molodezh'* organized dance evenings, musical concerts, balls, debates, and meetings with veterans and other notables.

The Party also supplied literature and a variety of new toys for children; put on plays; produced movies, radio programs, and television shows like the popular *Spokoinoi nochi, malyshi*; and engaged youth in communist celebrations such as parades. This patriarchal approach endeavored to supply an amalgam of fun and ideological inculcation, while striving to fulfill the Party's promise to give all Soviet children a "happy childhood," with intermittent success. For adults, traditional modes of leisure continued to predominate in the early post-1917 era, though many middle-class establishments were closed. Nevertheless, the *Proletkul't*, a state-funded organization for workers, did supply engaging leisure, and adults participated in parades. In the mid-1930s and especially the postwar period, middle-class, and to a lesser extent, working-class citizens benefited from increased state investments into entertainment, including clubs, sport complexes, radio, and television.

The post-1945 period witnessed the appearance of style-seekers—youth fascinated with Western leisure, fashion, and music. In response, the Party launched a campaign in the mid-1950s to control youth leisure, which included state-sponsored youth patrols that attempted to violently impose "proper" leisure behavior, with limited effectiveness. Fascination with Western-style leisure culture increasingly pervaded Soviet society and came into full bloom during *perestroika*, as officialdom ceased persecution of previously underground leisure. The Soviet demise brought a new authoritarian government to Belarus that renewed the controlling, patriarchal approach to leisure, cracking down on Western-style leisure. Contemporary play in Belarus continues to be divided by social status and geographical location, combining traditional and Communist-era forms.

See Also: Play as Entertainment, Sociology of; Russia; Ukraine.

Bibliography. Verena Fritz, *State-Building: A Comparative Study of Ukraine, Lithuania, Belarus, and Russia* (Central European University Press, 2007); Catriona Kelly, *Children's*

World: Growing Up in Russia, 1890–1991 (Yale University Press, 2007); Stewart Parker, *The Last Soviet Republic: Alexander Lukashenko's Belarus* (Trafford Publishing, 2007).

Gleb Tsipursky
University of North Carolina, Chapel Hill

Belgium

Historically, Belgium was controlled by the Habsburgs of Austria and Spain. It was then a part of France, and from 1815, it was a part of the Kingdom of the Netherlands. In 1830 Belgium became independent. Traditionally one of the wealthiest parts of Europe and one of the most industrialized, Belgium has had varied types of play from simple toys and pursuits to sophisticated games with elaborate rules. Certainly as early as 1379, there were playing cards in the region, which were noted in the writings of Johanna, Duchess of Brabant, and Wenceslaus of Luxemburg.

Young children in Belgium played many of the largely universal games such as Hopscotch, Skipping, Skittles, Marbles, and Hide-and-Seek. Some of these can be seen in the paintings of Pieter Bruegel the Younger, who was born in Brussels and spent most of his life in Antwerp. He includes in his works scenes of children, mainly boys, involved in street games such as Leapfrog (which was generally known in Flanders as Sheep-Jumping), Fighting on Horseback, playing with hobby horses, and also the game Trip Him Up. In one painting, Bruegel portrays a peasant mother teaching her children how to take part in a country dance, and in one of his winter scenes, he shows local men involving in skating, curling on a frozen lake, and boys with toboggans.

The French influence in the region has resulted in older people playing boules, with both younger and older people taking part in recreational golf. The country has many golf courses, such as the Royal Club at Tervuren, which has hosted a number of professional tournaments. Soccer has become an important part of life for the country, with the population playing it as a recreation in school fields and courtyards across the country. In rural parts of Belgium, *pelota* is played, harking back to the historical connections with Spain.

Since Medieval times, puppeteers have been popular in village and town festivals and markets. Most perform for small children and tell moral tales. In the Middle Ages, pageant plays were staged; they have had a recent revival with small theatrical groups helping to enliven market days. From the late Middle Ages, the wealth of Belgium, largely made through selling wool, meant that it became home to many printers—it is not surprising that it became a center for printing playing cards.

The town of Turnhout, near Antwerp, has been known for printing and selling playing cards since 1826, and later became involved in making card games and games including dice. In 1970 the three remaining game companies amalgamated to form Cartamundi, which still produces packs of cards for casinos around the world. There have been several editions of the board game Monopoly, some using bilingual boards in Flemish and French and some in just one language. All of the games represent the entire country of Belgium, not just a particular city.

A surviving Flemish painting from the 15th century shows a woman playing Chess against a man with a number of onlookers. The Flemish painter Lucas van Leyden (1494–1533), who also lived in Antwerp, painted a scene showing a woman and a man playing Chess. This painting now hangs at the Gemäldegalerie in Berlin, Germany. Chess remains popular in Belgium—the Fédération Royale des Échecs de Belgique (The Royal Chess Federation of Belgium) was established in 1920, with its headquarters in Anvers. An annual Belgian Women's Championship has been held since 1946 and an Annual Belgian Championship since 1949.

There has also long been a great interest in model-making, especially of trains, with Belgium having had a central role in the manufacturing of trains throughout Europe. The many wars that have been fought on Belgian soil have helped nurture an extensive Wargaming culture among boys and men. The availability of many miniature figurines for wars fought in Belgium—the Revolt of the Netherlands, War of Spanish Succession, Napoleonic Wars, World War I, and World War II—has enabled Wargamers in Belgium to conduct their pursuits through school groups and clubs, and also on the internet. The Battle of Waterloo in 1815, fought in Belgium, is one of the most popular Wargame scenarios in the world, and the result has been that many Wargamers from overseas visit Belgium to study the battleground. There are regular reenactments held on the battle site that bring in many people from all over

Belgium and overseas. The large number of memorials and battle sites for World War I have similarly attracted many wargamers to Belgium. Outdoor pursuits such as hiking, cycling, and boating on the canals also remain popular in the country.

See Also: Chess and Variations of; Hide & Seek; Napoleon; Wargames.

Bibliography. Eugeen van Autrenboer and Louis Tummers, *The Turnhout Playing Card Industry 1826–1976* (Ministry of Foreign Affairs External Trade and Cooperation in Development, 1976); Demetrius Charles de Kavanagh Boulger, *The History of Belgium: Part 1. Cæsar to Waterloo* (Adamant Media Corporation, 2001); Harry Golombek, *Chess: A History* (G.P. Putnam's Sons, 1976); Michael Rayner, "The 100 Days," *Miniature Wargames* (February–June 1988).

Justin Corfield
Geelong Grammar School

Bezique

Bezique was originally a French card game dating back to the 17th century; it is similar to Piquet, from which it is derived. It is, in its basic form, a two-player game, although there are variations for more players. It is very similar to Pinochle, which developed from the standard two-hand Bezique.

Bezique's peak of popularity was during the 19th century, when it was well known enough to be mentioned in novels. For example, when Emile Zola conducted research for what would be his novel *Nana*, he investigated the lives of courtesans and found that typically these women could be expected to squeeze in a game of Bezique after lunch during their busy day.

Bezique was popular enough for several variations to come into existence. There is the two-handed variation, known as Rubicon Bezique, which uses four decks for play and has certain variations in the scoring. Three-Handed Bezique uses three decks and allows triple scoring; Four-Handed Bezique uses six decks for its four players. Six-Deck Bezique is also known as Chinese Bezique and was said to be a favorite pastime of Winston Churchill. It is similar to Rubicon Bezique, although it uses more cards and has its own scoring. Finally, Eight-Deck Bezique, similar to the six-deck variety, but has eight decks and some scoring differences.

Bezique is not played with a standard 52-card deck. The Bezique deck (sometimes referred to as a Piquet deck, in reference to its earlier form) is a 64-card deck. There are two of each value card, from seven through the ace in each suite. The two through six cards are not used in any of the variations. Ranking of the cards, from highest to lowest is ace, 10, king, queen, jack, nine, eight, and seven.

In the basic two-person version, the dealer deals three cards to the other player and then three cards to himself. Two cards are dealt to the nondealing player and two to the dealer, followed by three cards dealt to each player. The remaining cards are placed face down. Sometimes this stack is referred to as the talon. The top card is turned face up. That card's suit becomes the trump suit.

The nondealing player now plays any card, face up, and then the dealer plays a card. If the dealer's card is the same suit as the nondealer's card, but a higher value, he wins the trick. The dealer also wins if the played card is of trump suit. With each trick, the winner takes the cards and places them in his or her own separate stack. During each trick a player may declare a meld, a pairing of cards such as a king and queen of clubs, and is awarded points for each meld. At the end of the trick, the players take cards from the talon so that they have eight cards in their hand until the talon is exhausted.

The winner of the last trick takes the last card from the talon, and the other player takes the upturned card that determined the trump suit. They then play the last eight tricks, and at this time they must follow the suit placed on the table. If the second player cannot follow suit, he or she can play a card of the trump suit. If he or she cannot play the same or the trump suit, he or she can play any other card. This continues until the last trick is played.

Now the players review their cards. Ten points are awarded for each ace or 10, That total is awarded in addition to whatever points were received from the melds earlier in the game. In two-handed Bezique, the first player to score 1,000 points wins. One of the distinguishing characteristics of the different forms of Bezique (aside from the number of cards) is the number of points required to win the game as well as points awarded for different combinations.

Scoring is done using Bezique markers, paper and pencil, or a cribbage board.

See Also: Europe, 1800 to 1900; History of Playing Cards; Pinochle; Piquet.

Bibliography. BBC, "Bezique," www.bbc.co.uk/dna/h2g2/A646724 (cited September 2008); Frederick Brown, "Zola and the Making of 'Nana,'" *The Hudson Review* (v.45/2, 1992); David Parlett et al., *Card Games* (McGraw Hill, 1995); David Parlett, *A History of Card Games* (Oxford University Press, USA, 1991).

Robert Stacy
Independent Scholar

Bicycles

Leonardo da Vinci sketched a facsimile of the modern bicycle in 1490 but never built it. Another precursor was the celerifere of 1790, which lacked steering. The first bicycle was Baron Karl Drais von Sauerbronn's wooden *Draisienne,* which debuted in Paris in 1818. Also called the hobbyhorse or running machine, the *Draisienne* was steerable and had two in-line wheels on a frame that the rider straddled as he walked.

In 1839 Kirkpatrick Macmillan, a Scottish blacksmith, created a wooden self-propelled bike that weighed 56 pounds and used swinging cranks on the front wheel to power rods linked to levers on the rear wheel.

Pierre and Ernest Michaux built the velocipede, or boneshaker, in 1865—a two-wheeled riding machine with pedals on the front wheel. Also made of wood, with wooden tires initially and metal tires later, the velocipede was a rough ride on the era's cobblestone streets. For some time, the velocipede was considered the first bicycle, but the *Draisienne* now gets that honor. The velocipede was renamed "bicycle" in 1869.

Once metalworking techniques advanced enough to make strong small parts, the first all-metal bicycle appeared. It was the 1870 high wheel, with pedals attached directly to the front wheel and no freewheeling mechanism. Tires were made of solid rubber, and the long spokes of the front wheel served to absorb some of the shock. As manufacturers learned that a larger wheel produced greater distance per rotation, the front wheels became larger and larger, stopping only at the length of

In 1986 bicycling was the third most popular U.S. participation sport, after swimming and general exercise. Biking enthusiasts ride for exercise, transportation, and as a way to "get back to nature."

the rider's leg. With the rider high above the machine's center of gravity, any abrupt stop because because of a rut, stone, or stray dog would cause the machine to rotate forward on the front axle. The rider's legs became stuck under the handlebars, and the rider landed on his head, "taking a header."

At half a year's working-class wages, the high wheel was the preserve of young men of means. Its heyday was the 1880s. The adult tricycle was the sedate alternative for the woman rider, restrained by corsets and long skirts, as well as clergy, doctors, and other dignified persons. Tricycle manufacturers introduced band brakes, rack-and-pinion steering, the differential, and other devices later used by automobile manufacturers.

To reduce the risk of "taking a header," some bicycles were made with the small wheel in front. These were "safety bicycles," and the older models were "ordinary bicycles" or ordinaries. The English high ordinary bicycle was also called the Penny Farthing because the large and small wheels resembled a penny and a farthing set together, dating from 1871.

Improved Bicycle Technology

Improved metalworking techniques allowed bikes with two same-sized wheels with a metal chain, sprocket, and gear system to allow one rotation of the pedals to generate greater distances. The first chain-driven bike dates to 1884. The Rover Safety, popular between 1885 and 1900, had a saddle, handlebar grips, and a crank axle in the rear and was easy and safe to ride. Still, without shocks and with hard rubber tires, it offered a rough ride. The League of American Wheelmen, the precursor of today's League of American Bicyclists, worked in the 1880s and 1890s for better roads.

John B. Dunlop's pneumatic tires, an 1888 innovation, meant the end of the high wheel. A mass-produced, comfortable bicycle was affordable by the working man and modest for the ladies. Bustles and corsets went by the wayside as bicycling became the hot fad.

By 1910 the automobile made bikes less popular among adults. Smaller bikes for children debuted that year, but failed to catch on until after the end of World War I in 1918. Makers included Mead, Montgomery Ward, and Sears & Roebuck. Schwinn later began manufacturing bicycles. Children's bikes incorporated elements from motorcycles and automobiles and weighed up to 65 pounds. The children's bike boom began after World War II. The design remained popular into the 1950s with added design elements reminiscent of jets and rockets.

In the 1960s lightweight bicycles became the fashion. The three-speed bicycle dates from the 1950s, and the 10-speed derailleur, common in Europe from the turn of the 20th century, became popular in the 1970s. The environmental surge of the 1970s made bikes popular, and in 1978 U.S. bike sales surpassed those of automobiles. In 1986 bicycling was the third most popular U.S. participation sport, after swimming and general exercise. In 1996 mountain bike competition was featured at the Olympic Games.

Mountain bikes appeared in the 1980s. Manufacturers made bikes with 15, and then 18, 21, and 24 speeds. At the beginning of the 21st century, the mountain bike became popular.

Global bicycle sales in 2007 were $61 billion, with 100 million bikes built—mainland China produced 73 million. European Union bicyclists bought 70 percent, with sales up almost 15 percent over five years. U.S. sales were up 9 percent in the same period. The lightest bike made to date, a carbon fiber model weighing 13 pounds and manufactured by China's Giant, sold for $7,100 in 2007.

See Also: United Kingdom; United States, 1876 to 1900; United States, 1900 to 1930; United States, 1930 to 1960.

Bibliography. Suman Bandrapalli, "Pivotal Dates in Bicycle History," *Christian Science Monitor* (February 13, 2001); Mary Bellis, "Bicycle History," inventors.about.com/library/inventors/blbicycle.htm (cited October 2008); Bicycle Pedaling History Museum, "A Quick History of Bicycles," www.pedalinghistory.com/PHhistory.html (cited October 2008); David V. Herlihy, *Bicycle: The History* (Yale University Press, 2004); Ralph Jennings, "As Fuel Prices Climb Higher, So Do Bicycle Sales," *International Herald Tribune* (May 14, 2008).

John Barnhill
Independent Scholar

Billiards

The term *billiards* is believed to have derived from the French word *billart,* meaning "mace," which was used in the 15th and 16th centuries as a striking implement in lawn games such as troco and croquet. It is generally thought that the indoor game of billiards evolved from these outdoor games. Although the term *billiards* is used in the United Kingdom to refer exclusively to the game of English Billiards, in the United States it is usually used as a more generic term for all games played on a cloth-covered table with a cue (striking implement) and balls, otherwise known as "cue sports." Cue sports include a variety different games which then fall under a number of subdivisions. Furthermore, many subdivisions of these games have their own geographically disparate sets of rules and etiquettes. The term *billiards* will be used only in conjunction with the British definition.

Carom billiards is the overarching title of a family of cue sports that were originally played on tables without pockets, or holes in to which balls can be "potted." The object of most carom games is to score points by striking one's own ball, or "cue ball," against the opponent's, and for it to then strike the third, "object ball"; this sequence of collisions is known as a "carom."

Carom billiards is believed to have originated in France during the 18th century. Included under the heading of carom billiards are the disciplines of three-cushion billiards, American four-ball billiards, and English billiards. English billiards differs from the earliest forms of carom billiards in that it is played on a table with pockets. Six pockets are located at each corner of the rectangular table and opposite each other half-way along the long sides of the rectangle. As well as scoring points by caroming, or "cannoning" (as it is now more commonly known in the contemporary games of snooker and pool), points can also be scored by potting the balls.

Pocket billiards is the collective name for games that are now known more commonly as pool. Pool includes various versions including eight-ball (commonly associated with an English variation), nine-ball, straight pool, one-pocket pool, and pyramid pool. The name *pool* is believed to have derived from the 19th-century American pool rooms, where people would meet to pool their money and gamble on horse races. Because the pool halls often provided carom billiards tables, the term *pool* became synonymous with the particular offshoot of the game that became popular in these establishments.

Snooker is a cue sport that was developed in India toward the end of the 19th century. Cue sports, and in particular, pyramid pool, were very popular pastimes among British Army officers stationed in the country at the time. One variation of pyramid pool was devised by officers in Jabalpur in 1874 by adding colored balls to the already existing 15 red balls. The variation became known as "snooker," which was originally a military term used to refer to inexperienced personnel. It is believed that Colonel Sir Neville Chamberlain of the Devonshire regiment was playing this new variation of pyramid pool when his opponent failed to pot a ball, and Chamberlain called him a "snooker."

The types of balls required to play cue sports vary from game to game. Carom billiards balls are larger than pool balls and come as a set of two cue balls (one colored or marked) and an object ball. American-style pool balls come in sets of two suits of object balls, seven solid-colored balls and seven striped, an eight ball and a cue ball; the balls are positioned on the table differently for different games.

The English version of eight-ball pool uses sets of red and yellow balls instead of solids and stripes and the balls are smaller than American-style balls. Snooker balls are also smaller than American-style pool balls, and come in sets of 22 (15 reds, six "colors," and a cue ball). Cue sport balls have been made from many different materials since the inception of the game, including clay, bakelite, crystalite, ivory, plastic, steel, and wood.

Just as with the balls, the size and style of cue sport tables varies from game to game. However, all tables are generally rectangular and twice as long as they are wide. Most pool tables are either seven, eight, or nine feet long. Nine-foot tables are most commonly used for American-style pool. English eight-ball pool tends to be played on the shorter tables. High-quality tables have a bed of thick slate to prevent warping and changes because of humidity. All types of of cue sport tables are covered with a woven wool or wool/nylon blend cloth called "baize." The cloth of the billiard table has traditionally been green, believed to reflect the games' origins in the lawn games of the 16th century.

Unsurprisingly, the implement used in cue sports to strike the ball is called a "cue." A cue is usually either a one-piece tapered stick or a two-piece stick divided by a joint of metal. The widest point of the taper is referred to as the "butt" and is gripped in the players' hand. The narrowest end of the taper is referred to as the "ferrule." A small leather pad, known as the "tip," is affixed to the ferrule; this is the only part of the cue that makes contact with the ball. High-quality cues are generally made from a hardwood. Pool players tend to favor cues made from maple, whereas snooker players tend to favor ash wood cues.

See Also: Bocce; Croquet; Europe, 1200 to 1600.

Bibliography. D. Alciatore, *The Illustrated Principles of Pool and Billiards*, (Sterling Publishing, 2004); Robert Byrne, *Byrne's New Standard Book of Pool and Billiards* (Harcourt Brace & Co., 1998) C. Everton, *History of Snooker and Billiards* (Partridge, 1986); I. Shamos, *The Illustrated Encyclopedia of Billiards* (Lyons & Burford, 1993).

Mike Wragg
Leeds Metropolitan University

Bingo

Bingo is game of chance in which players race to be the first to form a specified pattern of pieces on a grid. Although there are many variations of Bingo that do not involve financial gain, the game originated as a form of lottery and is in its most popular form today a form of gambling. Like lotteries, Bingo is acceptable to a larger segment of society than games involving direct betting (such as those involving cards or dice). It is often used as a fundraising tool for churches and nonprofit organizations, and its popularity has led many casinos to develop Bingo halls as well.

American Bingo uses the numbers one to 75, and the cards feature the numbers in a 5 x 5 grid.

The Origins of Bingo

In a 1957 *New York Times* article, Robert Daley wrote that playing Bingo predated the pyramids of ancient Egypt. However, while this may have been a common origin story at the time, no known archaeological evidence supports this claim. The Egyptian origin story may have evolved in the 1800s, when both Bingo-styled games and modern Egyptology became a part of popular culture in Europe and the United States. The mystique of ancient Egypt was often used to validate the legitimacy of an idea or activity at this time; for example, it was a popular misconception that ancient Egyptians created Tarot cards, even though the origins of Tarot can be traced back to Italy in the 1400s.

Italy is also now generally credited with the origin of Bingo, since the Bingo game mechanic appears to have evolved from the Italian lottery. The Italian National Lottery today works similarly to other number-picking lotteries, but the game invented in 1530 closely resembled Bingo. Early games of *Lo Giuoco del Lotto D'Italia* involved calling out numbers and placing markers on cards containing a random assortment of numbers. The first player to cover a complete row on the card was declared the winner. Originally developed in Florence as a means of raising funds for the city's public works projects, the Italian National Lottery now brings in over $75 million for the government each year.

During the 1700s, the Bingo-like rules of the *Lotto D'Italia* spread through Europe as a recreational game under the Italian name Lotto. Although an exact date of development is unknown, in 1778, a French news item reported that *Le Lotto* had become a popular pastime. These early versions of Lotto, as Bingo would be called for the next 150 years, used an identical structure to the Italian game. Each card contained nine columns and three rows, with each column containing one to three numbers from a 10-number range (1–10 in the first column, 11–20 in the second, etc.); in total, 15 of the squares contained numbers, while the other 12 squares were free spaces. The first player to cover all numbers in one of the three rows was declared the winner.

In 1700s Mexico, the Bingo game took on a new form—*Lotería*—with illustrations replacing numbers. In the Mexican version of the game, players each attempt to form a four-piece pattern on a 4 x 4 grid. The patterns are not limited to straight lines but may also include diagonals, all corners, and small squares of four. The caller (the person who randomly selects and reads out the next piece in all versions of Lotto/Bingo) selects one card from a 54-card deck containing one of each of the *Lotería* symbols and reads out either the name of the card or a riddle that indicates the card's identity. Sometimes a number is provided along with the pictures to ease the challenge of finding a match. Among Bingo games, *Lotería* is unique in its cultural significance as an art form. Like the Tarot, *Lotería* has inspired many artists to create unique decks illustrating the 54 standard symbols, including the Rooster, the Little Devil, the Sun, the World, Death, and the Little Black Man.

Educational Lotto games, still popular worldwide today, began in the 1800s. The simplest educational Lotto games were developed to help young children recognize numbers and amounted to nothing more than a simplified Lotto board with illustrations surrounding each number. These games are some of the earliest examples of the simpler square boards commonly used in Bingo today. More advanced educational Lotto and Bingo games put answers to questions in each square; players must know the correct answer in order to fill in the square. This form of the game is popular for classroom review in subjects including math, spelling, reading, and even Egyptology.

Modern Bingo

Today, Bingo games are almost universally called Bingo. Citizens of English-speaking countries primarily play two variants. The British version more closely resembles the Italian *Lotto*, while the U.S. version more closely resembles the Mexican *Lotería.* Both versions involve a caller drawing numbers from a bin until someone calls out "Bingo!" Generally the cards are sold to the players before the game begins, and a portion of the purchase price of the cards goes toward cash prizes for the winners. The most popular mechanism for drawing numbers in public Bingo games involves lightweight balls, each printed with a unique number within the range used in the game. To ensure fairness in commercial Bingo games, a machine generally handles ball randomization and selection. These machines are sometimes designed to look complicated so that ball selection becomes part of the entertainment. Similar machines are also used in many lottery drawings, especially those broadcast on television.

The version of Bingo played in the United Kingdom and some former British territories, sometimes called Housey Housey (or just Housie), uses the 3 x 9 grid from Lotto, with similar objectives involving covering horizontal rows. However, often in the United Kingdom, callers will sometimes use slang terms (often similar to Cockney rhyming slang) to refer to the numbers. For example, seven is "Lucky for Some," 17 is "Never Been Kissed," and five is "Man Alive" (an example of rhyming slang). Although these rhymes almost resemble the riddles of the *Lotería,* the British slang is not as standardized as the Mexican riddles. The amount of slang used varies widely; the slang for one and 90 are the most frequent embellishments. Some callers also prefer to call out the numbers as separate digits followed by the number as read: for example, "One and six, 16."

The version of Bingo played in the United States is like *Lotería* in its game play, but instead of the Mexican pictures, American Bingo uses numbers from one to 75, laid out in a 5 x 5 grid. Like *Lotería,* a range of 15 numbers appears in each column, but American Bingo adds the labels B, I, N, G, and O to the five columns. This means the numbers called are B1 through B15, I16 through I30, and so on. The lettered column labels were added aid players in looking for matching numbers, since many Bingo players do not realize that the column determines the numeric range and would otherwise search the entire card.

Although the name Bingo is now used internationally, it originated in the United States. In 1928, a carnival pitchman discovered the game of Lotto in Germany. He adapted it into a carnival game, renaming it Beano. A year later, Ed Lowe, a traveling toy salesman, attended a carnival in Jacksonville, Georgia, and saw how popular and addictive the game could be: players, he reported, kept insisting on one more game until well after closing. Ed Lowe brought the game back to his faltering toy company in New York and began playing it with friends. According to Lowe, a woman who won in an early playtest called out "Bingo!" instead of "Beano!" and he immediately realized that would be a name under which the game would become popular. Lowe realized that it was impossible to patent a game that had come out of the public domain, so instead he asked the imitators who soon began competing with him to also call their games "Bingo." He charged only a dollar a year for the privilege of using the name Bingo, realizing perhaps that having Bingo become the generic name for the game was more valuable to his sales than any profits he could realize from licensing.

Bingo's popularity as a parlor game soon led to its adoption by churches and charitable organizations as a fundraising tool, but technically it was a form of gambling and therefore illegal in most of the United States. In 1952, the New York State County of Appeals overturned charges against Edward P. Burns, a Niagara Falls Bingo operator who had been indicted for conducting a lottery. In 1954, New York City police stopped ignoring Bingo games and started charging Bingo organizers with criminal offenses. Citizens immediately began lobbying to legalize the game, arguing that the 1952 Court of Appeals decision set a precedent. Eventually, most states began to regulate Bingo (and similar fundraisers like lotteries and raffles), requiring organizations to provide proof of nonprofit status and to register for an operating license.

Since its legalization, commercial gambling operations have embraced Bingo. Many casinos in the United States have Bingo rooms, often with state-of-the-art electronic boards for the players. Bingo is also now a popular online pastime, with many games operated for profit (thanks to the difficulty of enforcing gambling laws internationally). Some online Bingo games even let the player opt to have the computer do all the work, from marking cards to calling "Bingo!", making it perhaps one of the most efficient forms of gambling on the internet.

See Also: Gambling; Italy; Parlor Games; Play in the Classroom; United Kingdom; United States, 1930 to 1960.

Bibliography. Avery Cardoza, *The Basics of Winning Bingo* (Cardoza, 2003); Rene Colato Lainez and Jill Arena, *Playing Loteria* (Luna Rising, 2005); Roger Snowden, *Gambling Times Guide to Bingo* (Gambling Times, 1986).

Jay Laird
Northeaster University

Blackjack

Blackjack, also known as Twenty-One, is played in more casinos in the world than any other game. Although the game is, at the core, one of chance, the skillful player can take advantage of a number of options to increase his chances of winning. The goal is quite simple: taking one card at a time, accumulate the highest possible hand without exceeding a value of 21. Blackjack, like other banking games, pits each player against the dealer, making it a game more suited to formal betting environments like casinos than for recreational play among friends.

Origins

Blackjack originated in France in the 1700s, where it was known as *Vingt-Un* or *Vingt-Et-Un*, French for Twenty-One. It is unknown exactly when the game came to America, but the rules as most widely used today were refined in Indiana in 1912. Most of the rule variations created by American casinos involved changing the payouts for various hands. The first of these bonuses to become popular was the "blackjack": if a player was dealt the ace of spades and a black jack (aces are worth 11 and face cards are all worth 10), then the player received 10 times his original bet. The promise of such a high payout made the game more popular, but also a bad investment for the casinos, so the rule didn't stay around long. In 1912, U.S. casinos reduced the payout to 3:2 (or 150 percent of the original bet) but made it easier to obtain by offering the payout for any "natural" 21 with an ace and a 10.

Despite the removal of the high payout for a black jack 21, the name *Blackjack* became the standard for the American version of the game. The name is now used in many parts of the world, with other older names mostly reserved for less-popular variants. The British play both American Blackjack and Pontoon, a variation thought to be an English bastardization of *Vingt-Un*, as well as a completely different game called Black Jack, which more closely resembles Crazy Eights. In Australia, Pontoon refers to a copyrighted game known as Spanish 21; the name was changed so that it could be used without being licensed from the publisher. The original French *Vingt-Et-Un*, now seldom found in casinos, has simplified rules and is more often treated as a social game.

Rule Variations and Customs

In Blackjack, each player and the dealer receive two cards. Player card visibility varies by game: some allow the first two cards to be dealt face down, so only the player can see, while others require all cards to be dealt face up. In all variations, the dealer has one face-up card and one concealed (or sometimes as-yet-undealt) card, and all subsequent cards dealt to any player are left face-up on the table. Because the players are not competing with each other, none of these variations affect game play, but they have become an important enough part of the social norms of the game to be considered rules.

If, on the first two cards, the dealer has a natural 21, any players who do not also have a natural 21 immediately lose the hand. Otherwise, the dealer works from one side of the table to the other, playing out each player's hand. At any point in the game, if a player ties the dealer's score, the hand is a "push," meaning that player and the dealer are tied. However, except in the case of the dealer's natural 21, every player has an equal chance for victory or defeat against the dealer, regardless of others' outcomes.

Players have five basic options, each represented by a hand signal. Some casinos prefer that players only use hand signals in order to prevent verbal miscommunication; others ask players to use specific terminology when communicating a decision. The most common two options are "hit" and "stand." A hit, signaled by touching a finger to the table, is a request for an additional card. A stand, signaled by moving the hand to one side on the table or by sliding the cards under one's chips, ends a player's turn. If the player exceeds 21 in his hand, he "busts," and his turn ends, losing him his bet.

The other options a player may pursue are only available at the beginning or end of a hand. If the two cards the player has been dealt are of the same rank (or, in some places, value, meaning that 10 through king are counted as equivalent), the player may, before taking any cards, split his hand into two, doubling his bet by placing chips next to the original bet and holding up two fingers. If a player is convinced that he has a losing hand before he's taken any action, some casinos offer the option to "surrender" (by making a chopping motion over the bet), in which case the player loses only half the bet and gives up the hand. Finally, if the player believes that one more card will cause him to win the hand, he may "double down" by placing more chips on the table and holding up one finger; this also signals the dealer that the next card will be the player's last, so this can only be the player's final decision.

Although there are many small variations that affect payouts or add an additional reward or restriction to play, the most common is a sixth start-of-game option, "insurance." If the dealer's upcard is an ace, then the players, under this rule, may make a separate bet that the dealer has a natural 21. The bet is limited to half the player's original bet, but it pays out at 2:1, so the player can effectively "break even" in what would otherwise likely be a losing situation. However, if the dealer does not have a natural 21, then the insurance bet is lost, and regular play of the hand continues.

This winning hand of an ace (sometimes used as a "soft" card) and a 10-point face card is a "natural" 21 in Blackjack.

One unusual aspect of Blackjack is that the ace can have a value of either one or 11. It is referred to as a "soft" card, since its value changes to whatever is most advantageous for the player. Since the goal is to have the highest-scoring hand without exceeding 21, the ace is counted as 11 until doing so would "bust" the player. At that point, the ace is counted as one, and the "soft" hand (because its value could change) becomes a "hard" hand with a fixed value.

The dealer is essentially the game's referee, with a strict mechanical function that could be replaced by a computer, but the culture surrounding Blackjack has kept the game played primarily at casino tables. When playing out his hand, the dealer does not have any choices. The dealer may not split or double down but may only hit or stand. A rule made visible to all players dictates at what point the dealer must stand, even if it means he'll lose. If the dealer busts, then all players who have not "busted" win twice their bets back.

Rules that affect game play and payouts are marked on each Blackjack table. For example, every table is marked with one of two rules: "Dealer stands on all 17s" or "Dealer hits soft 17." The first rule states that as soon as the dealer has reached a total of 17, he must stop dealing himself cards, even if another player has exceeded that value. The second rule states that if the dealer has reached 17 but there are aces involved, the dealer must continue to hit. In addition, the table may have rules about payouts for naturals, availability of insurance, and other variations.

On the other hand, rules about playing customs—for example, cards in hand versus cards face up, hand signals versus verbal ones, and so on—are not generally posted. Players are expected to follow the etiquette of those around them, but the dealer will generally correct a player who makes a mistake as long as it does not affect the game's outcome.

Card Counting, Cheats, and Casino Countermeasures

Although, because of the limited decisions available to the player, Blackjack has a large element of luck, there is enough skill involved that casinos must carefully monitor the odds of the dealer winning and the resulting payout. Since the dealer's role is dictated by casino rules, this mostly involves monitoring player behavior and changing table rules or payouts if the current setup proves to be unprofitable. However, players who come armed with knowledge of the probabilities associated with a Blackjack hand can develop up to a 2 percent advantage over the casino. This number becomes more significant when you consider that the house (the casino) has a 5 percent advantage over the players when only basic rules and play strategies are used.

While basic playing strategy involves estimating the likelihood that the dealer has a higher total by comparing one's own point total to the dealer's visible card, more sophisticated composition-dependent strategies involve analyzing the specific cards in the player's hand as well as the other cards up on the table. If there are more low cards face up on the table, for example, then the player may wish to avoid taking an additional card, since that means there is an increase chance of being dealt a high card. According to WizardOfOdds.com, a composition-dependent strategy can at best reduce the house advantage by approximately 0.04 percent in a single-deck game.

Card counting is a more popular, complex, and controversial strategy. Various card-counting strategies and systems have been developed since 1962, when Edward O. Thorp proved mathematically that Blackjack could be beaten by card counting and published his results in the book *Beat The Dealer*. In general, card-counting systems do not require the player to memorize exactly which cards have been played. Instead, the card-counting player adds up point values as cards are revealed in play and bases his betting on the current value of the entire table.

The controversy around card counting is that although it is not a form of cheating (since it relies on the player's skill in manipulating public information), local laws sometimes forbid it. Further, it is technically legal in most places, but since casinos, like other private businesses, have established the right to refuse service to anyone for any reason, players who are suspected of card counting are often banned. It is, however, illegal in most places to use any form of device for card counting, since then the player is receiving technical assistance to improve his odds.

Thorp's work on card counting was originally modeled on a computer, correlating the Kelly criterion, a formula used to maximize long-term profit over repeated plays of a given game, with a probabilistic analysis of card occurrences in a single-deck Blackjack game with a varying number of players. Thorp, working with his colleague Claude Elwood Shannon (the "father of information theory"), developed the first wearable computer, which was used to test these probabilities in a given game. However, the high price of electronics in the 1960s prevented such devices from proliferating; by the time such technology would have been cost-effective, the bans were already in place.

Another strategy popularized in the 1970s by professional gambler Ken Uston involved team play. A Blackjack "team" consists of players "working" different tables, making small bets on their hands while counting cards. As soon as a card count turns favorable, the player signals another player to join the table and make big bets. As long as the dealers and pit bosses (the managers of the dealers and the first line of casino security) do not notice the signals, this is a far safer way to count cards than increasing ones' own bets at a table over time. However, the "big players" on such teams rarely last long, as they are eventually barred from casino play. From 1979 until 2002, various incarnations of the MIT Blackjack Team, inspired by Uston and Thorp's work, played in casinos worldwide; generally an incarnation of the team would only last for a period of months before being banned in too many casinos to continue.

In order to reduce the effectiveness of such card counting and other strategies, many casinos have moved to primarily "shoe-based" Blackjack games, in which multiple decks are shuffled together and played through. The use of multiple decks reduces the player's ability to gain a significant advantage: six or more decks shuffled together reduce the player's statistical advantage to zero, and therefore is the preferred size. A few casinos still offer single-deck Blackjack games, but these are considered "advanced" games, as the standard way of playing involves players concealing their card values, thereby preventing the dealer from assisting them with questions. A dealer will never advise a player on what move to take, but will sometimes remind beginners of their options.

At least with Blackjack, casinos must walk a very fine line between giving players the feeling that a game is winnable and ensuring that they make money. Consider, in contrast, a slot machine: the player generally feels that the machine is "in control" and expects that the outcome is a matter of luck, while with a Poker game, the player generally feels that the game is primarily skill-based, and therefore chalks up losses to poor judgment. With Blackjack, however, players differ widely in their beliefs in luck versus skill. The casinos prefer players who believe in luck, while those who play too skillfully may be asked to leave for making too much money.

In certain notable cases, the casinos have even ejected players without giving them an opportunity to cash in their chips. However, Ken Uston is also famous for winning a lawsuit against an Atlantic City casino that had barred him for card counting; he argued that it was prejudicial to bar a "skilled player" who used no visible means of cheating. The New Jersey decision unfortunately did not set a national precedent, but as of 2008, Atlantic City casinos still must allow card counters, although they have now other rules-based measures in place to prevent players from obtaining too much of an advantage.

Blackjack in Popular Culture

The publication of *Beat the Dealer* in 1962 greatly increased Blackjack's popularity as people attempted to apply the system outlined in the book. Since then, many Blackjack systems have been developed, causing occasional publishing frenzies of books that promise players a reliable method of winning. Since 2003, Blackjack has experienced a resurgence in popularity thanks to two bestselling books by Ben Mezrich, *Bringing Down the House* and *Breaking Vegas,* which together tell the story of two generations of the MIT Blackjack Team.

In 2008, Kevin Spacey produced the movie *21*, based on Mezrich's book. Many of the exciting elements of the story, including players sneaking hundreds of thousands of dollars in cash across the country and wearing disguises to avoid casino intimidation, were based on true events. While the film was a box office hit, Asian-American groups criticized the producers for changing the principal characters' ethnicities from Asian to Caucasian.

See Also: Europe 1600 to 1800; France; Gambling; History of Playing Cards; Luck and Skill in Play.

Bibliography. Ben Mezrich, *Bringing Down the House: The Inside Story of Six M.I.T. Students Who Took Vegas for Millions,* (Free Press, 2003); William Poundstone, *Fortune's Formula* (Farrar Straus and Giroux, 2005); William N. Thompson, *Gambling in America: An Encyclopedia of History, Issues, and Society* (ABC-CLIO, 2001); Edward O. Thorp, *Beat the Dealer: A Winning Strategy for the Game of Twenty-One* (Random House, 1966).

Jay Laird
Northeastern University

Blind Man's Bluff

Blind Man's Bluff, as the game is known in thse United States, has been played by both children and adults under a variety of names and in a variety of ways for at least 2,000 years. In its most familiar form, the game consists of a blindfolded player who attempts to catch one of the other players who are silently running around, touching and teasing the blindfolded person. Once the "blind man" catches someone, he must identify that person, usually by touching the face and body to see if he can recognize the individual, and, if he can correctly do so, then that person becomes the next blind man.

Though its exact origins are unknown, Blind Man's Bluff has been played around the world for centuries and is known as Blind Man's Buff in England, as *La Gallina Ciega* (Blind Hen) in Spain, and as *Mosca Cieca* (Blind Fly) in Italy. The game can be played in numerous ways, and some versions include tying the hands of the "blind man" behind his back, blindfolding all players except one, having the players make the sounds of different animals, and incorporating elements of other games, such as the decreasing number of seats from Musical Chairs.

Blind Man's Bluff reached the height of its popularity between the years of 1837 and 1901, when it was played as a parlor game in Victorian England and America. During this time, the game, formerly played by children, was appropriated by adults, where it developed new meanings and connotations. As a game for adults, Blind Man's Bluff, like many other parlor games, purported to help adults return to the supposedly more innocent and carefree times of childhood, but the physical touching that is an integral part of the game provided adults with a culturally permissible justification for physical contact and flirtation with members of the opposite sex. After all, the rules of Blind Man's Bluff do not specify how much or how little touching is necessary among players, and Guessing Blind Man, one of the many versions of Blind Man's Bluff, even calls for men and women to sit publicly on one another's laps, an action that was only sanctioned in Victorian times as part of innocent and wholesome entertainment.

At the end of the Victorian era, the popularity of parlor games among adults waned, and Blind Man's Bluff was returned to the grammar schools and playgrounds, where the game is often taught to young children. In addition to the amusement and exhilaration that it provides them, Blind Man's Bluff helps children learn to rely on senses other than sight in navigating through their surroundings. Adults also frequently impart Blind Man's Bluff to children with a certain amount of nostalgia for bygone, simpler pleasures and pastimes, but children find ways to add fresh elements to the game that help to keep it current and relevant for them. For example, the water game Marco Polo has its roots in Blind Man's Bluff, and through such evolutions and variations, as well as its earlier forms, Blind Man's Bluff will continue to exist as a game in many children's play repertoires.

See Also: Marco Polo; Parlor Games; Play as Entertainment, Psychology of; Play as Entertainment, Sociology of.

Bibliography. Patrick Beaver, *Victorian Parlor Games* (Thomas Nelson, Inc., 1974); Roger Caillois, *Man, Play, and Games* (University of Illinois Press, 2001); Sarah Ethridge Hunt, *Games and Sports the World Around* (Ronald Press Company, 1964).

Ramona Anne Caponegro
University of Florida

Blinky Bill

Blinky Bill is both the title and protagonist of a series of classic children's books by New Zealand–born Australian author-illustrator Dorothy Wall in the 1930s. Though the first book has passed into the public domain, all three books—*Blinky Bill: The Quaint Little Australian*, *Blinky Bill and Nutsy,* and *Blinky Bill Grows Up*—have remained in print for over 70 years, as well as inspiring television series and computer games.

Wall (1894–1942) had moved to Sydney from New Zealand at the age of 20 years for a job in journalism; given the mild regional rivalry between New Zealand and Australia, it's interesting to note the "quaint little Australian" subtitle of the *Blinky Bill* book. Quaint or not, Blinky Bill—an anthropomorphic koala bear in red dungarees—frequently misbehaves throughout his adventures. He's not just rambunctious or curious, like many children's book protagonists—he's a bully, and even a bit of a misanthrope, scowling and whining throughout. The books themselves are darker than children's books of the 21st century, with frank discussion of the numbers of koalas who were killed by hunters. The widescale death of koalas—most killed for their fur (the meat is poisonous), some killed as pests—was the first environmental issue to receive public attention in Australia, a few years before Wall wrote her books. Long before Australians worried about the destruction of koala habitats, they were startled into action by the news that nearly a million koalas had been killed in a single hunting season. The books presented a general conservationist moral.

There have been several adaptations of *Blinky Bill.* From 1984 to 1991, Australian television ran *The New Adventures of Blinky Bill*, which took four characters from the books—Bill, Mrs. Magpie, Angelina Wallaby, and Walter Wombat, but not Bill's adopted kangaroo sister Nutsy—and paired them with new Australian anthropomorphic animals: Charlie Goanna, Eric Anteater, Sybilla Snake, and Kerry Koala. The animals were played by puppets, interacting with human characters like Ranger Barry in Bollygum National Park. Not long after *The New Adventures* left the air, an animated series was made in 1993: *The Adventures of Blinky Bill* adhered more closely to the books, including all of Bill's family in the cast of characters in a little town called New Greenpatch, presided over by the birdbrain Mayor Pelican. Though more faithful to the books than the 1980s series in some respects, *Adventures* was criticized for being brighter and lighter in tone;

Bill is cheery and wide-eyed, cutely mischievous instead of a bully, and the conservation angle is all but ignored.

This tamer Blinky Bill features in some recent computer games: Blinky Bill and the Magician and Blinky Bill Kindergarten are educational games for young children, presenting and grading performance on simple puzzles.

See Also: Australia; Bullying; Daydreaming.

Bibliography. Dorothy Wall, *Blinky Bill and Nutsy, Blinky Bill Grows Up*, and *Blinky Bill: The Quaint Little Australian*, (Angus & Robertson, 1933); Dorothy Wall, *Blinky Bill*, nla.gov.au/nla.aus-an3281107 (cited October 2008).

Bill Kte'pi
Independent Scholar

Blocks

With their economical shape and scale, blocks beg for little hands to touch and arrange them. To the untutored eye, this is mere play. But to experts in developmental science, block play sets the foundation for numeracy, spatial skill, and creative thinking.

Blocks are perhaps the simplest yet most profound toys ever devised. Founded on a few basic shapes but rendered in dozens of materials, a modest palette of blocks can come to represent nearly anything in the hands of an imaginative child. While playthings have been among human artifacts since antiquity, the archetypical building block apparently became popular starting in the mid-19th century. That was when Friedrich Froebel created the "Gifts," the first block set based on a philosophy of learning and designed for use in the classroom.

Children will learn about gravity and balance by stacking, lining up, or fashioning blocks into structures.

Blocks' elegant simplicity makes them accessible to toddlers and older children alike. In children's hands, blocks are tools to probe the laws of the physical world. Building with blocks is a means to symbolize (represent) in three-dimensional space and to engage children in active problem solving as they figure out how, for example, to provide roofs for houses and just the right overall shapes to recreate scenes from their real life experience. Two-year-olds start stacking or lining up wooden blocks to implicitly investigate gravity, balance, and cause and effect. Larger blocks allow preschoolers to build structures like boxes and bridges, providing opportunities for pretend play. Working together to create larger, more complex designs, 5- to 7-year-olds engage in social play that elicits cooperation, planning, and problem solving. Telling stories about the meaning of their constructions cultivates language and the creation of narratives. Block play with others allows children to learn about communication and perspective taking—behaviors key to future successful participation in the work force.

A decline in playtime in American society—up to eight hours less discretionary playtime in 2008 than in 1998—suggests that children may have less experience with blocks than earlier in our history. Yet, the American Academy of Pediatrics called blocks "true" toys and urged parents to continue to buy them for their children.

The geometric nature of blocks invites inquiry about the role of block play in fostering visual-spatial and mathematical reasoning. Unit block sets, with pieces that are multiples of a basic shape, demonstrate proportionality, which may underpin development of number sense, measurement, and recognizing patterns and relationships. Unit blocks play a central role for many early childhood education centers, and could play a much greater role in families if their value was better appreciated.

Research into the educative function of block play blossomed in the early 1970s. Early studies were primarily descriptions of block constructions. Throughout the following decades, research explored the connections between block play and developments in language, spatial sense, and quantitative concepts like counting and addition. Researchers looked for links with curricular touchstones in literacy and science, technology, engineering, and math disciplines. For example, one recent study identified a relationship between the ability to rotate objects in the mind's eye and performance in geometry.

The timeless simplicity of blocks is the key to their broad and enduring appeal. For children, they embody limitless creative possibilities. Educators see in them diverse learning opportunities. The capabilities that block play invite foreshadows many of the learning tasks children will face in school and life. This is what gives blocks their power.

See Also: Academic Learning and Play; Cooperative Play; Erector Sets; Froebel, Friedrich; Lincoln Logs; Play and Learning Theory; Pretending; Toys and Child Development; Unstructured Play.

Bibliography. Beth Casey et al., "The Development of Spatial Skills Through Interventions Involving Block Building Activities," *Cognition and Instruction* (v.26/3, July 2008); Howard P. Chudacoff, *Children at Play: An American History* (New York University Press, 2007); David Elkind, "Can We Play?", *Greater Good*, (v.4/4, Spring 2008); Kenneth R. Ginsburg and the Committee on Communications, and the Committee on Psychosocial Aspects of Child and Family Health, "The Importance of Play in Promoting Healthy Child Development and Maintaining Strong Parent-Child Bonds," *American Academy of Pediatrics* (v.119/1, January 2007); Karyn Wellhousen and Judith Kieff, *A Constructivist Approach to Block Play in Early Childhood* (Delmar, Thompson Learning, 2001).

Wilkey Wong
Roberta Michnick Golinkoff
University of Delaware
Kathryn Hirsh-Pasek
Temple University

Bocce

Bocce is a precision sport and a widespread game, whose name is the plural form of *boccia*, the Italian word that indicates the kind of ball used in the game itself. Its rules and characteristics are similar to those of bowls and Provencal *pétanque*, although bocce is more popular in Italy and other Mediterranean countries.

Archaeological research has found evidence of games similar to modern bocce in ancient Egypt and in Rome. The idea of throwing an object as close as possible to a fixed target has remote origins and has appealed to people from all social backgrounds. According to findings in the Roman city of Pompeii (Italy), the Romans introduced balls in the place of previously used stones and contributed to the diffusion of the game, especially among soldiers. Apparently, Emperor Augustus was a skilled player.

During the Middle Ages and early modernity, various games involving ball throwing on different surfaces were popular all around Europe. Thanks to their simplicity, such games were enjoyed by the rich and the poor alike, even though they have often been forbidden, as they were thought to bring disorder into the lives of peasants and soldiers. Bocce was included in Bruegel's masterful *Children's Games*, which is one the most suggestive representations of folk life by the great Flemish painter. Famous personalities such as Galileo, Francis Drake, Luther, and Calvin were said to be passionate players of early versions of the game.

Modern Bocce Emerges

However, modern bocce made its appearance later. The famous French *Encyclopaedia* (1751) laid down the basic rules of the game, which in France was known as *boules*. Two years later a learned Italian, Raffaele Bisteghi, published a codification of rules in Italian, *Il Gioco delle Bocchie* (The Game of Bocce). Whether played singularly or by teams of two or three people, bocce was a simple and inexpensive game, which did not require major structures or sophisticated equipment. During the 19th century, it spread across continental Europe, especially into France and Italy. In such countries it had strong roots in areas of the countryside characterized by small landholdings. Landowners used to meet in market towns to sell their goods, drink wine, and enjoy some common life, often by playing bocce. With the advent of the industrial revolution, bocce moved from the countryside to urban areas.

It became popular in southern France, around Lyon, and in northwestern Italy, where Italian industrial growth actually started. In France several different games developed out of *boules*: *boule lyonnaise* and *pétanque* became the most popular ones. In Italy, bocce received official recognition with the foundation of the first society, which took place in 1873 in Turin. Among the members of the *Cricca bocciofila* (the bocce lovers' gang) there were also exponents of the new urban bourgeoisie, such as the writer Edmondo De Amicis, who believed in the value of this game for the mind, the soul, and the body. Bocce became an occasion of social gathering and exchange of ideas, too. The liberal state and rising entrepreneurs felt threatened by the game, which was often seen as a vehicle of socialist thoughts.

In this sense, governments and some entrepreneurs reacted by cooperating in the organization of workers' spare time—as would become usual in America in the 1920s with the diffusion of Fordist management principles. In the meantime, the earliest groups of bocce lovers in Piedmont (the region around Turin) met in Rivoli in 1897 and laid the ground for the foundation of the first regional federation.

At the beginning, bocce was only played outdoors and with wooden balls. At the national level, the first organization, the UBI (Unione Bocciofila Italiana, the Italian bocce-lovers union), was founded in 1919 and led by a lawyer from Turin, Massimo Cappa.

With the advent of fascism (1922), the new regime wanted to take control over recreation, which, because of its popularity among the working class, was suspected to be a vehicle of socialist or antifascist ideas. Since 1929 bocce has, thus, been included in the fascist organization for free time, that is, the Opera Nazionale Dopolavoro (OND, the National Afterwork Opera). Fascism, however, contributed to the diffusion of the game on the national territory.

After World War II, bocce remained a popular game, although several questions and disputes have since occurred. The existence of two versions, the more agonistic *volo* (played in Piedmont) and the more recreational *raffa* have often brought about problems of organization and membership. In wider terms, bocce has become always more of a sport, whose players participate in the Olympics, rather than a game. The latter has sometimes been associated with older adults or retired people and a modest youth involvement. In the last decades, however, remarkable changes have occurred. Bocce has enjoyed increasing popularity among women; furthermore, it has spread to countries with high Italian immigration, such as the United States and Australia, and regained popularity in other

The oldest organized bocce league in the United States is thought to be in Philadelphia, and the Bocce League of America was established in 1935. Public bocce courts are found across the United States, particularly on the East Coast.

Mediterranean ones, like Croatia and Slovenia. Finally, bocce is becoming increasingly popular as a source of good health and an incentive to develop self-discipline and respect for colleagues and competitors; all these qualities had been envisaged as early as in ancient Greece and are still the core grounds that help keep alive this ancient game and sport.

See Also: Boules; Bowling; Europe, 1600 to 1800; France; Italy.

Bibliography. BocceBallRules.net, www.bocceballrules.net (cited October 2008); Daniele Di Chiara, *Storia Delle Bocce in Italia e Nel Mondo—Dalle Origini ai Tempi Nostri* [History of Bocce in Italy and the World—From its Origins to Current Times] (Poligraf, 2005); Rico C. Daniele, *Bocce: A Sport for Everyone* (Authorhouse, 2000).

Ernesto Gallo
University of Turin/University of Birmingham

Boggle

Boggle is a word game designed by Allan Turoff in 1972 and is trademarked by Parker Brothers/Hasbro. Boggle is played with 16 letter dice that are shaken in a container and spread into a 4 x 4 square grid. During a three-minute round, players seek to construct words using adjacent letters and record these words privately. After each round players read their lists, and words that appear more than once are eliminated from scoring. The longer the word the more points received, and the player with the highest point total is the winner. The sides of each die have one letter, except for Qu, as a Q would be unusable in most English words without a U following.

In the last decades variations of Boggle have been manufactured such as Boggle Deluxe with a 5 x 5 grid, Travel Boggle, and Junior Boggle, with the later two being the only remaining Boggle games remaining in production. Today word games based on the same premise are readily available via the internet for casual play.

Boggle, while never obtaining the cultural following of Scrabble, has earned a place in American game culture. Boggle clubs, though few, appear at various colleges in the United States, such as Dartmouth College, Berkeley College, and Grinnell College. References to Boggle have appeared in various television programs, including *Seinfeld*, *King of the Hill*, and *Friends* and in the lyrics of the Beastie Boys. A brief Boggle television game show hosted by Wink Martindale appeared in 1994.

See Also: Crosswords; Hasbro; Play and Learning Theory; Scrabble; Word Games (Other Than Crosswords).

Bibliography. Boggle Word Game: How to Play, http://www.centralconnector.com/GAMES/boggle.html (cited October 2008); Philip E. Orbanes, *The Game Makers: The Story of Parker Brothers, from Tiddledy Winks to Trivial Pursuit* (Harvard Business School Press, 2003).

Daniel Farr
Randolph College

Bolivia

This landlocked South American country is one of the poorest countries in the Americas. It has borders with Argentina, Paraguay, Brazil, Peru, and Chile, the latter of which managed to defeat Bolivia in war in 1879 and removed its access to the sea. Unlike most other countries in Latin America, Bolivia has an indigenous majority, most being from the Quechua and the Aymará, with those of European descent making up 15 percent of the population of over 9 million (2007).

Many of Bolivia's indigenous people inherited traditions and customs from the Incas, with playing music, singing, and dancing being very important. Many musical instruments were made from wood or hollowed out llama bones. Some people in Bolivia still play the Inca game in which contestants flip pottery counters, similar to the game of Tiddlywinks. There is also another game called *Picha* in which players use dice. There are also two Inca board games called *Tacanaco* and *Chuncara,* in which dice are used, and as a result of the score achieved, colored beans or seeds are moved around the board. Spinning tops are still popular with many children, as is playing with dolls and making models.

The Spanish brought an introduction of Spanish musical instruments, especially the guitar, as well as many of their customs. Because of the geography of the country, although there was horse-riding, it was never on the same scale as in neighboring Argentina. For manufactured toys, the Spanish elite were, and indeed still are, the major market for goods made or imported into the country. Until 2006, they also controlled the government, and they still dominate economic life. Wealthy Bolivians are involved in following many of the same pursuits as people in the West—Wargaming, making model airplanes, trains, battlefield dioramas made from model kits, and playing elaborate board games. Chess, Backgammon and card games form an important method of relaxation. Soccer is the main recreational sport in the country, although because of the cheap cost of living, many foreign tourists have visited the country to hike, which has since become popular with the locals.

There also existed the Afro-Bolivians, many of whom, up until the 1952 revolution, lived in near-slave-like conditions. They brought with them percussion instruments, heavy rhythm beats, and the chanting that has come to symbolize *saya* music—now incorporated into many chants at soccer matches and the like. There is also a small Japanese population, mainly from Okinawa, and this has led to the introduction of Japanese games such as *Go*. Some youth clubs offer billiards and play music with juke boxes. Because of the poverty of the country, there is still little use of computer games.

See Also: Chess and Variations of; Peru; South Americans, Traditional Cultures.

Bibliography. Bob Cordery, "Chaco," *Miniature Wargames* (v.13, June 1984); Robert Pateman, *Bolivia* (Marshall Cavendish, 1995); Michel Peltier, "Des Loisirs Pour une Civilisation," *Écrits de Paris* (v.345, 1975); Mariano Picon Salas, *A Cultural History of Spanish America: From Conquest to Independence* (University of California Press, 1962).

Justin Corfield
Geelong Grammar School

Bosnia and Herzegovina

The now-independent nation of Bosnia-Herzogovina was once part of the Yugoslav Republic. With the disintegration of that country in the early 1990s, Bosnia declared its own independence in 1992. That declaration was followed by a three-year conflict among Bosnia's ethnic Bosniacs, Croats, and Serbs. Along with every other aspect of life, leisure and play in all its forms were severely disrupted. In the years since the Dayton Accords were signed in 1995 ending the conflict, play in all its forms has made a tentative return and in some cases has helped to rebuild the country.

In the years before the conflict, perhaps the most popular form of group play had been soccer. Throughout Bosnia, soccer has always been very popular, whether it was children playing informal pickup games in the streets or amateur or semiprofessional leagues of varying degrees of skill. Nearly every village had a soccer field. Soccer, like every other aspect of life in Bosnia between 1992 and 1995, was affected, however, by the fighting. First, many of the leagues and even teams broke up. Where different ethnic groups had been able to play together in the years of the Yugoslav Republic, the new situation prohibited that kind of play. Further, although this did not happen everywhere, soccer fields were sometimes the places where executions took place, and practice areas around several soccer fields became cemeteries. By 2000, however, there was some movement toward ethnic groups playing together, with Bosniac and Croat league play beginning in that year. Two years later, Serbian leagues began to play as well.

As was the case in much of the old Yugoslav Republic, basketball was very popular in Bosnia. As was the case with soccer, play flourished on many levels, but, as was also the case with soccer, playing in integrated groups stopped during the conflict. In 2001, the U.S. State Department sponsored a series of basketball clinics held in different locations—some of which, like Sarajevo and Tuzla, had been battlegrounds—throughout the country. Led by Don Casey, who had coached the New Jersey Nets and Los Angeles Clippers in the National Basketball Association, the program reached an estimated 500 young players of all Bosnian ethnic backgrounds. In various other areas, rebuilding parks and playgrounds has become part of an extensive effort to bring life back to normal. Other team sports at various levels of play and organization included hockey and volleyball, and these are still popular.

In Yugoslavia's history, there was a great deal of emphasis on group activities, although individual activities flourished as they always had. Many of these pursuits are being revived, and not only by the Bosnian population. The Bosnian government is hoping to use these pastimes as a means of encouraging sport tourism. These include swimming and scuba diving, mountain climbing, hiking, skiing, biking on roads as well as mountain biking, fishing, hunting, sailing, and canoeing.

A very old form of individual play in the city of Mostar had been for young men to jump off the city's famous bridge into the water below. That bridge was destroyed in 1993 during the conflict, not to be rebuilt for another 10 years. Once it was rebuilt, it once again became the scene of the very individual game of bridge jumping.

See Also: Europe, 1960 to Present; Serbia and Montenegro; Soccer (Amateur) Worldwide.

Bibliography. Paul Bennett, "Bosnia Rebounds: Playgrounds and Sports Fields Help Heal a War-Torn Country" *Landscape Architecture* (v.89/4, 1999); Patrick Gasser, "Breaking Post-War Ice: Open Fun Football Schools in Bosnia and Herzegovina" *Culture, Sport, Society* (v.7/3, 2004); U.S. State Department, "U.S. to Co-Sponsor Basketball Clinics in Bosnia-Herzegovina," www.state.gov/r/pa/prs/ps/2001/2388.htm (cited July 2008); Craig Zelizer, "The Role of Artistic Processes in Peacebuilding in Bosnia-Herzegovina," *Peace and Conflict Studies* (v.10/2, 2003).

Robert Stacy
Independent Scholar

Boston

Boston is a card game using the standard 52-card deck. It's a trick-taking game, a Whist variant that incorporated elements of Quadrille and developed over the 18th and 19th centuries. The game was supposedly developed in the early days of the American Revolution, when Bostonians wanted a game not as associated with the British as Whist was; this may or may not be true.

Some of the key developments in Boston include the mid-18th century adoption of the *misere* bid, a bid to lose all 13 tricks. This negative or reversed approach is not found in many widespread trick-taking games, outside of Hearts, but as a possible bid it had been introduced in a variant of the game Hombre and soon spread to Quadrille, Boston, and Tarot. In addition to *misere*, other possible bids included *petite misere* (making one discard followed by losing 12 tricks), *piccolissimo* (winning one and only one trick), *piccolo* (winning two tricks), and *misere ouverte*, in which the player plays with his hand exposed on the table. This approach to negative and precision bids was passed on to games like Skat, Solo, and Norwegian Whist.

Misere and *petit misere* were—legend has it—named after the islands Little Misery and Big Misery off the coast of Marblehead (near Boston). The use of French is sometimes explained by Benjamin Franklin's love of the game and introduction of it to the court at Versailles, but these are unlikely explanations. What is true is that Boston rose in popularity quickly, before its niche was usurped by Bridge; variants and alternate names of Boston are attested all over the English-speaking world.

Boston can also refer to Eight-Ball, the billiards game most Americans refer to simply as pool.

See Also: Billiards; Bridge and Variations; History of Playing Cards; Skat; Whist.

Bibliography. G. Abrahams, *Brains in Bridge* (Horizon Press, 1962); Elliott Avedon, *The Study of Games* (Krieger, 1979); Roger Caillois, *Man, Play, and Games* (University of Illinois Press, 2001); Johan Huizinga, *Homo Ludens* (Beacon Press, 1971); David Parlett, *The Oxford Guide to Card Games* (Oxford, 1990); Brian Sutton-Smith, *The Ambiguity of Play* (Harvard University Press, 2001).

Bill Kte'pi
Independent Scholar

Boules

The term *boules* is used in a number of different ways around the world. Derived from the French word for ball, the word *boule(s)* can be used interchangeably to describe a number of different lawn bowling games, as well as to refer to the balls used during game play. Most commonly, the term refers to the popular French game *pétanque*. A few of the many similar games and game variations include boules, bowls, *boule lyonnaise*, *jeu provençal*, *boule de fort*, *boule nantaise*, *boule des berges*, *boule des flandres*, *boule bretonne*, *boule en bois bocce/boccia* (including *volo* and *rafa* styles), *varpa*, flat green, crown green, and indoor bowls. Play is usually outdoors or on indoor courts often found in pubs and/or restaurants.

The game of *pétanque* (pronounced PAY-TONK) is one of the more popular versions of boules. Played enthusiastically around the world by members of diverse ethnic groups, it is especially popular in France, where it was developed in the early 1900s, and in French-speaking communities.

Families play it as an informal backyard game, French social club members play it at picnics and other gatherings, and some individuals join pétanque clubs. Local pétanque clubs are affiliated with Federation of Pétanque USA, and others are part of the Fédération Internationale de Pétanque et Jeu Provençal (International Federation of Pétanque), which has branches in 50 countries. Members in the formalized pétanque organizations take part in league play, tournaments, and world championships. The organizations also maintain sport standards that include acceptable gear standards, player behavior, and rules.

Pétanque is played with metal balls or boules on any hard-packed dirt surface. Individuals can play the game as singles or in teams of two or three members. Six boules are used per team except during one-on-one games, when the two players each use a set of three boules. The player starting the game draws a small circle on the ground and, with both feet in the circle, tosses the small (often wooden) target jack or cochonet to a distance of six to 10 meters.

Players then throw, not roll, the boules toward the jack to score points. When necessary, distances are measured carefully to determine which boule is closest. Unlike in other similar games, in pétanque the jack is not fixed. As a result, game play is dynamic, and the outcome of a game can change quickly. Points are gained for every ball that is closest to the central jack. Rounds are played until a team reaches a total of 13 points. Matches routinely consist of a total of three games.

Despite a more or less standardized way of playing the game, many folk versions abound, and most players learn the game by word of mouth or by example by playing the game with more experienced players. The boules are usually commercially made, heavy metal balls (usually steel), inscribed with a pattern to tell the teams apart. Players often make their own handmade scoreboards and measuring devices and carry cloths on their belt loops to wipe their hands often.

Playing the game takes on social importance at gatherings such as family picnics and Bastille Day events. Players customarily celebrate after the game with picnic food and wine. Workers might gather for games during the lunch hour in city parks. In this tradition, local clubs often sponsor free lessons and provide gear for games during weekday lunch hours in public parks.

In the United States, the game is enjoying a new popularity among French-ethnics, French-speakers, and non-French speakers alike. While groups playing pétanque advocated to park agencies for years to designate dedicated grounds for pétanque playing, this agenda now has a national importance as players formalize the game more and promote the game as a recreational pursuit within public parks. Boules-type games have a long and rich history of play. This is a testament to the fact that in many cases these games evolved from simple stone-throwing contests. These games continue their popularity today in part because of the social nature of their play and because people of all ages and capabilities can take part. Additionally, gear is relatively inexpensive and easily sourced. Like other lawn games such as horseshoes and croquet, boules provides players with ample opportunity for leisurely competition and social interaction.

See Also: Bocce; Bowling; Croquet; France.

Bibliography. Discover France, "Petanque: The French Game of Boules," www.discoverfrance.net/France/Sports/DF_boules.shtml (cited October 2008); Pascal Leroy, *Jouer aux Boules* (De Vecchi, 2006).

Jennifer Adler
City University of New York
LuAnne Kozma
Michigan State University Museum

Bowling

There are many varieties of bowling, which is played for recreation as well as at the tournament level. The three basic types are lawn bowls, indoor bowls and 10-pin bowling. The archaeologist Sir Flinders Petrie uncovered evidence of bowling as early as 5200 B.C.E. in Ancient Egypt, as a ball and pins were found in the tomb of a child from that date. It was played in Ancient Greece and during the Roman Empire, and it was also played by the ancient Polynesians, including those who migrated to New Zealand.

In the Middle Ages, bowling, often with stones, was popular in village and town communities, often involv-

The American Bowling Congress, photographed c.1905, was formed in 1865 in New York City.

ing the throwing of stones in a game possibly closer to shot put. It was a test of strength, as shown by William Wallace in the film *Braveheart* (1995), set in Scotland. In 1361, King Edward III of England passed an edict that prevented the hurling of stones, as it would take away time that young men should spend practicing archery. The most famous historical incident connected with bowling was with Sir Francis Drake, on July 19, 1588, exclaiming, after he had been brought news of the arrival of the Spanish Armada, that there was plenty of time to finish the game and also defeat the Spaniards. It is thought that Drake was playing on the sand at low tide. The earliest lawn prepared specifically for bowling seems to have been that at Holyrood Palace in Scotland during the reign of King James IV (r.1488–1513).

Many of the legal restrictions on bowling introduced by Edward III were not rescinded until 1845, and a committee was established in 1848 to establish a set of rules for bowling in Scotland. This led to the establishment of the Scottish Bowling Association in 1892. By this time there were already groups involved in bowling in England, including the Northumberland and Durham Bowling Association from 1882. The London Parks Bowling Association was established in 1901, and the English Bowling Association was formed on June 8, 1903, with the cricketer W.G. Grace as the first president.

It was not long before bowling clubs and associations were established around the world, particularly where there were British communities, with the establishment of the Imperial Bowling Association. However, with many members in countries outside the British Empire, this association was transformed into the International Bowling Board, which held its first meeting on July 11, 1905. By 1915 there were bowling greens in Kobe and Yokohama in Japan, and in Shanghai and Kowloon in China. During the 1970 Commonwealth Games, 18 countries took part in bowling activities—the recreation having been recognized as a sport.

The popularity of lawn bowling led to the start of indoor bowling, with many of the same rules. The reason for its establishment was largely because of inclement weather, as shown by the name of the first organization, the Edinburgh Winter Bowling Association, formed in 1905.

Bowling on carpet took place soon afterwards at the Crystal Palace, and soon there were indoor bowling arenas in many British cities, the most well-known being that run by the Paddington Bowls Club at Maida Vale. There were also indoor bowling venues built in Switzerland, as well as in Canada, the United States, and Australia.

Ten-pin bowling was very much a U.S. recreation, although its origins may date back to Ancient Egypt. Legend has that church cloisters were used in the Dark Ages in Germany, and King Henry VIII of England condemned the game (although he did play skittles). Its modern popularity goes back to the early years of the 19th century, when it was played in New York City, with Washington Irving's character Rip Van Winkle, in the book of the same name published in 1818, complaining about the noise from "little men" bowling. The game had attracted gambling by 1841, when it was banned in Connecticut. In 1875 there were attempts to establish an international bowling association based in New York, but this only led to the formation of the American Bowling Congress in 1895.

During the 20th century, bowling alleys were built in many parts of the world, especially in the more prosperous countries, and these alleys have become a venue for many teenagers and young people to meet. Initially, "pin-boys" were employed setting up the pins, but in 1952, machines were invented to do this automatically, which sped up the game and led to its greater popularity. There are now bowling alleys in many countries of the world, including in Africa, and in the 1980s it began to become popular in East Asia, and bowling alleys were built in North Korea. The governing body for this recreation or sport is the Fédération Internationale des Quilleurs, based in Helsinki, Finland.

See Also: Skittles; Team Play; United States, 1930 to 1960.

Bibliography. George Allen and Dick Ritger, *The Complete Guide to Bowling Principles* (Tempe Publishers & Ritger Sports Co., 1986); George T. Burrows, *All About Bowls* (Mills & Boon Limited, 1915); Ray Nelson, *A History of the A.B.C.: American Bowling Congress* (n.p., 1984); Herman Weiskopf, *The Perfect Game: The World of Bowling* (Prentice Hall, 1978).

Justin Corfield
Geelong Grammar School

Boys' Play

Boys' play has been conceptualized within three main research areas: sex/age differences in gender/maturity-typing of play; play as a gendered site, and thus as a site for the study and critique of young masculinities; and cultural-commercial articulations of play culture(s) as boyhood culture. What constitutes boys' play, or "boyish play" or "games boys play," therefore invites ethical, clinical, commercial, literary, ethological, and historical-anthropological approaches. Sex differences in and gender-typing of play have been studied for various reasons, mainly developmental, pedagogical, clinical, and feminist. Most of this research is limited to Western classrooms, playgrounds, and more experimental settings, and to the later half of the 20th century. A lesser-developed area of research addresses differences in father and mother play styles and related aspects of gender/maturity typing in intergenerational play.

Sizable sex differences in spontaneous toy choice are noted at the early age of 12 months. Even with otherwise attractive toys, preschool children like toys less if they are labeled as being intended for the other sex, and they expect other girls and boys to do the same. Toy preference on the basis of gender-typing is frequently found to be more rigid for boys than for girls. For instance, a late 1990s American study revealed a strong pattern of gender-typing in children's toy requests to Santa. Boys asked for boy-typed or neutral (according to kindergarteners and first graders) toys almost exclusively, with preferences being strong across all ages, as opposed to a curvilinear pattern, peaking at age 5, found for girls.

According to research, in the second and fourth grades and in relation to peer girls, boys progressively engaged in more aggressive and rough and tumble play as well as more functional, solitary-dramatic, exploratory, and group play and were more likely than girls to prefer adult-absent, peer-oriented situations. In comparison to girls' group play, boys' group play at age 10 to 11 years has been found to be more complex in role differentiation, interdependence between players, size of play group, explicitness of group goals, number of rules, and team formation; it also allows more age-heterogeneity. In 1970s research, fifth-grade boys played outdoors more than girls, played more competitive games, "played" less and "gamed" more, and were less likely to engage in cross-gender-typed play.

Boys play more with three-dimensional toys such as blocks and other toys that invite manipulations and transformations (object-oriented play), and they build more structures as compared with girls. Preschool-aged boys engage in fantasy play both less frequently and at less sophisticated levels, and among boys such play tends to be more fantastic and physically vigorous, often including play-fighting and superhero themes. Whereas girls may be more likely to create imaginary companions, boys may be more likely than girls to actively impersonate characters.

Physical and Sex Differences

Boys are known to be engaged more in exercise play, play fighting and play chasing, and rough-and-tumble play. At least in experimental, single-sex settings, boys are observed to engage in slightly more physical play solicitations than girls; not much is known about cross-sex play fighting. Research suggests that such often unstructured, nonobject play allows expression of care and intimacy, development of social signalling and leadership skills, rehearsal of combative and cooperative strategies, dealing with hierarchical roles and competition, establishing/displaying social dominance in a safe way, and optimal musculoskeletal development. In early adolescence, play fighting may be subjectively associated more with the establishment of dominance than with playful interaction, and in this age group indeed seems related to displays of dominance and of aggression. This primacy of competition has been observed across play contexts, for instance, in the internal power structures that characterize "clans" of young adolescent male online gamers.

Primary anatomical sex differences are unlikely to be of much concern in early play except for cases of micturation contests and sex play, where genitalia may be explicitly thematized. In Western taxonomies, sex play is more maturity-typed than gender-typed, tends to be homosocial at least until pubescence, may be group-based ("circle jerk"), and, in rural settings, may involve animals.

The dividing line between sex play and experimentation, as between genital play/exploration and masturbation, is difficult to draw even where male virginity is culturally marked, and thus depends for its recognition on such arbitrary elements as successful penetration or consummated coitus. The clinical significance for boys seems minimal in cases of age parity. Sexologist John Money, however, provocatively aligned early "sexual rehearsal play" with the necessity for prehuman male juveniles to practice correct mounting posture. In some cultures, sexual indulgence and sporting excellence may be judged incompatible even for boys, for instance according to Western medical consensus about onanism even up to the 1930s.

The discrete analytic categories to which sex differences are usually restricted (object play, fantasy play, social play, sex play) may not say much about the usually synthetic play outside experimental settings. Moreover, gender-typing is frequently reported to vary significantly with specific conditions of the play situation and copresence of supervisory figures. Some studies find no sex differences, and others find the reverse of expected patterns. Even the strongly boy-typed superhero play, research suggests, is found to be attractive to girls, who may explore agency and autonomy through such play and actively position themselves as women within narratives of heroism. Interestingly, functionalist reflection on boys' perusal of the superhero has usually been less positively formulated, for instance, as a conduit to express and "work through" feelings of hostility and aggression, to sublimate "primitive impulses," and compensate for object loss and/or maternal rejection that would otherwise manifest itself in displaced aggression toward the external world. Furthermore, differences in which girls and boys evaluate performance goals, relationship goals, and avoidance goals are not consistently found even within the Western world.

Historically, boys have engaged more in exercise play, play fighting and chasing, and rough-and-tumble play.

Studies on the relation between gender-related evaluative judgments and age also seem inconsistent. Systematic studies in which play- or toy-mediated gender violations related to appearance, activity, morality, and perceived physical laws are distinguished and compared are few. Contemporary research examining 3- to 11-year-olds' knowledge of and beliefs about violating several gender norms suggests that most toy- and play-related violations appeared not especially devalued in either sex, and that evaluations of gender norm violation vary greatly across particular items. In other words, the extent to which, and how, boys' play can be studied in terms of gender norms requires ongoing reflection.

Psychological Studies

Clinical relevance of boy-typed play for boys and girls has nonetheless been debated extensively. American clinical psychology during the 1960s to 1970s expressed sincere interest in "gender deviance," "sissies" and "gender-disturbed" or "effeminate" behavior. Retrospective studies find that self-identifying homosexual and bisexual adults report more boyhood dress-up doll play, cross-gender role-playing, cross-dressing, seeking girls as preferred or exclusive playmates, and active avoidance of rough-and-tumble play. Self-identifying lesbians report taking male-identified roles in play or fantasy and rejecting girl-typed items of dress and play. Transsexuals often report patterns of cross-stereotyped play preferences in childhood.

However, what should constitute "cross-gender typed" play depends largely on the invocation of traditional stereotypes and binaries, or on the insistence on norms and the assumption of their historical continuity, monolithic nature, and functional necessity. It also tends to be analytically tied to the gender-typing of play forms and themes rather than play styles and roles within play scenarios. Another question here is that of gender as an identifier of identity. For instance, according to a 1970s study, 63 percent of a junior high sample and 51 percent of adult women reported having been "tomboys" in childhood. Of the adults, 65 percent preferred active, outdoors ("tomboyish") games to quiet, indoors games.

Functional interpretations suggest boy-typed play equips boys with the social skills needed for masculine-typed occupational careers, while comparative interpretations suggest play has been subjected to selection pressures over the course of mammalian evolution as well as more proximal ecological constraints. This would link early sex differences in play, observed across species and cultures, to a primordial division of postjuvenile labor: hunting, conflict resolution, and territorial assertion versus gathering and mothering. In clinical and experimental settings, sex differences have often been related to sex hormones, neuro-anatomical sex differences, or sex-differentiated positive and negative reinforcement based on selective stimulation, reward, accomplishment, and punishment. It is generally accepted that play styles and preferences answer to a complex reverberation of said factors, only some of which are likely to be phenomenologically salient.

It is, however, a recognized problem in this literature how to distinguish aggressive from assertive, agonistic, and energetic elements in play, and in turn, to distinguish such elements from behavioral categories not considered play and not consistently known for sex differences in incidence ("fighting"). Studies suggest that post–second wave feminism women are more likely than men to interpret boys' agonistic interactions as aggression if they have to choose between aggression and play. In sum, categorization issues may confound theorizing of play as typical of boys, of boys' behavior as play, and of typical boys' play as typically male, as functional, as necessary, as beneficial, and as open or entitled to pedagogical recognition or intervention.

Play and Young Masculinities

Since the 1980s, a forum of gender theorists has characterized boys' play as instrumental in the tentative effectuation, negotiation, and contestation of cultural stereotypes and politics of not male tasks or roles but masculinities—male identities. Rather than typing play as boyish or boys' play as gendered, here boyish play is conversely taken to inform gender typologies. Sport, especially, has been recognized as a critical canvas for masculinity's hierarchizing, identitarian, and existential properties. Sports are considered the quintessential testing or cultivation ground of civilized modern masculinity, functions that have rendered Western masculinity a critically pedagogical, developmental, and performative notion.

The infrastructure of amateur and institutional sport is also frequently likened to a stage for masculinity as a collective project, providing uniform contexts for bonding, fraternalism, mateship, claims to privilege, and the articulation of gender difference. Games, then, may often be culturally elaborated as masculine both, and paradoxically, in terms of a continuity of their salience across male age strata (from boys to old boys and from sons to fathers) and in terms of an alleged biographic discontinuity implied by discourses of games' "man-making" properties. According to one study, German grade school boys were more likely than girls to list sports celebrities as "role models" (placing them on the same level as that of cinema figures and of actors), however, only 50 percent of children stated that they had such models, with no significant sex differences.

Boys' play is often conceptualized as preparatory and anticipatory, and thus, as a psychological necessity with regard to "gender development," or maturation more generally. Anthropological reports suggest that peripubescent transgressive play by boy troupes may not only be functionally (e.g., "backyard rampages" observed in Portugal) but also emically deployed as expressing initiatory efficacy (e.g., *kunyenga*, sexual acts among South African street boys).

However, to conclude that boys' play, in the absence of overarching ritual paradigms, naturally takes on ritualistic, preparatory, or initiatory meanings, and thus that such play amounts to an anthropological imperative, seems to be stretching theory too far. Given the importance of matters, what is thought to introduce boys to adulthood or manhood, or to corresponding indigenous forms of status, is rarely identified by indigenous notions equivalent to play or games.

Examples that lend themselves to anthropological debate on this issue include *Correr el gallo* or cock race (Spain), *el encierro* or bull-running (Pamplona, Spain), *Evala* or the traditional fight festival in the Kabye region of Togo for male youths, and scepter throwing as part of the *Junii Brasovului*, or The Feast of the Youth in Brasov, Romania.

A Historical View

In ancient contexts, traditional training schemes that led up to manhood in terms of civil entitlement and military office included competitive "sports," of which the Athenian *ephebeia* and its domain of the *gymnasion* may be the best documented. As the Spartan annual festival of *gymnopaedia*, this institute has elements both of formalized training regimes and of heroic, aestheticized athleticism. Comparably, rock lifting is assumed to have been partial to boys' admission ceremonies into farmer communities of Korea, and also of premodern Sweden, where it is still part of Strongest Man competitions.

Fighting or sparring customs for boys commonly appeal equally to native categories of play, contest, dramatization, and ritual and may be better characterized by the Geertzian interpretation of "deep play." Examples here include *ói'ó* (a Xavante club fight custom) and cross-sex stick-fighting partial to the Zulu *Thomba* (male puberty) ceremony. Initiatory customs generally characterize masculine-typed cultural dramas that transcend the modern, pedagogical idea of sport (e.g., blooding in British hunting and the *alternativa* in Spanish bullfighting).

Current ethnographic research on playgrounds suggests that gender is "done" via a variety of conduits: language, apparel, playmate choice, role play, and inclusions and exclusions from teams, play areas ("borderwork"), or activities. This element of performativity applies to participation but also extends to spectatorship and fandom, especially as instrumentalized by television and internet. Games, sport, and physical activity are identified as informing the diverse "identity slots" of masculinity/boyishness attested especially in school environments, and to the culturally exalted archetype of the male coach. In high school, gendered hierarchies are heavily informed not so much by who plays a sport but about what sport is being played. In the Anglophone world, the symbolism of the Jock has elaborate status, such that playing esteemed and varsity sports provides "Jock insurance" compensating for more feminine-typed activities.

Verbal play includes examples of traditional, strongly gender-coded games of verbal duelling observed among ethnic minorities (e.g., the dozens) and in non-Western settings. In Turkey, boys aged 8 to 14 years were reported to exchange insults, the foremost goal of which appears to be to force the opponent into a passive, feminine role. According to folklorists, this behavior can be seen as a quasi-rite of passage of a culturally specific, paradoxical relation to authority (bravery and courage versus submission to the older male) as well as an expression of male solidarity among the age group.

Western history shows scores of examples in which boys' play became elaborated with regard to programmatic, religious, or nationalist causes. Sports were conceived as socializing interventions to shape boys into colonizers, muscular Christians, national socialists, and more generally, gentlemen. Public schools, the YMCA and the Boy Scouts were frameworks that heavily depended on sports, games, and play activities.

Historians relate the transformation of British men from being loutish fistfighters in the early 19th century to more fair-minded, chivalrous gentlemen obsessed with games and sports in the late 19th century to a new morality that came to the public school system around 1850. Key figures like Thomas Hughes and Charles Kingsley stressed the moral and physical beauty of athleticism epitomized by rugby, rowing, and cricket. The notion of the gentlemen, then, is historically bound up with boyhood socialization through forms of competitive play that thus emerged as specifically British.

The "masculine games ethos" is shown to have had lasting repercussions across the colonial landscape from tribal New Guinea and India to South Africa and the Caribbean. Games and modern sports, gender, and nationalism often became interwoven facets of the politics of identity. Historical studies, for instance, attest to the highly gendered nature of the games of hurling and Gaelic football (U.S. soccer) and the relationship of these games to conceptions of nationalism, the body, and anticolonialism. Through the discourses surrounding these games, and other facets of the Irish renaissance, a nationalist conception of Irish masculinity emerged that distinguished Irish men from English men, Irish boys, and Irish women. The linguistic equation between "boys" (of the nation) and "men" is interestingly found both in war and in team sport. For instance, the members of the male Italian team at the 1932 Los Angeles Olympic Games were affectionately called "Mussolini's boys" in the press, reflecting both the times' growing militarism and the contemporary Fascist idea of the "new man."

Spectator team sports are still recognized as pristine arenas for, or major signifiers of, masculine performance. In contemporary Britain, playground football has been conceptualized as a series of ritualized performances, associated with the active exclusion and belittling of girls and nonparticipating boys, with heterosexuality as a social imperative, and with a key role for the body as spectacle of skill and strength. The sporting context would also, however, provide adolescent boys with an acceptable and nonthreatening medium for discussing and comparing their bodies with other males.

In canonical writings, "play" has figured as an important characterization of the way children engage in the wider hierarchical ordering of masculine/feminine styles ("masculinities," "femininities"). There is reason, however, to be critical of strict phenomenological distinctions between "gender play" (childhood), "trying on gender" (adolescence), and "doing gender" (adulthood); the same caveat applies to "sex play," "sexual experimentation," and "sexual activity." The analytic application of the ludic in this sense seems ethnocentric and developmentalist; boyishness and boyhood may not be reduced to gender codes or species of "masculinity." To see boys' play and play culture as prefiguring, or as symptomatic of, a masculine habitus and patriarchal order, then, remains importantly contingent on analytic preconceptions.

Play Cultures as Boyhood Culture

The theme of boys playing in a garden was an established subject in the paintings of China's Song dynasty (960–1279). It continued to be a favored theme among artists and craftsmen of the Ming (1368–1644) and Qing (1644–1911) dynasties. Variously known as *yingxitu*, "pictures of boys at play," and *baizitu*, "pictures of a hundred boys," these themed illustrations appear frequently in the decoration of Ming and Qing porcelain and other minor arts. A transhistorical view suggests that the iconicity of boys' play changed markedly as it reflected major cultural preoccupations, from a basic preoccupation with male progeny and later concerns over social rank to a more contemporary generalized interest in good fortune.

In the 21st century West, by comparison, play culture as a representational domain has become a major site for political rough-and-tumble over problems associated with masculinity as "hegemonic" but also informs debates more directed at what should constitute boyhood culture. It has been the feminist contention that early intervention into perceived sex-stereotyping would aid in the reconstruction of a more gender-sensible society.

Specific contemporary debates revolve around the progressive hypermuscularity of action figures of late 20th century (would relate to later body dysmorphic disorder and testosterone use), promotion of mixed-sex teams in sports (would enhance sex equity), sale of toy guns (would subvert gun control efforts), and war toys/games generally (would undo pacifist goals in pedagogy). Other issues include the banning of playground games like tag (would reduce sexual harassment), sexist/sexual/violent/racist content in digital games known to have a largely young male audience, and explicit celebrations of traditionally gendered childhood pastimes, such as the 2007 bestselling *Dangerous Book for Boys*. Furthermore, the contemporary American rubric of Attention Deficit and Hyperactivity Disorder has been interpreted as medicalizing a play style normal to boys if not to childhood generally.

Play wrestling is another example where the "sex roles" tradition of inquiry is in need of a more cultural focus. The late 1990s craze of "backyard wrestling" among adolescent boys and young adults seems to be an emulation of the mass televised mock genre of professional wrestling more than an extension of the less structured play-fights typical of middle and late childhood. The backyard phenomenon is mostly associated with American fandom, home videotaping and online hosting of video files. Even in American childhood, play fighting has long been influenced by Asian martial arts (1970s) as well as popular wrestling genres (1990s).

The gendered nature of play culture has been documented widely by historians. Toy soldiers in turn-of-the-century Britain, for instance, reflected a particular view of the nature of war by stressing the ethos of the competitive game, with its overtones of manliness, rules, and discipline. Yet research also suggests boyhood culture deserves intersectional approaches that go beyond a strictly ethical focus on masculinities.

For instance, especially after the 1920s and early 1930s, the United States has seen an emphasis on highly-organized sports for preadolescent boys, sport teams, leagues, and championships. This development was based on the rise of sport itself in all parts of the country, and more specifically the inclusion of sport in the school curriculum, as well as the rise of boys' work organizations as a new branch of social welfare. To Americans, competitive sport promoted physical fitness, democratic living, general education, citizenship, and sportsmanship, which qualified it as among the best preventive measures for juvenile delinquency and the most important ingredient for the overall character development of children. The historical corollary was not just increased participation but also an intergenerational male culture based on fandom, spectatorship, multi-mediation, collector frenzy (player cards, autographs), and dress codes.

An early 1970s study reported that American second-grade boys classified their own play activities as falling into three categories: "games," "goofing around," and "tricks." Recent technological formations may revolutionize the way in which boyhood, play, and gender will be cross-categorized and cross-theorized. Illustratively, contemporary research on videogaming suggests that the traditional dialectic of "boyhood/girlhood" and of "boyhood/manhood" may increasingly refer to juxtaposed subjectivities coproduced by and in turn validating the digital imaginary, a reciprocity between gamer- and avatar-based representations, without a determining role for age or sex.

See Also: Action Figures; Girls' Play; Inter-Gender Play; Play Fighting.

Bibliography. Jack W. Berryman, "From the Cradle to the Playing Field: America's Emphasis on Highly Organized Sports for Preadolescent Boys," *Journal of Sport History* (v.2/2, 1975); Gary Allen Fine, *With the Boys. Little League Baseball and Preadolescent Culture* (University of Chicago Press, 1990); Conn Iggulden and Hal Iggulden, *The Dangerous Book for Boys* (Collins, 2007); Brian Nankervis, Roy Slaven, and H.G. Nelson, *Boys and Balls* (Allen & Unwin, 1994); Anthony J. Papalas, "Boy Athletes in Ancient Greece," *Stadion* (v.17, 1991); Barrie Thorne, *Gender Play: Girls and Boys in School* (Rutgers University Press, 1993); Wendy Varney, "Of Men and Machines: Images of Masculinity in Boys' Toys," *Feminist Studies* (v.28/1, 2002).

Diederik Floris Janssen
Independent Scholar

Brag

Brag, a card game that dates to the latter part of the 18th century and is similar to Poker, originated in Britain. The game spread to the United States in the 19th century and was extremely popular. The first known reference to it was in 1835, in a book titled *The South-West*, authored by "a Yankee." (At the time *south-west* was the term used to designate Louisiana, Mississippi, and Arkansas.) The author describes a place where gambling was conducted: "the tables were surrounded with players, at two of which they were dealing 'faro;' at the third playing 'brag.'" Brag is almost identical to an Indian card game, *Teen Pathi* (also known as "three card").

Brag is played with a standard 52-card deck. The dealer deals out three cards (face down) to each player after the players have anted up. After the cards have been dealt, players, in sequence, have the option of increasing the bet or dropping out ("folding"). If the player does not match the bet, they fold. The betting continues until there are only two players. These players show their hands, and the winner (whose winning hand is sometimes referred to as a "bragger") takes the entire pot. If there is a tie, the player who "saw" the last bet loses.

A winning hand is determined in the following way: the best hand is three of a kind (known as a "prial"), with three three-cards holding the first rank, which beats a straight or "running" flush (the best of these being ace, 2, 3), a "straight," a flush, a pair, or the high card. The rankings on each of these are similar to those in poker.

While playing with three cards and anteing up once is the basic and most popular version, there are variations with four, five, seven, nine, and 13 cards per hand. In the four-card variant, players would use the best three of the four cards they were dealt, and in the five-card version, players would discard their two worst cards. Other variations include being able to ante more than once or having multiple sets that may be played. There was also a variant known as "bastard brag," played with three cards per hand with the variation of having a set of three cards face up as the communal set, and each player must, before showing their cards, remove one from their hand and replace it with one of the three communal cards. As with many card games, wild cards are sometimes called as part of the play.

Brag was not only very popular among the American civilian population in the first half of the 19th century but was one of the most common ways that soldiers on the frontier spent their time. Some of the officers who played Brag became generals in the Civil War. Ulysses Grant was a frequent, although generally unsuccessful, player. In one extended game he lost $5 (then a substantial amount of money) to James Longstreet, who later became a Confederate general. Not long before the Civil War, Grant met up with Longstreet and paid him the money he had lost a few years before. The next time Grant and Longstreet would meet would be during the surrender of the Confederate Army at Appomattox. After the surrender, the victorious Grant approached Longstreet and asked him if he would care to play a hand of Brag to recall the old days on the frontier army.

See Also: Faro; Poker and Variations of; United States, 1783 to 1860.

Bibliography. Brag Rules, www.pagat.com/vying/brag.html (cited September 2008); John T. Krumpelmann, "Ingraham's 'South-West' as a Source of Americanisms," *American Speech*, (v.18/2, April 1943); P.J. Moran, "Grant and Longstreet," *New York Times* (June 12, 1890); Pagat.com, "Brag," www.pagat.com/vying/brag.html (cited October 2008).

Robert Stacy
Independent Scholar

Brazil

The largest country in South America, Brazil was a Portuguese colony until the Napoleonic Wars, when the King of Portugal had to flee to Rio de Janeiro, Brazil's largest city, and at that time its capital. His son declared Brazil independent in 1822, and the Empire of Brazil lasted until 1889, when a republic was proclaimed. Many indigenous people survived in Brazil, and the original migrants to the country were Portuguese. Great prosperity under Emperor Pedro II resulted in over 100,000 Europeans a year migrating to Brazil in the late 1880s. There had long been a large African slave population, with slavery only abolished in 1888. Brazil was the last major country to abolish slavery.

Historically, there have been large differences between the types of activities followed by the members of various communities. Indigenous people played traditional games and made heavy use of the *pife*, a flute fashioned from bamboo, and the *maraca*, a hollow wooden handle with dry seeds inside, serving as a rattle. Portuguese settlers brought with them some of their European pursuits, and wealthy Brazilians have taken to horse riding, being involved in rodeos, and enjoying Western-style theater, music, puppet shows, and the like.

The African community in Recife and Salvador, especially males whose ancestors came from modern-day Angola, often play *capoeira*, a form of judo and wrestling by which two players show their strength. The original concept came from slaves being punished for fighting who had to develop a method of testing their strength and prowess in a manner that would not attract the attention of their owners.

All communities in Brazil pursue recreational sports, with *futebol* (soccer) being the most popular game in the country, with boys and young men playing soccer in school playing fields, courtyards, and barren patches of land in every city and town in the country. With Brazil's teams doing well in international soccer events, many poor children hope to emulate Edson Arantes do Nascimento (Pêlé) and rise from humble origins to become a world superstar. With about 90 percent of Brazilians living along the coast, swimming, surfing, yachting, and fishing remain extremely popular. Along beaches, there are always soccer games and people playing volleyball, riding bicycles, or being involved in windsurfing. Other sports that attract many Brazilians include boxing, tennis, basketball and also auto racing. Brazil has produced a number of important race car drivers.

Dancing and music, especially playing in the *bateria* percussion bands, can be seen in frequent festivals, especially during Carnival, where the samba music attracts a large audience. Children as well as adults are involved in dressing up for the *Festa do Divino* held on Pentecost Sunday, especially in the towns of Alcântra and Paraty, where children don costumes fashioned after 16th century clothes.

Board games in Brazil were popular in the 1960s and 1970s, with a Brazilian version of Monopoly called *Banco Imobiliário* (Real Estate Bank), with some street names from Rio de Janeiro and others from Sao Paulo. The game also varies from the original as it does not have the utility companies but instead has six railway stations.

Wargaming has also been strong with boys and young men from Brazil's middle class. Most of it was based on traditional themes such as the classical world and Napoleonic Europe, but the situation changed with the manufacture of miniature figurines for the War of the Triple Alliance, in which Brazilian armies, along with those from Argentina and Uruguay, invaded Paraguay in the late 1860s. There has also been recent interest in Brazil's military involvement in World War II, with some Brazilian companies now making Brazilian army figurines for reenactments of battles in the Italian Campaign of 1943–45. *Dungeons & Dragons* was popular in the late 1970s and early 1980s, but the hand-drawn version has long been overtaken by the computer version.

See Also: Argentina; Chile; *Dungeons & Dragons*; Portugal; Soccer (Amateur) Worldwide; South Americans, Traditional Cultures; Venezuela.

Bibliography. Janet Lever, *Soccer Madness* (University of Chicago Press, 1983); Robert Levine, "Sport and Society: The Case of Brazilian Futebol," *Luso-Brazilian Review* (v.17/2, 1980); Christopher Richard, *Brazil* (Marshall Cavendish, 1991); Rhoda Sherwood, *Brazil* (Gareth Stevens Publishing, 1988).

Justin Corfield
Geelong Grammar School

Bridge and Variations of

Bridge is a trick-taking card game played by four players with a standard 52-card deck. Though there are both current and historical variations, when we say simply Bridge, we are referring to Contract Bridge, which in the 1920s replaced Auction Bridge as the default form of the game. Because the game is played by two pairs, with each partner seated opposite the other, traditionally the players are referred to as North and South, East and West, in reference to their seating positions and complements.

History

Modern Bridge is a refinement of trick-taking games that developed in the 16th century after the introduction of the Italian tarot deck (and its concept of "trump" cards). Other games in this broad family include Euchre, Hearts, Pinochle, Rook, and Spades, as well as Whist, Bridge's direct antecedent. All trick-taking games revolve around a finite play-unit called the trick: each player in turn puts a card from his hand into play, and when every player has done so, the trick is completed and removed from play, and a winner determined according to the rules. The first player in the turn is said to have made the lead; the lead in the first

Aces are high in Bridge, followed by kings, queens, jacks, and numerically down to twos, the lowest card in each suit.

trick of the game is the opening lead. Both leading and being last have advantages: The lead sets the suit for the trick, while the last player is the only one who knows exactly what the outcome of his play will be.

Key to trick-taking games are the trump cards, derived from the word *triumph*. In the early games using the Tarot deck introduced in Italy, the Major Arcana—those cards that were not part of any suit—were essentially a permanent trump suit, outranking all other cards. In games using the traditional 52-card deck, particular cards will be designated as trumps, meaning they have been elevated above their usual rank. Usually this is done by designating an entire trump suit, such that diamonds beat clubs, hearts, and spades (for instance). In some games, the trump suit is determined by the rules and is always the same; in other games it is determined in the course of play and may be changed during play.

There are four broad subfamilies of trick-taking games. Evasion games—what David Parlett calls reversed or trick-avoidance games—are those in which players seek to avoid taking the trick. In final-trick games, the goal is to take the last trick of the game, while the tricks preceding it are of diminished consequence. The oldest form of trick-taking is the race game, which persists in Euchre, Whist, and some variations of Spades. The goal in a race game is simply to take a certain number of tricks before anyone else.

The race game that was the forerunner of Whist—and is thus Bridge's grandfather—is Ruff and Honors, an 18th century Anglophone adaptation of the French game Triumph. In Ruff and Honors, the player with the trump-suit ace could "ruff" the stock (the four cards left after dealing 12 cards to each of four players), which meant to take all four cards while discarding four of those in his hand. The Honors of the name refers to the extra points gained for playing face cards of the trump suit, a practice retained when Whist developed from the game. Whist was the first trick-taking game to become both popular and rigidly defined, codified in Edmund Hoyle's books of game-playing rules; previously, most card games had varied greatly by region and context (gambling, social game, children's game).

Although variants of Whist were just as popular, the existence of those rigidly defined rules helped its reputation as a game that called on skill more than it kowtowed to chance—a game that, like Chess, could be studied, practiced, and pondered. This is the context in which Bridge budded from Whist's stem. The first form of Bridge was called Biritch or Russian Whist, and when played or referred to today is usually called Straight Bridge or Bridge Whist. Biritch retained the card values from Whist, as well as a number of its rules, with some significant changes: the trump suit in Biritch was chosen by the dealer, whose partner's hand became the dummy hand (exposed face-up on the table), and a call of no-trumps or biritch was introduced. The earliest written mention of Biritch comes in 1886, a time when card games were undergoing a sea change, especially in the United States, where Poker threatened the popularity of older games, and Boston's status as the nation's game was about to be supplanted by Bridge.

With the introduction of Auction Bridge in 1904, the fourth family of trick-taking games was born, the contract family. In contract trick-taking games, players make bids—guesses—about the tricks they will take, either their number or their point value. The bid chosen for the contract becomes the one players have to meet, or prevent other players from meeting. This is the basic form not only of Bridge, but of Spades and Pinochle. In Auction Bridge, the highest bid becomes the contract.

Auction Bridge provided the basic rules for bidding and play, and from that basis Contract Bridge was developed by players such as Harold Vanderbilt, the great-grandson of Cornelius Vanderbilt. A Harvard lawyer who ran some of his family's railway companies, Vanderbilt was an avid Bridge player who wrote extensively about the game, continuing the Whist-family's tradition of thinking about games, strategizing with them, and modifying them. The major change was that only the contracted tricks were counted below the line toward a grand or slam bonus; other scores were tweaked to balance the game. Contract Bridge was popularized so quickly that unadorned "Bridge" soon became synonymous with it.

Bridge tournaments became popular around the time Contract Bridge was being refined, and in 1937 smaller officiating organizations unified to become the American Contract Bridge League, which remains the principal officiating authority for tournaments in North America. The World Bridge Federation was founded 20 years later, governing bridge internationally.

Bidding

Bridge is played with partners, and communication between them is strictly restricted: there are no closed communications (any information passed between them is shared with opponents, by the nature of its disclosure), and so communication is done only through calls made and cards played. At the same time, the bidding system is such that each team must attempt to bid a contract they can actually make, without either partner knowing which cards the other partner has. This is one reason Bridge is a game that invites such contemplation and rewards attention and experience.

Bridge requires a minimum bid of seven tricks, so a long-held practice is to subtract six from your bid. A bid of four spades, then, proposes a contract of winning 10 tricks, with the suit of spades as the trump.

Bidding systems have developed as a way for partners to communicate back and forth about their hands in order to propose a contract. In natural bidding systems, most of the bids made relate directly to the hand. In artificial bidding systems, bids are essentially used as code for other information, like the one-club bid in the short-club bidding system, which is used to indicate that the bidder has a strong hand (and not that the bidder necessarily wants to bid clubs). Although it sounds like we are talking about secret ciphers here, conventions—the artificial calls in a bidding system—must be known to all players, and any opposing player can ask the bidder to explain the meaning of his bid. One of the best-known artificial calls is the Blackwood convention, which is used to talk about the number of aces in one's hand.

One partner bids 4NT (four no trump) in order to ask the other partner how many aces he has. The other partner, recognizing the signal, responds with a bid of five, with the suit determined by how many aces he has: clubs for no or all aces, diamonds for one ace, hearts for two aces, spades for three aces. Such conventions date back to Vanderbilt's time, and the original strong club system was named for him.

Bidding systems and their conventions complicate strategy as much as they assist, because even asking a particular question—phrased in the manner of the convention—reveals something about your hand, just as asking for threes in a game of Go Fish reveals that you have threes.

Scoring

If a contract is made, points are given for making the contract, for tricks above the contract's requirements, and for various bonuses if applicable. If it is not made, points are awarded to the other team for every "undertrick," that is, for every trick less than the contracted bid made by the team attempting to make the contract. The amount of contract points are determined by the number of tricks in the bid, multiplied by 20 if the trump suit was minor (diamonds or clubs) and 30 if the trump suit was major (hearts or spades) or if a bid of no-trump was made (the first trick in no-trump is worth an additional 10 points).

The four level bonuses available are partscore (for a contract worth less than 100 contract points), game (for a contract worth 100 points or more), small slam (a bid of six tricks), and grand slam (a bid of seven tricks).

A scoresheet in the variant game Rubber Bridge is divided into two columns, one for each team of partners, as well as being horizontally divided by "the line." Points scored for meeting a contract are recorded below the line. Points scored by other means are recorded above the line. Rubber Bridge also revives the practice of honors from earlier games in the family tree, awarding bonuses for particular cards.

Duplicate Bridge

In Duplicate Bridge, played in clubs and tournaments, the same arrangement of cards is used by multiple groups of competing teams, in order to reduce the effect of chance on relative performance. For instance, Bridge boards will be used to hold hands in place so that they can be passed to other players, and North/South players will stay at the tables while East/West players move from one table to another, with the boards passing in the opposite direction, so that every team plays every hand and every East/West team plays every North/South team. Bidding boxes are often used in order to allow for silent bidding, to cut down on noise.

Contract Bridge Maxims

A number of sayings have developed common beliefs and advice among Bridge players:

Prefer length to strength. A weak long suit is better than a strong short suit.

Prefer majors to minors.

If in doubt, lead a spade.

Play into weakness.

Play through strength.

Second hand plays high.

Third hand plays low.

Singaporean Bridge

A variant of Bridge invented and popular in Singapore—so popular there that many Singaporean players are unaware that it is a variant, but so obscure in the rest of the world that few online game servers offer it as an option—is simply called Singaporean Bridge. Partners are not determined until the end of bidding, which eliminates any need or usefulness for the traditional bidding systems and conventions. The winner of the bid "chooses" his partner by declaring that his partner will be the holder of some specific card the winner does not have—the ace of clubs, for instance—and although the partner can reveal his identity, it usually is not discovered until the course of play, when the partner plays the card in question.

See Also: Boston; Casino; Casual Games; Euchre; Hearts; History of Playing Cards; Luck and Skill in Play; Organized or Sanctioned Play; Pinochle; Preference; Whist.

Bibliography. G. Abrahams, *Brains in Bridge* (Horizion Press, 1964); Elliott Avedon and Brian Sutton-Smith, *The Study of Games* (Krieger Publishing, 1979); Roger Caillois, *Man, Play, and Games* (University of Illinois Press, 2001); James Carse, *Finite and Infinite Games* (Ballantine Books, 1987); David Parlett, *The Oxford Guide to Card Games* (Oxford University Press, 1990); Brian Sutton-Smith, *The Ambiguity of Play* (Harvard University Press, 2001).

Bill Kte'pi
Independent Scholar

Bulgaria

Located in southeast Europe, bordering Romania, Serbia, Macedonia, Greece, and Turkey, people in the Republic of Bulgaria have been influenced by all of their neighbors, and also by Russia. Great sporting events took place in medieval times, with competitors from some other countries participating. In 1980, in a bid to win the 1992 Olympics, these events were detailed by Bozhidar Peichev in a booklet highlighting these games. Jousts and other tournaments were also held, testing battle skills.

Under the rule of the Ottomans, a number of Turkish games were introduced, such as *Tavla*, a version of Backgammon. Chess also became popular, as did card games. Bulgaria gained its independence in 1878, and a move to Westernize the country followed. Games from Western Europe were introduced, including bowling and skittles. The poverty of much of the population meant that most children had to play far simpler games such as Hide-and-Seek, skipping and Marbles. The increase in education during the 1930s led to more children participating in recreational sports, such as soccer, basketball, and netball. There was also interest in cycling and hiking, with some foreign tourists visiting the country. The British-born Elizabeth Mincoff, who married a Bulgarian diplomat while living in Sofia from the 1900s until the mid-1940s, wrote about Bulgarian lace, folksongs, and other elements of local lore.

After World War II, the Communists took over Bulgaria, and it was largely cut off from Western Europe. Much money was spent on sporting facilities, and many playgrounds, adventure playgrounds, and the like were built around the country, including ice skating rinks. Children were heavily involved in the Young Pioneers movement, taking part in annual camps and hikes. Some foreign visitors to Bulgaria were involved in speleological activities such as caving and potholing (exploring vertical caves), and a local interest in this began. Chess became a very popular pastime, with the establishment of the Federation Bulgare des Echecs. After the end of Communism in 1990, there was a revival of many pre–World War II folk customs following the return of many exiles. There was also an increase in tourism to the country, and there are now amusement arcades and bowling alleys in Sofia, the capital, and other cities. Wargaming has changed to reflect the different political climates promoted by governments.

During the late 1920s and 1930s wealthier Bulgarians tended to use games and scenes from the Balkan Wars of the late 19th and early 20th century, and the birth of modern Bulgarian nationalism. In the period of Communist rule, Wargaming focused on the medieval period, with interest in Byzantium and medieval Bulgaria; and from the 1990s on, the Wargames groups have covered all periods, including the politically sensitive ones such as World War I and World War II. However, the popularity of Wargaming among teenage boys has largely given way to playing computer simulation games.

See Also: Basketball (Amateur); Bowling; Chess and Variations of; Hide & Seek; Netball; Skittles; Soccer (Amateur) Worldwide; Wargames.

Bibliography. Bozhidar Peichev, *The Olympic Games in 14th Century Bulgarian Literature* (Sofia Press, 1980); R. Petrov, "Wrestling in Bulgaria," *Olympic Review* (v.199, May 1984); Zahari Staikov, "Sociology of Sport in Bulgaria," *International Review for the Sociology of Sport* (v.1, 1966); Zahari Staikov, "Labour, Leisure and Physical Culture: A Bulgarian Perspective," *International Review for the Sociology of Sport* (v.20/1–2, 1985); I. Vassilchev, P. Bankov, and K. Vilichov, *Mass Physical Education and Sport in Bulgaria* (Sofia Press, 1986).

Justin Corfield
Geelong Grammar School

Bullying

Bullying, while varying in definition and situation, is broadly defined as the infliction or threat of physical harm, verbal harassment, and coercive methods to manipulate and control peers. Bullying may be considered a form of play for those that bully. This behavior among children may begin at young ages, but becomes particularly common as children enter middle school and through high school. Some argue that this behavior becomes more common during this time span in part because of hormonal changes, but it is also profoundly influenced and reified by the frequent and numerous social transitions that occur during this period of maturation. Ultimately, the issues of bullying range from the childhood schoolyard to the hazing and initiation rituals affiliated with fraternities.

One of the most prominent researchers on bullying is Dan Olweus, and he, more than any other researcher, has put bullying on the map as a major area of research. In general, research addressing bullying among youth has addressed its occurrence within developed nations such as the United States, United Kingdom, Norway, Sweden, Japan, and Australia. The experience of being bullied has been affiliated with increased risk of suicide. In recent years, being the victim of bullying has also been suggested as a factor influencing various teen retaliation killings such as those of the 1999 Columbine High School massacre. The disenfranchised bullying victim may retaliate in extreme physical and violent fashions.

Two Forms of Bullying

Bullying may be direct or indirect in form. Direct forms of bullying would be characterized by a victim receiving bodily harm from kicking, hitting, pushing, or shoving. Indirect forms of bullying are often indicated by mental, emotional, and psychological harm through name-calling, rejection, gossip, threats, or insults. These two forms of bullying may occur separately or in conjunction. When examined in this duality, nearly every adult recalls having been the victim of bullying as a child at some point. A difficulty when examining bullying is the conflation of bullying with harassment. Gender and sexual harassment may be regarded merely as bullying or vice versa. Currently, sex and gender are not well understood in the context of bullying.

Traditionally, bullies were often boys. Today, increasing numbers of girls are also enacting bully identities. The subjects of bullying are often social outcasts in one or multiple fashions—one may be gender nonconforming, believed to be nonheterosexual, engaged in stigmatized social groupings with interests in the arts, music, or sciences. Statistically, the victims of bullying are equally distributed between the genders, but with boys having greater risk for direct bullying and girls having greater risk for indirect bullying. The roles of bully and victim are not mutually exclusive—one may be bullied by one person, but may themselves be the bully of another. Among middle-school students in the United States it is estimated that approximately 27 percent of students have been bullied at least sometimes, with 10 percent being bullied weekly or more often. By high school the numbers decline to 10 percent bullied sometimes and four percent bullied weekly or more often. At particular risk of bullying and harassment are gay, lesbian, bisexual, and transgender students, with many reporting daily incidents.

In recent years bullying through the use of internet and digital resources, such as Web sites, community sites such as Facebook.com and Myspace.com, emails, and text messaging, has increasingly occurred. This cyberbullying accompanies the increasing number of youth who own and use computers and cell phones. In the United Kingdom, 6 to 7 percent of students report having received a nasty or threatening text or email message. Among these students, girls reported higher incidences of this sort. In the United States, a survey of youth 10 to 17 years old found that in the last year, 12 percent had been aggressive to someone online, 4 percent were targets of aggression, and 3 percent were both aggressors and targets.

The iconic role of schoolyard bully has been noted in various films and television programs. In the movie *Billy Madison,* the O'Doyle family members are noted as bullies; in the *Karate Kid* films, Johnny Lawrence personifies a bully who is socially and physically aggressive, but is not significantly larger physically. The character of Nelson Muntz on *The Simpsons*, while complex, demonstrates many of the stereotypical characteristics of a bully. He is personified as less intelligent, physically larger than his peers, and disrespectful of authority and of high-achieving peers.

Bullying behavior, while more prevalent among youth and teens, continues into adulthood. Bullying in the workplace may manifest in various forms ranging from health-harming mistreatment or verbal abuse to threatening, humiliating, intimidating, or sabotaging behaviors. This form of bullying is believed to be more prevalent than illegal discrimination and far more prevalent than workplace violence. It is estimated that one in six experience workplace bullying, with illegal or undocumented workers being at particular risk. Bullying is also noted in other adult institutions such as fraternities and sororities, sports teams, prisons, and the military.

The satisfaction coming from controlling and bullying others is what helps explain bullying; there is no evidence that bullying can be explained by those who bully having low self esteem. If anything, bullies seem to have a high regard for themselves. Also, bullying is a symptom of a community problem, since bullying is not found as much in schools or communities where adults pay close attention and work hard to make community-building a central part of the curriculum.

See Also: "Bad" Play; Boys' Play; Play and Power, Psychology of; Play as Competition, Psychology of; Play as Competition, Sociology of; Playground as Politics.

Bibliography. Ann Frisén, Anna-Karin Johnsson, and Camille Persson, "Adolescents' Perception of Bullying: Who is the Victim? Who is the Bully? What can be Done to Stop Bullying?," *Adolescence* (v.42/168, 2007); Gregory Green, "Bullying: A Concern for Survival," *Education* (v.128/2 2007); Dan Olweus, *Bullying at School: What we Know and What we Can Do* (Blackwell, 1993); Peter Smith et al., "Cyberbullying: Its Nature and Impact in Secondary School Pupils," *Journal of Child Psychology and Psychiatry* (v.49/4, 2008); Nan Stein, "Bullying, Harassment and Violence Among Students," *Radical Teacher* (v.80, 2007); M.L. Ybarra and K.J. Mitchell, "Online Aggressor/Targets, Aggressors, and Targets: A Comparison of Associated Youth Characteristics," *Journal of Child Psychology and Psychiatry* (v.45, 2004).

Daniel Farr
Randolph College

Bungee Jumping

Bungee (or sometimes bungy) jumping is the first and probably the best-known of the 20th century's extreme sports—so ubiquitous that it has become a standard metaphor for risky behavior, like rocket science for intellectual challenge or sliced bread for great ideas.

This high-wire game of chicken was inspired by a Polynesian rite of passage called the *N'gol*, practiced on Penticost Island in the Vanuatu archipelago. Polynesian society is a case study in risk taking. Beginning in the Fiji islands around 3,500 years ago, the Polynesians moved inexorably eastward in a remarkable human colonization that ended just short of South America. They set out without a single compass, map or assurance that there was anything beyond their shores but ocean.

Along the way, each island developed its own variations on the rituals of the protoculture. *N'gol*—land-diving—is one of these variations. At its root is a myth about an abused wife. To escape her husband, she jumped from a high tree, tricking him into following her. Unbeknownst to him, she had tied vines to her ankles, allowing her to survive while he jumped to his death. What was desperation for her became a death-defying male ritual. Every April, when the vines are at their most supple, the men on the island build jumping towers, flinging themselves off headfirst toward the ground below. While boys begin with 12-foot platforms, the most accomplished men might climb as much as 100 feet high. The last diver's success—or cataclysmic failure—would determine the success of the all-important yam harvest.

Ironically, land-diving is on the wane in Vanuatu, while bungee jumping has crossed continents. It offers the heart-pounding opportunity to display the same combination of bravery and self-affirmation of land-diving without the religious and cultural context.

Bungee cords consist of hundreds of continuous-length rubber strands, encased in a nylon sheath.

Bungee cords are heavy strands of rubber, braided together to create a strong and flexible rubber rope. Long cords, matched to the weight and height of the jumper, are attached at one end to a harness. The harness is usually wrapped around the jumper's legs below the knees at one end, and at the other to a high platform. Leaping off the platform, which can be mounted in any clear, open space, the jumper experiences a massive adrenalin rush and the sensation of freefall—hopefully without the otherwise tragic collision with earth's gravity. The elastic cords halt the fall before impact, producing a bouncing recoil that provides a second, less-elevated rise.

The first recorded bungee jump took place in 1979 as an April Fools Day stunt by a member of the Oxford Dangerous Sports Club in England. It was a dry run for the legendary jump by a group of club members in tuxedos and chest harnesses off the edge of San Francisco's Golden Gate Bridge six months later.

Many people were driven to replicate the experience in the 1980s, sometimes with fatal consequences. However, it was not until 1988 that skier and bungee enthusiast A.J. Hackett opened the first permanent, commercial bungee jumping site at the Kawarau Bridge outside Queenstown, New Zealand. Since then, bungee jumping experiences can be found throughout the world, wherever bridges can be licensed or high cranes rigged.

As extreme sports go, bungee jumping has matured into an experience that provides thrills without significant serious risk. Jumpers at the Hackett site in New Zealand have ranged in age from a boy of 10 years to several octogenarians. Studies of jumpers have found an assortment of postjump minor physical complaints ranging from headaches and whiplash to pulled muscles and dizziness, all of which dissipated fairly quickly. Serious injuries and fatalities are few. Most are attributable to lack of care and experience by either the company offering the jump or by freelancers jumping in unsafe areas or with faulty equipment.

See Also: New Zealand; Play as Catharsis; Play as Rehearsal of Reality; Risk in Play.

Bibliography. John Chambers, *New Zealand and the South Pacific Islands* (Interlink Books, 2007); Martin Lyster, *Strange Adventures of the Dangerous Sports Club* (The Do-Not Press, 1997); Vanuatu National Tourism Office, "Pentecost and Maewo Islands," www.vanuatutourism.com (cited September 2008); Craig Young, "Is Bungee Jumping Safe?" *Western Journal of Medicine* (v.170/5, May 1999).

Cynthia L. Baron
Northeastern University

Caillois: *Man, Play and Games*

Roger Caillois (1913–78) was a French sociologist and philosopher, whose study *Man, Play and Games* has, since first appearing in 1958, greatly contributed to the understanding of the relationships among play, games and culture. For Caillois, playing is a central trait of all cultures, which is why their values, customs, and beliefs are expressed in the games they play. While playing, defined by Caillois as a free and creative activity separated from ordinary life by its rules and demarcated spaces, is a universal phenomenon, games and play experiences differ both within and across cultures. He therefore qualifies different ways of playing, from unstructured to highly controlled, as well as four types of games based on the general attitude of the players: competition, chance, simulation, and vertigo. In doing so, Caillois delivers a profound lesson on the playful diversity of human culture.

Relation of Huizinga

Man, Play and Games can be read as a response to the work of another influential play theorist, the Dutch cultural historian Johan Huizinga, whose seminal study *Homo Ludens: A Study of the Play Element in Culture* appeared in 1938. Caillois praises *Homo Ludens* for its bold claim that culture derives from playing: Huizinga suggests that studying historic changes in play provides important insight into the evolution of human societies. He indicates that modern cultural values and institutions, such as law, science, and art, stem historically from playful challenge, exhibition and improvisation. Specific forms of culture developed as archaic play became more formal and elaborate: riddle contests and word play evolved into written poetry and philosophic argumentation, verbal battles in reserved spaces evolved into juridical processes, and tribal dances evolved into theatre performances.

Caillois also embraces most of the basic characteristics of play that Huizinga argues are common to different cultures and epochs. Huizinga sees playing as a voluntary activity, carried out for its own sake and therefore lacking any worldly motivation, such as monetary interests. Play takes place outside ordinary life and obeys specified rules and limits in time and space, whether these are marked by the chessboard, the tennis court or the playground. Further, play creates bonds between players, giving rise to collectives of like-minded persons who tend to exclude the uninitiated. As researcher of urban culture Ian Borden indicates in his inspiring study *Skateboarding, Space and the City*, skateboarders often demarcate their group identity through a certain use of clothing, space, and body language, thus maintaining their own enclosed "play-community," whose activities and aesthetics an outsider may initially find difficult to comprehend.

Unsurprisingly, Huizinga and Caillois suggest a relationship between play and religious rituals. After all, religion is often practiced in temples, churches, and other self-contained spaces, where ideal rules and codified movements bracket the activities off from ordinary life. Much like sacred rituals, play absorbs its practitioners, captivating them through a shared sense of beauty and exaltation. In his earlier study *Man and the Sacred*, Caillois argued against Huizinga's tendency to fully assimilate playing and rituals, though both clearly regard play as a special cultural realm that it is important to protect from the monotony and imperfections of the outside world.

Nevertheless, although Huizinga explores different play characteristics, such as theatricality, virtuosity, and improvisation, for him they serve mainly competitive behavior. As Caillois points out, Huizinga has for example forgotten to consider gambling, which is an important part of everyday play, from lotteries and slot machines to betting. This has also lead to the misplaced claim that play excludes economic interests. Even though it does not directly produce wealth or goods, Caillois argues that play often involves an exchange of property in the form of winning and losing money.

Another problem is that Huizinga leaves unexplored the possibility that play may satisfy varying individual impulses and result in divergent experiences among the players. Maneuvering a horse in show jumping hardly equals horse track betting. Likewise, a rollercoaster ride does not necessarily involve the same bodily actions and sensations as performing a skateboard move down a flight of stairs. While being identifiable as play, these suggest shifting degrees of competition, chance, and excitement, as well as a panoply of other activities and experiences that seem impossible to capture in one definition.

Classification of Games

Play may have certain universal features, such as being free, separate, and regulated, but there are also various forms of games that involve quite diverse attitudes. If these are not explored more fully, there is a risk that we fail to understand the cultural meaning and significance of playing. Caillois therefore takes the theorizing of play a step further by devising a fourfold classification of games: *agôn* (competition), *alea* (chance), *mimicry* (simulation), and *ilinx* (vertigo). Each of these categories is based on one dominant attitude or drive among the players, which at the same time distinguishes them from other games and their players. The four games also take place in specific arenas, such as stadiums, casinos, theaters, and amusement parks.

Agôn stands for the category of competitive games, where rivals seek to excel one another in pursuits requiring physical skill or ingenuity, such as Chess, golf or football. Competitive play is often rule-bound in order to ensure an equal footing for different players to prove their skills. At the beginning of a chess game, for example, both contestants have the same number of pieces, and sometimes the less experienced player can be given the advantage. An ideal winner in agonistic play is thus someone who conquers by pure merit and, in doing so, reminds the observer of the hard work and commitment that winning a competition entails.

Alea is a category of games that invokes an element of chance and therefore seemingly negates the skill and practice of *agôn*. Roulette, lottery, and the game of Dice all involve an expectant attitude, even a sense of abandonment to destiny, as the outcomes are hard to affect. Caillois claims that winning and losing money is an important part of games of chance. He also adds that *alea* can at times come close to *agôn*, as both seek to escape the individual differences of ordinary life by creating conditions of equality between players, whether this involves the same possibilities for proving one's superiority or the same chances of winning money.

Mimicry represents games of simulation, where one takes on a stylized role, wears a disguise, or identifies with another person, as in theatre, masquerades, or video game playing. Watching competitive play, such as a sporting event, one is often identifying with the competitors and therefore also engaging in *mimicry*. This can range from wearing the shirt of a favorite football team to body movements echoing actions on the playfield. But in contrast to the clear-cut rules of *agôn* and *alea*, simulation relies on an element of improvisation, as the player needs to inventively maintain the illusion of being another.

Ilinx includes games that involve a desire to be seized by a sense of disorder, intimating a partial loss of control and balance, an alteration of perception. Whereas feelings of vertigo can be produced by the most mundane activities, such as spinning around or sliding down an ice-covered slope, they are also part of specific cultural arenas dedicated to vertigo. One of these is the amusement park, where one can experience the visceral effect of being powerlessly thrown around or momentarily transported to staggering heights in a rollercoaster or another contraption. *Ilinx* may at times echo the attitudes of *mimicry,* as both are less bound by rules than other forms of games.

Every category also includes a continuum between *paidia* and *ludus*, where *paidia* stands for unstructured and anarchic and *ludus* for structured and institutionalized play. *Paidia* and *ludus* describe different ways of playing games, and the variations in restraint and freedom, rules and improvisation among players. While, for example, some forms of *agôn* proceed along more undisciplined lines, such as when children play with a ball on the beach, other forms, such as football, operate with specified rules and take place on limited playing fields that often add more challenge to the game. Although Caillois shares Huizinga's view that uncontrolled play usually evolves into more elaborate forms, with *ludus* slowly replacing *paidia*, he suggests that improvisation is an equally important feature in play, especially when rules are seen as restricting by players.

Caillois' fourfold categorization would be unthinkable without *ludus*, which "purifies" play experiences. The rules and institutionalization of games guarantees that play and ordinary life remain uncontaminated from each other. This is crucial, because the ideal rules and separate arenas of *agôn*, *alea*, *mimicry,* and *ilinx* discipline the powerful drives on which they are based. Everyday life contains elements of competition, chance, simulation, and vertigo, but they are often unrefined and therefore potentially destructive. If play and reality are confused, the pleasures of playing easily result in the "corruption" of games, breeding obsession and anxiety, as when *alea* turns into superstition, *mimicry* leads to alienation from oneself, and the pursuit of *ilinx* shifts into substance abuse.

Everyday Playing

The next step is to explore in more detail how *agôn*, *alea*, *mimicry,* and *ilinx* relate to each other in everyday playing. Caillois claims that this not only provides insight into the diversity of play experiences but also indicates the variable position of play in different cultures and epochs, as well as brings out how different forms of games shape and express cultural values, customs, and beliefs. But he is no more suggesting that games can tell us all about a culture than that other forms of culture can tell us all about play. Rather, Caillois argues that play is a special realm of culture that is in constant interaction with other spheres of culture, as if they were mirror images of each other. Play and reality may express the same basic drives and attitudes, but they are still separate realms as much as Wargames are different from real war or playing Monopoly from commerce.

As Caillois then claims, the four categories only emerge in six possible pairs that can be further divided into three classes. Some of the categories are complementary (fundamental relations), whereas others occur together more rarely (contingent relations) or seem altogether incompatible (forbidden relations). The self-abandonment of *ilinx* is, for example, in stark contrast with *agôn* and its valorization of control and skill, as much as the visceral effect of a roller coaster ride is different from the concentrated attacks of fencing. *Ilinx*, then again, is occasionally related to *alea*, as in situations where gamblers become possessed by the game, losing control over their behavior and money.

Caillois is especially interested in two fundamental relations between games, as he claims these are crucial for the transition from archaic to modern societies: *mimicry* and *ilinx* on the one hand, and *agôn* and *alea* on the other. For example, the magical rituals and festivals in traditional Australian, African, and American cultures would regularly gather people to turn their daily lives into a collective vertigo through dancing and donning terrifying masks to emphasize their possession by mystic forces. This combination of role-playing (*mimicry*) and ecstatic states (*ilinx*) was important for social cohesion, as it provided a release of collective energies and thus contributed to reinvigorating social life.

Against this, the rational and calculative worldview already present in ancient Greece and, more broadly, in modern societies has displaced the eruptive rituals with more institutionalized and controlled social practices. Whether it be the struggle between political parties or the competition for market share, education, or jobs, *agôn* emerges as the dominant cultural form, seen as providing an equal opportunity for all to prove their skills and expertise.

But rules, whether in reality or in games, do not always guarantee a fair outcome. Only small differences in players determine the winner, no matter how much perseverance and talent the other competitors possess. Likewise, despite social policies, laws, taxation, and other forms of regulation, people born into certain socioeconomic backgrounds may find it difficult to advance in society. This is why *alea* gains such a strong foothold. It balances the agonistic spirit by introducing a sense of hope in the face of the eventualities of life: Lotteries and betting games, for example, open up equal opportunities of success for all the players, regardless of their background.

The element of hope is also present in the figure of the "superstar" or the "hero," where *agôn* and *alea* come together: the superstar personifies both the hard work and good luck needed to reach the top. Interestingly, the superstar reintroduces an element of *mimicry*, as people identify strongly with the triumphs of the superstar, even wanting to become one themselves. Caillois further suggests that *ilinx* is still necessary in the modern world, as amusement parks and festivals form a desired contrast to the monotony of ordinary life. Despite the domination of the *agôn-alea* pairing, then, *mimicry* and *ilinx* continue to have an importance for modern societies and their play practices.

Taken together, *Man, Play and Games* not only provides a useful classification and analysis of different types of games (*agôn*, *alea*, *mimicry*, and *ilinx*) and ways of playing (*paidia* and *ludus*) but also lends insight into historic and modern world cultures through the study of their games and playing practices. Claiming that play is a cultural realm in its own right, Caillois shows that it both shapes and expresses the beliefs, values, and rules of every society. Anticipating play researcher Brian Sutton-Smith's important argument in *The Ambiguity of Play*, Caillois suggests that playing does not fall neatly into a single category and is therefore by nature ambiguous, exceeding our attempts to know it definitively.

This also means that *Man, Play and Games* is necessarily open to revisions, prompted by recent changes in playing and understandings of play. For example, the strong distinction between "play" and "reality" appears unwarranted today, with portable technologies such as mobile phones, laptops, and digital games, blending leisure and work, play and reality. Many forms of play also seek to conquer and change the realm of everyday life, such as skateboarding, where practitioners inventively turn urban spaces that are otherwise seen as uninviting into a large playground full of new opportunities, as Ian Borden points out. Where playing begins and ends is therefore only something the players themselves know.

Further, some combinations of games Caillois deems unfeasible, such as the skills of *agôn* and the passivity of *ilinx*, are common today. Extreme sports like skateboarding and surfing are precisely based on a shifting relationship between competition and vertigo, skill and abandonment, a feeling of both "moving" and being "moved" by the circumstances. Digital games can even display multiple combinations of Caillois' categories in the same game, allowing players to identify with characters, encounter surprises, be swept away in fast machines, or perform complex actions.

Because of these minor lacunas, *Man, Play and Games* may actually take on an even greater significance for our attempts to understand play as a cultural phenomenon: It encourages more detailed exploration of the way we theorize playing. Rather than settling with the masterly analysis laid out by Caillois, we should venture to play with *agôn*, *alea*, *mimicry*, and *ilinx*, seeking new combinations and categories, new ways of both playing and theorizing.

See Also: Gambling; *Homo Ludens* (Huizinga); Play as Competition, Sociology of; Rhetorics of Play (Sutton-Smith); Skateboarding.

Bibliography. Ian Borden, *Skateboarding, Space and the City. Architecture and the Body* (Berg, 2001); Roger Caillois, *Man and the Sacred* (University of Illinois Press, 2001); Roger Caillois, *Man, Play and Games* (University of Illinois Press, 2001); Johan Huizinga, *Homo Ludens: A Study of the Play-Element in Culture* (Beacon Press, 1955); Brian Sutton-Smith, *The Ambiguity of Play* (Harvard University Press, 2001).

Kim Kullman
University of Helsinki

Cambodia

Located in southeast Asia, the precursor of modern Cambodia was the Empire of Angkor, which exerted control over the region in medieval times. Before then, the Empire of Funan, located in southern Cambodia and Vietnam, became renowned in China for musical instruments in the 3rd century C.E.. When the Chinese traveler Zhou Daguan visited Angkor as part of a Chinese Embassy in 1296–97, he did not mention any of the games there, and historians have surmised this might be because they were so similar to those in China at the time that they did not merit a mention. Certainly there is evidence that playing music, kite flying, skipping, and model making were all pursued.

In 1432, the city of Angkor was sacked, and Phnom Penh later became the capital. When Cambodia became a French Protectorate in 1863, it was still a small town, with the vast majority of the population living in villages scattered across the countryside. Entertainment was provided by theatrical groups and dancing, which took place around the year to celebrate various events in the agricultural calendar—the Water Festival and the August Ploughing are the two most important ones.

The French community, and also the urban elite, started to pursue many of the games that were popular in France. By the 1920s, boules, a bowling sport, was played in streets in Phnom Penh, and Croquet in people's gardens; also popular were games involving dice. By the 1930s, playing cards became almost as popular as Mahjong, which was still largely only played by the ethnic Chinese, or Sino-Cambodians.

It was not until independence in 1953 that the school system was expanded to provide primary education for all children. Secondary education remained in the French language until 1971, and as a result, French games tended to predominate for older children, with soccer rapidly gaining a large following. One game called *Mik* in Cambodian, which the French called *Marelle,* was similar to Hopscotch and popular with younger children. There were also other games such as Hide-and-Seek, Marbles, and miming. Model making, especially of animals and musical instruments was a pastime of older children and adults. Scrabble (with words in French or, later, in English) was very soon the preserve of teenagers and adults who were fluent in another language.

As well as the foreign expatriates in the country, and the Cambodians who had traveled overseas, some older school students also started playing Chess—both Chinese Chess and the European version. In the late 1960s and early 1970s, children from wealthier families started making models and taking part in elaborate Wargaming, as well as playing with dolls and Legos. Until 1969, most of the foreign imports into Cambodia came from France or former French colonies, but later it became more common to import games from the United States. Although gambling in private, such as in Mahjong games, remained common, the only casinos in the country were government owned or regulated and were located in Phnom Penh or at Bokor in the countryside.

During the rule of the Khmer Rouge, from 1975 until 1979, imported items were unobtainable, and with a large part of the population living in near-starvation conditions, most adults were concerned about the daily battle for survival. For children, however, with little or no organized schooling, there were opportunities for play and amusement without toys, following pursuits not dissimilar to children around the world.

The war that followed the Vietnamese invasion of Cambodia in 1978 led to many Cambodian refugees settling in the United States, France, Canada, and Australia. Russian technicians who worked in Cambodia in the 1980s played Chess regularly, and it became popular again with many people. When the war ended in 1991, and many of the refugees returned to Cambodia, they brought with them Western habits. There are now adventure playgrounds, amusement centers, bowling alleys, and casinos, as well as groups involved in military reenactments, Wargaming, and *Dungeons & Dragons.* The Artillery Park in Phnom Penh continues to be popular with foreign tourists—machine guns, grenade launchers, and even heavy artillery can be fired by those happy to pay in foreign currency.

See Also: Chess and Variations of; *Dungeons & Dragons*; Hide & Seek; Kite Flying; Scrabble.

Bibliography. Charles R. Joy, *Young People of East Asia* (Oldbourne, 1962); Glenn Kirchner, *Children's Games Around the World* (Benjamin Cummings, 2000); Someth May, *Cambodian Witness: The Autobiography of Someth May* (Faber & Faber, 1986).

Justin Corfield
Geelong Grammar School

Camping and Hiking

Both camping and hiking are leisure activities that bring participants into close proximity with nature. While the former can refer to organized, goal-oriented group living in the outdoors, in which young participants are supervised by trained leaders, in this case camping signifies temporarily living and sleeping in the out-of-doors in a mobile or makeshift shelter, such as a tent, in a nonurban location, like a campground, a national park, or crown land. Hiking, on the other hand, refers to an extended walk for pleasure or exercise generally undertaken in the country. The two activities can take place in concert, as in the case of a multi-day backpacking trip, or independently of one another. Camping can also be combined with watercraft such as canoes and kayaks, or with automobiles, such as recreational vehicles (RVs).

Hiking as a recreational activity finds its origins in the 18th century and coincides with the development of a "taste for nature" that compelled people to venture outside to walk for pleasure, as well as to creates spaces, such as trails and parks, in which to walk, and eventually to hike. Later attempts to privatize such spaces precipitated political protest. In Britain, for instance, the rambler movement, which emerged in response to the 19th-century Enclosure Acts, saw hikers take to the countryside to protest these changes. The origins of recreational camping are more difficult to pin down. Camping out for utilitarian purposes has a long history in settler colonies such as Canada, the United States, and Australia. The history of the fur trade, gold rushes, pioneer settlement, and conflicts such as the American Civil War, for example, could not be told without reference to camping. At what point people began to make their way into nature to camp out for pleasure, however, is unclear. That it was happening at least by the mid-19th century in the United States and Canada is evidenced by the emergence of the summer camp movement.

Participation in both activities increased as a result of the anxieties brought on by industrialization, urbanization and the rise of corporate capitalism in the closing decades of the 20th century. In particular, concerns about the ills of modern life impelled individuals out of urban centers for "authentic" encounters with nature. Men, in particular, engaged in outdoor activities for the physical challenges that were believed to counteract the seemingly emasculating effects of modernity. Following the designation of Yellowstone in the United States as a national park in 1872, a number of Western nations followed suit in developing national park systems, which in turn created new opportunities for camping and hiking. Such opportunities were increasingly sought after in the postwar era as a result of the democratization of recreation and travel brought on by relatively widespread prosperity, the increasing accessibility of automobiles and the development of lightweight and more streamlined equipment.

Motivations

In contemporary Western culture, the primary appeal of both camping and hiking is the opportunity to be in nature, which itself has different meanings for different groups. For some, nature has religious significance, as a sanctuary or a place to commune with God. For others, it is the solitude offered by being in nature or the sense of escape from "civilization" that compels them to camp or hike. Then there are those who cite the educational benefits of the nature experience afforded by camping or hiking. That camping trips have been employed in teaching a diverse range of scholastic subjects including biology, geography, and history is yet another manifestation of "nature as instructor."

Being in nature also has aesthetic appeals. This is particularly true of hiking, an activity that by emphasizing the journey over the destination has encouraged participants to appreciate the landscape through which they are moving, but also to be on the lookout for wildlife and birds. The aesthetic ideal sought after by hikers has long been associated with the breathtaking views and grandeur popularized by 19th-century authors and painters, such as Ralph Waldo Emerson and J.M. Turner.

Beyond the appeal of nature, there are other motivating factors for strapping on a pair of hiking boots or packing up a tent and camping supplies. The physicality of the experience, for example, furnishes the appeal for some, who emphasize the health benefits or physical challenges of camping and hiking. While for others, activities often associated with camping and hiking, such as hunting, fishing, or birdwatching, compel them into the out-of-doors.

While some are attracted to the perceived seclusion offered by camping and hiking, the reality is that both activities are generally undertaken in groups. The intimacy afforded by the small participant base, the breakdown of social barriers as a result of decreased formality, and the tendency toward interdependence amongs participants creates unique opportunities for relationship building. For some such activities offer a way to reconnect with friends and family or to make new acquaintances. The social potential of experiences in nature, such as those offered by camping and hiking, in conjunction with the belief that wilderness can have a lasting impact on the individual, is the rationale behind wilderness therapy, which aims to encourage new patterns of behavior in participants and to transform conceptions of the self. This practice primarily targets at-risk youth, psychiatric patients, and inmates.

See Also: Canada; Canoeing and Kayaking.

Bibliography. Stephen Kaplan, "Psychological Benefits of Wilderness Experience," *Human Behaviour and Environment* (v.6, 1983).

Jessica Dunkin
Carleton University

Canada

While Canada has some sports and other leisure activities in common with the United States, many forms of play are very much a product of both the environment and history of the country. If there is one distinguishing characteristic about play in Canada, it might be the great extent to which it is outdoors. Skills that were required for sustenance and survival in the earliest days have evolved into individual and team events.

Canadian Sports

Of all the sports in Canada, it is perhaps hockey that is most associated with the country. The sport as it is currently played came into being during the 19th century. Hockey is played throughout Canada by men and women and all ages on a wide variety of levels. According to Hockey Canada, which governs amateur play, there are over 4.5 million Canadians who play, coach, officiate, or otherwise support the game in an administrative or other capacity.

With over 3,000 hockey arenas throughout the country, Hockey Canada also estimates that as of 2007 more than 1.5 million games are played each year, with a further 2 million practices held.

While hockey is considered Canada's national winter game, another sport of Canadian First Nation origin, lacrosse, is very popular and is considered the nation's official summer game. Lacrosse is played formally and informally throughout the country in three major venues. There is box lacrosse, which is played indoors, and men's field and women's field lacrosse.

While baseball is not as popular in Canada as it is in the United States, it still has a wide following. Baseball Canada, which governs the sport, states that there are currently more than 400,000 Canadians who play the game in 13,000 teams, with 62,000 coaches and 13,000 umpires.

Curling is a team sport in which a shaped and polished stone is pushed and then slides toward a target known as a "house." As the stone travels down the ice, team members use brooms to remove rough ice "pebbles," in an effort to steer the stone toward the target. The game, played by a four-person team, is Scottish in origin and dates back at least to the 16th century. It is extremely popular in Canada. According to Curling Canada, 2.7 percent of the entire Canadian population plays the sport—over 754,000 people. It is most popular in Canada's prairie provinces, and perhaps 12 percent of the population in that region have tried the sport. Another interesting statistic from Curling Canada states that at least 40 percent of all curlers pursue other active sports in the off-season such as golf, fishing, camping, or regularly working out.

Football is widely played in Canada on all levels. While it is similar to American football, there are some differences. Canadian football fields are larger than American, being 10 yards longer and almost 12 yards wider. Canadian teams also have three instead of four downs. Despite these and other differences, Canadian and American high school teams adjust easily to playing according to either set of rules, depending on which side is hosting the game.

Diminishing Leisure Time

In common with both the United States and the rest of the industrialized Western world, Canada does have a problem with diminishing time available to pursue all of the recreational opportunities that exist. A nationwide study conducted in 2007 by Canada's Institute for Research in Public Policy reported that the number of hours that both fathers and mothers spent working had increased, cutting down on the time they could spend in playing with their children. The average time spent each week working rose from 44.6 to 46.3 hours. The amount of time available for play declined from 31.5 hours to 29.5 hours. The only province to show a departure from this trend was Quebec.

A similar study conducted in the province of Nova Scotia by the API Atlantic Research Group in 2008 reported the same results. The study found that workers in the province were working a months' more paid time than they had 10 years earlier. In addition to this tendency to have less leisure time, the findings reported

Curling at Rideau Hall in Ottawa, Canada, in an 1875 photograph by W.J. Topley. According to Curling Canada, 2.7 percent of the Canadian population plays the sport, and there are over 1,600 curling clubs across Canada.

on how that time was used. At least 40 percent of leisure time was spent watching television, and only 20 percent was spent on sports and active pursuits.

Canada's heritage of active play, as is the case in the United States and an increasing number of places, is being reduced by more passive pursuits such as television watching and the increasing use of electronic games.

Indigenous Play

Among the forms of play are those developed by the Inuit (commonly and mistakenly referred to as Eskimos), who live throughout northern Canada. Inuit play is very physically demanding and is based on having to develop strength in order to merely survive in the arctic. Another interesting characteristic of Inuit play is that most Inuit games take place indoors and, except for the blanket toss and jumping games, take place within what would be an area the size of an igloo. Musk-Ox fighting is a form of wrestling with the players on their hands and knees facing each other and their heads tucked under the other's collar bone.

In this position they attempt to push each other out of a designated circle. Another form calls for the players to lie on their stomachs, facing each other with a loop of canvas around both their heads. At a signal they try to pull each other over a line. There are also a large number of jumping and kicking games. The games, which were a form of training and building strength, now have a new importance in that formalized contests are seen as a way of preserving the Inuit heritage. There are six such competitions, known as the northern games, conducted in Canada's Northwest Territories. The winners of these competitions go on to compete in the International Arctic Games, which are held in Russia, Finland, Greenland, or the United States (Alaska).

The use of games and play to reinforce identity is, in fact, a major concern. Inuit life, as is common throughout the world, has been affected by television, electronic games, and other games such as basketball. A governmental organization, Statistics Canada, reports that both Inuit and non-Inuit children (aged 4 to 14 years) engage in about the same degree of physical play. Approximately 65 percent play sports of some type at least once a week. The same survey also indicated a baseline of three or more hours a day watching television and two or more hours a day playing video games.

Popular Pastimes

Other popular activities include paintball; downhill and cross-country skiing; snowboarding; deep sea, lake, and river fishing; hunting; snowshoeing; dog sledding; and hiking. Cycling and mountain biking, swimming, and other water sports are also popular.

Team Sports

Team sports played at all levels include basketball, rugby, soccer, and cricket. Like curling, this sport, which is not native to Canada, has a surprisingly wide following, although it is not as popular as it was at the beginning of the 20th century. Provincial associations throughout Canada claim that approximately 40,000 cricket players are registered, while another 50,000 play the informally but regularly. School programs are also adopting cricket as a sport.

Canada's wide array of sports and active pastimes and their ability to spur sport tourism have for a long time been looked on as an important means of national income. For several years, the Canadian Congress on Leisure Research has provided a forum for discussion and proposals to encourage sport tourism.

See Also: Arctic Play (First Nations); Cricket (Amateur); Curling (Scottish); Fishing; Hockey (Amateur); Play as Learning, Anthropology of; Snowboarding; Team Play.

Bibliography. Paul Arseneault, *The Great Canadian Hockey Phrase Book* (Nimbus Publishing, 2007); Baseball Canada, www.baseball.ca (cited July 2008); Canadian Lacrosse Association, www.lacrosse.ca (cited July 2008); Cricket Canada, www.canadiancricket.org (cited July 2008); Hockey Canada, www.hockeycanada.ca/index.cfm/ci_id/6698/la_id/1.htm (cited July 2008); William Humber and John St. James, eds., *All I Thought About was Baseball: Writings on a Canadian Pastime* (University of Toronto Press, 1996); Douglas Maxwell, *Canada Curls: The Illustrated History of Curling in Canada* (Whitecap, 2002); James Opp and John C. Walsh, *Home, Work, and Play: Situating Canadian Social History, 1840–1980* (Oxford University Press, 2006); Wayne G. Pealo, *Canadian Sport Tourism: An Introduction* (Recreation and Tourism Management Research Institute, 2003); Stephen G. Wieting, ed., *Sport and Memory in North America* (Frank Cass, 2001).

Robert Stacy
Independent Scholar

Car and Travel Games

Contemporary car and travel games are played by people of all ages, primarily as a way to occupy themselves and avert boredom while traveling long distances via automobile, bus, train, or airplane. Often games are suggested by parents to restless children while on long trips, but these games are not exclusively for children.

Some of the games that people play while traveling are niche games that have originated in the specific context of the highway. Some are adaptations of games that are found in other contexts, such as I Spy, or Car Bingo. Other games, such as Car Cricket, are loosely based on the rules of other games and applied to the context of travel.

What is common to all games that people play while they travel is that they can be played within a confined space over long periods of time. There are differences between games that can be played in cars and buses and those that can be played in other forms of long-distance transportation, such as trains or airplanes. Games that have originated in the context of cars or buses are of particular interest from a sociocultural perspective because they demonstrate the influence of environment on play and can be used to illustrate how culture contributes to and is influenced by niche games.

Cultural Influences

The common characteristic of games that are specific to car or bus travel is the reliance on observation and rules that allow for extended play. Many of the games can be played alone, and others require interaction. From a sociocultural perspective, car and travel games are influenced by culture. The games arose with advances in automotive technology, which allowed people to make long-distance trips. Culture also influences the content of car and travel games. For example, a game such as Car Cricket is only possible with specific environmental features, and is consequentially only found in specific cultural contexts. Car and travel games have also influenced popular culture, such as in the case of the term *Punch Bug* becoming an alternative name for the Volkswagen Beetle. There are numerous variations of all car games, from those that are for amusement, to those that are competitive, to those that are elicit or erotic.

There are games that can be distinguished as car or travel games because they make use of the environment that is unique to highway travel. All of these games involve varying degrees of observation on the part of the players.

Some examples are I Spy games, Car Bingo, Car Cricket, alphabet games, and number plate games. In addition, there are car travel games that involve discrete observations, such as the observation of specific makes of cars such as Volkswagen Beetles (in a game that is often called Punch-Buggy), or of a car that has one broken headlight (in a game that is sometimes called Padiddle).

I Spy, Bingo, and Cricket

I Spy games can be played in almost any context and are well suited for play in a car or bus. At least two players are required to play the game. There are no props or scoring cards needed. This game makes use of what is available in the immediate environment of the car or the landscape, as players take turns guessing what the other is observing based on his or her descriptions. The game is best played during highway travel, where there is a broader view of the landscape. The game requires skilled observation and the engagement of players.

Car Bingo is a variation of standard Bingo. The car version of Bingo requires players to observe objects or animals that would be seen on a road trip and match them to these objects on a Bingo-style card. Items on a Car Bingo card might include a cow, a stop sign, a truck, or a gas station. This game may be played by a single player or as a competition between several players. Car Bingo games are manufactured and sold, but they could also be made. Car Bingo would be suited to car travel on the highway or local roads in most of the world but would not be effective in desolate areas such as the desert or thick forest. The game requires moderate skill in observation but is primarily a game of chance.

Car Cricket is loosely based on the rules of Cricket, but does not require any physical movement or any materials to play. The game makes use of the context of car travel by requiring the players to observe the names of pubs they see along the way, scoring or getting "out" for features of the name of the pub. There are variations of the game, but basic rules are that a player scores a point for each leg that would correspond to a person or animal in the name of the pub.

For example, a pub named Henry IV would score two points, because the king had two legs; likewise, a pub named the White Horse would score four points. Zero points are given for inanimate objects such as The Free Press. A person is called out when the name of the pub contains "head" or "arms," as in The Carpenter's Arms. The game is played primarily in the United Kingdom, where there are many pubs with these types of names. The game is thought to be decreasing in popularity as the road system is being converted to large motorways that do not allow for observations of pub names. This is a good example of how a car game emerged from a specific cultural context and is changing as a response to changes in the human-made environment.

Car Games

Some games played by car passengers involve finding letters of the alphabet in road signs or billboard advertisements. There are numerous variations of this game, but basic rules are for players to find the letters of the alphabet in sequence. Similarly, there are varieties of games that make use of car number plates. These games might involve finding numbers or letters. In North America, where there are distinctive number plates for each of the states, provinces, and territories, the game may involve the quest to find as many different plates as possible. This game might be played within the time frame of a single car trip and continued on subsequent trip. The game could be played alone or with others, for amusement or competition.

One of the only car games that can be played at night is a competitive game to be the first to identify a car that has a broken headlight. This is sometimes called Padiddle, which is a nonsense word. Variations of the game include slapping or kissing the person who did not spot the Padiddle. Other variations may include removing an article of clothing for each time a player did not spot a Padiddle, presumably for players who are on a romantic date. This is an example of a car game that uses the context of the nighttime driving environment to facilitate interaction among players and, especially in the latter example, as a form of foreplay.

Similarly, there are car games that involve pointing out when a player has spotted a specific make of a car. The most common version in the United States involves the Volkswagen Beetle and has become a pop culture phenomenon.

Variants of the game do extend to other makes of cars. Similar to Padiddle, this game requires only that the player observe and call out their observation. In the case of observing a Volkswagen Beetle, players commonly deliver a mild punch to the arm of their fellow player upon the revelation that they have spotted the car, leading to the name Punch Buggy for the game, and causing some people to begin to call the Beetle a Punch

Bug. This is a good example of how a simple car game spread mimetically through popular culture.

See Also: Bingo; Cricket (Amateur); I Spy.

Bibliography. Elliott M. Avedon and Brian Sutton-Smith, eds., *The Study of Games* (John Wiley & Sons, 1971); Thomas M. Malaby, "Beyond Play: A New Approach to Games," *Games and Culture* (v.2/2, 2007); Jaipaul L. Roopnarine, James E. Johnson, and Frank H. Hooper, eds., *Children's Play in Diverse Cultures* (SUNY Press, 1994).

Suzanne M. Flannery Quinn
University of South Florida

Casino

Casino (or Cassino) is a card game played with a traditional 52-card deck, for two to four players. An English-language descendant of the Italian game *Scopa* (played with Italy's 40-card deck), it is the only common card game in the English-speaking world to use fishing instead of trick-taking. The basic mode of play is that of matching outplay: each player plays a card that matches one in play on the table in order to capture it.

The term *fishing* for a game like Casino is coined by the Chinese, for whom fishing games are the norm, as trick-taking games are the norm in the West. Cards are dealt face-up on the table in a pool, from which players attempt to capture cards by matching them with a card from their hand—any turn in which they are unable to, they instead increase the size of the pool (and the odds of anyone being able to capture a card from it) by dealing one of their cards into it. The first player to 21 points—each round has 11 points available—wins, with the Big Casino (the 10 of hearts) and Little Casino (two of spades) carrying special point values.

Though fishing games are more common in the East, it's only the terminology that's borrowed intercontinentally; European fishing games crop up here and there throughout history, one of the earliest being the French game Culbas, played on a triangular table in the early 17th century. Casino is described a century later, in the 1797 edition of Hoyle's. Scopa, to which it is likely related, is named for the way the player "sweeps"—or "scoops up"—the pool, while Casino is probably named for the Italian city of Cassino. Casino elaborates on the fishing games that had come before it—*Culbas*, Scopa, and the 1730 French game *Papillon*—with the concept of "building."

There are two types of building. A player can "build five" (or any other value) by taking a two from his hand and placing it on top of a three in the pool—provided he has a five in his hand to then use to capture it. He has to announce the build, and any other player with a five can then capture the built card instead—which explains why Casino does not simply become a game in which players build small cards into larger cards to capture. Built cards can be further built upon, but the builder must always have a card of the appropriate type at any stage of building—you cannot build a seven by playing two twos on a three unless you also hold a five in your hand.

The second type is natural building and reflects games' fascination with doubles (as seen in dice and dominoes games). Natural building works like regular building, except that cards of equal value are stacked up and combined without adding their values—two fives become one five.

Building greatly complicates the game, especially among experienced players, who can read a pool and see not simply its cards, but also its potential cards to be built, as a Chess player can read a board and see moves and outcomes. Building is an American innovation in Casino, developing—probably in New York—around the years of the Civil War. It remained a regional or occasional variation until the 20th century, when it was incorporated into all accounts of the game.

There are some variant rules of Casino. A five-player game can be made by removing the twos of hearts, diamonds, and clubs and dealing an extra card to each player on the last deal. Under the trailing royals rule, face cards are eligible for building with, and orphaned face cards are awarded to the player who makes the final capture.

A similar game, *Pasur*, is played in Iran—but like Scopa, it lacks Casino's building innovation.

See Also: China; Fish; History of Playing Cards; Italy.

Bibliography. Elliott Avedon, *The Study of Games* (Krieger Pub., 1979); Roger Caillois, *Man, Play, and Games* (University of Illinois Press, 2001); David Parlett, *The Oxford Guide to Card Games* (Oxford University Press, USA, 1990); Fyodor Soloview, *Six Generations Card Games/Playing Cards: Immigration from Europe to America Edition* (Six Generations Publishing, 2004); Brian Sutton-Smith, *The Ambiguity of Play* (Harvard University Press, 2001).

Bill Kte'pi
Independent Scholar

Casual Games

Electronic video games were divided into two categories—hard-core and casual games—in the 1980s. Although both began as simple arcade games of this era, the two types have evolved in radically different directions and primarily serve different purposes and populations.

Hard-core games branched from arcade games like Space Invaders but have become substantially more violent and immersive—an elite performance activity for the young, mostly male demographic. The most popular hard-core games require special consoles, fast reactions, and a substantial time commitment. Novice gamers must master arcane rules and conventions before gameplay becomes rewarding.

In contrast, casual games are democratic. They can be played anywhere on almost any form of electronic device, with no special skills or knowledge. In addition, they generally maintain the simplicity and family-friendly vibe of the famous Pac-Man.

Most casual games conform to patterns from one or more time-tested analog game types: knowledge/trivia quizzes (Jeopardy!), word grids (crosswords and other word games), pattern-based puzzles (jigsaw, Rubic's Cube), logic puzzles (matrixes and mazes), card games (Solitaire), and hand-eye coordination challenges (Pinball and other traditional arcade games). With such a wide range of possibilities, it is not surprising that the Casual Games Association documents hundreds of new game launches every year.

Although the variety of forms is dizzying, casual games share several conventions. All are at heart single-player games. Gameplay is simple and intuitive—rules of play can be explained in a sentence or two. The player quickly builds confidence and comfort with initial stages that are designed to be easy to win. The game advances with only one or two modes—typing or single clicks rather than complex keyboard and modifier combinations.

Many casual gamers play in unstable environments, such as at work or on public transportation, so gameplay is easily interruptible and can usually be suspended without penalty. Gameplay tends to be open-ended—progressive but not sequential. There is often no "final" goal that marks the finish line, just a series of more challenging levels marked by higher scores. Each succeeding puzzle is a variation on a familiar theme. These characteristics make it possible to find a comfortable game and replay it frequently, building strong user loyalty for the game and the site on which it was found.

In practice, the term *casual games* reveals itself as a misnomer. These games are casual only in that they can be accessed easily and with no planning. Successful casual games, like Pop Cap's Bejeweled or Zuma, are actually highly addictive. Although designed for short bursts of gaming, a popular casual game can hold a player hostage for hours—a perfect way to relieve stress and wind down from work during lunch or at the end of the workday.

Despite their extensive online dominance, casual games have long been the underrated stepsister of electronic gaming. This opinion has changed as Nintendo Wii's impressive sales figures made it clear that a powerful underserved demographic had been ignored or misunderstood by the hard-core-game–driven gaming world. The demographics of casual game players conform more closely to those of the Wii than to most console games. They tend to attract an older audience dominated by women over the age of 40 years, most of whom would never answer to the gamer label. In fact, although consumers are fairly evenly divided by sex, women over 35 years old represent about 70 percent of those who actually pay for game downloads rather than just use them online.

See Also: Arcades; Checkers and Variations of; Crosswords; Go; Puzzles; Word Games (Other Than Crosswords).

Bibliogaphy. Dean Takahashi, "PopCap Games Executive Interview: Don't be Stupid, Have Fun," www.venturebeat.com (cited July 2008); Seth Schiesel, "Video Games Conquer Retirees," *New York Times* (March 30, 2007); Casual Connect, "Casual Games Market Report 2007," www.casualconnect.com (cited July 2008).

Cynthia L. Baron
Northeastern University

Central American Nations

Central America consists of the countries in the southernmost tip of the North American continent: Belize, Costa Rica, El Salvador, Guatemala, Honduras, Nicaragua, and Panama (which, because of the Panama Canal, literally straddles North and South America). With the exception of Belize—formerly British Honduras—the Central American nations are all former Spanish possessions. Because of its proximity to the Caribbean Sea, there is a good deal of cultural interchange between Central America and the Caribbean; the Caribbean nation of the Dominican Republic is a member of the System for Central American Integration (SICA), a nascent European Union–like organization.

Cat and Mouse

Cat and Mouse is a Costa Rican children's game for at least seven players and is therefore good at parties and school. Two players are designated the cat and the mouse; the rest form a circle around the mouse, holding hands, singing "*Alla viene el gato y el raton, a darle combate al tiburon*" (the cat and rat are coming to fight the shark).

The cat tries to break through the circle to catch the mouse, while the children in the circle try to stop him by moving together to close the gaps between them or lowering their hands.

Crazy Seven

Crazy Seven is a memory and counting game played throughout Central America, with five or more players. One player begins counting one, the player to his left counts two, and so on around the circle. At seven and every multiple of seven, players clap their hands in unison and counting resumes in the opposite direction. Players who fail to clap are out of the game.

Wall Bounce

Especially popular in Guatemala, Wall Bounce is played with a tennis ball (or racquet sport ball of some kind) for each player. Players line up a short distance from a wall, and bounce the balls against it while reciting the game's chant in time with following the directions indicated by the chant—anyone who makes a mistake is out of the game. The American game Russia, with chants like "onesies" and "twosies," is very similar.

The Wall Bounce chant is:

Sin moverse (without moving)
Sin reirme (without laughing)
Sin hablar (without talking)
En un pie (on one foot)
En una mano (with one hand)
Adelante (clap your hands in front before the catch)
Atras (clap your hands behind you)
Torbellino (whirl your hands like a "whirlwind"—torbellino—before the catch)
Caballete (clap your hands under one knee like a "little horse")
Ahora sí ("right now"—hold your arms straight in front of you to catch)
Media vuelta (turn around halfway)
Vuelta entero (turn all the way around)

The Blind Hen

The Blind Hen is a Salvadoran game for a large group of players. The player who is "It" is blindfolded and spun around, while other players circle him or her (holding hands) and chant, "Little hen, what are you looking for?" The "hen" replies, "A thimble and a needle," only to be told, "We have it, but we won't give it to you." The hen must then try to tag another player while the group tries to avoid any of its members being tagged and at the same time taunting the hen and hinting at where they are with their voices.

La Rayuela

La Rayuela is a Hopscotch game in Honduras, where the days of the week are marked on the Hopscotch board. Players kick a marker (a rock, stick, piece of tile, etc.) onto a square, hop into that square, turn and kick the marker out, and hop out.

The Pilgrim

The Pilgrim is a hopscotch game played in Panama using a board unlike the one familiar with Americans: A rectangle is divided into six segments by drawing a square in it, with an X in the square (four segments in the square, plus the segments north and south of the square). Each player kicks his or her marker into square one, hops into it, kicks it into square two, hops into it, and so on, alternating directions while moving forward through the board.

See Also: Bahamas and the Caribbean; South Americans, Traditional Cultures; Spanish America; Tag.

Bibliography. Arnold Arnold, *World Book of Children's Games* (Fawcett, 1972); Elliott Avedon, *The Study of Games* (Krieger Pub., 1979); Jesse Hubbell Bancroft, *Games* (MacMillan, 1937); Roger Caillois, *Man, Play and Games* (University of Illinois Press, 2001); Patricia Evans, *Rimbles: A Book of Children's Classic Games, Rhymes, Songs, and Sayings* (Doubleday, 1961); E.O. Harbin, *Games of Many Nations* (Abingdon Press, 1954); Sarah Ethridge Hunt, *Games and Sports the World Around* (Ronald Press Company, 1964); Glenn Kirchner, *Children's Games Around the World* (Benjamin Cummings, 2000); Nina Millen, *Children's Games from Many Lands* (Friendship Press, 1943).

Bill Kte'pi
Independent Scholar

Central Asia, Ancient

In the modern world, Central Asia broadly refers to the western Chinese provinces (such as Xinjiang, Tibet, and Qinghai); the former Soviet republics of Kazakhstan, Kyrgyzstan, Tajikistan, Turkmenistan, and Uzbekistan; and the nations of Afghanistan and Mongolia. It has historically been inhabited by Turkic peoples, with Russians forming a significant minority in the modern age and Tajiks (a Persian-speaking Iranian people) making up much of the population of Afghanistan, Tajikistan, and Uzbekistan. When we speak of ancient Central Asia, we are speaking principally of these Turkic peoples (and possibly related groups such as the Mongols), living in the steppes north of the Ancient Near East and the easternmost reaches of the Indo-European peoples.

In earliest times, the area was inhabited by nomadic and seminomadic groups who domesticated the horse and the camel. In the last two millennia B.C.E., as empires came to power in the ancient Near East, the steppe people provided a constant source of trouble for them; Herodotus chronicles the doomed efforts of the Persians to conquer the Scythians, for instance.

Ancient Sports

The steppe peoples were well-known for their proficiency with horses—the Huns and Mongols were famous for it—and horseback riding and racing were popular (and practical) pursuits. One of the earliest sports in the region developed out of this proclivity: polo, probably first played in nearby Persia in the last couple of centuries B.C.E. Like many games, polo was a form of simulated warfare, sometimes played with as many as 100 horsemen on each side. The "game of kings"—in Persia it was almost exclusive to the nobility—spread across Central Asia as far west as Constantinople and as far east as Tibet, where the word *pulu* for ball gave the sport its name, later corrupted by the British (who discovered it through India) into polo.

Unlike in Persia, across the steppes polo was the game of the people—all the people. Those who could ride could play, hitting the ball as they rode with curved sticks similar to field hockey sticks. Leather shields were sometimes used to protect players' legs from being struck by the sticks, and vulnerable parts of their steeds' anatomy were likewise protected. The sport grew in popularity fast enough that rituals evolved in some parts of the world devoted to one or another god of polo, and the oldest surviving polo ground in the world dates to 33 B.C.E., in the Manipur state of India.

The game of field hockey is much like polo without the mounts; while one did not necessarily evolve from the other (stick-and-ball games are common around the world), the Daur people of Central Asia developed their game of *beikou* sometime after the spread of polo through the region. *Beikou* is a short (roughly half an hour), intense game played between two teams of men fighting over an apricot root with long sturdy branches.

While polo passed from the elites to the commoners, the sport of *cuju* began in the army and was eventually adopted by the royal courts of China's Han dynasty. Probably beginning sometime in the 5th century B.C.E., *cuju* was very similar to football. A ball stuffed with feathers was used, with six goal posts on the field, some with nets between them, and some freestanding. Professional players played the game for the royal court, but it was an exceptionally popular sport among people from all walks of life—including women.

Many illustrations survive of women playing *cuju*, along with records of a teenage girl beating a military team in a match. The sport evolved over time, and in the Song dynasty the six goals were reduced to one, in the center of the field (giving both teams equal access to it, with points accruing according to the team member who made the goal). But the game died off because that interest encouraged a commercial aspect, and the Song's usurpation of the sport led them to shore up the professional players by requiring amateur players to hire a professional to train them—making it no longer a sport that could be played for free, or in which skill was more important than license.

Another stick-and-ball game, resembling golf more than field hockey, was *chuiwan*, which originated in the Song dynasty of China and spread as far as Europe when the Mongols discovered it. Little today is known about its rules beyond the hitting of balls into shallow holes in the ground from a distance—a simple game of skill that is easy to adjust for both children and adults.

Early Games

At the same time that cuju developed, the Chinese invented the board game *xiangqi*. It may have been related to *liubo*—not much is known about liubo's rules to be sure. The word *xiangqi* means "figure game," but may indicate a connection to the constellations; the "river" on the board is referred to as the "heavenly river" in some literature, which would imply the Milky Way. The movements of pieces on the board may emulate, or suggest, the movement of celestial objects in the night sky. Though a military strategy game, *xiangqi* had a strong following among the people as an engrossing game that rewarded attention and concentration. Like Chess and possibly *liubo*, *xiangqi* used a variety of figures—seven types—with different point values and different methods of movement, which is one reason the game in the modern day is often called Chinese Chess.

The earliest Go board has been discovered in northwest China, from the Han dynasty—around 246 B.C.E.—but while the game was likely known on the steppes, it did not spread west with the same success as other pursuits.

The Chinese were especially fond of puzzles, which were a pursuit of both children and adults. The disentanglement puzzle now known as *baguenaudier* was invented by the 2nd-century general Zhuge Liang and is sometimes known via its variant the Impossible Staircase. In the puzzle, a double loop of string must be disentangled from a series of rings on pillars. Many similar puzzles abounded in the era, across the steppes; unlike modern board games, such puzzles could often be created on the spot from items at hand, which could then be reused for their original purpose later.

The Chinese board game *liubo*, dating from early in the 2nd millennium B.C.E., was popular in the area until about the 500s B.C.E. A strategy game or "battle game" like Chess, its rules are not known—rarely in antiquity were rulebooks of games written—but it involved moving figures across a grid of squares and an accumulation of "fish" or "stones" representing points. It could have been as involved as Chess, as deep as Go, or as simple as Checkers.

See Also: Afghanistan; Africa, Traditional Play in; Ancient China; Ancient Egypt; Ancient Greece; Ancient India; Ancient Rome; Go.

Bibliography. Elliott Avedon, *The Study of Games* (Krieger Pub., 1979); Robbie Bell and Michael Cornelius, *Board Games Round the World: A Resource Book for Mathematical Investigations* (Cambridge University Press, 1988); Roger Caillois, *Man, Play and Games* (University of Illinois Press, 2001); Patricia Evans, *Rimbles: A Book of Children's Classic Games, Rhymes, Songs, and Sayings* (Doubleday, 1961); E.O. Harbin, *Games of Many Nations* (Abingdon Press, 1954); Sarah Ethridge Hunt, *Games and Sports the World Around* (Ronald Press Company, 1964); Glenn Kirchner, *Children's Games Around the World* (Benjamin Cummings, 2000); Nina Millen, *Children's Games From Many Lands* (Friendship Press, 1943); Brian Sutton-Smith, *The Ambiguity of Play* (Harvard University Press, 1997).

Bill Kte'pi
Independent Scholar

Charades

The tension in the game of Charades comes from trying to help the audience guess the meaning of the charade, but not to guess too quickly. There is no dramatic tension, and hence no fun, if the charade is solved without a comic detour. For hundreds of years, charades were guessing games with riddle clues, often given in rhyme with a two-part or two-syllable answer. In France the game is still played this way. In the United States and the United Kingdom, Charades are typically performed silently as an acting game for guessing.

Literature on Charades is split between books on guessing games and books on silent theater or tableaux. The former is rooted in the European game tradition of courtly entertainment, most notably the *petits jeux* of the court of King Louis XIV, the latter, in the people's theater of mumming and mime. Philosophical treatises on the complexities of silent enactment go back to Plato's *Cratylus* (360 B.C.E.), as Socrates speculated on our potential, like the deaf, for using head, hands, and body for basic communication.

Books still exist from the 1700–1900s about the enormous popularity of American and British Charades. These games were created for group entertainment, either for royalty or for one's own parlor. They typically had poetic clues to proverbs or were riddles, often with the formula "my first," "my second," "my whole," indicating a hint at the first syllable, the second syllable, and the whole proverb or compound phrase. Air-gun, archbishop, court-ship—books often contained alphabetized answers to each riddle. For example: "My first has weight; my second, humor. My whole I only know by rumor: It's tastes, they tell me are aquatic, It's manners, lively and erratic. Answer? Gram-pus" (A whale). The charade sometimes included a tease about its solvability. "My first means provisions, my second yields drink, my whole's a good whish—what is it d'ye think? Fare-well."

Charades began to include what was called "dumb show" or silent enactment along with the clues in the early 1800s. Nonverbal theater itself goes back to ancient Greece, ancient Egypt, and Asia and was associated with religious ritual, dance, and pageantry. Although charades are done with pantomime, they are different from "pantomimes," which are scripted comedies often performed for Christmas and other festive occasions. Charades may appear to be like a signed language; however, charades contain conventions, but no grammar.

Today the acting game is played in teams, or with a single, silent performer acting in front of a group. The performer either makes up a clue title, or is given one to perform. The one who guesses correctly gets to go next.

Standard gestures for the game include icons for the initial category: movie—turning of an old-fashioned movie camera; song—opening the mouth and silently singing; book—opening two hands together, imitating a book; and phrase—making quote marks with both first and second fingers moving up and down. Other variations include celebrities, plays, television shows, Web sites, and video games.

Titles that include double-entendre are the most popular in any genre. Clues can be literal or visual puns. Touching the ear can suggest "sounds like." Pointing to something suggests "looks like." Pointing to one's lower arm indicates a syllable, harkening back to the split-syllable tradition of the earlier rhyming charades. The enthusiastic touching of the forefinger to the nose indicates the answer is correct, or "on the nose." Incorrect answers or misunderstood clues often lead to giggling.

Charades became popular in America in the 1940s and 1950s and have been incorporated into British and American television shows, and coopted by educators for teaching history and other subjects. It has been packaged into numerous variations as a board game since the 1960s, along with its recent pencil-and-paper variation, Pictionary. Most recently, scholars of animal behavior have suggested that orangutans in captivity play a charades-like game to communicate preferred foods. There is no report of the orangutans giggling, however.

See Also: France; Parlor Games; Pretending; United States, 1930 to 1960; United States, 1960 to Present.

Bibliography. Elliott M. Avedon and Brian Sutton-Smith, eds., *The Study of Games* (John Wiley & Sons, 1971); L.B.R. Briggs, *Original Charades* (Scribner and Son, 1891); Annette Lust, *From the Greek Mimes to Marcel Marceau and Beyond* (Scarecrow, 2000); A. Mayhew, *Acting Charades, or Deeds, Not Words: A Christmas Game to Make a Long Evening Short* (D. Bogue, 1852); Peter Puzzlewell, *A Choice Collection of Riddles, Charades, Rebuses, Etc. (1859)* (Kessinger Publishing, 2008); St. Andrews University in Scotland, "Orangutans 'Play Charades' to Communicate with People," *National Geographic News* (August 2, 2007).

Anna Beresin
University of the Arts

Checkers and Variations of

Checkers is not a single game but a family. Checkers (or Draughts as it is known in England) may have been played in Ur, modern-day Iraq, as early as 3000 B.C.E. Archaeologists carbon dated a game that resembled modern Checkers, although the board and number of pieces are different and the rules are not fully known.

Less cloudy is the history of *Quirkat*. Egyptian inscriptions and paintings as early as 1600 B.C.E. contain references to a game like Checkers, and Quirkat was played throughout Egypt in 1400 B.C.E. Even temple walls held depictions of the game, which was played on a 5 x 5 board. Although pieces moved along the intersections of lines, rather than diagonally as in the modern game, it used flat circular pieces in light and dark colors and had the same objective—take the opposing pieces. Plato and Homer refer to the game, and Ramses III and a female are shown on a Theban wall painting using pieces modeled after Trojan war heroes such as Achilles and Ajax.

As Quirkat, the game arrived in Spain with the Arab/Berber armies of Tariq in 711. It first appears in written history in Abu al-Faraj Ali's *Kitab al-Aghani* (Book of Songs) c. 950 C.E. From Moorish Spain it spread through Europe, Hispanicized as *Alquerque*. An incomplete set of rules for Alquerque is in the *Libro de Acedrex, Dados e Tablas* of Alphonso X, an illuminated manuscript created between 1251 and 1282.

Variations

Around 1100, the old Arabic game of Alquerque was adapted onto an 8 x 8 chessboard in the south of France. The larger board required expansion of the number of pieces to 12 per side. The name of the game was *Fierges,* and the pieces were *ferses.* Fierges had no compulsory jumping. The mandatory capture rule came into being in 1535 in France to add challenge to the game; the new variation was called *Jeu Force,* and the older Fierges, now relegated to women's play because it was less of a challenge, became known as *Le Jeu Plaisant de Dames* or *Dames.* With Jeu Force, by the middle of the 16th century the basics of the modern game were in place.

This form became Draughts in England. Scotland, Australia, and New Zealand also refer to the game as Draughts. The English mathematician William Payne wrote a work on Draughts in 1756. The Dutch refined the game in the 18th century by enlarging the board to 10 x 10 and using 20 pieces a side. In this form it moved to North America and became Checkers.

Checkers and Draughts games all use two types of pieces (called stones): soldiers and kings. Initially all pieces are soldiers. Players take turns moving their pieces either into blank squares or jumping and thereby capturing enemy pieces.

Captures are single or multiple and are generally mandatory, with no option of ending a jump before taking all available enemy pieces. Soldiers become kings by reaching the enemy's back row. Soldiers move diagonally; kings have more options, depending on the variant being played. Victory comes to the first player to stalemate the other, either by blocking all moves or taking all opposing pieces. If neither can prevail, the game is a draw.

American Checkers

Draughts or American Checkers plays on an 8 x 8 board with 12 soldiers a side, and limits soldiers to moving forward only, allows kings short jumps, and has other variations. Continental or international Checkers uses a 10 x 10 board with 20 pieces a side. Soldiers can capture forward or backward, and kings have longer jumps. In Poland this game is sometimes played on the 8 x 8 board. Brazil and Sweden also use the Draughts configuration for international rules. Since good players often draw, Killer Checkers is sometimes played; in this variant a player must stop at the next cell after the last jumped piece if the piece is a king. Local variants apply also in Portugal, Spain, and the Czech Republic. Thai Checkers uses eight pieces a side. Italian Checkers bars soldiers from capturing kings and sets other restrictions on jumps. There is a variant called Pool Checkers that was played in the southern United States in the 18th century. Its background is either Spanish or French, possibly both, and it resembles Russian Checkers.

Other Versions

Canadian Checkers uses international rules and 30 stones per side. It is popular also in Sri Lanka and India. Frisian Checkers is played mainly in Holland and, as Fri-

Although some regard Checkers as a simple game for kids, there are an estimated 500 quintillion possible positions.

sian Draughts, was first used by innkeepers in the 18th century to draw in customers. Turkey also has a distinct Checkers variant with 16 stones on an 8 x 8 board not separated by blank squares at play's beginning. Stones can move forward or sideways. A variant is called Kens.

J. Boyler has developed a Checkers game in which red has 10 pieces and black 20. The game is called, naturally, 10 vs. 20. Red has to take all black pieces, while black's objective is to stalemate red. Other games are Albuquerque, dating probably to the American Civil War; Christopher Elis's Give and Take; and the Italian Kharberg/Damma played on a 5 x 5 board with 12 stones per side and, thus, virtually no empty spaces in which to maneuver. Peter Aronson offers Ring Board Checkers, and Matthew Burke uses two interconnected sets of Checkers to play Activator Checkers.

Remco Industries developed Fascination Checkers in 1962. In Losing Draughts, the player unable to move wins the game. Other variations include Hide, Board Draughts, Contract Checkers (created 1935), Chip (created 2002), Surround Checkers, Fractagonals, and Polarity. The game remains popular and attracts creative players always seeking a new means of keeping the challenge in the game.

Tournament Play

The first world Checkers championship occurred in 1847. Tournament play began in 1847, with world championships following. Tournaments have strict rules and emphasize strategy. Soon it became apparent that certain openings were inevitably advantageous, and tournament players had two move restrictions, later increased to three moves.

Andrew Anderson of Scotland defeated James Wyllie, also of Scotland, in the first world championship match in 1847. Playing Go-As-You-Please style, they had previously played four matches. Wyllie outlasted Anderson to win the title. In 1859 Wyllie lost to Robert Martins of England, but Wyllie recaptured the title in 1864 and again in 1872 defeated Martins. In 1873 and 1874 Wyllie won matches against the American W.R. Barker.

In 1876 Robert Yates of the United States won the title and defended successfully in 1877 against Martins. Then he retired, later dying at sea at age 24. Wyllie regained the title and defended successfully until he lost to James Ferrie of Scotland in 1894. Ferrie lost to fellow Scot Richard Jordan in 1896. Jordan beat Robert Stewart of Scotland in 1897.

By this point the play was producing an inordinate number of draws, so the Two-Move Restriction came into being. The initial two moves of a game were taken at random from a list of legitimate moves. Six two-move openings were banned as too advantageous to one of the players. Two of them cost a piece at the onset.

American Charles F. Barker, brother of W.R. Barker, tied Jordan in 1900, but Jordan retained the title, defeating Harry Freedman of Scotland in 1902 before resigning the title in 1903. Ferrie became champion.

International team play began in 1905. England and Scotland had competed previously, but this was the first competition outside Britain. Great Britain bested the United States easily. The second international match in 1927 went to the Americans over the British easily. The Americans won the third match in 1973, again easily, and they won the fourth in 1983 in similar fashion. The fifth match in 1995 again went to the Americans.

Alfred Jordan of England (not related to Richard Jordan, although some sources contend they were cousins) offered to play anyone in the world for his title in 1912. Ferrie declined. Stewart accepted, but the match never took place. In 1914 American Newell W. Banks tied Jordan. Jordan was regarded as world champion although he never won the title. Banks defeated him in 1917, and Jordan moved to America where he placed second several times in the American championship but never won the title. Banks lost to Stewart in 1922, then several times sought a rematch that Stewart refused. Banks claimed the title in 1934 because Stewart refused to play. Banks lost the title to American Asa Long the same year in the first match to use the Three-Move Restriction, which made the first three match moves by random selection from an approved move list.

The British regarded Stewart as champion and two-move restriction as the order of play, so they refused to recognize the outcome. The British and Americans had separate champions into the 1960s, when they rejoined competition.

Champion Checker Players

Championship players could compete for a long time. In the American championship, Long defended against Edwin Hunt of the United States in 1936 but lost to Walter Hellman, another American, in 1948. Hellman tied Willie Ryan in 1949 and defeated Maurice Chamblee in 1951 and Basil Case in 1953. He lost to Marion Tinsley in 1955. Tinsley beat England's wheelchair-bound Derek Oldbury, who ignored the ban on British competition in American events, in 1958. When Tinsley retired, Hellman reclaimed the championship. Hellman defended against Long in 1962, Oldbury in 1965, and Eugene Frazier of the United States in 1967. Hellman died in 1975, and Tinsley took the title, defending against Elbert Lowder of the United States in 1979 and Long in 1981.

Again in 1985 Tinsley defeated Long (recall, Long was champion first in 1934 and qualified to challenge in 1985 by winning the U.S. tournament). Tinsley defeated American Don Lafferty in 1987 and retired in 1991. Oldbury beat Richard Hallett to claim the title; Hallett had been retired from Checkers for 30 years before that match. Oldbury died in 1994, and Ron King of Barbados became champion in a match against England's William Edwards. Ron King tied Don Lafferty to hold the title in 1996. The most recent championship was in 2003, and Alexander Moiseyev dethroned King. Tinsley, who died in 1995, lost only seven games in 45 years and is regarded as the greatest Checker player in history.

The first women's championship took place in 1986. The winner was England's Joan Caws, who defended several times before losing in 1993 to Patricia Breen of Ireland, the current champion. By the turn of the 21st century the American Checkers championships included Two- and Three-Move Restriction, Go-As-You-Please, 11-Man Ballot, Mail Play, and women's. The World Checkers Draughts Federation also held man–computer competitions and junior championships. In 2003 the reigning computer world champion was Nemesis.

Early Checkers Computer Games

The first computers and the first computer Checkers game appeared before World War II. Alan Turing, the famous computer pioneer, was the first to apply computer logic to a well-defined, rule-driven game. Because the first computers were not sophisticated or powerful enough to handle his game, Turing simulated play by making paper and pencil computations.

Arthur L. Samuel wrote the first Checkers program in 1952, a learning program rather than a game-playing one. Within a few years he was playing two copies of the program against each other, eliminating the loser, and pitting the winner against yet another version. Over time, the program improved, and eventually it appeared capable of master-level play. The program famously beat a blind Connecticut Checkers master, Robert Nealey, but later it became known that Nealey was not as good as reputed. In 1966 the Samuel program lost eight games in a row to Walter Hellman and Derek Oldbury. Still, given the slow speed of computers at the time, the program was remarkable, and it was the first that could improve itself without the aid of a human.

The Duke Checkers program, developed in the 1970s by Tom Truscott, Alan Bierman, and Eric Jensen, beat Samuel's program in a two-game match and lost to Elbert Lowder with two losses, two draws, and a win. Lowder was careless and should have not have lost a single match. The Duke programmers challenged Marion Tinsley, but the match never took place, and the Duke program was shelved.

Chinook

Jonathan Schaeffer's Chinook began in 1989. Schaeffer was working on computer Chess but decided to change to Checkers. He assembled a team that included Norman Treolar as the game expert, Robert Lake for databases, and Martin Bryant as the creator of an opening book. Many graduate students and faster computers were also essential. Chinook introduced the endgame database to Checkers. This allowed the computer to know all possible positions with eight pieces or fewer on the board.

The database was six gigabytes, compressed. The Schaeffer team had its match with Tinsley in 1992, but lost four to two without the eight-piece database. For the 1994 rematch they had the full database, and the match featured six draws before Tinsley retired because of ill health (he died shortly thereafter). Chinook beat Don Lafferty, second best in the world to Tinsley, in 1995. The match featured 31 draws and a single victory. Chinook won the 1996 U.S. national tournament. The team had proved all it had wanted to, so it retired Chinook and made the database public. The database was the PC standard for years thereafter.

PC games include Gil Dodgen's Checkers and Martin Bryant's Colossus from the early 1990s, which was probably the best PC game because it used the Chinook database as well as Bryant's opening book. Dodgen worked with Ed Trice to develop World Championship Checkers. English players also entered the game scene: Adrian Millet's Sage, Murray Cash's Nexus and Nemesis, and Roberto Waldteufel's Wyllie. Roberto had a seven-piece database at a time when Chinook was holding onto its seven- and eight-piece databases. Cash and the Trice/Dodgen pair developed the eight-piece database in 2001, as did Martin Fierz, and Schaeffer released the eight-piece database in 2002. In late 2007, one book contained 1,869,199 moves. Also in 2007, a 10-piece endgame book was available for purchase.

Modern Computer Programs

Modern programs can show every possible combination of moves when eight pieces are left on the board (some say the programs can do this at 10 pieces); the result is that computer Checkers is more a game of database searching than of strategy. The programs consistently play the best Checkers players to a draw and sometimes defeat them. The game remains popular worldwide and provides training in logic and thinking, as well as providing a great deal of fun.

Although some people regard Checkers as a simple game for old men and small children, estimates of the number of possible positions reach 500 quintillion. Expert players can spend years mastering play, developing favorite strategies for both defense and attack. They study long series of forced jumps, known as strokes, that have attained classic status. Famous strokes include the Boomerang, Wyllie's Switcher Winder, and the Goose Walk. The Canalejas Cannonball strategy is 350 years old and still can end a game in only five moves.

Checkers is a worldwide game with local variations in rules, board, and pieces, but the same basics. A sign of the popularity of Checkers and the seriousness with which players regard it is the development of the online Checkers history museum, started as a means of preserving images lost in the fire at the Petal, Missouri, International Checker Hall of Fame in 2007. The World of Checkers Museum is in Dubuque, Iowa, and the American competitive Checkers organization posts online news of tournaments, as well as rankings, transcripts of championship matches, and educational material about the game and how to become more proficient at it.

See Also: Chess and Variations of; France; Play as Competition, Psychology of; Play as Competition, Sociology of; United States, 1860 to 1876; United States, 1900 to 1930; United States, 1930 to 1960; United States, 1960 to Present.

Bibliography. Robbie Bell and Michael Cornelius, *Board Games Round the World: A Resource Book for Mathematical Investigations* (Cambridge University Press, 1988); College Sports Scholarships, "A Brief History and How to Play Checkers," www.collegesportsscholarships.com/checkers-draughts.htm (cited July 2008); Martin Fierz, "A Brief History of Computer Checkers," www.fierz.ch/history.htm (cited July 2008); Martin Fierz, "Checkers," www.fierz.ch/checkers.htm (cited June 2008); Neto, Joao Pedro, "The Checkers Family, The World of Abstract Games," homepages.di.fc.ul.pt/~jpn/gv/checkers.htm (cited July 2008); Online Museum of Checkers History, "Promoting the Future of Checkers, by Glorifying its Past," www.online-museum-of-checkers-history.com/ (cited July 2008); Usacheckers.com, "World Championship Results," www.usacheckers.com/worldchampionshipresults.php (cited July 2008); World Checkers Draughts Federation, wcdf.wz.cz/index.htm (cited July 2008).

John Barnhill
Independent Scholar

Chess and Variations of

Chess has always been a fascinating game. It has a long history, with roots in ancient India. Besides the game in practice, there is a long history of literature recording past developments and tactics. Furthermore, this game has been an interesting object of theoretical speculations in psychology, sociology, linguistics, semiotics, and philosophy. It is known as the game of the kings and is not a game of chance. This led to its identification with intelligence in early computer science, whereas modern literature has shown that its self-referential logic is linked to insanity. More prominently, Chess is present as a symbol in fine arts and cinema. For these reasons, Chess could perhaps be the greatest game created by humankind.

Origins

As with every other creation, Chess gives the impression of having had an inventor, as in myths in which a god creates languages or other cultural artifacts. The first known tale about Chess's creation is found in a Muslim legend that dates back to pre-Muhammadan days, according to the historian Murray. It reports the history of Qaflan, a Persian philosopher who was asked by the Queen Husiya, daughter of Balhait, to invent "war without bloodshed." The philosopher asked the Queen to give him a gift in grains of corn upon the squares of the chessboard. On the first square one grain, on the second two, on the third square double of that on the second, and in the same way until the last square. The total of the geometrical progression is 2^{64}-1, or 18,446,744,073,709,551,615—a quantity that would cover England to a uniform depth of 38.4 feet in grains of corn. Poets never ceased to write legends about Chess: in 1763 Sir William Jones wrote a poem on Caissa, the nymph who was the means of teaching Chess to mankind.

Legends apart, *Chatrang Namak* (8th century B.C.E.) is the first written source explaining Chess rules and attributing its origins to India. Earlier sanskrit sources refer to *Chaturanga* (four angles), an early Chess ancestor in which four armies battle on a chessboard. Archaeological findings like the Butrint "King" (465 B.C.E.) are often uncertain. Because of their differential value, we need at least two figures to identify them as Chess pieces. Linguistic data are more interesting; the evolution of the term *Chaturanga* led to Persian *Chatrang* and Muslim *Shatranj*. The etymology of English term *Rook* is related to Sanskrit term *Ratha*, meaning "chariot." War chariots were used in Indo-European armies before they learned how to ride (as described in epic poems like the *Iliad*). Chess history can be useful in reconstructing ancient Indo-European institutions.

Starting from India, lexical data let us reconstruct how Chess spread across Asia to the Malay Islands, China, and Japan, starting new variants. The history of the term *queen* is interesting in understanding how Chess arrived in Europe. The piece was, in Sanskrit, the *mantrin*, meaning the *Raja*'s minister. The term was translated to Persian *farzin*, then became the arabian *firzan* or *firz*, meaning a vizier. This explains the Italian term *fersa*, which in the Middle Ages designated the piece we call the Queen. The term led to the French *vierge* (virgin). The feminization of the Indian piece *minister* was complete, and explains the modern Italian *donna* (woman). In Spanish and in English the vierge became a Queen, probably because of its position next to the King. Another explanation could be the political importance of Renaissance queens. The term remains *ferz* in Russian, thus indicating a possible second Chess route from Persia to Europe. A confirmation comes from *slon*, the Russian term for the bishop, which means "elephant"; like the Sanskrit *hasti*, persian *pil*, and Arabian *al-fil* (the elephant). The term became *alfil* in Spanish, in Italian *alfiere* (meaning ensign), and in French *fou*, meaning joker. The same linguistic data would seem to exclude an origin from the Byzantine game *Zatrikion*, which is similar to Chess. The link between the two routes has been found in Poland, where both European and Russian terms are present in Renaissance Chess, as in Jan Kochanowski's poem *Szachi*. Other hypotheses on Chess's relation with ancient Latin games, like the *Latrunculorum Ludus*, are neither proved clearly by archaeological findings nor supported by linguistic data.

Evolution

From *Chaturanga* to contemporary Chess, rules have different variants in relation to their geographical and historical development. In the Middle Ages, the old rules inherited from the Muslim world coexisted with modern innovations in codexes like the *Bonus Socius* (8th century). These codexes report a rich collection of Chess problems, often for gambling purposes. Some of them are classified as *Partito a la rabiosa*, referring to the modern movement of the queen. Still, the *Cracow Poem* (1422) reports many unfamiliar rules about the king's and queen's movement. Heterodox Chess, Chess variants, always coexisted with the official rules that represent just one of the ways in which the game evolved. We have heterodox chessboards, heterodox pieces like the Griffin and heterodox games like Kriegspiel. Nowadays, everyone can easily play old and new heterodox Chess, like Bobby Fischer's game on the internet.

Both the Catholic and the Orthodox churches condemned the game in the Middle Ages, thus proving the popularity of the game at that time. The Renaissance saw the standardization of rules across the European courts and international Chess activity began. Chess tractates developed Chess theory; in the 15th century, Juan Ramirez de Lucena wrote a treatise reporting both the old rules for the Queen's movement (*De Viejo*) and the new ones (*De dama*). Portuguese player Damiano published his chessbook in Rome (1512). Chess players attained a cosmopolitan reputation and often international contests were organized. At the court of Philip II of Spain, the great Ruy Lopez was beaten by Paolo Boi of Syracuse. The Italian player Gioacchino Greco was so popular that he was invited to England, France, and Spain to exhibit his talents. A lot of contemporary knowledge, openings (the first moves), and theoretical ideas in national schools of thought and traditions originate from this period.

Modern Chess

In modern Chess, theoretical innovations are related to the names of the greatest players and to the cultural

Chess has been popular since the Middle Ages, even though both the Catholic and Orthodox churches condemned it.

glories of their nations. The greatest players spoke Spanish and Italian during the Renaissance, French between the Enlightenment and Romanticism, English and German at the turn of the 20th century, and Russian after World War II. As the great world champion Aleksandr Alekhine noticed, these movements are related to artistic and cultural movement too. Philidor, a French composer and Chess player, first analyzed the pawn chains according to 18th-century rationalism; players like Labourdonnais or Mac Donnell developed the impetuous Romantic style, exemplified in historical games like Anderssen's Immortal or Evergreen. The positional school of Steinitz and Tarrasch posed some of the basis for modern Chess thinking and are related to Positivism; Aron Nimzowitsch, Richard Reti, and Aleksandr Alekhine developed the new "hypermodern" conception by reversing the value traditionally accorded to center occupation. In the same period, Picasso's Cubism posed a new representational convention, and Arnold Schoenberg invented the new dodecaphonic musical grammar.

In 1924, the World Chess Federation was founded, thus inheriting the experience of other informal organizations wiped out by World War I. At that time, the title of World Champion became formally recognized. Before that date, those considered world champions were Wilhelm Steinitz, from 1866 to 1894, Emanuel Lasker (champion 1894–1921), José Raul Capablanca (champion 1921–27), Aleksandr Alekhine (champion 1927–46, with a brief interruption by Max Euwe between 1935 and 1937). After World War II, Russian players Mikhail Botvinnik, Mikhail Tal, and Tigran Petrosyan took turns holding possession of the world title 1951–69. Boris Spassky obtained the title in 1969 and held it until 1972, when he lost the match to the American Bobby Fischer. This challenge inaugurated a new era in Chess and became a symbol of the United States–Russia Cold War. The young Fischer refused to play against Anatoly Karpov in 1975, probably because of psychological pressure. Karpov represented Russia until 1985, when he was defeated by Garry Kasparov. After the end of the Cold War, Kasparov broke his relations with the World Chess Federation (FIDE) and created his own organization. The world title was reunified in 2006, when Vladimir Kramnik defeated World Chess Federation champion Veselin Topalov. In 2007 Kramnik lost the title, beaten by Indian champion Viswanathan Anand.

Chess and Artificial Intelligence

In the 20th century, Chess became an interesting topic of discussion in research fields such as information science, linguistics, sociology, psychology, and philosophy. Chess is central in the pioneering research of Alan Turing, who wrote the first Chess program in 1951. Because of the lack of computers, he tested the algorithm manually against a young researcher, Alick Glennie. The machine lost. In the second part of the century, the Russian world champion Botvinnik, an engineer, worked on heuristic Chess algorithms; nowadays, brute-force calculus is more employed by programmers, thanks to the great improvements in computer execution time. In 1997, the purpose-built Chess computer Deep Blue won a match against the world champion Garry Kasparov. More recently, a commercial software program defeated world champion Vladimir Kramnik. During the World Title Match between Kramnik and Topalov, Topalov's coaches accused Kramnik of using a small portable chessboard during game breaks.

Both human and computer strength is measurable by the Elo score—the international standard of evaluation. Elo points are attributed or subtracted to a player's score in relation to opponent's strength and game result (win, draw, loss), using a complex mathematical formula invented by the american master Arpad Elo. The current World Champion Anand has a score of 2,800 Elo points, whereas contemporary software reaches an incredible score of 3,000. Nevertheless, Chess engines are not close to imitating human Chess logic: human players construct long-term plans, trying by method to start the antagonist on the way to the position they aim toward. Computers simply calculate every possible move to a certain depth: Beyond their calculus horizon, they know nothing.

Perspectives on Chess Meaning

In Saussure's work, Chess became a metaphor for the positional and differential conception of linguistic value. Hjelmslev developed the comparison with formalized languages like logic and mathematics. Chess became a model of meaning in early Structuralism. Even in the analytical tradition, Ludwig Wittgenstein was fascinated by the analogies between languages and Chess. He focused on rules; the failed attempt to reduce the rules of mathematics to ones of logic led the philosopher to consider the meaning of following the rules of different games in different situations. He argues that when one shows someone the king and says: "this is the king," this does not tell him the use of this piece unless he already knows the rules. With this model, like both Hjelmslev's and Saussure's, we are not capable of fully understanding how to choose between the possible strategies and plans permitted by the rules. A more suitable model can be found in Umberto Eco's works: According to him, in Chess, a given position conveys a series of optional moves, a set of possible responses, and a chain of foreseeable (or unforeseeable) solutions. The two players' evaluations can be, and effectively are, sensibly different. Eco agrees with Charles Peirce's pragmatic notion of meaning as "conceivable consequences."

The most important Chess philosopher was Emanuel Lasker. The World Chess Champion studied mathematics with David Hilbert and became a respected professor of mathematics at Heidelberg University. In his book *Struggle,* he developed many Chess ideas in his general philosophy. He noticed how Chess shows an aesthetic effect: what the move says, expresses, discloses, and announces—it is that which excites and stirs the spectator. The spectator enjoys not a game of Chess but the history and drama of the game in which a chessboard is merely the stage and the pieces its actors. He discovered a meaningful relation between position, game rhythm, and passions, and conceived the match as psychological warfare. He used to study his opponents' games in order to achieve a deep knowledge of their preferences about openings and game lines, thus discovering tactics psychologically disturbing to the enemy. In Alekhine's example, if a player prefers a defense because of its strength and security, then when the same defense is used against him, he will feel in trouble.

Lasker's concept of psychology was related to Brentano's theories and as such are perhaps outdated. Psychoanalysis discovered an importance in Chess quite early on; in 1931 Ernest Jones presented to the British Psycho-Analytical Society a work on the great American champion Paul Morphy. In a Freudian perspective, Chess is the sublimation of both aggressive and homosexual impulses. The great Chess player and New York psychoanalyst Reuben Fine extended this point of view, analyzing the life of many modern Chess champions. He also trained the young champion Bobby Fischer. His psychoanalytic point of view is rather old-fashioned. In spite of this, he underlined the relationship between Chess and mental disease, present in the works of contemporary psychiatrists like Dextreit and Engel.

However, contemporary cognitive psychology is more interested in the role of vision and memory with respect to Chess position, or in so-called intuition. Both psychological and sociological studies investigate the greatest champions' careers or Chess expertise in children. The gender problem is a good matter of discussion; sources report that in the Middle Ages, aristocratic women used to play Chess. In spite of this, Chess became a traditionally male competition. Nowadays, women are often seen as weaker players than men, and a women's world tournament exists. Still, the Hungarian Chess grandmaster Judit Polgár, the only woman on FIDE's 2008 Top 100 players list, currently refuses to participate in women's contests. However, differences between men and women at playing Chess are not cognitive but cultural, such as the aggressive attitude of many players and the sexism of the traditional Chess training environment.

Literature

Since the Middle Ages, Chess has been present as a theme in many epic or courtly love poems, as a symbol of either conflict or seduction. In *Tristan* (12th century), Tristram and Yseult play Chess on their journey to King Mark's court, during which they become lovers. The romance *Les Eschez Amoureux* describes in considerable detail a game in which a lady beats her suitor. In *Floire et Blanchefleur,* the hero is able to enter the Saracen prison in which Blanchefleur is held, thanks to winning a game against the porter. This poem became the model of many novels across Europe—an example is Boccaccio's *Philicopo.* The cliché of Chess as seduction existed even up to modern times, for example in the drama *Una Partita a Scacchi* by Giuseppe Giacosa (1875).

In modern times, the essay by Edgar Allan Poe, *Maelzel's Chess Player,* anticipated his detective stories and revealed that the famous Chess automaton known as the Turk, which also beat Napoleon, was a fraud. The absolute self-referential game logic is often parodied in novels; Lewis Carroll's *Through The Looking Glass* is a model for further thematic developments, as in Massimo Bontempelli's *The Chess Set in the Mirror.*

The same logic is perhaps the key to understanding the link between Chess and insanity, such as in works like *The Luzhin Defense* by Vladimir Nabokov and *The Royal Game* by Stefan Zweig. The latter is considered, by players, the best novel about Chess. At first, the reader sympathizes with the mysterious challenger against the arrogant world champion, but then is compelled to take the champion's side when the challenger shows signs of insanity. The theme of Nazism is also present in the short story, as in other novels like *The Luneburg Variation* by Paolo Maurensig, which was probably inspired by true World War II episodes, such as the death of many Jewish players, like the Polish player and problematist David Przepiórka (1942). In the same period, many of the world's great players became instruments of Nazi propaganda, and the same Aleksandr Alekhine was forced to write a delirious article on "Jewish and Aryan Chess," in 1941. Chess is present also in popular literature. Raymond Chandler, another Chess addict, characterizes his detective Philip Marlowe as a Chess lover in the *The Big Sleep.*

Fine Arts

From Arabian to Western middle age manuscripts, Chess is often represented in miniatures, having the same symbolic values attributed to the game in novels. Depicted Chess positions are often readable and testify to the game's evolution. Chess is a typical theme in *Still Life: In The Five Senses* by Lubin Baugin (1630)—chessmen enclosed in a Chess case are a symbol of the sense of touch. The theme also is present in contemporary still-life paintings, such as *The Queen,* by Audrey Flack (1976). *Chess Players* is another common theme in artist's works, from Ludovico Carracci (1590, now in Berlin, Gemaldegalerie) to Honoré Daumier (1865 Paris, Musee du Petit Palais).

Contemporary artists are more interested in Chess's geometrical features than in their symbolic meaning. Chessboards were present in the art of Kandinsky after he adhered to the principles of Bauhaus; we can find the same use in Paul Klee's *Super Chess* (1937). Avant-garde Chess sets were designed by both Man Ray and Yves Tanguy. Chess is a central path in the life and work of Marcel Duchamp, who was also a strong Chess player and a member of the French Olympic Chess team, captained by Alekhine. More recently, David Pelham created a minimalist acrylic Chess set in 1970; Cy Enfield created a commemorative Chess set for the occasion of the Fischer–Spassky match. However, Chess set design exists in every culture, from the abstract geometrical Muslim tradition to the realistic representation of middle age warfare in the Lewis Chess set (12th century), depicting Viking warriors, and the so-called Charlemagne set (11th century), probably realized in Amalphi.

Cinema

Like in figurative arts, Chess was also present in the origins of cinema: *A Chess Dispute* by Robert W. Paul dates back to 1903. Chess characterizes both the avant-garde, like the Expressionistic *Das Wachsfigurenkabinett,* by Paul Leni, in 1924, and in commercial films such as *The Lodger* by Alfred Hitchcock (1927), or *The Smiling Lieutenant* by Ernst Lubitsch (1931). In this period, *Chess Fever* by Vsevolod Pudovkin (1925) uses an avant-garde language to parody Chess obsession. The film also featured many Chess champions: Capablanca, Grünfeld, Marshall, Reti, Spielmann, Torre, and Yates.

A possible explanation for the presence of Chess in films could be that many famous actors and directors were known Chess addicts. For example, Humphrey Bogart is represented alone while studying a Chess position in Curtiz's *Casablanca.* Similarly, Stanley Kubrick inserts a game between a human and a machine in his *2001: A Space Odyssey* (1968); the position came from a real game (Roesch-Willy Schlage, Hamburg 1910). We find the same inquietude in *Blade Runner* by Ridley Scott (1982), where an android beats its human father at Chess, and then kills him. The metaphor of a Chess game can be found in other works by Scott, such as *Black Hawk Down* (2001). But the most interesting movie about Chess is perhaps *The Seventh Seal* by Ingmar Bergman (1957), in which a crusader—a knight—plays Chess against the Grim Reaper during the Black Plague. In this film, the game becomes a second narrative structure, a counterpoint to the plot. As in Kubrick's *Odyssey*, an actual game can be found in *Harry Potter and the Philosopher's Stone* (Jovanovic-Manzardo, Imperia 1967).

See Also: Ancient India; Game Theory; Human Relationships in Play; Inter-Gender Play; Luck and Skill in Play; Memory and Play; Play and Literacy; Russia.

Bibliography. Aleksandr Alekhine, *Ajedrez Hipermoderno* (Editorial Castilla, 1945); N.J. Cooke, R.S. Atlas, D.M. Lane, and R.C. Berger, "Role of High-Level Knowledge in Memory for Chess Positions," *American Journal of Psychology* (c.106/3, 1993); H.A. Davidson, *A Short History of Chess* (Greenberg, 1949); Umberto Eco, *A Theory of Semiotics* (Indiana University Press, 1976); Reuben Fine, *The Psychology of the Chess Player* (Dover Pub., 1956); Mike Fox and Richard James, *The Complete Chess Addict* (Faber and Faber, 1987); A.D. de Groot, "Intuition in Chess," *International Computer Chess Association ICCA Journal* (June, 1986); Louis Hjelmslev, *Prolegomena to a Theory of Language*, (University of Wisconsin Press, 1961); Andrew Hodges, *Alan Turing: The Enigma* (Burnett Books, 1983); D.D. Horgan, "Chess Expertise in Children," *Applied Cognitive Psychology* (v.4/2, 1990); Israel Albert Horowitz, *From Morphy to Fischer: A History of the World Chess Championship* (Batsford, 1973); N.V. Krogijus, *Psychology in Chess*, (R.M.H. Press, 1976); Emanuel Lasker, *Lasker's Manual of Chess* (Dover, 1925, repr. 1960); Edgar Allan Poe, "Maelzel's Chess Player," in *Complete Works* (Harvard University Press, 1902); P. Saariluoma, "Visuospatial and Articulatory Interference in Chess Player's Information Intake," in *Applied Cognitive Psychology* (Routledge, 1992); Ferdinand de Saussure, *Course de Linguistique Générale* [Course in General Lingustics, 1922] (Open court Classics, 1998); H.A. Simon, and F. Gobet, "Templates in Chess Memory. A Mechanism for Recalling Several Boards," in *Cognitive Psychology* (v.31/1, 1996); Gareth Williams, *Master Pieces* (Quintet Publishing Limited, 2000).

Francesco Galofaro
Bologna University

Chile

This South American country stretches along the Pacific Coast of South America, measuring 2,650 miles from north to south, but is, on average, no more than 110 miles wide. There had been a small indigenous population there for at least 11,000 years, with the first Spanish explorer arriving in 1535. The town of Santiago, now the country's capital, was founded six years later. Initially, settlers established farms using the local population as slaves to farm them. Chile became independent in 1810. Nearly 90 percent of the population lives in cities or towns.

The indigenous population used traditional musical instruments such as the *zampona*, the *bomba*, the *charango*, and the *quena*, and the "creole" population was involved in organizing masked dancing ceremonies. Many of the early migrants from Spain were from the Basque region, and this influence was seen by the playing of *pelota*, although today few people play this instrument. Horse riding and rodeos also date from this period. From the 18th century, flying kites became a popular amusement of wealthier Chileans, especially from September until March—it was said to have been introduced to the country by Roman Catholic monks. Gradually, kite flying came to be enjoyed by powerful people as well. There is a Chilean Kite Fliers Association, and in some competitions, five people compete against each other. There are also kites that have two lines so that two people can handle them. Activities were often organized by clubs and professional societies called *gremios*.

Later, during the 19th century, there were quite substantial numbers of English, Irish, and Scottish immigrants, especially in southern Chile around Puenta Arenas, and at the port of Valparaiso, near Santiago. The British established the Vina del Mar Lawn Tennis Club in 1881, opening tennis courts at the Valparaiso Sporting Club in 1910. The latter was also the location of the Valparaiso Golf Club when it opened in 1897, with the British community establishing another golf course in Santiago in the Prince of Wales Country Club. At around the same time, other games were introduced, including cricket, polo, horse racing, rugby, and soccer.

The first soccer game was played between British residents in Santiago in 1891, with a Briton called John Ramsay later deemed the "father of Chilean football"—the game at that time being entirely recreational. Since then, soccer has become the major recreational sport in the country, with boys and young men playing it in school teams and also in cities, towns, and the countryside. Other outdoor pastimes enjoyed by Chileans include jogging, basketball, beach volleyball, hiking, orienteering, and in the colder parts of the country, snow skiing, snowboarding, and tobogganing. Water-based activities, such as fishing, surfing, and water-skiing, are also popular.

French migrants brought *boules* to Chile, and Italians brought *bocce*. In the mid-19th century there was also a large number of immigrants from Germany, and they brought with them German customs and folklore festivals. Late in the 19th century, there was a sizeable migration from Russia and other parts of Eastern Europe. This led to Russian games and traditions, with the playing of Chess becoming popular in schools, and the establishment of the Federacion Deportiva Nacional de Ajedrez. For the board game Monopoly, there was a Chilean version called *Metropoli*, which featured important streets in Santiago.

The national folk dance, the *cueca*, involves dressing up by both men and women, and people trying to emulate the role of a rooster stalking a hen. The best examples of the *cueca* are said to be those on Chiloé Island on Independence Day each year, where there are also other festivities including log splitting.

Wargaming has also been popular since the 1920s, especially with wealthier and better-educated families. Initially there was great interest in the Napoleonic Wars, and also in the Wars of Independence, as well as Chile's War against Peru.

During the Pinochet dictatorship, because of Pinochet's great interest in Napoleon, Wargaming for the Napoleonic Wars again became popular. Since then there has been renewed interest in Conquistador-Inca Wargaming and also, more controversially for some Chileans, Che Guevara and various guerilla campaigns in Latin America.

The increased prosperity of Chile from the late 1980s—the middle class was estimated at about 35 percent of the population at this time—has led to the establishment of ice-skating rinks, bowling alleys, amusement arcades, and clubs that have billiards, darts, pinball machines, and jukeboxes. Computer games have also become extremely common, especially in urban areas.

See Also: Billiards; Bowling; Soccer (Amateur) Worldwide; South Americans; Traditional Cultures; Wargames.

Bibliography. Fernando Larraín Mancheno, *Fútbol en Chile* [Football in Chile] (Federación de Foot-ball de Chile, 1945); Him Webster, "The War Between Chile and Peru 1879–81," *Miniature Wargames* (June-July, 1984); Jane Kohen Winter, *Chile* (Marshall Cavendish, 1991); Gertrude Matyoka Yeager, "Chinganas (Saloons), Bailes Máscaras (Masked Balls) and the Prensa Chismosa (Gossip Press): Three Aspects of Creole Culture in Nineteenth-Century Santiago de Chile," *Studies in Latin American Popular Culture* (v.1, 1982).

Justin Corfield
Geelong Grammar School

China

Many of the games played in China date back to ancient times, and while some of them have detailed and complicated standard rules, others remain relatively simple, or have regional variations. Since ancient times, children have played with marbles, rattles, dolls, model soldiers, and kites. Other games such as Hide-and-Seek and the Cat's Cradle would also have played for centuries. During the Han dynasty (206 B.C.E.–220 C.E.), more complicated games came to be played, and many of these were developed during the Tang dynasty (618–907) and the Song dynasty (960–1279). Many children are still involved in making large kites, sometimes as big as 16 or 18 feet across.

Although traditionally made from paper or cloth, many kites nowadays are made from plastic, and can be used to twist and soar in the wind, with competitions in which kites are made to resemble birds, dragons, and sometimes fish, ships, or wild animals.

Certainly one of the best-known games played by Chinese people has been Mahjong. While rich people had Mahjong pieces made from ivory, it was also possible to make them from bone, bamboo, or wood. Played on square tables, Mahjong sessions lasted anywhere from an hour to days, and traditionally the game has involved gambling, with people often playing for high stakes. Certainly in early modern China—and in some stories from as recently as the early 20th century—people were known to gamble all their possessions, including their house, their families, and even commit themselves to years of servitude on the outcome of a game. This led many people to become critical of the game, as its gambling aspects came to be seen as more important than merely the skill and luck required to win.

In the eyes of some of the public, Mahjong became associated with the corruption of the era of the warlords in the 1920s and 1930s, and it was banned by the Communist government in China from 1949, although it continued to flourish in Taiwan and among the overseas Chinese communities.

Secret Mahjong

In spite of its ban, Mahjong continued to be played secretly during the 1950s and 1960s, although the noise of "shuffling" the pieces usually alerted neighbors to any game. From the 1930s on many Westerners associated with China started playing Mahjong in Western Europe and North America, sets being sold in the United States by Abercrombie & Fitch. So popular was it among non-Chinese in the United States that Eddie Cantor even recorded the hit single "Since Ma is Playing Mah Jong."

It is now, once again, played widely in China, with technology allowing for the making of more readily affordable pieces, and although gambling does take place, many people play it without any monetary stake in the outcome of the game. Indeed, in 1998, the China State Sports Commission published a new set of rules for mahjong that officially removed gambling and the consumption of alcohol and allowed players to compete in pairs, as with the card game Bridge. For people travelling, Mahjong sets often came in boxes, but to help increase the patronage of the game, from the 1980s, some plastic playing card manufacturers started producing Mahjong pieces on long rectangular playing cards; however, they lacked the character of the traditional pieces, which are now often made from plastic or resin.

Although Mahjong was certainly heavily associated with gambling during the 1920s and the 1930s, this was also the period where gambling dens and casinos flourished, with illegal betting taking place often with the connivance of the police or corrupt officials. This was especially true of the International Settlement of Shanghai, and more so the French Concession in Shanghai, where many laborers toiled all day to make money and doubled their wages or lost them all in games of Mahjong. This gambling permeates the novels of Andre Malraux set in Shanghai, and also the landlord class in the novels by Pearl S. Buck and Lin Yutang.

Chinese Chess

Another Chinese game that has also proved popular is *Xianqi*, or Chinese Chess. This game has some similarities with Indo-European Chess, except that the board has a river—symbolically the Yellow River—across the middle of it, and there are also cannons that can be fired from one end of the board to the other. This has led to the modification of Indo-European Chess called Gun Chess in which pieces can be taken without the need to move the piece doing the taking.

The other major variation from traditional Chess is that the king and his guards are not allowed to leave the palace, and there is no powerful queen. Xianqi pieces are generally made of wood (and nowadays of plastic) with the Chinese figure on each piece denoting its place in the game. Overall, the game became heavily associated with battle tactics, and although it was played by members of the ruling class in China, it was also extremely popular with poor people.

Indo-European Chess was played heavily in the Westernized parts of China and was so popular with the White Russian community in Shanghai that the world Chess champion Alexandr Alekhine even visited the city while on a tournament in the Pacific in 1933.

By contrast with Xianqi, the game Go became more closely associated with the ruling class in China, and it became expected that scholar gentlemen should be able to play. This was largely because of the use in China of a board with 19 horizontal and 19 vertical lines and 181 black and 180 white counters, providing a very high number of possible moves. Go was certainly being played in ancient times and is mentioned in the Analects by the great Chinese sage Confucius (551–479 B.C.E.).

By legend, it was supposed to be a game inspired by an ancient Chinese emperor to try to discipline his son, and the oldest games found by archaeologists date from the Han dynasty. The way in which you surround other pieces was seen by tradition as being the method used to control flooding, and certainly this representational use of it has become associated with the game. However, the game is certainly not unique to China and was played, with some variations, by the Incas and also as Mancala, by many Africans, who used stones or grain seeds.

During the Tang dynasty, the game Go started to be played in Japan, and indeed it is still often thought of in North America and Western Europe as a Japanese game. This is largely because of the role of Oscar Korschelt, a

A young Chinese boy plays with a Western-style notebook computer (note the Qwerty keyboard). The introduction of a vibrant capitalist economy in China in the late 20th century revolutionized daily life—and play.

German engineer, who helped popularize it in Europe after having worked in Japan from 1878 until 1886. His description of the game, first published in 1880, was the first detailed account of the rules published in Europe, and when sets were manufactured in Western Europe from the 1950s, its association with Japan, rather than China, led to some confusion over its country of origin. The Chinese were also, probably, the first to play the game Shogi, a form of Chess in which pieces are not taken but turned to work for the player who captures them. Again this game was transmitted to Japan and is often thought of as a Japanese game.

Playing With Pets

As with people all over the world, many Chinese kept pets and enjoyed playing games with them. However, since 1949, in order to reduce the population of stray dogs and cats in cities, the only animals allowed to be kept by people in urban areas were birds, and many of these are kept in elaborate cages. Owners teach the birds to sing, and the birds—in their cages—are often taken on walks, especially on particular days to parks, where the cages are placed near other birds in cages, and the birds compete with each other in songs and chirping. In Imperial China there was also a tradition by which scholars and members of China's ruling class, the Manchus, had crickets as pets. Indeed, the Emperor Hsuan Tung (Pu Yi, 1906–67) kept his own crickets, as did many of the officials at the Imperial Court. These were kept in small containers the size of a large coffee mug, which were often made from cane, and were allowed out under close watch, occasionally being used to take part in cricket "races" or sometimes "cricket fights" at which gambling often took place. This tradition has largely faded in China, although old cricket "cages" can sometimes be found in regional markets.

Sports tended to follow the traditional tests of strength and prowess, as with most other countries in the world, such as archery and wrestling. Some of the wrestling was similar to that in Central Asia, but martial arts such as taekwondo and judo had more firmly established rules and were as much for self-defense and fitness as recreation. There were also influences from the Mongols, who ruled China during the Yuan dynasty (1271–1368), and the Manchus in the Qing dynasty (1644–1912), who both came from a culture heavily reliant on horses, leading to many games and activities involving tests of horse riding skills.

Recreational Sports

It was not until the early 20th century that the school curriculum in schools across China started to introduce competitive and recreational sports. This curriculum has seen many Chinese boys and girls become active in these sports, with table tennis (or ping pong) becoming one of the most popular of these games. Ping pong was introduced into China in the 1950s, and it was in 1971 that a match between the Chinese and U.S. teams helped lead to an easing of tensions between the two countries.

China's great success in table tennis has seen it emerge as a game played by children and young people all over China, used as a test of agility and fitness rather than solely strength. Badminton and volleyball have also proven popular, and many boys play a variation of badminton that involves a much heavier shuttlecock, with the players standing in a circle and using their feet to keep the shuttlecock airborne.

Another similar game involving a ball has one child throwing the ball as high as he can into the air and naming a friend, with the other players having to stand around in a circle. The friend then has to catch the ball, go into the middle of the circle, and do the same again. If somebody does not catch the ball, they have to stand still while the ball is thrown at them.

The influence of the European powers in China during the 19th century did lead to many European and North American games coming to be played in China. Tennis and Croquet were both popular in the "Treaty Ports"—the ports where the European concessions were located. These were areas that were under European jurisdiction, and where most of the foreigners in China lived apart from many of the Chinese people until World War II. Many of these areas boasted their own tennis clubs, and some of the large European houses in Shanghai had their own tennis courts or Croquet lawns in the gardens. Indeed, there was even a tennis court in the Forbidden City in Beijing (Peking), and Pu Yi was playing a game there when news arrived in 1924 that he was to be evicted from the Imperial Palace, forcing him to move to Tianjin (Tientsin). In Hong Kong, controlled by Britain until 1997, and where there has always been a large European and North American population, there have been cricket and rugby clubs. In nearby Macao, gambling has long flourished, with some of the most lavish casinos in the world located there.

The construction of swimming pools in China in major cities from the late 1920s, and in many parts of the country from the 1960s, and the teaching of swimming at schools increased the number of people in China who take part in recreational swimming. During the 1960s, the Chinese leader Mao Zedong himself regularly swam in the Yangtze River, doing much to popularize swimming by older Chinese.

Although European games have become popular in China, traditional martial arts have tens of millions of adherents, and Chinese, especially older ones, can often be seen in the early morning exercising using deep breathing and hand movements to perform qigong, an exercise seen as increasing body strength and prolonging life. Some Western customs and games were introduced by missionaries and teachers during the 20th century, with people like Gladys Aylward (1902–70) using her initiative to keep the children occupied as she led 94 of them to safety away from the invading Japanese, a story retold in her book *The Small Woman* (1957) and the film *The Inn of the Sixth Happiness* (1958). The British academic and sinologist Joseph Needham (1900–95) was also involved in helping a group of schoolboys escape from the Japanese, having also to keep them occupied with various games as they made it to Chongqing (Chungking).

Playing cards were traditionally parts of games played by the wealthy, and some elaborate ones from late Imperial China have survived. For children from poor families, the equivalent of cards were often fashioned from paper, leaves, or bark and games of snap could still be played with even the most simple of items. As the manufacture of playing cards has become cheaper, from the 1970s, these became more and more accessible to most people in China, and with, from the 1980s on, factories printing playing cards for exporting overseas, playing games with cards has become more and more common. Indeed, there are a number of card games largely played only in China, and these include Atom, which involves three packs of cards; Bashi Fen ("Eighty Points"); Chinese Blackjack (similar to European/North American Blackjack but with slightly different ways of scoring); Fan-Tan, which traditionally involved heavy gambling; Four Color Cards; Gnau, which remains popular among the Chinese in Malaysia; Tichu, which combines aspects of Bridge and Poker; Tien Len, which originates in southern China and Vietnam; Winner; and Zi Pai, which uses a specially printed deck of cards.

In Shanghai, Bridge clubs operated during the colonial period, and older people there and in Tianjin and other former Treaty Ports still play Gin Rummy, Patience and Solitaire.

Storytellers and Puppets

In villages throughout China, some of the high points of the year were the visits by the itinerant storytellers, puppeteers, travelling theaters, and circus performers. These engendered in generations of Chinese a great interest in folklore and historical epics, and small children are regularly involved in role playing from some of the more famous stories such as that of Monkey, and also the heroes of the "Water Margin" during the Song dynasty, when villagers banded together to fight corrupt officials in a story not dissimilar to that in England of Robin Hood. These shows inevitably led to children playing with puppets—both glove puppets and marionettes—and also, for wealthier boys, Wargaming.

During the 1920s and 1930s, among families of expatriates in China and those of Westernized Chinese, the playing of European-style Wargames became important, with lead figures being used to reenact battles from Chinese history, and also from European history. These, and also model trains, aircraft, and other toys, were sold in hobby shops in Shanghai and other large cities, with the young J.G. Ballard in *The Empire of the Sun* (1984) devoting hours to making his model aircraft. Meccano also gained a large following during the same period, but after 1949, importing these toys became impossible, although they continued to be used in Taiwan, Hong Kong, and Macao. For the board game Monopoly, there was a Hong Kong version with streets in both Chinese and English, and in 2008 production of a world edition of Monopoly with Beijing, Hong Kong, Shanghai, and Taipei all represented began.

Youth Movements

The Boy Scout movement was established in China in 1912 by the Reverend Yen Chia-lin, and it was followed by the Girl Guide movement, with the General Association of the Scouts of China founded in Nanking in 1934. Both the scouts and the guides initially drew heavily from the European and North American expatriate population in China, especially in the Treaty Ports, but also from the children of Westernized Chinese families, and in particular Christian Chinese, and by 1941 it had 570,000 registered members. However, under the rule of Generalissimo Chiang Kai-shek in the 1930s, there was competition from the New Life Movement, which was established in 1934 as an adjunct of the Kuomintang (Nationalist) Party.

This movement involved boys and girls helping in the community, but also—on a political front—promoted modern ways and explained better hygiene standards and spoke out against foot binding and the like, as well as emphasizing Confucian values. During World War II, boys and girls from the New Life Movement were involved in work for the Nationalist government against the Japanese. After 1949 the new Communist government in China banned both the New Life Movement and also the Scout Association and the Guide Association, but the latter two organizations continued to flourish on Taiwan and in Hong Kong.

In Communist China, the Young Pioneer movement and the Communist Youth League were both established along the model of the Soviet Union, with its members symbolically wearing a red scarf, and these youth groups undertook similar activities to those of scouts and guides, although there was a political element to the training of the Young Pioneers. The Young Pioneers of China took over from various youth movements operating in Communist-held parts of China, and during the Cultural Revolution the group became known as the Little Red Guard movement, with the members of the Communist Youth League becoming the Red Guards as the social and recreational movement became intensely political.

Since the establishment of the market economy in China, and with increasing prosperity, there has been a decline in the number of children involved in the Pioneers, and many Chinese children are now involved in computer games, which have proliferated around the country. The increasing ease of access to computers has seen large numbers of Chinese children and youth involved in computer games; many games are now available with Chinese legends, with the stories of Monkey and the Water Margin being translated from folk tales and actual role-playing into a virtual setting. Also, from about 2004 on, some Chinese earn an income by playing these games and then selling the scores they have received to people overseas, who can then play these games at a higher level than would otherwise be possible.

See Also: Ancient China; Mahjong.

Bibliography. Stewart Culin, *The Gambling Games of the Chinese in America* (Kessinger, 2007); W. H. Fan and K. T. Fan, eds., *From the Other Side of the River: A Portrait of China Today* (Doubleday, 1975); Peggy Ferroa, *China* (Marshall Cavendish, 1991); Fung Shiu-Ying, *Chinese Children's Games* (ARTS Inc., 1972); William Hinton, *Shenfan: The Continuing Revolution in a Chinese Village* (Secker & Warburg, 1983); William Kesen, ed., *Childhood in China* (Yale University Press, 1975); Michael David Kwan, *Things That Must Not Be Forgotten* (Flamingo, HarperCollins, 2001); H. T. Lau, *Chinese Chess: an Introduction to China's Ancient Game of Strategy* (Tuttle Publishing, 2003); Li Cunxin, *Mao's Last Dancer* (Viking, 2003); Matti A. Pitkanen and Reijo Harkonen, *The Children of China* (Carolrhoda Books Inc., 1990); Sally Rodwell, *A Visitor's Guide to Historic Hong Kong* (Odyssey, 1991); Frances Wood, *No Dogs and Not Many Chinese* (John Murray, 1998).

Justin Corfield
Geelong Grammar School

Chinese Checkers

Chinese Checkers is a board game for two to six players that has its origin in the European game Halma. In 1928, the game came to the United States and was very popular throughout the 1930s. Players enjoy using various strategic skills to advance their marble game pieces to the opposite corner of their starting position, especially using their critical thinking, analytical, and motor skills. Chinese Checkers continues to be popular among game enthusiasts.

Halma was created in 1883 by a professor at Harvard Medical School named George Howard Monks. Monks called the game Halma, since it is the Greek word for jump, and because of his brother Robert's fondness of the British game Hoppity.

Chinese Checkers and Halma have three main differences. The players in Chinese Checkers typically use marbles as game pieces, the game board has holes instead of squares, and the game board has a six-pointed star shape, not a square design.

German Patent

The prominent German game company Ravensburg published and patented Chinese Checkers in 1892. The game was marketed with the name Stern-Halma, to incorporate *stern,* the German word for "star," and to emphasize the game board's hexagram shape. In 1909, game manufacturer Spears and Sons promoted Stern-Halma in England and had some modest success with British sales.

Chinese Checkers came to the United States in 1928 with J. Pressman and Co. as the Hop-Ching Checker Game. Brothers Bill and Jack Pressman later changed the name to Chinese Checkers to reflect the growing worldwide interest in the Far East. At this time, events like the finding of King Tut's tomb in 1922 and the introduction of Mahjong in 1923 contributed to the public's attraction to Chinese Checkers.

Chinese Checkers became widely popular in the United States in the 1930s. During this period, many toy companies produced the game and marketed it under such intriguing names as Man Dar-In, Mah Tong, and Ching-Ka-Chek.

One particular game manufacturer, the Topeka company called L.G. Ballard, marketed their own highly successful brand called Star Checkers. The various names of Chinese Checkers continued until 1941 when game manufacturer Milton Bradley received a patent on Chinese Checkers. Even with this patent, modern versions of Chinese Checkers still exist, such as the game Rubido. Rubido has similar game pieces and board design, but has four levels of difficulty.

Like other board games, Chinese Checkers requires some strategic planning by players to win. Since the object of the game is for players to move all of their game pieces to the opposing corner, it is advantageous for players to

A vintage set of Chinese Checkers, which was at the height of its popularity in the United States in the 1930s. It teaches critical thinking, analytical, and motor skills.

advance quickly by jumping over other game pieces to an empty space. Some players like to make the game even more challenging by playing the fast-paced version of Chinese Checkers, where players can move their game pieces over nonadjacent pieces, or the capture version of Chinese Checkers where the pieces that are hopped over become captured and collected by players.

Many players consider Chinese Checkers a classic game, since it has been around for so many decades and can be enjoyed by families. It is suitable for young players and is relatively easy to learn. In addition, it teaches critical thinking, analytical, and motor skills. The most important aspects are that Chinese Checkers is fun and continues to delight game enthusiasts.

See Also: Checkers and Variations of; Mahjong.

Bibliography. Frank Hoffmann, Martin Manning, and Frederick J. Augustyn, Jr., *Dictionary of Toys and Games in American Popular Culture* (Routledge, 2004); David Parlett, *Oxford History of Board Games* (Oxford University Press, 1999).

Dorsia Smith
University of Puerto Rico, Río Piedras

Cityscapes as Play Sites

The city as a place for children's play is a barometer for changing perceptions about safety, community, and trust in any society. The city as a place for adult play is a barometer for changing perceptions about leisure, adult pleasures, public decency, and morality. The two are inextricably linked. Where a cityscape transforms itself into a public arena for adult-only forms of play, whether in the shape of casinos or lap-dancing clubs, that city's urban environment's suitability for children's play of course declines proportionally. Where playgrounds or other opportunities for children's play survive in cityscapes, they are increasingly compromised by parental fearfulness of escalating risks to children from other city dwellers, whose interest in children cannot be trusted. Cities as places where adult "play" pushes the boundaries of moral acceptability cannot also afford spaces for "innocent" childhood play without significant tensions existing.

These tensions are often mapped onto cityscapes as differentiated territories, where "red-light" districts are geographically as separate as possible from "child-safe" areas, with various recognizable gradation zones in between, and where socioeconomic distinctions differentiate neighborhoods on the basis of social class, wealth, deprivation, crime rates, level and kind of policing, and so on.

Free Running and Parkour

In the literal and figurative border zones created in this way, hybrid forms of play often thrive, as most remarkably with so-called Free Running and Parkour (an activity with the goal of moving from one point to another as efficiently and quickly as possible, using mainly the abilities of the human body). Free runners and Parkour practitioners, called traceurs (male) or traceuses (female), use their athleticism to move at speed through cityscapes, where walls, fences, gaps between buildings, and so on, are obstacles to be gracefully negotiated.

Largely young person's pursuits, Free Running and Parkour exist in a liminal zone between childhood and adulthood and typically reclaim the cityscape for a pure form of playfulness, uncompromised by the tension between adult-only interests and children's safety. It does not matter to a free runner or traceuse whether the cityscape being traversed is the rooftops of a downtown red-light district or a children's playground in the suburbs. The cityscape is reduced to obstacle course, undifferentiated by socially determined meanings.

With worldwide numbers of practitioners limited, not least by the extraordinary level of agility required, Free Running and Parkour are revealing instances of an extreme transformation of cityscapes into play sites that is partly explicable as a cultural response to the compromising of more conventional play sites by adult fears about unsafe urban environments. Free Running and Parkour resonate as distinctive early 21st-century cultural inventions because they transcend such tensions by reducing the cityscape to an abstraction. Meanwhile, media-based leisure pursuits, especially the playing of computer games, have moved most children indoors and out of the real public cityscapes.

Trend Toward Indoor Play

The widespread relocation of play indoors throughout the developed world was an inexorable trend of the late 20th century, as technologically mediated forms of play developed from the growing attractions of burgeoning mass media and then accelerated exponentially in the era of the computer and internet. For a period in the late 1970s and early 1980s, these technologies also underpinned the explosive development of video arcades, which concentrated new forms of semipublic electronic play in urban spaces, leading in some societies to a "moral panic" about the supposed effects on young people and the associated risks of congregating in these places, reinforced by sensationalized stories of long hours spent on obsessive or addictive behavior.

But the rapid development of computer game technologies quickly moved this form of play beyond the unwieldy arcade games cabinets onto personal consoles and computers in the home. Fears about supposed effects and addictive behaviors persisted of course, but these quickly became domestic issues and had increasingly less to do with concerns about new forms of "dubious" public space for these new forms of playful activity.

So urban public space by the end of the 20th century, in much of the developed world, had been largely evacuated as far as children's play was concerned, except where fenced and monitored playgrounds persisted in appropriate neighborhoods, and even those tended to be used by parents at specific times of the day, when safety in numbers delivered some sense of collective security. The enticements of technologically enhanced forms of play in convenient domestic settings rendered children themselves complicit in this widespread retreat from the cityscape, with the latter becoming increasingly itself the object of dystopian visions in popular culture, such as several of John Carpenter's unnerving films (e.g., *Assault on Precinct 13* and *Escape from New York*).

The way in which American popular culture in particular, at this period, amplified dystopian fears of the cityscape's imagined decline into sordid, crime-ridden haunts for the morally suspect reveals the degree to which the real cityscape had been deeply compromised as a hospitable environment for any playfulness other than adult leisure pursuits.

Urbanism and Play

Three concomitant phenomena have arisen from this in relation to urbanism and play: (1) an increasing emphasis on creating new kinds of "child-safe" play spaces within the proliferating urban regeneration initiatives that are reclaiming the cityscape from those dystopian visions, underpinned as they were by the reality of socioeconomic decline in postindustrial economies; (2) a growing interest in the make-believe urbanism of computer game cityscapes, as a displacement from the real into the virtual; and (3) some promising experiments with taking the digital back out into the real cityscape again in some newly playful ways.

The first of these emergent phenomena frequently redefines children's play in urban environments within the framework of new community arts. The regenerated cityscape typically includes the outcomes of cultural regeneration policies, not just urban planning per se, and new community arts initiatives are encouraged by the creation of new spaces and facilities. Throughout the developed world, urban community cultural development schemes have blossomed, with community arts projects for young people often high on their agendas.

From the Village of Arts & Humanities in North Philadelphia, Pennsylvania, to Artmakers Trust in Hamilton, New Zealand, place-making and community art-making are being combined in an applied playfulness that gives young people new places to go in the cityscape. "Playing" via community arts significantly redefines what we mean by play, of course, but the reclamation of urban places for young people engaged in pleasurable forms of making and doing of these sorts is distinctly different from the more highly codified appropriation of play as sport, the other way in which the regenerated cityscape's improved facilities can offer somewhere for young people to play.

Virtual Reality Play

The increasingly hyper-real make-believe urbanism of computer games affords an entirely new understanding of the cityscape as a play site. Cinematic realism and three-dimensional graphic sophistication are producing imaginary cityscapes of increasingly immense proportions within the computer or games console, and multiplayer online games provide for an increasing sense that these virtual cityscapes are actually inhabited. Where the computer game and the virtual world merge, the digital cityscape becomes an intriguing blend of recognizable reality, social interaction, and fantasy. Still at a fairly early stage of development, this phenomenon of make-believe urbanism is likely to intensify, with consequences as yet unseen for our understanding of how real and virtual cityscapes may increasingly impel each other's development.

In the meantime, a number of innovative experiments have deliberately taken the digital out into the cityscape in order to clarify where we might be headed. One of these, a project of the Patchingzone initiative associated with the V2 media research centre in Rotterdam, focused specifically on play and gaming. Called "Go for IT," this 2009 project was based on an "Interactive Urban Game," played in a public space in the south Rotterdam city district of Feijenoord, and engaged young people in a series of interconnected encounters with "wearable" digital technology, e-fashion, and mobile communications. Projects like this are an indication that play is finding its way back out onto the streets.

See Also: Adventure Playgrounds; Playground Movement, U.S.; Psychological Benefits of Play; Unstructured Play.

Bibliography. Joy Keiko Asamen, Mesha L. Ellis, and Gordon L. Berry, eds., *The SAGE Handbook of Child Development, Multiculturalism, and Media* (Sage, 2008); Sheridan Bartlett, et al., *Cities for Children: Children's Rights, Poverty and Urban Management* (Earthscan Publications Ltd., 1999); F. von Borries, S.P. Walz and M. Böttger, eds., *Space Time Play: Computer Games, Architecture and Urbanism, the Next Level* (Birkhäuser, 2007).

Dan Fleming
University of Waikato

Civilization (I, II, III, IV)

Civilization is a computer and video turns-based strategy/simulation game series developed by Sid Meier and first published in 1991 by MicroProse. It is one of the most successful strategy game franchises of all time, selling over 8 million copies and spawning four sequels, several expansion packs, and innumerable clones. Civilization has been released on numerous game platforms, including Atari ST, Amiga, Super NES, PlayStation, PlayStation 3, Nintendo DS, and Xbox 360, but its most famous incarnation is as a PC and Mac game. It remains popular, appearing third in IGN's top 100 games of all time 2007, the second highest position for a computer game after Tetris.

The game traces the emergence of embryonic civilizations from their prehistoric origins (4000 B.C.E.) through to the nuclear age and beyond. After adopting a nation, players compete against other computer-controlled nations on a randomly generated world map. The game begins with only one or two settler units, which can be used to explore the local environment, transform the landscape, and found cities. Once founded, the resources of cities can be diverted toward different activities, such as creating more playable units of different kinds including military units, creating city improvements such as temples, harbors, and later power stations and airports; improving the wellbeing of citizens; and researching new technologies.

At first the game is invariably spent establishing and managing a handful of cities, setting research and development targets, and revealing more of the map through exploration, allowing the local environment to be converted into productive land. But sooner or later the embryonic civilizations in the game-world encounter each other, and competition over the limited resources—pursued through both war and diplomacy—commences. Victory is achieved either by destroying all other civilizations, reaching the end of the modern era with the highest score (2100 C.E.), or developing the technology to build and successfully launch a spaceship that reaches Alpha Centauri.

One of the most distinctive features of Civilization is its knowledge and technology mapping system. By devoting resources to research, civilizations eventually "discover" new technologies that can be exploited in different ways. These discoveries are dependent on one another in a hierarchical tree; thus the player cannot begin working on advanced technologies, such as nuclear power, before working their way through more basic technologies, such as the alphabet, navigation and map-making, and later metallurgy, chemistry, and nuclear physics. Technological development holds the key to exploiting the game world, allowing the player not only to develop more advanced combat units, but also to keep their citizens happy and their civilization well-managed. Thus the game is more a matter of a race for knowledge than a race for power and military domination. But this pursuit of knowledge is tempered by the necessity to maintain and develop functioning city-states. The player must therefore also devote resources to developing civic amenities, building wonders of the world, and developing trade and diplomacy. Different forms of governance can also be deployed through periodic revolutions to help maintain the emerging civilization.

Civilization was widely praised on its release for its ambitious scale, absorbing game play, and vast historical scope. Its potential educational uses were also widely discussed. Sequels were met with similar acclaim, each retaining the general game play, while strengthening the game mechanics, adding detail, and improving the audio and visual appeal. The original top-down map of the game world was superseded by an isometric map in Civilization II, and by a fully-rendered three-dimensional map in Civilization IV. Anomalies in the game mechanics that allowed ancient combat units to defeat modern combat units were removed in Civilization II.

Culture was introduced in Civilization III, with each city rated for its cultural attainment and influence, allowing conquest of other cities through cultural takeover. Civilization III also introduced new ways of winning, including cultural domination. Civilization IV made religion a more central component of the game, with seven world faiths replacing the generic temples of the original game, changing the balance of diplomacy within the game. It also introduced a multiplayer mode, allowing players to compete against one another online.

See Also: Academic Learning and Play; Age of Empires; Amiga; Play and Learning Theory; Sim City; Tetris.

Bibliography. David Choquet, ed., *1000 Game Heroes* (Taschen, 2002); Guinness World Records Ltd., *Guinness Book of Records Gamer's Edition 2008* (Guinness World Records

Ltd., 2008); J.C. Herz, *Joystick Nation: How Videogames Gobbled Our Money, Won Our Hearts, and Rewired Our Minds* (Abacus, 1997); IGN Entertainment, *IGN's Top 100 Games,* http://top100.ign.com/2007 (cited July 2008); King, Lucien, *Game On: The History and Culture of Videogames* (Universe Publishing, 2002); Kurt Squire and Henry Jenkins, "Harnessing the Power of Games in Education," *Insight* (v.3, 2003).

Luke Tredinnick
London Metropolitan University

Clapping Games

Throughout history, some elements of children's play have remained universal. Children bounce balls, jump rope, clap hands to rhythmic sequences, but the way they play or the chants they chose recite tend to be particular to their own countries and customs. Children, especially in urban environments, adopted clapping games when resources were minimal. Gender often shaped play: while boys received resources to play ball games, girls adopted hand-clapping games because no equipment was required. Whether waiting for class, sitting on a stoop, or just passing time, girls could break into spontaneous clapping rhyme games or hand rhythm sequences, embellishing rhymes that have sometimes been traces back in history for hundreds of years. All that was needed was a friend who either knew the rhymes and moves or was willing to learn them.

Classic clapping games, which were learned after finger and singing games, often had unknown origins and endured from generation to generation. Some clapping games, call-and-response songs, and dances are derived from African music and traditions. Environment dictates the rules of most street games, and clapping games do not just involve playing a game—they involve social interaction and concentration. Unlike organized sports, street games provide children the opportunity to make up the rules and create new chants relevant to their experiences. Although simple rhymes that do not require coordination and communication skills can be played by toddlers two years of age and older, girls often learn chants at about five years of age, and continue to learning more intricate rhythms from partners.

The finger game Pat-a-Cake, Pat-a-Cake, Baker's Man, has been attributed to 17th-century English writer and poet Tom D'Urfrey. The 19th-century American writer Lydia Maria Child described a variant form of the clapping game: "Clap the hands together, saying, 'Pat a cake, pat a cake, baker's man; that I will, master, as fast as I can;' then rub the hands together, saying, 'Roll it, and roll it;' then peck the palm of the left hand with the fore-finger of the right, saying, 'Prick it, and prick it;' then throw up both hands, saying, 'Toss it in the oven and bake it.'" The fundamental essential for clapping games has always been two individuals sitting opposite of each other.

Then, each person begins by clapping their hands together at the same time, then, each person reaches out with the right hand to clap her partner's right hand. Then, each person claps her hands again and then reaches out with the left hand and claps her partner's left hand, and then the sequence repeats, clapping on the beat. Some games require that players pat shoulders, hands, or thighs, alternating with clapping hands with a partner. Clapping one or two hands at a time, backs of hands, the palms of hands, double claps, hands up, and hands down, are all variations that made each rhyme distinctive. With some clapping games, the goal is to progress to a faster pace both in the song and claps. Repetition, coordination, and duration give the chants used in clapping games rhythmic conviction and power.

See Also: Africa, Traditional Play in; Finger Games; Girls' Play; Singing Games; Spontaneous Group Play; Street Games.

Bibliography. Lydia Maria Child, *The Girl's Own Book* (Edward Kearney, 1843); Thomas D'Urfey, *The Campaigners* (Chadwich-Healy, 1996); Joanna Cole and Stephanie Calmenson, *Miss Mary Mack and Other Children's Street Rhymes* (Morrow Junior Books, 1990); Kyra D. Gaunt, *The Games Black Girls Play: Learning the Ropes from Double-Dutch to Hip Hop* (New York University Press, 2006); StreetPlay.com, "Clap and Rhyme," *Street Rhymes Around the World,* www.streetplay.com/thegames/clapandrhyme.htm (cited August 2008).

Meredith Eliassen
San Francisco State University

Coleco

While Coleco Industries produced a wide variety of toys and games until its bankruptcy in 1988, including the

Cabbage Patch Kids dolls, the company is best known for its home videogame system, ColecoVision. As such, Coleco had a lasting and meaningful impact on the landscape of video games during the early 1980s. Coleco Industries, which was originally named the Connecticut Leather Company, was founded in West Hartford, Connecticut, in 1932 as a shoe leather company by Russian immigrant Maurice Greenberg. Moving into plastic molding in the 1950s, Coleco eventually sold off their leather business and became a publicly traded company. By the beginning of the 1960s, the company was one of the largest manufacturers of above-ground swimming pools. In 1976, after an unsuccessful attempt to enter the dirt-bike and snowmobile market, they released Telstar, a clone of the home PONG unit being sold and marketed by Atari.

Despite the fact that Coleco was certainly not the only company releasing home PONG clones, they enjoyed moderate success and went on to produce nine more varieties of the Telstar unit. In 1978, unfortunately, as the home videogame market moved to programmable, cartridge-based game units, Coleco was forced to dump over a million obsolete Telstar machines at a nearly crippling cost of more than 20 million dollars.

Coleco president Arnold Greenberg ignored this near disaster and directed his research and development team to begin work on a new home videogame system, the ColecoVision, which he felt would set the standard in graphics quality and expandability.

Released in the summer of 1982 at a retail cost of $199, the ColecoVision had the ability to display 32 sprites on-screen at the same time, along with a 16-color on-screen palette, out of a total of 32 colors. In addition, the ColecoVision featured three-channel sound. The key to this new system's success, however, as with many of the new home systems being released at this time, was the included cartridge. In the case of the ColecoVision, Coleco successfully negotiated the right to release the smash arcade hit Donkey Kong.

Beyond Donkey Kong, 12 additional cartridges were released along with the ColecoVision. While Atari had pioneered the licensing of arcade games for home play with Space Invaders, Coleco made this a key part of their strategy, aggressively seeking licenses for coin-operated games instead of concentrating on developing original games.

Hitting the market in the midst of the public relations war between Atari and Mattel, the ColecoVision sold for around $100 more than the Atari 2600, but $35 less than Mattel's Intellivision. The price point, combined with the inclusion of Donkey Kong, made the ColecoVision an instant success. The first run of 550,000 units sold out almost immediately. By Christmas of 1982, one million of the systems, along with more than eight million cartridges, had been sold.

After the initial release of the ColecoVision in 1982, Coleco immediately released the Atari 2600 Converter. Selling for $60, the Atari 2600 Converter allowed users to play Atari 2600 cartridges on their ColecoVision. The Atari Converter was amazingly popular, and went on to sell 150,000 units in the first three months after its release. However, as one would expect, its release resulted in a flurry of litigation, starting with a $350 million lawsuit from Atari over patent infringement. Coleco countersues for $550 million, claiming that Atari was infringing on U.S. antitrust laws. The two companies eventually reached a settlement, resulting in Coleco paying royalties to Atari on every Atari Converter unit sold.

By the end of 1983, the ColecoVision had sold more than 1.5 million units, surpassing the number of units sold by the Atari 2600, the Mattel Intellivision, and Atari's new 5200 Supersystem. In addition to the Atari Converter, the 29 game publishers who were producing cartridges for the system give the ColeoVision the largest game library of any console on the market at the time.

After the success of the ColecoVision, Coleco decided to invest not in the production of a new home game system, but in a home computer system instead. This was a logical step for Coleco as they, along with the other major home videogame system developers, were beginning to suffer financially as consumers turned to home computer systems, such as the Commodore VIC-20 or the the Commodore 64. Coleco's answer was the ADAM computer. The ADAM computer was released as two separate versions. One version of the ADAM was a stand-alone unit, while the other version, called Expansion Pack #3, involved a series of add-ons to the existing ColecoVision game system.

The hardware for both units included 64k of RAM and 32k of ROM (expandable to 144k). Interestingly enough, the hardware also included a built-in word processor. The stand-alone system featured two game controllers, and an external cartridge slot into which ColecoVision cartridges could be inserted and played. Both systems included a full-sized keyboard, a digital tape drive, and a large printer that also served as the unit's power supply.

By late 1983, Coleco had received a delayed approval from the FCC on the ADAM design, and the company frantically began mass production to meet the 400,000 preorders that retailers were demanding before the pivotal Christmas season, with a retail price of $600 for the stand-alone unit, and $400 for the ColecoVision add-on package. Unfortunately, public reaction to the ADAM was mass indifference. Sales were vastly below what Coleco had originally predicted. Out of the preorders, only 100,000 eventually sold. The primary problem for the ADAM's low sales was that it was remarkably buggy. One of the most dramatic problems was that the machine emitted a magnetic pulse when it powered up, erasing any tapes accidentally left in the drive. Matters were made worse by the fact that many of the ADAM manuals instructed users to put the tape in the drive before actually turning the computer on.

Eventually, 60 percent of all ADAMs were returned to stores as defective. In 1984, with the rest of the home videogame market in a downward spiral, the consumer electronics division of Coleco lost over $258 million dollars. In an effort to bolster sagging sales, the retail prince of the standalone ADAM unit was reduced to $300. However, not even this price reduction, in addition to a billion dollars in Cabbage Patch Kid sales, could save the company from the losses it incurred as a result of the abject failure of the ADAM. By 1985, the ADAM and ColecoVision line of electronic devices was abandoned by Coleco. Shortly thereafter, in 1988, Coleco itself filed for Chapter 11 bankruptcy.

See Also: Arcades; Dolls, Barbie and Others; Mario.

Bibliography. Winnie Foster, *Encyclopedia of Game Machines Consoles, Handhelds & Home Computers 1972–2005* (Magdalena Gniatczynska, 2005); Steven Kent, *The Ultimate History of Video Games: From Pong to Pokémon* (Prima Communications, Inc., 2001).

Ethan Watrall
Michigan State University

Colombia

This country, located in the northwest of South America, has a population of 44 million (2007), with 6.7 million living in the capital Santa Fe de Bogotá (generally known as Bogotá). Over half the population has an indigenous background, and as a result some pre-Columbian games and pursuits are still played in the country.

Some of these—similar to Tiddlywinks—involved the use of clay flippers, now often replaced with plastic in bright colors. There are also board games similar to those used by the Incas in Peru, where dice are thrown and the score allows contestants to move colored seeds or small shells around a board, the winner being the person who encircles the other. Musical instruments were similar to flutes or recorders made from hollowed wood. Many of the skills taught to boys involving the use of slingshot and hunting have long ceased to be practiced except in rural areas.

The arrival of the Spanish changed society in Colombia by introducing many European customs and musical traditions. The great wealth of the Spanish settlers in Bogotá and Cartagena saw a sophisticated society where there were regular balls—even masked balls—and theatrical performances. Chess has been popular with both wealthy and poor, and in 1939 Dr. Alexsandr Alekhine played a "blindfolded" tournament at Buenaventura in March 1939 during his tour of Latin America. The Federacion Colombiana de Ajedrez still oversees Chess in the country.

Although children in Colombia have played universal games such as Marbles, Hide-and-Seek, and Hopscotch, with the increase in schools in the early 20th century, there was a move toward organized activities and a promotion of recreational sports, including soccer, which has now become the most popular recreation with boys and young men throughout the country. Boxing is common in poor communities, with some seeing it as a potential career after the success of some Colombian boxers.

There was a Colombian version of the board game Monopoly—each color group represented streets in Bogotá, Cali, Cartagena, Medellín, and other cities. However, the popularity of board games has declined with the emergence of youth clubs that encourage playing pool, skateboarding, and rollerblading. There have been a number of amusement arcades and bowling alleys built, but even these have had a decline in popularity with the emergence of computer games. Traditionally, Wargaming was popular among the Spanish elite, and much of this focused on European scenarios such as the battles in medieval Spain and the Peninsula War in Spain. In more recent times, there has been greater interest in Colombian history, including role playing for the Conquistadors such as Gonzalo Jiménez de Quesada.

See Also: Bowling; Peru; South Americans, Traditional Cultures; Wargames.

Bibliography. John Bale, "International Sports History as Innovation Diffusion," *Canadian Journal of History of Sport/Revue Canadienne de l'Histoire des Sports* (May 1984); Clive Gammon, "Cradle of Champions," *Sports Illustrated* (November 1980); Sarah Ethridge Hunt, *Games and Sports the World Around* (Ronald Press Company, 1964); Glenn Kirchner, *Children's Games Around the World* (Benjamin Cummings, 2000).

Justin Corfield
Geelong Grammar School

Common Adventure Concept

The common adventure concept emerged in the 1970s. Focusing on mutuality and democratic "leaderless" outdoor activity at the lowest possible cost, it has remained a model of noncommercial group activity since. While every group activity that shares cost, planning, and responsibilities without having a designated and compensated leader could technically be called a common adventure, the model is used mainly by clubs and universities who want to encourage their students or members to go on outdoor trips.

An early form of the common adventure concept was developed almost simultaneously at various American universities beginning in the late 1960s and early 1970s. Most notable among the early proponents of the concept is Gary O. Grimm, who served as Outdoor Program Coordinator at the University of Oregon. Grimm wrote a paper titled "Union Outward Bound: An Educational Experiment" in 1970, which can be regarded as the first theoretical basis for the common adventure concept. The paper draws on B.F. Skinner's psychological theories and is based on an antiauthoritarian belief in the benefits of a "learner-controlled" environment. While the paper does not mention the term *common adventure*, many of the ideas that inform the concept can already be found in his paper.

The term *common adventure* was first introduced in 1972, when Richard A. Wyman wrote a paper focusing on the legal ramifications of the common adventure concept for University of Oregon. Wyman takes the term from the 1930s court decision *Murphy vs. Hutzel*, in which the judge decided not to grant any damages to the suitor on grounds that both the plaintiff and the accused had been "common adventurers" and had thus shared responsibility. Wyman argued that stressing the aspect of a joint enterprise might protect the university's outdoor program from lawsuits. He did not, however, recommend relying on this exclusively, pointing to the weakness of his defense and the possibility of charges of negligence that could be brought, if the court ruled that the university program did not provide its participants adequate supervision and leadership. As a result, Wyman advised that program personnel should not be paid by the university in order to avoid claims of negligence under common carrier law, one of the aspects Wyman was most concerned about.

Both of Wyman's suggestions were later misunderstood, leading others to develop two principles coming originally from a legal perspective but entering the level of general ideology of the common adventure concept. These principles stated that personnel could not be paid for their participation in common adventure trips (if they were employed by a university or club they had to participate in their off time) and that personnel could not share their expertise while on a trip.

Not only did the latter go against the original idea underlying the concept, but both of these points were invalidated on a legal level in a court decision in the 1980s, when the court ruled that participating in trips was a "natural extension" of the program personnel's job. As a result, many universities introduced written waivers signed by the participants. The misconceptions going back to Wyman's paper, however, still remain in the common adventure community.

Outdoor Education Programs

The term *common adventure* entered the wider field of college and outdoor education programs when it was used in a paper cowritten by Gary Grimm and Harrison H. Hilbert, the founding director of the Idaho State University Outdoor Program. The paper, which is entitled "An Operational Definition and Description of College Outdoor Programs," was read at an international conference of the Association of College Unions in 1973. The paper not only introduced the term, but also brought the concept to a wider base and attempted to give guidelines to other colleges who wished to establish similar programs.

The common adventure concept's rejection of "authoritarian" leaders on trips runs throughout this paper: The underlying idea Grimm and Hilbert formulate is that people who are trained accordingly are capable of solving problems on their own rather than relying on somebody else. They consider an outdoor environment the perfect area for self-guided problem-solving. The training Grimm and Hilbert refer to happens on trips or in preparation as members who already possess certain skills teach untrained members.

Moreover, since every member on the trip has different skills, "natural leaders" emerge from the group in situations where their expertise is needed, only to reintegrate afterwards. The antiauthoritarian approach of the common adventure concept goes so far that people who come up with ideas for trips and advertise them on special message boards are referred to as "trip initiators" rather than as leaders. This is to ensure that it is not "their" trip, but rather the group's, and that they have no special role on the trip. They merely provide the initial idea, which, however, may be modified to something quite different during planning, as Watters points out.

See Also: Anti-Competition Play; Cooperative Play; Experiential Learning Definitions and Models; Hobbies; Kayaking and Canoeing; Organized or Sanctioned Play; Original Play; Play and Sports Education; Play as Education; Play as Entertainment, Sociology of; Sociological Benefits of Play.

Bibliography. Gary O. Grimm, *Union Outward Bound: An Educational Experiment* (University of Oregon, 1970); Harrison H. Hilbert and Gary O. Grimm, "An Operational Definition and Description of College Outdoor Programs," www.isu.edu/outdoor/great.htm (cited June 2008); Ron Watters, "Revisiting the Common Adventure Concept: An Annotated Review of the Literature, Misconceptions and Contemporary Perspectives," *Proceedings of the Annual International Conference on Outdoor Recreation and Education* (Association of Outdoor Recreation and Education, 1999).

Johannes Fehrle
Albert-Ludwigs-Universität

Congo, Democratic Republic of

The third largest country on the African continent, Congo occupies over half of the Congo River basin. It was, as the Congo Free State, a possession of King Leopold II of Belgium. Earlier, in 1908, it became a Belgian colony called the Belgian Congo, and after independence in 1960, it became the Republic of the Congo. From 1971 until 1996, the country was known as Zaire.

There have been many traditional games in the country, and perhaps the best-known is *Mankata,* which involves making a hollow in the ground and then placing stones around those of one's opponent in order to capture their pieces. It is very similar to the Ethiopian game *Gabata,* and the Japanese game *Shogi,* and there are several versions of it in different parts of the Congo. Other Congolese games that have survived are *Nzango, Minoko,* and *Mangola.* Collecting shells used to be more than a hobby, with some shells serving as the local currency in the Kingdom of the Kongo in the 15th and early 16th centuries.

There are also many local crafts involving metalwork and bronze casting—gold and ivory were rarely used—but much of it is concerned with wood carving, especially fashioning large wooden masks known as *mbuya,* which were then used for dancing. The masks for the Pende tribe are particularly grotesque and are believed to be the inspiration for paintings by the Spanish artist Pablo Picasso.

Many are decorated with raffia, leaves, and feathers. The Bakuba and the Liba tribes have slightly different customs and very different masks. Music accompanying the dancing has also been very popular, with jazz and recordings of local vocalists thriving since the 1950s. For girls and women, sewing, embroidery, and weaving brightly colored cloth remain popular pastimes.

During the period of Belgian rule, the country was a rich source of rubber, which was used to make bouncing balls and other toys, initially used mainly by Belgians. The colonial society led to the introduction of Wargaming using lead figurines, Meccano sets, and also Chess and card games. In 1940, there were 10 social and sporting clubs in Leopoldville (now Kinshasa). Since independence, these games have been followed by the Zairean elite, especially those who have studied or lived abroad. Many of the children of the elite, and large numbers of poor boys and young men, follow or play soccer, and makeshift soccer games can be found in every town and most villages in the country.

See Also: Africa, Traditional Play in; Belgium; Chess and Variations of; Soccer (Amateur) Worldwide.

Bibliography. François Bontinck, "Les Makuta Dans le Passé" [The Makuta in the Past], *Zaire-Afrique* (June–July, 1987); S. Comhaire-Sylvain, "Congolese Games," *Zaire* (April, 1952); Pius Théophile Muka, *Evolution du Sport au Congo* [Evolution of Sport in the Congo], (Editions Okapi, 1970); Peter Townshend, *Les Jeux de Mankala au Zaire, au Rwanda et au Burundi* [Mankala games in Zaire, Rwanda and Burundi], (Centre d'Études et de Documentation Africaines, 1977).

Justin Corfield
Geelong Grammar School

Cooperative Play

Cooperative play can be conceived of as an entertaining way to obtain readiness for life, work, and love. In a more historical sense, it can be defined as a quick sketch of society's most sublime and ridiculous desires and dreams.

According to the rules of evolution, selection takes place when different types of individuals compete against each other to survive. Certain kinds of individuals outcompete others by reproducing faster and transmitting their characteristics to the next generation.

For many authors, this mechanism is called *survival of the fittest*, a term coined by Herbert Spencer in his *Principles of Biology* and used later by Darwin as a synonym for natural selection. This metaphor is no longer used by modern-day scientists, who prefer to use the term *natural selection* to describe the resulting process by which those who are better prepared tend to survive. The term *better prepared* can have many interpretations. Some people equate the term *survival of the fittest* with survival of the strongest or survival of the most aggressive. However, it is not true that competition is humankind's first law. It is acceptable to use the term *survival of the most cooperative* under certain circumstances. The goal for evolution is selection, not the mechanisms by which it is achieved.

Life requires a dynamic combination of competition and cooperation, yet few studies have systematically evaluated that combination. Cooperation is a biological and social process of achieving results by combining the actions of different agents. In a broad sense, agents do not have to be either rational individuals or friends in order to cooperate.

Competition and cooperation do not necessarily have to be divergent strategies. Agents can be groups, sport teams, bacteria, or enemies in a war. Although those who cooperate tend to exhibit higher levels of trust, all that is needed to develop cooperation is a previously unknown number of interactions between participant agents. In sports teams, whether they are formally constituted or not, a problem arises when the quest for self-interest by each participant leads to a poor outcome for the whole group.

On a sports team, players are supposed to compete against each other for a place in the next match, but at the same time, they have to cooperate with teammates in order to win that match as a group. In this type of a situation, self-benefit is mediated by the benefit of others. It is not infrequent that the temptation to defect from others is stronger in terms of the short-term rewards for the defector. This is known as a social trap, occurring when individual agents betray partners to

On a sports team, players compete against each other for their place in the next match, but have to cooperate to win.

get the best slice of the cake, with negative long-term effects. In these cases, we should not blame the defector, attributing his defection to "weakness of spirit" or a poor system of values. Social order, in the form of formal or informal rules, normally defines the system of rewards for each social situation. People learn how to evaluate those rewards and act accordingly. If competition is—according to capitalistic rules of social organization—the engine for social life, then specific activities in every sort of life are meant to be devoted as manifestations of that goal.

The Effect of the Future

The secret for cooperation to thrive without central authority is what Robert Axelrod calls "the shadow of the future." This means that the weight of the next state, relative to the current situation, has to be large enough to make the future important. In other words, in a determined situation an agent cooperates only if he or she sees that there is a future possibility for getting rewarded because of his or her present act. That reward has to be large enough to make this agent delay his or her complete satisfaction now and wait for the next several interactions. What makes agents cooperate is merely the possibility of future encounters.

Following this reasoning, another way to define cooperation is by describing it as the process under which two or more agents combine their actions and work together, once it is defined that the payoff for an infinite number of interactions will be higher than the payoff for just one or a few present interactions. In other words, there is a higher probability for future payoffs from working together than exists if everyone works for their individual interests only.

Is this a selfish approach to relationships between agents, whether they are human beings or not? Probably yes. But it can be viewed as a realistic approach. In essence, every human being gets into situations under a selfish rationale: to win, to have fun, to show off, to defeat others, and so on.

There is nothing beyond human nature and social organization there. But people learn very quickly that the possibility to stay and play for an extended periods of time only occurs if they cooperate with others. For most children, cooperation during playtime works, and rewards them in the long term, in the form of friendships or avoided punishments. If kids can share a swing, they can enjoy it longer. As stated before, society normally defines the rewards for each situation, and people learn very quickly how to gain those rewards. The current organization of society rewards immediate gratification to the detriment of future payoffs: Act now, call now, win now! People are continuously forced to live in the fast track, a never-ending present of instant gratification and consumption. This model of social organization is good for the economy, but not for its people. The effect of this way of thinking has been destructive in terms of the environmental effects.

Play reflects this reality. A sort of social autism, in the form of a lack of subjective awareness of others' intentions, is prevalent in most everyday play activities. Cooperative play has to be fostered because of its intrinsic dilatory individual gratification. Put in brief, in a world of egotists competing against each other to survive, who needs to play cooperatively?

Survival and Cooperation

What society believes in and acts upon is not a series of genetic programs, triggered by individual cells and DNA. Beliefs and behaviors are the result of historical interactions between agents. The relation between human beings and the environment is characterized by mutuality and reciprocity: human beings (in fact, all organisms) seek out and at the same time actively adjust their behavior to environmental features or affordances. During this process, the environment is transformed by human beings on a very active and never-ending interplay. Interactions with the world are recorded in the form of cultural meanings.

There is no human activity out of social boundaries of meaning and ideology. From a phylogenetic point of view, human beings developed strategies to overcome genetic fates as competition long ago. Nowadays, a social order based on pure competition between individuals, groups, or societies is the result of historical injustices in the way the means of production are distributed. It is not only the result of genetic forces against which human beings are helpless.

As asserted by Aristotle in his *Metaphysics*, cooperative construction of truth is indeed the construction of an organized world of meaning. Activities in which people have the chance to interact, with or without rules, serve themselves as "natural" opportunities to nurture and reproduce both cooperative and competitive practices using different strategies. Cooperation plays an important role in survival. This phenomenon influences the basic mechanisms of reproduction, mutation, and selection as much as competition does.

Cells have to cooperate in order to generate organisms and in turn, organisms do cooperate to get healthy groups and species. In the case of human beings, nature has become social. Natural order is the social order. An ecological scale of social events should consider only whole organisms, not sets of attached biological entities. For example, senses are not only light input channels but interrelated active systems that provide and seek meaningful information from other social agents. This active process makes adaptation and living in the world possible.

Social Skills

One of the major contributions of John Dewey to American education is the assertion that children can learn social skills by working together in cooperation. Of course, those social skills are constructed within a system of meanings inserted into a specific ideology. Play is always attached to a particular historical moment, as in the case of a ball game played by ancient Mayan and Aztec cultures in Mesoamerica. The social meaning of that game is very different from Maya beliefs to modern soccer organizations, since both social situations have very different cultural roots and meanings. As exemplified by Jerome Bruner, children from Tengu, New Guinea, play competitive games that end up with no winners. The aim is to have fun and exhibit certain social skills, not to defeat the opposite player. Bruner believes that this dynamic could be an explanation as to why adults in Tengu society do not compete against each other in the way adults in Western societies do. For Bruner, children's play reflects prevailing ideals in adult society.

Cooperation demands that a new system of beliefs about what is important for society be developed and transformed into play situations. For example, diversity is a consequence of cooperation between any sort of individuals who have different ways of interpreting and living in the world. Nonetheless, many people prefer that schools break students into ability-based groups so that students can progress at different rates and get the kind of academic help they need. At first glance, this differentiation between human beings with different abilities or conditions sounds appealing and rational. However, solidarity arises when everyone understands that it is for the well-being of humanity that we have to face our common problems as a group. Hiding out individual differences is useless in play situations. Rewarding bunches of "differentiated and talented" individuals is not helpful in fostering cooperation. In terms of evolution, diversity is healthy and is an asset for social capital that, in turn, plays a vital role in the development of more cooperative relationships within groups and organizations. Cooperation improves the mechanisms to develop effective self-direction.

Cooperative Play Defined

Cooperative play is a sequence of activities between two or more agents in which every piece of activity is harmonized in order to achieve a previously negotiated goal. It is different to parallel play, where agents share objectives but not activities, and to associative play, where agents share activities as affordances but not objectives. During an activity involving cooperative play, every playing agent has to not only be aware of the activities displayed by the rest of agents, but also be aware of the common goals the participants agreed upon. The emphasis is on play rather than competition.

Some additional conditions must be met in order to consider an activity as cooperative play: first, it becomes clear from the beginning of the interaction that the pursuit of self-interest leads to a poor outcome for all participants. In cooperative play, the rules are defined as being strongly dependent on each other's strategy, and the payoffs consequently depend on the movements of every player.

Environment fosters the characteristic habits of expansive thinking and complex problem solving. In most situations, environment can be characterized as the others that are a vital part of one's strategy. In the case of human agents, intellectual curiosity can easily be satisfied if cooperative play is required. Each participant normally seeks paths of inquiry and interest with the help of others. There is a decisive need for open-mindedness as a tool that combines flexibility for problem solving and accepting differing points of view as viable solutions. Critical thinking and respect for evidence as a valid way to reshape one's own opinions, in the form of "what if," can be easily fostered by cooperative play.

It can also be established that a connection exists between the extent of cooperative tendency of play and the level of role reversal and mind reading. In role reversal, every player has to figure out or assume what the other player would do in a particular situation (walking in someone else's shoes), witnessing his or her own behavior from another side. Consequently, role reversal can convey significant insight and transformative learning during play. Mind reading is the capability to think in advance about what others are about to do. This natural empathy is greatly exercised during cooperative play.

In cooperative play, the payoffs for players need not be the same or symmetrical. The theoretical distribution is defined at the beginning of the interaction, in the form of rules, and is controlled afterward by the very dynamics of play. This attribute emphasizes that every player is rewarded in terms of his or her own subsequent interactions and based upon his or her level of participation and, in the case of human agents, the level of compromise with predetermined rules.

Does cooperative play promote mediocrity? It may, in the form of self-limiting activities in which players might minimize their own performance, seeking out obstacles as causes for failure. This can happen because of a need for risk avoidance, maintaining a minimum level of control, and protecting self-esteem. But this can occur only with intense competition, where the biggest or strongest agent always wins and everybody agrees with that uneven outcome. There may be competition involved in play, but the outcome of the competition should not be losing and sitting out the rest of the game. When everyone knows how to win and has the same opportunity to do so, cooperative play guarantees the same level of excitement and compromise as competitive play, and all this can be done without the frustration and sense of abandonment that competitive play supposes. For example, switching teams ensures that every player eventually ends up on a winning team.

Cooperative play need not be considered desirable from the point of view of the society. Most forms of corruption are excellent examples of cooperative play, and school bullying is cooperative most of the time. In the beginnings of the capitalist system, trust in commercial transactions was based upon an implicit recognition of mutual dependence and cooperation. This was not necessarily meant to be a fair relationship between the poor and the rich.

To this extent, it is recommended that a central authority exists to define which forms of cooperation are valid, depending on environmental, social, and historical conditions. Cooperation cannot be individually defined, and it can be hard for an isolated individual to foster cooperation in a hostile environment. For example, many schools have eliminated grades or student ranking, since this sort of classification system works against the very spirit of cooperation.

Cooperative play defines participants as belonging to a group in which everyone shares a set of goals and activities, emphasizing participation, challenge, and fun, rather than having the goal of defeating someone. With a central authority, participants learn how and when to "cooperate" with other participants, doing the same kinds of activities and viewing them as "more fun" when everyone has a role in the activity.

In conclusion, cooperative play can be conceptualized as a way to change the modes by which society reproduces relationships between human beings and with the rest of the world's species. Cooperative play can be oriented toward the goal of promoting peace, justice, respect for individual differences, quality of life, solidarity, and mutual understanding among human beings.

See Also: Academic Learning and Play; Fantasy Play; Game Theory; Play as Learning, Anthropology of; Team Play.

Bibliography. Robert Axelrod, *The Evolution of Cooperation* (Basic Books, 1984); Jerome Bruner, "Play, Thought, and Language," *Peabody Journal of Education* (v.60/3, 1983); K.H. Rubin, *Children's Play* (Jossey-Bass, 1980); Robert Wright, *Nonzero: the Logic of Human Destiny* (Vintage Books, 2001).

Mauricio Leandro
City University of New York

Cossacks (Napoleonic Wars)

The first title in the Cossacks series was released in April 2001 by Strategy First Inc. and later re-released in April 2002 by CDV Software Entertainment AG. The game was developed by Kiev-based GSC Gameworld. Cossacks is a real time strategy (RTS) game set in 17th- and 18th-century Europe. In terms of gameplay, Cossacks follows the established conventions of the RTS genre: Players gather resources (gold, wood, food, stone, iron and coal) and use them to construct buildings and military units, which are then sent out to attack enemy armies and buildings.

Like other RTSs, Cossacks places a particular emphasis on resource management, but unlike the majority of RTSs, units require constant feeding of resources. If the faction runs out of resources, a penalty is applied. If a player runs out of gold, for example, military units that require maintenance will mutiny. One aspect of the game that sets it apart from the majority of RTSs is its historical setting. Players can choose from one of 16 factions: Algeria, Austria, England, France, Netherlands, Piemonte, Poland, Portugal, Prussia, Russia, Saxony, Spain, Sweden, Turkey, Ukraine, and Venice. Each faction has its own selection of military units that adequately matches their historical equivalents in function. Military units are divided into four categories: infantry, cavalry, artillery, and naval.

Like their historical counterparts, infantry form the backbone of the army, and though they are not as fast and maneuverable as the cavalry or as powerful as the artillery in the damage they inflict, infantry can withstand considerable punishment and are essential for taking over enemy villages.

One of Cossacks' main selling points at the time of release was its ability to field up to 8,000 units simultaneously. Another important feature of the game was the use of organized unit formations. Aside from titles in the Total War series (that are not strictly RTSs as they have both a turn-based and real-time component to them), no previous RTS offered the opportunity to form individual units into larger formations. In Cossacks, players can assign a specific number of individual units to a formation of 15, 36, 72, 120, or 196 units, as long as a commanding officer and musician are included. These can be controlled as a single entity, and once troops are grouped in the correct numbers, players can form their troops in line, column, or square formations that have an important impact on their performance on the battlefield. This creates a very different brand of tactical engagement from the RTSs of the time. With previous titles like the popular Age of Empires series, combat was more of a messy affair, with players sending out groups of units at their foes without having control over how the troops are ordered while moving or in combat.

Cossacks II: Napoleonic Wars is the first full-blown follow-up to Cossacks, released in April 2005 by CDV Software Entertainment AG and developed by Strategy First Inc. Napoleonic Wars automates the resource-gathering aspect of the game, leaving players to focus more on troop movement and battles. But the biggest leap forward in terms of game-play comes in the way troops are managed on the battlefield. Napoleonic Wars delivers a more decisive simulation of battles in the period by grouping units into corps of 120 troops each and putting greater emphasis on the importance of timing volleys correctly than its predecessor. The game does a great job of delivering the feel of Napoleonic warfare: thousands of brightly colored, tightly packed ranks of troops unleashing volleys of musket fire in clouds of billowing smoke at oncoming walls of bayonets.

See Also: Civilization (I, II, III, IV); Wargames; Warhammer; World of Warcraft.

Bibliography. Cossacks II: Napoleonic Wars Official Site, www.cossacks2.de (cited July 2008); Daniel Mackay, *The Fantasy Role-Playing Game: A New Performing Art* (McFarland & Company, 2001); Lawrence Schick, *Heroic Worlds: A History and Guide to Role Playing Games* (Prometheus Books, 1991); Andreas Jahn-Sudmann and Ralf Stockmann, eds., *Computer Games as a Sociocultural Phenomenon: Games Without Frontiers, Wars Without Tears* (Palgrave Macmillan, 2008); J. Patrick Williams et al., eds., *Gaming as Culture: Essays on Reality, Identity and Experience in Fantasy Games* (McFarland, 2006).

Gordon Calleja
IT-University of Copenhagen

Costumes in Play

When we hear the word *costume*, most of us think of young children dressing up as their favorite superhero or cartoon figure while engaging in fantasy play, but the use of costumes in play does not belong solely to the young. In fact, costumes can be a large and vital part of the culture of play from infancy through adulthood. If we ask ourselves the question, "How does one pretend to be something or someone else?," the answer might likely include the use of a costume. Most of us have made use of a costume during fantasy play or as part of a holiday celebration as children or as adults.

The definition of the term *costume* used throughout this writing refers to a style of dress or components of dress worn to portray the player as a particular character or genre of character other than their regular persona in informal and formal play experiences. In this sense, the role of costumes in play experiences is that of a tangible, concrete support tool that scaffolds the game or transports the player into the chosen role. It is through an examination of play over a lifetime that we can see the importance of costumes unfold in many forms and uses.

Children and Costimes

In childhood, children engage in fantasy and dramatic play, often utilizing a costume during play experiences. In her classic text *A Child's Work*, Vivian Paley illuminated the important role of fantasy play in early childhood. Paley's rich, descriptive stories involve the reader in the look and feel of young children's fantasy play. The roles of play props, including costumes, make their appearance as a mechanism for assisting the child at play—a device allowing the player to delve deeply into their play role or character. As Bodrova and Leong noted, in early childhood, most children prefer to engage in play that has a topic that is familiar to them and, as such, may often make use of costume materials that are representative or realistic in nature. The wide utilization of commercially available prop boxes in early childhood education classrooms reinforces the use of representative costume play; a firefighter box includes the necessary costume pieces, which differ from the costumes in the box used for playing storekeeper.

In addition to representative costume use, young children often utilize their creative capacities by employing the power of their imaginations to create costumes out of everyday items; for example, a blanket can be used as a superhero cape or as a veil for a bride on her wedding day. During childhood, costumes appear in impromptu and structured play experiences and during secular and nonsecular holiday celebrations as children seek to explore the world, including the world of imagination.

Adolescents and Adults

As children grow, play during the adolescent and adult years continues to explore the use of costumes. As with children, adult use of costumes can be seen during holiday celebrations or during informal and formal play experiences. Adult costumes can be prepackaged, manufactured sets or a variety of items brought together for use by the player. A Star Trek convention in the United States or a Manga gathering in Japan are just two examples where one can find adolescents and adults exploring the use of costumes in play. In fact, a relatively new genre, titled Cosplay, delves into the costume and play experience of adolescents and adults. Cosplay, a contraction of the English-language words costumes and play, describes a performing art experience where a player takes on the persona of a character, utilizing costumes and other relevant props. Players can engage in cosplay at both formal and informal events with other cosplay enthusiasts.

Another genre of adult play and costumes can be seen at virtually every major sporting event: the team mascot. Sport team mascots are a part of virtually all levels of professional and student genres of sporting activities and typically involve the use of costumes in interactive play experiences that can be either structured or impromptu. As the player takes on the role of a character or mascot, the costume serves to scaffold the play experience by transforming the player into the desired role. The benefit of the costume use can be experienced by others beyond the player, as the costume serves to alert play observers to the play roles under performance.

The Role of the Costume

Crossing the generational lines of childhood and adulthood, one can examine the role of costumes in the performing arts, spanning the genres of dramatic theater, improv theater, and musical theater. The role of the costume in these venues can be as much about the audience's perception of the character as well as the artist's perception of the character or play role. From informal dramatic play experiences in early childhood to the formal genre of musical theatre, the use of costumes assists in creating rich, visual, and imaginative experiences for the players and their audience. Costumes have a role in transporting players and audience members into new ways of thinking, speaking, perceiving, and acting.

If costumes are chosen and/or created by the player, the costume, as well as the play experience, is intimately related to the very definition of the player. However, costumes chosen for use by someone other than the player may not necessarily be considered part of a pure play experience. Pure play, or play for play's sake, is something that can only be defined by those at play. Costumes, as a part of the pure play experience, are a supportive tool employed by the player as part of the overall experience. The role of the costume, as play itself, needs to bear personal meaning to the player. In crafting an understanding of the role of supportive play materials, the significance of a costume in play is best left to the role of the player.

As a player dons the red blanket that serves as a superhero cape or the manufactured animé cosplay costume, it is the player's prerogative to explore the costume's many affordances; perhaps even those beyond the original intent. In this manner, the costume can further the player's opportunity for self-expression and overall enjoyment of the play experience. Depending on the play experience and the player, the choice of costume can be a spontaneous decision or a carefully crafted selection based upon the needs of the player, the play experience, and the play character. Costumes provide players, as well as play observers, with a tangible entry point for beginning a play experience or extending a play script in new directions.

See Also: Fantasy Play; Play as Catharsis; Play in the Classroom; Pretending.

Bibliography. Elena Bodrova and Deborah Leong, *The Tools of the Mind Project: A Case Study of Implementing the Vygotskian Approach in American Early Childhood and Primary Classrooms.* (International Bureau of Education Publising, 2001); Vivian Gussin Paley, *A Child's Work: The Importance of Fantasy Play* (University of Chicago Press, 2004); Lenore Terr, *Beyond Love and Work: Why Adults Need to Play* (Scribner, 1999).

Angela Eckhoff
Clemson University

Counter-Strike

Counter-Strike is a multiplayer first-person shooter game (FPS), initially developed as a modification (mod) for Half-Life, one of the most acclaimed single-player FPS games of all time, by Minh Le and Jess Cliffe in 1999. The game rapidly gained popularity with the online FPS community, leading Half-Life developers Valve to employ Le and Cliffe to further develop the game and eventually bundle it with later versions of Half-Life, distributed on Steam, Valve's digital distribution platform.

Counter-Strike is an online multiplayer game with no single-player content (although a single-player version called Counter-Strike Condition Zero was released in 2004). The game takes place on a series of "maps," or small areas in which two teams, Terrorists and Counter-Terrorists, compete over a number of short rounds (usually lasting two to three minutes) to complete a particular objective. The two most common objectives are: bomb defusing and hostage rescue. In the bomb defuse scenario the terrorist side has to plant a bomb, which is carried by one of the players to one of two bomb sites situated on the opposite end of the map from their spawn point, while the Counter-Terrorists try to defend the two bomb sites from being bombed. If the Terrorists plant the bomb, the Counter-Terrorists have a predefined number of seconds to clear the bomb site of Terrorists and defuse the bomb.

A spawn point is the area where players start off after dying. In some online FPS games, spawning is continuous, meaning when a player dies, they automatically return (respawn) in a predefined or self-chosen (depending on the game) location. In Counter-Strike, once a player dies they have to wait for the next round to respawn and rejoin the game. In hostage rescue scenarios, Terrorists need to defend a number of hostages, while the Counter-Terrorists attempt to rescue the hostages and bring them back to their spawn area. In all scenarios, a team can also wipe out the opposing team, unless that team has planted a bomb, in which case the bomb has to be defused for the Counter-Terrorist side to claim victory.

At the start of each round players may buy a primary weapon, a sidearm (pistol), armor, grenades, and other equipment such as night vision goggles or defusal kits. Both teams start with a basic pistol and 800 credits, allowing them to buy a better pistol, flak vest, grenade, or piece of equipment. The outcome of the first few rounds tends to tip the balance in the favor of one team, as the amount of money each player has depends on their performance in the previous round, mostly related to the amount of kills they attained, and modified by whether their team won or lost. All other things being equal, the losing team will find it harder to catch up, since it will have inferior weapons and equipment to the opposing team.

Counter-Strike maps are relatively small. The severity of damage incurred from even one shot can be fatal. When these qualities are combined with the fact that players do not respawn in the same round they are killed, it makes for a sense of consequence to one's actions that is unmatched in most popular multiplayer FPSs, and that allows for continuous respawning on bigger maps.

Movement in Counter-Strike consists of running (the default mode), walking, crouching, and jumping. Players cannot lean sideways, throw themselves on the ground, or sprint, as is now becoming commonplace in most FPSs games. The most recent version of Counter-Strike, titled Counter-Strike Source, has not changed the game play in any significant way. These factors have not, however, dissuaded the online Counter-Strike community, and the game is still considered one of the most popular and widely played games around the world, with a regular presence at all major pro-gaming tournaments.

See Also: Mortal Kombat; Play Fighting; Team Play; Wargames; Warhammer.

Bibliography. Daniel Mackay, *The Fantasy Role-Playing Game: A New Performing Art* (McFarland & Company, 2001); Lawrence Schick, *Heroic Worlds: A History and Guide to Role Playing Games* (Prometheus Books, 1991); Andreas Jahn-Sudmann and Ralf Stockmann, eds., *Computer Games as a Sociocultural Phenomenon: Games Without Frontiers, Wars Without Tears* (Palgrave Macmillan, 2008); J. Patrick Williams et al., eds., *Gaming As Culture: Essays on Reality, Identity and Experience in Fantasy Games* (McFarland, 2006).

Gordon Calleja
IT-University of Copenhagen

Cracking the Whip

Cracking the Whip, or versions of it, have been popping up in schoolyards and backyards for centuries, as paintings from as far back as the 1500s depict contestants of all ages taking part in the action. Also known as Smack the Whip, it is an outdoors-only and wildly tuned-up version of Follow the Leader (Whether He Wants You to or Not!).

The premise for the game is quite simple, and yet more than a bit complicated at the same time. One person is chosen to be the leader, and several others line up behind him or her, each holding on to one another (the second person in line holds on to the leader). As the game begins, the leader attempts to shake off his or her followers by running quickly or slowly, twisting, turning, doing double-back movements to fake them out—anything that can be imagined and physically performed. His hangers-on do everything they can to hold on, but must copy his movements. Should any player lose their grip and fall off, they are eliminated, as are any other players behind them. Those that manage to hold on until either a predetermined period of time passes or the leader gets too tired are declared the winners. Should the leader shake everyone off, he or she is the victor. For obvious reasons, it is best to play this game outside, in an open area—preferably one that is not too wet or muddy.

One of the first recorded images of this contest comes from the Fleming artist Pieter Bruegel's 1560 work *Follow the Leader*, which depicts several people in a row, holding on to one another. A few centuries later, in 1872, Winslow Homer put together his own painted canvas creation. Titled *Crack the Whip*, it pictures several young boys running along, joined at the hands. Both of these paintings extol the long-lasting aspect of the game, probably because of its simplicity—just about anyone can play it at any time, provided that everyone is about the same size and there is enough open space to have fun.

Because of its unchallenging nature in the social and psychological senses, Crack the Whip is more commonly found as an undisciplined schoolyard competition rather than in the more organized setting of a classroom or physical education class. The game does not allow for a great deal of social interaction, except for children encouraging one another to hold on so no one gets thrown off. Children may learn the social aspect of congratulations, giving each other a "way to go!" message for either throwing all others off or hanging on all the way through.

The psychological benefits of the game are not many, but they are important. For example, a youngster might plot out his or her movements ahead of time, trying to out-think his opponents in the back. The fact that he or she must throw them off to escape gives extra incentive to try new things (movements) to escape or put more and more effort into old motions. The followers have their own mental game to play as well, as holding on to the last might impress their friends and classmates with their intestinal fortitude. Being thrown off may undermine their "toughness" in the social setting.

See Also: Boys' Play; Original Play; Play and Power, Sociology of; Play and Sports Education; Play as Competition, Psychology of.

Bibliography. Joan Baxter, *The Archeology of Childhood: Children, Gender and Material Culture* (AltaMira Press, 2005);

Elliott Avedon Museum and Archive of Games, "Crack (or Snap) the Whip," www.gamesmuseum.uwaterloo.ca/VirtualExhibits/Brueghel/whip.html (cited July 2008); Barrie Thorne, *Gender Play: Girls and Boys in School* (Rutgers University Press, 1995).

Jason Norman
Old Dominion University

Cribbage

No one knows exactly when Cribbage was invented. The rules were formalized in the 17th century by English poet Sir John Suckling. Cribbage is a game that uses a standard deck of 52 cards and a board with holes in it and pegs to keep score. Games are normally played to 60 or 120 points. Cribbage can be a two- or four-player game, with the two-player version generally being more popular. The four-player version uses two teams of two.

It is possible that the game of Cribbage was invented before the 17th century, but it is from this time that the first recorded version of the game exists. Although Sir John Suckling is given credit for inventing Cribbage, it is more likely that he just codified the rules and committed them formally to paper. Cribbage shares common elements with the French game of *Piquet*, especially the use of pegs to keep score. Piquet is considered to be more complex then cribbage. Cribbage also has more luck involved in it then piquet. Cribbage may also be related to an English game called Noddy, and it is possible that Noddy was the original name for Cribbage. The peg board was most likely taken from early dice games.

English settlers in America brought Cribbage with them when they colonized America, and the game caught on there, especially in New England. From there it became popular with sailors and fisherman, since only two players were required. During Victorian times, the four-player version was very popular and appears in Charles Dickens's story, *The Old Curiosity Shop*, in which the character Mr. Quilp not only plays, but cheats at Cribbage. Cribbage was also popular in the U.S. Navy during World War II.

The name is believed to been derived from the extra hand the game has, which is called the "crib." This extra hand, made up of cards discarded by the players, is scored by the dealer each round.

The board, which has either 60 or 120 holes on it, is used to keep track of each player's (or team's) score. Two pegs are used in a leapfrog fashion to record each side's score. This allows the other side to see whether the score was recorded correctly or not. Cribbage boards can be very elaborate. Eskimos made Cribbage boards to trade with sailors and fisherman, using the ivory from walrus tusks for parts of the boards. Originally souvenirs for the sailors, these boards are now museum pieces. King Gustavus IV of Sweden signed his abdication on a Cribbage board.

Each round of Cribbage consists of three parts. First, cards are dealt to each player, who then discards cards to the "crib." The second part involves the players taking turns playing cards and scoring points for certain combinations. The final part consists of each player totaling the points in their hands for certain combinations of cards. To make the game more interesting, one card is pulled from the deck (not all the cards are dealt to the players), and this card can be combined with cards in the player's hand during scoring.

Of course, this card is not revealed until after players have discarded their cards to the crib during the first part of the round. During the third part is when the dealer gets to score the points for the cards in the crib. Once this is done, the deal is passed to the next player. Play continues until one player (or team) scores the required number of points. Gambling is possible in Cribbage by placing a wager on the difference in each side's score at the end of the game.

See Also: Dice; Europe, 1600 to 1800; Gambling; Peg Boards; Piquet; United Kingdom.

Bibliography. American Cribbage Congress, www.cribbage.org (cited August 2008); Douglas Anderson, *All about Cribbage* (Winchester Press, 1971); Dan Barlow, *Play Cribbage to Win* (Sterling Publishing Co., 2000); Jack Botermans et al., *The World of Games: Their Origins and History, How to Play Them, and How to Make Them* (Facts on File, 1989); Frederic V. Grunfeld, ed., *Games of the World: How to Make Them, How to Play Them, How They Came to Be* (Holt, Rinehart and Winston, 1975); John Scarne, *Scarne on Cards* (Crown Publishers, 1973).

Dallace W. Unger
Independent Scholar

Cricket (Amateur)

Cricket is a team game devised in Britain and recognized from the 18th century on, then introduced to various segments of the British Empire. It is a game that is played across the ages, from schoolboys to village elders, and it has played a part in a developing British society over the last few centuries.

A cricket game comprises two teams of 11, with two umpires on an oval-shaped field. One team is batting and the other is fielding, and then they trade positions. Runs are scored while batting during an inning, which is further divided into overs, which consist of six balls being bowled. There are variations now, including Twenty20, which is based on limited overs and played by county cricket teams, while indoor cricket is played during the winter. It is one of the few games, like golf, that can take most of the afternoon, including a break for afternoon tea. It has a language of its own—"silly mid off"—some of which has entered general language use, such as being "on a sticky wicket," while often being portrayed in art and literature as a gentleman's game.

The Origins of Cricket

The origins of cricket are not clear, but it is believed to have developed out of folk games played by children living in the Weald before it was taken up and played by the gentry and aristocracy, mainly between 1660 and 1830, and involved a considerable amount of betting—for example, around £20,000 was bet on a series of games between Old Etonians and England in 1751. In 1677 there was the first recorded instance of a member of the aristocracy attending a cricket match, and by 1700, its popularity ensured the game was mentioned in local press. This took the form of advertisements of forthcoming matches.

Close fielders put pressure on the batsman during a game of cricket, as one of the two umpires observes the action.

Gambling was an important part of these matches as they were played by gentlemen who had plenty of time and money to spare. As previously suggested, the first part of the evolution of cricket from a medieval folk game to the modern sport took place in Kent, Sussex, Surrey, and Hampshire, under the patronage and direction of wealthy landowners. Cricket moved out of these boundaries in the second half of the 18th century. Consequently this meant the center of cricket was Hambledon until the MCC (Marylebone Cricket Club) was formed in 1787. It was the MCC that laid down the code of laws that were adopted throughout the game, and even today, they have custody and are the arbiters of the laws of cricket throughout the world. The Georgians played cricket for fun, but during Victorian times, cricket became very important, and they played for their spiritual and mental regeneration. It was legalized by the English parliament in 1845, which was also the period when county cricket was instigated, followed later in the 19th century by international cricket.

Victorians felt playing cricket would give them strength of character and a positive image. It was seen as incredibly important because its values were used by politicians, philosophers, preachers, and poets, while it provided a sense of stability during a period of social, political, and technological flux. This meant that the village cricket team was seen as a release from the tedium of agricultural and industrial labor. However, laborers were barred from playing with the bourgeois and aristocratic teams; therefore, they had to play among themselves. This later evolved into professional teams, while the amateur teams remained the bastion of the upper classes. By the turn of the 20th century, the cricket ground and club within an English village was as important to the community as the church and pub.

As the British Empire expanded, the colonizers introduced cricket to India, Pakistan, Australia, New Zealand, West Indies, and South Africa, among other regions, as the colonial communities associated cricket with gentility and "civilization." The Indians and Pakistanis refused to accept the Christian and other gospels that were being preached to them by the British colonizers, but they did adopt cricket, and were determined to play it at least as well as the colonizers. As can be seen in contemporary competitions, they are very successful at it.

During Victorian times, women were discouraged from taking part in cricket in any serious way, as it was deemed a "male-only" sport and not suitable for women, because it involved running and other perceived unladylike behavior. The Women's Cricket Association began after World War I and the drive for women's emancipation. It was established in 1926 but is still not as widely supported as the male version. Cricket now has to compete with soccer and, to a certain extent, rugby and golf as a leading sport, certainly in Britain, though it is a game still played in schools and villages at an amateur level.

See Also: Boys' Play; Gambling; India; Pakistan; Spontaneous Group Play; Team Play.

Bibliography. Christopher Brookes, *English Cricket: The Game and its Players Through the Ages,* (Readers Union, 1978); Neville Cardus, *English Cricket* (Collins, 1946); Brian Stoddart and Keith P. Sandiford, eds., *The Imperial Game* (Manchester University Press, 1998).

Vanessa Harbour
University of Winchester

Croatia

The Republic of Croatia was, until 1991, a part of the Federal Republic of Yugoslavia, but historically it has had close ties with Italy. The region was dominated by Venice during medieval and early modern times, and then was a part of the Austro-Hungarian Empire until the end of World War I. With its own cultural identity stretching back to medieval times, a vast 90 percent of the population are ethnic Croats, and 96 percent speak Croatian.

Many traditional Eastern European games and pursuits were played until the early 20th century. Men were involved in woodwork, metalwork, and leatherwork, spending much time with their boys, teaching them about crafts. Josip Broz (Tito) spoke of his childhood in the village of Kumrovec in Croatia in the late 1890s and 1900s, during which he said he was involved in playing with other boys from the village, fighting Slovene boys from nearby, fishing and hunting for hickory, and also taking part in gymnastics at school. He also spoke fondly of *pikusa,* which was a combination of hockey, cricket, and golf, with five boys on each side.

Although small girls often played in streets with boys, women and girls predominantly remained in the family home, where they would be involved in spinning, weaving, and sewing, making some of the costume that has come to represent Croatia, from the pill-box cap to the loose pants worn by men. Indeed, it was the brightly colored ties made in Croatia that became known in France as cravats before becoming fashionable throughout the world. Lace and quilting are also popular. For men working in the fields, especially shepherds, the playing of flutes, a instrument that resembles the bagpipes, and also yodeling were common.

Traditional Game

One traditional game, which celebrates the victory of the Croats over the Turks, is the *Sinjska alka,* which takes place in August and involves horsemen dressed in 18th-century clothing. Another great historical and cultural event is the Split Carnival, where there is much storytelling and folk reenactment.

With more children attending school since the 1920s, there has been a great emphasis on recreational sports, such as table tennis, soccer, volleyball, basketball, and netball, as well as hiking and camping. Scouts from Croatia were active starting in 1913, and the Yugoslav Scout Movement was one of the founding members of the World Organization of the Scout Movement; however, its membership ended in 1948. During the Communist period, boys and girls joined the Young Pioneers Movement and were involved in civic activities as well as camping and hiking in other parts of the country, and the Savez Izvidaca Hrvatske (Scout Association of Croatia) has been reestablished. Playing cards and Chess are both popular, the latter being heavily promoted in schools by the Croatian Chess Federation. The most popular recreational sport in the country remains soccer, with the country doing well in recent international tournaments, and overseas Croatians dominating other teams, such as that of Australia.

See Also: Bosnia and Herzegovina; Chess and Variations of; Fishing; Slovenia; Soccer (Amateur) Worldwide.

Bibliography. Phyllis Auty, *Tito: A Biography* (Longman Group Ltd., 1970); Vladimir Blaskovic, *Croatia* (Speltar, 1974); Croatian Chess Federation, www.crochess.com (cited July 2008); Vladimir Dedijer, *Tito Speaks* (Weidenfeld & Nicolson, 1953); Milos Velickovic and Ljubomir Milojevic, *Sport in Yugoslavia* (Sportska Knjiga, 1952).

Justin Corfield
Geelong Grammar School

Croquet

The exact origins of Croquet are unknown, but it was certainly played in the 16th century. King Louis XIV of France played a game called *Le Jeu de Mail,* which involved hitting a ball through several hoops with a mallet. In the British capital, a similar ball game was played known as Pall Mall, but this involved hitting the ball through a raised arch, making the game far more difficult. Because of the area in London in which it was played, it is the origin of a street named Pall Mall.

Playing continued intermittently in England, Ireland, and France under a number of rules until 1857, when the Briton John Jaques, a manufacturer of sports equipment in Britain, wrote a book about the game. In 1867 Walter Jones-Whitmore wrote about Croquet in the magazine *The Field* and organized the first Croquet championship, which was held at Evesham, Worcestershire. This proved very popular, and in 1870 the British championship was held at Wimbledon at the All-England Croquet and Lawn Tennis Club (as it was then styled). The size of the Croquet court was increased from 48 feet to 50 feet, and the set-up of the hoops was agreed upon as the Hale Setting, which continued until 1922. The Croquet Association was formed in 1896, with organizations established for Croquet in Australia, New Zealand, and South Africa. In 1900 Croquet was offered as an Olympic sport, and was the first to allow women to compete—but it was never again offered in the Olympics, although Roque, a variation, was played in the 1904 Olympics.

Although there are professional Croquet games and a tournament, most often Croquet is played as a social game, and has been very popular in England and with anglophiles around the world. The U.S. president Rutherford B. Hayes spent $6 from government funds to purchase some Croquet balls, creating a minor scandal at the time. Gradually, Croquet scenes started appearing in paintings by the U.S. artists Winslow Homer and Norman Rockwell, the French Impressionist Édouard Manet, and the post-Impressionist Pierre Bonnard.

The "American" six-wicket version of Croquet is widely played in both the United States and Canada.

Croquet gradually became a social game and was enjoyed by the British upper class. Gerald Hugh Tyrwhitt-Wilson, 14th Baron Berners, donned a turban made from brocade when he played Croquet with Diana Mitford and her sisters, and Winston Churchill replaced the tennis court at Chartwell with a Croquet lawn. Mention should also be made of references to Croquet in fiction. In Evelyn Waugh's *Brideshead Revisited* (1946), Sebastian Flyte injures his foot while playing Croquet, and P.G. Wodehouse, in his last book, *Sunset at Blandings* (1977), has a scene with the Chancellor of the Exchequer playing Croquet at Blandings, shadowed by his security guards.

As well as the upper class, many houses of the British and American upper middle class started installing their own Croquet lawns, with the game's popularity mirrored in the literature of the time. Agatha Christie grew up in Ashfield, Devon, a house with its own Croquet lawn, and Croquet appears in some of her murder mystery stories, and John Galsworthy mentions Croquet rules in *The Forsyte Saga* (1906–21). H.G. Wells wrote *The Croquet Player* (1936), in which he uses the game as a metaphor for a man who ponders his existence.

As a pastime, Croquet has risen and fallen in popularity because of coverage in the press. There was renewed interest in the United States after an American polar explorer played Croquet near the South Pole; and in 2006, after the British deputy prime minister John Prescott appeared in the press playing Croquet, there was a 300 percent increase in the sales of Croquet sets at a leading British superstore. It still remains popular at many holiday resorts around the world, including in India and the West Indies.

See Also: Bocce; Boules; Bowling; Tennis (Amateur) and Variations of.

Bibliography. James Charlton, *Croquet: The Complete Guide to History, Strategy, Rules and Records* (Turtle Press, 1977); David Drazin, *Croquet: A Bibliography* (Oak Knoll Press and Roefield Press, 2004); Nicky Smith, *Queen of Games: History of Croquet* (Trafalgar Square, 1991); Charlton Thompson, *Croquet: Its History, Strategy, Rules and Records* (Penguin, 1988).

Justin Corfield
Geelong Grammar School

Crosswords

The crossword puzzle is the most universally played puzzle game worldwide, and the most familiar and ubiquitous word-based game in history. According to the U.S. Department of Census's 2006 Compendia, when adults are quizzed on their frequent leisure activities, over 30 million Americans pick up a crossword puzzle occasionally every year, and almost 13 million of those do so at least twice a week. Crosswords can be found in close to 100 percent of the world's daily newspapers. With the addition of reprints in magazines, solvers anthologies, and the thousands of puzzles available on the internet, the number of people who solve crossword puzzles, at least occasionally, is probably incalculably large.

History

Invented at the turn of the 20th century by Arthur Wynne, the editor of the "Fun" section of the *New York World* newspaper, and initially named "word-cross," the first crossword puzzle was a simple affair. It was vaguely reminiscent of an ancient mystical word puzzle called a word square. Word squares have been found engraved in walls as far back as Roman times, and one was excavated in Herculaneum, the second city lost to the Vesuvian eruption of 79 B.C.E.

The word square is a block of letters filling an equal number of columns and rows. Words appear twice, once horizontally and once vertically, in the same order left to right and top to bottom. Later variations on the word square were played as puzzles and did not require identical words on both axes; the words simply needed to interlock using all the grid spaces. Wynne borrowed this concept, which he recalled from puzzle books of his childhood in England, but rotated the square into a diamond with a hole of blanks in its center. The grid squares were numbered to indicate where the horizontally and vertically interlocked solutions began and ended. Clues were simple definitions of short, common words.

Soon after the introduction of the word-cross, a compositor's error fortuitously renamed the puzzle "crossword," and the name stuck. Within three years crossword puzzles had become an American cultural mania. Anyone who has followed the history of Sudoku, the latest puzzle phenomenon, would recognize the pattern, although compared with crossword's enormous cultural effect, Sudoku is still a mere fad.

Puzzle Structure

This basic structure that Wynne created slowly evolved into the familiar American crossword puzzle, which conforms to several basic structural rules. In theory, a grid can be made to any size dimension. In practice, American crossword sizes range from 13 x 13 to 25 x 25, and tend to be built with an odd number of squares in the rows and column grid. The puzzle is always symmetrical on the diagonal. That means that if there is a black square in the fifth grid box from the left in the top row, there will be one at the fifth grid box in the bottom row, reading from the right. Or, more simply, if you flip the puzzle upside down, the grid will look the same both ways.

Puzzles are expected to contain more white squares than black ones. The proportional guideline has become more flexible in recent times, but most well-designed

FUN'S Word-Cross Puzzle.

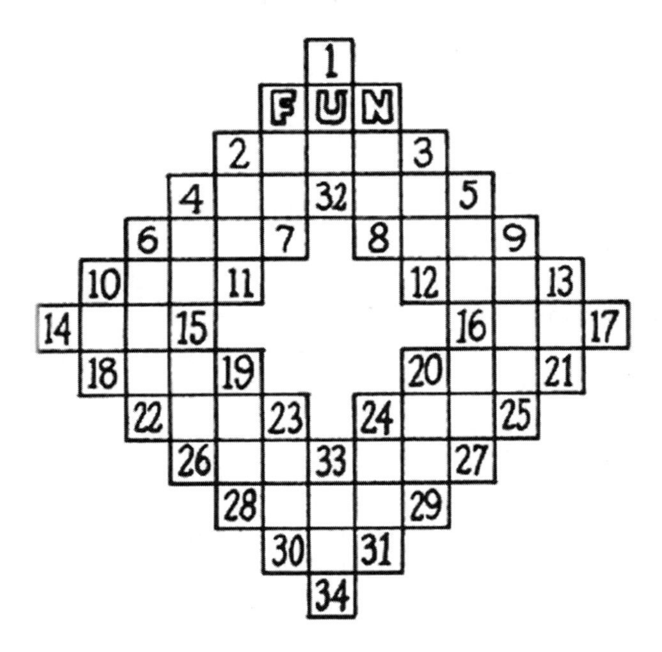

FILL in the small squares with words which agree with the following definitions:

2-3. What bargain hunters enjoy.
4-5. A written acknowledgement.
6-7. Such and nothing more.
10-11. A bird.
14-15. Opposed to less.
18-19. What this puzzle is.
22-23. An animal of prey.
26-27. The close of a day.
28-29. To elude.
30-31. The plural of is.
8-9. To cultivate.
12-13. A bar of wood or iron.
16-17. What artists learn to do.
20-21. Fastened.
24-25. Found on the seashore.
10-18. The fibre of the gomuti palm.
6-22. What we all should be.
4-26. A day dream.
2-11. A talon.
19-28. A pigeon.
F-7. Part of your head.
23-30. A river in Russia.
1-32. To govern.
33-34. An aromatic plant.
N-8. A fist.
24-31. To agree with.
3-12. Part of a ship.
20-29. One.
5-27. Exchanging.
9-25. Sunk in mud.
13-21. A boy.

The first crossword puzzle was created by Arthur Wynne and appeared in the New York World *on December 21, 1913.*

puzzles still conform to an approximately 6:1 ratio in what is referred to as an "open" grid. All of the white squares must connect with at least one other group of white squares—there can be no white boxes in an island of black squares, and every across definition must have at least one letter in it that is used in a down definition as well. In addition, the puzzle's white squares must all connect—you cannot have a puzzle with self-contained white grids divided from each other by black squares. Solving a puzzle is, by design, a cumulative process. Each solved word adds information about the longer or more obscure clues as the interlocking grid provides multiple entryways into the puzzle.

There are no fixed rules about the puzzle clues themselves, although there are many accepted conventions. Clues are usually "straight," i.e., definitions and descriptions. They are salted with fill-in-the-blanks on the easy side and pun/wordplay clues (usually indicated with a question mark) on the more difficult side. All words must be at least three letters long, and none should repeat in a solution (although some clever puzzle constructors have been known to use the same definition for different solutions). Definitions and answers should maintain parallel grammatical forms—if the clue's definition is in the plural form or is couched in the past tense, the answer should be as well.

In addition to accepted conventions, there are predictable patterns that become obvious to frequent solvers. In American-style puzzles, short obscure words and names, like "ort" or "Otto" with a multiplicity of strategically useful vowels appear frequently enough that many solvers think of them as puzzle words.

Cultural and Language Aspects

Unlike Sudoku, which easily crosses countries, classes, and professions intact, crossword puzzles depend on command of the language and general popular knowledge. A puzzle designed for a *TV Guide* reader, considered unchallenging by another American solver, might be completely opaque to an accomplished New Zealand crossword puzzle lover, despite the common language.

Although not thought of as a level game, the crossword puzzle is easily configured as one. That is because crossword difficulty is not solely determined by the answers, many of which will be common short words and abbreviations even in moderately difficult grids. In easy puzzles, word definitions are extremely straightforward and can usually be looked up in dictionaries by newbies. Easy puzzles also provide helper hints, like letting the solver know that the solution contains a phrase, or even how many words to use.

But knowing the definition of a word is less than half the battle of mastering the crossword. Languages are rich and often have words that are spelled identically but mean different things. English is particularly full of ambiguity. So many English words are synonyms of other words, or have multiple and often contradictory definitions. A seemingly innocuous clue can have many equally possible interpretations, effectively obscuring the answer. As a result, a puzzle creator can create many puzzles out of one grid. By substituting different clues the grid could be geared to the casual player or designed to stump an accomplished cruciverbalist—the Latin-derived description (*cruces* = cross; *verbus* = word) that the crossword puzzle elite use to describe their avocation.

Will Shortz, the editor of that gold standard of American crosswords, the *New York Times* crossword puzzle, has been a popularizer of a once-infrequent crossword puzzle element, the theme. Themes can be hinted in the title of a crossword, or be alluded to in a clue in the puzzle itself. Many rely on puns, but others involve word-play that substitutes, transposes, or alters familiar phrases with alternative words, or even with graphic symbols. Discovering the theme increases the likelihood of solving the puzzle, which may remain completely obscure otherwise. This strategy tends to localize crossword puzzles even more, as people with less familiarity with the language, or with American popular culture and slang, may find them tough going.

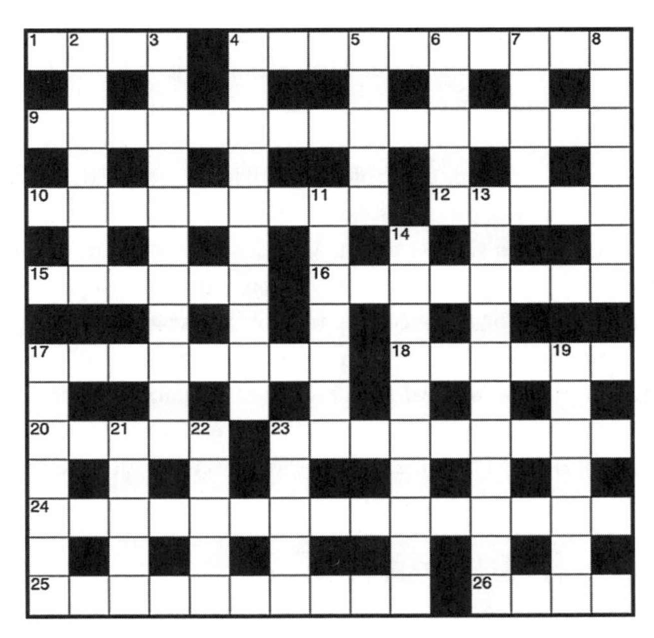

A British crossword grid has a higher percentage of black squares to white, and a basketweave visual pattern.

The British Crossword Puzzle

To their respective devotees, the crossword puzzles of the United Kingdom (UK) and the United States are hardly mentionable in the same breath. Americans maintain that the UK versions are not really crossword puzzles at all, but another form of word puzzle entirely. UK puzzlers disparage the U.S. puzzles as simple quiz games, with no real intellectual challenge. In either case, puzzlers of each type tend not to overlap.

There is little question about the genesis of the UK version, as the American crossword puzzle was firmly established as a popular mania in the United States years before it crossed the Atlantic. The migration took place in 1924, when the *Sunday Express* reprinted one of Arthur Wynne's puzzles with several clues adapted for the UK audience. But the crossword in the UK (and in many Commonwealth nations) quickly morphed into a different animal. Within a year of the first American puzzles reaching England, a challenging alternative became the rage among readers of the Tory Sunday newspaper *The Observer*. The puzzle was created by the British linguist Edward Powys Mathers, whose use of the alias Torquemada (the most infamous head of the Spanish Inquisition) revealed his penchant for difficult and painfully obscure cluing. This variant, cleaned up and shorn of the most unfair and esoteric clues, eventually made its way to other UK newspapers and pushed out the American version completely.

British grids are also squares and conform to many of the same basic structure rules as American grids, with one notable exception. Their grids contain a much higher percentage of black squares to white ones—from 25 to 50 percent of the main square—making a "closed" grid. The visual pattern tends to create alternating rows like a basketweave, where the first row is almost full of white boxes and the next row only contains white boxes to continue a down clue. The result is twofold: there are few letters in common between horizontal and vertical clues, and there is a larger proportion of longer answers to short ones. Determining one or two crossing clues is much less helpful than it is to an American solver.

The most striking differences between the two types of crossword puzzles are found in the clues themselves. British puzzles never contain straight clues. That's why they are called "cryptic"—as in the definition "having a hidden meaning." The name comes from the same root as "cryptography," the study of codes. This label both explains the nature of the clues and characterizes their unfathomability to the majority of American crossword puzzlers. Each clue is a self-contained riddle. As any child who has read the Harry Potter books knows, word puzzle riddles are more popular and prevalent pastimes in Britain than they tend to be in the United States.

Because the clues must be decoded before the puzzle can be solved, it is harder for a new solver to find an easy opening to a cryptic puzzle.

UK puzzles often define parts of the word, using puns and anagrams. For example "Coldplay" might be defined in a simple UK puzzle clue as "icy birth of Ibsen." "Birth" is a code word similar to the American question mark or word form—a hint that "icy" will provide the first part of the answer. For the second part, you'd have to know that "Ibsen" was a playwright. A common clue pattern is the hidden word—a word that is stashed in plain view in the clue itself, usually by dividing it between two clue words. Usually a word that precedes or follows the hidden word is the "straight" definition of it. However, even an experienced solver can misinterpret a cryptic clue and mistake a hidden word clue for an anagram.

An inexperienced or non-UK solver can simply miss the definition when the word itself is not familiar. The differences in names of common objects in British and American English can create a barrier as well. For example, lorry = truck, boot = trunk, and roundabout = rotary, to name just a few better-known differences. Add to these complexities the same cultural knowledge required in an American puzzle, and it is not surprising that there is as little crossover in crossword types as there is between devotees of American football and British rugby.

Modern Culture

A variety of memorabilia from the golden age of crosswords in the 1920s testifies to the era's obsession. Memorabilia with the distinctive crossword grid, songs with titles like "Cross Word Puzzle Blues," and some books were even written with crossword themes. By the 1930s, crosswords had joined Mahjohng and other Roaring Twenties manias as persistent but no longer ubiquitous interests.

Today, at the turn of the new century, crosswords are experiencing a small rebirth as a visible element of popular culture. At least two marriage proposals in the 1990s were delivered (and accepted) through clues in *New York Times* puzzles. *Wordplay*, a documentary about the world of crossword puzzles and *Crossworld*, about puzzle competitions and the crossword obsession, have helped to spark interest.

Crossword puzzles are diversions with automatic bragging rights, as those who routinely complete the *New York Times* Sunday puzzle can testify. But some argue that they are good for more than a Sunday morning break with coffee. They are seen as a comparatively painless way to deliver information and hone mental acuity.

Benefits of Crossword Puzzles

The type of mental gymnastics and omnivorous memory for trivial details that make a good cruciverbalist have led people to study whether doing crossword puzzles (or other mind-exercising tasks) might stave off age-related dementia. Newspapers have been quick to publish the work of psychological researchers who adhere to the "use it or lose it" credo. As a result, a host of self-help authors have recommended crossword puzzles as a way to keep the mind active and alert. The jury is still out on whether such mental puzzles can really help to maintain cognitive brain function in the aged or those afflicted with Alzheimer's disease, as other studies have indicated that crossword puzzles measure general knowledge better than they arrest mental deterioration. However, the ranks of crossword puzzlers have swelled as many senior citizens turn to the daily crossword puzzle for mental aerobics.

Crosswords are also used to convey new information. Several computer programs have been developed to automate the more tedious elements of designing a new crossword puzzle, like creating the symmetrical grid and numbering the clues. All that is required to create a simple puzzle is a list of words. Besides helping professional constructors develop a puzzle more quickly, this software has brought crossword puzzles into the classroom.

The most obvious beneficiaries are elementary school children. Web sites for elementary school teachers frequently share lesson plans for using crosswords as a painless gateway to understanding new words and spelling them correctly. Because the software is so accessible, students can not only solve puzzles the teacher creates but also build their own puzzles and share them. Their familiarity in classrooms has encouraged children story authors to incorporate crossword puzzles in fiction once again. In 2003, *Who Sent the Valentine, Rachel?*, a children's mystery novel that centered around a Valentine's Day card with a puzzle enclosed within it, was serialized in the *Los Angeles Times*.

What works for children's acquisition of knowledge may work equally well for adults. Crosswords, being a visual grid, can provide a link between word and image to help people acquire a second language. Studies have also shown that crossword completion offers an enjoyable mnemonic format for supporting standard classroom lectures.

See Also: Scrabble; Sudoku; United States, 1900 to 1930; Word Games (Other Than Crosswords).

Bibliography. Michelle Arnot, *What's Gnu. A History of the Crossword Puzzle* (Vintage Books, 1981); Patrick Creedon, *Wordplay* (Grinder Productions, 2006); David Z. Hambrick, Timothy A. Salthouse, and Elizabeth J. Meinz, "Predictors of Crossword Puzzle Proficiency and Moderators of Age-Cognition Relations," *Journal of Experimental Psychology: General* (v.128/2, June 1999); Anthony Mollica, "Crossword Puzzles and Second-Language Teaching," *Italica* (v.84/1, Spring 2007); George W. Rebok, Michelle C. Carlson, and Jessica B.S. Langbau, "Training and Maintaining Memory Abilities in Healthy Older Adults: Traditional and Novel Approaches," *The Journals of Gerontology, Series B* (v.62/3-1, June 2007); Marc Romano, *Crossworld* (Broadway Books, 2005); Kate Ruder, "The Aging Brain, How to Keep Your Mind Sharp," *Diabetes Forecast* (v.60/6, May 2007).

Cynthia L. Baron
Northeastern University

Cuba

The largest island in the Caribbean, Cuba was occupied by the Spanish from the early 16th century until 1898, when U.S. troops invaded as part of the American-Spanish War. The United States pulled out its soldiers in 1902, establishing a number of military bases there. In 1954 Fidel Castro began a guerilla campaign against the Cuban government, taking power on January 1, 1959. Since then, the Communist Party has been in power in Cuba.

Of the many influences in the country, the most important are Spanish, African, and North American. The Spanish and African lifestyles encouraged music, and Afro-Cuban music—both playing instruments and listening to it—remained a very popular pastime in the country. The U.S. influence on Cuba can still be seen through the popularity of baseball. It started early in the 20th century with some U.S. teams having scouts in Cuba who signed up promising young players such as Adolfo "Dolf" Luque who went to the United States to play for the Cincinnati Reds. Baseball is now played at schools throughout the country, and by members of youth groups, university teams, and the like. Boxing is also heavily promoted and because the Cuban boxers did not play in professional competitions, they were allowed to compete in the Olympic Games, where they achieved remarkable success winning many gold, silver and bronze medals.

Of the other sports, the main recreational one is basketball, known locally as *baloncesto*. Some of the elite used to play tennis and squash prior to the Communist takeover, but neither has retained much of a following. Even soccer, which remains the most played game in the rest of Latin America, does not attract many of Cuba's youth, although cross-country running and athletics have become popular in recent years, as have swimming and diving. A local game that has developed is *Jai alai*, which involves tossing a ball and catching it in a basket attached to one player's hand. This developed from the Basque game *Pelotari*.

Prior to 1959, there were casinos, nightclubs, and golf courses that attracted wealthy North Americans and others. However, these were closed down by Castro, and sport and activities have been influenced by the state rather than by the private sector. The lack of contact that most Cubans have had outside their own country, until recently, has also led to improvising with traditional games such as jigsaws, Hide-and-Seek, and building blocks.

Under the Communist government, more daycare centers were established throughout the country, catering to children as young as 3 or 4 months old. This allowed both parents in many families to go to work, as compulsory education was enforced, and even older Cubans were encouraged to attend night schools. The increase in the school population led to far more organized sporting activities, and with boys and girls in the Young Pioneers Movement, many take part in hiking and camping. Because of the trade blockade against Cuba, there are local industries making sports equipment such as baseball bats, gloves, and balls.

Chess has had a very large following in Cuba, and José Raul Capablanca was the international Chess champion 1921–27. The establishment of cultural ties with the Soviet Union led to an increase in the profile of Chess throughout the country, coordinated by the Federacion Cubana de Ajedrez. Dominoes is also played by many people throughout the island, with slightly different rules that follow the Spanish ones. These involve taking scores up to double nines.

Board games have never made much of an impact on Chess and Dominoes, although some of them have had a strong following. During the 1930s to the 1950s, Wargaming was popular with many boys and men reenacting important battles, especially those having to do with the Spanish Reconquista and the Spanish Civil War. Interest in the latter continued after the Communist takeover, although with a totally different emphasis, but there has never been much interest in Cuba for games about the wars of Che Guevara in Latin America or the Cubans in Angola.

See Also: Baseball (Amateur); Basketball (Amateur); Chess and Variations of; Dominoes and Variations of; Wargames.

Bibliography. Joseph L. Arbena, ed., "Sport in Revolutionary Societies: Cuba and Nicaragua," *Sport and Society in Latin America: Diffusion, Dependency, and the Rise of Mass Culture* (Greenwood Press, 1988); Emily Morris, *Cuba* (Heinemann, 1990); P. Parsons, "The Battles with Ché," *Miniature Wargames* (January, 2001); Paula Pettavino and Geralyn Pye, *Sport in Cuba: The Diamond in the Rough* (University of Pittsburgh Press, 1994); Ana María Váquez and Rosa E. Casas, *Cuba* (Childrens Press, 1987).

Justin Corfield
Geelong Grammar School

Curling (Scottish)

Historians do not agree whether Curling began in Scotland or in continental Europe, nor do historians agree when the sport was invented, though *Time* magazine records it as originating in 1500. Evidence dating from the 15th century in the form of paintings and old Curling stones support the earlier existence of this remarkable game or sport.

This ice sport is played with two teams in which members slide "stones" (weighing under 44 pounds) at targets on the ice. Curling is similar to other games such as Quoits, Lawn Bowling, and Shuffleboard. It is now usually played on artificial ice instead of frozen lakes. Besides the Olympics, other tournaments are held for juniors (under 21), seniors (50 and up), and women, who have played since the 1890s. In 2006 the Winter Paralympics introduced Curling with specialized wheelchairs with which the players enjoyed Curling.

According to the Royal Caledonian Curling Club, founded in 1838 in Edinburgh, which is the national governing body of this sport, Curling's first written record is from February 1541. John McQuinn, a notary, wrote the account of the match between himself and a monk at Paisley Abbey, across the ice.

Curling is often considered Scotland's game, as can be witnessed by the intensity with which Curling is played, and its popularity since at least the 1500s, as well as its immortalization in poet Robert Burns's *Tam Samson's Elegy* in 1786. Curling spread worldwide, first being picked up by Canada, and then by the rest of the world. Curling has been part of the Winter Olympics since 1998.

Bonspiels, known as Grand Matches, were two- to three-day events initially held outside until the first indoor rink was constructed in Glasgow in 1907. The first Grand Match was held January 15, 1847, and the last was held February 7, 1979, on the Lake of Mentieth. The Bonspiel was played between North and South Scotland. These tournaments were excellent chances to socialize with other Curlers during a weekend celebration of food, drink, and game.

Today, Curling championships continue and clubs are still strong in membership across the world. Clubs offer a chance to socialize with different social classes and friends with similar interests. This Scottish winter sport has found popularity among young and old, men and women, the able and disabled alike.

See Also: Canada; Europe, 1200 to 1600; Europe, 1960 to Present; Team Play.

Bibliography. Am Baile, "Curling Bonspiel," www.ambaile.org (cited July 2008); K. Lee Lerner and Brenda Wilmoth, eds., "Curling," *World of Sports Science* (Thomson Gale, 2007); K. Lee Lerner and Brenda Wilmoth, eds., "Wheelchair," *World of Sports Science* (Thomson Gale, 2007); Dorothy Jane Mills, "Curling," *International Encyclopedia of Women and Sports* (Macmillan Reference USA, 2001); Morris Mott, "Curling," *Berkshire Encyclopedia of World Sport* (Berkshire Publishing Group, 2005); Morris Mott, "Curling," in *Encyclopedia of World Sport: From Ancient Times to the Present* (Berkshire Publishing Group, 1996); Royal Caledonian Curling Club, "Grand Match," www.royalcaledoniancurlingclub.org (cited July 2008); Royal Caledonian Curling Club, "History of the Game," www.royalcaledoniancurlingclub.org (cited July 2008); David B. Smith and Bob Cowan, "Curling History," curlinghistory.blogspot.com (cited July 2008).

Michelle Martinez
Sam Houston State University

Cyprus

The fourth-largest island in the Mediterranean Sea, and the largest in the Eastern Mediterranean, Cyprus has long historical ties with Greece, with Greeks colonizing the islands as early as 1200 B.C.E. In later years, Phoenicians, Egyptians, Persians, Romans, and the Venetians held the island, with it being conquered by the Turks in 1571. It was placed under British administration in 1878, and when Turkey entered World War I, it was annexed by the British. They held it until 1960 when Cyprus gained independence.

In 1974, following a military coup in Cyprus, Turkey invaded to safeguard the Turkish population, mainly located in the northern part of the country. This led to the establishment of what has become the Turkish Republic of Northern Cyprus, although it has only been recognized by the Turkish government.

Many of the traditional ancient Greek sporting events such as running, archery, and wrestling were certainly popular in Cyprus in ancient times, when boys heavily practiced the use of a slingshot. This continued through the various occupations, with the Romans establishing gladiatorial arenas and using the island as a source of wild animals for some of their events on the Italian mainland. Under the Venetians, some Italian pursuits were introduced such as falconry, Chess, and the use of playing cards, but their culture never succeeded in making much of an impact beyond the coastal region, and even then it was restricted largely to the elite.

It was during the long rule of the Ottomans that, gradually, pastimes such as playing cards and Backgammon started to be played in villages throughout the island. With the British came many British toys and games, and it was not long before the heavy Army and Navy presence on the island developed a great interest in Wargaming, still popular with many boys and men. Much of it has traditionally focused on the Crusades, with Cyprus having played such an important part in them, but gradually the availability of different types of miniature figurines led to a greater interest in Byzantine military history. The British presence also led to the establishment of the Girl Guides Association of Cyprus in 1912, and the Cyprus Scots Association, established in the following year.

After the Turkish invasion, differences gradually emerged in Cypriot society, with the northern Turkish population, generally already more conservative, becoming isolated and remaining playing Backgammon, cards, and Dominoes. They have been allowed, since the early 2000s, to engage more in international trade, resulting in newer games being introduced and the establishment of groups such as the Northern Cyprus Turkish Scouts. The Greeks in the rest of the island, through greater engagement with the West and increased prosperity, took to computer games from the early 1990s, and amusement arcades, halls with pinball machines, and bowling alleys can be found in Nicosia.

With a warm climate, Cyprus has long attracted many tourists, especially from Britain and northern Europe, and a number of these have settled in the country. As a result, there have been many recreational sporting clubs catering to sailing, fishing, badminton, cricket, cycling, golf, soccer, squash, tennis, and skiing in the winter.

See Also: Arcades; Backgammon; Dominoes and Variations of; Greece; Turkey; Wargames.

Bibliography. Adrian Fleetwood, *Getting a Life in North Cyprus* (Rustem Bookshop, 2006); William Mallinson, *Cyprus: A Modern History* (I.B. Tauris, 2008); Ulf Metzker and P. Hadjiagelis, *The Socialization of Adolescents in Cyprus* (Pedagogical Institute, 1982).

Justin Corfield
Geelong Grammar School

Czech Republic

The Czech Republic was created from the splitting of Czechoslovakia in 1992 into the Czech Republic, with its capital Prague, and Slovakia. The region has been wealthy since medieval times and as a result there have been many forms of play. Good King Wenceslas, from the Christmas carol of the same name, was based on the Czech king Václav, who was murdered in 929 B.C.E. During the Middle Ages, great tournaments were held in Prague, which included jousting and other tests of strength and military prowess.

Boys from wealthier families spent their time as pages, with many working to master heraldry. Descriptions of fairs from the late Middle Ages mention juggling, fire-breathing, bear-baiting, fortunetelling, the sale of "lucky" potions, and other forms of entertainment. Puppets—both hand puppets and string puppets (or *marionettes*)—were also common throughout the region then known as Bohemia. Festivals such as the *Fastnacht* are celebrated each year before the Christian period of Lent, with folk-dancing in the streets, fancy dress parades, and general merriment.

Because of the wealth of Prague, from the 16th century on, many games such as those involving playing cards became common among the wealthier people, and an increase in schooling led to the start of school-organized sporting events including rowing. In spite of the devastation of the region during the Thirty Years' War (1618–48), the region recovered economically, and as part of the Austro-Hungarian Empire until World War I, Bohemia became the center for much of the culture of central Europe, including music, theatrical performances, and the manufacture of toys such as dolls for girls and mechanical items, which came to interest generations of boys. Chess in particular was a popular pastime, with many Chess pieces in Bohemia made with "Crowsnests"—raised thick platforms. From the 1930s, some of the Czech Grandmasters were internationally recognized as being among the best in the world. The Sachovy Svaz Ceske Republiky still oversees the playing of Chess in the Czech Republic.

The country—as Czechoslovakia—was an independent country after World War I, and from after World War II until 1990, it was controlled by a Communist government. During the years of independence, there was a heavy emphasis on school sports and pastimes, with soccer becoming popular, as well as tennis, golf, hockey, and other recreational sports. Hiking and cycling also attracted many people, and the Sokol movement organized gymnastic performances.

During the Communist period, there were close ties with the Soviet Union, and it became hard to get Western games in the country, although circuses and dancing remained popular, and there were a number of ice-skating rinks built in the country. The situation changed completely in 1990, and many Western European–style amusement arcades were established, as well as there being an increase in ice-hockey stadiums, 10-pin-bowling alleys, and a Grand Prix circuit built in the city of Brno.

During the Communist period, children were encouraged to play with electrical circuit boards at schools, and there has long been an interest in robotic toys, remote-controlled cars, and airplanes, which has continued to the present day. There was a Czech version of the board game Monopoly, with the streets all depicting Prague. However, board games lost their popularity during the 1990s, with many children taking to computer games. Wargaming for the events of the Hussite Wars, the Thirty Years' War, and the Seven Years' War has long been popular, and there are now many computer games that refer to that conflict and others involving the Czech Republic.

See Also: Amusement Parks; Chess and Variations of; Monopoly and Variations of; Wargames.

Bibliography. Paul Grace, "Brazen Hussites: A Wargamers' Guide to the Hussite Wars 1419–1434," *Miniature Wargames* (October, 2001); Rob Humphreys, *Czech Republic* (Wayland Publishers Ltd., 1997); MaryLee Knowlton and David K. Wright, *Czechoslovakia: Children of the World* (Gareth Stevens Publishing, 1988); Mick Nichol, "The Campaign of Prague, April–May 1757," *Miniature Wargames* (March–April, 2001); Lundek Pachman, *Checkmate in Prague* (Faber & Faber, 1975); Michael Peters, "Lion of the North: Fast Play Rules for Combat During the Thirty Years War," *Wargames Illustrated* (no.127, April 1998); F.A. Toufar, *Sokol: The Czechoslovak National Gymnastic Organisation* (George Allen & Unwin, 1941).

Justin Corfield
Geelong Grammar School

D

Darts

The game of Darts, in which spiked darts are thrown at a circular target, remains a popular game in Britain, especially in public houses (hotels) and in British communities around the world, although now people in many other countries also play the game.

The first record of the game Darts took place in the town of Dartford, in Kent, in the southeast of England. It is believed that the original dartboard might well have been the cross section of a tree, or the end of a wine barrel. Some people have suggested that the original darts were arrows that boys threw at the target board to test their skills. Certainly, the game seems to have been used for training by archers in the Middle Ages when practicing, and was said to have been practiced by English archers before the Battle of Agincourt in 1415. At around the same time in Japan, the Ninjas had used much larger darts called throwing spikes to attack their opponents, but there was never a move toward their use in Europe.

King Henry VIII of England played Darts, and a set of "Biscay elaborated darts" was given to him by his second wife, Anne Boleyn, in 1530, three years before they were married. Anne Boleyn's father had lived in France, and she grew up there, so it is possible that her darts were of the style used by the French who lived on the Bay of Biscay. As a game, Darts continued to be played by many people, and it has been reported that the Pilgrims played Darts on the *Mayflower* while sailing to America. The game was largely played in Britain and North America until the mid-19th century, when interest began in the countries in the British Empire, later spreading to other countries. In about 1900 the rules for the game started to be standardized, with a target made out of paper being patented in the United States, and leading to the current board being patented in Britain in 1906.

The game is still played in public houses throughout Britain, mainly by men, and also in schools, again mainly by boys. In the 1920s the first Brewery Leagues were established in Britain, and it was not long before a national Darts association was established. In 1927 the London newspaper *News of the World* established a nationwide competition, and by World War II, the game was regularly played by British soldiers. The *News of the World* Individual Darts Championship started up again in 1947, and the British National Darts Association was established in 1954.

There are regular tournaments in England and around the world. The game has also been televised in some countries, not just in pubs and hotels, but also in youth clubs and schools. Because of a concern of possible injury when children play, new versions have been made using magnets instead of pointed tips.

Because of its portability, it was not long before the game of Darts was being played around the world, and many recreational groups took it up, often using different dartboards that have sometimes been decorated with the faces of well-known politicians or other public figures.

There are now many Darts groups around the world, including the American Darts association, the Darts Federation of Australia, the National Darts Federation of Canada, the Czech Darts Organization, the Danish Darts Union, the Dutch Darts Organization, the German Darts Organization, the Hungarian Darts Federation, Italian Darts Association, the Norwegian Darts Organization, the Polish Darts Federation, the Swedish Darts Organization, and the Swiss Darts Association.

See Also: Europe, 1200 to 1600; Play as Entertainment, Sociology of; Team Play.

Bibliogaphy. Dan William Peek, *To the Point: The Story of Darts in America, Including a History of the Sport in Great Britain & Ireland* (Pebble Publishing, 2001); George Silberzahn, *How To Master The Sport of Darts* (Totem Pointe Books, 2004); Paddy Whannel and Dana Hodgdoon, *The Book of Darts* (Henry Regnery Co., 1976).

Justin Corfield
Geelong Grammar School

Daydreaming

Psychologists use the term *task-unrelated images and thoughts* (TUIT) to describe daydreaming episodes. A daydream can be triggered by a situation, a memory, or sensory input and is considered to be an aspect of the imagination connected with the emotions. A daydream, or series of daydreams, can precede episodes of creative innovation. Athletes, musicians, and other performers utilize a form of daydreaming when they practice visualization. As the individual prepares for a competition or performance, they form a mental picture of the desired successful outcome. The unique characteristic of daydreaming is that it occurs in solitude. However, if the daydreamer begins to confuse these mental images with reality, the daydream is considered to be a hallucination.

Psychologists estimate that one-third to one-half of a person's thoughts while awake are daydreams, even though a single daydream rarely lasts more than a few minutes. Psychologist Jerome L. Singer argued, "probably the single most common connotation is that daydreaming represents a shift of attention away from some primary physical or mental task we have set for ourselves, or away from directly looking at or listening to something in the external environment toward an unfolding sequence of private responses made to some internal stimulus." The daydreamer experiences an inner process creating pictures in the mind's eye of mental sequences of an event or a situation or creatively constructed images that he or she has never actually experienced or may have varying degrees of probability for taking place. The daydreamer may use these *monologues intérieurs* or inner voices to escape from reality temporarily, to overcome a frustrating situation, or to satisfy hidden wishes.

Psychologists have been interested in the cognitive or information-processing model of daydreaming, for what it reveals about the complexity of human motivation. William James (1842–1910), in his *The Principles of Psychology*, introduced the term *stream of thought* to describe daydreaming as a process of waking awareness that comprises the experiences of direct perceptual responses, and the complex interplay of such responses with associated phrases, memories, fantasies, fleeting images, and inner voices. Daydreaming can reveal how experiences and memories are internally organized. Daydreaming and make-believe play in children can be considered to be manifestations of a natural cognitive capacity at certain developmental stages from circumstance and events in a child's environment.

According to Sigmund Freud (1856–1939), daydreams are derived from the primary process mechanisms of condensation, displacement, and pictorial representation that link to wish fulfillment. Freud asserted, "The psychical process of constructing composite images in dreams is evidently the same as when we imagine or portray a centaur or dragon in waking life." Freud uncovered a link between dreaming and imagination, while Carl Jung (1875–1961) took the dream-thoughts of directed daydreams and reduced them to archetypes. Freud felt that people who experienced daydreams were unfulfilled and that daydreaming and fantasy were early signs of mental illness.

Defining Daydreaming

The semantics of daydreaming, synonymous with "reverie," has changed over time. Philosopher John Locke

(1632–1704) considered a daydream to be "when ideas float in out mind, without any reflection or regard of the understanding." British essayist Joseph Addison (1672–1719) asserted, "If the minds of men were laid open, we should see but little difference between that of the wise man and that of the fool; there are infinite reveries and numberless extravagancies pass through both." Lexicographer Samuel Johnson (1709–84) did not define *daydream* in his *Dictionary of the English Language,* but he defined the word *toy* as a "wild fancy; irregular imagery; odd conceit." Johnson also defined the term *revery* [sic] as "loose musing; irregular thought."

Daydreaming in Literature

During the late 18th century and early 19th century, the perception of daydreaming in men was seen as simple reflections or meditations that were not expected to have some objective outcome, or an intellectual process involving the imagination. However, daydreaming in women was associated with laziness and novel reading. American lexicographer Noah Webster (1758–1843) developed *The American Spelling Book,* also known as the "Blue-Backed Speller" as a means to standardize spelling and punctuation in the United States. Webster's 1787 edition contained a story about a female daydreamer called "The Country Maid and her Milk Pail."

"When men suffer their imagination to amuse them, with the prospect of distant and uncertain improvements of their condition, they frequently sustain real losses, by their inattention to those affairs in which they are immediately concerned. A country maid was walking very deliberately with a pail of milk upon her head, when she fell into the following train of reflections: The money for which I shall sell this milk, will enable me to increase my stock of eggs to three hundred. These eggs, allowing for what may prove addle, and what may be destroyed by vermin, will produce as least two hundred and fifty chickens. The chickens will be fit to carry to market about Christmas, when poultry always bears a good price; so that by Mayday I cannot fail of having money enough to purchase a new gown. Green—let me consider—yes, green becomes my complexion best, and green it shall be. In this dress I will go to the fair, where all the young fellows will strive to have me for a partner; but I shall refuse every one of them, and with an air of disdain, toss from them. Transported with this triumphant thought, she could not forbear acting with her head what thus passed in her imagination, when down came the pail of milk, and with it all her imaginary happiness."

Daydreams of future wealth and glory were part of a gentleman's leisure activities. Washington Irving (1783–1859) first use of the word *daydream* in relation to play appeared in 1820 in his *Sketchbook: The Voyage* when he described, "one given to daydreaming, and fond of losing himself in reveries." During the second half of the 19th century, there was a rebellion against the Industrial Revolution when crowded cities became unhealthy places for families. Poor families could not dispense with their children's labor, but new middle-class families could and did forego the contributions of children.

Children's literature reflected this change, when authors such as Charles Kingsley (1819–73) who wrote *The Water-Babies,* and Kenneth Graham (1824–1905) who wrote *At the Back of the North Wind,* began creating alternative imaginary landscapes in stories for children. The adult concept of romanticized and cherished childhood was once seen as just a preparation stage for adult life. While rural and working class children retained their working role within families, the lives of middle-class children were increasingly set apart from adult responsibilities. Industrialization, immigration, and urbanization worked to distill the distinctions between classes. By the 1860s, there was a truly poor underclass and a working class employed in factories or as hired farm labor that contrasted with a growing middle class layered by levels of education, wealth, and occupation.

Modern Studies

Dutch anthropologist Karl Groos (1861–1946) wrote about the role of fantasy play in children and how it was built around taking on adult roles as parents, teachers, and adventurers. Interpreted from this perspective, daydreaming became an important tool for information processing for a child to integrate complex external environments into a set of organized memories. In the beginning of the 20th century, educators studied daydreaming in conjunction with secretiveness in children, examining what young children kept secret and the motives for such secretiveness. Daydreaming presented a need for secretiveness when the daydreamer anticipated the impossibility of explaining; the uselessness of explaining; the fear of being misunderstood; the fear of discouragement, of disillusion, of disbelief, or of lack of interest; or the fear of ridicule, displeasure, of being thought foolish, of being made to feel ashamed, or having pride wounded, of losing another's good opinion, of disgrace, of curtailment of liberty, or punishment.

In the 1960s, textbooks used for training teachers provided strategies for combating daydreaming that included language similar to texts that described drug use. By the late 1980s, most psychologists considered daydreams a natural component of the mental process for most individuals. Individuals may not admit to daydreaming because it presents a window into the workings of the inner mind and the sense of one's own personality and the individual's desire to preserve privacy. Daydreaming first occurs during childhood, sometime before age 3, as part of the origins of thinking that are linked to make-believe and pretend play that all humans experience.

These early daydreams set the pattern for adult daydreaming. Children who have positive, happy daydreams of success and achievement generally continue these types of mental images into adulthood. These daydreamers are most likely to benefit from the positive aspects of mental imagery. Daydreams related to play become an impetus for problem-solving, creativity, and accomplishment, whether children are playing with dolls or playing games that can be used to practice skills that will be later needed in adult life. Daydreams can be a form of visualization that the daydreamer acts out in real life. The child left alone tries to imitate the actions and behaviors of adults. As children grow to adulthood, they gradually internalize make-believe games and play them out privately in their own imaginations.

See Also: Fantasy Play; Maypole Dancing; Play as Entertainment, Psychology of; Playing Alone; Pretending.

Bibliography. Sigmund Freud, *The Freud Reader* (W.W. Norton & Company, 1995); Karl Groos, *The Play of Man* (Appleton-Century Crofts, 1901); William James, *The Principles of Psychology* (Harvard University, 1981); Jerome L. Singer, *Daydreaming and Fantasy* (George Allen & Unwin Ltd, 1976); Jerome L. Singer, *The Inner World of Daydreaming* (Harper Colophon Books, 1976); Jenny Tyrrell, *Power of Fantasy in Early Learning: A Connective Pedagogy* (Routledge-Falmer, 2001).

Meredith Eliassen
San Francisco State University

Denmark

Denmark, with a population of only six million people, has made significant contributions to the development of play theory, research, policy, and practice. In 1961 the International Play Association was formed in Denmark. Danish children are required by state policy to have multiple play breaks throughout the school day. Many innovations in play were born in Denmark such as child-built adventure playgrounds. Opportunities for play abound in Danish culture and civil society. Play facilities exist in public spaces such as airports, shopping centers, museums, and town squares. School grounds and parks with playing fields and play equipment are in neighborhoods throughout Denmark. Role-playing has made an impact on Danish educational opportunities. Danish culture and society see play as a critical social experience for children and adults to develop independence and willingness to take calculated risks. This strong cultural orientation has influenced play in Denmark and abroad.

The International Play Association has deep roots in Scandinavia and Denmark in particular. Early in the 1930s the movement to preserve and support children's right to play gained momentum. As a result, Danish children were encouraged to build their own play habitats or adventure playgrounds. Today, play and the right of the child to play are taken seriously by educators and municipal leaders. *Naturlegepladsen i Valbyparken* (nature playground in the Valby city park) in a southern suburb of Copenhagen was designed by Helle Nebelong and is recognized as being one of the best-designed playgrounds for children in the world.

It includes natural and built elements such as hills, elm tree branches and trunks, huts and towers of metal and wood, sand, and gravel areas all brought together by a circular wooden bridge that is raised a few feet from the ground and runs through and around the play areas. *Madsby Legepark*, the largest playground in Denmark, is in Fredericia. Typical Danish playgrounds include both built and natural elements and allow for considerable open-ended play. Museums such as the *Vikingeskibs Museet* (Viking Ship Museum) in Roskilde and the *Københavns Bymuseum* (Copenhagen City Museum) have extensive play areas for children that allow for dress-up; play with toys, artifacts, and replicas; playing of period games; and movement through thematic playscapes.

Throughout the world children and adults covet Danish-developed LEGO bricks building toys. The word

The LEGO brick building toy is an iconic Danish invention, launched in its present form in 1958.

LEGO is derived from the Danish expression *leg godt* which means "play well." The world-famous LEGO-LAND amusement park is in Billund, Denmark. This unique park facilitates play through miniature train rides, a mock driving school for children with small electric cars, roller coasters, and other such amusements. The most intriguing feature of the park is the opportunity to play with huge numbers of LEGO blocks and to see displays of the hundreds of imaginative options one can explore through playing with LEGO.

Denmark is home to an extensive network of role-play game players. There are many role-playing conferences each year in Denmark. The two largest are *Fastaval in Århus* in the spring and *Viking-Con* in Copenhagen in the fall. This excitement for role-play as a forum for fun and learning has lead to the development of the *Østerskov Efterskole* secondary boarding school in Hobro, which has a comprehensive curriculum completely taught through role-playing. Subjects are combined according to inspiration and relevant themes.

Veterans from the Danish role-playing scene and designers of educational as well as entertainment games, Malik Hyltoft and Mads Lunau developed and founded *Østerskov Efterskole*. Enrolling about 100 students per year, this innovative school conforms to governmental standards regarding the subjects taught and final exams, but it uses alternative pedagogy. The organizing theory behind this school is that the flow of the games and role-plays will induce students to learn.

See Also: Amusement Parks; LEGOs; Play and Learning Theory; Role-Playing.

Bibliography. Diane E. Lang, "Free to Play Outdoors?: A Cross-Cultural Comparative Study," *Play Rights Journal: An International Journal of the Theory and Practice of Play* (v.29/4, December 2007); Markus Montola and Jaakko Stenro, eds., *Playground Worlds: Creating and Evaluating Experiences of Role-Playing Games* (Ropecon RY, 2008); Helle Nebelong "Nature's Playground," *Green Places* (May 2004).

Diane E. Lang
Manhattanville College

Dice

Dice are one of the most common elements of chance in games, and one of the most ancient. Dice have been revered as divine messengers that offer a glimpse of the future, and reviled as the source of gambling, cheating, and ultimately spiritual decay. Legal and moral concerns aside, dice are, at their core, random number generators.

The numbers that can be generated by a set of dice depend on the markings, faces, and number of dice thrown. The most common modern die is six-sided, with sides numbered one through six by means of painted indentations that have come to have a set, recognizable pattern of positioning. In gambling, dice are commonly thrown in pairs, but in other games, especially war games, a player may be required to throw as many as 20 dice on a turn.

Dice are thought to have evolved from the astralagus, a fortune-telling device made of an animal's hoof that, when thrown, lands with one of four faces up. However, the astralagus is not the earliest method of divination through randomness. There are earlier references in history to drawing lots, flipping coins, and dividing yarrow sticks into arbitrary piles as methods of determining a random value.

The use of random number generators for divination may have led to the use of random number generators for unbiased decision-making. References to randomness as an unbiased decider can be found in ancient records recording judgments. If no fair means of deciding a case could be determined, a random number would make the decision. Using randomness

The most common die is six-sided, with painted indentations to indicate the numbers one through six.

for decision-making led to betting on the outcomes of the random decision, or gambling.

An aspect of fatalism often came into play. Tacitus, the Roman historian, writes that in the 1st century C.E., Germanic soldiers were so committed to dice gambling that they would, upon losing all of their money, make a final bet wagering their freedom. The result of losing such a bet was to be sold into slavery, but the soldiers considered it an honor. Another mention of Germanic soldiers states that they would decide the fates of their captors—whether to kill them or sell them into slavery—based on a roll of the dice.

Even in modern times, dice still are linked to the debate over free will, captured famously in the quote attributed to Albert Einstein: "God does not play with dice." Einstein believed that the mechanics of the universe could be explained through scientific means, but this quote takes the careful path of not denying God's existence, instead only asserting that God would not make any decision randomly. Einstein asserts that any event that appears random actually has a chain of causality leading up to it.

Dice have been present in the humanities, especially mathematics, philosophy, and literature, since their invention. Plato asserted that God plays with dice, perhaps inspiring Einstein's opposing view. Aristotle's students explored probabilities using dice in *Problematica*, and mathematicians including Fermat and Pascal studied statistical projections using dice.

In literature, God is often portrayed as judging people for playing with dice. These are most often morality tales, however, having to do more with defying God or cheating or making gambling a priority above everything else. In the *Mahabarata*, an early masterwork of Indian literature, battling families bet their fates on the roll of loaded dice.

Sometimes, however, God is on the side of the dice player. A legend of Olaf Haraldsson, an 11th-century king of Norway, tells how he wagered his kingdom on a roll of the dice against the King of Sweden. Although the Swedish king rolled a 12, the highest possible roll on two dice, Olaf claimed that God would let him roll higher. Upon his rolling, one of the dice split in half, resulting in both its six and its one side landing face up, which when added to the other six, resulted in a score of 13. St. Olaf is now the patron saint of Norway, perhaps more for his folkloric feats than his historic ones.

Dice and Corruption

At various points in history, societies have outlawed dice in order to prevent the corruption of their citizens. The two main points of moral disfavor for dice games were the loss of property (and sometimes liberty) from gambling and the prospect of cheating. *The Compleat Gamester*, written by Charles Cotton in 1680, decries the moral decay caused by game of Hazzard, a forebear to Craps. The author describes how men would become addicted to the game, losing interest in everything except the prospect of winning, often leading to ruination of their lives. This social concern led to dice falling out of moral favor in mid-18th-century England.

Games produced during this time often substituted a "tee-to-tum": a cube with a stick running diagonally through it to create a spinning top that worked very much like a die in determining random values, but was regarded as "family friendly." The "tee-to-tum" continues its existence today as the dreidel, a spinning top used in a popular Jewish holiday gambling game. However, the substitution of a different form of die did not prevent the other form of moral corruption: cheating. According to apocryphal sources, dice as far back as ancient Pompeii were "loaded." Prosecution for dice scams is documented back as far as the 14th century. At the end of the 16th century, Queen Elizabeth ordered police searches to track down loaded dice. Two common methods of cheating with dice are weighting one side so that the opposite face comes up more, and placing only the three most favorable numbers for a game twice each on a cube.

Early Uses of Dice

Archaeologists have uncovered many earlier versions of dice; as of 2008, the earliest known dice are estimated to date back to the 24th century B.C.E., from a tomb in Mesopotamia. The ancient Greeks created the standard for dice used today, in which the numbers on opposite faces of the die total seven (six plus one, five plus two, three plus four). The symmetry gave players assurance that the markings of the die were evenly distributed across the faces so that no subtle weight differences from the markings could interfere with "true randomness."

The 15th-century philosopher Desiderius Erasmus observes that in early uses of dice, the quantity of counters on the divining surface represented the current state of the prediction, and that this led to the use of tokens to track winnings in gambling. The notion that a counter representing each player's score could be moved along a numbered track presented an easier means of spatially perceiving who was ahead, and this led to a cognitive shift in game play. Erasmus says that with this change, players' attentions began to focus on the movement of the counters, regarding the dice as the means of movement. This shift in focus led to the concept of "race games," a classification coined by David Parlett in 1999 for games in which there is movement from start to finish in a linear fashion. Senet, a precursor to Backgammon that represents the spiritual journey through the underworld, is the earliest known game to use random number-based movement; a copy of the game was found in the tomb of the pharaoh Hesey (2686–2613 B.C.E.).

In addition to being the first known game to use counters for movement, Senet is also the earliest known game to incorporate the idea of each player controlling multiple pieces in the race from start to finish. In giving the player the choice of which piece or pieces to advance each turn, an element of strategy was introduced to the game space. This eventually led to the development of games such as Chess, in which the magnitude and direction of each piece's move is predetermined by the rules, so that strategy, rather than luck, determines the winner.

Although many pure strategy games such as Chess represent a battle, Wargames since the 18th century have often used dice to determine the outcome of combat, the high or low roll of the dice representing the victory of one set of troops over another. This randomness is a substitution for having to determine the outcomes of potentially thousands of individual conflicts, but it is no mere shortcut. Statistical models (for which dice are a popular topic of study) often employ randomness to similarly simplify overly complex systems, in a reversal of Einstein's idea: For simulation purposes, God does play with dice.

Role-Playing Games

Role-playing games, a 20th-century invention, are an outgrowth from Wargames. In role-playing games, the focus is on storytelling, with each player taking on the role of one or more characters undertaking a quest. In these games, the roll of the dice determines not only skill in combat, but also wisdom, luck, charisma, and other nonphysical characteristics. Unlike in Wargames, where a single roll of the dice generalizes the results of many individual encounters, in *Dungeons & Dragons*, each roll determines success or failure in applying a character's skill to one task. The level of determinism dictated by the dice recalls the original application of dice: to determine future fates as dictated by the gods.

See Also: Diplomacy; *Dungeons & Dragons*; Gambling; Game Theory; Risk in Play; Spinning Tops; Wargames; Warhammer.

Bibliography. Deborah Bennett, *Randomness* (Harvard University Press, 1999); Jack Botermans, *The Book of Games: Strategy, Tactics, & History* (Sterling Publishing, 2008); Charles Cotton, *The Compleat Gamester* (Imprint Society, 1970); Ricky Jay, *Dice: Deception, Fate, and Rotten Luck* (Quantuck Lane Press, 2003); David Parlett, *Oxford History of Board Games* (Oxford University Press, 1999); F.R.B. Whitehouse, *Table Games of Georgian and Victorian Days* (Peter Garnett, 1951).

Jay Laird
Northeastern University

Diplomacy

Avalon Hill's Diplomacy is a military strategy board game set in pre–World War I Europe. It not only underscores but also demands the shrewd and often deceitful making and breaking of alliances between would-be superpowers vying for domination of the continent.

Allan Calhamer developed Diplomacy throughout the 1950s while a student of 19th-century European history, political geography, and law at both Harvard University and Harvard Law School. The game achieved its final form in 1958 and saw mass production in 1960. In a 1974 essay written for *Games & Puzzles*, Calhamer recalls drawing inspiration for his game from an article in *Life* magazine contending that a world government constituted by multiple Great Powers of relatively equal strength would provide a system of checks and balances adequate for maintaining world peace and allaying geopolitical aggression. "Regardless of whether such a plan would have worked or could have been brought about in the real world," Calhamer writes, "the system of multiple and flexible checks and balances offered itself as a possible basis for a strategic parlour game of some depth and colour."

Diplomacy unfolds on a map of circa-1900 Europe, which is divided into 76 discrete land and sea "provinces." Seven players represent diplomats from major military powers—France, Great Britain, Germany, Austria-Hungary, Italy, Russia, and Turkey—who order armies and fleets to both defend and capture provinces with the aim of controlling at least half the board by game's end. Certain provinces contain supply centers whose capture infuses more resources into the controlling power's forces (in the form of additional pieces deployed on the board).

Unlike similar military strategy games (for example, Risk or Axis & Allies), conflict in Diplomacy is resolved without rolling dice; therefore, combat outcomes are not left to chance. Instead, players privately compose written orders for their units, which can move into unoccupied adjacent provinces, attack neighboring enemies, defend secured territories, support advancing units controlled by any power, or convoy units across bodies of water. When orders are revealed, unit movement occurs simultaneously (not in the turn-based fashion more common of the Wargame genre). These moments of revelation are filled with tension not because players worry about the caprices of dice, but because they can never be entirely confident their human ally-opponents have acted as anticipated.

Diplomacy's eponymous core element occurs between players in seclusion, often behind locked doors in hushed whispers. Playing the board game indeed means spending a significant portion of game time—hours, minimally, but entire weekends, more frequently—away from the board in clandestine negotiations. Calhamer wanted Diplomacy to be a game "principally of manoeuvre rather than annihilation." It is notoriously cutthroat, predicated on a striking paradox: No player can accumulate resources and territories without the support of other diplomats, yet winning the game necessitates emerging as a single dominant superpower. Thus, diplomatic sessions inevitably involve duplicity; all seemingly good-natured gestures of collaboration are nevertheless motivated by rapacity. "Loyalty, honesty, frankness, gratitude, chivalry, magnanimity—these are the hallmarks of the good friend, the good husband and father, the nice guy we all hope our daughters will marry," writes Richard Sharp in *The Game of Diplomacy*. "In the amoral world of Diplomacy, however, they are the hallmarks of the born loser."

Because units' starting locations are prescribed by Diplomacy's rule book and not randomly assigned, players have developed diverse, nuanced opening, and mid- and end-game strategies (similar to the treatment afforded chess). Postal play began in 1960. Three computerized versions of the game have existed since the 1980s, yet serious players prefer email as a tool for corresponding via the computer over long distances. More than 50 years after its invention, Calhamer's "strategic parlour game" enjoys enduring worldwide support through fan publications and an annual international championship competition, the World Diplomacy Convention.

See Also: Avalon Hill; Games of Deception; Risk, the Game; Wargames.

Bibliography. Allan Calhamer, "The Invention of Diplomacy," *Games & Puzzles* (January, 1974); Fernand Gobet, *Moves in Mind: The Psychology of Board Games* (Psychology Press, 2004); Richard Sharp, *The Game of Diplomacy* (A. Barker, 1978).

Bryan G. Behrenshausen
Kutztown University of Pennsylvania

Dodgeball

Dodgeball is a game many American and Canadian youth are exposed to at an early age, often during elementary school during gym class. Students are divided into roughly equal-sized teams and compete to remove players of the opposing team by hitting them with a ball. The goal of this game is two-fold—to hit the other team's players and to dodge the balls that are thrown at you. Players may return to play if a teammate catches a ball. Often this type of game continues for extended periods of time given the flow of players in and out of play. Numerous versions of this game exist dictating the number of balls in play, various additional physical skills such as shooting the ball through a basketball hoop, and whether players out of play just sit on the sidelines or are engaged in other activities.

This game has been a mainstay of elementary physical education, and to lesser degree middle and high school, over the course of the last century, given the simple rules and low cost of sports equipment. Many children thrill in playing this game that in some manners feels like a free-for-all, a game with few rules and much running and dodging. However, many adults reflect upon the Dodgeball play of their youth with disdain, recalling the sting of the ball and the boredom accompanying sitting on the sidelines while out of play. Despite the positive and negative recollections of Dodgeball it remains an iconic game of American childhood play. Indeed, the traditions of this game have entered into the media, with episodes of *Freaks and Geeks* (1999) and *South Park* (1998) addressing the violent nature of this game. The iconic status of this game was additionally demonstrated by the 2004 film *Dodgeball: A True Underdog Story*. This comedy demonstrated both the violent aspects and the positive team-centered aspects of this game.

In recent years this game has become subject to significant critique and debate in the health education field. Some physical education teachers argue that the game teaches valuable fleeing and dodging skills, while encouraging running and other athletic engagement. Yet, the least-athletic students, who may benefit most from more activity, are often the first students knocked out of play. Indeed, a fundamental critique of Dodgeball is the elimination nature of this game. The targeting of the least-athletic and least-skilled players first puts these players out of play early. This perpetuates a system of social stratification and stigmatization of the less skilled while simultaneously limiting their engagement in physical activity.

Another critique is that children should never be made into targets, particularly among their peers. Such targeting may encourage and engage students in bullying. Indeed, some students, especially the more skilled athletes or dominant boys, may delight in "pegging" a fellow classmate. If a student is "beaned," they may be teased and stigmatized, especially if one cries because of the physical pain of a particularly hard throw. However, others embrace this game as one of the few "reality" games left that gives students a peek at the adult world of competition. As more and more children are engaged in athletic games where everyone is a winner, it can be important to also note the competitive nature of the social world.

See Also: Play and Sports Education; Play as Competition, Sociology of; Team Play.

Bibliography. Michael T. Shoemaker, "Is There a Place for Dodgeball in Physical Education?" *The Journal of Physical Education, Recreation, & Dance* (v.72/4, April 2001); National Amateur Dodgeball Association, www.dodgeballusa.com (cited June 2008); Pamela Powers "Beyond Dodgeball, Kickball, and Duck Duck Goose," *Independent School* (v.66/4, Summer 2007); Rawson Marshall Thurber, dir. *Dodgeball: A True Underdog Story* (20th Century Fox, 2004).

Daniel Farr
Randolph College

Dolls, Barbie and Others

Dolls are commonly understood to be small figures that model the human form. Generally used as children's toys, dolls help to explain the educational and cognitive, social, and emotional values of play. As dolls have become more clearly tied to children and play, a wide array of types of dolls has emerged. Many of these dolls spring from the increased merchandising and marketing of the 20th century. However, dolls are often used within adult contexts, as collectible items and objects in religious and spiritual rituals. All of these dolls exist in a multitude of forms, with wood, wax, papier-mâché, porcelain, bisque, china, rubber, celluloid, plastic, and cloth offering options for their production.

Playing with dolls, most commonly believed to be a type of girl's play, indicates healthy psychological development. Whether it involves rocking a baby doll to sleep or dressing up a Barbie, playing with dolls is a means of learning about the world. In an educational sense, this socialization results from being able to transform activities normally associated with work, to reconcile reason and pleasure, to conquer the demands of time, to express desire, and to exercise imagination. Those cognitive abilities are tempered by the social value of play, which attempts to mold children into good citizens by allowing them freedom within limits and by teaching them gender expectations. Through playing with dolls, children learn to be parents (most commonly, girls learn to be mothers), to groom, and to accept changes in relationships. An emotional value of play joins these two

African-American dolls were introduced to the line of Barbie dolls in 1967, which now includes many ethnicities.

forces, offering the ability to develop coping skills, work out problems, and assess and deal with trauma. When combined, these three values of play mean that the act of playing with dolls carries educational, formative, and recreational purposes.

Dolls for Play

Dolls designed as children's playthings are far more common than either ritual or fashion dolls. Presumably created since the beginning of time, these objects of play became even more prevalent during and after the Victorian era, when childhood was first accepted as a distinct and separate stage of life. Instead of seeming like miniature adults, children were allowed the first 12 to 14 years to develop as individuals. They were still expected to learn appropriate gender roles and social practices, a process in which dolls could help. From the 19th century dolls, frequently took the form of babies and young children. Although adult figures did remain, they were less common.

The French *bébé*, which appeared in the late 1870s, is a fine example of this simultaneously educational and recreational feature. Modeled on healthy and generally chubby children, baby dolls were used to teach girls how to be mothers and sisters. In coaching girls to rock, diaper, clothe, and feed their baby dolls, adults instructed them in the art of motherhood. Since women have often been delegated to the home, this training—along with playing house—was much like an apprenticeship program.

Playing with baby dolls is also a means of explaining how to deal with real babies. Baby dolls are commonly offered to girls when their mothers are expecting another baby. With the doll, a child can act out its frustrations at no longer being the only or youngest child. The child can mimic her mother's actions and feel part of the process of caring for the new child.

Before the invention of the Barbie doll, baby dolls were among the most common toys sold. Changes in their appearance occurred as new technologies became available. Baby dolls that could sit were introduced in Europe beginning in 1860. They were followed by baby dolls with celluloid heads (1862) and the advent of the American market for baby dolls (1865) with the Horseman Company's dolls.

Other dolls take on the appearance of a slightly older child or an adult. These dolls offer girls a chance to develop friendships and to explore their own personalities. Although some care of the doll is still necessary, dolls modeled on older children and adults allow for conversation, tea parties, and virtually any activity a girl might undertake with another child. That imaginary play is another important form of socialization: the girl learns how to behave with other girls by playing with her dolls.

One of the most famous of this type is Barbie, who has intrigued little girls, worried parents concerned with their daughters' body image, and succeeded in capturing the market for dolls modeled on adult women or sophisticated teenagers from her debut at the New York Toy Fair in 1959. Created by Ruth Handler, this doll was based on the concept of paper dolls, which could be dressed in any fashion and whose clothes could be changed quickly. Noticing her daughter Barbara's interest in creating grown-up worlds for her paper dolls, Handler decided to design a teenage fashion model doll. The result was an 11 1/2-inch-tall rigid plastic doll wearing a black-and-white striped swimsuit and sporting a ponytail of blonde hair.

Selling for $3, this original Barbie (named for Handler's daughter) became the staple product of Mattel, the corporation Handler and her husband Elliot founded to market and produce the doll.

The Handlers were not content to leave Barbie alone in this fashion world. Within the first two years, five different versions of Barbie were created. Originally joined at the neck, arms, and legs, these first versions offered slight variations in features and great alterations in available clothes. Vinyl soon replaced plastic as the material used to create the dolls, and a whole host of friends joined Barbie. In 1961, Ken, a 12-inch-tall male doll with a six-piece, jointed body, became Barbie's male escort. He was joined by Midge (1963), marketed as Barbie's best friend, and Skipper (1963), Barbie's little sister; while Midge was modeled on the same basic proportions as Barbie, though with individualized features, Skipper displayed a nine-inch-tall, six-piece jointed body. Two friends for Skipper—Skooter, who could pass as Midge's younger sister, and Ricky, who could pass as Allan's (Ken's best friend and Midge's boyfriend) younger brother—were also introduced in 1963. Allan first appeared in 1964. Later, in 1966, Barbie's more modern cousin Francie, an 11 1/4-inch-tall, more buxom version of the original doll, was produced along with Tutti and Todd, Barbie's twin sister and brother (six and a quarter inches tall each). An African-American Francie doll followed in 1967.

These variations on the Barbie theme have continued to the present. A variety of ethnic Barbies, including Hispanic, Filipina, Native American, and African American versions, have been released. Collectible Barbies have also become increasingly popular. Fashion designers ranging from Yves St. Laurent to Christian Dior, Versace to Jean-Paul Gaultier, have designed clothes for the collectible versions of Barbie to wear. Ties to movies have also been made, with dolls based on characters like Scarlett O'Hara, Wonder Woman, Dorothy from *The Wizard of Oz,* Jo from *Little Women,* and Belle from *Beauty and the Beast*; dolls based on famous entertainers like Lucille Ball, Elizabeth Taylor, Audrey Hepburn, Elvis, and Cher; dolls based on historical figures like the Empress Eugenie and the Empress Josephine; and dolls devoted to the glamorous life (including countless princesses and fashion models).

While baby dolls have been tied to learning nurturing skills, Barbie dolls seem to be tied to different social skills. With extreme and sexualized body proportions—her measurements would work out to 39"-18"-33" on a 5-foot-9-inch real woman—parents and teachers worry that Barbie provides an unrealistic ideal of beauty. In response to that complaint, Mattel altered the doll's proportions to reflect a smaller chest measurement (36 inches) and a larger waist measurement (23 inches). While there is no empirical research that supports the assumption that Barbie or any other doll might create problems later on, questions about the effect Barbie has on girls' self-esteem and body image continue to be debated.

Fashion Dolls

Like Barbie, fashion dolls tend to focus on the significance of appearance and clothing style. From the 14th century, these dolls were used to introduce and support costume style. Monarchs and courtiers alike made presents of fashion dolls, offering a vision of the latest fashions in couture and coiffeur. In many ways, these dolls served as catalogs; sent to faraway ports from Paris, the fashion doll modeled fashionable life for those who could not be in the city. Russian princesses and American colonists alike could learn what the well-dressed European woman was wearing by ordering and looking at a European doll. So valuable were these dolls as fashion models that special regulations for exporting them were passed in Paris; rather than focusing on economic concerns, these regulations governed the specifications for measurements of the dolls and their clothes, an attempt to make life-size copies of the clothing possible.

With that purpose in mind, the need for fashion dolls to appear lifelike seems only natural. Springing from the German tradition of wooden manikins used as models for drawing and painting, this doll has a more realistic body that approximates the human form, which allows for the accurate modeling of clothes. When that accurate modeling was not possible, two-dimensional paper dolls could fill the gap. Drawings of realistic-looking men, women, and children could be dressed with cut-outs designed to fit their bodies. Although these paper dolls were not particularly useful as artists' models, they did allow for a vision of how certain costumes and hair styles would look when placed on the human body.

Among the most famous modern fashion dolls are those created between the 1930s and 1960s, notably Winnie and Binnie Walker, Cissy, Miss Revlon, Toni, Ginny, Jill, and Barbie. Each of these dolls allowed girls to dress them, style their hair, and, occasionally, apply their makeup. In emphasizing the processes of grooming, the dolls do have an educational purpose. However, their principle purpose has often been to display the fashion trends of the era.

In the 19th and 20th centuries, fashion dolls have become collectible items. Generally produced from more breakable materials like china, porcelain, and bisque, the fashion doll has maintained its emphasis on high-style couture. Collectors categorize them according to those styles, but also according to the shape and material composition of their heads and bodies.

Spiritual and Relic Dolls

The earliest examples of dolls had very few recreational uses. Instead, dolls were used as relics and idols. Imbued with a spiritual or ritual significance, these figures from ancient Egypt, Greece, and Rome might have been used as children's playthings, though they seem to have been more firmly attached to fertility and fecundity. Marriages were consecrated with dolls (as they still are in India); achieving sexual maturity (Africa) and reaching marriageable age (Syria) were signaled by giving and displaying dolls. In these instances, the doll serves a broader societal and ritualistic purpose.

The Katchina doll of the Hopi Indians functions as a symbol of blessing instead of as a toy. Believed to be the representation of the spirit beings (Katsinam), the doll—importantly not an idol—is given to a young girl. She and her family then hang the Katchina doll in their home as a physical symbol of the blessing given to the girl and her family. Though not an object of worship, the Katchina doll is offered respect.

Crèche dolls fit into the same category. Designed to physically illustrate the birth of Jesus, these dolls range from highly elaborate figures to primitive representations. Whatever their style, crèche dolls depict Mary, Joseph, and the baby Jesus, along with a variety of animals, shepherds, and wise men or kings. Depending on where they were created, the dolls can be made of materials as varied as wood, terracotta, wax, and porcelain. Their clothing also differs, with different makers choosing to use the representative dress of their own time and place or the dress they believed contemporary to the nativity. Given their religious significance, crèche dolls were rarely if ever used as toys. They were displayed in churches, museums, and homes (especially during the Christmas season) to denote the owners' Christianity and social status.

No single material was used to make these earlier dolls. Wax, wood, clay, ivory, marble, bone, leather, cloth, and wood dolls have all survived. Nor do their forms show a consistent style. Some, like the Egyptian paddle-shaped dolls, offer hair made of clay pellets, voluptuous curves, and fertility symbols as decorations. Others, like the terra cotta figures discovered in Grecian temples dedicated to Demeter and Persephone, Aphrodite and Artemis, display jointed figures, contemporary styles of headgear, dress, and musical instruments.

Doll Forms

Over time, dolls for play have taken a variety of forms. Wooden dolls were popular from the 17th century, when they were fashioned by artisans in England and Germany. Early versions of wooden dolls offered a turned body, hand-carved features with paint and gesso finish, and painted eyes. Generally, the heads of these dolls were disproportionately large. When compared to later dolls, these wooden dolls seem particularly crude. Ironically, the dolls' quality deteriorated over time, as less care was taken with each individual doll.

A specialized version of wooden dolls—nesting dolls—seems exempt from that deterioration of form. Russian in origin, nesting dolls stack dolls within larger dolls. The human form appears only through the brightly-painted exteriors. Although nesting dolls have evolved to include a variety of images, they were originally meant to celebrate motherhood and fertility.

Wax dolls were also available to children in the 18th century. Not as common as wooden dolls, these were widely available in Catholic countries, whose doll makers used wax to create crèche dolls. Wax dolls were available

Dolls can range in craftmanship from a simple cloth or cornhusk doll to an intricate fashion or porcelain doll.

in either a child or adult form, with the adult form tending to be more of a collectible or display item than a toy.

Papier-mâché dolls, whose heads were created from soaked paper that was thickened with a hardening agent and adhesive, became economical and practical in the 1820s. By attaching the papier-mâché head to a cloth body with wooden arms and legs, doll manufacturers could relatively quickly turn out dolls for sale.

By the 1840s, another relatively inexpensive doll joined these. The rag doll, which was officially patented in 1873, was created entirely from fabric. Layers of glued cloth were pressed with dies to create the doll's head, which was then stuffed and painted. The head was then attached to a stuffed cloth body, to which hand-modeled and hand-stitched legs and arms were sewn. Particularly popular in America, the rag doll has become a symbol of folk art and folk toys. Like cornhusk dolls, rag dolls were often made by women who could not afford to buy dolls for their daughters. These home-made toys were fashioned out of the materials available.

Porcelain dolls, on the other hand, were considerably more expensive. Although examples from the 1840s still exist, the porcelain doll's beginnings are unknown. The dolls tend to be more delicate and fragile than their wooden, wax, and cloth predecessors. China and Bisque, both variations of porcelain, were used primarily to make doll heads, arms, and feet, all of which were then attached to a cloth body. Occasionally, however, an entire doll was created out of porcelain; given their extreme delicacy, these dolls were rarely intended for use as playthings; instead, they were meant to be collectible items for display.

Toward the end of the 19th century, dolls became more realistic. Features were changed, with fixed glass eyes, jointed limbs, and lifelike proportions becoming increasingly more common. When combined with improved methods of mass production and increased world trade, these advances in doll making allowed for the marketing and merchandising of particular dolls. With the 20th century came named dolls, available in exactly the same form to children around the world. Some of the most famous of these dolls help to tell the story of all of the types that preceded them.

Doll Trends

The Kewpie doll illustrates the popularity and significance of baby dolls. Designed by Rose O'Neill, the Kewpie doll—whose name comes from a diminutive version of "cupid"—first appeared in bisque in 1913. Modeled on O'Neill's baby brother, the Kewpie doll quickly became popular. Many other materials were used to manufacture the dolls, who also sprang to life in stories and who were featured in merchandise as varied as clock cases, inkwells, and jewelry. By the 1920s, the Kewpie doll, now made principally out of celluloid, was the doll to have. Immensely popular, the doll offered a baby for whom a little girl could care.

Similarly, Raggedy Ann and Andy became friends for the girls who owned them. John Barton Gruelle, a political cartoonist, created the first Raggedy Ann for his daughter Marcella by drawing a face on an old rag doll. When Marcella delighted in the doll, Gruelle applied for a patent based on his hand-drawn illustrations of Raggedy Ann. Soon after receiving the patent, Marcella died and Gruelle began to publish stories that featured Raggedy Ann and Raggedy Andy. The first dolls were produced by the Gruelle family in 1918 and were used to promote the stories. The stories were successful (and are still in print), and the dolls have enjoyed constant popularity.

Depression and Wartime Dolls

As the 1920s passed, Americans were able to buy fewer dolls. The Great Depression severely limited the ability of families to purchase new dolls. So important were dolls, though, that new doll clothes continued to be made and given as gifts. Even in the heart of a catastrophe, the doll's significance was underscored. Manufacturers, too, persisted in marketing dolls, focusing on a few, "must-have" dolls. Although unavailable to the masses, these dolls served as models for the dolls that would follow. The DyDee doll and Betsy Wetsy introduced dolls who could drink form a bottle, wet a diaper, and blow bubbles; their realism emphasized the manner in which dolls could be used to teach childcare principles to girls. Another type of dolls—paper dolls—suggest a means of dealing with a lack of money. Paper dolls could be cut from magazines, where they and their clothes were preprinted, or drawn and cut from old newspapers. Created for centuries, S. & J. Fuller of England produced the first manufactured paper doll in 1810; J. Belcher of Boston followed with an American version in 1812.

Increased marketing of dolls also started during the Depression. One brand of dolls—the Madam Alexander dolls—began to gain popularity. Taking their inspiration from celebrities and current events, these dolls became especially popular after the 1934 birth of the Dionne quintuplets in Canada; the Madame Alexander versions of the babies helped to boost doll sales to $22 million in 1936. Another increase in sales figures came from dolls based on movies (like the 1937 Snow White dolls released to accompany the Walt Disney movie) and cartoons (like the Little Lulu dolls introduced in 1939.) Shirley Temple dolls figure into the same phenomenon. Not particularly educational, these dolls used the actress' fame and movies to market a model for maintaining optimism while overcoming the adversity of everyday life.

With the advent of World War II, doll production and sales decreased. Cloth dolls replaced their rubber and celluloid counterparts as those materials became increasingly necessary for the war effort. With the end of the war, doll making entered an era widely known as the golden age of dolls. Increased spending power and consumerism also led to the practice of owning more than one doll. With dolls that spoke, smiled, clapped, and danced, it was not difficult to encourage parents to buy one more doll for their daughters.

The Golden Age of Dolls

Three types of dolls appeared in this golden age. The first type included baby dolls like Tiny Tears (1950), Bonnie Braids (1951), Sister Belle (1961), and Chatty Cathy (1960s); the second included dolls based on movies and television shows, like Mrs. Beasley (1967), a doll who appeared in the television sitcom, *Family Affair;* the third were a variation on fashion dolls. These dolls encouraged girls to play dress up and to learn about current trends in fashion. Unlike more traditional fashion dolls, these were marketed as playthings, for which a wide array of clothes, fashion accessories, houses, and furnishings could be purchased. Virtually every doll manufacturing company released a doll like this: Vogue produced the Ginny doll (1951); Madame Alexander created Wendy (1953) and then Winnie Walker (1953), Binnie Walker (1953), and Cissy (1955); Ideal offered Miss Revlon (1956), Little Miss Revlon (1958), and Toni Walker (1958). None of these dolls created the same sensation as the Barbie doll, though.

New types of dolls have been developed continually since this golden age of dolls. Among the most famous of these dolls are Cabbage Patch Kids. Invented by Xavier Roberts in 1976, they allowed children to "adopt" a doll. Throughout the 1980s Cabbage Patch Kids enjoyed immense popularity. Many other new dolls have addressed the growing concern with displaying the ethnic diversity of the United States and the world at large by producing dolls of every color. One doll that addresses that concern is Chatty Cathy (1984), an African-American version of Mattel's 1960s-era Chatty Cathy. Still other dolls have celebrated the popular culture of the time, building on the possibilities first noted with the Mrs. Beasley doll. Rainbow Brite, Strawberry Shortcake, and the Smurfs are examples of dolls that gained increased popularity because of their exposure on television.

See Also: Girls' Play; Human Relationships in Play; Mother-Child Play; Playing "House"; Toys and Child Development.

Bibliography. David Cohen, *Development of Play,* 2nd edition (Routledge, 1993); Carolyn Goodfellow and Faith Eaton, *Ultimate Doll Book* (DK Adult, 1993); M.G. Lord, *Forever Barbie: The Unauthorized Biography of a Real Doll* (William Morrow and Company, 1994); Yona Zeldis McDonough, ed, *The Barbie Chronicles: A Living Doll Turns Forty* (Touchstone, 1999); Juliette Peers, *Fashion Doll: From Bebe Jumeau to Barbie* (Berg Publishers, 2004); Helga Teiwes, *Katchina Dolls: The Art of Hopi Carvers* (University of Arizona Press, 1991); Susan Waggoner, *Under the Tree: The Toys and Treats that Made Christmas Special 1930–1970* (Stuart, Tabori and Chang, 2007).

Anastasia L. Pratt
State University of New York

Dominoes and Variations of

Dominoes evokes the image of an interconnected system, the elements of which aid and determine one another. The image was given shape by an idle variation of the game of Dominoes in which rectangular tile pieces are put on edge in long lines, then the first tile is toppled causing the rest in line to fall in a precise and predictive manner. The outstanding legacy of this image in the 20th century, besides a common analogy referred to as the *domino effect* (often quoted in the context of global warming, for instance), meaning a chain of small events that cause similar events leading to catastrophes, is the so-called *domino theory*. A geopolitical theory that emerged in the United States during the 1950s and 1960s, from the analogy first proposed by President Eisenhower in 1954 to justify military intervention in Vietnam (and reiterated in the 1980s by Ronald Reagan to justify intervention in Nicaragua), the domino theory states that if one country comes under Communist control, the neighboring countries will also come under Communist control. Needless to say, the fall of Communist regimes in eastern Europe after 1989 illustrated a reverse of the pattern. These theoretical applications do have a connection to the games of strategy encompassed by Dominoes in their different variations and demonstrate that sometimes games have the role to synthesize real-life situations on a larger scale. Granted, the correlation of matching numbers is replaced by physical implications, but this goes to show how a certain tradition (in this case Asian) is usually translated into the Western canon.

The logical effect wanted by the individual or collective games played with Dominoes (the deck or pack of a domino set) is matching one end of a piece (also called bone, card, tile, ticket, stone, or spinner) to another piece identically or reciprocally numbered. The standard set comprises 28 pieces, marked from double six (six-six) to double zero (0-0). The pieces having a common end constitute a suit, and the quality of the pieces is expressed in weight: the bone with most dots is the heavier. The game is known throughout the world in different variations.

In China Dominoes are known as early as the 12th century, but the dotted cards of the Chinese had no blank faces, as do the ones familiar to contemporary players. On the European continent, dominoes first appear in the middle of the 18th century in Italy and then in France. It is difficult to determine what the connection is between the modern game of Dominoes and these initial manifestations or whether the Chinese model was "borrowed" by Italians. Keeping in mind that the missionary activity of the Catholic Church to China developed in the 17th century and was very intense in the first half of the 18th century, as well as the visits of secular Europeans to the Asian continent, it is not improbable that this is the channel through which the Domino game entered Europe. The game is not characteristic of European types of card-games; based on principles of numerology and mathematics, the Domino game is an Asian heritage, inspired by the Indian cubic dice. The principles of this "matching" game have generated, as shown above, deterministic clichés.

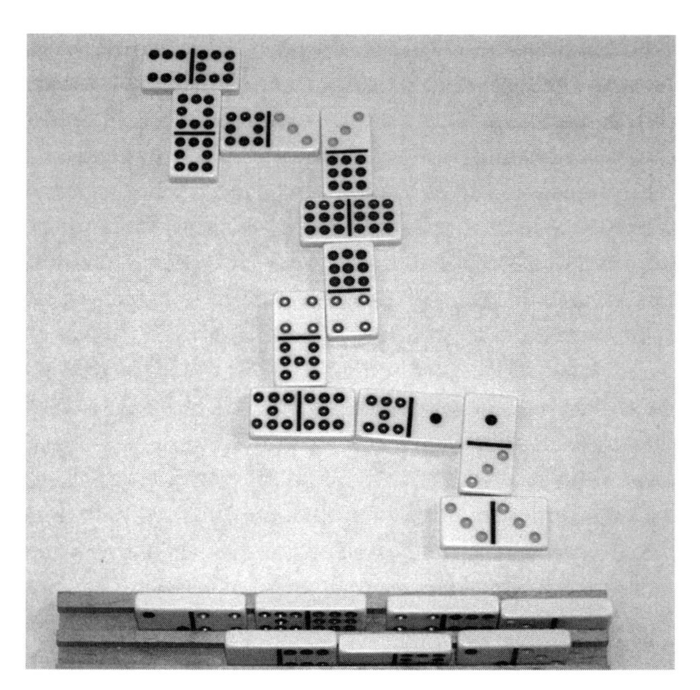

Most commercial domino sets are made of synthetic materials that approximate the look and feel of ivory.

The most spectacular manifestation of these clichés is an internationally acclaimed event—the Domino Day. The purpose of this event, initiated by the Dutch Robin Paul Weijers in the 1980s together with Endemol, is to set a world record in the number of falling domino tiles. The aim of the game is not only to establish new records, but to put on a majestic show that demonstrates the interconnections between the pieces. The participating teams invest great efforts to set up the tiles in a physically viable manner, so as to also produce an aesthetic outcome. Domino Day is indicative of the way in which Western European culture transforms a set of rules and game principles from a distinct tradition and, minimalizing its logical prerequisites, turns them into a game of illusions. However, this was not the initial procedure, as a glimpse into the different variations of Domino games show.

Modern Variations

At the outset, in Europe as well as in America, Dominoes was played according to the original model, taking on different forms to suit the social context. The most commonly played variations of Domino games are Domino Whist, Matador, and Muggins (all fives). The Whist is a Domino game for four players and is inspired by the notorious card-game. Each player has seven bones, and the game ends when one player has exhausted the last bone or the ends are blocked. The Matador is a common draw game with the usual object of going out first and collecting points based on the bones still in one's opponents hands. In Muggins points are earned when a player plays a bone, with the result that the count (the sum of all open ends) is a multiple of five. A special variation emerged in Texas, called 42, a trick-taking game played with a standard set of double-six dominoes.

This game was created in 1887 in Trappe Springs by two young boys, members of a strict conservative Southern Baptist sect who were forbidden to play cards. It is often referred to as the "national game of Texas" and continues to be very popular in much of the state. Tournaments are held in many towns, and the State Championship tournament is held in Hallettsville the first Saturday of March each year. Other popular variations of Dominoes include Bendomino, Chickie Dominoes (Chicken Foot), Concentration, Double Fives, and Domino Trains. Dominoes, similar to Poker, is played at a professional level, and matches and tournaments are often televised in Latin America. Organizations and clubs of amateur Domino players exist around the world. Some organizations, including the International Federation of Dominos and the Fédération Internationale de Domino (FIDO), organize international competitions.

See Also: All Fives; China; Dice; Play and Power, Sociology of.

Bibliography. Edmond Hoyle et al., eds., *Hoyle's Rules of Games*, 3rd edition (Signet, 2001); Dennis Roberson, *Winning 42: Strategy and Lore of the National Game of Texas* (Texas Tech University Press, 2004); Sarah Ethridge Hunt, *Games and Sports the World Around* (Ronald Press Company, 1964).

Ilona Denes
Central European University

Donkey

Donkey is a children's card game played with a traditional 52-card deck, in which cards are exchanged between players (instead of being played into a pool as in more complicated games). Special Donkey decks are often sold, with various animals in place of the usual four suits. The goal is to collect four of a kind in a four-card hand by discarding one card at a time. Each discarded card passes to the player to the left, who can keep it if he wishes, so long as he discards another card so as to keep his hand at four cards.

Once someone has four of a kind, they have won the game and should lay their hand down as quietly as possible. The other players then need to react by laying their cards down, whether they have a set or not. The last player to put his cards down loses the hand. This gives him a letter "D." If that player should lose more hands, he collects letters to spell the word *Donkey*. The game is lost when one person "collects" the letters to spell the word *Donkey*. A similar version of this game is called Pig. Instead of laying the cards down, a finger is laid aside your nose indicating that you have your four of a kind. The last person to notice this gesture is dubbed the "Pig."

See Also: Casino; Fish; History of Playing Cards.

Bibliography. Elliott Avedon, *The Study of Games* (Krieger Pub., 1979); Roger Caillois, *Man, Play and Games* (University of Illinois Press, 2001); David Parlett, *The Oxford Guide to Card Games* (Oxford University Press, 1990); Brian Sutton-Smith, *The Ambiguity of Play* (Harvard University Press, 2001).

Bill Kte'pi
Independent Scholar

Dozens, Playing the

The expression *the dozens* refers to dramatized exchanges of insults between two opponents, most typically involving the other's mother as indirect referent, and with a variable stress on overall performance, diction, phrase rhythm, or rhyme. It is part of 20th-century African-American urban speech culture, with likely but disputable roots in African history, as well as enduring resonance in contemporary pop culture, particularly television game shows (MTV's *Yo Momma*, running 3 seasons in 2006–08), standup comedy (e.g., comedian-audience interactions), and Web sites. What qualifies as its historically salient properties, functions, merits, and hence, what informs its status as "game" or "play," has been assessed variably across academic disciplines and their timeframes, ranging from 1930s–1960s social psychology of the lower-class black family and folklore to intersectional research into race/ethnicity, gender, life phases, language, and contemporary media.

The Dozens (a range of etymological suggestions has been proposed) have been variably known as being "played" or "talked," as "giving" or "putting" a person in the Dozens, as "yo' momma fights" or as featuring "yo' mama jokes," or as (involving) trash-talk, cussing, blowing, snapping, sounding, woofing, dissing, capping, cracking, bagging, hiking, joning, ranking, ribbing, serving, signifying, slipping, wolfing, sigging, or screaming. In some attested taxonomies, the Dozens typically amounts to a contest based on repertoire and verbal audacity that takes place between young children as they recite formulaic rhymes, while joning, among older participants, though sharing stylistic features with the Dozens, has rather a direct recognizable relationship to context and occasion, and is more directed at the individual, more improvised, and not expected to amount to a clear-cut contest.

Dozens are commonly classified "clean" or "dirty," referring to the inclusion of sexual slurs; accepts any public space as its natural setting; and has a traditional *dramatis personae* of befriended male peers, set against the background of a responsive audience. Themes of innuendo may include the full spectrum of sexual transgression, from female promiscuity, infidelity, and homosexuality to bestiality, and address the opponent or his family, most typically his mother or sister. The practice has been ethnographically attested as early as in third grade, among girls and across ethnicities, but is widely recognized as reaching its ultimate form among male black youth.

Audiences play a critical and triple role: to stir up and arbitrate (by being responsive to perceived verbal agility, improvisational skill, humorous content, and overall efficacy to top the opponents' turns and hence to entertain), as well as to bear witness to victory and loss. Thus, the Dozens fits within the urban ethnic template of street "battling" (compare rap and breakdance).

Anthropologically, the Dozens has been examined within a range of analytic contexts: insult-based oral genres, mediation and ritualization of in-group conflict (insults rather than violence, if a potential prelude to violence), and (less satisfyingly) joking relationships and kinship systems more generally. To categorize the Dozens as play usually pertains to its folkloric classification as informal contest or to its providing of a passive or active socializing context, either in terms of form (humor, agonistic speech, public speaking, ethnic speech patterns) or content (semiformal reiterations of a sexual order). Theorists have offered divergent functional interpretations, which variably highlight elements of humor, gender/masculinity, aggression, "ritualization," socialization, racial history, subcultures, peer group systems, and language in use.

Functional interpretations have ranged from psychoanalytic (management of child-adult separation anxiety, sublimation of aggression, catharsis) to social-pedagogical (male initiation, verbal skills training, sex education) and psycho-cultural. Some culture-based interpretations suggest that the Dozens, along with other genres such as "performing the Toasts" (long narrative poems that detail the exploits of heroes, badmen, and tricksters), inscribes a meta-social commentary on ghetto life and thus amounts to "deep play" (Clifford Geertz), a game with stakes superlative to the "mere" play it appears to be, in particular the persona of the male ghetto survivor. Others argue that the Dozens provides a dynamically adaptive conduit for the consolidation of group ties. For instance, humor would relate to the negotiation of gender-sexual hierarchies and masculinities within pupil and peer cultures.

At this point controversy exists whether to see the Dozens as positive coping strategy or as maladaptive symptom. Some interpretations stress ethnic/racial and personal resilience and conflict resolution, while others suggest the practice elaborates an internalized racial self-hatred or "neurosis." The Dozens in mass cultural representations has been criticized for its potential for the cultivation of misogyny as well as racist auto-stereotyping and denigration of black facial and body features.

See Also: Play as Competition, Psychology of; Play as Entertainment, Sociology of; Social Psychology of Play; Teasing.

Bibliography. Lige Dailey, *Playing the Dozens: A Psycho-Historical Examination of an African American Ritual.* Ph.D. Dissertation (The Wright Institute, 1986); Alan Dundes, ed., *Mother Wit from the Laughing Barrel: Readings in the Interpretation of Afro-American Folklore.* (Prentice Hall, 1973/1990); Thurmon Garner, "Playing the Dozens: Folklore as Strategies for Living," *African American Communication & Identities: Essential Readings*, Ronald L. Jackson, ed. (Sage, 2004).

Diederik Floris Janssen
Independent Scholar
Ilona Denes
Central European University

Dragon Quest

There are two significant games carrying the name Dragon Quest: the first is a pen-and-paper or tabletop role-playing game (RPG), the second a computer RPG. The RPG's name is conjoined: DragonQuest. In the United States, the digital game had to change its name to Dragon Warrior because of the trademark conflict, though the demise of the pen-and-paper game meant the name of the digital game later changed in 2003.

DragonQuest the RPG was published in 1980 by Simulations Publications (SPI). It was one of the second generation of RPGs, which helped advance the genre out of the wargame-based, combat-heavy roots established by the first versions of *Dungeons & Dragons*. DragonQuest used a skills system to allow detailed character creation, one of the first games to do so. By allowing players to create characters that do not follow a set class, but rather have more breadth and depth, the rules directed players toward putting more thought into the characterisation of their creations than previous games.

From a ludic standpoint, DragonQuest is interesting because of the way it handles damage taken by characters in combat. Very experienced characters are not very much more durable than novices. Tactically, this means that the "tank" approach to combat (when one very durable character takes the punishment the enemy is dealing out) does not work, which results in very active participation in conflict by all characters. This system also means that experienced and less experienced characters can mix more easily—in most RPGs the potent characters would not be challenged, or the weak ones would be killed instantly, or at least be unable to do much. In general, combat, though heroic in nature, tends to be more realistic than in the games that preceded it. However, DragonQuest's rule structure has greatly influenced modern games.

Magic is split into a number of "colleges," each providing different spells. Examples include the various elemental colleges (air, earth, fire, water) and less obvious ones (summoning, rune magic). This is another example of the way the game seeks to add flavor and character, and it broke with what many saw as the mechanistic magic common to early RPGs.

DragonQuest is presently owned by Wizards of the Coast, who acquired it when they purchased TSR, who in turn acquired it when they took over SPI. The trademark has been abandoned, allowing Square Enix to take it up, implying that the game is moribund, and indeed has been out of print since 1987. In spite of this, the game still has many devotees worldwide.

The computerized version of Dragon Quest is a long-running series with nine core games and various spin-offs. It was developed in Japan by Chunsoft and published by Square Enix. In the United States, the game was known as Dragon Warrior to avoid trademark infringement. Numerous versions of the game have been released for a slowly increasing complexity of console. All essentially follow the common tropes of computer RPGs: players battle monsters and solve puzzles, become more powerful as they do so by gaining experience, and find gold, which they spend to buy better equipment.

The series is incredibly popular in Japan, though overshadowed in the West by other Square Enix offerings, most notably, the Final Fantasy series. The soundtrack of the game is orchestral and has a following of its own. As a very early example of an RPG, many of its features (notably its two-dimensional top-down perspective) have gone on to become standard for the genre.

See Also: *Dungeons & Dragons*; Japan; Role-Playing; Wargames.

Bibliography. Daniel Mackay, *The Fantasy Role-Playing Game: A New Performing Art* (McFarland & Company, 2001); Lawrence Schick, *Heroic Worlds: A History and Guide to Role Playing Games* (Prometheus Books, 1991); J. Patrick Williams, et al., eds., *Gaming As Culture: Essays on Reality, Identity and Experience in Fantasy Games* (McFarland, 2006).

Justin Parsler
Brunel University

Dragon Warrior

The electronic videogame Dragon Warrior was originally titled Dragon Quest when it was released to Japanese audiences in 1986. It was released for the Japanese game console the Nintendo Family Computer, or Famicom. In 1989 the game was released for North American audiences and the Nintendo Entertainment System, or NES. The game was later ported to several other Nintendo console platforms, including the Super Famicom, Game Boy and Game Boy Color, and Japanese cell phones. The importance of the game in the context of the Japanese mobile sector has been noted by Dean Chan. The game was later used as a promotion for the Nintendo publication, *Nintendo Power*. The first game spawned a series of subsequent Dragon Warrior titles in North America and Dragon Quest games in Japan. It was not until 2005 that North American Dragon Warrior titles took on the title Dragon Quest because of a naming conflict with the North American role-playing game Dragon Quest, a competitor to *Dungeons & Dragons*. Copies of Dragon Warrior were given to subscribers, and the magazine devoted long articles over several issues to the game.

Dragon Warrior is an early and notable example of an electronic role-playing videogame. As the player progresses through the game they are awarded experience points and gold for the successfully defeating enemy creatures encountered along the way. As experience points are gained, the player increases in levels, which in turn increases their character's abilities. Battles occur in a turn-based fashion, where the player and encountered enemy take turns taking action against one another. Players have the ability to fight an enemy in combat, attempt to run away, use an item, or cast a magical spell. This turn-based approach is very similar to how play is structured in pen-and-paper role-playing games like *Dungeons & Dragons*.

The narrative of the game is also one that is pervasive throughout videogames and role-playing games in particular. The princess, or love interest, of the main character has been captured by the game's villain, and the main character must advance and save her from peril. Frequently this opponent also poses as a threat to the broader populace of the world. In the process of defeating the villain, the player acquires new skills necessary to defeat this ultimate enemy. By defeating his foe, the hero not only rescues the princess, but also rids the land of a malevolent tyrant.

The game used an overhead, two-dimensional, style of display, which has carried over to many electronic role-playing videogames even now. This style of visualizing a game has become so recognizable that many gamers explicitly associate it with electronic role-playing games immediately. It has been recognized by many game players and game developers as having had a significant impact on the electronic role-playing videogame genre.

Developed by the Japanese videogame development company Chunsoft, the game originally featured spell names that were largely nonsensical in Japanese. When an English version of the game was created, it was translated into a stylized version of early English. Spells were given names related to their function, and references to Arthurian literature were added to the games narrative. One instance of "Puff puff" being offered to a player was also removed from the U.S. version of the game. While Dragon Quest has spawned numerous sequels in Japan, only a small number have been localized for the U.S. and European markets.

Because the hardware of the NES made it difficult to generate pseudo-random numbers similar to the rolling of dice in role-playing games, Dragon Warrior made use of numerous other mechanisms to generate apparent randomness. An example of this can be found in how the name of the character chosen at the beginning of the game affects how quickly the player's skills adjust as levels are gained through the awarding of experience points.

See Also: Dice; Dragon Quest; *Dungeons & Dragons*; Fantasy Play; Play as Entertainment, Sociology of; Role-Playing.

Bibliography. Dean Chan, "Convergence, Connectivity, and the Case of Japanese Mobile Gaming," *Games and Culture* (v.3/1, 2008); Dustin Hubbard and Dwaine Bullock, "Dragon Quest Shrine: Dragon Warrior" www.dqshrine.com/dw (cited July 2008); Lawrence Schick, *Heroic Worlds: A History and Guide to Role Playing Games* (Prometheus Books, 1991).

Casey O'Donnell
University of Georgia

Dungeon Lords

Dungeon Lords is a role-playing game (RPG) released for the PC in 2005 by Heuristic Park. The game is usually played by a single player, although multiplayer options also exist. Dungeon Lords borrows heavily from successors such as the Oblivion series, the Baldur's Gate games, and even earlier, from games such as Might and Magic. It is known for being one of the most disastrous video games ever launched.

Dungeon Lords is very similar to many games in the fantasy roleplaying genre that have continued in popularity throughout the history of digital games. The game uses a first-person or distanced perspective whereby the player sees their avatar from behind and slightly above. The world within which a player moves is large and three-dimensional; scale is usually depicted through the use of maps that the player can access. Fantasy themes are common, and magic is usually a reality within each world. Players must guide their avatar through a narrative-orientated fantasy world, carrying out quests and slaying monsters. These actions reward them with experience points, and more specifically to Dungeon Lords, advantage points. Using points to boost a character's statistics makes them grow as a character, and allows them to specialize their abilities within a chosen class. As with most RPGs, the classes available in Dungeon Lords are based on an approximation of the classes originally used in *Dungeons & Dragons*.

Dungeon Lords was not a success and is known for its complex interface, poor performance, and bugged game play. When the game was released, it was heavily criticized for pre-emptively distributing a game for commercial retail when many features were incomplete, missing, or did not work. The box for the game also had the wrong specifications listed, meaning that many computers could not run the game, as they did not fulfil the memory or graphical requirements. A review of the game stated, "Dungeon Lords marks a new low for how incomplete a game can be and still get released." To give an idea of how poor the game was upon release, many buttons in the tutorial did not work, items disappeared from the player's inventory, and NPCs (nonplayer characters) were frequently bugged, did not offer rewards when prompted, or simply disappeared.

Later reviews acknowledged the faults inherent within the game, but also argued that Heuristic Park had done a great deal to remedy these aspects. As with many games released on the market, the company improved content with subsequent patches and editions, which aimed to correct the majority of early problems. However, when the company collapsed in 2005, no further support was available and much of the game remained unfinished.

Dungeon Lords seems to have suffered both from overambition and poor implementation of the innovative ideas it tried to implement. As a result the player is confused rather than enthused by the new directions the game attempted to take. Dungeon Lords' preemptive release may have been a result of Heuristic Park's internal problems, or as a response to the phenomenal success of massively multiplayer online role playing games (MMORPGs). By 2005, World of Warcraft already had five million active users, and with Oblivion IV as a strong contender for the single-player market in the same genre, Dungeon Lords may simply have been an attempt to corner some of the market by default.

See Also: *Dungeons & Dragons;* Role-Playing; Wargames; World of Warcraft.

Bibliography. Dungeon Lords Official Web site, www.dungeonlords.com (cited July 2008); Daniel Mackay, *The Fantasy Role-Playing Game: A New Performing Art* (McFarland & Company, 2001); Reviews of Dungeon Lords, www.metacritic.com (cited January 2009).

Esther MacCallum-Stewart
University of East London

Dungeons & Dragons

Dungeons & Dragons (D&D) is a tabletop fantasy role-playing game (RPG). It was initially published by Gary Gygax and Dave Arneson in 1974 and has since gone through several editions that have tweaked or otherwise updated the rule system. The game is single-handedly responsible for modern RPGs; although it grew from several similar games and systems, its combination of statistical game-play and imaginative role playing means it is a truly original text and one of the most influential games ever developed.

It is estimated that over 20 million people have played *Dungeons & Dragons*, and that it has 5.5 million active users; however, the influence of D&D is far more widespread than these figures would suggest. D&D rules, characters, and class systems are still used as a basis for many games of all genres. *Dungeons & Dragons* is the progenitor of literally thousands of spin-offs within the genre as well as having tremendous influence upon, if not actually being the origin of, the realms of computer gaming, live-action role-playing, fantasy literature, and online gaming. An example of this influence might be the 150 million accounts created on Runequest, the 11 million active users in World of Warcraft, or the 4,480,000 hits generated from entering "Dungeons & Dragons" into a Google search.

D&D is a structured game that somewhat paradoxically also depends on free-form action on the behalf of the players to succeed. Players adopt the roles of characters within a narrative setting and are allocated points for various social and physical attributes relating to their character. These are grouped roughly by strength, dexterity, constitution, charisma, wisdom, and intelligence. These statistics govern other abilities, such as how fast a character can react, or what are known as "modifiers"—numbers that determine how well or badly a character can respond to other circumstances. Characters come from various races and have a class that defines what type of action they can perform. Combat and other actions that require skill or luck are decided by dice roles, which are then modified according to each player's relative skills; otherwise, the game is played largely without pieces, although figures, maps, props and exterior elements such as music are all frequently introduced by enterprising players, and there is a flourishing subindustry to provide elements such as map paper and miniature figures to represent the player. Despite this, the bulk of the action takes place primarily within the players' collective imagination.

D&D Hierarcy

The game itself is run by a Dungeon Master, or DM, who decides on the form of the narrative. Events such as encounters with monsters or NPCs (nonplayer characters), the environment and narrative setting, and any trials, quests or actions that need to be performed are created by DMs, who also act as arbitrator and chairperson for the play session. The players (one or more—an average group is usually between five to seven people) decide the substance of play through their actions and decisions, visualizing and describing how their characters act in each situation as part of a consensual narrative. These actions may vary greatly from the DM's initial intention as the game is deliberately not linear in form and is instead determined by player decisions rather than a driven narrative. In fact, one of the beauties of the game is the ability to solve (or not) the problems created by this dynamic.

Game Variations

Dungeons & Dragons is a game that is hugely open to interpretation. Many players engage in extremely ludic versions of the game, where dice, statistics, and detailed movements are all charted in high detail while the game takes place. Others play very narrative versions, where characterisation is key, and the ludic elements merely facilitate this. The game is such that both extremes may also take part in the same game at the same time—D&D is very much up to the interpretation of the individual, and it is this capability within the game that seems to account not only for its enduring success, but also for the multiplicity of influences and spin-offs it has produced.

The initial fantasy setting has been reinterpreted within many other genres, with science fiction, horror, established worlds such as the Buffyverse, Westerns, and time periods such as the 1920s or Dark Ages all being some examples of how the game can be reinterpreted. Popular reinterpretations of D&D through slightly different rules or settings have spawned the tabletop role-playing genre (so called because a flat surface is usually needed to place dice, character sheets, and miniatures, but no other equipment is required) and include systems such as GURPS (Generic Universal Roleplaying System), Call of Cthulhu, Vampire the Masquerade, and Warhammer.

Player Interactivity

One of the core elements that has made D&D so successful is the open-ended nature of game play, which positions the player as hero travelling through a continuous landscape, rather than focusing on specific winning conditions. While players are encouraged to engage cooperatively together, the game emphasizes the role of the individual in situations that are more reminiscent of action adventure films or fantasy novels than simply adhering to a game of rolling dice and sliding statistics. Rather, the game dynamic enables a situation in which characters are able to perform extraordinary deeds and take active roles in the development and mythology of whatever world they are taking part in. Campaigns—games that last over several sessions—allow for character development both statistically and psychologically. A great deal has been written about the relative immersion and agency given to characters within these games by players—their ability, quite literally, to shape their own destinies and to map out lives through imagined selves is one of the core strengths of the game, and has also allowed D&D to develop in such multifaceted directions as a result.

The Influence of D&D

Although the game itself is still immensely popular, its influence can be seen in many other texts. Several popular fantasy series have been developed from characters initially played in D&D or similar games—George R.R. Martin's Wild Cards series, Feist's Magician, and the

Dragonlance series are all strong examples of novels or series that originated directly from campaigns in which the author played or was DM, and used the source material for their novels. Long-haul series such as Robert Jordan's The Wheel of Time and the Eddings's Belgariad sequences all contain archetypal D&D characters who, while they may not be directly sourced from games, are easily recognizable to their audiences.

The tropes created by the character class system in D&D have also had lasting influence on digital games, founding the RPG genre and enabling staple elements such as the selection of fundamental character class, the dependence on leveling up by gaining experience points, statistics allotted to abilities such as strength, intelligence, a pool of health, and mana points available to the player, armor and clothing that is class dependent and grants statistical benefits when worn, and turn-based combat systems. This common language has provided a fundamental basis to the genre. When Gygax died in 2008, thousands of obituaries appeared online on blogs, forums, and news pages. The dedication of patches and content updates in World of Warcraft and Ultima Online was testimony to the acknowledgement by the gaming community of the importance that *Dungeons & Dragons* has had in the fantasy genre, and *The Guardian* described Gygax as "the father of role-playing games ... one of America's most talented writers and game designers."

See Also: Fantasy Play; Maple Story; Role-Playing; Runescape; Silkroad Online; Warhammer; World of Warcraft.

Bibliography. *Dungeons & Dragons* Official Homepage, www.wizards.com/dnd (cited July 2008); Daniel Mackay, *The Fantasy Role-Playing Game: A New Performing Art* (McFarland & Company, 2001); Lawrence Schick, *Heroic Worlds: A History and Guide to Role Playing Games* (Prometheus Books, 1991); J. Patrick Williams et al., eds., *Gaming as Culture: Essays on Reality, Identity And Experience in Fantasy Games* (McFarland, 2006).

Esther MacCallum-Stewart
University of East London

E

Ecarté

Ecarté is a trick-taking card game, typically played by two people using a 32-card deck with all cards between two and six removed. In Ecarté, the ace ranks between the 10 and the jack, leaving the king as the highest-ranked card. As in Euchre, trump is determined at the beginning of each hand, but in Ecarté, the card values remain the same when trump. Ecarté gets its name (literally, "discarded") from its unusual system of proposing and discarding. After the cards are dealt, the nondealer has the opportunity to trade cards from his or her hand with cards in the deck by proposing to the dealer. If the dealer accepts, then both players may trade in any number of cards from their hands. This process continues until either the nondealer is satisfied with the hand or the dealer refuses the proposal.

Ecarté developed from a game called Triomphe, but should not be conflated with the Triomphe referred to frequently in texts by French writers as far back as the 15th century. Although it shares the same name as the Ecarté predecessor, the term *triomphe* (meaning triumph, from which we get the word trump) likely indicated an entire class of trick-taking games with a trump system that eventually codified into the ancestors of later games such as Euchre, Loo, Whist, and Ecarté. A text from the 17th century describes a four-person game played with a 52-card deck called Triomphe that was ubiquitous in France. In the 18th century, Triomphe referred to a two-person game played with a modified deck that developed into the modern version of Ecarté in the 19th century.

Despite its relative obscurity in the 21st century, Ecarté was widely popular in both Europe and the United States in the 19th century. Although the game requires a fair amount of skill, its chance elements and fast-paced game play made Ecarté widely popular as a gambling game. During the Restoration period in France, after the battle of Waterloo, Ecarté became extremely fashionable in Paris salons and casinos. In 1820, Ecarté was introduced to the United States, and although the game never achieved the status in the United States that Euchre acquired, the game was prevalent enough to be the subject of several treatises written by American authors.

Most of these authors, writing near the turn of the 20th century, decried the gambling aspect of Ecarté and the tendency of many players to cheat at the game. Overturning the king when deciding trump or merely possessing the king of trumps immediately scores the player a point, a fact undoubtedly taken advantage of by experienced cardsharps. Despite the censure by these writers of Ecarté's association with gambling, they all assert that the game is enjoyable for its simple rules and capacity to be played by amateurs and experts alike. These same authors attempted to highlight Ecarté as a "scientific" game that could be exhaustively explored through statistical analysis and probabilities. They formulated a set of hands that would likely win three tricks, termed *jeux de règle*, on which the player should bid.

Ecarté is largely unknown to modern card players. As a gambling game, Ecarté survived in French casinos into the 20th century before being replaced by Blackjack and Baccarat. Never as popular as in Europe, Ecarté in the United States was eclipsed by Poker early in the 20th century as the premier card game for gamblers. In modern times, Ecarté enjoyed popularity in Germany until the 1960s and is still played in isolated gaming circles in France.

See Also: Euchre; History of Playing Cards; Loo; Whist.

Bibliography. Cavendish, *The Laws of Écarté Adopted by the Turf and Portland Clubs: With a Treatise on the Game* (Thos. De La Rue, 1897); E.O. Harbin, *Games of Many Nations* (Abingdon Press, 1954); David Sidney Parlett, *The Oxford Guide to Card Games* (Oxford University Press, 1990).

Steve Stanzak
Indiana University

Ecuador

This South American country is located on the equator and has borders with Colombia and Peru. With a population of 13,700,000 (2007), about 2 million live in the port city of Guayaquil, and 1.4 million live in Quito, the country's capital. Descendants of the Spanish account for only 7 percent of the population, with an additional 3 percent being of African descent. Many indigenous customs and games survive. These include Inca games that involve flipping counters—originally made from clay, but now more often from brightly colored plastic. *Picha*, another Inca game, involving dice, was also common, as were the two Inca board games, *Tacanaco* and *Chuncara*. Both of these involve throwing dice and moving colored beans, seeds, or in coastal regions, small shells, to various parts of the board.

Jívaro music, played by many indigenous people, involves flutes made from hollowed pieces of wood or bones from llamas. Archaeologists have also found small spinning tops in the region, as well as statuettes, some of which were made for religious reasons, but others perhaps as toys. Boys were certainly involved in learning hunting skills, with the use of the slingshot, or archery.

The Spanish settlers in Ecuador formed a wealthy but small society and introduced European musical instruments, such as the guitar, now popular in Ecuadorian society. Board games imported from the United States, Peru, Argentina, and Europe also have a small following, including games such as Backgammon, Bridge and Chess; Chess is overseen by the Federacion Ecuatoriana de Ajedrez. The small African population brought with them customs that included making percussion instruments and the marimba, with Afro-Ecuadorian music becoming increasingly popular throughout the country.

In Quito, Guayaquil, and other urban centers in the country there are youth centers that offer pool tables, and simple bowling, as well as listening to jukeboxes and playing pinball machines. With some growing prosperity in the country, these centers have increased in number, size, and popularity. Since the early 20th century, recreational soccer has been popular throughout the country. There has also long been a following for Chess—the French world champion Alexsandr Alekhine performed famous "blindfolded" Chess tournaments at Quito and Guayaquil in March 1939.

See Also: Boys' Play; Chess and Variations of; Peru; South Americans, Traditional Cultures.

Bibliography. Paulo Carvalho Neto, *Diccionario del Folklore Ecuatoriano* [Dictionary of Ecuadorian Folklore] (Editorial Casa de la Cultura, 1964); Elizabeth Jane Townsend, "Festivals of Ecuador," *Américas* (v.3/4, 1978); Judith Wilgus de Isas, "Fiestas Folklóricas Ecuatorianas" [Ecuadorian Folk Festivals], *América Indígena* (v. 34/3, 1974).

Justin Corfield
Geelong Grammar School

Egypt

Play has been an important aspect of Egyptian society from ancient times until the present. Recreational activities in ancient Egypt were an important part of children's lives, and when adults took part in recreation,

Ancient Egyptian musical instruments ranged from the very simple, such as percussion instruments, to the very complex, such as harps. Singers were an integral part of Egyptian music, accompanied by drums, reed-pipes, or one-stringed fiddles.

their activities often combined both relaxation and productivity, such as fishing. In the Middle Ages, recreational activities were geared for the enjoyment of both adults and children alike, such as storytelling. Egyptian children and adults today usually engage in recreational activities along class and gender lines.

Children in ancient Egypt had carefree periods in their lives dedicated to play until they reached their teens, when they were expected to marry and bear children of their own. The types of games children played when they had carefree time after work varied from physical activities such as wrestling, throwing stones at targets, playing Tug-of-War, swimming in the Nile, Leapfrog, racing, and dancing, to imaginary activities such as using small doll-like figures of animals and boats made out of clay, wood, or stone. Balls were made of leather skin filled with dry papyrus reeds. Children in ancient Egypt were also encouraged to spend their free time doing arts-and-crafts projects, such as making charms honoring their favorite gods, playing with pet dogs and birds, or playing with spinning tops.

Ancient Egyptian adults enjoyed leisure activities as well. Noblemen and pharaohs held parties in which they were entertained by musicians, dancers, and singers. Wealthy families often had their own garden next to their house in which they could relax and be kept cool by fanbearers waving palm-frond fans. For common people, their pastime was often activities that were both relaxing and yet productive, such as fishing in the Nile, or hunting. Some adults played a game in the river in which men in light reed boats tried to tip the opponent's boat with poles. People of all ages and classes in ancient Egypt played boardgames such as Mancala, Mehen, Game of 20 Squares, Hounds and Jackals, Senet, and the Royal Game of Ur.

Egypt's Middle Ages

During the Middle Ages, Egyptian children and adults in all strata of society, rural and urban, often participated jointly in leisure activities, which were primarily storytelling and music. Popular literature recited in public was usually impromptu, not written, and handed down orally. There were also shadow-plays performed by puppets or hands in front of a light and behind a screen. The most widespread genre of stories was that of romance, and among the most popular collections of stories was *The Thousand and One Nights*. At the heart of stories about adventure and travel was the hero overcoming forces of evil, whether men, demons, or personal passions. Poetry writing was an important activity in the lives of educated men, and recitations of poetry were performed for the wealthy and rulers.

Music during the Middle Ages in Egypt figured into all aspects of life, from pure leisure time to work time. In addition to ceremonies and important occasions, songs accompanied harvest and work. Songs for ceremonial entertainment were sung unaccompanied or accompanied on drums, reed-pipes, or one-stringed fiddles. Men, women, and children often danced spontaneously in lines or groups along with the music at these festivities. In courts, the musician was a regular figure, playing for the ruler and marking his distance by concealment behind a curtain. Men of religion often condemned music and defined the conditions on which performing and listening to music were permitted, forbidding music that aroused temptation or used blasphemy and obscenities.

Modern Egypt

In Egypt in modern times, socioeconomics greatly define the type of play in which children and adults engage. Soccer is the most popular sport in Egypt, particularly among men and young boys in cities and villages alike. Class differences shape the type of organized play and recreation in which children and adults partake. Families with some means are often members of various sporting and social clubs, where they can participate in such activities as soccer, karate, handball, swimming, yoga, and horseback riding. The more exclusive clubs also have dog-walking areas. Extracurricular activities are rare for most children; a 2004 United Nations Development Programme survey found that 67 percent of Egyptian schoolchildren had never participated in extracurricular activities.

For families that can afford them, video games are very popular among children. Egyptian television offers cartoons and learning programs for children, including the Arabic-language production of *Sesame Street*. Children in urban areas have very little outdoor space for play because of the density of buildings; however, there is a widely visited public zoo in Cairo as well as a recently constructed 74-acre hilly park called Al-Azhar, built on what was once a landfill and now made available at reduced prices for the surrounding neighborhood, which is among the poorest in Cairo. In rural areas, children often play in the Nile, the contaminated water of which is the primary source of the high levels of the parasite bilharzias infecting Egyptian children.

Activities for adults outside of work are often divided by gender. Men tend to spend their free time playing board games, like Backgammon, and watching soccer matches in cafés. It is rare to find women in cafés outside of the upper-class areas, which include many Western café chains. Women often spend their free time visiting indoors with extended family. Many Egyptian women follow closely the popular soap operas on television, and all Egyptians eagerly look forward to the special radio series that are produced during the month of Ramadan. Unmarried male and female youth socialize in groups.

See Also: Ancient Egypt; Backgammon; Music, Playing; Soccer (Amateur) Worldwide; Spinning Tops.

Bibliography. BBC, "Leisure Time in Ancient Egypt," www.bbc.co.uk (cited July 2008); Marcelle Duschesne-Guillemin, "Music in Ancient Mesopotamia and Egypt," *World Archeology* (v.12/3, February 1981); Albert Hourani, *A History of the Arab Peoples* (Harvard University Press, 2007); Martin Rowe and Helen Rizzo, "Egypt," in *The Greenwood Encyclopedia of Children's Issues Worldwide* (Greenwood Press, 2008).

Heidi Morrison
University of California, Santa Barbara

Erector Sets

In 1912, Dr. Alfred Carlton Gilbert developed the Erector Set. A miniaturized version of the girder system used to build railroads, the toy envisioned a new version of childhood and endeavored to teach boys the principles of engineering. Hugely successful, the Erector Set became a mainstay of American toys.

Gilbert developed the Erector Set in the same era that saw the invention of Meccano and Tinkertoys, after watching construction workers erect the electrical system of a railroad with steel girders and rivets. Convinced that a childhood version of that system would allow boys to learn more about engineering, Gilbert developed a toy that he first called the Mysto Erector Structural Steel Builder, which included actual metal tools—the girders and rivets of the construction trade—in smaller sizes. As Erector Sets developed, those tools came to include a variety of parts: metal beams with regular holes, nuts, screws, bolts, pulleys, flanges, motors, and gears.

By offering these tools for building, Gilbert hoped to encourage construction and engineering abilities among America's boys. He believed that the ability to solve problems and create structures, no matter how small, would prevent boys from descending to the level of aimless, pessimistic, disaffected youth without skill or purpose. His Erector Sets and his *Erector Tips* magazine attempted to shape boys into efficient men by giving them the ability to build. Indicative of the Progressive Era that witnessed the emergence of an energized and activist nation, this focus on solving what he called "the boy problem" made the Erector Set one of the most successful educational toys in American history.

First offered at a time when skyscrapers were becoming popular and engineers were earning more money a year than doctors, playing with the Erector Set seemed like the first step toward a lucrative career. Businessmen and industrial psychologists touted the Erector Set's ability to encourage constructive instincts; parents paid a considerable sum to buy the toy and invest in their sons' futures. Americans saw the Erector Set as a means of producing the next wave of scientists and engineers who could continue to make life better and easier.

Innovative Advertising

In part, that message was relayed through advertising. Beginning with the 1913 New York Toy Fair, the advertising campaign for the Erector Set also made history. This was the first toy to have its own ad campaign. Using the slogan "Hello, boys! Make lots of toys!" the Erector Set took to the pages of *Popular Mechanics*, *Good Housekeeping,* and *The Saturday Evening Post.* By choosing magazines with such a varied readership, the campaign effectively targeted every demographic within the family. Fathers and grandfathers could be inspired to buy this engineering toy for their sons and grandsons when reading about science, mechanics, and engineering; mothers and grandmothers when reading about how to improve their household and its efficiency. The boys themselves could be stirred by the *Youth's Companion* or by a more family-oriented periodical. In asking for the Erector Set, boys seemed to reinforce society's hope for technological advancement and their parents' dreams for their financial success. That advertising strategy proved incredibly successful: Within three years, sales had reached $1 million; by 1935, more than 30 million Erector Sets had been sold.

"A Good Investment"

Given the costs of buying the Erector Set, that number is staggering. Prices varied in the early years, with the cheapest sets selling for 50 cents and the most expensive for $25. In the 1920s and 1930s, the Erector Set cost $70, which was more than a month's wages. Prices did begin to drop by the 1940s, when one version (the Gilbert All-Electric Erector Set) cost $19.95.

Seeming less like a toy than a tool, the Erector Set was durable and seemed a good investment. Made of actual steel before and after World War II, during which it was made of wood, the Erector Set was sturdier and more realistic than the Meccano set. Steel beams with a slight lip along the edge were bent at 90 degree angles to allow for the creation of very sturdy, square, hollow support beams when four were nested side-to-side. These bigger beams could then be combined with other tools to create a seemingly infinite number of structures. Even when the specific components shipped in the distinctive red metal boxes (which replaced the original wooden boxes in the mid-1930s) changed, nuts, screws, and bolts could always be counted on to fasten pieces together and build simple machines.

Collectors have identified three main types of Erector Sets. The first type was built between 1913 and 1923. A cruder version of the modern Erector Set, this type used a 1 1/8-inch-wide girder as its main building part. These sets were numbered from No. 0 to No. 8, with each set offering a different number of parts and costing a different amount: the cheapest set—No. 0—provided a handful of parts in a cardboard box for 50 cents; set No. 1 provided enough parts to create 27 models for $1; set No. 2 could produce 39 models for $2. The prices continued along that vein, though sets No. 5–8 also included toy motors. At the top of the line, set No. 8 provided six gears, four propeller blades, 14 axles, 24 pulleys, five tires, three pinion gears, 32 perforated strips, 230 small screws, 200 12-inch girders, 222 shorter girders, a screwdriver, and a motor—all for $25.

To test the market, A.C. Gilbert sponsored contests that asked young builders to send photographs of their creations to his company. Offering prizes like cars and ponies, the contests encouraged young boys to use their imaginations and to build beyond any instruction book or set of plans. The contests also served as an ingenious form of market research. A constant stream of new ideas for projects and models arrived in the form of entries to the contest; these new ideas then resulted in increased marketing of sets and projects specifically focused on boys' interests.

New Erector Sets

In part these new ideas also led to "The New Erector" set, typical of the period 1924 to 1962, known by collectors as type 2 sets. The redesigned steel girders in this type were 5/8 inches wide instead of the original 1 1/8 inches. More realistic in appearance, these sets included additional parts, including plates of a variety of shapes and sizes and models to use within a larger design. The largest and most elaborate sets were produced between 1924 and 1932. They peaked in 1931 with a shipping weight of 150 pounds for a wooden box measuring 2 1/2 feet square and eight inches thick. This enormous version of the Erector Set had enough parts to make hundreds of models, including a Hudson steam locomotive four feet long and a five-foot-long zeppelin.

The Great Depression and World War II changed the Erector Set by limiting the elaboration of parts and sets, yet production of the sets did not stop. During the Depression, the Erector Set could seem like a ticket out of despair, a plan for the future. Familiar models like the Ferris Wheel, Parachute Jump, and Refrigeration Plant helped the toy gain momentum, and innovations like the electric train set, which replaced the Hudson Locomotive model in 1938, brought new attention to the product. Further changes needed to occur during World War II, when steel was in short supply. Erector sets from that era were created in wood, a change that did not last past the end of steel rationing.

In 1948, another retooled version of the Erector Set appeared. Featuring the ability to create a Walking Giant (approximately two feet tall), the set weighed in at 40 pounds. For the next decade, no new sets appeared, though robots and space-related models were added in the 1960s as the United States entered into a Space Race with Russia.

By 1963, type 3 Erector Sets were being produced. Created by the Jack Wrather Company, which took over the A.C. Gilbert Company after Gilbert's death, these sets were redesigned by the Product Design and Development Company. Instead of trussed girders, the sets now featured strips of steel with evenly spaced holes. More plastic parts were introduced, and fewer models were illustrated in manuals. These Erector Sets, which span the period of 1963 to 1988, offered a Powermatic motor and a two-drum hoist. Changes in packaging accompanied these more fundamental design changes.

The Erector Set has become a mainstay of American construction toys. Mentioned in countless patents, including those for Flexible design construction toys, toy building elements, construction toys, and interlocking blocks, it is seen as a forerunner of toys designed to teach spatial thinking and to encourage mechanical and engineering pursuits. It has also served as a useful tool for adults making models for larger products. Besides its obvious use in planning buildings, robots, and other steel structures, the Erector Set has been used in projects like that of William Sewell, Jr., and William W.L. Glenn, two medical students at Yale University who used a set to create a heart pump in 1950. That pump was successfully used in experimental bypass surgery on dogs.

See Also: Blocks; Hasbro; Legos; Lincoln Logs; Meccano; Playskool; Tinker Toys.

Bibliography. William M. Bean and Al M. Sternagle, *Greenberg's Guide to Gilbert Erector Sets: 1913–1932* (Greenberg, 1993); William M. Bean and Al M. Sternagle, *Greenberg's Guide to Gilbert Erector Sets: 1933–1962* (Greenburg, 1998); Susan Waggoner, *Under the Tree: The Toys and Treats That Made Christmas Special 1930–1970* (Stuart, Tabori and Chang, 2007); Bruce Watson, *The Man Who Changed How Boys and Toys Were Made* (Viking, 2002).

Anastasia L. Pratt
State University of New York

Estonia

Located in the Baltic, Estonia was a part of the Russian Empire until it gained its independence in 1920. Occupied by the Russians, then the Germans, then again by the Russians, it was incorporated into the Soviet Union, only becoming independent again in 1991. With the majority of the population speaking Estonian, a language unrelated to others in the region, it has not been as heavily influenced by the Russians and Germans as other countries in the region.

Culturally aligned to Scandinavia, many of the pastimes of early medieval Estonians had much in common with those of the Vikings. Many games involved practicing for prowess in battle such as axe-throwing, chopping wood, archery, running along the oars of boats, and the like. Adventure playgrounds, popular with boys in this country, are a reminder of past history. The country is windy for much of the year, and kite-flying and ballooning are popular.

Much Estonian folklore was preserved in singing and music, and both of these were popular pastimes for adults as well as children. In Estonia, large choirs sung, sometimes numbering in the thousands of people. The first Estonian national song festival held in 1869 was a major event in the country's history. Bell-ringing—both hand-bells and church bells—has also been a traditional pastime.

Because of the pleasant summer weather in Estonia, many people enjoy camping or going to the beaches, with winter pastimes including skiing, skating, snowboarding, and tobogganing. As the climate for over half the year can be bleak, indoor games are popular, and chief among them is Chess, run in the country by the Eesti Maleliit. Paul Keres (1916–75) was born in Narva, which was then in the Russian Empire, on the Estonian-Russian border, and went on to become the European Chess champion three times after participating in his first public Chess competition at the age of 13.

With Keres, Estonia ended up in third place at the eighth Chess Olympiad at Buenos Aires in 1939. Keres's book, *The Theory of Chess Openings*, published in three volumes between 1949 and 1958, remains one of the standard works on the subject. Other prominent Chess players from Estonia include Friedrich L.B. Amelung (1842–1909), who published some 230 endgames; Andreas Ascharin (1843–96); Leho Laurine (1904–98); and Johannes Türn (1899–1993). The county's best-known living Chess player is now Jaan Ehlvest (b. 1962). Backgammon, card games, Darts and Dominoes also have a great following in the country.

Throughout the Soviet period, Wargaming societies flourished, with groups involved in replaying battles fought in medieval times or the wars between the Swedes and the Russians. Since independence, the battles in World War I and World War II have become more politically acceptable and have risen in popularity. With the increased Westernization of Estonia, and the return of some Estonian exiles, there has been a rise in the number of amusement arcades, bowling alleys, and other entertainment centers. As more Estonians speak a Western European language (mainly German or English), the importing of foreign games has also become more common, with clubs formed for *Dungeons & Dragons* and Warhammer. An Estonian version of the board game Monopoly exists, with the important streets of Tallinn marked.

See Also: Chess and Variations of; Finland; Latvia; Lithuania; Wargames.

Bibliography. Peter J. Babris, *Baltic Youth Under Communism* (Research Publishers, 1967); Glenn Kirchner, *Children's Games Around the World* (Benjamin Cummings, 2000); Michael Spilling, *Estonia* (Marshall Cavendish, 2000).

Justin Corfield
Geelong Grammar School

Ethiopia

The northeast African nation of Ethiopia has a population of 76.5 million, of which only 13 percent live in urban areas. Many people in the countryside (as well as large numbers in towns and cities) live in poverty. Traditional lifestyles focus around the village, and because of its distinct heritage, there are a number of games that are unique to Ethiopia. One of these is *Kwosso*, in which two teams with up to 100 men in each team, compete for possession of a ball made from goat skin. The game can last for an entire day, and most men only wear loincloths because of the heat—and with tackling and collisions, injuries do occur. It is often played in the sandy plain in the desert near the Afar (or Denakil) Depression in the north of the country, close to the border with Eritrea. Another popular Ethiopian game is *Feres Gugs*, or *Yeferas Guks*. Participants ride on horses, with the attacking team armed with wooden staffs, with the task of unseating the defenders, who have wooden shields covered with hides. This game as well can lead to serious injuries.

A more sedate game is *Gabata*, which is believed to have been played since medieval times. It is similar to the Egyptian (and Inca) game *Mancala* and the Japanese game *Shogi*, and it involves players using different-colored seeds to surround and capture the seeds of the other player that are then—unlike in the Japanese version—placed in a storage bin. The Ethiopian version of Hide-and-Seek played by children is *Debebekosh,* and the Ethiopian version of jacks is called *Kelelebosh.* A type of field hockey known as *Ganna* is also popular, but has nowhere near the following of soccer, which was introduced to the country by the Italians in the 1920s. The first soccer club in the country was the St. George Sports Association, founded in 1935, just before the Italian Invasion. The Allies drove out the Italians in 1941, and two years later, under British tutelage, the Ethiopian Football Federation was established, with Ethiopian soccer players competing against teams from Egypt and Sudan in 1957. Soccer continues to be played around the country by boys and young men, who compete as part of school or community groups.

Athletics have also become popular, with many boys involved in cross-country running, inspired by the success of several Ethiopian Olympic gold medal winners. Other young people in Ethiopia are involved in volleyball, tennis, boxing, swimming, and basketball, with cycling and hiking growing in popularity. Few girls or women participate in sports, generally remaining involved in indoor games and handicrafts, although the Ethiopian female runner Fatuma Roba won an Olympic Gold Medal in 1996. The Italian connection with Ethiopia, dating from well before their invasion in 1936, can still be seen by older men playing *bocce.* Card games, Draughts, and Checkers also attract many people.

Chess has clearly had a long history in the country. The British political servant Henry Salt (1780–1827), when visiting what was then known as Abyssinia, found a version of Chess being played that had three differences from the European version: pawns could only advance by one square, bishops could only move three squares, and pawns could not be exchanged for another piece when they reached the end of the board. Welled Selasse, the Ras of Tigre, gave Salt a collection of Abyssinian chessmen made from ivory, and they are now displayed in the British Museum. When the British Consul Walter Charles Metcalf Plowden later went to Abyssinia, he became a good friend of Emperor Tewodros (Theodore) II and followed the Chess game in more detail. Plowden discovered a number of other variations that he outlined in his book *Travels in Abyssinia* (1868). The Abyssinians believed that checkmate using two rooks was not honorable, but using two bishops was. They also found that if a player only had the king, the opponent had only seven moves to avoid a checkmate.

The Italian influence in Ethiopia led to the introduction of Wargaming, with the Italians preferring to play reenactments of their invasion in 1896, which had culminated in their defeat at Adowa. This later became a common theme in games played by Ethiopians.

See Also: Africa, Traditional Play in; Chess and Variations of; Wargames.

Bibliography. David Buxton, *The Abyssinians* (Thames & Hudson, 1970); Frank Catinella, "The Italian Wars Against the Dervish," *Miniature Wargames* (April, 2003); Steven Gish, *Ethiopia* (Marshall Cavendish, 1996); Imbakom Kalewold, *Traditional Ethiopian Church Education* (Teachers College Press, 1970); Richard O. Niehoff and Bernard D. Wilder, *Non-Formal Education in Ethiopia* (Institute for International Studies in Education, 1974).

Justin Corfield
Geelong Grammar School

Euchre

Euchre is a trick-taking card game typically played by four people in two partnerships. Originally played with 32 cards, Euchre now uses a deck of 24, with all cards between two and eight discarded. Its most distinctive characteristic is a trump system in which the jack of trump (called the right bower), followed by the jack of the same color (the left bower), are elevated to the highest-ranking cards. From the mid-19th to the early-20th century, Euchre and Poker were regarded as the national card games of the United States. Although its popularity in the United States has since declined, Euchre retains a strong following in certain regions, particularly the Great Lakes. The game also remains popular in Australia, Canada, New Zealand, and the United Kingdom.

Many writers at the turn of the 20th century speculated that Euchre came from the similar game of Ecarté played by French settlers in Louisiana. Other sources hypothesized that it developed from the French game

Triomphe, or was adapted from Ecarté by American sailors who named the right and left bowers after the main anchors of a ship. More recent scholarship suggests that the game is an offshoot of the Alsatian game *Juckerspiel*, likely brought by German immigrants to America in the late 17th or early 18th century. Euchre made a lasting contribution to card decks by introducing the joker, likely in the 1850s. In Euchre, it outranked both bowers as the highest trump. The name of the card came from name of the game, *Jucker*, rather than from the card's design; the joker card was initially blank. However, by the end of the 19th century, the traditional jester image became prevalent.

Euchre has gained the reputation as a game played by the lower class, as opposed to more formal and complex games, such as Bridge, that are regarded as indicators of social accomplishment. This concern with status is inherent in the structure of the game itself in its elevation of the bowers (from the German *bauer*, meaning farmer) above the royalty. This meaning also works in English, *jack* being the designation for common man. In modern practice, this association with farming and the lower classes is embraced in certain regional folk traditions, particularly in scoring rituals. For example, scorekeepers will often slightly uncover a pip on their scorecard so that it is "sprouting." In another scoring custom, when one team reaches nine points and is considered "in the barn," the occasion is marked by vocalizations of barnyard animals. At the score of 10, the players "enter the barn" and pantomime milking a cow.

Euchre has also been associated with sociability and playfulness since its introduction to the United States. Near the turn of the 20th century, the game was touted as an alternative to Poker, Whist, and Cribbage because it was simpler, more casual, did not involve gambling, and could be played by experts and amateurs alike. Less formal in its game play, players often gossiped, flirted, and told stories in-between or even during hands—a practice that would have been frowned upon in many other games. Progressive Euchre, a tournament-style variation of the game, emphasizes Euchre's social aspects.

A large group of players form temporary partnerships that last the duration of one game before they move to a new table and switch partners. The hosts coordinate the movement of players, introduce guests to each other, and facilitate conversation. Although Euchre has lost its place as the preeminent social game of the United States, the informality and sociability that characterized the game a century ago is still common among modern players.

See Also: Bridge and Variations of; Ecarté; History of Playing Cards; United States, 1783 to 1860; United States, 1860 to 1876; United States, 1876 to 1900.

Bibliography. Sarah Ethridge Hunt, *Games and Sports the World Around* (Ronald Press Company, 1964); David Parlett, *A History of Card Games* (Oxford University Press, 1991); David Sidney Parlett, *The Oxford Guide to Card Games* (Oxford University Press, 1990).

Steve Stanzak
Indiana University

Europe, 1200 to 1600

Play in medieval Europe was considered to be an educational activity for children to learn adult roles. Play was ephemeral—a passing entertainment—designed to instruct naturally. Between 1200 and 1600, Europe experienced sustained urbanization as a result of a series of population explosions. Between the 11th and 13th centuries, Christians traveled in military expeditions to win the Holy Land from Muslims.

Exploration and migration brought new paper and printing technology to Europe that was used to produce the first board games and playing cards. During the late 1390s, the Great Plague killed an estimated 30 to 60 percent of Europe's population, irrevocably altering its social structure. With such a loss of manpower and resources, there was little time, nor inclination, to play. Feudalism allowed for the emergence of city-states that extended trade and cultural exchanges throughout the Mediterranean. The Renaissance, the transitional movement in Europe between medieval and modern times beginning in the 14th century, brought a resurgence of nationalistic spectacles filled with mock battles, processions, athletic competitions, citywide celebrations, revelry for a saint's days, and pageantry for visiting dignitaries.

Early Games

Wandering minstrels traveled and performed songs with lyrics that chronicled romances from distant lands. These itinerate musicians and storytellers declaimed tales of his-

In Pieter Bruegel's 1559 painting Children's Games, *children are depicted playing with dolls, hoops, tops, dice, and a hobby horse, and riding on rails and barrels, performing acrobatics, climbing trees, giving piggyback rides, wrestling, and swimming.*

toric events and carried news. Wandering minstrels were often retained by nobility to entertain like jesters and played lutes, harps, violins, bagpipes, pipes, and drums. When the songs ended, jugglers and acrobats performed. From the 1200s to 1400s, troubadours (lyric poets) of knightly rank replaced minstrels in southern France and northern Italy, promoting a sensibility of courtly love.

Doll play was not restricted to children. Peddlers sold miniature ceramics, jugs, and cookware, as well as utensils. Girls played with dolls to develop practical skills like sewing, along with imagination, role-playing, and imitation. Hobby horses and imitation horses were popular with boys and girls. Metal models of knights in armor have been found that date back to 1300. Playing with marbles developed dexterity. Games such as Dice, Cards, Checkers, and Chess were popular because they developed strategy and memory. Play often incorporated ordinary materials and foodstuffs in games like cherry stones, marrow bone, buckle-pit, spurn point, cobnut, and quoiting. With cobnuts, the objects were used in game play as well as for currency for measuring gains and losses. The popular guessing game Handy-Dandy was played with a small object hidden in the palm of a hand behind the player's back.

With widespread illiteracy, the Catholic Church encouraged parish priests to act out scenes from the Bible. As time passed, the scriptural stories were embellished, so the Bible drama became a form of entertainment. Play also reflected the activities of changing seasons and church calendars. Prior to Lent, boys held cockfighting games on Shrove Tuesday, and children played with tops during Lent. During spring and early summer, holidays including Rogation Week, Pentecost, and Midsummer Day festivals provided occasions for communal play. On Midsummer's Eve, children gathered to entertain each other with music and songs. From late June to September, children participated in the harvest season. Nutting—seeking and harvesting nuts—became popular group play accompanied with bonfires and games. All Saints Day, November 1, came at the time of the pig slaughter, and pig bladders were used to make balls that were used in playing Croquet, Shuttlecock, Skittles, and tennis.

Latter Games

Archery was a popular sport in medieval times, along with fishing and bird hunting. Parents encouraged boys to learn military skills by enacting battles using bows and arrows, so violence was part of boy's play. Quintain was a military training drill that entertained spectators. A post was fixed upright in the ground, and a young knight on horseback dressed in armor and carrying a shield rode past and struck the post (or objects affixed to the post) with a sword. Cock-Stele was a cruel throwing game where a chicken was buried up to its neck in the ground, and young men threw sticks or arrows (cock-steles) at its head. However, boys were discouraged from tormenting other animals by throwing sticks and stones at birds, dogs, pigs, or horses.

Board games can be traced back to ancient times and were introduced in Europe during the 14th century as a form of educational play. Draughts, also called Ladies' Game and Game of Ferses, along with Merelles (also called The Mill) and Backgammon, became popular toward the late 1400s. In Draughts, a form of Checkers, two people alternated moves on opposite sides of a playing board. One played dark pieces, and the other played light pieces. Most commonly, the board alternated between red and black squares. In 1300, Jacques de Cessoles, a French Dominican friar, wrote a treatise on Chess as it related to human affairs, written in Latin and published in Genoa. The object of a Scandinavian board game called Fox and Geese was for the geese to surround the fox so he could not move; the fox could win by capturing a number of geese so that he could not be trapped.

Flemish artist Pieter Bruegel the Elder, in his painting *Children's Games* (1559), depicted over 200 children and adolescents playing a variety of games during the summer in different configurations. Some children played alone, while others played in pairs or groups. Much of the play represented games that were imitative or that required skill or athleticism. Objects depicted in the painting include dolls, hoops, tops, dice, windmills, a mask, and a hobby horse. Boys can be seen spinning tops with pear-shaped peg-tops. Active play included dancing, riding on rails and barrels, acrobatics, tree climbing, piggyback riding, wrestling, and swimming. Rattles, children's bells, noisemakers, and other children's percussion instruments are also depicted. Early windmills (similar to pinwheels) consisted of a piece of cardboard cut like a cross with a pin placed at the end of stick, so that when the child ran the pinwheel against the wind, the wheel would twirl. Children in this era would fly kites that were sails affixed to one end of a pole. Tops, prills, and whirligigs remained popular throughout the Middle Ages.

A handball game similar to the Roman game, using a leather-covered, inflated-bladder ball, was played by players who wore a hollow wooden brace over their arms and hands to give them more power in their hitting. Goff, an early version of hockey, was played with a curved club, and the object of the game was to drive the ball between two small sticks pounded in the ground some distance away. Stool-ball, which was later transported to the New World, was a game played by setting up a three-legged milking stool and having players roll three stones toward it, attempting to hit the stool. A defender stood near the stool, attempting to block the shots. Stool-ball later evolved into cricket. A wicket substituting the stool, a club was introduced to the game to hit the ball, and each hit counted as a point for the defender. The following rhyme depicts how stool-ball was an Easter game played for small stakes, such as a tansy or Easter-cake.

> At stool-ball, Lucia, let us play,
> For sugar, cakes, or wine;
> Or for a tansy let us pay,
> The loss be mine or thine.
> If thou, my dear, a winner be,
> At trundling of the ball,
> The wager thou shalt have, and me,
> And my misfortunes all.

Indoor games, including Blind Man's Bluff, Piggy in the Ring, Hand-In-and-Hand-Out, and Penny-pricks, were introduced in Europe during the Middle Ages. Shove-Groat was played on a table or board, with a number of parallel lines positioned about an inch apart. Playing cards were introduced in Europe in the last quarter of the 14th century. The earliest cards were expensive, as they were painted by hand. Printed woodcut decks were introduced during the 15th century, and suits varied in different regions. In Germany, the suits developed were hearts, bells, leaves, and acorns—still used today for Skat, while Italian and Spanish cards of the 15th century had swords, batons, cups, and coins. A tarot deck was introduced to Europe from the Middle East during the early 15th century, but the cards were not necessarily used for divination.

The board game called Goose, developed by Grand Duke of Tuscany Francesco de Medici (1541–87), became popular at the end of the 15th century. This game consisted of a card printed with a large spiral track of 63 squares in the form of a snake. Fourteen of the squares bore a picture of a goose, two dice were used, and the counters were moved according to throws from the tail to the head, and if the counter landed on a picture of the goose, it moved on the same number of squares given by the last throw, repeating until it reached a space without a goose. Some squares bore obstacles that might make the player lose ground or have to return to the beginning. The object of the game was to be the first person to reach the end of the journey.

See Also: Bowling; Checkers and Variations of; Chess and Variations of; Cricket (Amateur); Hobby Horses; Marbles; Maypole Dancing; Music, Playing; Skat; Tennis (Amateur) and Variations of.

Bibliography. Hugh Cunningham, *Children and Childhood in Western Society Since 1500* (Longman, 1995); Andrea Immel and Michael Witmore, eds., *Childhood and Children's Books in Early Modern Europe, 1550–1800* (Routledge, 2006); Glenn Kirchner, *Children's Games Around the World* (Benjamin Cummings, 2000); Iona Opie and Peter Opie, *Children's Games With Things* (Oxford University Press, 1997); Nicholas Orme, *Medieval Children* (Yale University Press, 2001).

Meredith Eliassen
San Francisco State University

Europe, 1600 to 1800

In 17th-century Europe, rich and poor alike shared a passion for play. Men and women from all rungs of social hierarchy bowled, played tennis, played cards, gambled, danced, and went to town fairs. The majority of Europeans still lived in rural areas, worked on small farms, and followed the seasonal rhythms of the year. Working in groups, they sang songs, told stories, or played games to relieve the monotony of shelling, spinning flax or wool, hoeing, mowing, and harvesting. Though people adhered to traditional recreations, economic changes, political upheavals, and religious contests transformed play. A more commercial, secular, urban, and individual-oriented life spawned novel, affordable games for children and adults. New sports, holiday resorts, cultural events, and literature enriched, and also erased, traditional forms of play. Increasingly, Europeans produced goods for national and international economic markets, rather than local communities. These economic changes sharpened the distinction between work time and playtime, childhood and adulthood, and play itself became a commercial opportunity. "Leisure" acquired new valences of meaning in English, French, and Italian. The 18th century witnessed the birth of the "modern" world, and with it, modern conceptions of play.

Sports in the 17th and 18th Centuries

Europeans played an array of sports, some more physically demanding than others, throughout the 17th and 18th centuries. Bowling continued to be a perennial favorite, in addition to skittles and croquet. Variations of football were played in Paris, London, and Florence. Enthusiasm for particular sports could dwindle rapidly. In 1600, tennis was one of the most popular physical games among all ranks of society in France. At the end of the 17th century, 114 tennis courts existed in Paris. By 1700, only 10 remained open in the city. Europeans recognized both the pleasurable and the practical purposes of playing sports, though they exercised to achieve different ends than we do today. A European gentleman would ride horses, fence, and dance in order to exhibit his body's "natural" grace and self-control, not his physical strength.

By playing sports, one could strive to attain the 18th-century ideal of being a "polished," "polite," and "genteel" person. In the 17th century, books about leisure pastimes and sports such as *The Compleat Gamester: or, Instructions How to Play at all Manner of Usual and Most Gentile Games, Either on Cards, Dice, Billiards, Trucks, Bowls, Chefs, also the Arts and Misteries of Riding, Racing, Archery, Cockfighing*, portrayed the activities of the aristocracy. In the 18th century, aristocrats, noblemen, and royalty could no longer claim propriety over leisure. Sports such as horseracing—formerly a roughly organized, spur-of-the-moment affair—became spectator events by the 18th century. In the 1600s, newspapers in Britain started advertising the dates and locations of horse races. By 1722, 112 cities and towns were holding race meetings. A racing calendar was established in 1727, and special racecourses were built for spectators. Audiences of thousands watched professional jockeys, gambled on horses, and generated large profits for the racecourse owners. England exported horseracing to France, and then to America.

Cultural Amusements

In addition to sports, urbanites living in Paris and London, as well as the villagers in the countryside, could attend musical performances or theatrical productions in their own neighborhoods. The expansion of the theater in England provides a striking example of how rapidly the availability of leisure activities increased in a century. During the reign of Charles II (1649–85), the English theater was popular but poverty stricken. In the first half of the 18th century, 1,095 new plays were written, and the number doubled to 2,117 during the second half. Provincial towns kept apace with theater construction in urban centers, leading one historian to state that by 1770, England had more theaters than it does today. In 1660, true opera and ballet did not exist in England.

A century later, audiences could watch pantomime, puppet shows, comic operas such as Gay's *Beggar's Opera,* ballet, and even an equestrian circus in London, replete with wild animal trainers, conjurers, jugglers, and trapeze artists. The 18th century witnessed the advent of the tourist industry. Guidebooks instructed tourists who visited Paris to attend the theater at the Palais-Royal or the Faubourg St. Germain, where people played billiards, cards, and ball games. In England, towns like Bath and Tunbridge Wells, long visited for the healing power of the water and the spas, turned into holiday towns replete with dancing, theater, and music. One could eat, listen to music, look at paintings, and dance in the famous Vauxhall and Ranelagh gardens in London.

Early modern Europeans also shared a rich literary culture. In the 18th century, publishers printed fiction and plays; books on cooking, gardening, and hunting; and children's literature. The malleable and affordable chapbook, an inexpensive 24-page publication, provided literature to suit all tastes: chivalric romances, pious tracts, jest books, folktales, abridged novels, and recipes. People found tales about criminals particularly fascinating. They bought glossaries of the "canting" speech spoken by criminals and printed versions of the lives and confessions of prisoners, always published after a round of hangings. The almanac, which included a monthly calendar, astrological predictions, and saint's days, was the best-selling publication in Britain. By end of the 17th century, over 400,000 copies were sold annually. But the growth in printed materials often perpetuated and preserved oral traditions. Children of the wealthy and the poor alike grew up listening to the stories, rhymes, and songs—the "old wive's tales"—of mothers and nursemaids. An abundance of 17th-century "commonplace books," notebooks that young people used to record proverbs and expressions, which they would later employ in speech, still exist in Spain, Italy, and France. People collected ballads and songs and pinned them up on alehouse walls. Songs popularized by cheap print would be heard the day after publication in the streets and in taverns.

Gambling, Games, and Politics

If Europeans enjoyed physical and intellectual games, they also liked to play with their money. In early modern Europe, people from all walks of life gambled. The French court had no inhibitions about gambling. Parents used playing cards to teach children geography, history, and classics; they were an educational toy that caught on in England. Gambling was also the form of play that received the most scrutiny from local officials. In England and Spain, towns designated particular alehouses or other places where people could gamble legally.

An abundance of legislation against gambling in Barcelona attests to the popularity of this recreation in the city. Regulations existed in Florence against playing Dice, cards, or shooting at targets at certain times and in certain places. The "reformation of manners," a broadly defined effort to reform traditional culture, resulted in increased disciplining of people that shirked their religious obligations to attend church on Sunday to bowl, play tennis, dance, or bet at cards and dice in alehouses and taverns. In 1698, 32 societies for the reformation of manners were active in London.

In Britain, games became a key source of political animosities. Charles I reissued the *Book of Sports* in 1633, allowing "our good people's lawful recreation" on Sundays after church, which included dancing, archery, leaping, May-games, Whitsun-ales, Morris dances, and Maypoles, but forbid bull and bear baiting, and bowling. The king's support of leisure activities intensified the religious and political antagonisms that led to civil war in Britain, and to Charles I's beheading. Though strict restrictions on play died out in 1730s, the reformation of manners morphed into the moral philosophies that dictated social behavior in 18th-century Europe. As the "middling sort" gained access to a variety of leisure activities, they sought to imitate the aristocracy and to distinguish themselves as part of a "polite" and genteel culture. In the 16th and 17th centuries, the courts of Queen Elizabeth I and Louis XIII were entertained at court by bear baiting. In the 18th century, the same games provoked criticism from people who sought to empathize with the pain and suffering of all living creatures.

Festivals and Fairs

New games, books, and holiday resorts coexisted with traditional forms of communal recreation in Europe. Carnivals, festivals, feast-days, religious holidays, and fairs punctuated the early modern European calendar. Festive celebrations included the 12 days of Christmas, Lent, early May, Pentecost, the feast of Saint John the Baptist, Our Lady of mid-August, and All Saints' Day. Eating, drinking, and dancing during these celebrations reinforced the social glue between inhabitants of a particular village or city. Though the main events of festivals might be serious religious processions and church services, the fun would start afterwards.

In 17th- and 18th-century Catalan towns, festivals began with a civic procession and illuminations, and were followed by three days of dancing. In 17th-century Spain, towns would hire musicians to accompany the church mass and the civic procession. The musicians would continue to play all night for the townspeople. According to 18th-century writer Henry Bourne, English people sang carols on Christmas and on New Years at the doors of wealthy people in return for gifts. Children actively participated in festivals. For example, on Twelfth Night, described by one historian as the greatest festival of the year, a child hid under table and an adult cut a piece of the Twelfth Night cake and asked the child which adult at the table should be given the piece of cake. During the second part of the Twelfth Night festival, everyone drank a toast to the person who found the traditional bean in his portion of the cake. This person became the "bean king"—a scene that Flemish and Dutch painters often depicted.

Festivals and fairs featured an array of activities. For example, festivals such as those in Lyon, France, involving masking, costuming, hiding, charivaris (a ritual of wearing masks and making noise to shame someone in a community), parades, collecting money, poetry, bonfires, playing games and athletic contests, occurred throughout Europe. One historian claims that the list of games played at festivals would include more games than Pieter Breughel depicted in his famous 17th-century painting *Children's Games*. At fairs, such as the famous Bartholomew Fair in London, crowds enjoyed musical performances and watched plays, clowns, and rope-dancing while consuming copious amounts of drink and meat. Dress up, now relegated to the play of children, used to be an activity enjoyed by all ages during festive events.

The American children's holiday Halloween is a vestige of the pleasure that people of all ages derived from donning costumes, disguising themselves, and participating in rituals in early modern Europe. In both Britain and continental Europe, men and women participated in mumming, a tradition in which they cross-dressed or dressed like government officials and went to neighbors' houses to dance and sing in disguise. Twelfth Night, Shrove Tuesday, and the November festivals also offered opportunities for Europeans to enjoy costuming.

Festivals and fairs served a myriad of complex, and seemingly contradictory, purposes in addition to the pleasure of socializing over food, drink, and dance. Rituals of play also challenged authority, contained an element of unpredictability, and might ferment political unrest. A well-orchestrated procession of local leaders during a festival reinforced their authority, but it also exposed them to critique. Wearing costumes and disguises could also serve political purposes.

In France, numerous royal and local edicts were passed against masking and mumming in order to stave off potential criticism of political leaders, fighting, conspiracy, and seditious activities. The festival could even lead to revolt and bloodshed. For example, an uprising against the royal tax officers was staged as a masquerade in Dijon, France. The Catholic Church slowly eliminated one festival, called the Feast of Fools, during which a child would be elected bishop and perform a mock-mass, but young men adopted its rituals, forming "fool-societies" or "play-acting societies."

Evidence of these youth societies of "misrule" has been found in France, Switzerland, Germany, Italy, Hungary, England, and Scotland. In London, a group known as "Lady Holland's Mob"—an unruly crowd that assembled at the Hand and Shears tavern on the eve of the opening of a fair—parodied the official administration of the fair and contested the city's authority. The ritualized practices of these youth societies could have darker aims. They led public ceremonies to punish and humiliate people who committed sexual crimes such as fornication, wife beating, and infidelity, or who transgressed gender roles, such as domineering women.

Perceptions of Play

Though the carnivalesque culture of the fair and the festival persisted into the 18th century, ideas about what constituted appropriate play, and who should participate in it, were changing. In 1600, a sharp distinction between the world of the adult and the child did not exist. The diary written by the doctor of Louis XIII, future king of France, provides evidence of a culture of play that both children and adults participated in.

As a young boy, Louis took part in court ballets and watched farces and comedies, wrestling matches, bullfighting and bear fighting. He sang and played the violin and the lute and participated in the collective religious and seasonal festivals. Unlike Louis XIII, the majority of adults and children lived in the countryside. Instead of attending plays and sporting matches, children helped adults with agricultural work, tending livestock, fetching water, or gathering firewood, and like adults, they combined work with play. Young shepherds went swimming, carved wood, and climbed trees. Children roamed the woods and the fields and played Hide-and-Seek, Blindman's Buff, and Tug-of-War. They delighted in toys such as marbles, whip-top, battledore-shuttlecock, kites, and footballs. They also imitated the violence found in adult life and engaged in more devious activities. They shot at birds or stole their eggs, tormented other animals, and played games like "bait the bear" or "badger the bull."

In 1692, John Locke challenged a long lineage of thought that defined play as idleness, wasted time, and even sinful, in his publication *Some Thoughts Concerning Education*. Locke construed play as a fundamental activity for children, and his views gained wide currency in 18th-century Europe. French philosopher Jean Jacques Rousseau published *Emile* in 1762, a guide to raising the ideal citizen, starting in infancy. The child, viewed as an incomplete and inadequate adult in the 16th century, would become a sentimentalized object of innocence and purity in the 19th century. In the 17th century, a single French word, *bibeloterie* (knick-knackery) described the miniature toys, "German toys," and "Italian baubles" that both adults and children collected. Even in 1730, no shops existed in England that manufactured toys specifically for children. By 1780, toyshops were everywhere. The ubiquity of the toyshop serves as a marker of transformations in the meaning of play. The ideal childhood, separated from the adult world and defined by playing games, redefined play itself as the activity of children and made the time to "play" more ephemeral. The 18th century marked a turning point in the history of play. Though more adults could attend concerts, visit parks, and cheer at sporting events, "playing games" increasingly described the activities of children. Over the course of the next century, the saturnalian carnivals and the festivals of misrule, where people of all ages could enjoy moments of playfulness together, would quietly disappear.

See Also: Blind Man's Bluff; Costumes in Play; Croquet; Europe, 1200 to 1600; Europe, 1800 to 1900; Europe, 1900 to 1940; Europe, 1940 to 1960; Europe, 1960 to Present; Folk Dancing; France; Gambling; History of Playing Cards; Horse Racing (Amateur); Ireland; Italy; Kite Flying; Maypole Dancing; Morris Dancing; Play and Literacy; Reading; Soccer (Amateur) Worldwide; Tennis (Amateur) and Variations of.

Bibliography. Philippe Ariès, *Centuries of Childhood; A Social History of Family Life* (Alfred A. Knopf, 1962); Hugh Cunningham, *Children and Childhood in Western Society Since 1500* (Pearson Education Limited, 2005); Natalie Zemon Davis, "Youth Groups and Charivaris in Sixteenth-Century France," *Past and Present* (v.50, 1971); Adam Fox, *Oral and Literate Culture in England, 1500–1700* (Oxford University Press, 2000); Colin Heywood, *A History of Childhood: Children and Childhood in the West from Medieval to Modern Times* (Polity Press, 2001); Majorie Keniston McIntosh, *Controlling Misbehavior in England: 1300–1600* (Cambridge University Press, 1998); Neil Mckendrick, John Brewer, and J.H. Plumb, eds., *Birth of a Consumer Society* (Indiana University Press, 1982); John Mullan and Christopher Reid, *Eighteenth-Century Popular Culture* (Oxford University Press, 2000).

Christine M. Walker
University of Michigan

Europe, 1800 to 1900

Europe endured seismic challenges and changes in the years between 1800 and 1900, as a series of political, social, and economic revolutions swept across the continent. Industrialization and urbanization, which began in the late 18th century and exploded in the first decades of the 19th century, changed the daily lives of tens of millions of people across the continent. These twin forces led to the expansion of both the middle class and the industrial working class and established the modern system of exchanging labor for cash wages.

These changes had an impact on sports and play. Agrarian societies live by the seasons; urban societies live by the clock. The shift to urbanization altered how Europeans viewed time, with sharp lines now drawn between "work" time and "leisure" time. Organized team sports, for example, gave working-class men an opportunity to get physical exercise in the outdoors after days spent doing repetitive work in airless factories. Urban middle-class men and women were encouraged to spend time in the out-of-doors to encourage good health, while indoor games and other amusements were part of building social communities and personal mental acuity. For middle- and upper-class children, the idea of childhood as a time of play and education was almost entirely an invention of the 19th century. This philosophy was aided by a growing commercial sector that began to churn out games and toys at an expanding rate throughout the second half of the century.

Sports and Play

The 19th century saw the rise of competitive sports in both Europe and the United States. Most of the spectator sports we enjoy today have their roots in the period between 1800 and 1900, as does that premier international showcase of athleticism, the Olympic Games.

The development of modern sports was aided not only by the growth of the middle class and changes in how people viewed leisure time but also in the dominant philosophical trends of the period. Romanticism, for example, emphasized communion with nature, helping spur the popularity of outdoor sports like hiking and mountaineering. Classicism was even more influential, given the interest in Greek and Roman principles of the strong body as the necessary adjunct of the strong mind. Millions of young men sought physical perfection in a growing variety of team and individual pursuits.

While some sports, like cycling, were the result of new inventions, the vast majority derived from preexisting sports that found new forms or were introduced to new audiences. What were once purely regional sports now spread out across the continent. Pursuits once open only to the aristocracy or upper class became available to the middle class. Routine pursuits were recast as leisure activities. Team sports became a stand-in for combat in the long, mostly peaceful period between the 1870s and the start of the World War I in 1914.

For centuries, fencing was a sport of the nobility. It was, in the strictest sense, a martial art—a practice that encouraged discipline, athleticism, and the adoption of a strict code of honor, but also had practical applications in combat or in settling issues of "honor" on the dueling field. By the mid-19th century, dueling was on the decline. Rather than abandon the practice, it was slowly shifted to a nonlethal sport, much as children are sent to practice karate or tae kwan do today. Fencing was popular among the upper and middle classes, particularly those who attended private schools, but never really filtered down to the working class. It was prevalent among the French, Germans, Italians, and Hungarians beginning in the early part of the 19th century and was one of the first Olympic sports. The sport's governing body, the Federation Internationale d'Escrime, was established in France at the turn of the 20th century.

Skating is a good example of the practical turned into the pastime. Historians are not sure when the people of northern Europe first learned to attach blades to their footware to slide across the winter ice. The oldest known pair of blades were found at the bottom of a Swiss lake; carved from the leg bones of an animal and meant to be tied on with leather straps, they were dated to about 3000 B.C.E. Iron skates originated around 1250 B.C.E. Skating became particularly important as transportation in the Netherlands, becoming the fastest way to move up and down frozen canals in the winter. This eventually led to the development of speed-skating, which by the end of the century had become a popular wintertime sport across Continental Europe.

The English picked up skating from northern Europeans but soon modified it to fit their geography. Unlike the Netherlands, England had few rivers or canals to use as speed-skating straightaways. Instead, they were confined primarily to small ponds. So they began to skate in geometric patterns, or "figures." The growth of figure skating was helped by the development of the steel skate in the 1840s. In this newer model, the skate blade was built into the shoe, allowing for turns and flexibility not available in older, strapped-on versions. Figure skating was carried back to the Continent, where the French and other cultures moved away from the strict geometry of the "English style" to embrace the more flowing, dance-like approach evident in the sport today.

Regional sports also became a pathway for cultural continuity in an era when millions of Europeans were setting out for North America and parts beyond. Bocce, a bowling game, had been enjoyed by Italians since the days of ancient Rome; by the 19th century, it was mostly a passion of the peasant class. Bocce was carried to America by those immigrants who arrived in huge numbers in the wake of a series of natural and political disasters in Italy beginning in the 1870s. More than a century later, bocce remains a popular sport in some Italian-American communities and is often seen as a tie to the mother country.

Historians see both the paths of cultural transfer in the development and movement of sports throughout the 19th century, but they also see the ways in which different cultural attitudes toward sports were indicative of the different approaches to the world as a whole. For example, in Great Britain, the focus was more on team sports, such as rugby, rowing, and early forms of soccer, where the point was to work together to dominate and defeat the opposing team. It is impossible not to see echoes of the nation's aggressive pursuit of colonial domination in their preference for rough team play. Less than 100 miles across the English Channel, Continental Europeans tended to prefer individual sports, such as swimming, diving, skating, skiing, and fencing. These differences were not static—there were plenty of Europeans who played soccer or joined rowing teams, just as there were plenty of Englishmen who enjoyed gymnastics and tennis and skating—but the preferences were clear.

At a time when the divisions between the aristocracy, the upper class, the middle class, and the working class were becoming ever more stark, there was a real separation between "amateur" and "professional" athletes. Professionals were often working-class men who earned money in the rougher, less respectable sports like prize-fighting and horse-racing. Amateurs, even those who spent most of their time training or competing in tournament play in dozens of sports, were seen as more pure and wholesome. This attitude found its highest form in the rebirth of the Modern Olympic Games in the final years of the 19th century.

The Olympic revival was the brainchild of a French aristocrat named Pierre de Frédy, the Baron de Coubertin. He had devoted his life to reforming the French educational system and believed that physical education was a critical component of building both strength and character. On a visit to Great Britain in 1890, he learned about the Wenlock Olympian Games, an annual competition organized by a local educator named William Penny Brooks in the rural Shropshire town of Much Wenlock. In 1850, Brooks had proposed the event "for the promotion of the moral, physical and intellectual improvement of the inhabitants of the town and neighborhood of Wenlock and especially of the working classes, by encouragement of outdoor recreation, and by the awards of prizes annually at public meeting for skill in Athletic exercise and proficiency in intellectual and industrial attainments."

Children run home from school in a photograph from the late 19th century, thought to be of either England or Ireland.

Taking this idea and drawing on the interest in the ancient Greek games spurred by archaeological digs at Olympia, Coubertin called for a congress at the Sorbonne in Paris in June 1894 to discuss the possibility of a universal sports competition. By the end of the meeting, the members had established the International Olympic Committee, elected Coubertin as president, and set a date for the first games. The first Olympiad was held in April 1896 in Athens, with 241 athletes representing 14 countries in athletics, cycling, fencing, gymnastics, shooting, swimming, tennis, weightlifting, and wrestling.

Non-Athletic Games

Not everyone in the 19th century wanted to take up rugby or swimming: Then, as today, the exercise of the brain was considered more interesting than the exercise of the body. As in sports, the games favored by people in the 1800s were often the same as those played by their ancestors for centuries, but even old amusements, like cards and board games, became more widely available as the years progressed.

Advances in Printing

Much of this was because of industrialization and advances in printing. Prior to the 19th century, board games were mostly handmade. The development of the industrial printing press by English and German industrialists in the early years of the century, and the increasing availability of cheap, wood pulp paper, lowered the costs of printing, while the adoption of chromolithography by the middle of the century made it possible to cheaply print multicolored prints, rather than relying on hand painting. All of this drove costs down and flooded the market with thousands of different games. The American-based Milton Bradley Company alone produced more than 400 games and puzzles by century's end.

Many of the new board games were variations on foreign games brought back to Europe by colonial adventurers. The British, in particular, were fond of bringing back versions of games from lengthy stays in India and Asia—sometimes so highly modified that only cultural anthropologists can see the shadows of the original games in their Westernized forms. The exchange of games had been going on for centuries, but mass production and competition between game manufacturers greatly accelerated the process.

Card games increased in popularity as playing cards became less expensive. Like board games, there were relatively few innovations in card gaming; most were variations on the same games that had been played, in one form or another, for centuries. However, with the growth of cheaper, mass-produced books that explained what had once been regional games, players were able to draw from a much larger pool.

For those who did not like to play cards, parlor games were another way to pass the time with friends and family in those decades before the radio and the television. Anyone who has seen a production or read Charles Dickens's *A Christmas Carol* might remember the scene where Ebenezer Scrooge and the Ghost of Christmas Present are watching his nephew Fred Holliwell and his friends play games; in Dickens' original story, a singing game called Glee is followed by Blind-Man's Bluff, then a word game called Yes or No. Parlor games could be quite intricate and often relied heavily on knowledge of history, literature, the Bible, and the pop culture of the times. Popular books were also helpful—*Cassell's Book of In-Door Amusements, Card Games and Fireside Fun*, published in 1881, gave rules for some 300 games. Some of these are still familiar today: Russian Gossip, for example, would today be instantly recognized as Telephone. Cassell's and countless other game books also detailed games for children, who were becoming a major consumer market by the 1850s.

For centuries, childhood had been treated as an apprentice adulthood. At least for those outside the aristocracy, more time was dedicated to learning trades than playing games. (After the Protestant Reformation, there were also fears that too much time spent in idle play was dangerous to the soul.) Children had always had toys and games, but they tended to be homemade and small in number. The growth of the middle class created a new class of children: those who did not have to go work in the factories or the fields and who were not members of the aristocracy. They were born into families that believed in the power of education to lift an individual to a new station in life. More emphasis was put on a child learning how to expand their minds, both in the schoolhouse and in their idle hours. The majority of early board games, for example, were based on literary or historical themes. The first jigsaw puzzles were usually maps pasted to a stiff board and cut around the borders as a way to teach geography.

While there would always be an emphasis on educational toys, as the century progressed, they also came to be seen as a way to teach children about larger social issues, including gender roles and modern advances in technology. Little girls learned about their place in life while playing with new toy stoves and tea sets and dolls, while little boys played with toy trains and tin soldiers. Middle-class parents usually had spending money and a desire to show their status: The purchase of the latest in toys and games for their children became not just a way to show love to a cherished child but also another way to display wealth. This became easier as mass production lowered the cost of goods in the final quarter of the century.

See Also: Bicycles; Blind Man's Bluff; Europe, 1200 to 1600; Europe, 1600 to 1800; Europe, 1900 to 1940; Europe, 1940 to 1960; Europe, 1960 to Present; History of Playing Cards; Horse Racing (Amateur); Puzzles; Reading; Skating; Tennis (Amateur) and Variations of.

Bibliography. Robert Crego, *Sports and Games of the 18th and 19th Centuries* (Greenwood Press, 2008); Patricia Evans, *Rimbles: A Book of Children's Classic Games, Rhymes, Songs, and Sayings* (Doubleday, 1961); Colin Heywood, *A History of Childhood: Children and Childhood in the West from Medieval to Modern Times* (Polity Press, 2001); Glenn Kirchner, *Children's Games Around the World* (Benjamin Cummings, 2000).

Heather K. Michon
Independent Scholar

Europe, 1900 to 1940

Playing is important part of growing up, but at the beginning of the 20th century, childhood lasted far shorter than it is believed to today. Children were compelled to grow up and mature far more quickly. That was largely because of the fact that children in the villages and poorer children in the towns had to start work at a very early age and had little free time. That is why children entered the adult world at a very early age, and the nonexistence of a clear border between the world of children and the world of adults was also reflected in the games they played. In large families where several generations lived together, children's rights were not as respected as today, and parents did not believe that children had a need to play. On the contrary, they considered play as a waste of time, being of the opinion that it was far more useful for children to perform one of the many household tasks.

In infancy and early childhood, play was the activity through which children learned to recognize colors and shapes, tastes and sounds. It was not until the second half of the 20th century that it was considered that the right to play was a child's basic right. The beginning of the century, with its dark overtones of war, shortages, and social upheaval, also contained the seeds of change, which would bloom in later years.

Changes with regards to the nature and needs of children became visible, and a child's environment was considered to be important for healthy development and their right for self-expression. Data on European children's play include descriptions of toy collections, games, and orally transmitted folklore and has been gathered mostly by folklorists, ethnologists, or art historians. Literature on adult play appeared much later in the second half of 20th century and mainly included descriptions of gambling games, card games, and the like.

Play and Learning

In infancy and early childhood, play was a learning activity and also provided pathways to social connections. Elementary school children used play to learn mutual respect, friendship, cooperation, and competition. For adolescents, play was a means of exploring possible identities, as well as a way to blow off steam and stay fit. Even adults had the potential to unite play, love, and work.

As it was the setting for play, education, and sometimes sleeping, having a nursery became common in 18th-century Victorian houses. It had direct connections to the family bedrooms or kitchen through a special corridor. This spatial separation of children in the middle-class home paralleled the rise of a specialist servant—the nanny—to care for them. The removal of children from the best rooms in the house was the evidence that children were seen as unique beings, rather than simply as tiny versions of adults. Special furniture, china, and toys support this notion, as do small playhouses built by famous architects. Most 20th-century houses, especially those built after World War I, were smaller and servantless. With the disappearance of servant quarters and with the identification of the kitchen with the mother (rather than with a servant) came an increasing integration of children's spaces into the heart of the house. Bedrooms for children were next to parents' bedrooms; bathrooms were shared. In general, the early 20th century saw a relaxation of social regulations.

In the early 20th century, kindergartens became more common. In England, they tended to take the form of a specially shaped classroom attached to a primary school, while in the rest of Europe the kindergarten tended to be a distinct building. This was associated with the Waldorf School Movement, which began in 1919, when Rudolf Steiner started Die Freie Waldorfschule for the children of the workers at the Waldorf-Astoria cigarette factory in Stuttgart. More common in the 1920s and 1930s were kindergartens designed in a modern style, like the 1934 nursery school on the outskirts of Zurich, where direct access to the outdoors, ample lighting, and light, moveable furniture, scaled to young children, were provided.

In the early 20th century, Progressive pedagogical theorists (like Karl Popper in Germany) began to apply the basic philosophy of the kindergarten movement—attention to the development of the whole child—to primary and secondary school students. In Europe, progressive educational reform attempted to bring students into closer communion with the natural landscape. Early in the 20th century, open-air schools—with neither heating nor glazing—were built primarily for tubercular children; the first of these was the Forest School established in Charlottenburg, Germany, in 1904. By the 1920s, open-air schools were recommended for nontubercular children as well.

In Frankfurt, Germany, architects designed decentralized schools called pavilion schools, with one-story wings disposed over large open sites to increase light and air circulation. Although there were some French pavilion schools, like in Suresnes, France retained a tradition of density, building multistory blocks with outdoor space on rooftop terraces. The first known use of sand for play is the heaps of sand called *sand bergs* in the public parks of Berlin in 1850. The kindergarten movement in Germany included sandboxes in their design in the latter half of the century, and in 1889 the newspaper of the Pestalozzi/Froebel children's houses described how to build a sandbox. From the earliest photographs of sandboxes in Europe, we can see that they had wheelbarrows, rakes, buckets, and spades, and molds of animals and other shapes. Today, implements are usually limited to smaller tools made of plastic rather than metal.

The Growth of Toys

Toys became important tools of play. From the early 20th century, depictions of toys were still mainly found in portraits of children of the middle and upper classes. The toys that appear in these paintings are not there to emphasize the person's affluence but merely attributes that designate a child. The same difference existed in the first decades of the 20th century between paintings and photographs. On occasions worth being preserved for posterity, children were set in an imaginary environment of luxury, and toys were added to make the scene perfect. Even if we do not know to whom the toys actually belonged, these images provide us with useful information, because the toys in the pictures had to be modern, popular, and something the children would be proud to possess.

For most of history, the majority of toys had been made at home. Wood, clay, and lead were the earliest toymaking materials for cottage industries, while jewellers and goldsmiths made toys for the very rich. Soon after each inventive advance in the industrial revolution, mass production provided toys at consumable prices. Means of mass distribution were also in place by the beginning of the 20th century, and there has been much change in the course of this century. The traditional source of all toys at this time was Germany—Britain was also well established—but World War I ended German dominance in the toy export trade. The British and French toy industry was given a boost because of the absence of German imports during World War I, although it remained very much a home market.

World War II again severely disrupted the European toy industry. After the war ended, manufacturers began to use synthetic fibers. The expanding market for factory-made goods changed the world of child's play. Children who grew up playing with folk toys of the conventional form like dolls, balls, carved animals, wheels, or discarded objects, such as sticks or rags, were slowly converted into entertainment all over Europe. Before the mass production of toys, play was seen as an expression of the natural spirit of childhood and not of bonding with objects. Its focus was more social than material interaction. It was not assumed that children needed a profusion of toys. They were a specialty product, mainly enjoyed by the upper classes, and were part of folk culture. These objects were crafted by parents, relatives, and children. Occasionally, they were made by local toymakers as gifts for special occasions.

Most children from the beginning of the 20th century did not have purchased toys. The first toy factories and toyshops appeared around the end of the 19th century, and dolls, wooden horses, wooden trains, and balls could be bought in those shops. But, as the toy industry was not on a large scale, toys were usually handmade and very expensive, and only wealthy, urban families could afford them. Most children made their own toys, mainly from natural materials, using wood or paper. The first marbles were fashioned from hardened earth, and balls were formed out of discarded articles of clothing, most often socks or pig bladders blown up and later layered with leather taken from old shoes. Kites were made from parts of maize, and other toys were made from paper pasted together with a mixture of flour and water instead of expensive glue. Large-scale toy production did not begin until between the two world wars, and it was only after World War II that more children could acquire bicycles, rollerskates, ice skates, scooters, and leather footballs.

At the beginning of the 20th century the toy industry was heavily rooted in German manufacture, as it had been throughout the 19th century. Despite this, there were several well-established toy businesses flourishing in Britain. Conservative by nature, the toy business was not adventurous. Toys that had been favorites in the 19th century remained firm favorites until the outbreak of World War I in 1914. Among these, selected according to the gender of the child, were clockwork toys, dollhouses, spinning tops, magic lanterns, push and pull toys, puzzles, rocking horses, and dolls.

The new century brought with it two new toys, which became phenomenally successful. The first of these, Meccano, was designed by Frank Hornby in 1899 to encourage his son's interest in mechanical engineering. It was highly innovative, because it was made of metal as opposed to wood, which was usually used for making construction kits. The industrial advances of the previous century had made educators aware of the importance of encouraging technical training for young men, and the advantages of this new toy as an instructive and amusing hobby were very clear. The second of the new toys, designed by Richard Steiff in 1902, was the first soft toy bear, which became known by its familiar title, the Teddy Bear, after 1906.

Learning Through Play

With infants, rather than giving their children toys, adults taught children simple games to teach them to walk; to make them aware of their hands, fingers, and toes; and to teach babies to concentrate and communicate with eye contact, facial expressions, and voice. Rhymes and games were taught in the home or in the infant school; children also learned them directly from one another when playing outside together. Children's folklore, such as rhymes, jokes, and riddles, were purely oral in transmission, circulated rapidly, and showed both continuity and variation. Riddles, for example, lightened the strain of heavy work. Boys all over Europe enjoyed teasing girls with sexual riddles, but riddling was also a contest of wit.

Preindustrial society required children to do their share of the farmwork. What free time they had after these responsibilities could be spent playing games such as various forms of Tag, Hide-and-Seek, ball games, and Hopscotch. Counting rhymes were utilized to determine the role of participants in games. Children came to understand their environment because of the songs and games they were involved in. Children's folk games reflected the inner life of kids, their gifts, and their preferences. Many categories of folk games were played in Europe: amusing (funny); satirical; counting out items (versified or not); songs dedicated to animals and plants; games related to nature's calendar (invoking rain, sun, rainbows, or wind or driving away thunder or rain); games related to the major events of human life, sometimes played with playing objects too; and tongue twisters or puns.

Street Games

Children's street culture was passed from one generation of city children to the next and between different groups of children as well. It was the most common in children between the ages of 7 and 12 and was the strongest in urban working-class industrial districts, where children could play on the streets for long periods without supervision. Because in most cases it is difficult and perhaps inaccurate to equate a certain age group with certain games, except when we divide games in children's games and adult's games, they are divided by the action that is performed. Games are usually grouped in games of competition, combat games, chasing, tag games, counting out games, guessing games, games of dexterity, games of strategy and chance, clapping games, singing games, parlor games, party games, role play games, and so forth.

A vintage German teddy bear. Richard Steiff designed the first soft toy bear in 1902, after sketching bears at the zoo.

In games of competition, children competed either in knowledge and skills taught at school or physically with or without the aid of requisites. Such games were popular in villages and towns. They usually comprised running, hiding, and testing physical strength. Village children had more space to play such games, and town children were deprived of many games because of the lack of physical space and the danger of breaking things in the home. But even town children had more space than they do today, because cars were few and far between until the 1950s, and children could play safely in most town streets. In winter, steep streets were transformed into perfect toboggan slides, and with a little extra effort put into treading down the snow and pouring water over it, entire streets were transformed into ice skating rinks.

Competition and tag games like jump rope, Hopscotch, Hide-and-Seek, and chasing, demonstrated a combination of skills, strength, endurance, and patience. Hopscotch, which originates in Britain, was also known in Slavic and Romanic language cultures. Clapping games were thought of as girls' games, although boys and adults played as well. They were thought to be a part of oral culture and were accompanied with singing or reciting a rhyme. After World War I, it became common to celebrate children's birthdays in urban areas. Invitation cards became collector's item in the 1920s, functioning as social souvenirs. Girls started collections of paper napkins, often brought home from birthday parties, beautiful packaging, including matchboxes, tin boxes, and fancy bottles; boys collected more "manly" items.

Role Playing

Role-playing games most often imitated characters with authority and responsibilities. Games that imitated the adult world, in which the roles are separated, were imitated by children. They were normally restricted to young children and, aside from their straightforward purpose of fun, could sometimes also serve the purpose of allowing children to explore adult roles and relationships. Role playing revealed a lot about children's psychological state, their perception of gender roles, home life, incomes, and their interpretation of the world around them. Children imitated jobs or professions they come into contact with, such as hairdressers, salespeople, car mechanics, or teachers, or made their own little theatres. The main goal of playing Doctor and Patient was to discover each other's bodies, especially "forbidden" parts, and this game even involved experiments with sexual play. Little girls often imitated their mothers, emulating jobs they saw performed around the home: they cooked, sewed, and made toys in the form of furniture, thus creating the impression that they had their own little home. While acting like a family, they learned about family relationships and other family arrangements. Boys liked to emulate their fathers, doing what was considered men's jobs, but they often played War too.

The 20th-Century Effect of War

The enemies have changed during the 20th century; cowboys and Indians or cops and robbers have been replaced with enemies from real 20th-century wars. Fascist and Nazi youth associations attracted large majorities of young people in Italy under Mussolini's rule and in Germany under the Nazi dictatorship. In these state-sponsored movements, young people found a variety of leisure opportunities, a strong national identity, and clearly defined gender roles. Because leaders encouraged members to put youth group duties above all other responsibilities, many youth joined in order to undermine the traditional authority of parents, school, or church. This practice reinforced their core beliefs that individuals owed primary allegiance to the state, and that youth and not their elders would shape the future. Through the Hitler Youth, the Nazi state controlled virtually all educational, vocational, and recreational opportunities and effectively coordinated propaganda, peer pressure, and intimidation techniques to claim, at its peak, more than 95 percent of German youth as members. On the other side, communist organizations in eastern, central, and part of southern Europe worked to educate young people in communist values and to aid the party to build communism.

They provided political education for young people, sponsored communist cultural events and literacy campaigns, oversaw a range of activities in the schools, and served as a training ground for future membership in adult parties. With the Russian revolution in 1917, interest in children and youth crested. The state hoped to mold children to create the new Soviet citizen, though officials also reflected the older aristocratic interest in childhood as a time of learning. Education spread widely. As the birthrate dropped, many parents devoted great attention to their individual children, providing tutoring or private lessons in dance or acrobatics. Highly competitive schools and opportunities for advancement within the Communist Party beckoned to successful children, and many parents tried hard to protect their offspring and encourage them to excel. Then, after a decade or two of peace after World War II ended, young people returned to characters from the novels of Karl May. Gendered-based games that imitated the adult world have been preparing young boys and girls to the roles designated to them by their sex.

Because the prewar village children had little time to play, they usually played while working in the fields or in the short breaks. As children were usually looking after the livestock if they lived in mountainous regions of Europe, there were a number of games they played during long hours spent looking after livestock at pasture. Those games involved running, hiding and seeking, making swings, and carving toys or instruments from wood. Only children from richer families had a specific time designated for play, usually after having done their homework. The children, who spent much of their days outside, played in a natural playground without boundaries or fences, surrounded by trees, fields, creeks, and ponds, and playing with rocks, pieces of wood, mud, living structures, or animals.

Games Across Europe

A traditional children's party game was Blind Man's Bluff, known under this term in United Kingdom and Ireland and other names elsewhere in Europe (such as Blind Mice in Slovenia). The game was a variant of Tag, played in a spacious area, such as outdoors or in a large room. The most popular games in southeast Europe were Crooked Wolf, Hide-and-Seek, and Leapfrog in Bulgaria, and a sort of baseball was taught in schools in Romania. Under the Communist regime, schools would take children from towns into the country to teach them seasonal agricultural work. Greek children played guessing games, like Blind Man's Bluff, Ring a Ring o' Roses, the Flea Flies, and Have You a Light. There were also older games, which were a combination of singing and reciting certain words and movements. In Hungary, as in other countries, children in towns jumped rope and played hula-hoop, while in most countries that emerged after the breakup of former Yugoslavia, the favorite games were Hide-and-Seek, Piggy in the Middle, Leapfrog, and Hopscotch. One of the most popular older games was a kind of a precursor to today's cricket, the aim of which was to hit a wooden object as far as possible with a wooden bat.

Adolescents preferred party games, in particular ones with an erotic charge, and these games provided them an opportunity to find and test potential mates. Games were a form of amusement at festivals, especially Christmas, New Year's Eve, Lent, and at weddings. Dancing and singing were often part of games. Card playing, and in some settings drinking and gambling, flourished among the lower classes in pubs and bars. Card playing was part of a men's world, but later the whole families and children had their own card plays to relax. Sports, such as wrestling, were also practiced by young men in Slovakia, Georgia, and elsewhere. Ball games, ice skating, skiing, and sledding were common in Northern and Central Europe or in other parts with temperate climate. Games using animals, especially bullfighting, and ball games such as football were widely practiced in Spain. Bullfighting was viewed as a symbolic representation of human struggle against death, as well as an explicit expression of the overt sexuality associated with the Spanish male. In Greece, a form of shadow-theater, usually performed in the open air with a small orchestra of musicians, was very popular.

Although games had different names in different countries, they were similar, and their ultimate aim was to demonstrate the most skillful, the quickest, and the most astute.

See Also: Blind Man's Bluff; Boys' Play; Bulgaria; Europe, 1940 to 1960; Europe, 1960 to Present; Greece; Hide & Seek; Ireland; Romania; Russia; Slovenia; Spain; Toys and Child Development.

Bibliography. William M. Clements, *The Greenwood Encyclopedia of World Folklore and Folklife: Vol. 3, Europe* (Greenwood Press, 2006); Brady Eilís, *All In! All In! A Selection of Dublin Children's Traditional Street-Games with Rhymes and Music* (Comhairle Bhéaloideas Éireann, 1984); *Encyclopedia of Children and Childhood in History and Society*, www.faqs.org/childhood/index.html (cited October 2008); Iona Opie, *The People in the Playground* (Oxford University Press, 1993); James Opie, Duncan Chilcott, and Julia Harris, eds., *A Collector's Guide to 20th-Century Toys* (Wellfleet Books, 1990); Halina Pasierbska, *Must-Have Toys: Favourites of the 20th Century* (Museum of Childhood Bethnal Green, 2004); Milan Ristoviæ and Dubravka Stojanoviæ, eds., *Childhood in the Past: 19th and 20th Century* (Association for Social History, 2001); Tanja Tomažiè, *Igraèe* [Toys], (Slovenski Etnografski Muzej, 1999).

Mojca Ramšak
Center for Biographic Research

Europe, 1940 to 1960

The war years from 1939 to 1945 meant great shortages of every kind, and the life of Europeans was subject to many restrictions. Between 1941 and 1945, children were killed in huge numbers throughout Europe during military operations and in concentration camps. Overall, 1.5 million Jewish children; children from Greece, Romania, Hungary, Albania, Bulgaria, Poland, Yugoslavia, France, and Germany; gypsy children; Slavic children; children who had the wrong nationality or religion or whose parents had the wrong political affiliations; or those who did not fit Hitler's concept of the Aryan race, died in the concentration camps of the Third Reich. Gypsy children and physically disabled children suffered pogroms and murder under the Nazis. Children took part in military conflicts through their activity in resistance movements in German- or Italian-occupied countries. Older children were occasionally used as informants or took part in sabotage actions. Others were told how to behave in case of an inspection of the home, remaining silent about illegal persons living in the house or apartment.

In Germany during the last period of the German defense in fall 1944 and spring 1945, many boys between the ages of 12 and 16 years were drafted as German troops on both the Eastern and Western fronts. During World War II, about 10,000 underage German boy soldiers were imprisoned in the largest Allied camp for child soldiers in France. Just before the end of World War II, about 70,000 German refugee children under the age of 15 were sent to Denmark, where they received inadequate medical care. It is estimated that in 1946, almost all refugee children under the age of 2, and in total about 7,000 refugee children, died in camps in Denmark of malnutrition and lack of medical care. Huge armies of orphans were left without parental care—left to the mercy of the state or relatives, or on the street.

The traumas and psychological scars resulting from a wartime childhood have been suffered by generations, and they were forced to grow up quickly, their childhood having been wrested from them by war—they were not able to have a normal education. When war becomes a part of everyday life, with its overt and covert violence, it cannot help but change children's lives and their concept of the world. Rationing, introduced early in the war, continued long after the war ended. World War II devastated many urban areas in Europe, and children in these areas began creating their own play spaces in bombed-out areas in their neighborhoods, using whatever materials and equipment could be found. Most children played with toys that had been handed down from older children or made at home.

The misuse of children for political and propaganda purposes was mainly linked to the 20th century and mass political parties and movements such as Nazism, Fascism, and Communism. Sports, culture, and other organizations for children and young people became tools in the hands of national political and religious movements and leaders (such as Benito Mussolini in Italy, Adolf Hitler in Germany, Francisco Franco in Spain, Josip Broz Tito in Yugoslavia, Enver Hoxha in Albania, Nicolae Ceausescu in Romania, Todor Zhivkov in Bulgaria, and Josip Visarjonovi Stalin in Russia). Political leaders in European countries were represented as spiritual fathers, teachers, and protectors of all children in their countries.

Post–World War II Environment

In the period immediately following World War II, children had the use of several key rooms in their homes, especially the multipurpose or living room. Other important spaces for children's play were basements and backyards. Postwar basements were spaces of escape from parents, especially for teenagers, and were the ideal setting for listening to music and playing games such as ping pong, which required too much space to fit into the upstairs rooms. In 1945, recreation programs evolved from a relatively minor area of government and grew to an enormous, complex, and profit-seeking enterprise. In the 1950s there was a rise in the birthrate, and children and youth were flooding schools and recreation centers.

Immediately after the conclusion of World War II in 1945, the growing divide between the Eastern and Western forces set in motion the wheels that would escalate into what would later be known as the Cold War. After such a brutal and bloody conflict in the first half, the latter half of the decade was dominated by enforced social upheaval as soldiers returned to their homelands, demanding government recognition for their sacrifices. Countless thousands of refugees sought return to their lands or to new homes abroad, and the slow process of recovery began to take place.

Europe was far from wealthy before or after the war ended, and in the 1950s, materials for toy making were still in short supply. There were restrictions on imports, and rationing continued to be a problem for all industries. Britain still had a toy industry, whereas German manufacturers were badly affected by the war. During World War II, toy production in Europe decreased, and some factories began to manufacture munitions instead. At this time, many homemade toys were produced, using materials that were available. One of the recurrent themes in the progress of toymaking since 1940 was the search for realism in toys. To make a true model of something takes a great deal more time and trouble than to make an approximation, and therefore miniature toys are often judged by how true to life they are. The advent of plastic made it so much simpler to produce realistic-looking models, and plastic model kits were a growing area of the toy industry from the 1940s onwards.

Although materials continued to be difficult to obtain for many years after the war, the potential of the new synthetic fibers as useful and economically priced replacements for silk boded well for the future of soft toys. Plastic educational toys, in prewar form, became available again in limited quantities. Toys played a part in the rebirth of postwar Europe as vital objects of trade and as educational tools. Postwar European societies were about to experience the beginning of the consumer age. At home, the demand for toys rapidly increased and was probably fuelled by the shortages that families had suffered for so long. Children still played with the toys that their parents had played with—teddy bears, guns, building kits, scooters, dolls, dollhouses, and tea sets. Model vehicles were top sellers, and the production of die-cast toys was a huge business on an international scale.

Cultural Expectations

Nevertheless, the phrase "first work and then play" was still present in daily lives of children and many of them lived by the rule "never play before you finish your homework." This rule pertained to both boys and girls, as school had been mandatory for both since the second half of the 19th century. What had changed was the attitude and strong awareness that girls would not be useful for postwar society if they remained illiterate. By the late 1940s, European child experts also advised parents to avoid superstitions—which were still firmly present, especially in rural areas—and to help children get rid of shyness and to encourage greater independence. Shy children risked being rejected by their peer groups as being too submissive. After the war, the definitions of appropriate masculine and feminine behavior started to change slowly.

For instance, when there was a shortage of food before the war, especially in some rural patriarchal areas, girls and women were given less to eat than boys and men. This attitude had changed, and equality of the sexes became more and more visible. European cultures with strong Catholic or orthodox religious traditions that were patriarchal fostered sharp gender divisions, whereas more egalitarian protestant cultures offered greater role flexibility for both males and females. Spain, Italy, Greece, and Albania, for example, emphasized gender roles more than Denmark, Netherland, Sweden, and Norway. Through explicit and unspoken messages, girls were encouraged to model themselves on their mothers and other women they knew or encountered in stories, schoolbooks, and television programs. Boys were encouraged to model themselves on their fathers and other male figures.

The 1950s was a decade of conservatism, following the mass upheavals of the war and a time when redevelopment and urban growth, including nurturing the ideal of the nuclear family, really began to take hold. Many modern cultural phenomena, such as the generation gap, started in the 1950s, stimulated by the Beat Generation and their works, which contrasted drastically with the conservative society of the decade. This decade also revolutionized entertainment, with the mainstream introduction of the television, the rapid growth of the recording industry and new genres of music, and movies targeted to teenage audiences. Many modern toys like hula-hoops and Frisbees were also invented in the 1950s. Because of the conservative nature of the era and the sometimes violent suppression of social movements, seeds of rebellion grew and were manifested through rock-and-roll music, and movies emphasized rebelliousness. These precedents would serve as the forerunners to the social revolution of the 1960s.

Marketing to Children

In the 1950s, the first mass-marketing strategies and television advertising to the world of toys appeared in the most developed countries of Western and Northern Europe. Previously, advertising was only minimally important, and marketers were not aware of children's consumption practices or their influence on their family's spending habits, and thus took little interest in them. Toy manufacturers were achieving success through efficiencies in the production process, without mass market advertising. Children loved collecting stickers with famous names from history, especially actors and actresses, political figures, famous thinkers, comedians, nasty characters, and sports figures. Marketers introduced a new strategy, including collector's items for children with products for adults. Cigarettes, soap, coffee substitute, chewing gum, and many other products contained collectibles for children. Before World War II, the Walt Disney Company in the United States launched a strategy of integrated consumption of trademarked goods, which appealed to young consumers and collectors.

Film, magazines, cards, posters, soap figurines, bubble gum, printed napkins, and toys built up a total universe of desirable objects and experiences. This strategy was so successful that it turned much later into the contemporary business of merchandising, which puts trademarked characters on wallpaper, videos, computer games, towels, schoolbags, pencils, erasers, and clothes, as well as in fast food. Even though such collecting worried some adults because of its prearranged character and the way it commercialized childhood, it mirrored the conditions of modern culture that also affected the adult world.

Children were included in international conventions for the first time in 1949, when the rights and protection of children in war—as part of the civilian population—were mentioned in the fourth Geneva Convention. With the war having recently ended, there were calls to ban toy weapons. Boys, in particular, had for centuries played with weapons of all sorts, improvised or store-bought, playing Robin Hood and Cowboys and Indians as part of everyday life. After 1953 such war toys were discouraged, but between the world wars the German companies produced a large range of resin figures, representing soldiers from many countries, although the majority of toys represented German soldiers and Nazi party leaders, such as Adolf Hitler and Hermann Göring.

Furthermore, growing concerns about toy safety in general were forcing firms to rethink some of their products in the 1950s. The concern about the potential health hazard of lead gradually induced firms to switch to plastics. Soft-toy makers had to be scrupulous about the safety of their own products, and all imports of dolls and soft toys had to be tested for hygiene. This was because earlier items had been found to be full of stuffing that was far from safe for small children.

New toys included LEGOs, launched in 1932 in Bilund, Denmark. In 1949, the company produced around 200 different plastic and wooden toys, including automatic binding bricks, a forerunner of the LEGO bricks we know today. At first they were sold exclusively in Denmark, and in 1955 the first real exporting of LEGO began with shipments to Sweden. By the end of the 1950s, the company expanded to Germany, Switzerland, France, Great Britain, Belgium, and Sweden, and by the end of 1960s to Finland, the Netherlands, Italy, Austria and Spain. LEGO products were developed in such a way that there was something for all ages and stages of development: from toddlers, schoolchildren, and teenagers to young-at-heart adults, whether they preferred creating their own designs or building predesigned models.

Western Influences

Plastic hula-hoops became popular in Europe in the late 1950s and early 1960s. Soon shaking one's hips and twirling hoops around their waists became popular in gym classes and acceptable to do in public for both girls and adult women. Similarly famous was another toy for all ages, a flying disc called the Frisbee or Frisbie. In the 1950s most children's toy dolls were representations of infants, but this changed when the Barbie doll was invented in 1959 in the United States. Ruth Handler, who created Barbie, believed that it was important for the doll to have an adult appearance, and early market research showed that some parents were unhappy about the doll's chest, which had distinct breasts. Barbie, with her clothes and accessories, was a status toy for girls—Barbie had become a cultural icon.

At the same time, the popularity of Play-Doh was rising—a nontoxic modeling clay compound similar in composition to bread dough and available in several colors. Large, bright, colorful, hygienic, and safe toys were made relatively cheaply for the preschool market in particular. The advantages of new technology and the question of toy design were then addressed in various ways. The toy industry was still unconvinced that it could be desirable to bring in marketing professionals and child psychologists when working on a new product line, particularly if it was connected with educational toys.

Radio and Television

In the 1940s, when radio was still regarded as a new medium, special children's programs were broadcast in order to attract young listeners. As such programs became popular, production increased. Children and teenagers took pleasure in listening to programs specifically aimed at children, as well as other programs. As with other electronic media, radio was met with worries from the adult world. In Sweden, as in other countries, it was a common fear that too much listening could make children passive and less eager to play. In the 1940s, Swedish teachers expressed worries about being regarded as mere loudspeakers by children accustomed to passively listening to radio.

However, compared with reactions to other electronic media, radio seems to have incited relatively few moral panic attacks. This can be explained in part by radio's supposed usefulness in education. In the 1950s, when television was introduced, researchers in Britain came to the conclusion that television reduced radio listening more than it reduced any other activity. In spite of this, one in three children said that if they had to do without radio, they would miss it quite a lot. The study also noticed that children who had been watching television for several years listened a little more often to the radio.

This was described as a revival in line with reports of adults' media behavior. While radio programs could not compete with television programs, other types of programming held listeners' interest, including panel games, discussions, music, and sports commentaries. In the 1960s people in villages of southern and central Europe were brought together by radios and television sets.

Communal village or family listening and watching of telecasts died out in the 1980s, when these activities became individual, even in demographically challenged rural areas. The consumer society that followed World War II provided parents with the tactic of disciplining children by denying toys or the right to watch a favorite television program. Adults set firm boundaries and rules and punished with time-outs and isolation. While more and more parents worked to survive or to achieve or maintain middle-class status, many children were on their own without parental guidance much of the time. Television became their nanny.

See Also: Denmark; Dolls, Barbie and Others; Europe, 1900 to 1940; Europe, 1960 to Present; Frisbee; Germany; LEGOs.

Bibliography. Duncan Chilcott and Julia Harris, eds., *A Collector's Guide to 20th-Century Toys* (Wellfleet Books, 1990); Jaipaul L. Roopnarine, James Ewald Johnson, and Frank H. Hooper, *Children's Play in Diverse Cultures* (SUNY Press, 1994); LEGO Corporate Web site, *LEGO Timeline,* www.lego.com (cited October 2008); Halina Pasierbska, *Must-Have Toys: Favourites of the 20th Century* (Museum of Childhood Bethnal Green, 2004); *When We Were Kids,* www.wwwk.co.uk (cited October 2008).

Mojca Ramšak
Center for Biographic Research

Europe, 1960 to Present

Today, play is considered to be a key part of the daily care of infants. Current child-rearing literature emphasizes the importance of early-childhood development for achievements later in life. As a result, parents in industrialized societies often feel a real sense of urgency in stimulating their children enough, often through toys. Since the 1960s, many books have been published on infant play, most consisting of suggestions for activities and games for parents and babies, such as singing songs, making the baby laugh, offering a variety of objects for the baby to examine, and popular games. While it can be assumed that parents everywhere have entertained and interacted with their babies in similar ways, such books reflect how modern theories of child development became mainstream during the 20th century.

Most recent child-rearing manuals recommend almost exactly the same types of toys for different stages of development. Mobiles, for example, are considered to be ideal toys for babies from 1 to 3 months, giving the baby a stimulating object to look at. Toys for newborn babies are designed to gently stimulate the developing senses of sight, hearing, and touch. Unbreakable crib mirrors are also very popular playthings for newborns, based on research showing that babies are most interested in faces.

As the baby's vision develops, experts suggest the introduction of objects with high-contrast colors. Floor gyms are also popular toys, giving babies something to look at and reach for before they learn to sit up (between 6 and 8 months). Throughout the first year, rattles, musical toys, soft balls, and toys are recommended to follow babies' growing comprehension of the world around them. By the end of the first year, as infants learn to crawl and acquire more small motor skills, toys like stacking cups, plastic telephones, busy boxes, board books, blocks, and push-pull toys are considered to be more appropriate. Books for babies are often grouped with toys, and more and more picture book classics have been transferred to the more durable board book format. Other formats created for very young children are the bath book and the cloth book. Many of these books are nearly indistinguishable from other stuffed toys.

Toy Production

Lower costs and wider production of toys were facilitated by the rise of factories, which meant that basic toys were more broadly integrated into everyday life, appearing in schools, clubs, and family leisure activities. Wood gave way to synthetics, including plastic and nylon, as the preferred materials, replacing the organic imagery of handcrafted toys. New materials and methods of production and the resultant uniformity of the product were a reflection of industrial values. Though new materials appeared, the overall themes in toy industry stayed the same as in the beginning of the 20th century. Dolls were given brand names; tin toys were replaced by die-cast or plastic; toy trains disappeared, banished to a more specialized model market; and toy soldiers became spacemen or superheroes. The major differences were in the materials and production of toys themselves, and in the influence of mass media, particularly television and computer games.

Plastic has become the preferred material for dollmakers (replacing bisque and composition); for toy soldiers, animals, and figures (replacing lead, wood, and composition); and for cheap and ephemeral amusements (replacing paper or card). Even in the area of soft toys, soft plastic has made an impact, although here the traditional filled fabric still reigns.

Television has dramatically changed the toy industry, and since it has been possible to advertise toys on television, the best toys have reached their marketplace with efficiency. The most popular construction toy of the last three generations, LEGOs, have taken over the role performed in the first half of the century by Meccano. Perhaps the biggest impact of plastic has been in the category of toys for very young children, where beautifully shaped and colored toys are now safe to put in a child's mouth, because even when the toys are painted, the paint is plastic-based instead of lead-based. Mass marketers focused on children as consumers, as their buying habits were being formed. Advertisers learned the best methods, mediums, styles, and symbols for reaching these customers and realized the importance and influence of the peer group in persuasion and social involvement. The commercialization of childhood transformed the toy industry and children as well.

The Influence of Licensing

Some of the most lasting memories of childhood involve the television. Children were enchanted by it, and the advent of color television in the late 1960s increased that magic. In some southern and eastern European countries, black-and-white television appeared in the late 1960s, because economic development was not equal throughout Europe. Children's television programming developed and grew in the 1970s, though some shows appeared as early as the 1940s and 1950s. The popularization of television created a demand for child actors, who, like adult entertainment celebrities, spurred a fan culture. A new generation of children's series was ushered in with the 1960s, including those featuring puppets and animation. In the mid-1960s there was a change in the broadcast pattern, with children's programs airing before noon or in the early afternoon, or sometimes both. Many children watched television at a playgroup or with babysitters while their mother went out to work. The preschool time slot continued through the decade, firmly cemented in its postlunchtime slot.

And by the early 1990s, there was hardly a children's toy advertised on television that did not have a personality associated with it. Plastic figures endowed with social identities become the dominant symbols in children's lives and the supreme emblems of their dearest pleasures.

Home Life and Childcare

In the period following 1975, children have typically occupied nearly every room in a middle-class home, with the exception being the living room. The family room remained the heart of family life, with the television at its center. Kitchens became larger centers, intended to facilitate cooking by more than just mom and to accommodate children doing homework, and sometimes containing computer facilities. Bedrooms remain gender- and age-specific and continue to function as important places of solitude and self-expression for children of all ages.

Also significant in this era was the rise of building daycare facilities. Daycare was sometimes accommodated in spaces such as churches, schools, and community centers or was sometimes integrated into large workplaces, such as office buildings and hospitals. In most cases, new daycare facilities draw directly on the language of domestic architecture, employing regional building materials, pitched roofs, bright colors, and easily legible room shapes. Daycare facilities typically comprise a series of small classrooms arranged along both sides of a corridor, as well as administrative offices and kitchens. Exterior play spaces, like the postwar private backyard, commonly feature equipment to encourage safe group play. Increasingly, security has become a concern in daycare centers because of perceived increases in urban violence and child abductions, and as a result, daycare centers are frequently surrounded by fences and entered only by workers, parents, and guardians.

The idea that city governments should organize and provide recreation programs, services, and facilities became widely accepted in the 20th century, with laws authorizing governments to operate structured recreation programs, and many important nonprofit organizations serving youth were formed. Numerous public departments have contracted with private businesses to operate swimming pools, golf courses, tennis complexes, marinas, community centers, and other facilities under contractual agreements that govern the standards they must meet and the rates they may impose.

Outdoor Recreation

Organized recreation has now moved from the public sector to the private, as profit-making businesses now provide structured opportunities for children's play and recreation. The former natural environment of toddlers and juniors who were playing outside became sophisticated and almost replaced with specially designed play systems and items like rockers, playhouses, slides, and trampolines. We find them in parks, on children's playgrounds, in front of schools, and increasingly in the yards of private residences. Ball courts for different ball games, climbing walls, special climbers, space nets and frames, cable ferries, and cable rides are becoming frequent urban environment play structures. Indoor or outdoor swimming pools are also equipped with different water tables, spirals, pumps, troughs, and much more.

Teenagers also receive attention in today's play industry, and play systems for them provide both physical challenges to stretch and the possibility to show off and socialize. Modern play systems combine both social and active elements like seating areas, towers and climbing walls, high slides, and basketball hoops. Active elements range from a single basketball hoop to a complete court. Social areas are carefully designed with informal seating and roofs that keep the elements out. Today, to play is every child's right, and every child should have equal access to good play opportunities, regardless of whether the child is able-bodied or has any form of disability. Invisible inclusivity became the leading politics in European playground designs. Of course, there are still many worn out and unsafe play areas, or areas with no play space, all over Europe, especially if town councils are not able or willing to take care of playgrounds or if the majority of local inhabitants are immigrants.

Perhaps the most significant public spaces designed for young people in the 20th century are entertainment parks like Disneyland in Paris; Gardaland, near Verona in Italy; LEGOLAND in the United Kingdom; Billund in Denmark; Gunzburg in Germany; the London Aquarium; and the London Eye, which is the world's tallest cantilevered observation wheel. Entertainment parks were inspired by cartoon characters and are composed of a series of fantasy landscapes with rides. A sophisticated system of pedestrian-only circulation, based on subtly miniaturized buildings, grants children a greater feeling of control than they might experience in real urban environments.

Unoccupied Free Time

On the other hand, several studies have shown the decline of children's free, self-initiated play, which is the result of technological innovation, rapid social change, and economic globalization. Increasing numbers of children and youth now have significant periods of unoccupied free time available and are lured by the attraction of adults' recreations, including drinking, gambling, and boisterous lawbreaking. The misuse of free time by children came to be viewed as a widespread social problem, and the provision and regulation of wholesome play activities became an instrument of social reform.

A number of reformers sought to develop agencies and institutions to solve the emerging social problems created by this new era, in which children now had too much unsupervised play time. Public demands for increased structured play opportunities and supervision became more frequent and vociferous. Technological innovations have led to the all-pervasiveness of television and computer screens. An unintended consequence of this invasion is that childhood has moved indoors. Children who might once have enjoyed a baseball game in an empty lot now watch the game on television, sitting on their couches.

The Modern European Child

There is a general similarity in child behavior between some European countries. Overall, 20 percent of children between ages 5 and 12 own a mobile phone, 36 percent have games players, and 44 percent have a television set; the United Kingdom shows highest ownership of all three, but Spain has the highest level of computer ownership (39 percent) and the highest percentage of internet access (21 percent). Germany has the highest level (18 percent) of DVD player ownership. Those who monitor what is "hot" for 3- to 8-year-olds and for tweenagers (8 to 12 years old) report high uniformity between countries, since they watch the same television channels.

Tamagotchi and Neopets remain popular, and pink, girlie-style Barbie dolls are less popular now. The tweenage group is difficult to market to, as it falls between the child and teenage worlds, but their technology-filled bedrooms are important to them. Meanwhile, single and working parents now outnumber the once-predominant nuclear family, in which a stay-at-home mother could provide the kind of oversight that facilitates free play. Instead, busy working parents outsource at least some of their former responsibilities to coaches, tutors, trainers, martial arts teachers, and other professionals. As a result, middle-income children spend more of their free time in adult-led and organized activities than any earlier generation.

Low-income youth sometimes have the opposite problem, because their parents may not have the means to put them in high-quality programs that provide alternatives to playing in unsafe neighborhoods. Preschool tutoring in languages, music, and sports, which emphasizes daily drills, became increasingly popular among urban populations in developed European countries. In such a world, play has come to be seen as a waste of precious time. By pushing young children into team sports for which they are not developmentally ready, we rule out forms of play that once encouraged them to learn skills of independence and creativity. Instead of learning these skills on their own in backyards, children are only learning to do what adults tell them to do. Play areas in restaurants, airports, and shopping malls have spread from Scandinavia to the rest of the Europe.

In Europe, there are also several children's museums in Germany (Berlin, Wolfenbuttel, Nürnberg, Bielefeld, Frankfurt am Main, Sachsen Anhait, München, Hamburg), the United Kingdom (London, Stratford, Halifax), Ireland (Dublin), Austria (Vienna, Graz), Norway (Oslo), Switzerland (Bern, Baden), Netherlands (Amsterdam, Rotterdam), Portugal (Lisbon), Italy (Rome, Milano, Udine), France (Paris), Belgium (Brussels), Turkey (Istanbul), Kosovo (Priština), Bulgaria (Sofia), Greece (Athens, Thessaloniki), Slovakia (Bratislava), Slovenia (Celje), and Russia (Moscow).

Many European national museums have permanent children's exhibitions, and there are also several toy museums or private toy and model collections. The first European children's museums were opened between the world wars and it was only much later, in the 1960s or 1970s, that they became particularly interested in promoting museums as resources for children. It was only in the 1990s that children's museums became widely popular. Children's museums today engage children in educational and entertaining experiences through innovation and excellence in exhibitions, programs, and use of their collections. They are unique places of learning, creativity, and play where childhood is respected, nurtured, and celebrated; they are fun learning experiences for children, families, and school groups.

Today, most children's museums tend to exhibit authentic specimens and artifacts from the fields of games, play, and toys. Children's museums are institutions committed to serving the needs and interests of children by providing exhibits and programs that stimulate curiosity and motivate learning. Children's museums bring children and families together where play inspires lifelong learning, and they play an important role in the lives of children and families within their diverse communities.

A Changing Demographic

The main changes in play of European children in the second half of the 20th century were important, because unstructured play was often replaced in modern times by organized activities, academics, or passive leisure activities such as watching television and playing video games. Toys have changed as well, because in the past, toys helped to socialize children into social roles, vocations, and academic tool skills, but today they often encourage brand loyalties, fashion consciousness, and group thinking. Technological advances, which already have their place in classrooms all over Europe, spread to babies and preschoolers who are not yet able to comprehend two-dimensional representations.

Parent peer pressure causes parents to engage in hyperparenting, overprotection, and overprogramming.

Media-spread fears about everything from kidnapping and molestation to school shootings and diseases cause parents to forget that children can play safely without adult organization, as in the past. Sexual emancipation during the 20th century has gradually shifted from adult culture, to youth culture, to child culture. The sexual emancipation of youth followed the youth revolution of the 1960s, when premarital sex became the norm rather than the exception. In the final decade of 20th century, sexuality is breaking through to the realm of childhood, which cannot be explained solely by the fact that puberty now starts at the age of 12 years instead of 14.

As adult sexuality becomes increasingly more visible to the child, sexuality becomes an explicit theme from the age of 8 years, and the presence of pornography in the public domain has allowed it to enter the children's room also. Despite efforts by puritan parents, sexually provocative clothes, an in-depth knowledge of sexual matters, and games involving sexual roles are all communicated to young children by older children, by the media, and by an industry that has helped to make children's culture a poor copy of adult culture. This is a big concern because there is a connection between children assuming adult roles inappropriate for their age and a longer struggle after puberty to overcome infantile personality traits.

Globalization reduced some differences among European children, even between advanced industrial and less-developed countries. A new concept of adolescence emerged, and at least in urban areas, an interest in romance as part of the youth experience developed as well. Shared youth culture had a wide impact in many otherwise different societies after 1950, thanks to the spread of rock music and common sports and media idols.

Common interests in the Internet, with which children were more adept than most adults, aligned the interests of young people in Europe. Computer technology had arrived in the world of play, a world in which reality had been replaced by fantasy and surreality. Video and computerized games were the fastest growing part of the toy industry in the 1980s. The new toys and the way that children played horrified those who felt that the new war toys were a threat to childhood, using replicas of sophisticated modern weapons as the main subject for play. Movements for peace play were founded to campaign against war toys.

The last decade of the 20th century was characterized by concerns and achievements for the growing awareness of environmental issues, though there was still a growing interest in video and internet games. Unlike children in 1900, today's European children are in the position of being able to choose from an abundance of toys and games, both recreational and educational, old and new. This is the result of the progress in the toy industry, benefiting from new technologies, modern marketing strategies, and stringent health and safety regulations. The future of play is in the fact that it has immeasurable importance to children's health and happiness.

See Also: Adventure Playgrounds; Amusement Parks; Boys' Play; Europe, 1900 to 1940; Europe, 1940 to 1960; Germany; Girls' Play; Meccano; Play as Mock War, Sociology of; Playground as Politics; United Kingdom; Wargames.

Bibliography. Barbie Clarke, "Children's Trends in Europe," *Young Consumers: Insight and Ideas for Responsible Marketers* (v.6/2, 2005); David Elkind, "Can we Play?" *Greater Good* (Spring 2008); Glenn Kirchner, *Children's Games Around the World* (Benjamin Cummings, 2000); James Opie, Duncan Chilcott, and Julia Harris, eds., *A Collector's Guide to 20th-Century Toys* (Wellfleet Books, 1990); Halina Pasierbska, *Must-Have Toys: Favourites of the 20th Century* (Museum of Childhood Bethnal Green, 2004).

Mojca Ramšak
Center for Biographic Research

Experiential Learning Definitions and Models

The term *experiential learning* (EL) commonly refers to active, action-based learning. That is, the individual learns through reflection on individual experiences and activities. EL may occur as the natural result of an individual experience such as learning more about playing football by playing a game of pick-up football, especially with oversized opponents.

Another usage of the term refers to engaging in activities and experiences planned by an adult or more knowable other. These may occur inside or outside the classroom and are typically designed for the individual learner. For example, children might cut a pumpkin open, dissect the seeds, and examine the pulp rather than read about it, or the children might engage in pretend play as they shop in a grocery store. The focus is thus on individual learning through hands-on experiences. Many refer to this as learning by doing because the focus is on the construction of knowledge by the individual.

EL contrasts sharply with traditional instruction. Traditional or didactic instruction (DI) used by teachers emanates from the Socratic method and uses oral discourse to inform a group of learners. The teacher or instructor stands in front of the class, and the learner/children listen or respond. DI involves more discussion by the instructor and less participation by the students. Most American schools rely on the didactic lecture-style instruction as the major instructional strategy with large and small groups even though scholarship supports the effectiveness of EL over lecture.

The value of EL for learning was initially recognized by John Dewey during the early part of the 20th century. Dewey, father of American education and the progressive approach in education, was among the first scholars to discuss the traditional versus experience based approach to instruction. He believed that children learn by doing and encouraged students to engage in carpentry, gardening, sewing, and cooking. He referred to these activities as experience-based activities and believed that these served as the foundation for experience-based learning. In school settings, these are typically referred to as concrete experiences and can occur through play.

Another supporter of EL, Carl Rogers, a noted psychologist in humanism, was among the first to use the term experiential learning. For humanists, all instruction could be divided into two areas, traditional and meaningless or experiential and relevant. Because humanist theory dominated the educational world in the 1960s and 1970s, this view of the world was popular in education. The model views the individual's desire to learn as the most powerful force in education and considers lecture-based instruction as meaningless.

David Knob applied the theories of Dewey and Rogers and others to adult learning and developed Experiential Learning Theory (ELT). Knob defined EL as "the process whereby knowledge is created through the transformation of experience. Knowledge results from the combination of grasping and transforming experience." He and Roger Fry were the first to develop a learning cycle based on EL. Their basic model used four stages: (1) concrete experiences; (2) observations and reflections; (3) formation of abstract concepts and generalizations; and (4) testing implications of concrete in new situations. The first stage is what most view as EL and requires the learner to be actively involved in a real, meaningful activity such as play with balloons as a way to demonstrate a state of matter. The first stage provides an opportunity for using concrete materials. This can involve real materials and real experiences.

The second stage requires the learner to engage in not just observation but also reflection. For example, after playing, the learner talks about what occurred and considers what could have occurred. This ranges from simple comments about what the young child played during play time to the complex statements of a chess player after a tournament.

The third stage allows the learner to connect the concrete experience to previous knowledge and concepts. Thus, the generalizations develop as the learner considers the broader implications. Finally, the learner tests implications of the concrete learning in different situations.

Variations of Experiential Learning Theory

To date, over 17 variations of the ELT have been developed. One approach developed prior to the ELT encourages preschool children to think about their play. This model was developed at the High Scope Organization in the early 1960s and was based on the work of J. Piaget. Children were encouraged to "plan, do, and review" their play on a daily basis. Critics of this approach believed that it placed too many parameters on the traditional play found in kindergarten classrooms.

It is important to note that the ELT describes and elaborates the processes involves in EL when the adult is creating the context for learning. The other side of EL occurs when the individual learns from experience. For example, when a young child plays with a set of keys, they may want to use the keys in an outlet in the same way that their parents have used the keys in a door.

For this reason, adults place protective coverings over the outlets because they do not want the child to learn through experience. Thus, the child plays safely, and adults know that they must create a safe environment for young humans who want to construct their own knowledge of the world. When individual learning is encouraged, risks may also occur. These may range from car accidents when adolescents learn how to control their car to Chess games that end in stalemate. For these reasons, a tension exists when using EL between encouraging a completely self-directed approach for learning to using a model that creates the context for learning.

EL has developed from a simple term used to describe the use of concrete experiences to an organized approach to learning and thinking that includes a developing body of research. Although the role of play in ELT has never been fully elaborated, it is difficult to imagine EL or ELT without play.

See Also: Academic Learning and Play; Piaget and Play; Play as Learning, Psychology of.

Bibliography. D.A. Kolb, *Experiential Learning: Experience as the Source of Learning and Development* (Prentice Hall, 1984); A. Kolb and D.A. Kolb, "Experiential Learning," *Academy of Management Learning and Education* (v.4/2, 2005).

Dorothy Justus Sluss
James Madison University

F

Fantasy Play

Imagine yourself walking into a restaurant and being seated by the hostess. Suddenly, the little boy at the table next to you jumps up in his chair and starts to point and shout "No, no, you can't sit there! That's where Curly Thomas is sitting!" The boy is outraged; his mother is visibly embarrassed. No Curly Thomas is in sight. What is going on? There are two answers. First, you have inadvertently stepped into a child's fantasy play, by sitting at the table where the little boy's imaginary companion was resting his legs and eating an imaginary lunch. Second, in reading and comprehending this scenario, you have exhibited what some researchers consider a long-term effect of childhood fantasy play: the ability to envision, and to form a mental image of, alternative possible worlds.

When we read, as well as when we daydream, remember, and replay scenes (perhaps changing the details, imagining ourselves or others doing or saying *x* instead of *y*), or fantasize (imagining oneself out sailing instead of at work, for instance), our consciousness fills with images in a way not so different from the mind of a little boy imagining Curly Thomas sitting in your chair eating his sandwich. Although young children engage in fantasy play in markedly different ways than adults, fantasy play reverberates across the human life span.

Piaget

Fantasy play, also sometimes categorized as pretend play, sociodramatic play, make-believe, and symbolic play, is most often associated with early childhood. According to developmental researcher Greta Fein, it has the following characteristics: familiar activities, such as baking a cake, performed without the actual material and/or outside the corresponding context; the activities may not result in the logical outcome, for example, no real birthday cake results; inanimate objects can be treated as animate, for example, a doll is treated as a baby; objects and/or gestures are understood to stand for something other than themselves, for example, sand is treated as flour and sugar; and children impersonate others, for example, bakers, mothers, animals, and even machinery, such as airplanes and cars. Although it overlaps with other kinds of play, such as rule-based games and object play, fantasy play involves a distinct set of abilities and has been linked to particular outcomes involving language, literacy, improvisation, political life, empathy, and morality.

According to Jean Piaget, who called it symbolic play, fantasy begins at about 18 months and ends when the child is about 7 years old, at which point, having developed sufficient cognitive mastery of symbolic representation, the child turns his attention toward games with rules. When children play, in the Piagetian view, they are assimilating new information and striving to integrate it within their relatively narrow range of schemas for understanding the world. In fantasy play, children may assign meanings to persons, social settings, and snippets of overheard adult conversation as a means of making sense of them. Fantasy play thus reflects children's learning about symbolic representation, an important cognitive ability. Later research has questioned Piaget's ideas on this subject, especially his treatment of fantasy play as a primarily individualistic enterprise and his claim that fantasy play ends around age 7, but it has tended to accept his fundamental insight that fantasy play is not frivolous, nor is it separable from children's developing ability to make sense of empirical reality.

Vygotsky

Through fantasy play, children also make sense of social reality. Fantasy play is a field for acting out roles, social scenarios, and the interactions among people. Lev Vygotsky, the developmental psychologist who considered social interaction to be the motor of children's development, considered imaginative play to constitute a "zone of proximal development" in which children could act, speak, and think in ways more intellectually and socially advanced than they could in real-life scenarios. To Vygotsky, make-believe play has two crucial features that distinguish it from other activities: first, it enables children to distinguish objects from meanings (allowing a stick to become a play horse), and second, it is rule-based play. It is rule-based inasmuch as roles contain rules: to play at being a mother, a little girl must follow the rules of maternal behavior, for instance. These features of play strengthen children's mastery of meanings and of social expectations. When they are engaged in fantasy play, as other observers have confirmed, children show abilities that they may not yet have in other activities.

Development of Fantasy Play

How does fantasy play develop? Very young children (age 2) tend to act out roles, pretending to cook dinner or put out a fire, usually single-handedly. Their play is often repetitive—the doll is rocked and put to sleep over and over, a road for cars is built and rebuilt. At this age, adults often play an important function in stimulating play: children younger than 3 years tend to prefer playing with their mothers and other caregiving adults to playing with peers. When they play with adults, very young children elaborate more sophisticated dramas, using more detailed actions and language. Later, around age 3, children engage in thematic play together, playing house, airport, or grocery store for instance. Children aged 4 to 5 tend to work out even more elaborate and fantastical narratives, saving princesses from dragons or blowing up enemy spaceships, often with highly creative, improvisational elements added to their stories. Sociodramatic play at this level requires children to make use of their increasing social and linguistic competency, as well as their understanding of symbolic representation. As children reach school age, their engagement in fantasy play of this kind declines and is replaced by other kinds of play, which nonetheless involve fantasy.

How able are children to distinguish make-believe from reality? In her work on imaginary friends, Marjorie Taylor argues that although very young children show some confusion about what exactly is real and what is fantasy, they have a much firmer grasp of the matter than adults tend to think. She points out that adults go to great lengths to convince children that Santa Claus is real—dressing up as elves in shopping malls, putting out cookies for Santa, sending letters through the mail—and yet children succeed in figuring out the ruse before long. Children show a noteworthy ability to shift quickly back and forth from reality to fantasy, explaining to an adult that an imaginary friend lives in the tree house, reminding the adult that "Rosabelle is really imaginary, you know," and then immediately saying that Rosabelle called from the North Pole just last week. Taylor also points out that although adults claim to have a clear-eyed view of what is real and what is fantasy, we also cry and feel genuine sadness watching sad movies and reading sad books, suggesting that the boundaries are not as sharp as we might think.

Children have presumably engaged in fantasy play for a long time, but such play rarely leaves a record, and only recently have adults treated it as worth recording. Toys provide something of a material history. We cannot say for certain what ancient Mesopotamian children did with toy wagons such as those archaeologists have found, or what young Romans did with model soldiers, but it seems a reasonable guess that they played out scenarios they saw or heard about adults engaging in. As historian Gary Cross points out, toys have long been a way for adults to pass on values to their children: Because toys are props for playing out certain kinds of themes, children's fantasy play, and the learning that goes with it, is influenced (though not simply determined by) the toys available to them. This does not mean that children will not make their own dolls or guns or horses or spaceships, but it does mean that the toys we provide our children send them messages about which scripts adults value.

Sources of Fantasy Play

Fantasy play tends to follow (with considerable improvisation) scripts children are familiar with, but children also glean stories from other sources, including peers, toys, and the media. Many scripts come from children's own observations of adult life, and fantasy play has often been considered direct preparation for adult roles. Hence, children in Western societies play store, house, school, doctor, construction site, and other familiar scenarios. In a time when children are watching large amounts of electronic media (and if not, are likely to spend time with peers who do), other scripts come from television shows, movies, and video games (which are, in turn, the production of adults' fantasies about what life is, could be, or should be). Walking into the free play of preschoolers, an observer is likely to hear variations on the latest superhero saga or Disney romance played out alongside housekeeping and building site.

This phenomenon is not new: Before television, children played out stories based on radio programs, and children have been overhearing, and later reading, adult-created stories for thousands of years. Scholarship on the intersection of toys, patterns of consumption, and the media, however, has pointed out that since the mid-20th century, children's playthings have become tools for fantasy play that is farther and farther from the real world of adult roles. Commercial toys used to support the reenactment of adult roles in fairly precise ways: baby dolls could be treated like real babies and toy kitchens used to act out homemaking, thereby preparing girls for roles as mothers and homemakers. Popular toys from early and midcentury such as model railroads, building sets, and model soldiers prepared boys for a particular conception of men's work.

In recent decades, such toys have been eclipsed by more fantastical novelty toys, including fashion dolls marketed to girls and extraterrestrial adventurers marketed to boys. By no means do toys and electronic media define the limits of children's fantasy play, but toys and electronic media—which, given the prominence of advertising and marketing in American life, overlap significantly—have an important influence on play, and as media and toy themes have shifted, so has children's fantasy play to some extent.

Around age 3, children engage in thematic play together, and can quickly shift back and forth from reality to fantasy.

The Effect of Television

Besides marketing toys and changing how children spend their time, what effects does television have on children's imagination? Dorothy Singer and Jerome L. Singer have studied the subject for several decades. In their most recent work they conclude that whether television has a positive or negative impact on children's fantasy play depends on factors including the amount watched, the quality of the programs, and whether or not adult caregivers help the child make sense of what he or she has seen by coviewing shows and discussing them with the child. At its best, Singer and Singer conclude, television and other electronic media, including video games and internet interactions, can provide children with productive new themes for fantasy play and new forums in which to engage their imaginations.

Toddlers who watched *Barney and Friends* (which deliberately emphasizes the delights of pretending), for instance, were more imaginative than a control group. High-quality children's programming can also suggest new themes and scripts for children to play out. At worst, electronic media can reinforce aggression, lead to identity confusion, and subject young people, who have a less firm grasp of reality and its dangers than their elders, to adults who do not have their interests at heart. Although studies have not found violent video games to have a negative influence all children, Singer and Singer cite evidence that about 10 percent of frequent players become more aggressive and less able to engage in other kinds of activities. More studies are called for to determine the effects of electronic media on children's long-term intellectual, social, and psychological development.

Although fantasy play is indubitably a critical aspect of children's development, this is no reason to assume it ought always to be cheerful, lighthearted and "fantastical." Fantasy play can involve children struggling to come to terms with difficult and painful realities. Jewish children at Auschwitz played "going to the gas chamber," a poignant example of children's need to make meaning of their situations, however horrible. African-American slave children played out master/slave games, including pretend back-talk and beatings. Since young children in bondage played with the children of their masters, some of this fantasy play involved both future master and slave playing out variations on their future roles, which should give pause to anyone who thinks fantasy play is always delightful fun. Like other kinds of play it has its darker elements as well. To children, it is serious business, which makes it quite useful to clinicians. Play therapists have harnessed fantasy play both to gain access to patients' experiences and to help them envision and ultimately realize alternative possibilities.

Debate Over Fantasy Play

Developmental psychologists have linked fantasy play to the highest academic achievements, but educational theorists including Rousseau, Froebel, and Montessori dismissed its educational purposes, although they held other kinds of play in the highest respect. Imagination, said Rousseau, is dangerous because it makes a person grasp for more than he can have, and therefore makes him dissatisfied with the goods within his reach. Children should be allowed to play, he advocated, but imagination should be discouraged.

Montessori considered fantasy a waste of time, at least as educators and parents conventionally treated it: as the realm of fairy tales and fables. Children should learn about reality first, she argued, because only once they have a grasp of the real world can fantasy have any meaning to them. If some progressive educators have taken surprisingly critical stands on fantasy, so have traditionalists, with contemporary educational policies stressing measurable results, test-taking, and narrowly academic learning, leaving no space for fantasy play. Fantasy play is left on the margins of education.

The separation of fantasy play from education is seriously misguided, most research on fantasy play suggests. Contemporary scholars have linked the fantasy play of childhood to adult literacy, improvisation, empathy, political life, and morality. As Jerome Bruner suggests, the ability to imagine alternative possible realities is inherently part of philosophical, artistic, and scientific thinking. Even those children who will not grow up to write symphonies or reconceptualize astrophysics need fantasy play, as it is essential to the everyday work of reading, as well as constructive engagement with other people, and the ability to resolve internal psychological conflicts. In the 1960s, developmental psychologist Sara Smilansky studied the sociodramatic play of Israeli immigrant children whom she categorized as disadvantaged. She found that these economically disadvantaged children were less encouraged to engage in fantasy play than native Israelis, and they were less successful academically.

When teachers trained to promote fantasy play intervened in the play of an experimental group of disadvantaged children, those children showed increased fantasy play and increased social and academic skills. Smilansky's research has been somewhat controversial. Some scholars and childcare experts cite it as a fine example of how fantasy supports academic and social skills. Other scholars point out that not all cultures uniformly value sociodramatic play of the sort Smilansky's study encouraged (or fantasy play at all), and the assumption that such play is an essential aspect of growing up may be ethnocentric. After all, many children have grown up to play positive roles in their communities without researchers showing them how best to play.

Western, contemporary societies do generally assume fantasy play to be an appropriate activity for children, and adults have many opportunities to engage in various types of fantasy play as well. Video games, fantasy sports leagues, magazines, and internet sites that follow the lives of Hollywood stars, as well as literature and work-related speculation (ranging from a plumber considering what type of pipe to lay to a professor dreaming up new research agendas), are all examples of adult engagement in fantasy. We tend to associate fantasy with the fantastical and small children, but at least for most of us it is an aspect of thinking that does not end with childhood.

See Also: Academic Learning and Play; Cooperative Play; Dolls, Barbie, and Others; Human Relationships in Play; Memory and Play; Montessori; Mother-Child Play; Piaget and Play; Play as Entertainment, Sociology of; Psychology of Play (Lev Semyonovich Vygotsky); Role-Playing.

Bibliography. Jean Piaget, *Play, Dreams and Imitation in Childhood* (Norton, 1962); Dorothy Singer and Jerome L. Singer, *The House of Make-Believe: Children's Play and the Developing Imagination* (Harvard University Press, 1990); Lev Vygotsky, *Mind in Society* (Harvard University Press, 1978).

Amy Shuffelton
University of Wisconsin, Whitewater

Faro

Part of the popular mythology of the Old West includes the image of cowboys playing Poker around a table in a saloon. In the mid-19th century, these Old West denizens would more likely be crowded around a rectangular table and playing a far more common gambling game called Faro.

Faro's origin is rooted in the 15th-century French game *Basset,* with likely influences from the earlier Teutonic game of *landsquenet.* It achieved its fixed form by the end of the 17th century, by which time it acquired its French name *Pharaoh.* The spelling was Anglicized as Faro, and the Faro decks eventually lost the image of an Egyptian king imprinted on the back of the cards. Over time, the game became popular throughout Europe, and it was likely introduced to America by British and French soldiers and immigrants during the colonial era. By the 20th century, Faro was the most common gambling game in the United States.

Faro is now an extinct casino game, although it had survived periodic bans until the ostensibly total ban on gambling in America by 1920. Faro is unlikely to be revived as a serious, or even legitimate, table game in contemporary casinos. It disappeared for two major reasons. First, Faro quickly earned a well-deserved reputation as a "sucker's game" because a Faro deck and table can be easily manipulated by card sharks. A bigger element of the game has kept the game from being reintroduced. Namely, Faro can be played with little or no house edge.

It is a relatively simple game of pure luck. There are variations, but the central aspect of the game involves betting on a denomination and waiting for a dealer to flip two cards over from a standard deck. If the second card matches the value of the bet, then the punter wins at even odds. If the first card matches, then the player loses the bet. If both cards match the bet, then this "split" results in the player losing half the wager. Other elements may come into play, as players can cover multiple bets as in Craps or Roulette. But the game's simplicity provides a crooked dealer ample opportunities to make Faro a fast-paced way for novice gamblers to lose money.

Because the game was so easy to learn, it became popular across the nation, and it has had a huge influence on American culture. Famous figures of the Old West, including Doc Holliday and Wyatt Earp, ran lucrative Faro banks, and techniques used in Faro, such as parlaying a bet, have been adopted in other gambling games. Numerous terms associated with Faro have also entered American English. Faro slang has given us standard terms and expressions such as keeping tabs, breaking even, in hock, stool-pigeon, playing on a shoestring, and even gambling chips.

Faro's colorful history also includes references within literature and film. Tolstoy includes Faro in *War and Peace,* and the game is a central element of Pushkin's brilliant short story "The Queen of Spades," which Tchaikovsky adapted into an opera. The game has also made a contemporary resurgence in feature films, most notably in the movies *Tombstone* and *Wyatt Earp* that were released in the 1990s. The game also has a presence in cyberspace. A Web site titled "Wichita Faro" provides an opportunity to play in a simulated gambling hall—no betting allowed.

See Also: France; Gambling; History of Playing Cards; Poker and Variations of; United States, 1860 to 1876; United States, 1876 to 1900.

Bibliography. Herbert Asbury, *Sucker's Progress: An Informal History of Gambling in America from the Colonies to Canfield* (Dodd, Mead & Company, 1938); Roger Caillois, *Man, Play and Games* (University of Illinois Press, 2001); Nigel E. Turner, Mark Howard, and Warren Spence, "Faro: A 19th Century Gambling Craze," *Journal of Gambling Issues* (April 2006).

Gregory A. Hansen
Arkansas State University

Female Aggressive Relationships Within Play (Putallaz)

The most significant recent research done on female aggression has come from Martha Putallaz and Karen Bierman. The main theories are that girls are more socially aggressive and less physically aggressive than boys, that abused girls grow up to be abusive, and that girls have less opportunity to work out aggression as part of team-building because of the different ways in which boys and girls playing (and particularly playing sports) are viewed and socially accepted.

Prevailing theory suggests that girls prefer social aggression such as gossip, name-calling, and making threats, rather than the physical violence of hitting and fighting exhibited by boys. Girls learn at early ages how to wound with words, and how to withhold favors such as attendance at a party or friendship, or even to invoke the infamous silent treatment unless the victim conforms to the requested behavior of the threatmaker. Although the wisdom of the ages suggested that sticks and stones might break our bones while names would never hurt us, current social research advises otherwise. The damaging effects female aggression cause can be summed up in a sarcastic remark made by the *Seinfeld* sitcom character Elaine. Instead of giving wedgies in locker rooms as the boys do, she says, "We just tease each other until one of us develops an eating disorder."

Socialization patterns differ significantly with male and female children, of course, with girls tending to be raised as more finely attuned to the needs of others, and quite possibly to how they can help fulfill those needs. This probably lends itself both to less physical or overt aggression and, simultaneously, to a deeper understanding of how to be socially aggressive—in essence, where the buttons are that can be pushed to harm, insult, or threaten another person.

Socially competent girls (those who are "popular") tend to be victimized less than those considered underdogs, and the reinforcement of this behavior makes the socialization process stronger as time goes on. While race and social status can be factors in which girls will be considered popular in what social contexts, they may not be the strongest indicators. When young girls play house (or other make-believe games), behavior as early as age 3 suggests which girls will be victims, which will be aggressors, and which will refuse to become aggressors or succumb to social threats. This differentiation seems personality based and dependent on the socialization of parents and early educators, as well as the quantity and quality of interaction with peers.

However, girls who are socially popular also tend to be more aggressive with one of the major forms of social bullying in which girls participate: gossip. Popular girls tend to gossip more, and their gossip is more evaluative of their targets, judging the choices made in clothing, friends, partners, and other social criteria. In short, popular girls may be less targeted, but they do more targeting.

At the same time, girls who are victims tend not to engage in victimizing when it is purely social violence directed toward them. "Picked-on" girls rarely fight back verbally or socially. Yet girls who are the victims of sexual or emotional abuse are likely to become violent; sexual abuse is the greatest indicator of delinquency and of violence (social and physical) by women, toward either women or men, and by adults to children. By the same token, girls who are physically pushed or slapped by a male or female are more likely to retaliate physically than to fight with words.

Female Relationships in Sports

For boys, organized sports are a strong facet of socialization, teaching them to pull against one another in oppositional goals of winning and losing, followed by social interaction that turns winning and losing into fodder for verbal good-natured camaraderie. Girls may not have the same socialization processes available to them for at least two reasons. Girls who seek to participate in sports that are perceived as more aggressive—tackle football probably represents the pinnacle of this group—can be viewed as less feminine. In experiments where men were shown videos of women involved in aggressive sports (such as mud wrestling or tackling), men actually became more aggressive and less social themselves than when they watched men engaged in similar activities. They also made comments suggesting acceptance of certain levels of violence toward women who engaged in such behavior, or women in general.

Women may also have no organized sports leagues available in the sport they wish to play. Body checking is a natural part of men's ice hockey, but it is illegal in women's. Men play baseball; women play softball. Female sports tend to be of a softer variety than male, and the aggression expected between males in sports is not as readily accepted in female sports, be that by coaches, by parents, or by spectators. This results in girls not being taught to compete with the detachment men are encouraged to show in such contests and afterward, and may be reflected in later years by career choices and advancement in competitive fields at management and executive levels.

Studying Aggression

However, when aggression is defined as a disruption of the social order, women may be getting away with more than men. Rachel Simmons, author of *Odd Girl Out: The Hidden Culture of Aggression in Girls*, suggested that female aggression often flies below the radar, resulting in neither bloody brawls nor actual disruption of classroom activities, as female aggression is often speech-based or involves threats of withholding affection. Girls may be aggressive and manipulative, but they lack accountability and the ability to change their behavior if such verbal threats and innuendos are not acknowledged as the actual disruptions of social order they can become, because their form of aggression is not recognized as potentially disruptive or dangerous.

In experiments with peer group entry, tables of board games were set up for children ages 7 to 9; once the groups were established, other children were observed trying to join in. Girl hosts were more likely to fuss over and welcome their guests than boys, while girls seeking to enter a peer group were likely to be less obtrusive and assertive than boys—a strong indicator of entry success. Most successful peer group entry strategies were female-oriented, using group statements or mimicking the behavior of the group, resulting in smoother and faster entry than aggressive demands to be allowed to join. Girls seeking to enter an all-female group were the most successful of any combination of genders.

A 2005 article on child development suggested that boys may be more aggressive physically because of environmental factors, while girls tend toward caretaking roles because of genetics. This theory has met with criticism and acclaim, as has the suggestion of Simmons that social aggression in girls is as present and as potentially destructive as physical violence among boys, and Putallaz and Bierman's assertions that females lead aggressive lives on several levels.

It is generally considered more acceptable for a girl to play in masculine ways than a boy to play in feminine ones; a girl called a tomboy is not insulted in the same way as a boy called a sissy. Thus it seems likely that girls will be accepted in aggressive sports before boys will be accepted in social situations that involve gossip and social hierarchies.

See Also: Athletics (Amateur); Boys' Play; Girls' Play; Play as Competition, Psychology of; Play in the Classroom.

Bibliography. Teresita Borja-Alvarez, Lynne Zarbatany, and Susan Pepper, "Contributions of Male and Female Guests and Hosts to Peer Group Entry," *Child Development* (v.62/5, 1991); Lyn Brown, *Girlfighting: Betrayal and Rejection Among Girls* (NYU Press, 2005); Martha Putallaz and Karen L. Bierman, eds., *Aggression, Antisocial Behavior, and Violence Among Girls* (The Guilford Press, 2004); Rachel Simmons, *Odd Girl Out: The Hidden Culture of Aggression in Girls* (Harvest Books, 2003).

Wendy Welch
University of Virginia, Wise

Finger Games

If play has always been a child's first teacher, then parents become a child's first toys. German educator Friedrich Froebel (1782–1827) asserted, "What a child imitates, he begins to understand." For a newborn's strong grasp reflex action, finger games provide the first play that can quiet a child. Finger games are derived from natural play between mother and infant and strengthen and develop flexibility. The actions are not as important as the interaction between parent and child. Newborns feel different sensations, but respond most affirmatively to soft stroking, cuddling, and caressing. Newborns are comforted when they suck their thumb or a pacifier, or when they hear the pitch of a parent's voice. Eye contact builds bonds between parent and child. Repeated sounds and motions form foundations for formulating memory. At the most elemental level, finger play is an individual's first lesson in living. By simply talking about ordinary actions, a parent can engage an infant in his environment.

Finger games do not educate through formula but, rather, through pleasant sensations. These games begin with the parent's touch and involve repetitive basic hand rhythm sequences. An infant associates meaning with the motion when variations of a finger game are repeated over time. One of the earliest developmental games can help a baby become accustomed to being turned over from back to stomach. A mother positions her baby on its back and sings as she goes through various motions: "Rub a baby belly—pat, pat, pat. Rub a baby belly—just like that!" Then rolling the baby over gently onto its belly, she chants: "Rrrooooll over baby!" Then she continues, "Rub a baby back—pat, pat, pat." Once the infant learns what is coming next, it soon anticipates the step, "Rrrooooll over baby!"

In fetal development the auditory system forms extremely early, and the ear is actually the first sensory organ to develop brain connections. When a baby is born, he or she soon recognizes familiar tunes and can distinguish between a parental voice and that of a stranger. Most infants (birth to 6 months) respond to music with body movements and wiggles. Newborns generally respond more quickly to a female voice than to a male voice, which may explain why people instinctively soften and raise the pitch of their voice when talking to infants. As an infant's hand-eye coordination develops (6 months to 1 year), he or she becomes more mobile and can grasp and manipulate objects. This means that when a baby shakes a rattle, he or she understands that the shaking causes a noise to occur.

Babies begin to clap their hands in response to music, so adults naturally encourage and demonstrate similar responses. Even toddlers (12 to 36 months) and young children smile when they see repetitions of finger games that they played in early developmental stages. Younger children tenaciously demand repetition of favorite activities. "Tell it again, and tell it just the same," and will correct the storyteller if there is even a slight deviation in the performance.

Some infant amusement has been traced back to medieval times. For example, in "Handy dandy, riddledy, ro, which hand will you have? High or low?" an adult invites a young child to guess in which hand the object is concealed in a fist behind his back. Most finger games played by children are derived, maintained, and continue to evolve through oral traditions. String figures (using one's fingers, and sometimes involving multiple people) to manipulate string to form designs evolved from indigenous cultures on many continents. Cat's Cradle is one of the best-known string finger games that utilizes a piece of cord or string. For older children, peers became the best source for learning finger games. Nineteenth-century American writer Lydia Maria Child advised young readers to "find some friend kind enough to teach her" string finger games. Likewise, Child included a section on shadow pictures, an ancient kind of finger game where players form pictures on a surface by forming various hand positions between a light source and the surface to form animal images.

See Also: Clapping Games; Froebel, Frederick; Mother-Child Play; Play and Learning Theory; Singing Games.

Bibliography. Mark Brown, *Hand Rhymes* (Dutton Children's Books, 1985); Lydia Maria Child, *The Girl's Own Book* (Edward Kearney, 1843); Friedrich Froebel, *Mother-Play and Nursery Songs: Poetry, Music, and Pictures for the Noble Culture of Child Life, with Notes to Mothers* (Lathrop, Lee & Shephard, 1906); Elece Hollis, "Playing Finger Games With Baby," kidsactivities.suite101.com (cited July 2008).

Meredith Eliassen
San Francisco State University

Finland

Located in Scandinavia in northern Europe, the climate of Finland—with its long, cold, and damp winters—has resulted in many pastimes involving snow or ice. Children from an early age take up skiing, skating, snowboarding, and riding in toboggans. Although people enjoy these on an amateur level, Finland has also produced large numbers of Olympic champions in winter sports. Cross-country and downhill skiing attract many—up to 10,000 people participate in the Finlandia Skiing Marathon. Sword-fighting and fencing have long been popular, and the Royal Academy of Turku has had an instructor in swordsmanship from at least 1640. One local game, *Mölkky,* has become the origin of the Cornish game Scattles, a version of Skittles in which all the pins are numbered.

In the summer, many young people enjoy hiking or cycling and, because of the Viking heritage shared by many, rowing. In some places the Viking sport of walking along extended oars of a boat is enjoyed. Whitewater rafting has become a popular pastime for young people in search of adventure and danger. There are also a wide range of activities including archery and *pesäpallo,* a type of Finnish baseball that is played by many adolescents in the summer. Because of the climate, many pastimes have to be pursued indoors. As well as indoor skating rinks and skiing, there are also many bowling alleys, amusement arcades, and indoor heated swimming pools and saunas.

Because of the Russian and German influences in the country, Chess has a large following, with outdoor Chess sets featured in Hesperian Park, Helsinki. Prominent Finnish Chess players include Eero Böök (1910–90), Carl Friedrich Andreyevich von Jaenisch (1813–72), Osma Kaila (1916–91), Kaarle Ojanen (b.1918), Anatol Tschepurnoff (1871–1942), and Heikki Markku Julius Westerinen (b. 1944). Wargaming has long been popular, with Finland having been part of the Swedish Empire, and then the Russian Empire until 1918 when it gained its independence. As a result, much of the Wargaming tended to focus on the various wars involving Russia, Finland, and Sweden, as well as more contemporary wars such as the Russo-Finnish War of 1939–40. Board games such as Monopoly proved popular in Finland—a Finnish version was released with the famous streets of Helsinki featured. Tove Jansson, probably the most famous Finnish writer, developed the lovable Moomintroll family, and many young children have toys based on characters from the books.

Many people also play card games, and large numbers of children learn musical instruments at school, although many do not continue with music in adulthood. A great pastime in the country is painting eggs, which is usually done before Easter. Because of the belief that witches might visit people over the Easter weekend, many people lit bonfires to frighten then, although now many schoolgirls use it as an opportunity to dress up as witches. In midsummer, there is a large festival when a giant pole is erected in towns that generally have a Swedish-speaking population, and people dance around them celebrating the good weather. The Linnanmäki Amusement Park in Helsinki was very popular during the 1950s and 1960s, and the Fédération Internationale des Quilleurs, the governing body for bowling, is based in Helsinki. However, increased access to computer games has dramatically changed the nature of play in Finland in recent years.

See Also: Chess and Variations of; Estonia; Skating; Skiing; Wargames.

Bibliography. Nick Dorrell, "The Battle of Palkane," *Miniature Wargames* (July 2006); Scott Elaurant, "Suomi!" *Miniature Wargames* (December 2001); Martin Hintz, *Finland* (Childrens Press, 1983); Tan Chung Lee, *Finland* (Marshall Cavendish, 1996); Mirja Liikanen and Hannu Pääkkönen, eds., *Culture of the Everyday: Leisure and Cultural Participation in 1981 and 1991* (Statistics Finland, 1994); Päivi Molarius, ed., *From Folklore to Applied Arts: Aspects of Finnish Culture* (University of Helsinki, 1993).

Justin Corfield
Geelong Grammar School

Fish

Go Fish (American) or Go and Fish (Great Britain and some of its former colonies) is a children's card game played with a traditional 52-card deck, or sometimes using special decks designed for the game (with animals or branded characters in place of the traditional cards). It can be played by two to 10 players, with seven cards dealt to each if there are only two, and five cards otherwise.

Each player in turn asks another player for a particular card (which the turn-holder must have in his hand), his turn ending when a player tells him to "go fish" because he does not have the card. Any time a pair of cards is formed, it is placed on the table; the game ends when all the pairs have been made, and the player with the most pairs wins. A simple game, easy to teach to children who need only to count to 10, it invites many variations: some groups may give each player only one turn regardless of whether he is told to go fish, in order to balance the game between players of different skill levels (which usually means children of different ages).

Some groups, especially in two- or three-player games, may fish until they have four of a kind instead of a pair. Some groups, in games with more than two players, may have the turn-holder announce their need—"Does anyone have any jacks?" instead of "Sheila, do you have any jacks?" This leads to a faster game, especially in large groups; indeed, if the game is filled to capacity with 10 players, the game would become too fast, with performance depending too much on the luck of the draw.

The strategic element is largely memory—a player paying attention will remember that Sheila had no jacks two turns ago and is less likely to have them now than she is to have some other card.

Fish can also refer to the six-player game sometimes called Literature, Russian Fish, or Canadian Fish. Literature uses a standard deck of cards with the twos removed (making 48). The players play in two three-player teams, each of which earns a point with each won set. There are eight sets: the "low" and "high" range of each of the four suits. Though players on a team cannot communicate among each other, a set is won when a player correctly declares that a set is in his team's possession, identifying which player has which cards in that set. This information can be guessed at, but is also revealed in play when players exchange cards as in Go Fish (but asking for specific cards—"the nine of spades"—rather than "any nines"). For this reason, it is against the rules to ask for a card you possess, which would be strategically useful in order to confuse the opposing team.

A well-used set of Little People, the popular peg-style figures released by Fisher-Price in the 1960s.

See Also: Casino; Donkey; History of Playing Cards.

Bibliography. Elliott Avedon, *The Study of Games* (Krieger Pub., 1979); Roger Caillois, *Man, Play, and Games* (University of Illinois Press, 2001); Johan Huizinga, *Homo Ludens* (Beacon Press, 1971); David Parlett, *The Oxford Guide to Card Games* (Oxford University Press, 1990); Brian Sutton-Smith, *The Ambiguity of Play* (Harvard University Press, 2001)

Bill Kte'pi
Independent Scholar

Fisher-Price

Founded in East Aurora, New York, in 1930, the Fisher-Price toy company has helped to shape the play of several generations of American children, as well as of children around the globe. The company's toys were intended to be bright, colorful, and durable; able to be passed down from sibling to sibling; and to possess an "intrinsic play value," according to the creed set out by company founders Herman G. Fisher, Irving Price, and Helen Schelle. Frequently backed by child development research and styled as educational toys, notable Fisher-Price products include push- and pull-toys, "little people" playsets, as well as a range of licensed-character toys. The company was purchased by Quaker Oats in 1968. In 1993 Fisher-Price came under the control of Mattel, which now markets all its preschool products under the Fisher-Price name. The company's growth into a multinational operation and one of the world's largest toy manufacturers shows the influence that the corporations and consumer markets have had on children's play and on the socialization function that toys play in contemporary society.

Initially, all Fisher-Price toys were made of wood, with the most famous toy being the wobbling Snoopy Sniffer pull-toy, of which five million were sold worldwide between 1938 and 1964. The post–World War II baby boom was a golden age for toy manufacturers. Fisher-Price produced a number of notable toys such as the Chatter Telephone and became an early pioneer in using plastic in toys. Little People playsets, which might feature a farm or castle, each with appropriate peg-style figures, were among the popular Fisher-Price toys of the 1970s. In 1983 Fisher-Price introduced Construx, a plastic beam connector-type toy, the company's first construction toy. Other notable toys of the 1980s were the Bubble Mower and the Puffalump doll. The Little People playsets were redesigned several times, most recently in 1997, when arms, hands, and clothing details were added. In recent years, nontoy products (such as strollers, high chairs, and play yards) have also been marketed under the Fisher-Price name. Infant toys such as rattles and mobiles are also popular company products.

The Fisher-Price company was an early leader in the use of licensed characters, beginning with the Mickey Mouse Band in 1935. Fisher-Price has also licensed Sesame Street preschool toys since the 1970s. At present, approximately two-thirds of Fisher-Price products use licensed characters (for example, Barney and Winnie the Pooh).

Development psychology researchers are also regularly involved in Fisher-Price product research. Each year, several thousand children take part in company focus groups or one-on-one sessions. Like the toy industry at large, Fisher-Price toys are not simply marketed as "age appropriate" but are increasingly styled as "interventions" and "tools" that advance children's and infants' cognitive and physical development. The first Fisher-Price electronic toys (a motion-sensitive talking doll and the Alpha Probe spaceship) were introduced in 1980.

In recent years, particularly given the success of Leapfrog toys and the "baby genius phenomenon," the company has begun to incorporate more electronics in its toys. For example, Little People playsets now feature sounds, lights, and electronic moving parts. From the company's founding, Fisher-Price toys were intended to be attractive and stimulating and possess both educational and play value. Though psychologists are partly responsible for the increasingly accepted view that learning and play are not at odds but rather two overlapping categories, the history of Fisher-Price shows that toy industry products and parent-directed marketing have also helped to create popular contemporary notions about the importance of educational play.

Fisher-Price has been an industry leader in the emergence of a "baby" toy market—products specifically geared for children aged 0 to 3 years. Though the company has long produced toys for this age range, the increased targeting of this "market demographic" has had a significant impact on children's play, particularly on how play figures into the relationships between children and adults. Some scholars have argued that many developmental and educational infant toys actually serve to give parents time away from their children and, by the power of marketing and the internationalization of the toy industry, promulgate globally what are in fact very culturally and socioeconomically specific child-raising patterns.

Despite the promises that mass-manufactured toys are beneficial for children, at times these toys have also ended up being quite dangerous to children. Like many other toy manufacturers, Fisher-Price has been involved in toy recalls because of safety concerns. In 1998 the company recalled 10 million Power Wheels vehicles, battery-powered ride-on trucks and cars that were reported to be involved in over 100 fires. For previously failing to report known safety defects, Fisher-Price was fined $1.1 million by the U.S. Consumer Products Safety Commission, the largest fine ever issued against a toy company. In 2007 Fisher-Price recalled around a million toys, including Sesame Street and Dora the Explorer toys, because they contained lead-based paint.

See Also: Play as Learning, Psychology of; Toys and Child Development.

Bibliography. Eric Clark, *The Real Toy Story: Inside the Ruthless Battle for America's Youngest Consumers* (Free Press, 2007); Bruce Fox and John Murry, *Fisher-Price: Historical, Rarity and Value Guide, 1931–Present* (Krause Publications, 2002); Patrick Hughes, "Baby, It's You: International Capital Discovers the Under Threes," *Contemporary Issues in Early Childhood* (v.6/1, March 2005); Stephen Kline, *Out of the Garden: Toys, TV, and Children's Culture in the Age of Marketing* (Verso, 1993); Susan Gregory Thomas, *Buy, Buy, Baby: How Consumer Culture Manipulates Parents and Harms Young Minds* (Houghton Mifflin, 2007).

Noah W. Sobe
Loyola University

Fishing

The subject of fishing, or the (attempted) capture of fish or other aquatic animals for commercial, subsistence, or recreational purposes, encompasses many disciplines. It has a rich and complex history and holds much significance for many reasons in a plethora of historical and contemporary cultures and civilizations. The earliest recordings of fishing for pleasure, recreation, and sport in Western society date back to the latter part of the 13th century.

The act of fishing is thought to have been practiced across the globe for over 40,000 years. It has a significant and complex sociocultural history, features prominently in the world's leading religions, and carries with it great symbolism and folklore. Many cultures and civilizations have traditionally placed high value on the practice of fishing as a means of survival and for its skill and artistry. Evidence of this can be found in the prominence given to depictions of piscatorial pursuits in prized archaeological artifacts, such as Peruvian Moche ceramics, Bolivian cave paintings, and Roman mosaics. However, fishing has not universally occupied a position of such high regard. Because of its perceived low social

Fishing for pleasure, recreation, sport, and as a food source is thought to have been practiced across the globe for over 40,000 years and was at one time viewed as a noble and gentlemanly activity.

status, fishing scenes were rarely represented in ancient Greek culture. And the modern pursuit of fishing for pleasure as opposed to survival or profit, which was at one time viewed as a noble and gentlemanly activity, is becoming increasingly considered, in Western society at least, to be a cruel and barbaric "blood sport."

The point at which fishing developed from an act of survival and economic necessity to a pursuit of pleasure and recreation is not definitively known, although some ancient Egyptian illustrations seem to depict fishing being practiced as a recreational pastime. The earliest English essay on recreational fishing was published in 1496, written by Dame Juliana Berners, prioress of the Benedictine Sopwell Nunnery. The essay was titled "Treatyse of Fysshynge wyth an Angle" and was published in the second *Boke of St. Albans,* a treatise on hawking, hunting, and heraldry.

Recreational fishing gained popularity in England and Western Europe during the 16th and 17th centuries. This was attributed mainly to the publication of Izzak Walton's *The Compleat Angler: or, The Contemplative Man's Recreation* in 1653. The book champions the position of the angler who loves fishing for the sake of fishing and was much read and often reprinted during the 16th century. More than 300 editions of *The Compleat Angler* have been published, which makes it one of the most frequently reprinted books in English literature.

Recreational fishing includes a variety of methods and equipment (or tackle, as it is commonly known), designed for specific prey and the environments that they inhabit. The most common form of recreational fishing is done with a rod, reel, line, hooks, and a range of baits or lures designed to entice and ultimately hook the fish through the mouth. Other devices are also used to compliment the presentation of the bait to the targeted fish. Some examples of such tackle include weights, floats, and swivels. This type of recreational fishing, with rod, line, and hook, is generically defined as angling. Laws and regulations managing angling vary greatly, often regionally, within countries. These commonly include the requirement to hold a permit or license, periods during which the capture of certain species is outlawed, and restrictions on types of tackle and on the numbers and sizes of fish that can be killed. The two most traditional methods of angling to develop in the United Kingdom and Western Europe are fly fishing and coarse fishing.

Fly fishing is a method most traditionally associated with the pursuit of trout, salmon, sea-trout, and grayling. It is also becoming more widely used as a method for catching a greater variety of species including pike, bass, and carp, as well as saltwater species, such as redfish, bass, tarpon, snook, and bonefish. Fish are caught by using artificial flies and lures. These are created by tying a variety of natural and synthetic materials onto a hook in order to imitate the prey attractive to the target fish species or to provoke them to attack.

Until the early part of the 19th century, recreational fishing was the preserve of the gentry who pursued salmon and trout, which were known as game fish. Other species of freshwater fish were dismissed as "coarse." Coarse fishing uses a variety of baits, which are presented to the fish by being either suspended in the water beneath a float or held on the river or lake bed by a large weight. Although the lower echelons of society did pursue the capture of fish long before the 19th century, this was usually for purposes other than recreation.

See Also: Anti-Competition Play; Europe, 1200 to 1600; Europe, 1600 to 1800; Unstructured Play.

Bibliography. J. Armitage, *Man at Play: Nine Centuries of Pleasure Making (*Frederik Warne & Co., 1977); O. Gabriel, K. Lange, E. Dahm, and T. Wendt, eds., *Fish Catching Methods of the World* (WileyBlackwell, 2005); S. Partner, *Coarse Fishers Basics: A Beginner's Guide* (Hamlyn, 2006); C. Waterman, *A History of Angling*, (New Win Publishing, 1981).

Mike Wragg
Leeds Metropolitan University

Flight Simulation

In the late 1920s, Ed Link worked for his father at the Link Piano and Organ Factory in Binghamton, New York, and became interested in the systems of bellows and pumps inside organs. On an airfield in Ohio in 1927, pursuing his passion for aviation, Ed had one of those moments of lateral thinking, when he realized that a similar pneumatic system might be constructed to move a wooden cockpit in a way that emulated aircraft movements in flight. In the basement of his father's factory, he connected an electric pump to some organ bellows, constructed a basic cockpit on top of the apparatus, and built his first "pilot trainer," patented in 1929.

Born in France of Morrocan parents and brought up by his mother on her cleaner's wages (after she left his abusive father), 33-year-old Zacarias Moussaoui was in the United States by 2001, paying for lessons on a Boeing passenger jet flight simulator at the Pan-Am International Flight Academy in Minnesota. He also had a flight simulator computer program on his laptop. When subsequently jailed for life as a September 11, 2001 (9/11) terrorist attack conspirator, Moussaoui's case inscribed in the popular imagination a link between computer simulations and terrorist attacks or other conspicuously public acts of staged violence. Though in fact a failed trainee pilot, and at most only peripherally involved in the 9/11 attacks, Moussaoui was symbolic of a perceived risk that led anti–computer game activist and attorney Jack Thompson to accuse Microsoft, maker of the world's most successful home computer flight simulation software, of aiding terrorists. (Thompson would later try to link the 2002 Washington, D.C., Beltway sniper to the computer game Halo and the 2007 Virginia Tech massacre to the computer game Counter-Strike.)

The cultural journey from Ed Link to Zacarias Moussaoui covers a remarkable transformation in attitudes about technologies of simulation, from aspiration to anxiety, in which simulation as play has become inextricably entangled. What is at stake here is the so-called "modality judgements" that people can make between reality and representation. In an important study in the 1980s of children's modality judgements in relation to television programming, Robert Hodge and David Tripp found a reassuringly acute capacity, even among young children, to make fine distinctions between the real and the represented. But the technologies of simulation have undoubtedly been affecting that capacity, based as they are on the ambition to blur the distinction between reality and representation as much as possible.

Flight simulation is the leading edge of these technologies, thanks to the long history of precomputer development that Ed Link inaugurated. But it was not until the advent of the personal computer that flight simulation definitively entered the realm of play. Combat flight simulation software remains a highly popular genre of computer game, with massively multiplayer options latterly available, thanks to the internet's capacity for interconnecting remote players within a shared simulated environment. So close is the convergence now between home computer simulation and professional pilot training systems that "Simpits" have become increasingly popular—the do-it-yourself construction of physical flight simulator cockpits around computerized displays driven by home PCs running commercially available software.

In a home-built Simpit, the line between simulation and playing breaks down completely. High-profile industrial designer François de Watteville, of New York design studio Chin de Watteville, has perhaps captured the zeitgeist with his "Rocket" Simpit design. A full-scale, stylized, polished aluminium, streamlined, single-seat aircraft body on a sculptural floatplane-like stand is lovingly and luxuriously crafted to look at home in a sophisticated domestic interior. The Rocket evokes H.G. Wells' *The Time Machine*, a Victorian backroom dream of technological release from mundane reality, while deploying the latest home computer technology and audiovisual systems to simulate the experience of flying a 1940s aircraft, based on the groundbreaking *IL-2* program by Russian software developer Oleg Maddox.

François de Watteville's vision is strikingly at odds with the moral panics fueled by Jack Thompson, evoking not a frenzied world of reality-blurring simulated violence but a realm of adult play where a newly attuned modality judgement places the Simpit experience somewhere else entirely—perhaps somewhere that Ed Link would have recognized—in a realm where technology supports a reverie, a creative daydream of imaginary flight precisely because of its increasingly uncanny reality-simulating powers.

Whether the increasing technological sophistication and "realism" of today's home audiovisual displays, matched by unparalleled computing power, will take us toward mass-market versions of de Watteville's Simpit vision, or whether the latter remains a one-time folly, as is more likely, it still evocatively reminds us of why flight simulations hold a particular fascination—reconnecting us as they do to the marvel of technologically mediated release from physical constraints that the Wright brothers achieved and that inspired Ed Link's own interest in the still-early days of aviation.

Maddox, top honors graduate of the Moscow Aviation Institute for aerospace engineers but victim of the collapse of the Soviet military machine that left him facing an uncertain professional future, is perhaps an early-21st-century equivalent of Ed Link, turning his talents not to real-world applications but to perfecting flight simulation software for play. His studio, 1C: Maddox Games, is responsible for the flight simulation games most revered by players for their aerodynamic realism and playability, from the original IL-2 to subsequent titles such as Pacific Fighters and Battle of Britain. Unlike the Microsoft Flight Simulator series and its early competitor Fly! (from Terminal Reality Inc., founded by an ex-Microsoft employee), which remained purely flying simulations, the Maddox titles (now themselves extensively emulated by other game companies) combine increasingly detailed flight simulations with historically well-researched aerial combat scenarios. As with Microsoft's industry-leading simulator, itself still the best-selling PC game of all time, various add-in modules allow Maddox games to be extended with new terrain and new aircraft, creating increasingly complex, internet-enhanced virtual worlds inhabited by armies of dedicated airborne "simmers'"

What the Moussaoui story makes virtually inevitable is an ongoing discursive slippage between those players and fears of another dedicated army—of somehow too easy movement from one role to the other, so that the spectre of another airliner piloted into a city by a flight simulation–trained terrorist remains one of the most evocative public fantasies, or large-scale failures in collective modality judgement, of our time.

See Also: Counter-Strike; Play and Power, Psychology of; Play as Mock War, Psychology of; Play as Mock War, Sociology of; Role Playing.

Bibliography. Robert Hodge and David Tripp, *Children and Television: A Semiotic Approach* (Polity Press, 1986); Alfred T. Lee, *Flight Simulation: Virtual Environments In Aviation* (Ashgate Publishing, 2005); Susan Van Hoek and Marion Clayton Link, *From Sky to Sea: A Story of Edwin A. Link* (Best Pub. Co., 2003).

Dan Fleming
University of Waikato

Folk Dancing

The Europe-wide folk revival at the turn of the 19th and 20th centuries saw folk dance as representative of a nation's heritage. Folk dance was linked to the national character, but more than this, it was valued as antiindustrial, its rural roots setting it against the decay of modernity. Cecil Sharp (1859–1924) and Mary Neal (1860–1944) were key in promoting the teaching of folk dance to children, something that began when Neal asked Sharp for dances to teach the girls in her Espérance Girls' Club (c.1905)—he pointed her toward William Kimber, a musician for the Headington Quarry Morris Dancers,

Dancing around a maypole on May Day become a key component of showing patriotism in England.

who travelled from Oxfordshire to London to teach her charges Morris dancing. After World War I, the work continued under the oversight of Sharp's English Folk Dance Society (founded 1911). Sharp lobbied the Board of Education to promote folk dance in schools, and in 1911 he established a summer school in Stratford-upon-Avon for school teachers. The English Folk Dance Society established an American branch in March 1915—now the Country Dance and Song Society of America.

The folk dance revival began under aristocratic patronage in the mid-19th century. For example, May Day festivities can be dated to the early revival of the 1840s, strengthening in the 1880s when it became a festival for children promoted by Sunday schools and other charitable bodies. By the Edwardian period, May Day had become a key component of patriotic Englishness, with healthy, happy children dancing around a maypole symbolizing the health of the nation as a whole. The link with a patriotic national identity became characteristic of the late-19th-to-early-20th-century folk revival. Sharp, for instance believed that folk songs and dances were original products of the English "race." Through them, children would come to love their fellow countrymen. This would make the child "a better citizen, a true patriot." It was therefore important to introduce genuine folk dance into schools. By 1913, most of those who had been taught and certified by the English Folk Dance Society, through the (voluntary) Stratford-upon-Avon program, were teachers. Official state recognition followed at the end of World War I.

During World War I, Cecil Sharp lectured, taught, and collected over 1500 folk songs and dances in the United States. It was at this point that the English Folk Dance Society established its American branch, now the oldest organization of its type in America. Subsequently, during the 20th century, folk and country dancing became an established pastime among adults in America, and all schoolchildren were taught English Country Dance and folk dance alongside traditional dances from other nations. English Country Dancing and Danish folk dances were especially prominent, alongside what were seen as the traditional American folk dances, the Contra and Square Dance. As in Europe, this was about heritage, citizenship, rural versus urban, and the natural versus the artificial. The Folk-Dance Committee of the Playground Association of America was said to have taught 250 folk dance teachers in girls' public schools by 1909; they went on to teach over 24,000 public school girls. Boys were also taught these dances, both as part of the school day and after school, often in association with specific festivals such as Thanksgiving.

See Also: Maypole Dancing; Morris Dancing; Playground Movement, U.S.

Bibliography. English Folk Dance and Song Society, www.efdss.org (cited July 2008); Roy Judge, "May Day and Merrie England," *Folklore* (v.102/2, 1991); Cecil J. Sharp, *English Folk Song: Some Conclusions* (Oxford University Press, 1907); Cecil J. Sharp, *The Country Dance Book,* Part V (Novello & Co., 1918); Daniel J. Walkowitz, "The Cultural Turn and a New Social History: Folk Dance and the Renovation of Class in Social History," *Journal of Social History* (v.39/3, 2006).

Karen Anne Sayer
Leeds Trinity and All Saints University

Football (Amateur)

The term *football* can refer to completely different sports depending on the geographic, cultural, and historical location in which it is being played. Football, for most, refers to a game that involves kicking a ball through the net of an opposing team. This sport is commonly referred to as soccer in North America. In Australia, the term *football* denotes a game that involves pushing a ball up an oval-shaped field through kicking, handballing, and running with the end objective to kick the ball through the goal posts of the opposing team. In Ireland, a form of football termed *Gaelic football* is played that involves a combination of carrying, kicking, and hand-passing a ball with the objective of kicking the ball through the uprights of the opposing team to score one point, or through the goal posts of the opposing team for three points. In various parts of the world, football can also refer to what North Americans generally refer to as rugby, which has numerous rule variations depending on where it is played, but generally involves moving a ball up a rectangular field through passing, running, and kicking, with the end objective of crossing the opponent's goal line.

In North America, the term *football* refers to a sport that is altogether different from the other meanings of football just discussed. The North American game of football is often referred to as American football or gridiron football. The term *gridiron* comes from the particular way that playing lines are positioned on the field. Gridiron can either refer to the field that the sport is played on or, in some countries outside of North America, it can refer to the sport itself. Gridiron football, and its various alternate forms, will be the central focus of this entry. While various forms of gridiron football do exist, the common features of each are generally that protective equipment is worn, the ball is passed forward by hand or by running from an ever-changing line of scrimmage through a system of downs, and the end goal is to pass the opponent's goal line or kick the ball through the opponent's uprights.

The different forms of football that have been discussed, including the soccer, rugby, and Gaelic forms, are all distinct and unique, although they also share a number of similarities that lend the same name of football to each sport being played. First, and most obviously, they each involve the use of kicking to advance a ball, thus inviting the name of football to describe the sport. The games are all played within a specifically designed space with a set time frame. Furthermore, they each involve scoring points by advancing the ball past an opponent's goal line or through an opponent's uprights. Lastly, each sport is immensely popular in the cultures in which they are played.

History of American Football

The development of American football is generally linked to early versions of rugby and soccer. While Native Americans played many ball games throughout history, the first records of organized football in the United States are from the early 1800s in intramural games at college campuses. At this time, the rules were not standardized, with each school abiding by their own set of rules. At Princeton, a game called "ballown" was played; at Harvard, an event called "Bloody Monday"; and at Dartmouth, a version called "Old Division Football." While the rule of each game varied, they all involved a violent struggle to advance a ball against an opposing team, with frequent injuries resulting. The games were so violent that some schools began banning the sport, with Yale banning football in 1860, followed by Harvard in 1861.

While banned on college campuses, various sorts of football became increasingly popular in American prep schools in the mid-1800s. The games had three distinct varieties involving: (a) advancing a ball by kicking it, (b) advancing a ball by carrying it, or (c) a combination thereof. Among the first games involving both kicking and carrying the ball was a game referred to as the "Boston game," which was named based on the location that it was developed. The game continued to spread and arrived back on major college and university campuses throughout the United States.

In 1873, representatives from several colleges and universities met in an attempt to create a standardized set of football rules for intercollegiate play. The rules that were tabled appear most similar to the contemporary game of soccer. Harvard did not participate in the rule-standardizing meeting; instead, they opted to keep playing the traditional Boston game that involved kicking and carrying the ball in a game that is most similar to the contemporary game of rugby. Harvard was unable to find American teams to play the Boston game, so they challenged a Canadian team from Montreal to a two-game series. In the first match, they played Harvard's Boston game, while in the second match they played Montreal's rugby game. Harvard took a quick liking to the rugby game and decided to adopt it for future play against American schools. The game caught on with other schools, leading to the formation of the Intercollegiate Football Association.

At the rule-formation meetings of the association, one member, named Walter Camp, from Yale is credited as the father of American football because of the various rule changes that he instituted. Some of his proposed changes included reducing the amount of players on the field to open up the game to make it faster and more exciting, establishing a line of scrimmage, and creating a snap from a center to a quarterback to start each play. These new rules were revolutionary in the formation of a unique game of football, which has since become what we now term American or gridiron football.

College Football

The immense popularity of gridiron football in the United States began on the fields of colleges and universities across the country. By the early 1900s, close to 50 schools had competitive intercollegiate football teams. The game of the early 1900s was excessively violent and often resulted in catastrophic injuries and even death. In the year 1905 alone, 19 football deaths were reported in the United States. This prompted President Theodore Roosevelt to threaten to terminate the game if changes were not made to ensure a safer playing environment. This led to several changes such as the rule that seven players must be on the line of scrimmage and the allowance of forward passing. These rules not only resulted in fewer injuries but also added a new level of speed and excitement for spectators.

While professional leagues began emerging in the early 1900s, the college game of football had the largest following. The professional game struggled to attract spectators because it lacked the excitement and energy of the college game, with bands playing and young, fast athletes. College teams also had the added advantage of a fan base comprising primarily alumni and current students. The professional game did not have such affiliations.

By the 1930s, the college game had spread across the United States, with various collegiate football conferences established across the country. Various bowl games were also established that all still exist today including the Rose Bowl, Orange Bowl, Sun Bowl, Sugar Bowl, and Cotton Bowl. There are now over 30 different intercollegiate bowl games played in the United States each year, revealing just how much the game has continued to expand over time. During the 1930s, the way the game was played began to evolve toward a game involving many more passing plays, as it does today.

By the late 1950s and early 1960s, the National Football League (NFL) had surpassed college football in terms of national popularity. The rise of television spectatorship and the development of the Superbowl sparked increased interest in the professional game. The NFL was also able to appeal to working-class individuals who had no university affiliation, which the college game was not particularly able to do. While the introduction of televised sporting events helped the growth of college football as well, it did not have the same impact as on the professional game.

Football Today

American gridiron football has become one of the most popular sports in the United States today in terms of participation and spectatorship. While it certainly has its largest following in the United States, amateur and professional football leagues have been developed in many other regions of the world including Canada, Mexico, Japan, and Europe. It has also become increasingly popular at younger levels, such as high school sport and various community leagues and programs, with players as young as 7 years old beginning to play. New variants of the game have also been developed such as indoor/arena football, flag football, two-hand touch, backyard football, Canadian football, and nine-man, eight-man, or six-man football.

See Also: Athletics (Amateur); Play as Competition, Sociology of; Rugby (Amateur); Soccer (Amateur) Worldwide; Team Play.

Bibliography. Mark F. Bernstein, *Football: The Ivy League Origins of an American Obsession* (University of Pennsylvania Press, 2001); Harford Powel, *Walter Camp: The Father of American Football* (Borah Press, 2007); Robert Stebbins, *Canadian Football: A View From the Helmet* (University of Western Ontario Press, 1987); Wiley Lee Umphlett, *Creating the Big Game* (Greenwood Press, 1992); John Sayle Watterson, *College Football: History, Spectacle, Controversy* (Johns Hopkins University Press, 2002).

Curtis Fogel
University of Calgary

France

Although play has always been a part of French society, its concept has drastically evolved throughout the centuries. Directly opposing the notion of work, free time was originally exemplified by the life of leisure the wealthy aristocratic elite led while the majority of the population had to work to survive. As a result, the aristocratic lifestyle became an idealized model deeply rooted in French society. The democratization of free time that has been taking place since the early 20th century has made leisure accessible to all. Additionally, the recent changes in lifestyle and values indicate a need and belief in pleasure. France has evolved into a secular society that views free time as an individual sacred right. With the combination of a shorter work week, a longer life expectancy, and a higher disposable income, the French can enjoy a substantial amount of free time for recreational and sports activities. Both adults and children still struggle to find an adequate balance between work and leisure. Even though most people feel that work is deemed an essential part of their existence, they ultimately view leisure as a necessary way of life

The Concept of Leisure

Two major paradoxical societal traditions have greatly influenced the concept of free time as leisure in France. Prior to the French Revolution, the aristocratic class tended to favor idleness over work, finding the latter particularly diminishing to one's individuality. Nevertheless, only the elite and the privileged were able to lead a life of leisure, while the rest of the population had to work to survive. Work was, therefore, seen as an unpleasant task given to the majority of the population, while the nobility could devote their time to artistic and intellectual pursuits. As a result, this lifestyle that only a very few could attain became an ideal that continues as a part of French society.

In the 18th and 19th centuries, the development of a new bourgeoisie class influenced by Protestant values also impacted the concept of leisure in France. Contrary to the aristocracy, the bourgeoisie welcomed work and saw it as a positive moral value that could give the individual a sense of accomplishment and pride, while also contributing to the enhancement of society. The bourgeoisie condemned aristocratic idleness, finding the need for leisure and pleasure undoubtedly immoral. Nevertheless, the 19th-century French bourgeoisie was somewhat envious of the wealthy aristocracy but could only attain financial freedom through work. As a result, contemporary French society carries tendencies from both conflicting traditions: the French are willing to work hard, even sometimes overtime hours, as long as they know they will be rewarded by a long period of vacation.

Vacation Time

With the reduction of work time (35 hours per week), accompanied by five weeks of paid vacation, the French enjoy more free time than many developed nations. The French have a specific and unique concept of summer vacation because unlike their European neighbors, they usually take a month off during July or August. This makes the French very proud not only because they take a break from work but also because it demonstrates their privileged and envied social status. From the Renaissance (the 16th century) until the early 20th century, the concept of vacation was exclusive to nobility and the high bourgeoisie, who would escape the oppressive heat of Paris and spend summers in the country or by the seashore.

Vacation as free time became a new social reality and a right when in 1936 a new law granted two weeks' paid annual leave to all French salaried workers. Additional laws in 1956 (three weeks' paid leave), 1969 (four weeks' paid leave), and 1982 extended the amount of paid vacation, bringing it to the current five weeks of paid vacation. Since the 1960s, the increase of disposable income and the availability of transportation have made traveling more accessible to a majority of French people, who often prefer vacationing within France.

Adult Leisure

Since the Middle Ages, the French have found pleasure through entertainment, while socializing with their compatriots. French literature attests to such a societal phenomenon and helps us better understand the evolution of games throughout the centuries. Social adult games were an important part of court life until the French Revolution and primarily acted as an entertainment for the nobility, a small portion of the French population. Verbal games, also considered intellectual games designed to demonstrate one's intelligence and wit were a major entertainment at the king's or queen's court.

Card games first appeared in France in the late 14th century and rapidly became popular among adults because they were thought to be more complex than Dice but simpler than Checkers. The cards also represented an equal representation of the four social classes: nobility (spades), clergy (hearts), bourgeoisie (diamonds), and peasantry (clubs). Moreover, specific card games even today still carry a social specificity. For example, *Belote* is popular and played in cafes with four players. Bridge is viewed as bourgeois and is often favored by intellectuals, who see chance balanced out by reason. *La*

Bataille (war) and *Le Jeu des 7 Familles* (family game) are played by both adults and children. *Les Patiences* or *Réussites* (similar to solitaire) are individual card games, nowadays mostly played electronically.

Additionally, games of chance have a long tradition in the history of France. Considered immoral, games involving money and gambling were originally condemned by the church and only existed illegally. In the 16th century, King Francis I authorized the first official drawing games after realizing the kingdom could benefit financially. In 1776, Louis XVI decided to unify these games by creating the "royal lottery," whose monetary gains became state funds. Since then, the lottery has been modernized, but its fundamental concept remains unchanged.

Today, games of chance are considered a business that each year generates billions of euros. La Française des Jeux was the new name given in 1976 to the governmental organization responsible for regulating all games involving money. Moreover, horse betting, officially operated by PMU (Mutual Urban Bet) since its creation in 1952, is the second most popular betting activity. Finally, casinos represent the third largest type of organization that profits from games of chance. Like their ancestors, many French play the lotto and diverse quick draw games in hopes of becoming wealthy and leading a life of leisure.

Adults enjoy many different sorts of social entertainment. Food is still at the heart of the social life of the French, who gather at home, in restaurants or cafes to enjoy one of life's most important pleasures. In addition, cultural outings to museums, concerts, theatres, cinemas, and sports events are regularly enjoyed but their frequency highly depends on the socioeconomical and educational level of the individual. The higher the level of education and wealth an individual possesses, the more intellectual the events he or she attends are.

At-home recreational activities have become indispensable to French daily life, especially with the increase in free time and better access to technology. The use of computers, the internet, and telephones has increased in recent years. One out of two households possess a computer at home. However, the use of technology varies highly according to age.

Watching television is still the most popular activity, and the average adult spends three and half hours a day in front of the television. News, films, and sports are the most frequently watched programs. The increase of television ownership has resulted in a decrease in cinema attendance. Additionally, the French listen to the radio every day and consider music an important cultural activity. Consequently, various music festivals are organized throughout the country. Finally, reading is another leisure activity that nonetheless presents socioeconomical disparity. Books are three times more likely to be read in middle- to upper-class families than in the working class.

Adults also take pleasure in tackling all different handy- or home-related projects. Gardening can be included in this type of activity, but tends to be more predominant among married and mature adults (age 40 to 50 years, and/or retired). Moreover, we note an increased number of women who undertake home repairs. Nature-related activities are linked to an overall need to create a comfortable yet pleasant surrounding environment, while feeling the self-satisfaction of creating something.

Child's Play

In today's France, play is viewed as an essential activity that starts from birth and continues until adulthood, but this was not always the case. The concept of play as a central element to a child's development has changed in the 18th century, with theories on childhood and education elaborated on by Jean Jacques Rousseau. Later, the birth of psychology in the early 19th century also contributed to redefining the role of play in the construction of a child's identity. Educational pedagogy has evolved in such a way that playing has been fully integrated as part of the learning process at school and at home. Because family is so central to French life, young children (newborn to age 3 years) learn first from the playing they experience with their parents, mostly their mothers, who tend to be the primary caregivers. The psychological relationship between child and mother is thought to be so crucial in France that the government has implemented a three-year parental leave, which allows a parent to care for his or her child during the first three years of his or her life.

Many traditional children's games are especially played at familial ritual occasions (birthday, wedding, anniversary, etc.). While the adults socialize among themselves, children are expected to do the same and generally play group games such as *Cache-Cache* (Hide-and-Seek), *La Marelle* (Hopscotch), *Le Jeu de Quilles* (Land Bowling), and *Colin-Maillard* (Blind Man's Bluff). Nevertheless, *Les Billes* (Marbles), a boy's game typically played at school during recess, is slowly disappearing. Additionally, children play badminton, fly kites, swing on swings, and jump rope. In urban settings, children who live in apartments play on public playgrounds generally after school rather than at home in their own backyard.

Children also develop their social skills with commercial toys and games. Parents' purchases are nonetheless very much dictated by traditional social rites. Therefore, children receive toys on Christmas, birthdays, and special occasions as a sign of reward or comfort. Commercial toys and games aim to please, entertain, and finally socialize the child. At home, the parents, while desiring to gratify the child, are likely to buy games with an educational purpose. Nonetheless, contemporary toys and games given to French children still reflect and mimic the sexual division of social roles. Consequently, girls are almost systematically offered toys that highlight their maternal and domestic functions (dolls, house games, etc.) while boys are directed toward more masculine toys (action figures, construction games, etc.). Ultimately, toys help the child acquire a better understanding of society's rules and values among which is the ambiguous relationship that exists between work and pleasure so unique to France.

Technology

The youth have their own concept of leisure and entertainment, which is directly linked to a profound desire for socialization. Technology has become the new way of socialization for this generation whose preferences are as follows: First, radio is listened to on a daily basis by most teenagers, who, no matter their socioeconomic level, are in possession of their own radio. Second, television is watched by all, even though lower classes indulge in this leisure more frequently than upper classes. Third, youngsters in particular enjoy spending time with new technology, such as computer and video games. Their accessibility has drastically expanded within the last 10 years and also presents a slight gender discrepancy.

Video games tend to attract boys, while girls favor verbal and nonverbal communication means (computer and phone). Fourth, reading is still an important activity, even though it continues to decline. Again, a gender divergence is noticeable. While girls choose novels, boys are more likely to read comics. If the need to socialize among themselves is deemed essential at various stages, it is certainly most frequent for the 15-to-18-year-olds who favor many group outings to cafes, parties, and concerts. Most recently, cell phones have become an easy and preferred method by which many French teenagers play.

Sports

The notion of sports as we know it today appeared as a result of 19th-century industrialization. While examining ancient games, Georges Vigarello states that physical exercise has always been a part of French society. In the 16th to 17th century, games revolved around competition and bets and presented some element of violence. From tournaments and duels to games of ball and mail (a cross between golf and croquet), players had to prove both their strength and adroitness. Additionally, ancient games followed traditional societal rites, whether related to Christian religious holidays or special occasions, such as marriage or the birth of a future king.

In the 19th century, a clear distinction between work and leisure was made, and a new sport system carrying specific rules was organized. The democratization of sport intended to make it accessible to all in an effort to develop a sense of collective spirit. Sport was therefore given both a moral importance and practical utility. In the 1980s, the element of competition added a new dimension to sports, which translated into the flourishing of many league teams, both professional and not. Vigarello further argues that organized sports offer secular French society central values of merit, social equality, and loyalty. Consequently, many French people gather to watch (whether live or on television) main sporting events: soccer, tennis (i.e., the French Open and the Paris Masters), bicycling (i.e., Le Tour de France), rugby, and race car driving (i.e., 24 Hours of Le Mans).

The pedagogue Pierre de Coubertin certainly had a tremendous influence on the way contemporary sports are nowadays viewed and structured. Not only did he redefine sport as both a competition and a spectacle, but he also contributed to the improvement of sports education. A variety of Olympic sports have been incorporated into the French educational curriculum. Youth are therefore exposed and also involved in a wider selection of sports than the adults. Additionally, they often practice sports as extracurricular activities to balance out the demands of school and family life.

Sports in France have also become an essential part of daily adult life, especially since the 1970s, when the upper class started to incorporate individual sports into their lifestyle. Overall, the notion of beauty and pleasure became applicable to the body and its representation. Today, the most highly practiced sports are as follows: hiking, bicycling, swimming, bowling, walking, running, and playing tennis. Interestingly enough, *La pétanque* (also named *les boules*) is a non-Olympic game that has been played since antiquity. Its popularity comes not only from its affordability—making this game accessible to all social classes—but also its collective orientation. Originally a more masculine game, more and more women find pétanque appealing. There are today about 7,000 French clubs with a total of 425,000 licensed players.

See Also: Boules; Europe, 1960 to Present; Sociological Benefits of Play.

Bibliography. Baudouin Eschapasse et al., eds., "D'où Viennent Les Jeux ... De Hasard, De Cartes, De Société ou De Plein Air," *Historia* (v.175, 2006); Martine Fournier et al., eds., "A Quoi Sert le Jeu?" *Sciences Humaines* (v.152, 2004); Gérard Mermet, *Francoscopie 2005* (Larrousse, 2004); Gabriel Langouët, *Les Jeunes et Leurs Loisirs en France* (Hachette, 2004); Nicole Samuel, "Free Time in France; An Historical and Sociological Survey," *International Social Science Journal* (v.38, 1986); Georges Vigarello, *Du Jeu Ancien au Show Sportif. La Naissance d'un Mythe* (Editions du Seuil, 2002).

Nathalie Degroult
Siena College

Freud and Play

Because of the writings and theories of Sigmund Freud (1856–1939) concerning play, as well as those of his daughter Anna (1895–1982), Austria, and particularly the Freuds' home of Vienna, where he lived from 1860 until their emigration to the United Kingdom in 1938, has a special place in the social history of play and its theories. Throughout Austrian history, games, play and sport have entertained and influenced the area's populace. Sports have been instrumentalized by political parties and have played important roles in the creation of a modern Austrian national identity. However, Freud's main contribution to the study of play is his observation that play can be a significant window on a child's emotional life and that in play, a child can, through repetition, better cope with difficult feelings.

Sigmund Freud lived through a tumultuous and trying time in the history of Austria. Soon after he and his family moved to Vienna in 1860 from his birthplace in Príbor (in the present-day Czech Republic)—a city also within the confines of the Austrian Empire of the period—the Austrian army lost a short war with neighboring Prussia. Austria began a long reorganization, which included the recognition of a semiautonomous Kingdom of Hungary (creating the Austro-Hungarian Monarchy). Freud grew up and studied in a Vienna now famous for its cultural ferment, as intellectuals and artists debated and interacted with the complex, shifting sociopolitical worlds known today as the *fin-de-siècle*.

Literary Works

It is during this period that Freud wrote about children's play in pieces such as *Three Essays on the Theory of Sexuality* (1905). In this piece, Freud theorized that children like games, such as rocking, carriage rides, swinging, and being thrown up in the air, because the repetition and mechanical agitation involved was tied to sexual excitation. He also was thinking about adult play, specifically wordplay, when he wrote *Jokes and Their Relation to the Unconscious* the same year. Two years later, Freud discussed play in his ruminations on the sources of artistic genius. In *Creative Writers and Day-Dreaming*, he asserted that children at play acted in the same way as writers, creating their own worlds in ways pleasing to them.

Most famously, Freud turned to thinking about play again after World War I left the Austro-Hungarian Monarchy dismembered and a new, shaky Austrian Republic in its wake. The father-figure emperor had been dethroned and a Social Democratic regime installed. Millions had died, and Vienna suffered in the hard transition from imperial capital to the seat of a controversial government ruling over a bankrupt state. The first year of the republic, 1919, saw Freud, who had spent some time treating war veterans who had recurrent nightmares that replayed their wartime traumas, watching his year-and-a-half-old grandson Ernst Halberstadt voluntarily, and even gleefully, reenact the departure of his mother from his sight. This famous game of "*fort-da*" (gone/here) led Freud into his disturbing speculations concerning the death instinct, the rival to its equal, the more acceptable *eros*. This was Freud's one step beyond, in his work *Beyond the Pleasure Principle* (1920). The repetition of an unpleasant experience enables the reenactor to be active, restoring (at least momentarily) the previous state of affairs, Freud argued. But the "big" past that ultimately was (and is) the most disturbing, he theorized, was the past before life: death. Self-preservation for the apparently disenchanted 60-something grandfather was still sex (to create life), but also the more limited actions tied to repetitious play: dying on one's own terms.

Freud After World War II

Ultimately, this limited freedom was to be denied to the elderly clinician and theoretician. After Austria's annexation by Nazi-led Germany in 1938, Freud and his daughter Anna fled to the United Kingdom. He died in exile shortly thereafter. Anna had begun her distinguished career in the field of child psychology and had chaired Vienna's Psycho-Analytic Society for a few years in the 1920s. Anna used play with children in ways analogous to the way psychoanalysts use the dreams of their adult patients. By the late 1930s, she too had turned to thinking about self-defense mechanisms and how children's play helped them adapt to their realities. Departure from her childhood hometown was not voluntary for the 43-year-old.

After the horrors of the Holocaust and World War II, before which the Freuds had fled, the Allies reestablished the Austrian republic in 1945, remaining as occupiers there until a decade later, when an international treaty was signed giving the second Austrian republic its independence. Two themes would mark the institutional histories of play and sport in this new Austria of the postwar era: desires to reconnect with the sporting and political landscapes of the pre-German period, and desires to create a sense of Austrian national identity.

Sport would play a particularly large role in the latter undertaking, particularly Alpine skiing and soccer. The country cohosted the European men's soccer championships in 2008, giving Austrians the chance to communally celebrate. The unprecedented economic prosperity of Austria of the late 20th century provided the opportunity for play and leisure activities in general on an unprecedented scale.

See Also: Play and Learning Theory; Play and Power, Psychology of; Play as Mastery of Nature; Play as Rehearsal of Reality; Psychoanalytic Theory and Play; Soccer (Amateur) Worldwide; Toys and Child Development.

Bibliography. Catherine Bates, *Play in a Godless World: The Theory and Practice of Play in Shakespeare, Nietzsche and Freud* (OpenGate, 1999); Peter Gay, ed., *Freud Reader* (Norton, 1989); Roman Horak and Georg Spitaler, "Sport Space and National Identity. Soccer and Skiing as Formative Forces: On the Austrian Example," *American Behavioral Scientist* (v.46/11, 2003); Ernest Jones, *Life and Work of Sigmund Freud* (Basic Books, 1961); Gilbert Norden, "Sport in Österreich: Entstehung, Verbreitung und Differenzierung (19. und Frühes 20. Jahrhundert)," *Historicum* (Winter, 1998-99); "Zwanzig Jahre Spielforschung," www.spielforschung.at (cited June 2008).

Joseph F. Patrouch
Florida International University

Frisbee

At first glance, a Frisbee seems like a fairly simple toy; a plastic disk with its edges curled under, it has no moving parts, is inexpensive, and is easy to use. A mere flick of the wrist sends a Frisbee gliding through the air, and anyone at almost any age can enjoy playing with a Frisbee. Yet its simplicity belies the versatility of the Frisbee, which can be used in a multitude of ways—from a backyard game of catch to professional competitions of such sports as Ultimate Frisbee and Frisbee Golf. A Frisbee can be used to perform a variety of tricks to show off various throwing and catching skills.

A game of Frisbee can include two players or even teams of players, with participants ranging in age from young children to adults. In addition to humans, many dogs also enjoy playing with Frisbees and can be trained to catch them and perform tricks just for fun and exercise or to participate in professional competitions with their human partners. The Frisbee is simple in design yet complex in the possibilities and applications that this toy provides players, from novices to professionals, who can use it in various environments to create everything from unstructured or spontaneous play to organized sports competitions, providing entertaining play or fierce competition between teams.

The question of who the specific inventor of the Frisbee was has been debated, but many attribute the name and origin to the Frisbie Baking Company, a Connecticut bakery that produced pies. When local college stu-

A Frisbee player makes an impressive horizontal catch while playing at the beach. Wham-O sold over 100 million Frisbees before selling the company, which at the time was the nation's leading toy manufacturer, to Mattel.

dents discovered that an empty pie tin had wonderful aerodynamic properties that made it ideal for playing catch, the game was dubbed "frisbie."

A plastic version of the Frisbee that could fly farther and be thrown more accurately was developed by Walter F. Morrison and Warren Franscioni in 1948; when the partners split, Morrison began producing a plastic Frisbee that he named the "Pluto Platter." Since Americans were becoming fascinated by UFOs at this time, Morrison tied the name of his toy into the popularity of UFOs, especially since the shape of the Pluto Platter made it look similar to an extraterrestrial vehicle.

The potential of this new toy did not escape the owners of a new toy company, Wham-O, who bought the rights to Morrison's Pluto Platter and began producing them in 1957. Wham-O later changed the name of the Pluto Platter to Frisbee after discovering that the terms *frisbie* and *frisbie-ing* were often used in connection to the toy. After the addition of a section of raised ridges to stabilize the flight of Frisbees and an innovative advertising campaign that promoted Frisbees as part of a new sport, Wham-O enjoyed spectacular sales of the Frisbee.

The connection of Frisbees and sports has evolved, limited only by the imaginations of Frisbee players around the world. Sports that are played with Frisbees include Ultimate Frisbee, Frisbee Golf, and Freestyle. Ultimate Frisbee began in 1968, the creation of a group of high school students in Maplewood, New Jersey. Ultimate Frisbee is influenced by other sports such as football, basketball, soccer, and hockey and is played in 42 countries around the globe. Ultimate Frisbee was also part of the World Games in Japan in 2001.

Humans are not the only ones who enjoy playing with Frisbees—dogs enjoy getting in on the action, too. Tournaments are held around the world in countries such as the United States, Japan, German, and the Netherlands, where dogs and their humans can participate in various types of competitions or show off their skills by performing tricks and stunts. Whether it is in a professional competition or just playing catch in the backyard, many dogs enjoy the exercise and companionship of playing Frisbee with their owners, and with a little patience, many dogs can be taught to master a trick or two involving a Frisbee.

Frisbees are a source of fun and entertainment for novices as well, and playing with a Frisbee is not only enjoyable but provides good exercise, especially for those beginners who spend a good deal of time running after the Frisbee that they were not able to catch or climbing onto the garage roof to retrieve one from an errant throw. Physical skills such as eye-hand coordination can be developed as one masters catching and throwing the Frisbee; in addition, Frisbees are also a great way to bring people of all ages together for shared play.

Players, whether they are skilled or not, can enjoy a game of Frisbee, which always seems to involve a lot of laughing, joking, and friendly competition during a casual game. For many people, picnics, beach parties, and other summer gatherings would not be complete without a game of Frisbee. Since Frisbees are easily portable, inexpensive, and available in different colors and sizes, they are the perfect addition to almost any get-together. These games can include the entire family, as even a young child can throw a Frisbee and participate in the fun or attempt some tricks. With its seemingly endless applications, which are limited only by the imaginations of players, the Frisbee remains popular.

See Also: Play as Competition, Sociology of; Play as Entertainment, Sociology of; Team Play.

Bibliography. About.com, "The History of the Frisbee," www.inventors.about.com (cited July 2008); Essortment, "History of Frisbees," www.essortment.com (cited July 2008); Victor A. Malafronte and F. Davis Johnson, *The Complete Book of Frisbee: The History of the Sport & the First Official Price Guide* (American Trends Publishing Company, 1998).

Allison A. Hutira
Youngstown State University

Froebel, Friedrich

Friedrich Froebel, the father of kindergarten, was perhaps the first person to use play as the central element of an educational method. Central to his method, which he named "kindergarten" or children's garden, was a series of educational play materials he termed "Gifts." He also created finger plays, a new type of musical and premathematical play for mothers to use with their young children. Rooted in play, kindergarten began early-childhood education as it is known today. His educational method, or "the Kindergarten Movement," spread around the world over the next century.

Born in eastern Germany on April 21, 1782, Froebel spent much of his childhood in the outdoors, becoming one with his natural surroundings. Later, he would include his love of nature and the outdoors into kindergarten. His early academic training in mathematics, architecture, and mineralogy could have led to a professorship at several prestigious universities; however, Froebel refused these opportunities and instead became a teacher. He began his teaching career in Switzerland under the tutelage of the renowned educator Johann Pestalozzi. In 1817 in Keilhau, Germany, Froebel opened his first school. Not until 1839 could he put into practice his dream of a new schooling for young children by founding the world's first kindergarten in the village of Bad Blankenburg, Germany. Froebel not only established and taught in this first kindergarten but also began many other similar schools and trained the first women teachers for his new form of education.

Because of its closeness to a young child's heart and mind, Froebel saw play as an act of the child's true spirit. He felt that the child needed to experience things directly in order to learn and that play achieved this firsthand experience. Froebel used his prior background in mathematics to create little number stories, called finger plays, for mothers to teach their children premath and language skills. He also created a series of blocks and other manipulatives he called Gifts. Block play became a permanent part of his kindergarten movement. His most famous gift, Gift Two, was composed of a sphere, a cylinder, and a cube; this versatile combination of blocks could be used for everything from lessons in geometry to dramatic play. Believing that children needed to use their own hands in learning, he also crafted a series of activities called Occupations for use with the Gifts.

Froebel's core belief, that play offered the child not just words but active experiences that promote learning, inspired several more of his lasting contributions In the new kindergarten, playful learning was the main conduit for the knowledge, so Froebel incorporated art, music, storytelling, finger play, nature experiences, and circle time. Froebel often led children's play activities outdoors, an innovation that was then criticized. In 1851, at Altenstein Park, Froebel invented the play fest, perhaps an early forerunner of the modern play day.

Even after his death in 1852, Froebel's dream of spreading kindergarten around the globe endured, and many schools today with kindergartens are indebted to Froebel's philosophy and methods. Froebel lived for children and their play, and in death he is remembered for his contributions to both education and play. Rising above his gravesite in Schweina, Germany, are sculptures of his beloved kindergarten blocks in the form of the famous Gift Two, the sphere, cylinder, and cube. This monument testifies that Froebel's greatest gift to children may have been the gift of play.

See Also: Blocks; Finger Games; Play and Learning Theory; Play as Entertainment, Psychology of.

Bibliography. Norman Brosterman, *Inventing Kindergarten* (Harry Abrams, 1997); Friedrich Froebel, H.K. Moore, and E. Michaelis, tr., *Autobiography of Friedrich Froebel* (Echo Library, 2007); Bertha von Marenholtz-Bulow, *How Kindergarten Came to America: Friedrich Froebel's Radical Vision of Early Childhood Education* (New Press, 2007); Mary Ruth Moore, "An American's Journey to Kindergarten's Birthplace," *Childhood Education* (v.79/1, Fall 2002); Brian Sutton-Smith, *The Ambiguity of Play* (Harvard University Press, 2001).

Mary Ruth Moore
University of the Incarnate Word

Galoob

Now part of Hasbro, for 40 years Galoob manufactured toys, most notably Micro Machines, Sky Dancer, and Game Genie. Lewis and Barbara (Frankel) Galoob founded Lewis Galoob Toys in 1957 as a distributor of stationery and toys. The company's first success was the Jolly Chimp, a battery-powered toy monkey that banged cymbals and nodded its head. During the 1960s and 1970s, Jolly Chimp photo albums, calendars, and stationery kept the company income stream steady if not spectacular. In 1970 Lewis Galoob became too sick to continue. His sons David and Robert took over and made the company into a $1 million business by 1976.

In 1976 the company bought a low-cost line of battery-operated radio-controlled cars and trucks that served as the basis for the company's growth for 20 years. By 1978 the vehicles produced sales of almost $5 million, but Galoob lacked a year-in-year-out surefire seller to absorb the boom and bust cycle of the fad-driven toy business.

In the 1970s product licensing became important to toy producers, and Galoob licensed Smurfs, which remained Galoob's major licensing venture until the licensing of television character Mr. T led to Galoob scoring sales of $28 million by 1983. Although Mr. T's popularity collapsed in 1984, other lines and intensive advertising almost doubled sales. In 1985 the company's earnings reached $100 million, thanks to the Animal, an off-road machine with claws to help it climb, and the first girl-oriented transformers, Sweet Secrets.

Galoob failures included Strobe-Dice, an electronic crap game. Baby Talk, Galoob's electronic talking doll, ran into the 1987 glutted market for electronic toys. Mr. Game Show, a $125 board game featuring a sarcastic voice, was another failure.

The slump in electronic toys and a shift of production to the People's Republic of China generated a net 1987 loss of almost $25 million with a 40 percent reduction in sales. That year Galoob found its surefire seller—Micro Machines—tiny toy cars. In 1988 Galoob's $140 million in sales included $60 million in Micro Machines. In 1989 the toys accounted for $135 million of Galoob's $228 million in revenues.

In 1990 the market went bust. Even Micro Machine sales slumped, as did sales of Bouncin' Babies, Galoob's 1989 hot-selling doll. The Federal Trade Commission then found Galoob guilty of deceptive advertising.

In the 1990s Galoob cut 17 percent of their workforce and ousted David Galoob, ending Galoob as a family company. Under Mark Goldman, the company committed to Micro Machines as its key brand. With five playsets and 155 machines in 40 collections, including Star Wars and Power Rangers, Micro Machine sales recovered from $43 million in 1991 to $113 million in 1994. In the 1990s

Galoob added Starship Troopers and Johnny Quest to its Star Wars and Star Trek licenses. Later Galoob would license Babylon 5, Aliens, Predator, and others.

Galoob's 1992 Game Genie gave Nintendo game players extra lives, speed, weapons, and other features not in the games themselves. Nintendo sued, but the court ruled that users had the right to modify copyrighted intellectual properties for their own use. Game Genie earned $65 million in 1992, but the video game market moved past it, and 1994 earnings were only $4 million.

Galoob's next big seller was the Styrofoam-winged, launcher-propelled twirling and flying Sky Dancer, introduced in 1993, and the number one girl's toy with $70 million in earnings in 1995. Galoob also sells Pound Puppies, DragonFlyz (the first flying articulated figures), dollhouses, and castles. In 1995 Galoob recovered to third place among U.S. toy makers, with sales of $220 million. In 1997 and 1998 Galoob was again losing money. Hasbro bought Galoob in 1998 for $220 million.

See Also: Hasbro; United States, 1960 to present.

Bibliography. Stevanne Auerbach, Dr. Toy's Guide, www.drtoy.org/1995/galoob_toys.html; Gary Cross, *Kids' Stuff: Toys and the Changing World of American Childhood* (Harvard University Press, 1999); Dan Fost, "Hasbro Adds Galoob to Its Toy Chest," *San Francisco Chronicle*, www.sfgate.com (cited July 2008); Funding Universe, Lewis Galoob Toys, Inc., www.fundinguniverse.com/company-histories/Lewis-Galoob-Toys-Inc-Company-History.html (cited August 2008).

John Barnhill
Independent Scholar

Gambling

Gambling, in its strictest sense, is the staking of any form of valuable item on a game of chance. By this definition, the staking of a bet on, for example, a game of football or pool is not gambling; however, in contemporary parlance it is widely accepted to be so. Gambling is often referred to as "gaming." In the United Kingdom, for example, the regulation of gambling takes place under the Gaming Act. The words are often used interchangeably, but technically *gaming* refers to the operators of gambling companies, as opposed to the individual games that they may offer; "The gaming company offers gambling services."

Under the definition offered above, services such as insurance and markets such as the stock exchange could be considered gambling. These are often not considered as such on the basis that an involved party has an interest in the outcome of the bet beyond the financial terms offered. For example, in the insurance of a house, it is assumed that the person needs a roof over their head, independent of the financial aspects of the insurance "bet" that has been entered into.

There are factors common to all forms of gambling, and these are the stake, the (predicted or definite) probability, and the odds on offer. Games are usually measured by their expected value, which is calculated by multiplying the stake and odds (in decimal form), and then multiplying this by the probability. For example, if you were to stake $100 on the flipping of an unbiased coin, and make this as an even money bet, the expected value is (100 x 0.5) x 2 = $100. If you were to be offered 2.1, the expected value is (100 x 0.5) x 2.1 = $105, and if you were to be offered 1.9, the expected value is (100 x 0.5) x 1.9 = $95, so you can see that depending on the odds, it is possible to make a profitable (+EV) or negative (–EV) value bet.

In sports betting, the overall expectation is usually expressed as the total percentage of the odds offered on any given market, be it a football match, tennis tournament, or any other market in which there is only one winner. This becomes more complex for markets that may have several winners; for example, the "Top 10" market in a golf tournament would be an equal proposition (for bookmaker and client) at 1000 percent. Traditionally in the United Kingdom, bookmakers priced a single-winner market to 117 percent, meaning that if you were to place a bet on each outcome to ensure the same result, you would lose 17 percent. A market priced to over 100 percent offers a bookmaker advantage, and a market priced to under 100 percent entails a player advantage.

History

Gambling has its roots in ancient civilizations. Evidence exists of gambling as an activity in both Ancient Rome and Ancient Greek civilizations. It has been contentious, at times being seen as a recreational activity used to pass the time or settle disputes and at other times as a sinful activity likely to produce social malcontents. Early evidence of regulating gambling exists primarily from

In the American colonies, gambling was a popular and accepted activity. Cockfighting, however, was illegal for many years because it was not considered a suitable game for gentlemen.

the Christian religions. Two of the oldest Canons of the Apostles banned games of chance, with the threat of excommunication to those partaking in them. In 1215 the fourth Lateran Council inserted in the "Corpus Juris" a declaration banning clerics from playing, or even being present at, games of chance.

More recently, in the United Kingdom the Gaming Acts of 1845 and 1892 declared gambling debts unenforceable in a court of law in an attempt to prevent them occurring, which failed. Since the widespread availability of betting services online, precipitated by the growth of the internet in the late 20th century, a more recent round of regulation has taken place. In the United Kingdom, the government abolished the previous 9 percent tax on all bets placed, replacing it with a 15 percent tax on bookmakers' profits, and in 2007 the government formed a new gambling commission to entice online venues to locate in the United Kingdom under friendly regulation terms.

In sharp contrast, between 2004 and 2006 many European countries enacted barriers against international operators, in many cases with the stated ambition of protecting their national, often governmental, betting companies and lotteries. In 2006, the European Union launched an investigation against nine European nations for breaching free market regulations and adopting protectionist policies; an issue that remains largely unresolved as of this book going to press.

The more problematic legislation, on a worldwide basis, came from the United States. In October 2006, the United States enacted the Unlawful Internet Gambling Enforcement Act of 2006 (UIGEA). The legislation was passed as part of the SAFE Port Act. The act made it illegal for any company to accept a financial instrument in conjunction with internet gambling. This means that it is illegal for a company to accept credit cards, checks, bank drafts, and so forth if these funds are to be utilized for online gambling. To date, the act has proved essentially ineffective, with the majority of gambling companies (outside of some European countries and Australia, and with a couple of notable exceptions) still accepting customers from the United States and, while incurring periodic small delays, still succeeding in sending and receiving funds from customers in the United States.

Expression of Odds

The expression of odds varies greatly depending on the region. In Europe, odds are generally expressed as either a decimal or fraction. The decimal version of these indicates your return on a one-unit stake; for example, odds of 2.00 represent even money, so if your bet is successful you would receive a return of two units. This is equivalent in fraction terms to 1/1, which is usually expressed as "Evs" or "Evens." In fractions, the top number refers to the profit and the stake is the bottom number, so for a bet at 7/4, you would stake four units to return 11 (seven plus your original stake), which is equivalent to decimal odds of 2.75. Bets in which the profit gained is less than the original stake (for example, betting 10 to win three, and thus return 13) are known as "odds on" bets. These have an implied probability of over 50 percent, but their odds are expressed in the same way. For example, 1/3 would mean that you stake three units to return four (one profit plus your original three), and this is equivalent to decimal odds of 1.33. Decimal odds are rounded to two decimal places, though companies will handle the extraneous decimals in different ways.

In North America, for parimutuel horse racing, odds are expressed in a fractional format. Parimutuel betting basically operates as a pool, where all money bet into that pool for any given race is paid out (minus a proportion held by the operator) to the customers who bet on that option, proportionate to the amount they invested in the pool. Thus, the odds offered are liable to change up to the post time (starting point) of the race. Curiously, the eventual payouts when displayed on screens at the track or for television are usually then expressed in the European decimal format. Parimutuel betting is known as "tote" betting in some countries, including the United Kingdom.

For sporting events, however, odds are expressed in what is known as "Moneyline" format. Where the implied probability is less than 50 percent, that is, the return is greater than even money, the odds express the profit to a stake of 100 units. For example +180 would return 280 (180 profit plus the original 100), and +1500 would return 1600 (1500 profit plus the original 100). For odds below the implied probability of 50 percent, they are expressed in the stake required to profit 100 units; for example minus 150 means you would have to stake 150 units to profit 100 (returning 250 units), and minus 415 means you would have to stake 415 units to profit 100 (returning 515 units).

Asian Odds

Occasionally an Asian bookmaker will only offer Asian-style odds. These are similar to the decimal format offered by European bookmakers and come in three principle formats. The first of these is the Hong Kong format, which comes in the form of a positive number rounded to two decimal places, and represents the units won in excess of the original stake were the bet to win. For example, Hong Kong odds of 0.75 mean that a player would collect 75 units on top of their original stake if they bet 100 units. Thus, it is equivalent to decimal odds of 1.75.

Indonesian odds can be both positive and negative. When they are positive, they are interpreted in the same manner as the Hong Kong odds described above. When the number is negative, it represents the number of units a player would need to stake to win one unit. So, for example, Indonesian odds of minus 2.00 indicate that you would be required to stake 200 units to return 100 units of profit (300 units in total). In this case, it is essentially equivalent to negative U.S. odds, but divided by 100 to show results to 1 unit rather than 100.

Finally, Malay odds are expressed as a number with a value no greater than 1. That is, they are found in the range $-1 \leq x \geq 1$. Where they are positive, they are the same as Hong Kong and Indonesian odds, as described above. Where they are negative, they represent the amount a bettor has to stake to win 1 unit. So, for example minus 0.2 would indicate the player would have to risk 20 units to win 100, meaning a wager of 100 units would profit 500 units and return 600 units.

The other thing that needs to be noted with sports betting is the concept of the handicap. This is found in most types of betting and is designed to create an even proposition. If, for example, the New England Patriots were playing the Tennessee Titans, and New England were heavy favorites to win the match, you may find they are approximately minus 300 on the U.S.-style moneyline, meaning the bettor has to place $300 to win $100. This sounds an unattractive proposition to many bettors, and so, in an attempt to increase the amount of money bet on the event, a handicap is offered.

In this case, the handicap would be minus 7. This means that you are offered the chance to place (usually multiples of $110 to win $100) a wager on New England winning by more than seven, or Tennessee losing by less than seven (thus including the possibility of them winning or tying the match). In North America, should New England win the match by exactly seven points, all wagers are usually refunded. When European (especially British) books took up this idea, they added the concept of the "tie handicap," meaning that you can bet on the game ending with New England winning by exactly seven points. This generally makes the bet a worse proposition and increases the hold of the bookmaker. In this case, if you were to bet minus 7 or +7, and the result finished at seven points, your bet would be considered lost.

In Asia, the concept of the Asian Handicap was founded, especially for soccer. This differs from the usual handicap in that it allows for the possibility of splitting your stake between two selections on a single bet. For bettors not used to this proposition it can be confusing, as in a game with binary scoring opportunities like soccer, the difference between a bet on Under 2.5 and Under 2.75 is not immediately obvious. The calculation that takes place in this situation is that if you bet Under 2.75, half of your stake is placed on Under 2.5, with the remainder being placed on Under 3, with both halves of the bet taking the advertised odds or juice.

Forms of Gambling

Gambling is generally divided into three broad categories. The first of these is casino games, the second is sports betting, and the third noncasino games. While there is inevitably some crossover between the first and the third, the method of play is likely to be different; for example, if a player is acting as the bank in a standard casino game played outside such a venue, then players usually alternate so that the house advantage is eliminated, and the game instead depends on elements of luck and possibly skill.

Casino gaming includes the majority of popular games associated with gambling. Among these are games in which it is possible to gain a player advantage (so as to be profitable) and those in which the house edge is impossible to overcome. Examples of the former are Blackjack, Poker, Slots, and Video Poker, subject to their payout tables and jackpots. Examples of casino gaming where it is not possible to overcome the house advantage include Baccarat, Roulette, Craps, Casino War, and similar games. There also exists a gray area here, with some arguing that, for example, Roulette can be beaten with wheel bias calculations or devices featuring magnets, and that craps can be beaten by using a technique known as "dice setting." The former is illegal in the majority of venues, while the latter has yet to be proven over a large sample, but it is worth considering that gamblers are always developing new methods to attempt to beat these games, as the payoff on doing so is likely to be substantial.

Sports betting is offered both in casinos (for example, in Las Vegas) and in dedicated venues (as is more often found in European countries like the United Kingdom). It encompasses betting on both horses and sporting events. In the United States and some other countries, horse and greyhound racing are usually offered on a parimutuel (or "tote") basis, whereby all bets are entered into a pool and, barring notable exceptions (such as a short-priced favorite that would otherwise have a payout below a state-defined minimum), the house hold is guaranteed. In Europe, and more recently in Australia, horse and greyhound racing are more commonly found contemporarily in fixed odds betting, as is the case with all other sporting events. This form of betting in recent years also includes events other than sports; for example, betting on politics and reality television or other notable events, and has expanded to include betting exchanges, where customers are able to place bets against each other, with the "house" taking a commission, often meaning players are able to bet into a 105 percent market as opposed to a 117 percent market.

Noncasino betting refers to those games more often played outside of licensed venues. These include games such as most card games, coin games, carnival games, and dice games such as Backgammon. These vary greatly by country; for example, in the United Kingdom, card games such as Whist and Rummy are popular gambling pastimes, while in Greece and Cyprus, Backgammon is more popular.

The other item worth considering here is arbitrage. This basically refers to the betting of all outcomes to ensure a profit, and is possible where the market, when considering all service providers offering a price to bet on a given event, sums to less than 100 percent. If you are able to bet into a 95 percent market for example, and stake your bets correctly, you would return approximately 5 percent of your initial stake as profit, regardless of the outcome of the event upon which your wagers were staked.

Psychology of Gambling

The majority of people gamble for entertainment. While they may enter the gambling session intending or hoping to leave with a profit, there are only a few who actually achieve this consistently, and then often only by using techniques that differ greatly from those utilized by the casual gambler. It is possible to unite the two approaches, however, by utilizing the economic principle of utility. Economists argue that any form of production (that is, the creation of anything, be it physical or emotional) requires the satisfaction of wants. It can thus be argued that whether valuables are at stake or not, the playing of a game is always a form of productive experience.

The professional gambler also receives satisfaction, but for those players the satisfaction tends to come from defeating the bookmaker or other players in the form of parimutuel betting or betting exchanges, resulting in a long-term profit for the player (even professional gamblers will lose in many short-term sessions because of mathematical variance. These players win in the long term as their often small advantage comes to the fore over a larger sample. In many cases, these players may not gain satisfaction from playing the game or taking part in the activity, even while playing in the same context as the casual players discussed above.

Gamblers join the individual gaming session out of their own free will and decide the size of the stakes that they bet. Gambling comprises a cyclical chain of events that move from a process of decision making to the placement of a wager, a resulting outcome that generates an emotional reaction and cognitive appraisal of one's actions within the context of the gamestate. In games where players can pull out after any round, there is, at this point, a decision to stay or leave the game (permanently or otherwise). If the player stays, the process is repeated again. The frequency of this cycle depends on the game being played or wagered on. Gambling is often thought of as a form of recreation, while to others it represents a source of regular income. For the majority, gambling is a controlled, willful activity, but there is a proportion of gamblers for which it becomes a source of addiction.

Gambling involves a social and competitive component. In card and board games there is an opponent, in casino games the dealer, at the race track the other betters, horses, and jockeys. Gambling also affords people the opportunity to brag about their prowess in front of others. Igor Kusyszyn frames gambling as a ritualistic activity where each game is programmed, yet the program is fluid and allows for variations among the ritualistic moves. The uncertainty of the event generates an element of risk that can lead to cognitive, emotional, and physical arousal of the individual. He also claims that gambling creates the sense of a safe environment, free from real failures and social punishment, and leaves the gambler in a comfortable state.

Gamblers tend to experience a heightened sense of arousal during the game involving an increase in heartrate and muscle tension. This arousal can be experienced as both positive and negative emotions, such as excitement, hope, joy, euphoria, fear, anxiety, nervousness, stress, sorrow, or despair. It further creates emotional states ranging from pride and self-esteem to guilt, anger, and at times even hostility, which can, in some cases, be externalized to other people—a spouse, other gamblers, jockeys, trainers, a quarterback, and so forth. All in all, gambling can be an emotionally intense activity, involving a wide range of emotions.

Gambling behavior can also be described through the psychological concept of "operant conditioning." In operant conditioning, a behavior is maintained through its consequences. Thus, a gambling activity that leads to winning a prize is likely to maintain the gambling behavior. Similarly, the excitement and heightened emotional arousal during gambling can itself be enough for the gambler to motivate the gambler to keep gaming. Naturally, gambling also often leads to negative consequences such as the loss of money or other valuables. For some, the loss of money can serve as a form of punishment for future gambling, as the person becomes intent on winning his or her money back.

Problem Gambling

Some gamblers may have limited control over their gambling behavior. Problem gambling (ludomania) thus involves an urge to gamble despite negative consequences and a desire to stop. Whether gambling is a problem or not depends on the consequences it has upon the gambler's life rather than the actual gambling behavior per se. Common negative consequences of problem gambling include loss of money and personal belongings, negative consequences for family members, loss of friends, loss of self-esteem, and depression. Severe cases of problem gambling can be viewed as a form of mental disorder, referred to as "pathological gambling." Pathological gambling was recognized as a mental disorder with the publication of the *Diagnostical Statistical Manual IV* (DSM-IV). Although the term *gambling addiction* is often used in popular parlance, pathological gambling is generally considered to share more similarities to impulse control disorders than addiction disorders, but it has also been shown to share similarities with both. Research has shown that pathological gamblers produce lower levels of norepinephrine than non-gamblers. From this perspective, gambling can be seen as an addiction based on increases in norepinephrine levels during the gambling process.

Toneatto describes a number of cognitive distortions observed among problem gamblers, such as the magnification of gambling skills, minimization of other gambler's skills, superstitious beliefs, anthromorophism, illusion of control over luck, temporal telescoping, reframing of losses, and interpretive biases.

A common form of interpretive bias is known as "the gambler's fallacy." The gambler's fallacy is the mistaken belief that the occurrence of an event or outcome decreases the probability of that event or outcome happening again in the near future. For example, if a coin is tossed repeatedly, and one side comes up many more times than the other, the gambler is likely to believe that this yields a greater chance for the other side of the coin to come up in the future. Thus, the gambler's fallacy involves making false predictions about future events based on a short-term sequence of random events.

See Also: Baccarat; History of Playing Cards; Parlor Games; Play as Entertainment, Psychology of.

Bibliography. Igor Kusyszyn, "The Psychology of Gambling," *Annals of the American Academy of Political and Social Science* (v.474, 1984); Marilyn Lancelot, *Gripped by Gambling* (Wheatmark, 2007); Tony Toneatto, "Cognitive Psychopathology of Problem Gambling," *Substance Use & Misuse* (v.34/11, 1999).

Gordon Calleja
Darryl Woodford
IT-University of Copenhagen

Gamesmanship

Sports, while having many goals, maintain winning as the most important goal. Indeed, winning as the primary function is written into the rules of many sports. This is evidenced by examining the objectives of various sports: In basketball, the team who scores more points in a certain timeframe wins the game; in tennis, the player or doubles team who wins the designated number of games and sets before the opponent does wins; and in baseball and softball, the team that scores the most runs in defined innings while also preventing the opposing team from scoring wins. Many other rules exist in sports that dictate how the sport is to be played to reach the primary objective of winning. And, while some rules are updated and clarified, it is impossible to have rules in place for every possible action that may occur within a sport. When athletes play or coaches act within the rules of the game, but in a questionable manner in an attempt to increase their chances at winning, they are engaging in gamesmanship.

Defining Gamesmanship

Gamesmanship is a concept that many who are familiar with sport know and understand, but it is difficult to specifically define. Most agree that actions that bend or push the rules but do not break them in an attempt to gain favorable advantage constitute gamesmanship. In gamesmanship, players or teams may introduce some type of "game playing" to gain an advantage in the real game. These actions typically occur within the rules of the game or are not directly covered by the rules, and thus they are not in violation of rules. It is important to distinguish gamesmanship from cheating. When someone cheats, they typically are breaking rules in an attempt to gain an edge. Those engaging in gamesmanship are typically not breaking rules; they are playing within the rules to try to gain some advantage by exercising actions that may either push the limits of the rules or not be directly addressed by the rules of the game. At its most basic, gamesmanship is a psychological strategy to gain an advantage. While it may involve actions taken on either a physical or psychological level, the intent is to psychologically impact the opponent to gain the advantage.

The main purpose of gamesmanship is to increase the chances of winning. This is done in several ways, which tend to play out psychologically as well as physically. A common gamesmanship strategy is to attempt

Some argue that the line between gamesmanship and cheating has been blurred in recent years.

to disrupt the flow of the game, either by distracting the opponents or by trying to intimidate them. An example of this would be a tennis player mimicking the routine of her opponent or questioning an opponent's call even though the call was obviously correct. In many other sports, instances abound of players taking time at inopportune times. Some of these instances are intentionally done to impact the opponents, and thus the attempt is to disrupt the flow of the game.

Types of Gamesmanship

Another way gamesmanship is evidenced is when players or teams interact with opponents in such a way as to give them a false impression of either their interest in the activity or their ability. For example, it is not uncommon for sport participants to compliment their opponents on their stellar play and natural abilities in the course of play as a way of presenting the impression that the opponent must be more skilled than the participant. The participant's goal is to get the opponent thinking about his/her skill level as being superior to the participant's and then hoping that the opponent spends unnecessary thought on this difference and how it is playing out in the current competition. Another example is when a player asks the opponent, during the course of the competition, for his or her advice about a particular style of play or type of competitor. Finally, some competitors will simply try to discount the value they place on winning the event, instead making sure their opponent knows they simply enjoy being on the same court or field with said opponent.

Another type of gamesmanship involves acting in a way that is contrary to typical and accepted actions in the sport. In American football, where toughness and masculinity are often admired, acting in a manner that would give the opponents an impression of weakness or femininity might be attempted to "psych out" or throw off an opponent. In another example, a basketball team may not engage in pregame warm-ups in an attempt to get the opponents thinking about the team's motives. That is, the opponents may start to give undue attention to the whereabouts of their opponents, rather than focusing on the warm-up. And then they may question why their opponents may not be warming up, wondering if it is a function of the value they place on the game or on their abilities as competitors.

Gamesmanship can vary with the type of sport being played, as well. Consider how the line between gamesmanship and cheating may be different based on whether a sports event is officiated by players themselves or by an officiating staff. In a self-officiated sporting event, players are responsible for calling rules violations on self and others. A deliberate rule violation with the intent of gaining competitive advantage in this situation would clearly constitute cheating.

But consider a similar situation in an officiated event (that is, when a coach or team deliberately violates a rule in an attempt to gain an advantage); in this case, it can be argued that rather than cheating, this constitutes gamesmanship, as the officials are the ones responsible for maintaining a fair and competitive environment. If they fail to do so, it is their responsibility, not the coach's or team's. Indeed, some argue that this line between cheating and gamesmanship is blurred. When a coach or team attempts to reassign responsibility to someone in charge, actions that might previously have been deemed cheating are now considered gamesmanship. An example of this would be when in basketball, the ball goes out of bounds on Team A, thus rendering possession to Team B. Team A takes a time-out, and upon returning to the floor before Team B, sends a player over to inbound the ball from the official. If the official does not catch the error, the ball is awarded incorrectly to Team A, and they maintain possession.

Rules and Customs

Some sports, in addition to having rules that dictate play, also have written codes that are designed to eliminate gamesmanship or at least specify specific customs and practices in the sport that in part help to eliminate gamesmanship. Tennis, for example, publishes "the Code," in addition to the rules of the sport. The U.S. Tennis Association indicates that the Code is needed as many instances beyond the specific rules arise in the game of tennis, and the Code dictates fair play based on custom and tradition. Many other sports specify codes of conduct for coaches and athletes. While many of these codes are focused on maintaining ethical behavior in sport, some also focus on eliminating gamesmanship.

Although it is difficult to say conclusively who tends to engage in gamesmanship, the argument can be made that typically, the team or athlete who perceives they do not have the skills or who is in the process of losing may be more likely to engage in gamesmanship. That is not to say that every team or individual who finds themselves behind will engage in gamesmanship, but it is in this instance where it is more likely to occur. Also, unless there is a previous history of intense competition or perceived gamesmanship or cheating with a particular opponent, it seems unlikely that a team would engage in gamesmanship prior to the start of competition. Most individuals and teams strive to win on the merits of their ability, rather than on the psychological impact of gamesmanship. However, in cases where it becomes clear that ability may not be enough, some choose to engage in gamesmanship in an attempt to meet the overall goal of winning.

See Also: Athletics (Amateur); "Bad" Play; Diplomacy; Play as Competition, Psychology of.

Bibliography. Leslie A. Howe, "Gamesmanship," *Journal of the Philosophy of Sport* (v.31/2, 2004); Angela Lumpkin, Sharon Kay Stoll, Jennifer M. Beller, *Sport Ethics: Applications for Fair Play* (McGraw-Hill, 1999); Stephen Potter, *The Theory and Practice of Gamesmanship, or The Art of Winning Games without Actually Cheating* (H. Holt, 1948); United States Tennis Association, *The Code* (USTA, 2008); Jerry Jaye Wright, "Gamesmanship or Cheating: How Far Should Coaches Go to Gain an Edge?" *Strategies* (v.6/3, 1992);

Jessie Daw
Northern State University

Games of Deception

Interpersonal deception is by tradition focused on the framework of a physical world, where there exists ethical principles that have been developed over a long time to restrain a person's actions. For example, truth is expected when dealing with people in everyday life. If someone is found to not be truthful, they are said to be lying, and their integrity comes into question, which can undermine relationships.

Lying happens in a dynamic interaction where the liar and the listener tap dance around one another, changing their thoughts in reaction to each other's moves. Lying behavior includes, but is not limited to, manipulating information to distance themselves from the message, so if the message is found to be false, they can extricate themselves. Thus, they use vague generalities and talk about other people or strategically control behavior to suppress signals that might indicate that they are lying. For example, their face may be more impassive and body more rigid. Other examples are image management, by smiling and nodding more, and omission, not exactly lying but keeping information from another person.

If you observe children who have discovered the ease of lying, they blame their siblings, put on their best "innocent" expression, and hold their hands behind their backs. At that age they are very impressionable and learn quickly. Before long they can pull the wool over their parent's eyes very well. Lying is a form of deception, but in what medium it is used subjectively makes it good or bad.

For instance, lying to one's mother's face is not considered to be good, while distorting your image online is considered not so bad. In person, lying or deception is subjectively seen as a lack of integrity and not a virtue. In the virtual world, in military war, and in strategy games such as Chess, deception may be the key to winning the game, battle, or war. In military war, this may be called a feint on the battlefield or possibly psychological operations to convince the enemy to focus their actions elsewhere.

Solid strategy and tactics usually require a certain amount of deception. They also require sacrifice, as pawns are called pawns for a reason. Deception can promote strategic planning and tactics—attempting to make your opponent think you are doing one thing when you are really trying to do another. A good example would be a sacrifice that you try to make look like a mistake rather than a clever ploy. It promotes the development of thoughtful planning and thinking abstractly in advance of a well-thought-out action. Deception is used in martial arts, military strategy, and play.

One game that has a long association with deception for its believers is the Ouija Board. The Ouija Board is commonly used as a game or as a way to attempt to communicate with a deceased loved one. Some users believe that demons lay in wait to gauge the vulnerability of the player and then deceive them by answering correctly. While the player may become convinced that a loved one is talking to them, the belief is that a demon could slowly work its way into the person, eventually gaining full control of their physical being. This thinking holds that "evil demons" pretend to be cooperative ghosts in order to trick participants into becoming spiritually possessed. The possession would not happen overnight but over a period of time as the demon tests the waters of their subject, and as the person gets more and more comfortable. Those who subscribe to such beliefs fear that as the entity applies more and more pressure, complete self control will be lost.

In a virtual world, such an expectation of truth is more flexible than in reality. For example, in some online games, it is acceptable for a player to win or to gain reward by deception, which does not contravene our moral standards.

Second Life

One game that allows users to play with deception is Second Life. Since its establishment in 2003, Second Life has turned out to be an explosive global phenomenon. It is inhabited by well over 5 million virtual residents. One of the odd things about Second Life is the ease with which one can, in various ways, shade the truth or flat-out lie. In a mostly text world, with avatars that type what one tells them to and blush, smile, and frown on cue, the listener is extremely dependent on the speaker for body language, which can be misleading, either because of self deception, or actual intent to deceive. Combine the ability to create multiple avatars, the lack of any tie between an avatar's appearance and real life, and the opportunity for confusion, and deception increases.

Almost every resident in Second Life approaches the balance between being a perfect copy of themselves and a created persona that is different. Some people exist as digital duplicates with avatars that closely mimic real life. Some chose avatars that are wildly different from their real-life appearance. Likewise, the role and persona people project varies wildly. Some immerse themselves in a role, to the point where they do not exhibit any connection to their real-life existence. There is also a teen version of the game in which teenagers can meet and create their own worlds, but it is more social in nature.

Tecmo Games

The Deception games are a series of console strategy role-playing games (RPGs) created and published by Tecmo for Sony's line of PlayStation consoles that have an emphasis on passive combat via the use of traps. There are currently four games in the franchise, Deception: Invitation to Darkness, Kagero: Deception II, Deception III: Dark Delusion, and Trapt. Deception is an action game with RPG elements, resembling the full motion video (FMV) genre of games, particularly Sega CD, such as Night Trap and Double Switch. The primary object of the series is to dispatch intruders through the positioning and activation of traps. What makes Deception so innovative is that moral judgment comes heavily into play. There is also a Chess Kombat Mode that allows players to partake in a game of Chess-like strategy.

The player takes on the role of an unjustly executed person who pleads to the devil to spare his life at the moment of his demise. The devil (explicitly referred to as Satan in the manual) grants his request and gives him command over the Castle of the Damned. Soon after the player takes over control of the castle, many visitors soon find themselves drawn to the new home—some for power, some for salvation, and some for something as simple as shelter.

The player (sometimes) has the option of either destroying the intruders or letting them escape, but both choices carry consequences; for example, the player may choose to either kill the parents who are out to find a cure for their ailing daughter, or let them escape to inform others of the demonic presence invading the mansion. Additionally, killing intruders is sometimes the only way to proceed and gain more Magic Points (earned by taking the victims' souls) or Gold (earned by killing the victims).

Game play is carried out by using a three-dimensional representation of the character. Traps can then be activated and set up within varied rooms of the castle and created before each respective level. The story can also take various paths depending on the choices the player makes.

Tecmo's Deception: Invitation to Darkness contains the following character descriptions:

Satan: Your sole existence in this game is to ensure the resurrection of this evil lord and to obtain his dark power. You must first make an unholy covenant with the devil in order to become the Master of the Castle.

Astarte: Satan's Messenger—she is the right hand of Satan who spared your life in its dying moments.

Souls: As you seek to revive Satan, you capture uninvited castle invaders and excavate their precious souls. Upon sacrificing their obtained souls, you must choose to exchange the value of their soul for magic or for money, or retain their carcass for your own diabolical monster creations.

Intruders: They may come for many reasons: some come to take your place as Master of the Castle, while others come to seek to rid the dark force of evil occupying their homeland. All of them want you dead.

Unrest: A once-united Kingdom of two differing nations grows restless. The sword-wielding nation of Angelio and the magically powerful nation of Zemekia had peacefully emerged from a war-ridden past.

Yurias: King of Zemekia, and your brother, who plotted the death of your father and framed you for it. He has seized the throne and your fiancée.

Fiana: Princess of Angelio—she is your beloved fiancée, who is unwillingly held by your brother.

Ardebaran: Contractor—he is the current Master of the Castle of the Damned. He will be your first enemy test. Defeat him to become new master.

Kagero: Deception II shifts the perspective to third-person and emphasizes trap combos. This iteration of the series formed the basis of current Deception titles and would be built upon in future titles, coming out two years after its predecessor. In it, players assume the role of Millennia, a young girl being used as a puppet and guard for a race known as Timenoids (or TMD, as the game abbreviates their race's name), who are like humans except immortal, and whose power is desired by the humans whose lives they govern. Millennia finds herself in the middle of the war between her own race and her captors, with her chosen side dictated by the player. One of the endings to the game heavily implies that Kagero is a prequel to Tecmo's Deception, and that Millennia will grow up to become Astarte from the first game; this interpretation is supported by the fact that naming the main character in Kagero "Astarte" lets you start with a hefty sum of extra Ark (the game's currency). However, Tecmo has not made it clear if that ending is canon.

Deception III: Dark Delusion expanded on the gameplay of Kagero by introducing a training mode, a mission mode, and trap enhancement through a series of crests and other artifacts. In the main story mode, players control Reina, a girl who, with her adoptive family, has been kidnapped and brought to the land of Burgenhagen to be sold into slavery. Reina must use the trapping powers she acquired to defeat her kidnappers and solve the mysteries of the pendant she wears, which other people seem to covet for unknown reasons.

In Trapt, players now control Princess Allura, a maiden who runs away from her kingdom after being framed for the murder of her father, and who enters into a similar demonic contract with a being known only as Fiend to get revenge on her pursuers. This game, aside from being the first entry on a next-generation system, utilized what were known as Dark Illusions—specialty traps that were contained within the room of any given castle, and that required a special sequence of triggers in order to be used, with the payoff being greater damage done to the invaders and a generally more spectacular presentation.

Furthermore, at certain points in the storyline, side stories could be explored that presented some alternate scenarios from the main plotline, providing more back-story on the game's events. Included in the game's menu was a Survival Mode, which pitted Allura against waves of invaders with only nine traps at her disposal—three ceilings, three walls, and three floors. Creating new traps necessitated the spending of Warl, like Ark and Dreak before it, and was done similarly to Kagero through the use of a logical tree. Secret traps and settings could be purchased with Warl by finishing the game and unlocking the three endings, collecting preset amounts of Ark, or by killing all encountered invaders.

Mortal Kombat

Another game that uses deception is Mortal Kombat. Mortal Kombat: Deception precedes Shaolin Monks (in release date only) and follows Deadly Alliance. Deception was released in two versions for PlayStation 2 and Xbox. The regular version for both systems, a Premium Pack for PlayStation 2, and Kollector's Edition for Xbox, both added a metal trading card and a bonus disc containing a history of Mortal Kombat, several video biographies of characters, and an "arcade perfect" version of the original Mortal Kombat.

The game is known as Mortal Kombat Mystification in France. Deception adds Chess Kombat and Puzzle Kombat game modes. Chess Kombat is similar to classical Chess, but uses player-selected characters as pieces, and pieces must engage in Kombat to take a piece (much like the 1980s computer game Archon). Puzzle Kombat is reminiscient of Super Puzzle Fighter II Turbo, a puzzle game by Capcom. The character roster for Puzzle Kombat is Scorpion, Baraka, Nightwolf, Ermac, Sindel, Sub-Zero, Bo' Rai Cho, Kenshi, Mileena, Jade, Kabal, and Raiden. Deception has highly interactive stages, with multiple levels, arena-specified weapons, breakable boundaries, and instant-death traps. Characters can no longer be slammed against walls, however. Deception also has a Combo Breaker system that allows players to interrupt combos up to three times per match. Weapon impalements are no longer in the game because of the introduction of death traps. Deception characters have two Fatalities and a *hara-kiri* suicide move.

Characters are more specialized as well, boasting unique (though sometimes held over from Deadly Alliance) throws, finishing poses, and rises after losing one round (e.g., Sub-Zero shoots ice to the floor to lift himself up, etc.). Deception is the first game in the series to assume that the "good guys" lost the battle of the previous game. The character Noob-Smoke switches character models instead of fighting styles (Noob fights with monkey style, Smoke with Mi Tzu), with no weapons style. They are playable after unlocking and appear in Arcade Mode as sub-bosses. Deception is the first Mortal Kombat to feature an extensive online mode. The GameCube version has Noob-Smoke, Jade, Li Mei, Kira, Hotaru, and Havik as already unlocked characters and Shao Kahn and Goro as playable characters; however, it does not support online mode. Deception marks the return of Stage Fatalities, which were absent in Deadly Alliance.

Games of deception come in many forms, from board games like Chess to virtual environments like Second Life and Mortal Kombat. The virtual world makes it easier for one to use deceptive maneuvers.

See Also: Age of Empires; "Bad" Play; Costumes in Play; Dragon Quest; Dragon Warrior; Dungeon Lords; *Dungeons & Dragons*; Fantasy Play; Gambling; Gamesmanship; Hide & Seek; Human Relationships in Play; Mortal Kombat; Ouija Board; Play as Mock War, Psychology of; Play as Mock War, Sociology of; Play as Rehearsal of Reality; Playground as Politics; Poker and Variations of; Pretending; Role-Playing; Sex Play; Street Fighter I and II; Street Games; Theology of Play; War; World of Warcraft.

Bibliography. Joey Cuellar, *Mortal Kombat?: Deception Official Strategy Guide* (Brady Games, 2004); Bruce Pandolfini, *ABC's of Chess* (Simon & Schuster Adult Publishing Group, 1986); Michael Rymaszewski, *Second Life: The Official Guide*, (Sybex, 2008); Amy Weber, *Creating Your World: The Official Guide to Advanced Content Creation for Second Life* (Sybex, 2007).

Miriam D. Dufer
Old Dominion University

Game Theory

This article presents general historical information on game theory and represents this topic in what is hoped to be language that is easily understandable to lay people without any prior knowledge of this subject. Also, there are explanatory definitions of general principles involved that have been developed in this field and further explorations of game theory attributes. Basic mathematics behind game theory are briefly touched on in a way that does not require too much technical knowledge for understanding how it works. For further clarification, examples are provided with some figures that demonstrate the applicability of game theory to various life circumstances.

Many may hear the words *game theory* and think that the term is referring to theories of game playing. However, this is not necessarily true, as game theory is about particular aspects of interactions between individuals or animals as they strive to achieve the ultimate outcomes from specific events. We often play "what if" games without being actively aware that we are doing so. Many everyday events can stimulate us to play "Chess matches" involving possible scenarios that depend on our actions in some combination with another party, and there definitely are different results on different occasions. Although this article appears in the *Encyclopedia of Play in Today's Society* and the implementation of game theoretical principles is certainly enjoyable and evokes playful qualities in human minds (at least that can be known), game theory is not simply about games that are played. It is about logical mathematical applications to strategic considerations of conflict scenarios involving player entities (both human and other animals), a method of determining a maximum benefit (or payoff) from the conflict for one or more of the players (via payoff matrices), and theoretical as well as literal implications of such episodes.

Game theory allows us to use formal logic to explain what is not typically discernable but is reliably true. Quite often, an individual who attempts to maximize his or her payoff must also simultaneously minimize the other player's payoff. According to David Barash, professor of psychology and zoology at the University of Washington, it might be said that the existence of other people who compete for similar interests that we want necessitates the reason for having game theory. Essentially, in game theory, players must necessarily account for not only their own interests but also others' behavior.

Formal Study of Game Theory

Game theory is actually the academic conceptualization of behavioral phenomena in strategic situations, typically accounted for by mathematical methods of logic. The formal study of game theory has been occurring since the publishing of John von Neumann and Oskar Morgenstern's 1944 book, *Theory of Games and Economic Behavior*. Game theory is generally considered in the domain of applied mathematics, but it is also primarily applicable to economics, biology, computer science, philosophy, and political science. There are numerous important features of game theory. Historically, game theory has been used by nuclear strategists, notably at the think tank RAND Corporation in California, to rationally calculate potential Cold War scenarios that approached perilous and realistic outcomes for the entire world. Additionally, David Barash mentions in *The Survival Game: How Game Theory Explains the Biology of Cooperation and Competition* that biologists and psychologists have been and continue to be able to model and predict the behavior of living things, and in particular more recent extensions to evolutionary strategies. Anatol Rapoport idealistically suggested in *Fights, Games and Debates* that game theory could contribute the most benefit to humanity by facilitating self-improvement and self-knowledge. Therefore, it may be important to become skilled in effectively managing conflict without violence.

Although extensive scholarly literature has been produced on game theory, the general public has not yet fully realized what it actually is. Paul Walker in the *History of Game Theory* lists two recent instances of public notoriety, albeit still possibly not considered in the "mainstream" media, that have occurred in which game theory was prominently displayed. In 1994, the Nobel Prize in economic sciences was awarded to John Nash, John C. Harsanyi, and Reinhard Selten "for their pioneering analysis of equilibria in the theory of noncooperative games." In 2005, the Nobel Prize in economic sciences was awarded to Robert J. Aumann and Thomas C. Schelling "for having enhanced our understanding of conflict and cooperation through game-theory analysis." Game theory oversimplifies reality, in particular where cooperation and competition are involved, and enhances mathematicians' ability to make a tractable analysis.

Game Theory Models

Making simple models to represent complex phenomena facilitates the process of determining answers to our speculations. In 1950, John Nash proved that every finite game, involving any number of players, has at least one (Nash) equilibrium, though there might not be any that involve only pure strategies for all players. When there is more than one equilibrium, and players cannot make binding agreements, they must try to coordinate to arrive at an equilibrium outcome. Many other criteria for equilibrium selection have been studied (e.g., focal points, subgame perfection, stability, and so on). An outcome is *Pareto optimal* (or *efficient*) if no agent can be made better off than that outcome without making another agent worse off.

There are zero-sum games, in which one player maximizes his or her payoff at the expense of the other player's payoff being minimized. Also, there are non-zero-sum games, in which there may be a joint benefit that emerges out of a conflict situation. Alternatively, there may be a joint loss that occurs for players who decided to act in certain ways that are counterproductive to their own interests, for example, in certain formulations of the classic Prisoner's Dilemma. Therefore, there are different types of strategic situations occurring with different interactions between players or agents. Consequently, other game theoretical approaches consider subjective probabilities that attempt to determine non-zero-sum solutions, whereby individuals proceed in a subjective way of estimating probable choices of others. This essentially enables individuals to reduce strategic interactions to a traditional single-agent decision scenario.

In game theory, rational behavior is assumed to enhance the opportunity for the most preferred payoff. Of course, the other player is simultaneously working toward that as well. Game theory does not care how the payoffs are ranked, just how rational the actions are. It must be noted that game theory is not concerned with the rationality of the value (or utility) undertaken, just in the most effective method. Consequently, even a player who intentionally loses a game gets his or her highest payoff because the criterion for his or her utility was determined to be met. The problem occurring with this phenomenon is that rational individuals must account for others' probable choices, which are also contingent on their choices as well.

The Prisoner's Dilemma

It is important to understanding game theory to briefly describe the following classic scenario. In a two-player, one-shot Prisoner's Dilemma, players can either plead guilty or not guilty to a crime (and both are actually guilty by the evidence). When both plead guilty, this results in the most jail time for each player. When both refuse to plead guilty, they receive the least jail time. One player pleading guilty and implicating the other will result in no jail time for that player, while the implicated player (who still pleads not guilty) will receive the greatest possible sentence. Typically, in this case, game theory rationality induces mutual defection, whereby both players (i.e., "potential" prisoners) are "suckered" in to a less desirable outcome because they suspect the other one will defect first. The Prisoner's Dilemma is just that, a dilemma. In this scenario, two players can either both benefit with the highest payoff (both pleading not guilty), both achieve the lowest payoff (both pleading guilty), or one of them benefits while the other does not (one pleads guilty while the other pleads not guilty). However, individuals' concepts of reality are not fixed. In an iterated Prisoner's Dilemma problem, players subjectively weigh a present advantage against possible future losses. Of course, this brings to mind an oft-repeated aphorism, "A bird in the hand is worth two in the bush."

There are numerous variations to two-player phenomena. The utility (or value) players place on outcomes affects what payoff (or gain) is ultimately the best in their given situation. When another player is considering the likelihood of your decision, which often is in complete opposition to his or her own preference, the resulting conflict provides an opportunity for a payoff. John von Neumann did demonstrate mathematically in *Theory of Games and Economic Behavior* that when two players interests are in complete opposition, there is always a rational course of action.

Other Game Scenarios

In other scenarios, similar interests are desirable. For example, those who are considering becoming short-term investors in the stock market have to decide if the given stock will be likely to appeal to other investors and lead them to buy stock and concomitantly increase the stock value. A player's objective is to maximize his or her long-term expected payoff. Learning takes place at each stage. The theory for determining maximum utility emanates from the Nash Equilibrium theorem that a set of actions has the property of no player being able to profitably deviate from that given course of action, given the actions of other players (i.e., no player has an alternative course of action that increases their payoff).

A point can be made that game theory acknowledges the other player's viewpoint, which is a separate matter from ascribing to their ideological position. Barash also intimates that sometimes being able to predict particular behavior can influence or cause it to actually occur, in what can be called a self-fulfilling prophecy. This has been referred to as the security dilemma in national security analysis. It is interesting that the Romans had a motto of *Si vis pacem para bellum* (if you want peace, prepare for war), which accounted for the longevity of their empire, until they forgot to think about the other players in the scenario and were sacked by invaders. Per game theory, conflict is very likely and usually inevitable.

Game theory is not concerned with the ethics or moralizing of who profits the most and who loses. Barash states that different actions result in payoffs that differ. Individuals optimally strive for the highest possible payoff. However, some individuals value their consequences for particular actions differently and have changing payoffs. Moreover, even the most altruistic players derive a personal, or "selfish," benefit. As William Poundstone wrote, "Shortsighted rationality forces players to subvert the common good."

Definitions

We will define a *game* as having the following aspects:

- There are two or more players involved.
- One or more players make decisions from a certain number of options.
- One decision creates different situations that can affect who makes the next decision and the options available.
- The decisions made by each player may or may not be known by the other players.
- There is an ending point, i.e., the game does not continue forever.
- Each combination of decisions determines a payoff to each player.

There are three different ways in which game theory can be applied. The first application is exploring games on a purely theoretical level and examining the problems that directly arise from the development of game theory. The second application of game theory is analysis of strategic interactions with the purpose of predicting or explaining the actions of the people involved. The third application is analysis of the logical consistency of certain arguments.

Attributes of Game Theory

In this section, the basic concepts in game theory will be discussed. Many times in game theory, a payoff matrix is used to represent a game. A payoff matrix shows the possible strategies available to each player and the payoff, amount of money, points, et cetera, that each player receives for his choice, depending on what the other players do. As shown in Figure 1, this information is put into a matrix, in the form (C, R), where C is the payoff to Player 1 when he plays the C strategy and Player 2 plays the R strategy, and R is the payoff to Player 2 when he plays the R strategy and Player 1 plays the C strategy.

Figure 1

		Player 1	
		C_1	C_2
Player 2	R_1	(C_{11}, R_{11})	(C_{21}, R_{21})
	R_2	(C_{12}, R_{12})	(C_{22}, R_{22})

Definition: Let C_{ij} be the payoff to Player 1 when he uses his i^{th} strategy of his m total strategies and Player 2 uses his j^{th} strategy of his n total strategies. If $\max_{i£m} \min_{j£n} C_{ij} = \min_{j£n} \max_{i£m} C_{ij}$, then (i, j) is a saddle point.

The saddle point is the best that either player can do, given that his opponent is a rational player. In other words, a saddle point is the element of the game matrix that is both a maximum of the minimums of each row and a minimum of the maximums of each column. A game matrix may have no saddle points, one saddle point, or multiple saddle points. When a saddle point exists, it is equal to the value of the game (i.e., the best outcome that both players can guarantee).

Definition: A zero-sum, or strictly competitive, game is a game in which the interests of the parties are strictly contradictory.

In other words, a zero-sum game is a game where it is impossible for the players to benefit from cooperation. Zero-sum games are named for the fact that we can represent the payments so that the sum of the payments to the players is zero, i.e., $C_{ij} + R_{ij} = 0$, where C_{ij} and R_{ij} are the payoffs to Player 1 and Player 2, respectively, when Player 1 plays i and Player 2 plays j.

The following example illustrates the phenomenon of zero-sum games.

Example 1: Consider a two-person zero-sum game in which one player, the chooser, chooses even or odd, and the other player, the guesser, tries to guess what was chosen. The matrix for this game is shown in Figure 2 below.

Figure 2

		Chooser	
		Odd	Even
Guesser	Odd	(+1, -1)	(-1, +1)
	Even	(-1, +1)	(+1, -1)

In Example 1, since there does not exist a payoff for either player that is both a minimum of its row and a maximum of its column, we can see that there are no saddle points.

We note that in a zero-sum game, the payoff to Player 1 is the opposite of the payoff to Player 2.

Definition: A non-zero-sum, or non-strictly competitive, game is a game in which the interests of the parties involved are not strictly contradictory.

Games that are not zero-sum games are classified as non-zero-sum games. In a non-zero-sum game, it is possible for the players to benefit from cooperation.

Example 2: Consider the two-person non-zero-sum game that occurs when two people are trying to decide what to do. Becky and Blake are planning to go out to eat. They talked about it but did not have time to make a decision. In fact, the only thing decided was that Becky wants to go to the Pasta Place and Blake wants to go to the Local Diner. Both Becky and Blake would rather go to the other place together than to go to their choice alone.

Figure 3

		Blake	
		Pasta	Diner
Becky	Pasta	(1,2)	(-1,-1)
	Diner	(-1,-1)	(2,1)

This is a non-zero-sum game because both Becky and Blake would benefit from cooperating with each other. Becky would benefit from going to Local Diner with Blake over going to the Pasta Place by herself. Likewise, Blake would benefit from going to the Pasta Place with Becky over going to the Local Diner by himself.

Basic Mathematics Behind Game Theory

The first attempt to create a mathematical theory of strategy for games was made by Emile Borel in 1921. Although the mathematical theory of games did not receive attention until J. von Neumann and O. Morgenstern published their book *Theory of Games and Economic Behavior* in 1944, Neumann proved the fundamental theorem of game theory, the minimax theorem, in 1928.

The minimax theorem, which is used to analyze zero-sum games, says that an equilibrium pair exists when there is a strategy that is the best for Player 1, regardless of what Player 2 plays, and there is a strategy that is the best for Player 2, regardless of what Player 1 plays. The pair of these two strategies is called an equilibrium pair. When an equilibrium pair exists, it is the value, or solution, of the game.

To create a mixed, or randomized, strategy for Player 1, we need to determine what percentages of the time he should play each of his strategies. A mixed, or randomized, strategy is a probability distribution over the whole set of strategies of a player.

Example 3: Consider two people, Brandon and Tiffany. They both enjoy each other's company, but neither can communicate with the other before deciding whether to stay at home (where they would not see each other) or go to the beach this afternoon (where they *could* see each other). Each prefers going to the beach to being at home and prefers being with the other person rather than being apart. This game can be represented by the following matrix form:

Figure 4

		Tiffany	
		Home	Beach
Brandon	Home	(0,0)	(0,1)
	Beach	(1,0)	(2,2)

Each player has a set of strategies ([Home, Beach] for both players in this example). Specifying one strategy for the row player (Brandon) and one strategy for the column player (Tiffany) yields an outcome, which is represented as a pair of payoffs.

In this example, going to the beach is a (strictly) dominant strategy for each player, because it always yields the best outcome, no matter what the other player does. Thus, if the players are both maximizing their individual expected utilities, each will go to the beach. So (Beach, Beach) is a dominant strategy equilibrium for this game. Because of this, Tiffany and Brandon, if they are rational, do not need to cooperate (make an agreement) ahead of time. Each can just pursue their own interest, and the best outcome will occur for both.

Example 4: Now consider Kim and Derek. Derek likes Kim, but Kim does not like Derek that much. Each knows this, and neither wants to call the other before deciding what to do this afternoon: stay at their respective homes or go to the neighborhood swimming pool. Here is the matrix form:

Figure 5

		Derek: Home	Derek: Pool
Kim	Home	(2,0)	(2,1)
	Pool	(3,0)	(1,2)

In this case, Kim's best strategy depends on what Derek does. But if she assumes Derek is rational, she will reason that he will not stay home, because going to the pool is a dominant strategy for him. Knowing this, she can decide to stay home. This is called iterated dominance. In this example, Kim gets higher utility than Derek because of their relative preferences, and Derek gets less utility than he would have if Kim wanted to be with him. In this example, Pool-Home (3,0), Home-Pool (2,1), and Pool-Pool (1,2) are all Pareto optimal outcomes. The equilibrium outcomes in both this example and the previous one are Pareto optimal.

Example 5: This is the classic Prisoner's Dilemma problem. Consider Baxter and Jerry, two prisoners who have each been offered a deal to turn state's witness (defect) against the other. They cannot communicate. They had originally agreed to remain in solidarity, i.e., not testify against each other, but since the agreement cannot be enforced, each must choose whether to honor it. If both remain in solidarity, then they will each only be convicted of a minor charge. If only one defects, then the state will throw the book at the other and let the defector go. If they both defect, each will get convicted of a serious charge.

Figure 6

		Jerry: Solidarity	Jerry: Defection
Baxter	Solidarity	(3,3)	(1,4)
	Defection	(4,1)	(1,1)

In this game, the strategy of defection is weakly dominant for each player, meaning that whatever the other player does, defecting yields an outcome at least as good and possibly better than remaining in solidarity would. Note that if the bottom-right cell payoffs were (2,2) instead of (1,1), then defecting would be strictly dominant for each player. Either way, Defection-Defection is a dominant strategy equilibrium. However, it is not Pareto optimal. Both players could be made better off if neither defected against the other.

This is an example of a social dilemma: a situation in which each agent's autonomous maximization of self-utility leads to an inefficient outcome. Such a situation can occur for any number of people, not just two. An agreement by two people to trade with each other (involving goods, services, and/or money) sets up a Prisoner's Dilemma–type game whenever the agreement cannot be enforced.

Example 6: The example of Brandon and Tiffany is now revisited. They are going to the same conference, and each is expecting the other to be there, but they have not seen each other yet. Each has a choice of two activities for the first afternoon: swimming or hiking. They both hope to see each other (if they do not they will have no fun), and each prefers swimming over hiking. They must each decide what to do before knowing where the other is going.

Figure 7

		Tiffany: Swim	Tiffany: Hike
Brandon	Swim	(2,2)	(0,0)
	Hike	(0,0)	(1,1)

The best outcome is obviously Swim-Swim, but going swimming is not dominant for either player. Both Swim-Swim and Hike-Hike have the property that each player's strategy is the best (or tied for the best) response to the other player's strategy in that pairing. This defines a more general equilibrium notion called the Nash equilibrium. The dominance equilibria of examples 4-6 are all Nash equilibria as well.

A third equilibrium exists in this game involving what are called mixed strategies. A mixed strategy is a probability distribution over the pure strategies (which are Swim and Hike for each player in this example). Note that the players do not have to have the same set of strategies available to them, even though that has been the case in all the presented examples.

As has been shown, game theory is actually the academic conceptualization of behavioral phenomena in strategic situations, typically accounted for by mathematical methods of logic. There are numerous important features of game theory that have been discussed. This certainly has not be an exhaustive discussion of this topic, nor even close to the technical precision with which stalwart game theorists apply to various scenarios under study at any given point in time. Hopefully, however, this has been an enlightening introduction that informs even the passive reader of at least some of what game theory really involves.

See Also: Human Relationships in Play; Play as Learning, Psychology of; Psychoanalytic Theory and Play; Psychology of Play (Vygotsky).

Bibliography. David P. Barash, *The Survival Game* (Henry Holt, 2003); R. Duncan Luce and Howard Raffia, *Games and Decisions* (Wiley, 1957); William Poundstone, *Prisoner's Dilemma* (Doubleday, 1992); Anatol Rapoport, *Fights, Games and Debates* (University of Michigan Press, 1960); Don Ross, *Game Theory*, Stanford Encyclopedia of Philosophy, plato.stanford.edu/entries/game-theory (cited May 2008); John von Neumann and Oskar Morgenstern, *Theory of Games and Economic Behavior* (Princeton University Press, 1944); Paul Walker, *History of Game Theory*, www.econ.canterbury.ac.nz /personal_pages/paul_walker/ gt/hist.htm (cited May 2008).

Brandon K. Vaughn
Frank W. Roberts
University of Texas, Austin

Georgia

One of the republics in the Caucasus, Georgia was an independent kingdom in medieval times, but from the early 19th century, it has been part of the Russian Empire and then the Soviet Union. In 1991 Georgia regained its independence; it shares borders with the Russian Federation, Azerbaijan, Armenia, and Turkey. As a result, many of the influences in Georgia come from its neighbors—Chess from Russia, Backgammon from Turkey, and card games from nearby Iran. During the Middle Ages, the influence of the Byzantine Empire led to much mural painting, some of which survives in churches, as well as sculpture.

Many men were also interested in metalwork and leatherwork, not just as a means of income but also for personal use, the latter being important for a society that relied heavily on people being able to ride horses. The national sport played on horseback was *tskhenbourti*; and there were also games involving strength and prowess such as the local version of wrestling known as *tchidaoba*.

Local folklore was imparted through poetry, much of it in the Persian (Iranian) tradition, and also through storytelling and theatrical and other shows, some using marionette puppets, that took place at markets and on holidays. Dancing and playing music were also popular pastimes. During these markets at Tbilisi, the port of Sukhumi, and towns such as Kutaisi and Rastavi, new games would be introduced. In 1801, Eastern Georgia became a part of the Russian Empire, followed by the rest of the country in 1810. By the late 19th century, Russian schools were built throughout Georgia, and boys and girls there were involved in playing with many other children their own age. During his time at school in the 1880s and early 1890s, Joseph Stalin (then Josef Djugashvili) was involved in forays in the countryside, where he and other boys would play Brigands, the local version of Cowboys and Indians.

During Georgia's period as part of the Soviet Union, the Young Pioneers Movement organized regular camps, hiking groups, and retreats, and at these and most schools, children played Russian games, including many involving cards, Wargaming—especially World War II battles—and with toy cars and trains. Soccer has become popular, as has recreational basketball, boxing, handball, and gymnastics. There were skating rinks, funfairs, and places to play with dodge'em cars. The Puppet Theater in Tbilisi was a great attraction.

Since independence, there has been a rebirth in Georgian cultural identity. With Georgia close to the Republic of Kamlykia (which has remained a part of the Russian Federation), the center of world Chess, many Georgians still play Chess and Georgia has produced a number of leading world players such as Iuri Akobia, Maia Chiburdanidze, Roman Dzindzichashvili, and Baadur Jobava. The Chess Federation of Georgia did much to encourage the country's youth. As Georgia interacts more with other European countries, there has been far more interest in recreational soccer in the country. There is now a small Scout association, founded in 1997, that has involved boys and girls in hiking and camping.

See Also: Armenia; Chess and Variations of; Russia; Soccer (Amateur) Worldwide; Turkey.

Bibliography. Michael Axworthy, "The Persian Army of Nadir Shah," *Miniature Wargames* (March–May, 2002); Isaac Deutscher, *Stalin* (Penguin Books, 1966); Peter Nasmyth, *Georgia: In the Mountains of Poetry* (Palgrave Macmillan, 1998); Roger Rosen, *The Georgian Republic* (Odyssey, 1991).

Justin Corfield
Geelong Grammar School

Germany

A country in central Europe, with the largest population of any nation in the European Union, Germany has much in common with both western Europe (it shares a border with France) and eastern Europe (it is also bordered by the Czech Republic and Poland). Once the center of the Holy Roman Empire, later the center of the Protestant Reformation, and briefly divided between communist East Germany and capitalist West Germany, the country is rich in cultural traditions from many sources.

Germany has long been called "the land of poets and thinkers" and was home to composers Ludwig von Beethoven, Johann Sebastian Bach, and Richard Wagner, painters Albrecht Dürer and Max Ernst; and philosophers Immanuel Kant, Friedrich Nietzsche, and Karl Marx. But it is the Brothers Grimm, creators of collections of orally collected German folklore, who have been adopted by Western culture as a whole.

Despite this intellectual tradition and the heavy foods of Germany's cuisine, athletics are extremely popular. Almost half of the country plays sports regularly, in teams or individually, and most of that half belongs to a sports club. Germany also has the third-highest Olympic medal count in the world. Association football (soccer) is far and away the most popular spectator sport—the two sports leagues with the highest attendance in the world are both German soccer leagues—and this carries over into widespread amateur participation in schools, amateur leagues, and informal recreation.

Other popular spectator sports include volleyball, basketball, cricket, hockey, and tennis. Cricket is one of the oldest organized team sports in Germany, the first cricket club having been formed in 1850 by Americans and Britons who introduced the sport to Berliners. Despite this, it was always an obscure sport until the 1980s, when amateur and university cricket clubs began to catch on, a trend continuing through the 21st century. Rugby, introduced by British students, is a fast-growing sport among both spectators and participants. As basketball becomes more and more popular across Europe, German basketball's popularity is propelled by the success of Dirk Nowitski, now a Dallas Maverick and consistently one of the best players in the NBA. Where once German basketball teams were dominated by American players—aging professionals and former college stars—far more players are now native, having grown up playing the sport. Winter sports are popular, and the northern parts of the country receive plenty of snow, as, of course, do the Alps. Germany is the only country with four bobsled, luge, and skeleton tracks, two of which are over a century old.

The last century has seen a revival of interest in fencing worldwide, with which Germany has a strong history. Though the popular imagination associates fencing with France, the German school of fencing has enjoyed considerable attention. Developed during the Renaissance, the German school emphasizes efficiency and simplicity and was designed for the longsword rather than the rapier.

Germany has long had a liberal attitude toward homosexuality. Since 2007, Berlin has been home to the Respect Gaymes, a teen athletic event designed to raise awareness and promote tolerance. Teenagers of all sexual orientations compete in soccer, streetball, and martial arts, while workshops and exhibitions are offered in dance, theater, boxing, and hip hop. The centerpiece of the Gaymes is a celebrity soccer tournament, featuring athletes, entertainers, and politicians.

Germany has been a world leader in the development of toys. From Froebels blocks to the present day, German-made dolls (e.g., Zapf dolls) and engineering toys (e.g., Fisher Technic), have been trendsetters. Furthermore, festivals such as the Nurenberg festival bring together toy retailers from around the world.

Children's Games

A popular children's game in Germany is *Alle Vogel Vliegen* ("All Birds Fly"). Children sit in a circle, while the leader of the game says (usually as quickly as possible), "All birds fly, all dogs fly, all airplanes fly," and so on, naming various animals and other objects that might or might not fly. Although the leader flaps his arms after each object, the players are supposed to flap their arms only after things that really do fly—birds and airplanes, but not dogs.

A 1920s German motorcycle toy, now a collector's item. Play in Germany has been influenced by the country's geographic location, bordering both western and eastern European cultures.

Though sometimes played in schools now, Alle Vogel Vliegen was originally a forfeits game. Most countries have some version of a forfeits game, in which children who make a mistake in the game have to forfeit something of theirs that they have brought with them, putting it aside or in the center of the circle in a common heap. This creates a second game that follows the first, once enough forfeits have accumulated. The forfeits game goes through the forfeited items one at a time, and everyone agrees on what must be done to reclaim the item. The tasks that need to be accomplished can sometimes seem ritualistic and other times resemble the dares in Truth or Dare, calculated to embarrass the forfeiter, usually in jest.

For instance, the forfeiter may be told to kiss every girl or boy in the game—or, worse, kiss only the one they love. They may be told to approach an adult on all fours, barking like a dog or crying like a baby. They may be asked to eat soap or lick a trash can, to walk backward around the room 13 times, or to perform some task that may have to be attempted multiple times before getting it right, like singing the alphabet backward in a short amount of time.

Hopscotch is another popular children's game, and while other countries have multiple versions of the game, sometimes favored in different regions, Germany has only one, called *Hinkspiel*. The seven Hopscotch circles are named for the days of the week: *Montag, Dienstag, Mittwoch, Donnerstag, Freitag, Samstag*, and *Sonntag*. Players drop a stone into Montag, hop into the circle, kick the stone into the next day, and so on, losing a turn for failing to complete this in any way (by kicking the stone into the wrong circle or hopping onto a line instead of inside the circle, for instance). Successfully completing Hinkspiel once allows a player to write her name in any unclaimed circle, making it her "house"—

in that circle and that circle only, she can rest both feet when she lands in it, and no other player can enter the circle without her permission. The game becomes more difficult with each round, as a player could conceivably be required to hop from Montag to Freitag. Play ends when all the circles have been claimed.

See Also: Hockey (Amateur); Soccer Worldwide (Amateur).

Bibliography. Arnold Arnold, *World Book of Children's Games* (New York, 1972); Elliott Avedon, *The Study of Games* (New York, 1979); Jesse Hubbell Bancroft, *Games* (New York, 1937); Robbie Bell and Michael Cornelius, *Board Games Round the World: A Resource Book for Mathematical Investigations* (New York, 1988); Roger Caillois, *Man, Play and Games* (Chicago, 2001); E.O. Harbin, *Games of Many Nations* (Nashville, 1954); Johan Huizinga, *Homo Ludens* (Boston, 1971); Sarah Hunt, *Games and Sports the World Around* (New York, 1964); Glenn Kirchner, *Children's Games Around the World* (Dubuque, 1991); Nina Millen, *Children's Games from Many Lands* (New York, 1943).

Bill Kte'pi
Independent Scholar

Ghana

The West African country of Ghana was the center of a wealthy trading empire from late medieval times. It was invaded by the British, and in 1901 the Ghanaian Empire became a full part of the British Empire as the Gold Coast. In 1957 it gained its independence under Kwame Nkrumah and became the Republic of Ghana.

The reason for the country being known as the Gold Coast was because of its rich history of making gold ornaments, which was associated with the Kingdom of Ashanti. There was a rich heritage in the country before the arrival of the Portuguese, the Danes, the Dutch, the French, and the British, who came in search of slaves. The Danes, and later the British, established settlements, and it was not long before scholars started studying the elaborate woodcarving and metalworking of the Ashanti. Boys and young men were involved in fashioning finely carved stools, and other ceremonial ornaments. The Ewé people, who live in modern-day Ghana and also in Togo, were involved in carving small figurines used by children to play, although particular ones were imbued with great symbolic and ritual importance and were sacred. Dancing and the playing of drums was also common.

For girls and women, spinning and weaving brightly colored cloth occupied much of their time, both for recreation and, obviously, to wear and to sell. Girls have been involved in skipping and playing Hide & Seek, and other similar games with boys. The introduction of many schools throughout the country from the 1930s led to most boys, and many girls, attending some form of school, where sports were a part of the British curriculum for recreational purposes. This led to the introduction of soccer, which is now the most popular game for boys and young men in the country, with Ghana's soccer team having achieved great results in various World Cup events. Boxing has also been heavily promoted through the success of the Ghanian boxer Roy Ankrah. Many of the schools follow a British-style curriculum, and as a result, many children play cards and also board games, with computer games becoming increasingly common, especially among the wealthier families. Cycling is also a common form of recreation, as is hiking. The Ghana Scout Association was founded in 1912, and the Ghana Girl Guides Association was founded in 1921.

Taking part in musical events and listening to recordings of Ghanian music has been very popular since the 1920s—the Ghanian band Kumasi Trio received attention in London in 1928. Other instruments played include the guitar and the saxophone, as well as a variety of drums, giving the music a feeling of the rhythm of jazz. Because so many people from Ghana were taken as slaves to the Americas, Ghanian music has been popular among African-Americans, and this, and the government campaign by Kwame Nkrumah beginning in 1957 has led to much more indigenous music.

See Also: Africa, Traditional Play in; Hide & Seek; Soccer Worldwide (Amateur).

Bibliography. G.L. Barnard, "Gold Coast Children Out of School," *Oversea Education* (January, 1957); John Collins and Ronnie Graham, "Ghana," in Simon Broughton, Mark Ellingham and Jon Lusk, eds., *The Rough Guide to World Music: Africa & Middle East* (Rough Guide, 2006); Barrington Kaye, *Bringing up Children in Ghana* (Allen & Unwin, 1962).

Justin Corfield
Geelong Grammar School

G.I. Joe

G.I. Joe (Government Issue Joe), also known as the "All-American Hero" or "America's moveable fighting man" was the first action figure to enter the world of toys. This action figure was also the first doll-like toy marketed specifically to the boy consumer market. Inspired in part by the success of Barbie, G.I. Joe was invented by Don Levine. Produced by Hasbro, G.I. Joe entered the market in 1964 and continues to be an iconic childhood toy for many men and boys.

Before G.I. Joe came to plastic life, he experienced an earlier existence as a comic book hero from 1951 through 1956, with 68 issues published. Informed by the success of Barbie and the accompanying market of accessories, Levine sought to develop a similar type of toy to tap the boy-based consumer market. Hasbro simultaneously produced four figures to represent the four armed forces as iconic heroes: Rocky the Movable Fighting Man (Army), Skip (Navy), Ace Fighter Pilot (Air Force), and Rocky (Marine). The generic name of G.I. Joe was created to encompass the entire collection to facilitate marketing and brand identification.

The name was inspired by the 1945 movie *The Story of G.I. Joe*. These first action figures were just under 12 inches tall, making them slightly taller than Barbie, and sold at $4 apiece. The full articulation of the figures' joints was innovative and drew much attention. These first figures were marketed with a variety of accessories available for purchase: guns, tents, rifles, mess kits, and holsters, for example. Given the difficulty of trademarking a human being, the figure's trademark scar on the cheek was added to distinguish the real figures from knock-offs. The first-year (1964) sales figures for G.I. Joe topped $16 million—Hasbro had tapped a new market niche.

In 1965 Hasbro introduced an African-American soldier to their line. This soldier was not a subordinate of the other figures, nor was he a mere friend—he too was a hero. This socially progressive move during an era of racial discord met with limited success, and this soldier was sold exclusively in northern U.S. states for the first several years. Inspired by the growing space program, an astronaut figure was added in 1966. Additionally, this year brought soldiers from other countries like France, England, and Germany, as well as the first talking G.I. Joe figures. An action girl nurse was added to the crew of figures in 1967 but was a failure. In 1970, flocked hair and beards (brown, black, red, or blond) were added to G.I. Joe figures. Lifelike upper bodies and chests were added to the figures in 1975 so the figures could be played with without their shirts. In the post–Vietnam War era Hasbro sought to reduce their affiliation with military and re-released the collection as the "Adventure Team."

G.I. Joe dolls from the 1970s included figures with flocked hair and beards, "Kung-Fu Grip," and "eagle eye vision."

In the early 1980s a relaunch of products introduced smaller 3 ¾-inch action figures that were met with success. This relaunch was bolstered by the success of similar-sized Star Wars action figures. Additionally, a television cartoon series was introduced, creating a synergistic marketing and consumer culture. While for much of G.I. Joe's history there was a lack of a foe or evil to fight, the cartoon was based on the adversarial relationship of the G.I. Joe team with the COBRA organization. This cartoon series also incorporated public service announcements at the end of each episode, where the G.I. Joes would teach a safety lesson to children or warn against risky behavior. These announcements ended with the recognizable phrase "Now we know!"

During the 1990s and 2000s, G.I. Joe experienced some renewed interest and introduced new lines of full-size and smaller figures. These new products were bolstered by the 30th anniversary and the interests of collectors. By this era many who had played with the figure as a child were now men who collected figures and accessories. Today, G.I. Joe and action figures at large have lost favor among boys as more interactive and video-type games have flooded the market. However, these figures persist as iconic masculine toys and markers of childhood.

See Also: Action Figures; Dolls, Barbie and Others; Hasbro; Play as Mock War, Sociology of.

Bibliography. Karen Hall, "A Soldier's Body: G.I. Joe, Hasbro's Great American Hero, and the Symptoms of Empire," *The Journal of Popular Culture* (v.38/1, 2004); Don Levine and John Michlig, *G.I. Joe the Story Behind the Legend: An Illustrated History of America's Greatest Fighting Man* (Chronicle Books, 1996); John Michlig, *G.I. Joe: The Complete Story of America's Favorite Man of Action* (Chronicle Books, 1998); G. Wayne Miller, *Toy Wars: The Epic Struggle Between G.I. Joe, Barbie, and the Companies that Make Them* (Random House, 1998).

Daniel Farr
Randolph College

Girls' Play

Girls' play encompasses play with toys and board games, playing games such as skipping with others, and changing, elastic concepts of femininity that dictate what is appropriate for girls' play. It is important to remember that ideals of play are not always put into practice by girls themselves, and that they may vary by class and culture as well as over time. Girls' and boys' toys have not necessarily been different historically; both girls and boys, for instance, played with hoops, bowling them along with sticks, but there are more toys, such as dolls, that have been traditionally aimed more at girls than boys. These toys have been those most likely to teach gendered roles, or those that have relied on the child's wish to imitate adults. In this way, toys provide material evidence of how childhood was perceived in the past—in this case, what adults believed girls should be like. This was more often than not framed by what a woman was supposed to be, and girls' play was shaped by expectations of her future. Time was as likely to be spent—even in the 20th century—helping out in the home as it was playing.

Historical Sources

Sources of information about boys' play are much more commonplace than those for girls' play. Many of the major celebrations reserved for children in the medieval period, for instance, such as that for the boy bishops—from St. Nicholas's Day (December 6) to Holy Innocents (December 28)—were almost exclusively associated with boys. However, even for that period, miracle stories; advice manuals such as *How the Good Wife Taught her Daughter* (c.1430); literary and visual sources; archaeological finds; laws and legal records, such as coroners' inquests, funeral accounts, and guild records; and the lives of Saints, all help us to fill out the details of everyday life.

By the Enlightenment, philosophers such as John Locke (1632–1704) and Jean Jacques Rousseau (1712–78) were beginning to provide advice to parents about the educational development of their children through play, based on observation. As we move into the 19th century, retail catalogs begin to advertise toys and games that reveal what items were bought by adults for girls and boys, especially in wealthier households. This kind of literature provides us with additional evidence of which toys and games were given to children to play with and also helps us to come to an understanding of society's expectations about the appropriate behavior of girls.

In the Medieval period, for instance, girls might play with miniature jugs, ewers, cups, and plates made out of lead-tin alloy, so that they could copy what they saw taking place in the home. Archaeologists have found small bowls, cutlery, and even cauldrons strong enough to have water heated in them dating to the 16th century. In Pieter Breughel's (1525–69) painting *Children's Games* (1560), two girls can be seen playing with dolls—dolls seem to have been the one toy most commonly associated historically with girls' play, an early dictionary defining them as "small images which maidens are wont to make in the form of girls and to wrap in clothes," though the doll was also an adult object—wax dolls were used, for example, as votive offerings at shrines and churches.

The Advent of the Doll

The word *doll* itself is a relatively modern word, dating from the 17th century. Before this they were referred to as "poppet," with variations such as "popyn" and "puppet." Poppet is derived from the Latin *pupa* or *puppa*, meaning girl, and also refers to small iconic images. As well as being made of wax, medieval dolls could be made of wood, earthenware, and cloth. Sometimes children made the dolls themselves, and parents may have made them for their children in poorer homes, but cheap manufactured dolls were widely available by the 16th century. They might have been painted or, in the case of more elaborate dolls, dressed in ways appropriate to the child's rank. There were simple everyday clothes such as those we see on the doll in Breughel's painting, which is wearing a wimple, with a black dress covered by a white apron, a manner of dress appropriate to nobility. An account from Sir Richard Grenville's 1585 expedition to Virginia recounts that native American girls were very pleased to be given dolls brought over from England.

The most common form of doll until the mid-19th century was in the image of an adult woman, and it was only after 1850 that European manufacturers began making and exporting dolls that looked like babies or children. In a climate of falling birthrates among established middle-class Americans, it was hoped by many commentators that playing with these baby dolls would promote motherhood to girls who might otherwise shy away from it or limit their family size.

Dollhouses were originally made for only the very wealthy and replicated the child's own home, often being made by several craftsmen who would normally have been involved in housebuilding. One very early example in the Victorian and Albert Museum in Britain dates from 1673 and was made in Germany for the family of an apothecary (chemist). Dollhouses at this time would have been important for teaching girls about their domestic responsibilities and household skills. Much larger houses that girls could actually play inside were occasionally built; for example, Queen Victoria and Prince Albert had a Swiss Cottage built for their children in the grounds of Osborne House on the Isle of Wight, United Kingdom (UK), which had child-sized furnishings.

The future Queen Elizabeth II similarly had access to a permanent playhouse in the style of a miniature Welsh cottage, called Y Bwthyn Bach, presented to her by the people of Wales on her 6th birthday in 1932. This last was copied by a toy manufacturer, Lines Bros. of Merton, Surrey, UK, and was sold as a dollhouse from 1935 on. In the 20th century, dollhouses, and play-, cubby-, or Wendy-houses (named after the character Wendy in J.M. Barrie's 1904 *Peter Pan*) designed to encourage imaginative role-play became much more widely commercially available, and remained an ideal means by which to identify and support gender-specific behavior.

Girls' Toys

On the whole, girls' toys by the 19th century, in Europe and America, were made out of delicate materials such as paper, papier-mâché, or porcelain and, as in the medieval period, tended to be small versions of homely objects like tea sets and music boxes. The expectation, certainly among the middle classes, was clearly that girls would play carefully and quietly indoors. Many objects were too delicate to withstand much play at all; girls from well-to-do homes fell back on dressing up homemade rag dolls in order to avoid breaking their more expensive fine wax or china dolls. Stories in girls' periodicals reinforced this with sad tales of the consequences of carelessness. Nineteenth-century girls' play always had a purpose.

Their toys encouraged them to learn nurturing skills and the skills of household management and to acquire a knowledge of fashion—the skills that they would need as they became eligible young women. But, even this was carefully overseen, as, though play was assumed to be intrinsically helpful and fitting for boys by this period, American and European society was more likely to encourage girls to develop accomplishments such as sewing, reading, or looking after younger siblings—all assumed to be more appropriate preparations for adult womanhood than play. There were variations between Europe and America. By this period, parents in the United States, for instance, were strongly advised against letting girls ride hobby horses, whereas this was acceptable for girls in France—the fear in America being that girls would enter too soon into sexual awareness if they straddled any toy, including rocking horses, bicycles, et cetera. And, in the interests of maintaining childhood innocence, no comfortable American parent wanted their little girl to become a tomboy, which this more physically active form of play might encourage. Children of both sexes were to remain naturally pure and innocent of sexuality—and therefore separated from one another in their play—for as long as possible.

Toy Preferences

Unsurprisingly, the 19th-century visual record shows that when girls under 7 years were depicted with a toy (which is actually relatively rare, only 20 percent of them being shown with toys at all and the rest standing by flowers or other feminine items), 80 percent were carrying a doll, while the other toys depicted in association with girls were all doll related, including miniature furnishings such as chairs, cups, and saucers. Girls themselves, however, did not necessarily choose to play according to the dictates of their parents. One survey in America, conducted in 1898, which asked children what their favorite toys were, found that only two-thirds of girls played with dolls and under a quarter listed dolls as their favorite toys. Only a few girls mention their dolls in diaries, while most record school gossip, descriptions of daily events, and fashion.

The hoop—also played with enthusiastically by boys—seems to have been their favorite toy. Others mentioned skipping with ropes and playing with balls. Hoops, which were made from wood or metal, were played with in the garden, the yard, park and around town, and even indoors if the weather was bad. Girls also record in their diaries and in memoirs snowball fights and sledding, playing on swings and seesaws, recollections of making dens, playing catching and singing games, running, and playing with scooters and tricycles. All of these were forms of play adults associated with boyhood rather than girlhood; there is also photographic evidence of young boys with dolls, as these were often the only soft toys available in much of the 19th century—most animal toys were made of wood and/or often mounted on wheels. Playing with dolls gave a child of either sex a sense of control over someone smaller than themselves in an adult world until the late 19th century, when soft toys became more widely available with the development of progressive educational theory.

Play and Good Health

In Europe and America, as the playground movement took hold at the turn of the 19th and 20th centuries, older working-class girls and boys continued to be separated or closely supervised. However, by this point girls and young women were also engaging in active play, in team games for example, to build strong bodies for the future. In many European states and America by the 1880s, many authorities stressed that woman's highest duty and calling was to reproduce a healthy race of good and valuable citizens who would contribute to the strength of the nation (in the case of America) and of the empire (in the case of Britain). In line with these concerns about national efficiency, girls were educated to become good homemakers and mothers, with a clear sense of their responsibility as citizens. Play itself was seen as a way of cementing patriotic values, and the working class and (in America) immigrants formed a special focus of concern.

The children of the poor already caused deep disquiet for philanthropists in the 19th century, as they did not seem to experience a childhood at all. One British reformer, Henry Mayhew (1812–87) described a girl he saw selling watercress on the streets of London as having "lost all childish ways," her "little face, pale and thin with privation, was wrinkled where the dimples ought to have been." These children now became the center of policymaking in Europe and America, and the lack of available resources for their play was seen as a grave concern. The spaces where they played—street corners, rough ground, and empty lots—and their makeshift toys were perceived as inadequate and dangerous, especially to girls who were at constant risk of a loss of purity and a fall into early sexuality. Instead, active physical play appropriate for girls was encouraged by progressive reformers, who campaigned and organized for playgrounds to be built in poor areas and for healthful activities to be held, such as gymnastics, volleyball, and relay races. Though there were some concerns that undue physical activity was unfeminine, and many assumed that girls disliked competition, these activities would, they believed, promote good health and friendship, grace, and beauty, if the focus was on the group and the development of general fitness.

The National Federation of Settlements *Study of Young Girls* (c.1921) argued that these activities would promote "sturdy, normal womanhood," "wise, efficient motherhood," and "worthy citizenship." Girls were seen as the mothers of the race, who must be specially guarded and guided, there was a moral responsibility for those supervising girls' games, and therefore much debate about what was appropriate. Reformers also discussed inappropriate forms of leisure for girls and young women, such as dance halls, and frowned upon undirected, unsupervised forms of play as potentially corrupting.

Post–World War II Play

After World War II, sex differences became less of a focus as definitions of childhood changed, though they persisted in the gendering of toys in the growing consumer market that characterized this period. Notably, Barbie and other mass-market hyper-feminine dolls were developed during this time, and related play was reinforced by their television advertising. Some gender markers expanded. Whereas girls' and boys' clothes had been relatively gender neutral in the 19th century—parents opting to almost obscure their child's sex, the child being seen as innocent of sexuality—girls' clothes, and therefore their toys and playthings, became color-coded pink for girls, blue for boys. However, at the same time, direct resistance to sex-stereotyping grew with a renewed interest in feminist politics in America and Europe from the late 1960s.

Play was less likely to be segregated by sex in formal situations and institutions such as playgrounds and school. Girls' participation in organized sports in the United States increased in the 1970s and 1980s after the institution of Title IX. When enshrined in international law, by Principle 7 of the United Nations (UN) Declaration of the Rights of the Child (1959), the right to play was also effectively made gender neutral.

As children began to attend school for longer, and were therefore no longer contributors to their families' income, working-class girls and boys had more opportunity for play. The evidence suggests that in poorer households, girls were still more likely than their brothers—who might still be out earning additional income after school—to be helping with domestic chores and child-minding. Nonetheless, as housing conditions improved, as the sense of childhood under threat grew, and as adult gender roles changed, girls and boys from all walks of life became more likely to play at home and to spend more time playing with their parents than their peers.

See Also: Boys' Play; Dolls, Barbie and Others; Playground Movement, U.S.; Toys and Child Development; Wendy Houses.

Bibliography. John Burnette, *Destiny Obscure: Autobiographies of Childhood, Education and Family From the 1820s to the 1920s* (Penguin, 1982); Karin Calvert, *Children in the House: The Material Culture of Early Childhood, 1600–1900* (Northeastern University Press, 1992); Hugh Cunningham, *Children and Childhood in Western Society Since 1500* (Pearson Longman, 2005); Barbara A. Hanawalt, "Medievalists and the Study of Childhood," *Speculum* (v.77, 2002); Colin Heywood, *A History of Childhood: Children and Childhood in the West From Medieval to Modern Times* (Polity, 2001); Henry Mayhew, *London Labour and the London Poor: The London Street Folk* (Griffin, Bohn and Co., 1861); The National Federation of Settlements, "Study of Young Girls," (c.1921) in M. Anderson Linnea, "The Playground of Today is the Republic of Tomorrow: Social Reform and Organized Recreation in the U.S.A., 1890–1930s," reproduced from the *Encyclopaedia of Informal Education*, www.infed.org (cited August 2008); Iona Opie and Peter Opie, *Children's Games in Street and Playground* (Clarendon Press, 1969); Iona Opie and Peter Opie, *The Lore and Language of Schoolchildren* (Clarendon Press, 1959); Nicholas Orme, *Medieval Children*, (Yale University Press, 2003); Peter N. Stearns, *Childhood in World History* (Routledge, 2006); Victoria & Albert Museum, Museum of Childhood, www.vam.ac.uk/moc (cited August 2008).

Karen Anne Sayer
Leeds Trinity and All Saints

Go

Go is a board game for two players, played with black and white game pieces on a 19 x 19 grid. The game originated in China, and gained popularity in Korea and Japan in the 1st millennium C.E. In Japan, the game flourished and became firmly embedded in Japanese culture. It has inspired Japanese philosophy, art, and literature, as well as popular cultural forms such as *manga* and *anime*.

While Go is the Japanese name for the game, its original Chinese name is *Wéiqí*. This term can be roughly translated as "the game of surrounding," which describes the game's basic mechanics; namely, to use one's own playing pieces (stones) to surround the opponent's stones or empty space on the board (territory).

The origin of Go is shrouded in legend, and it is impossible to say exactly when and where it was created. It is assumed that the game emerged in Central Asia before 1000 B.C.E. The first written reference to Go is found in the *Chronicle of Zuo*, which is believed to have been compiled no later than 389 B.C.E.

In the 8th century C.E. the game gained popularity at the imperial court of Japan and became widespread among the general public over the course of the subsequent centuries. In the 17th century, the game became a national institution when a Minister of Go was appointed, and players started to receive government subsidies.

In Japanese Zen Buddhism, Go became an important metaphor for the illumination of spiritual concepts. This is expressed well in the 13th-century Zen master Dogen Zenji's observation that "You play Go by yourself, the opponents become one." The language used to describe Go is also saturated with philosophical terminology: *shikatsu* (life and death), *aji* (flavor), and *ishi no nagare* (the flow of the stones).

This philosophical aspect also reflected in the great number of Go proverbs, some of which apply to life as well as the game (e.g., "Don't go fishing when your house is on fire"). This is undoubtedly one of the reasons why Go also became an important influence on Japanese art and literature. Images of Go abound in Japanese prints and paintings, particularly from the Edo, Meiji, Taisho and Showa periods. In literature, Go metaphors can be found in traditional *senryu* (short satirical poems) as well as in modern masterpieces such as Yasunari Kawabata's *The Master of Go*.

While Go had been known in the West since the 17th century, when it was described by Thomas Hyde in *De Ludis Orientalibus* (1694), it did not become popular in Europe until the 19th century. In the early 20th century, it was introduced in the United States. Today, the International Go Federation has 71 member states, and the number of Go players has been estimated at 27 million worldwide. An increasing number of people are playing the game online on sites such as the Kiseido Go Server (KGS) or the International Go Server (IGS).

While professional Go was dominated by Japanese players for much of the 20th century, many top Go players today are Korean. However, the culture and terminology of Go is still predominantly Japanese, and some Go terms have entered popular culture. Perhaps most famously, the American computer game developer and publisher Atari was named after the term that describes a group of stones in imminent danger of capture.

The game has gained renewed popularity, particularly among children, through Yumi Hotta and Takeshi Obata's manga series *Hikaru no Go,* which has sold more than 22 million copies in Japan and also enjoys widespread popularity in the United States.

See Also: Ancient China; China; Japan; Korea, North and South.

Bibliography. Walter Augustus de Havilland, *The ABC of Go—The National War Game of Japan* (Kelly & Walsh, 1910); John Fairbairn, "Go in Ancient China," http://www.pandanet.co.jp/English/essay/goancientchina.html (cited July 2008); Shirakawa Masayoshi, *A Journey In Search of the Origins of Go (Yutopian Enterprises, 2005);* Robert T. Myers and Sangit Chatterjee, "Game of Go: Culture and Science," *Science and Culture* (v.69/7–8, 2003); Peter Shotwell, Huiren Yang and Sangit Chatterjee, *Go! More than a Game* (Tuttle, 2003); Arthur Smith, *The Game of Go: The National Game of Japan* (Tuttle, 1956).

Julian Kücklich
University of the Arts, London

GoldenEye 007

The first-person shooter game GoldenEye 007, released by Rare in 1997, was the overall highest-selling game for the Nintendo 64 console and remains one of the most popular movie tie-in games to date. Although the game is based primarily on the narrative and settings of the James Bond film *GoldenEye* (Martin Campbell, 2005), it includes characters and situations inspired by the Bond series of films and books as a whole. The game is especially notable for its multiplayer mode, in which four players can simultaneously compete in a variety of contests. GoldenEye 007 occupies an important position in the history of the first-person shooter and the multiplayer console game; the popularity of its multiplayer mode represented a significant development in the mainstreaming of video games as a center for social activity.

GoldenEye 007 was released two years after its cinematic counterpart—an eternity in marketing years. Another Bond film, *Tomorrow Never Dies* (Roger Spottiswoode, 2007), was released in 1997 as well. The delay in the release of the GoldenEye game, combined with the possible confusion of a new Bond project rendering the GoldenEye title obsolete as a marketing tool, led to relatively low expectations for the game's release. The game was originally expected to be an on-rails shooter, in which the character is automatically moved through a level; this was partly because of that fact that the developers, early in the design process, did not have access to the Nintendo 64 control scheme and were thus unable to envision how player control might work in the game. GoldenEye 007 seems to have come together in a somewhat haphazard way: though it started as an on-rails shooter, the final product has an emphasis on navigation, exploration, and stealth; the game's missions were reverse-engineered from the gadgets and enactive options that designers wanted to include in the game, and its extremely popular multiplayer mode was, by all accounts, little more than an afterthought. The multiplayer mode was added to the game almost single-handedly by Rare employee Steve Ellis, who combined altered versions of environments from the one-player game with arenas unique to the multiplayer mode to create spaces for competition between game players.

The game was generally well-received on its release, but it took time for its massive popularity to build. The single-player mode proved popular and was rated highly by critics for repeat play because of the variety of tasks it asked of its players and the rewarding design of its different difficulty levels. Ironically, given its marginalization in the game's production history, GoldenEye 007's multiplayer mode drove much of the game's word-of-mouth popularity. The multiplayer mode is extremely versatile in the options it gives players, and its design encourages novel and surprising emergent situations. The social and competitive aspects of multiplayer gameplay facilitated exposure of new players to the game and motivated them to buy their own copies in order to improve their gameplay skills.

After the game proved popular, the rights to the James Bond franchise were acquired by Electronic Arts, meaning that the Rare team that designed GoldenEye 007 would be unable to produce a Bond-related sequel to the game. Members of the development team behind GoldenEye 007 worked on the similar Perfect Dark (Rare, 2000) and on the TimeSplitters series (Free Radical Design, 2000). Electronic Arts has produced a number of Bond games to mixed critical reception, some more successful than others, but none matching the popularity enjoyed by GoldenEye 007 in the late 1990s.

See Also: Play as Mock War, Sociology of; Play as Mock War, Psychology of.

Bibliography. Brady Games, *Totally Unauthorized GoldenEye 007: Strategy Guide* (Brady Games, 1997); Gary Alan Fine, *Shared Fantasy: Role Playing Games as Social Worlds* (University of Chicago Press, 2002); Martin Hollis, "The Making of GoldenEye 007," www.zoonami.com (cited July 2008).

Daniel Reynolds
University of California, Santa Barbara

Golf (Amateur)

Amateur golf is a unique sport that is played without supervision from officials. The overriding principle of amateur golf is the integrity of the game, which demands courtesy and sportsmanship. Derivatives of the sport of golf originated in Scotland in the 15th century, and today's game is still a prominent activity played by more than 60 million worldwide. The popularity of golf has been recognized by the International Olympic Committee (IOC), and bids to potentially add the sport at the 2016 Olympic Games are currently under review.

The sport of golf is structured into two divisions of professional and amateur play. Whereas most media coverage surrounds the professional ranks, the majority of participants are amateurs. In fact, professional golfers make up such a minority of all golfers that the number of professional golfers who earn their main income from competition is less than 5 percent. Professional golfers who earn their income through golf do so as a club or teaching professional. On the other hand, amateur golfers make up the main group that enjoys one of the mainstays of leisure activities across the world.

According to the National Golf Foundation, participation in amateur golf is approximately 26 million annually in the United States. According to statistics from 2005, 15 million amateur golfers play eight or more times per season, and there are approximately 4.6 million golfers that play 25 or more rounds per year. Golf participation is similar in Western countries as well and has grown tremendously in Asian countries. For instance, the People's Republic of China was nearly void of golf participation 25 years ago. Yet, amateur golf has recently grown 30 percent per year. Currently, China has one to five million golfers nationwide and possesses 400 golf courses, compared with 20 courses in 1995.

The governing bodies of amateur and professional play alike are the United States Golf Association (USGA), the Royal & Ancient Golf Club (R & A), and the International Golf Federation (IGF). The USGA is the governing body throughout the United States and Mexico, whereas the R & A operates within Europe, Asia-Pacific, and Africa. The IGF supports the international team championships and promotes the inclusion of golf with the International Olympic Committee as an Olympic sport. These organizations along with the World Amateur Golf Council help standardize play through rulings, etiquette, equipment standards, scoring, and a handicap system.

Amateur Status

Amateur is defined as a person who pursues an activity as a pastime rather than as a profession. Yet, the governing bodies of the USGA and R & A outline specific rules and definitions of the amateur golfer. Generally, the amateur golfer plays the game as a nonprofit endeavor and does not receive compensation for golf-related activities. Amateur golfers defined by the USGA are deemed to have established golf skill by competing at a national and/or elite level. The purpose of amateur status is to "keep the game as free as possible from the abuses that may follow from uncontrolled sponsorship and financial incentive." As a result, players must adhere to the rules regarding amateur status.

For instance, the USGA's rule 3.1, "Playing for prize money," states that "amateurs may play in professionally sanctioned events, yet must waive their right prior to participation." This rule manifested during the 2008 Nationwide Children's Hospital Invitational. Daniel Summerhays won the tournament but was a collegiate amateur and thus could not accept the prize of $135,000. Although the amateur status is dependent upon stringent criteria, certain exceptions do apply regarding financial assistance. Most notably, amateur golfers can win prize vouchers and retail prizes not to exceed $750. A common misconception is the monetary values for hole-in-one competitions. An amateur golfer still retains his/her status if the prize far exceeds the $750 limit for a hole-in-one competition.

Another notable regulation marks the line between professional and amateur status. A professional golfer is deemed to have a distinct advantage over an amateur by way of devoting him/herself to the game. Juxtaposed is that there are more opportunities for competitive amateur golf in the United States compared to professional golf. Thus, many skilled players must choose to actively pursue the ranks of professionalism either as teaching or club pro or touring professional. Often, very highly skilled amateurs choose the latter and attempt to earn their living as a touring professional. However, if unsuccessful in the endeavor, then the ruling bodies deem that players may reapply for amateur status.

Handicap System

The handicap system allows for men and women of varying skill levels a standard of equal play. The USGA establishes both a handicap index and a course index that signifies a player's skill level in relation to par. All amateur golfers with established indexes can play and compete on virtually any course. First, to obtain a handicap index, golfers must be members of an official golf club and post at least five peer-reviewed scores. The USGA establishes a player's handicap index by utilizing the tools of Course Rating and Slope Rating. The Course Rating is a score that a scratch golfer (zero handicap) would post under normal conditions based on yardage and obstructions. On the other hand, the Slope Rating is the difficulty of a course for nonscratch golfers. The maximum handicap index is 36.4 for men and 40.4 for women.

Each competing player establishes a course index by multiplying one's handicap index and slope rating and dividing by 113 (e.g., the lowest possible slope). Before play, each player then establishes a handicap allowance, which is the number of shots given or received. The greater the discrepancy between course and slope ratings; the more shots a nonscratch golfer will receive.

Consequently, the lower the difference between course and slope rating, the fewer number of strokes a player will receive. Lastly, there is an established system of handicap allowances. Each golf hole has a handicap rating based on difficulty, and differences between player's handicaps indicate the specific holes in which the handicap allowances are given. The scorecard from Bethpage Black, New York, host of the 2002 U.S. Open, helps illustrate the handicap allowance system. Two players with handicap indexes of 12.4 and 16.2, respectively, compete. The difference of four between the handicap indexes results in a handicap allowance of four strokes on the handicap golf holes of 13–16. Thus, according to the scorecard, strokes will be given on holes 17, 8, 18, and 2.

For amateur players, handicaps are established on two assumptions that align with the spirit of amateur play: 1) players post every round for peer review and 2) players try to make the best possible score. However, some research has revealed that cheating occurs fairly fre-

The World Amateur Golf Council standardizes play through rulings, etiquette, scoring, and a handicap system.

quently. In an online poll of over 7,000 golfers, 70 percent of amateurs admitted to cheating at golf. One of the ways that cheating occurs is the recording and utilization of false handicap indexes. *Sandbagging* is a term for when a golfer claims a higher handicap in order to gain an advantage. The most common egregious acts of raising one's handicap include reporting incorrect higher scores, not completing rounds to avoid posting a score, and playing more than one ball.

These players enter tournaments or competitions with inflated handicap indexes or play in lower flighted tournaments (A, B, C) in which they have an unfair advantage. Whereas the USGA empowers each golf club to have a handicap committee to ensure accurate posting of scores, infractions still unfortunately occur.

Amateur Competitions

Accomplished golfers with extensive playing experience often participate in various levels of competition. These can vary from local tournaments (i.e., club championships, city championships and/or county amateurs), state (i.e., state opens, state amateurs), regional (i.e., north/south amateur) and national based tournaments (i.e., western amateur). The USGA and R & A sponsor several national competitions and conduct three international competitions for the most proficient worldwide amateurs. The R & A, founded in 1754, established the first amateur championship at Hoylake, England, in 1885. Similarly, the USGA, formerly named the Amateur Golf Association and organized in 1894, played the first U.S. Amateur in Newport, Rhode Island. In 1895, the first U.S. Women's Amateur was played in Long Island, New York.

There are specific standardized entrant criteria for the amateur championships. First, the USGA national championships involve a specific handicap index. These handicaps range from 2.4 (U.S. Amateur) to 18.4 (U.S. Women's Senior Amateur). The handicap criteria signify the ability level of top amateur golfers.

To elaborate, the U.S. Amateur, one of the most prestigious amateur events, requires the same handicap index (less than 2.4) as the U.S. Open. Second, all amateur championships have an eligibility requirement that includes sectional qualifying tournaments. Also, each amateur competition varies according to specific entrant criteria; most notably, age.

For example, the U.S. Junior Amateur is participated in by those under 18 years of age with a handicap index of 6.4 or lower. The Mid-Amateur is played by those with a handicap index under 3.4 and over the age of 25, whereas the U.S. Senior Amateur is played by the best amateurs over the age of 55, with a handicap index fewer than 7.4. Other entrant criteria for high-level amateur events include golf course criteria. Specifically, the U.S. Public Links Championship can only be played by amateurs who are members of public golf courses. Gender is a linear eligibility requirement; female golfers can play in male events, but the USGA hosts female-only events.

The USGA and R & A host three international competitions for the most elite amateur golfers. These include the Walker Cup, Curtis Cup, and Men's and Women's Amateur team. First, the Walker Cup is a biennial competition that was first played in 1922. The Walker Cup is similar to the Ryder Cup, which features the United States of America against Great Britain and Ireland. The Curtis Cup was first played in 1932 and is similar to the professional competition of the Solheim Cup. The best female players from the United States compete biennially with the best from Great Britain and Ireland.

Forms of Play

The two most common formats of amateur golf and amateur championships are Stroke Play and Match Play. These types of play can be combined with most other types of formats. Stroke Play consists of playing the round in the fewest strokes possible, and the winner is the player with the fewest number of strokes. Match Play consists of playing one side against another and consists of playing holes instead of the total number of strokes. The winner of match play is determined by one side or player leading by a number of holes greater than the number of holes remaining. Other common formats played in the international competition include but are not limited to foursomes, four-ball, and best-ball. Foursomes, also known as alternate-shot, consist of a team of two players with only one ball in play. Each player in turn alternates between shots during each hole and alternates on the teeing ground for each hole.

Best-ball is also a team format competition in which each player plays his/her own ball. Best-ball can be played in teams of two, three, or four players, and the best score by each player is recorded for the hole. Four-ball is a two-person match play best-ball format, and the team counts the best score for the hole.

Additional amateur types of playing formats are the scramble and stableford formats. The scramble is the most popular type of amateur stroke-play format and consists of teams of two, three, or four players. Each player plays a tee ball, and the team determines the best shot and all players proceed to play their second shot from that spot, and so on, until the hole is completed. Typically the scramble format results in the lowest scores of any format.

The stableford format consists of stroke play in which the stroke total for a hole is associated with a specific score, and thus the highest score wins. For individual play, each hole has a fixed point total that may account for overall handicap. The stableford format is also popular with teams of two, three, or four. The fixed total coincides with a player's handicap index, and he/she must score more points than the fixed score. For example, a golfer with a handicap index of 15 would have a fixed score of 30 points that he or she must beat to order to win points.

History of Amateur Play

The USGA and R & A also host Open Championships (British & U.S.), in which amateurs compete with professionals. Although professionals typically dominate these events, amateurs have won both the British and U.S. Opens. Francis Ouimet became the first amateur to win the U.S. Open in 1913.

In all, five amateurs have won the U.S. Open and British Open; the last amateur winner was Johnny Goodman in 1933. Seven of these championships were won by perhaps the greatest amateur in the history of golf. Robert T. "Bobby" Jones was considered one of the last great amateurs due in part to his success on the course against top professionals.

He remained an amateur despite his success in the major championships, winning 13 out of 26 events entered. He won 13 "majors" in his short playing career between 1923 and 1930 and retired at the age of 28. His golf proficiency culminated in 1930 by winning the era's grand slam of golf, consisting of the U.S. Amateur, U.S. Open, British Amateur, and British Open. The greatest female amateur golfer is considered to be Glenna Collett Vare. She dominated her era of golf and won the U.S. Women's Amateur six times. Between 1928 and 1931, she won 16 consecutive victories. In 1924, her most impressive year, she won 59 out of 60 matches played. She was a member of the first Curtis Cup team, and in 1953, the LPGA created the Vare trophy for the golfer with the lowest scoring average of the year.

The largest numbers of participants within golf are amateurs. Although most will pursue golf as a leisure activity, some amateurs will play at more competitive levels through the inclusion of tournament play. Regardless of one's ability level, amateur golf still remains a self-regulated sport in terms of rules, yet the governing bodies also help to maintain the integrity of the game. The USGA and R & A standardize the handicap system that provides equanimity in terms of competition and regulate the financial incentives for all amateurs to enjoy the sport.

See Also: Athletics (Amateur); China; Gamesmanship; Play as Competition, Psychology of.

Bibliography. David Levinson and Karen Christensen, *Berkshire Encyclopedia of World Sport* (Berkshire Publishing Group, 2005); R. Hardin, "Creating Myth and Legend: O.B. Keeler and Bobby Jones," *American Journalism* (v.18, 2001); P. Hollander, *One Hundred Greatest Women in Sport* (Putnam Publishing, 1977); B. Pennington, "Shaving Strokes and Integrity," *New York Times* (July 14, 2008); P. Vitello, "More

Americans are Giving up Golf," *New York Times* (February 21, 2008).

Robert J. Bell
Ball State University

Gollywogs

The gollywog (spelled variously gollywog, golliwogg, golliwogg, etc.) was, like the teddy bear, a stuffed toy given to young boys throughout much of the 20th century, considered more appropriate for boys than feminine dolls or other stuffed animals. Gollywogs enjoyed the most popularity before action figures took a prominent position in the marketplace. Gollywogs were rag dolls, nearly always male, made to look like garish blackface caricatures.

The dolls were based on a character created by Florence Kate Upton (1873–1922), the New York–born daughter of English immigrants, who moved to England after her father's death in 1887. In order to pay for art school, she worked as an illustrator and illustrated a children's book written by her mother for the publishing company of Longmans, Green, & Co., called *The Adventures of Two Dutch Dolls and a Golliwogg*, which was released in Christmas 1895. Thirteen more Golliwogg books were published as collaborations between Upton and her mother, and they proved popular sellers through the turn of the century.

Despite the popularity of the books, no one thought to copyright the Golliwogg character. Not only were gollywog books by other authors and publishers produced, but gollywog dolls were manufactured to great success. The popularity of the dolls in particular spread throughout the English-speaking world, peaking in popularity with the children born in the years following World War II.

Upton's illustration was based on an actual doll she had had in New York, which her aunt found packed away: Dressed in brightly colored formal clothes such as a character in a minstrel show might wear, he had pitch-black skin, bright red lips, big white eyes, a wild untamed Afro, and crude features compared to the lithe and refined Dutch dolls in the story. *Gollywog* soon became a term for such "darkie" caricatures, and outside of Upton's books, they were often depicted as villains, menaces, or merely stupid. Gollywogs were used as product mascots in the United Kingdom, notably for James Robertsons & Sons jam (which was subject to a boycott in 1983 for racial insensitivity).

Despite the controversy surrounding racial stereotypes, gollywog memorabilia is still popular among collectors.

Gollywog and *wog* became racial epithets in reference to the toys, throughout the Commonwealth states. *Wog* tended to be inclusive of all dark-skinned people, including those of Middle Eastern or Mediterranean descent. The toys have fallen out of favor since the 1970s and 1980s, as sensitivity to racial prejudices and prejudicial depictions has gained currency.

See Also: Dolls, Barbie and Others.

Bibliography. Bertha Upton and Florence Kate Upton, *The Adventures of Two Dutch Dolls and a Golliwogg* (Dodo Press, 2007).

Bill Kte'pi
Independent Scholar

Grand Theft Auto

Grand Theft Auto (GTA) invites players to enter a world that allows them to vicariously live out fantasies that in real life would garner time behind bars. Fighting, stealing, and assaulting innocent bystanders are just a few of the many perks of deviant behavior that can be exercised in this controversial game. Players can take on the role of a criminal in a big city, typically a lowly individual who rises in the ranks of organized crime over the course of the game. Various missions are set for completion by the figureheads of the city underworld, generally criminal, which must be completed to progress through the storyline. Bank robberies, assassinations, and other crimes feature regularly, but occasionally taxi driving, firefighting, pimping, street racing, or learning to fly an airplane are also involved as alternate adventures, which can be done at any time during the game, with the exception of the periods performing main missions. Characters can even have sex with prostitutes in the game.

GTA is a computer and video game created by the Scottish company DMA Design (now Rockstar North) and published by BMG Interactive (a subsidiary of BMG Records) in 1997. The game allows players to assume the role of a criminal who can roam freely around a big city. There are currently nine games in the series, with a further two expansion packs for the original.

Grand Theft Auto, now known primarily as GTA 1, was the first game in the Grand Theft Auto series. Many GTA games have been made since, such as GTA Vice City and GTA San Andreas. Grand Theft Auto, the first title in the *GTA* series was released on PlayStation in 1997/1998 and also for Windows PCs. The game is set in three different fictional cities, Liberty City, San Andreas, and Vice City. These renditions of the cities are vastly different from their more well-known counterparts in the GTA III era. In the game, you can choose one of about six protagonists, and even change their names. It begins with only one level to choose from.

Grand Theft Auto: London 1969 was made as an expansion pack for GTA, and Grand Theft Auto: London 1961 was in turn an expansion pack for London 1969. Both of these games require the original GTA disc to work.

The second game in the series, Grand Theft Auto 2, was developed for Microsoft Windows, PlayStation and Dreamcast and released in 1999. Set in the indeterminable future, it featured updated graphics and somewhat different game play based upon the player's appeal to various criminal organizations. A reduced Game Boy Color port was also produced.

Grand Theft Auto III and subsequent games have more prevalent voice acting, and radio stations, which simulate driving to music with disc jockeys, radio personalities, commercials, talk radio, pop music, and American culture. There have been 10 soundtracks released for this game series, making the music an important character in the game.

The use of vehicles in an uncharted urban environment provides a basic simulation of a working city, complete with pedestrians who obey traffic signals. Players can pick their cars, steal their cars, and detail their cars however they like. This series of games makes it easy for a player to customize their gaming experience.

Grand Theft Auto IV (GTA IV) is the 11th GTA game in the series. The game was developed by Rockstar North, and was published and released by Rockstar Games for the Xbox 360 and PlayStation 3 console systems. It was released to widespread hype on April 29, 2008, scoring positive reviews from virtually the entire gaming press. Grand Theft Auto IV is set in 2008 in a redesigned Liberty City, a stylized recreation of New York City. The character Niko Bellic is an Eastern European (Serbian) who has come to America to find a better life, following the advice of his cousin Roman; however, when he arrives, he finds that Roman has been lying—he is not rich or popular, and he is in trouble. Niko has been duped into solving Roman's problems, and soon ends up in trouble himself.

See Also: Adaptive Play; Bullying; Fantasy Play; Female Aggressive Relationships Within Play (Putallaz); Girl's Play; Human Relationships in Play; Inter-Gender Play; Play and Power, Sociology of; Play as Catharsis; Play as Competition, Sociology of; Play as Entertainment, Sociology of; Play Community; Playing Alone; Playmate; Pretending; Rhetorics of Play (Sutton-Smith); Role-Playing; Social Psychology of Play.

Bibliography. Gary Alan Fine, *Shared Fantasy: Role Playing Games as Social Worlds* (University of Chicago Press, 2002); Lawrence Kutner and Cheryl Olson, *Grand Theft Childhood: The Surprising Truth About Violent Video Games and What Parents Can Do* (Simon & Schuster, 2008); Daniel Mackay, *The Fantasy Role-Playing Game: A New Performing Art* (McFarland & Company, 2001); J. Patrick Williams et al., eds.,

Gaming As Culture: Essays on Reality, Identity and Experience in Fantasy Games (McFarland & Company, 2006).

Miriam D. Dufer
Old Dominion University

Greece

A country in southeast Europe, the birthplace of democracy and the Olympic Games, heir to an ancient civilization and a long history, Greece has long been near the center of European culture.

Soccer and basketball have been prominent sports in Greece for years, and unlike much of Europe, Greece was one of the founding countries of the International Basketball Federation in 1932. Though the national team and professional basketball have only been prominent since the 1980s, amateur basketball enjoys a history nearly as old as the sport itself. The success of the national team since the 1980s has propelled the popularity of youth and interscholastic basketball, making it one of the most popular recreational team sports. Though soccer is more popular, arousing more passion in the professional arenas, the Greeks have been less successful there, going nearly 40 years without making it to the European Cup final.

Cricket and handball are common recreational sports in some parts of the country, and volleyball is popular nationwide. Because of the size of Greece's coastline, water polo is one of the nation's leading sports (and the national teams are some of the best in the world).

Among Greek children, a popular game is *Kukla*, which is essentially a tag game. Parallel lines are drawn, chalked, or otherwise indicated, about 10 feet long and 10 feet apart: a goal line and a throw line, with an empty can or other target places at the center of the goal line. Players line up at the throw line and toss bean bags at the can in an attempt to knock it over, while one player takes a guard position behind the can. The first player to knock the can over must run to retrieve their beanbag and return behind the throw line, while the guard must set the can upright again and attempt to tag the player before they reach the safety of the throw line. If a tag is made successfully, the player becomes the guard in the next round.

Thanks to the beauty and pleasantness of the Mediterranean and Aegean seas, water sports are especially popular in Greece. Sailing, yachting, and other boating activities are the pleasure of those who can afford them, and scuba diving is increasingly popular because of the clarity of the water.

The politics of commercial fishing discourage amateur fishermen—who must be licensed, pay a fee, and abide by certain restrictions—but the Greek islands abound with windsurfers, who enjoy some of the best conditions for the sport outside the tropics.

See Also: Ancient Greece; Basketball (Amateur); Soccer (Amateur) Worldwide; Water Play.

Bibliography. Arnold Arnold, *World Book of Children's Games* (Fawcett, 1972); Patricia Evans, *Rimbles: A Book of Children's Classic Games, Rhymes, Songs, and Sayings* (Doubleday, 1961); E.O. Harbin, *Games of Many Nations* (Abingdon Press, 1954); Johan Huizinga, *Homo Ludens* (Beacon Press, 1971); Sarah Ethridge Hunt, *Games and Sports the World Around* (Ronald Press Company, 1964); Glenn Kirchner, *Children's Games Around the World* (Benjamin Cummings, 2000); Nina Millen, *Children's Games From Many Lands* (Friendship Press, 1943); Sarah B. Pomeroy, *Ancient Greece: A Political, Social and Cultural History* (Oxford University Press, 2007).

Bill Kte'pi
Independent Scholar

H

Hand and Foot

Hand and Foot is a North American game that is similar to canasta and appeared in the 1980s. The game is always played with partners. Hand and Foot is a melding game where the objective is to meld all the cards you are dealt into stacks belonging to the partnership. Although there are many variations on the game, few are in print at this time. Because of the large number of variations, it is important to know the house rules that are being played with. Many of these variants are shared by players on the internet. The game uses more decks of cards than canasta, making it easier to play, especially for beginners.

Hand and Foot is normally played in teams of two players with either two or three teams. The number of decks of 54 cards (both jokers are included in each deck) used is commonly one more then than the number of players. For each hand, each player is dealt a hand of 11 cards and a foot (a second hand that is not immediately used) of 13 cards. (Some variants deal the same number of cards to both the hand and the foot, either 11 or 13.) A player continues to play from their first hand until they have played or discarded the last card from it. At that point they can pick up their second hand (the foot). If they played the last card from their hand, then they can continue to play. If they picked up the foot because of a discard, they have to wait until their next turn to play any of the cards from their foot. The round ends when one player has played all of his cards.

The main point of the game is the melding of cards into stacks of three (the minimum number of cards) to seven (the maximum) cards. Melds can consist of only cards of the same rank. Twos and jokers are wild and can be melded into any stack, however, the number of wilds is limited depending on the number of cards in the meld. Once there are seven cards in a meld, it is considered complete and called a pile. Piles can be clean (not wild cards), dirty (one or two wild cards), or containing just wild cards. A partnership must have a certain number of piles in order to end the round. Threes of each suit have special rules depending on the variant being played, but normally they cannot meld and count for a large number of points against the player holding them at the end of the game.

When the round ends, points are awarded for the cards melded plus completed piles. Points are lost for cards that have not been played (either in the player's hand or foot). Play continues to a certain number or points or a certain number of rounds. If playing a certain number of rounds, it is typical for each player to deal the same number of times.

Commercial card decks to play Hand and Foot have been produced since 1987.

See Also: History of Playing Cards; Team Play; United States, 1960 to Present.

Bibliography. Jack Botermans, Tony Burrett, Pieter van Delft, and Carla van Splunteren, *The World of Games: Their Origins and History, How to Play Them, and How to Make Them* (Facts on File, 1989); Merilyn Simonds Mohr, *The Games Treasury: More Than 300 Indoor and Outdoor Favorites with Strategies, Rules and Traditions* (Chapters Publishing Ltd., 1993); Pagat .com, "Hand and Foot," www.pagat.com/rummy/handfoot .html (cited July 2008).

Dallace W. Unger, Jr.
Independent Scholar

Hares and Hounds

The hunting game Hares and Hounds has a long history in the United Kingdom, France, the United States, and other parts of the world. Sometimes a few hares try to elude the hounds' pursuit; alternatively, hares and hounds comprise two teams. Names for this hunting game include Hounds and Hares, Hunts, Fox and Hounds, and Stag Hunting. In a variant of Hares and Hounds called Paper Chase, the hounds leave shreds of paper as clues for their pursuers. Another variant, a board game called Hares and Hounds or the French Military Game, can be found online. Motorcycle courses for Hares and Hounds races have become popular in recent years.

British accounts of Hares and Hounds show that the game has had a fairly consistent pattern since the 17th century. Since much running takes place, children usually play the game in the country, but it is also possible to play in parks or wooded areas of cities. Before beginning the game, hares plan where they will run. Hounds count to give hares a head start before pursuit begins. During the chase, hounds call out to the hares to check the hares' direction. If no hares answer, the hounds may decide to give up their pursuit. A hound who spots a hare shouts "Tally-ho!" to alert teammates. After capturing a hare, a hound may pat him or her three times on the head or on the back.

Toward the middle of the 19th century, Paper Chase became a common term for games of Hares and Hounds played at British schools. *Tom Brown's School Days* (1857) describes children's careful shredding of newspaper, carried in bags and left as clues. Nineteenth-century schoolchildren did not need to worry about littering, but 20th-century organizers of games told children to bring all the pieces of shredded newspaper home to avoid littering. This concern continues in the 21st century.

More self-contained and litter-free, the board game Hare and Hounds offers both children and adults a chance to develop complex strategies. In this game, one player represents the three hounds; the other represents the hare. If the hare makes its way to the left of the hounds, it succeeds, but if the hounds cut off the hare's escape, they win the game. Electronic versions of this game, written in Java, have appealed to many players.

In the United Kingdom and the United States, motorcycle races called Hares and Hounds have become elaborate competitions. The first motorcycle rider to set out on a marked off-road course becomes the hare, and those who follow that rider become the hounds. Races in California, Nevada, and Idaho involve two separate courses of about 40 miles each, with a break in between the loops for refueling and maintenance. Motorcycle races in the United Kingdom tend to be shorter, with only one course, but their off-road terrain is similarly rough and challenging.

The best-known analysis of Hares and Hounds by a folklorist is Alan Dundes's "On Game Morphology" (1964). Applying Vladimir Propp's structural theory, Dundes notes that Hares and Hounds has a double structure with different lacks, interdictions, violations, and consequences for Hares and Hounds. He observes that traditional folktales have a similar double-stranded structure, since heroes and villains have opposite goals. Besides folklorists, combinatorial games theorists have studied Hare and Hounds, exploring the range of moves that two players can make.

See Also: Boys' Play; Game Theory; Organized or Sanctioned Play; Play as Competition, Sociology of.

Bibliography. Thomas Hughes, *Tom Brown's School Days* (Adamant Media Corporation, 2005); Glenn Kirchner, *Children's Games Around the World* (Benjamin Cummings, 2000); Iona Opie and Peter Opie, *Children's Games in Street and Playground* (Oxford University Press, 1969); Joseph Strutt, *Sports and Pastimes of the People of England* (T. Tegg, 1801).

Elizabeth Tucker
Binghamton University

Hasbro

Hasbro is an American toy and game company, the second-largest such company in the world (after Mattel). Hasbro and its subsidiaries are responsible for some of the best-known American toys and games.

The company was founded in 1923 by Henry and Helal Hassenfeld (the Has bros). Originally a textile company that also sold school supplies, in the 1940s it began offering toys to its school supply customers. In 1952, its first major hit, its first iconic product, came about when the company purchased Mr. Potato Head from independent inventor George Lerner. Mr. Potato Head was, and remains, an enormous success, one of the most recognizable toys despite its several changes in body design.

Originally, multiple sets of accessories were sold, along with other Potato Head family members and Mr. Orange. (Originally, the characters were only accessories, to be attached to a potato or orange at home; the plastic potato was introduced in 1964). Though the accessory sets have been streamlined, the company currently produces a number of specially branded Mr. Potato Heads, including a Darth Vader (Darth Tater), a Spider-Man Potato Head, an Indiana Jones Potato Head, and so on.

The next major success was the sort that was so big, it created success for other companies at the same time: With the 1964 introduction of G.I. Joe, Hasbro coined the term *action figure* for boys' dolls. The market grew quickly, and by the start of the 1980s, action figures were enormous sellers for multiple companies, often featuring collectible lines with dozens of individual figures, accessories, and playsets. My Little Pony followed, a popular toy line for girls, and in 1984 Hasbro acquired the Milton Bradley Company, a major producer of board games (including Battleship, Connect Four, Life, Twister, and Yahtzee).

Major Hasbro subsidiaries include:

- Wizards of the Coast, a game publisher that acquired TSR, the makers of *Dungeons & Dragons*. Wizards of the Coast also makes Magic: the Gathering. Avalon Hill, a publisher of wargames and strategy games, is a subsidiary of Wizards of the Coast.
- Claster Television, the production company behind *Romper Room* and distributor of *Star Blazers, Transformers, G.I. Joe*, and *ReBoot*, the first all-CGI show.
- Coleco, makers of Cabbage Patch Kids and the Colecovision video game console that competed against Atari and Intellivision during the golden age of video games.
- Galoob, which until Hasbro's acquisition in 1998 was the third-largest toy company in the United States. Galoob is best known for Micro Machines and Pound Puppies, and it produced a number of media tie-in toys, such as those for the *A-Team, Blackstar, Men in Black,* and *Starship Troopers.*
- Kenner, founded in Cincinnati in 1947 and a leader in television toy ads. Makers of the Spirograph, Easy-Bake Oven, and the *Star Wars* action figures that made the 3.75-inch figure the standard of the toy industry.
- Parker Brothers, best known for Monopoly.
- Playskool, a manufacturer of toys for children up to 5 years old.
- Tonka, a toy truck manufacturer.
- Tiger Electronics, a maker of handheld electronic games.

See Also: Coleco; Galoob; Kenner; Parker Brothers; Playskool; Tiger Electronics; TSR.

Bibliography. Deborah Jaffe, *The History of Toys* (The History Press, 2006); Don Wuffson, *Toys* (Henry Holt, 2000).

Bill Kte'pi
Independent Scholar

Hearts

Hearts came about in the 19th century and is a negative (or avoidance of) trick-taking game, also referred to as a nullo game. The objective of the game is to have the lowest score. Points are accumulated for each heart card the player has at the end of the round. Hearts shares the idea of trick avoidance with other games such as euchre, whist, and skat.

The idea of trick avoidance is directly opposite of the game of bridge, in which the players are trying to take as many tricks as possible. There are a number of variations of Hearts. Basic Hearts is also referred to as Omnibus Hearts. Normally play is with four people, each playing for themselves. Variants exist that allow as few as two players and as many as six. However, even in these variants each player still plays for themselves.

A standard deck of 52 cards is used in all the variants, although in some cases, one or more of the twos has to be removed to make the deal work out so that all players have the same number of cards.

In each hand, points are accumulated for each heart the player takes (usually one point for each card). In one of the variants, points are also gained for taking the queen of spades. This variant is called Black Maria or Black Lady since the queen of spade usually scores more than one point. The exact amount depends on the rules being used. Common values are five and thirteen, the same as the total of all the heart cards.

There is an exception to the rule of scoring points for the hearts (and queen of spades). Called shooting the moon or going for control, if a player can collect all of the cards that score points, the player scores zero and all other players score the value of all the scoring cards.

Another standard feature of Hearts is passing three cards to one of the other players at the beginning of the game. The pass can be to the same person each round or can vary from round to round. If varied, a pattern is usually used, and it must be such that each player will pass to every other player at the table at some point. There is often a hold round where no passing takes place.

The game is played in hands until either a predetermined number of hands are played, or one or more players exceed a certain number of points. At the end of the game the player with the lowest number of points wins. If players are wagering on the game the losing players pay the winner. A common amount is a penny per point of difference in their scores.

There a numerous variations to Hearts. One variation changes the number of points scored for each heart card. Called Spot Hearts, instead of one point no matter what the card is, each card counts a number of points equal to its value, with the jack being 11, the queen 12, the king 13, and the ace 14. Another variant involves when the queen of spades can be played. One variant requires the queen to be played the first time the player does not have any cards in the suit that was led. There is also a variant that allows the player who takes the trick with either the jack or 10 of diamonds to lower their score by 10 points. Hearts is considered a more challenging game if the game is played without the passing of cards before the play of each round.

See Also: Bridge and Variations; Euchre; Gambling; History of Playing Cards; Skat; Whist.

Bibliography. Jack Botermans, Tony Burrett, Pieter van Delft, and Carla van Splunteren, *The World of Games: Their Origins and History, How to Play Them, and How to Make Them* (Facts on File, 1989); Merilyn Simonds Mohr, *The Games Treasury: More than 300 Indoor and Outdoor Favorites with Strategies, Rules and Traditions* (Chapters Publishing Ltd., 1993); John Scarne, *Scarne on Cards* (Crown Publishers, 1973).

Dallace W. Unger
Independent Scholar

Hide and Seek

One of the best-documented games of European children is Hide and Seek, in which a designated seeker pursues other children who hide. In the ancient Greek game *Apodidraskinda*, one player kept his eyes shut for awhile to let the others hide and then pursued the hiders. Each of the hiders tried to be the first to get back to the point of departure, in order to become the next seeker. Later versions of this game vary; in some, children compete for the role of seeker, while in others they simply try to avoid getting caught. Young children play Hide and Seek in circumscribed areas, while teenagers play in larger spaces, with elaborate planning before the game begins.

In Elizabethan England, children played a number of hiding and seeking games; some of these are better understood now than others. The game King By Your Leave or Old Shewe featured a blindfolded seeker, known as the king, who was replaced by the first hider who could run back to the base. Shakespeare's *Love's Labour's Lost* mentions an old game that began with the cry "All hid"; other than explanation of the cry in the fourth act, no other details appear in the play. Similarly, in act four of *Hamlet*, the Prince of Denmark tells Rosencrantz and Guildenstern, who are inquiring about Polonius's body, "Hide Fox, and all after." Since the game Hide and Fox appears to have been very similar to Hide and Seek, it seems likely that Hamlet is referring to the children's game that was well known to Elizabethans.

Iona and Peter Opie's classic *Children's Games in Street and Playground* (1969) lists a plethora of names for Hide and Seek; many of these are based on the cries of the game's players. One 19th-century name, Whoop, comes from *Every Boy's Book* by J.L. Williams (1841).

The children's game of Hide and Seek can be traced back to ancient Greece and is thought to appear in William Shakespeare's Hamlet. *The game emphasizes evasion, pursuit, and capture.*

Other 19th-century British names recorded by the Opies include Beans and Butter (Oxfordshire), Hide-a-Bo-Seek (Berwickshire), Hide-Hoop (Pembrokeshire), Hiders-Catch-Winkers (Hampshire), Huddin-Peep (Lancashire), and Salt Eel (Suffolk).

A popular variant of Hide and Seek documented by the Opies is Sardines, in which only one player hides at first; all the others cover their eyes and count to give that player a chance to find a good hiding place. The seekers' objective is to join the hidden player. Eventually a large group of hiders awaits the last seeker, who loses the game. Other names for Sardines include Squashed Tomatoes and Mexican Hideout. Both adults and children have enjoyed playing this game at parties in the United Kingdom.

Mary and Herbert Knapp's *One Potato, Two Potato: The Secret Education of American Children* (1976) identifies Hide and Seek as a game of metaphors, in which children can express their feelings about eluding authority figures and taking or avoiding "It" roles. The Knapps suggest that hiding, getting caught, being alone, and becoming independent are important aspects of childhood that emerge during game-playing. Since Hide and Seek and other children's games emphasize pursuit, isolation, and capture, it seems clear that these states of being are meaningful for children.

American children of upper elementary school and middle school age have played various versions of the Hide and Seek variant Manhunt, which involves careful preparation. Teams of hiders and seekers are prominent in Manhunt, but not all versions of the game emphasize teamwork. Depending upon the terrain in which young people hide, Manhunt can be a difficult or even dangerous game. Common sites for this game include backyards and neighborhood streets, but children who want to challenge themselves further may play Manhunt in abandoned buildings and allegedly haunted locales. Players of the more dangerous versions of this game generally do not divulge their plans to parents and teachers.

See Also: Hares and Hounds; Play as Competition, Sociology of.

Bibliography. Mary and Herbert Knapp, *One Potato, Two Potato* (Norton, 1976); Iona Opie and Peter Opie, *Children's Games in Street and Playground* (Oxford University Press, 1969); William Shakespeare, *Hamlet* (Penguin Classics, 2001); J.L. Williams, *Every Boy's Book* (Dean and Munday, 1841).

Elizabeth Tucker
Binghamton University

Highland Games

The Highland Games are events held worldwide in order to foster and restore interest in traditional dancing, piping, athletic achievement, and other aspects of Gaelic culture. This celebration of Scottish and Celtic custom especially reflects the rituals born in the Scottish Highlands, the rugged and mountainous regions of Scotland north celebrated for being one of the most scenic regions in Europe. Usually a one- or two-day event held in the late summer or fall, the Highland Games combine entertainment and athletic competitions grounded in Gaelic tradition.

The origin of the Highland Games is believed to predate recorded history, so exactly how the Highland Games began is largely a mystery. The modern Highland Games' history is most notoriously traceable to King Malcolm III of Scotland in the 11th century. Different accounts trace the games' history to trials of strength, speed, agility, and skill that took place in religious and cattle fairs, or as training for military battle. The Highland Games also more specifically served as a mode of training for the Scottish men in times of English rule. The English outlawed Scottish military training to prevent any uprising, so the Scottish instead replaced arms and weapons with the implements of the Highland Games.

Regardless of the beginnings of the Highland Games, the modern games are a Victorian invention, developed after the Highland Clearances, the brutally forced emigration of the Scottish Highlands in the 18th century.

The Games

The athletic events typically seen at the Highland Games are referred to as Heavy Events. Participants wearing a kilt compete in a number of contests, receiving points for individual performance, and the athlete with the most points wins the overall Highland Games. Many of the competitors in Highland Games events are former collegiate track and field throwers who find the strength-oriented Scottish games to be an excellent way to continue their competitive careers.

Each Highland Games may use its own unique list of contests. Some of the competitions, however, have become staples in Highland Game contests. One such event is the caber toss. The athlete balances a tall pine or log vertically and attempts to "turn the caber." Turning the caber successfully means that as the athlete throws the log, the smaller end of the pine or log the athlete was holding must hit the ground in the 12 o'clock position after the large end hits. The stone put is very much like the shot put event contested in the Olympic Games, but instead of a round shot put, the Highland Games competitors use a stone. Weight over the bar, or weight for height, is an event in which athletes must toss a 56-pound weight over a specified bar height. Athletes receive three attempts at each height. If an athlete misses all three attempts, they are eliminated from the competition. Other common events include the Scottish hammer throw, the weight throw, and the sheaf toss.

The Entertainment

The Highland Games have developed into more than just a series of athletic contests; they have become full-blown festivals with music and dance entertainment and, in some cases, serve as a means to display Scottish goods or see historical mock battles. The music performed reflects the Gaelic culture. The bagpipe instrument has become the most popular symbol of the Highland Games, with as many as 20 or more pipe bands playing together during the opening and closing of the games. At the modern Highland Games, spectators are able to enjoy two types of dancing: Scottish country dancing, a social dance, and Highland dancing, competition dances. The Highland Fling, the Sword Dance, and Scottish Lilt are examples.

See Also: Athletics (Amateur); Golf (Amateur); Play as Competition, Sociology of.

Bibliography. Francie Hall, *Scottish Highland Games* (Overmountain Press, 2002); Cowal Highland Gathering, www.cowalgathering.co.uk/index.asp (cited July 2008); D. Webster, *Scottish Highland Games* (Reprographia, 1973); Wikipedia, "Highland Games," en.wikipedia.org/wiki/Highland_Games (cited July 2008).

Larry Judge
Ball State University

History of Playing Cards

Playing cards resembling the "standard" 52-card deck used in Europe, the Americas, and Asia have been in use since the beginning of the 15th century C.E. The earliest known cards originated in China some time in the 1st millennium C.E. Cards from Egypt dating back to near the start of the 2nd millennium C.E. may provide the link to the first European and Indian cards, which have similar rank and suit characteristics. There is, however, no direct evidence linking these cards back to the early Chinese cards, which have a different rank and suit relationship.

Because of their portability and flexibility, playing cards quickly became a versatile instrument of recreation, not only for gambling, but also for other forms of play, education, art, and even divination. Today many other forms of card decks exist, including special decks for collectable card games, but the 54-card "French Deck" (often called a Bridge or Poker deck in the United States) and the 78-card Tarot deck are the two most common. When speaking generally about card decks, a 52- or-54-card deck with four suits and 13 ranks (and often two jokers) is called a "standard" deck, while variants such as Tarot are called "nonstandard."

Chinese, European, and Indian Origins

The oldest known playing cards are thought to date back to the Tang Dynasty (618–907). These cards, found in China, may have been used for playing "The Game of Leaves," but although there is mention of the game in writing from that time, the rules are unknown. Andrew Lo argues that this game was actually a board game of promotion and demotion, using dice and a series of reference pages ("leaves") to determine scores. However, Ouyang Xiu (1007–72) writes that card games were developed simultaneously with the use of sheets of paper instead of rolls, which occurred during this same period.

In 1895, W.H. Wilkinson proposed that these first cards may have also served as money, and thus were both the instruments of play and the stakes themselves. Early Chinese cards had four suits, all related to increments of money: coins, strings of 10 coins, myriads of string (representing 10 strings of 10 coins), and tens of myriads. Another way of looking at the values is 1 (coins), 10 (strings), 100 (myriads), and 1,000 (tens of myriads), which are common monetary denominations; it is further speculated that the card designs were originally created as copies of the paper money of the time.

There were two different types of early Chinese cards: Kwan P'ai and Lut Chi. Kwan Pa'i playing cards contained only the first three suits, with each suit containing nine cards, again suggesting an attempt to use the cards to generate numbers from 1 to 999. Each suit additionally contained an "honor card," the earliest ancestor of today's "face cards" or "trump cards." Lut Chi, found in the South of China, added the fourth suit.

It has been proposed that the early European suits, which included "wands" or "batons," might have evolved from a misinterpretation of the images of strings of coins from the Lut Chi cards. However, there is no direct evidence of a link between the development of cards in China and Europe; it is only known that Chinese cards were developed much sooner.

European cards have a similarly vague and varied set of origins. The earliest proposed date is in the 1200s; the latest possible date is in the late 1300s. The earliest references to what were once thought to be card games—"*games de rege et regina*"—now are more commonly thought to refer to Chess-like games. Further, in Francesco Petrarch's work "Phisicke Against Fortune" (1353–60), a treatise that deals with a variety of moral and philosophical problems including those around gambling, cards are never mentioned. This suggests the likelihood of the later date being more accurate.

Cards used by the Mamluks, Islamic slave soldiers who seized power in Egypt from 1250 to 1516, are the most likely inspiration for the European decks. The Mamluk deck contains the same numbers and classifications as what are now considered "standard" playing cards: 10 cards denoting a value from one to 10, and three ranked "face cards," each in four suits (sticks, coins, swords, and cups).

Indian cards, known as *ganjifa*, are commonly thought to have their origins in India in the 16th century. There is some speculation that Chinese and/or European cards influenced the creation of these cards, but they are in many ways a unique variation. The cards are circular in form, intricately hand painted, and have anywhere from eight to 32 suits. However, the cards share with European cards the ranking of 10 numeric cards plus a number of "face cards," usually two per suit. Many games were played with these cards at the time of their origin, but their use today is much more limited. The game of *Naqsh* is one of the most popular surviving games; the goal is to have cards adding up to various numbers, with the "face cards" counting as 11 and 12, again as with European decks. Today the word *ganjifa* is used to refer to "standard" Anglo-European cards as well as the original Indian decks.

Design Changes and Standardizations

From 1370 to 1400, playing cards grew in popularity across Europe. Writings from this period document card games being played in Spain by 1371, and in France and Switzerland by 1377. The early decks were handmade works of art available only to the rich, but the introduction of the mass production of paper around 1400, coupled with the popularity of woodcut printing, quickly led to the creation of inexpensive decks for general public consumption.

Even with mass production, the suits used in card decks did not become standardized across Europe until the 1500s. During the 1400s, decks often had five suits instead of four. The suits varied from country to country: Germans used hearts, bells, acorns, and leaves, while Italians used variations of the swords, cups, batons, and coins from the Mamluk decks; the "Latin suits," as they came to be known, also were used by the Spanish. The English used the Italian suits until after 1480, when the French adapted the German suits to create the four used in most places today: hearts, clubs, spades, and diamonds.

The ranking and number of cards was inconsistent as well: some decks contained a fourth trump card, the valet, who ranked below the knight; it is thought that these two cards merged to form the jack used today. A German deck from around 1440 even reversed the rankings on two suits, making the queen higher than the king, probably to reflect a historic royal lineage.

France provided the standard that became adopted throughout Europe, and eventually America and much of Asia. Two different French decks, both using the four common suits and 13 ranks per suit, rose to popularity, each distinguished by the design of their court (trump or face) cards. The court cards of decks manufactured in Rouen, in the north of France, became the standard in England, while the court cards of decks manufactured near Paris became the standard in France.

Eventually, even though Rouen had a geographic advantage over Paris in its proximity to England, the influence of the Parisian court card designs spread throughout Europe. The Parisian card designs continue to be used today, even in decks from Rouen.

The "Paris Court" imagery featured three trumps per suit, each depicting historic royalty, among them Alexander the Great and Julius Caesar. One-third of the trump cards appear to be inspired by the court of Charles VII, France's king in the period from 1422 to 1461, when these cards were likely designed. There are alternative historic interpretations for these four cards; it is unknown if the ambiguity was intended to flatter the king's court by drawing historic parallels with the likes of Charlemagne and the Biblical Rachel.

Until 1745, the portraits on court cards did not have vertical symmetry; this resulted in card players often being able to deduce who had trump cards based on people turning those cards "right side up" in their hands. While a French card designer is often credited with the concept, the French government regulated the design of playing cards and forbade this change. In 1799, Edmund Ludlow and Ann Wilcox patented reversible playing cards, which had risen to popularity in the preceding half-century. By 1802, this design was the standard upon which others were based.

The card known in English decks as the knave became the jack in 1864, when Samuel Hart published a deck using J instead of Kn for the lowest court card. The knave had been called a jack as part of the terminology of the game All Fours since the 1600s, but this was not common usage because the game and the word were considered vulgar. However, because the card abbreviation for knave (Kn) was so close to that of the king (K) it was easy to confuse them, especially after suits and rankings were moved to the corners of the card in order to enable people to fan them in one hand and still see all the values. The earliest known deck to place suits and rankings in the corners of the card is from 1693, but these cards did not become popular until the 1864 Hart deck reintroduced them along with the knave-to-jack change.

Another innovation from the Hart design is the joker, the 53rd card found in most decks. The card was created for the game of Euchre as a "trump card" that would beat any other one. The term *joker* was adapted from the original Alsatian name for the game, *Juker*; it does not relate to the fool from the Tarot deck, as is commonly thought. Some card decks now contain two jokers, often one in color and one in black and white; this enables players to create games in which one joker beats another. Manufacturers often trademark their jokers, as this is the one card value that does not have a standard form (or symmetry, for that matter). Sometimes the 54th card is, instead of a joker image, simply the manufacturer's logo.

Starting in the 1920s, paper cards were coated with plastic to produce a more durable product that was easier to handle and that would not fall apart. This was the final step in the development of the standard card decks that are still used today. After this, some manufacturers began to develop cards printed on plastic. However, while these were more durable than their paper counterparts, they have never reached the same level of popularity.

Cards and Society

Like dice, cards offer pleasure through a portable means of playing an infinite variety of games. The evolution of cards over the last millennium has been, to a large extent, to make play with cards more pleasurable—not only in terms of the graphic design considerations mentioned previously, but also in terms of the physical shape and size of the card. For example, most cards are now rectangular with rounded corners, and have a slick surface that makes them easy to manipulate. Certainly anyone who has ever played with a deck of "worn out" cards will recall how much more frustrating things like dealing and shuffling were. The pleasures of card games also often parallel other simple pleasures, such as forming collections or organizing or discarding things. However, those who feel that work is the solitary goal of this life have throughout history regarded pleasure with suspicion.

According to David Parlett, most games originally involved some stakes, and thus gaming and gambling are synonymous. In fact, playing games merely for recreation instead of personal gain is, according to Parlett, a relatively recent development. Protestant morality—not only the famed work ethic but also a belief that cards were "the devil's picture book"—was a primary contributor to early card bans.

Because cards have been associated with gambling since their creation, various cities and countries banned their use soon after their introduction. The earliest known ban was in Paris in 1377; two years later, cards were banned in Switzerland. Cities in Spain followed suit in 1382 and 1384. The city of Ulm, Germany, initiated a ban in 1397, only seven years after the first paper mill was established in Nuremberg. That same year, the prevot of Paris declared a workday ban on recreations that could distract workers; in addition to cards, dice, tennis, and all forms of bowling were named in the decree.

While these early bans were all lifted (or no longer enforced after a short time), various religions have continued to institute bans, including conservative Protestant sects, most notably Mormons Baptists in the United States. Conservative Baptists justify the ban as a means of addressing concern about corruption through gambling; the conservative Mormon ban is part of a larger prohibition of occult objects, fearing that any deck may be used for cartomancy (fortune telling).

The introduction of mass production of paper around 1400 led to inexpensive decks for the general public.

A number of "alternative" decks have been created to get around religious prohibitions. Kille cards, which contain pictures but no suits or numbers, experienced a brief popularity outside of Sweden for this reason. In 1906, Parker Brothers introduced the game of Rook as an alternative for Puritans who refused to play with regular cards. Rook contains 57 cards divided into four suits plus a "joker" (the titular rook), but there are no face cards (instead they are numbered one to 14) and the suits are colors instead of shapes. In addition to the game outlined in the Rook rules (which resembles trick-taking games like Bridge), religious families often use Rook cards to play other games, even ones that involve gambling for chips instead of money.

The invention of cartomancy, or card-based fortune-telling, created an additional mystique around cards. Some cartomancers claim that reading the cards started in Ancient Egypt with the god Thoth, but evidence suggests that cartomancy developed after playing cards were introduced in Europe in the 14th century. The earliest document mentioning card-based divination (using regular cards) is from a 1540 book titled "The Oracles of Francesco Marcolino da Forli." Although Tarot cards were invented in 15th-century Italy, from the 18th century to the early 20th century, "standard" playing cards were used as the primary fortunetelling device. In recent history, readings from the Tarot deck have become more popular than readings from playing card decks. The detailed imagery of many Tarot decks, combined with the common misconception that they are "older" than playing cards, adds to the appeal of having one's future story told with them.

Deck Variations

It is a common misconception that Tarot cards led to the development of the modern playing card deck. In fact, Tarot cards were developed some time between 1400 and 1430 in Italy. First, an additional rank was added to the "standard" 52-card deck, similar to earlier deck variants with the knight and the valet. Then an additional group of picture cards, known as *carte da trionfi*, or triumph cards, were added. These did not have a suit and superseded all other cards in rank; in other words, they "trumped" them. The earliest known description of such a deck is from Martiano de Tortona and dates back to the early 1420s. The deck he describes has 16 trump cards that represent the hierarchy of Greek gods. The earliest mention of today's standard 78-card Tarot deck is from 1491, though there have been expansions of such decks up to 97 cards, and down to as few as 42 cards.

Tarot Cards

Through the early history of the Tarot, because the cards were hand painted, they were only accessible to the wealthy. Their influence may have contributed to the lack of regulation on Tarot cards; these cards were not explicitly banned in most places, and sometimes they were even explicitly allowed, much as Rook cards are today. Another theory about the Tarot exception to card regulation is that they were regarded as divining objects and therefore players could get away with claiming to be fortune-telling when they were in fact gambling.

Although some believe something resembling cartomancy began even before the creation of playing cards, the earliest documents describing Tarot-based divination is from around 1750. The Tarot decks were originally developed for playing the game of Tarot, variants of which are still popular in Europe today. Because the various hierarchies of the 22 trumps (also called the major arcana) often drew from mythological symbols, the cards suggested a mystical authority that led to their adaptation for fortune telling.

In addition to the Tarot, other card deck variations are used worldwide for specific games. David Parlett classifies five notable European deck variations; while standard cards could be used to make any of these decks, such decks are specially designed for the particular game being played. In order to play Piquet, for example, the standard "French-suited" card deck is abbreviated to 32 cards, removing the values of two through six. German card decks, often still using the traditional German suits of leaves, acorns, hearts, and bells, may have 36 cards for the game of Tarock. Swiss card decks have a similar composition, but replace leaves with shields, and hearts with flowers. Spanish cards take a different approach, removing the high-numbered cards instead of the low ones, and changing the suits to swords, clubs, cups, and coins. Italian cards are identical to the Spanish cards in composition, but the symbol designs are significantly different.

Novelty Cards and Games

In the 19th century, artists began to create decks in which each card contained a unique picture. For these "transformation decks," artists started from traditional card symbols and layout and incorporated these into sets of 52 pieces of original artwork. In 1979, the Victoria and Albert Museum in London commissioned 52 artists to each produce a card interpretation; the paintings, drawings, and photos were then reproduced as an actual playing card deck. Today, novelty decks are still popular. These decks include satirical decks that have only the face cards changed to match current politicians and educational decks that contain a standard card grouping but also a fact to be learned on each card. There are also photo or art decks in which the card is mostly covered by a piece of art and only the corner index indicates the value of the card. Some 20th-century art cards also contained sexually suggestive images, intended to add an extra licentiousness to the already morally questioned practice of gambling.

The 20th century also brought about a revolution in card games using nonstandard decks. Many of these games, like Rook, still imitate the ranks and suits of standard cards, most often because the game rules call for similar actions as standard card games—i.e., matching numbers, colors, or suits and collecting or discarding sets. The game Uno, for example, is based on a variant of Crazy Eights, a game played with standard cards; Uno simply adds special "action" and "wild" cards to affect the order and actions of game play. Many Concentration games feature words and pictures to make the game educational or more appealing to children, but the rules are identical to the game played with regular cards. Decks of nonstandard playing cards have been used to create storytelling games, philosophical games, trivia games, word games, and a recent popular trend, collectible card games.

Although collectible card games have only become popular since 1993, the first collectible card game, the Base Ball Card Game, was published in 1904. By providing players with rules for competing via the statistics printed on each card, the game expanded the concept of baseball trading cards, which had already become popular in the previous two decades. However, the concept was not widely used until Richard Garfield created the fantasy card game Magic: The Gathering in the 1990s. The game immediately spawned imitators in many genres until 1997, when Richard Garfield's company received a patent on key aspects of the game mechanic and began to pursue companies, including Nintendo, for royalties on the patent.

In collectible card games, players prepare a deck containing an agreed-upon number of cards from their collections. Because the cards in such games are not printed in equal quantities, the rare cards appreciate in financial value over time. Each card contains descriptive text that tells the player what special rule applies to him when the card is in use. Although the scenario varies depending on the genre, generally players "battle" for cards. Often the prize for winning is to take the loser's cards into one's own collection permanently. This aspect of collectible card games brings the history of playing cards full circle, returning to the original Chinese concept of cards as both the mechanism and the stakes of play.

See Also: Ace-Deuce-Jack; Baccarat; China; Cribbage; France; Gambling; Play as Entertainment, Psychology of; Play as Entertainment, Sociology of; Pokémon; Solitaire and Variations of; Team Play; War.

Bibliography. Alliott M. Avedon and Brian Sutton-Smith, *The Study of Games* (Krieger, 1979); Henry Jones Cavendish, *Card Essays* (Thomas DeLaRue & Co., 1879); Stewart Culin, *Chess and Playing Cards: Catalogue of Games and Implements for Divination* (United States National Museum, 1895); Michael Dummett; *The Game of Tarot* (Duckworth & Company, 1980); Kaushal Gupta, *Gambling Game of Naqsh and Ganjifa Cards* (International Playing-Card Society, 1979); Catherine Perry Hargrave, *A History of Playing Cards and a Bibliography of Cards and Gaming* (Dover, 1991); Andrew Lo, *The Game of Leaves: An Inquiry into the Origin of Chinese Playing Cards* (Cambridge University Press, 2000); David Parlett, *The Oxford Guide to Card Games* (Oxford University Press, USA, 1990); Robert M. Place, *The Tarot: History, Symbolism, and Divination* (Penguin, 2005); W.H. Wilkinson, *Chinese Origin of Playing Cards* (American Anthropological Association, 1895); Yale University, "Cary Collection of Playing Cards online database," beinecke.library.yale.edu/carycards/default.asp (cited June 2008).

Jay Laird
Northeaster University

Hit the Rat

There are two types of Hit the Rat games, both of which are fundamentally tests of reflexes.

The first type is an operated game found at fairs and carnivals, especially in the United Kingdom. A target (the "rat," though real animals are not used) is dropped through a drainpipe over a spot in front of the player, who must hit it with a bat or stick in order to win a prize.

The second type is an arcade game, best known by the brand name Whac-a-Mole, though there are many brands. In this automated electric game, instead of a rat falling down a drainpipe, a rodent or other pest (there are, of course, other "nuisance" targets, including caricatures of public figures) rises out of one of four or more holes. The player must whack as many of the targets as possible within the allotted time with a cushioned mallet. The secret to the game is the algorithm used for the timing sequence, which is neither rhythmic nor identical with each play, making it impossible for the player to simply "get into the rhythm." The game therefore depends purely on reflexes, not on the ability to keep the beat. There are simplified versions of the game, with fewer holes, for younger players.

See Also: Amusement Parks; Arcades; United Kingdom.

Bibliography. Elliott Avedon, *The Study of Games* (Krieger Pub Co., 1979); Jesse Hubbell Bancroft, *Games* (MacMillan, 1937); Roger Caillois, *Man, Play and Games* (University of Illinois Press, 2001).

Bill Kte'pi
Independent Scholar

Hobbies

Hobbies are activities including crafting, sporting, or gardening that are carried on not as a regular occupation, but primarily for pleasure—as a pastime. The sensibility of having or developing a hobby is relatively new. It emerged during the 17th century, and the word *hobby* is derived from the term *hobby horse*. A hobby horse is a toy horse's head attached to the end of a stick, but in relation to *hobby*, it denotes having a hobby horse (a comfortable pastime, or a vocation) that one rides for hours and hours. A hobby is a pastime that occupies one's time in pleasant way—it is an activity that suggests that there is leisure time. During the 16th century, hobbies were indulgences of the very affluent when the vast majority of people existed at a subsistence level and did not have time, nor surplus resources to develop hobbies. During the 17th and 18th centuries, hobbies were practiced by the very young and the very old, since they were thought to inculcate moral values in the young, and foster serenity in the aged. During the 19th century, hobbies came to the forefront when urban services and industries freed up time for leisure activities, and during the 20th century, hobbies spawned new business industries.

Having time to pursue leisure or recreational interests is a relatively new phenomenon. In traditional societies, as contrasted with industrial, urbanized, and capitalist societies, there was relatively little change in family occupations over generations. Until the late 19th century, children had little choice in selecting careers; they generally followed family tradition by entering the family business. Since children provided labor to support family economies, they did not have discretionary time or resources for developing hobbies. If they did not want to practice their father's trade, they were sometimes placed in apprenticeships or indentured.

The history of hobbies is intertwined with the history of consumerism in the Western world. Practicing hobbies has had subtly negative connotations throughout history because they were thought of as amateur activities. In his book *Contemplations Moral and Divine* (1676), English jurist Sir Matthew Hale (1609–76) wrote, "Almost every person hath some hobby horse or other wherein he prides himself." During the 17th century, the advent of cheap manufactured goods started a consumer revolution, so "homespun" cloth was considered to be "coarsely" woven unmilled fabric rather than homemade.

The selection of hobbies throughout time has been largely based upon gender. In traditional agrarian societies, a woman's domain was connected with a repertoire of domestic manufacturing and processing tasks that were essential to maintain the well-being of her family. She controlled the household, the garden, the dairy, and the henhouse. A woman's days were spent processing the raw materials produced by her husband into usable items including food, clothing, candles, and soap. A woman's fertility was as essential as her productivity; childbearing consumed about 25 years of her life, because infant mortality was high and children were part of the labor force. Rural homes were functional and children played with discarded materials around the farm. By today's sensibilities, which foster cleaning, dusting, polishing, and decorating, homes in the 1600s would have seemed bleak and primitive. However, in the cities, a consumer revolution created an emerging merchant class. Cheap cloth and luxury items became available and cleanliness became the mark of urban sophistication, while industry and frugality gave way to delicacy, refinement, and attention to fashion during the 18th century.

Apprenticeships

Meanwhile, apprenticeships took up the formative years for many boys. Apprenticeship was a system of learning a craft or trade from one who is engaged with it, and of paying for the instruction by a given number of years of service, that harkened back to ancient Babylon and Egypt. Apprenticing was typical in medieval Europe where guilds supervised apprentice programs. Under the apprentice system, a master craftsman agreed to instruct a young man, to give him shelter, food, and clothing. In exchange, the apprentice would bind or indenture himself to work for the master for a given time, after which the apprentice would become a journeyman working for a master for a wage, or set up as a master himself. In the transition from agrarian cultures to production cultures, apprenticeships evolved. Between the late 1700s and mid-1800s, power-driven machinery allowed unskilled workers to perform the tasks of skilled hands in such occupations as sewing, weaving, and cabinet making. In the patriarchal structure of craft apprenticeship, boys served tradesmen and for husbandry, and girls were bound out to serve as housemaids. As the apprentice system eroded, once-specialized occupations, such as woodworking, became hobbies.

Perhaps the most famous example of an early-American apprentice-turn-hobbyist during this transition was Benjamin Franklin (1706–90), the son of a poor candle and soap maker. Franklin grew up in a large family that could not afford to send him for formal schooling. Franklin went into a Boston store that sold toys in 1713, when he was 7 years old, and purchased a whistle. Franklin's father Josiah withdrew him from his grammar school and sent him to a practical school that stressed writing and arithmetic. At the age of 10, Franklin returned home to learn his father's trade, but he was not engaged by his father's soap making trade, so he expressed an interest in going to sea. Josiah resolved to apprentice his 12-year-old son and took him to Boston to survey various occupational opportunities. At first Franklin was placed with his cousin Samuel, a cutler, but Josiah and Samuel argued over how to finance the apprenticeship. Later, he was placed with his older brother James, who was a printer. Franklin, who was arguably the most prominent hobbyist of the American Revolutionary era, learned the craft of printing, but left his apprenticeship early, causing a lot of family friction, and went to sea.

Nature study for entertainment became a popular pastime during the 18th century. Books drawing from medieval bestiaries for descriptions of animals both real and imagined were published, and accounts of exotic expeditions were condensed into popular literature for the monthly British digest of news and commentary called *Gentlemen's Magazine* (1737–1907). Nature study was also promoted in books written for children, including Mrs. Trimmer's *Easy Introduction to the Knowledge of Nature* (1780) and John Aiken's *The Calendar of Nature* (1784). Thomas Bewick's *History of British Birds* (1797 and 1804) was lushly illustrated with his own wood engravings. When fishing became popular in medieval Europe, making artificial flies for bait evolved as a recreational activity.

Women and Hobbies

Novelist Frances Burney (1752–1840) wrote in her diary on July 17, 1768, "I never pretend to be above having and indulging a Hobby Horse." During the 18th century reading, tambour, and other kinds of needlework were considered to be leisurely occupations for young ladies. Prescriptive literature, books, and magazines describing ideal lifestyles advised women on how to utilize leisure time to reflect their roles within home and society. Doing "fancywork" was a fashionable means for expression for women to demonstrate skill and artistry. Female hobbies employing needlework, leatherwork, painting, and decorating were never cultivated for profit, but rather for the benefit of family and friends.

Women were more likely to quietly find time to indulge in practical hobbies because if they tried to pursue careers in writing, they faced stiff opposition. *Godey's Lady's Book* (1830–78) was a popular magazine for women that included poetry, articles, and advice from prominent authors of the day. Issues contained the latest fashions in music literature along with plans for making dolls, games, and other amusements, along with patterns for elaborate needlepoint and sewing projects. As early as the 1840s, authors of child-rearing advice advanced the moral benefits of compiling scrapbooks, which were thought to teach children about reusing household fragments so precious resources would not be lost or wasted. American writer Lydia Maria Child (1802–80) advised young mothers in the 1830s to start boys and girls on paperwork making dolls and keeping scrapbooks, "Cutting figures in paper is a harmless and useful amusement for those old enough to be trusted with scissors; which, by the way, should always be blunt pointed, when placed in the hands of a very young child."

Hobbies For the Masses

Between the 1830s and 1850s, William S. Tower, a carpenter from Hingham, Massachusetts, began making wooden toys in his leisure hours. Tower soon accumulated a surplus of toys, and he established a cooperative guild consisting of 20 members who produced toys. Among the group, Joseph Jacob, proprietor of an axe factory, made toy tools; a local shipwright made toy boats; and a cabinetmaker designed furniture for dollhouses.

Hobbies were pursued as attitudes toward play and leisure changed when parents gave children memento albums in the early 1800s. Between 1840 and 1900, Europe and North America experienced a revolution in printing technology on literacy and play, the growth of a "chromo civilization," where the general public, not only the very affluent, could purchase and collect vibrantly colored images. Collecting, or acquiring things strictly for the sake of amassing them, dates back to the Renaissance when maritime trade brought new ideas and products to Europe. Collecting requires learning and study of some branch of knowledge such as a science, a specific event or period of history, languages, or special skills. This acquisition of knowledge can be

A 1902 photograph of a mother giving her daughter "Her first lesson in embroidery," a popular and practical hobby.

ephemeral in nature, capturing fads like collecting chromolithographed images in bookstores, or it can require developing an expertise, like identifying plants or butterflies. Becoming a collector of material objects can be associated with a broad range of interests including the study of nature, history, arts, crafts, and popular culture. Individuals collect everything from rocks, stamps, paintings, and coins to comic books and memorabilia.

For individuals with limited freedom of choice, hobbies can use and recycle discarded materials like wood and rags. Hobbies presented small opportunities to pursue something in which the individual was fully his or her own master. For slaves, there was very little opportunity for leisure time or play. Weddings provided the only real occasion for diversion with song and dance. Some masters allowed slaves to improve a small piece of ground by planting vegetables.

Slaves worked this land for themselves on Sundays and sold surplus crops at markets, using the profits to buy necessities. Sunday evenings were reserved for family, and men smoked tobacco, drank rum with friends, and whittled. Woodcarving—working wood by means of a cutting tool held in the hand into a sculptural ornamentation of a wood object—dates back to the Middle Ages in Europe and even further back to indigenous people. Whittling, to cut small bits or pare shavings from a piece of wood (to whittle a doll, for example) is performed with a light, small-bladed knife, usually a pocketknife. Carved toys were often made during New England's harsh winters, when men whittled a doll or carved out a whistle, and women sewed small dresses for cornhusk dolls for their children. Woodcarving is considered to be an art, and employs the use of chisels, gouges, and a mallet, while whittling is considered to be a hobby and utilizes a knife.

19th-Century Hobbies

During the 19th century, gardening became a hobby for ladies who wanted to craft a decorative landscape at home. Although gardens typically were laid out near residences, they also appeared in window boxes and on patios in densely populated areas. Gardens were also planted in nonresidential green areas including botanical gardens or zoological societies, where hobbyists shared expertise in clubs and societies. Prior to the California Gold Rush, Sarah Gillespie arrived in San Francisco with her husband Charles. Sarah was an expert gardening hobbyist who had traveled throughout the Pacific Rim collecting plant specimens. Once the Gillespie family settled in their new home, they erected an elaborate greenhouse, despite the scarcity of building resources. Sarah Gillespie—credited with introducing the first Australian acacias, raised from seed in California—entered her flowers in the first state flower show held in California in 1853.

In antebellum America, women had little opportunity for economic independence: They either married and started families or they became spinsters. But financial and emotional stability for many families was shattered during and after the war. Women were left to support families when men, fathers, brothers, and husbands were killed or disabled, with homespun skills developed as amateurs. Women did not have many options for supporting families; housekeeping and taking in boarders allowed women to remain at home; others sought acceptable female occupations derived from former hobbies including writing and hat making.

Women started writing stories for children before the Civil War. American authors would not be expected to earn a living by getting children's stories published, because it was considered to be a hobby or pastime. The war put a halt to publishing books because supplies were scarce, especially in the South. However, northern publishers concentrated on the lucrative family book markets, and after the war, American literature achieved an economic boost. The phenomenon of the family (or domestic novel) written by women authors for female readers not only documented hobbies in domestic settings. The most popular family stories were written by relatively unknown women and illustrated by itinerant artists.

Christmas was established as a national holiday in the United States in 1865, which spawned a practice of exchanging handmade or inexpensive gifts among a wide circle of acquaintances and charities. By the turn of the century, acquaintances received cards, and gift exchanges were chiefly among family and close friends. Children saved and displayed greeting cards, scraps, and embossed paper products in gift albums. In the United States, the McLoughlin Brothers produced products, such as paper dolls and puzzles, that appeared in magazines or that were packaged as sheets, in booklets, and as boxed sets where children's products were sold. When children did not have the means to purchase fine chromolithographed images, they scrounged around the house for materials and common household items from food containers, newspapers, and remnant advertising material garnered from door-to-door salesmen.

Development of Outdoor Hobbies

During the 1870s, devoting energy to outdoor hobbies was considered by some to be a waste of time, until William H.H. Murray (1840–1904) became the father of an outdoor movement when he wrote *Adventures in the Wilderness; or Camp-Life in the Adirondacks*, published in 1869. The literary quality of *Adventures in the Wilderness* promoted New York State's north woods as a popular destination. It also placed rustic woodsmen on a pedestal like noblemen because of their intimacy with the wilderness. Murray did not just encourage his readers to go camping as a way to go fishing or hunting, he inspired millions of Americans to travel to the wilderness for leisure and to discover the joys of outdoor recreation.

The term *Murray's Fools* in popular culture referred to city folk who packed specially outfitted railroad trains each weekend to pour into resorts developed in the Adirondacks during the 1870s. The Arts and Crafts Movement dating from 1875 to 1920 drove a resurgence in the artisan traditions of producing self-directed work over machine-produced objects. Parents felt modern life separated children from nature, and that integrating traditional skills into education would encourage a more authentic and balanced relationship with the material world. With the decline of traditional craft apprenticeships, craftspeople aligned with peers in other disciplines. Schools integrated craft projects into curriculum including shop class and home economics classes.

Amateur photography became popular during the second half of the 19th century, even though it was considered to be another expensive hobby like gardening. Since nature has often been a favorite subject of photographers, photography has been perceived as a healthful, exhilarating hobby. During the 1880s, "The Merry Tramps," a neighborhood bohemian group from Oakland, California, regularly traveled throughout northern California to camp in exotic locations, including Yosemite, that became national parks. The group pitched their elaborate tents in the California Redwood forests, and pursued hobbies including reading, painting, photography, hiking, quilting, playing guitars, and playing singing games. Gene Stratton Porter (1873–1924) grew up in the Limberlost area of Indiana, and she wrote natural history articles for magazines, illustrating them with her own photographs. In her book *A Girl of the Limberlost* (1909), Porter told the story of Elnora Comstock, a daughter of an unloving widowed mother, who finances her own high school education by selling moths that she has collected in the swamp as a hobby.

Youth Hobbies

Parents encouraged children to develop hobbies to fill spare time as well as to grow intellectually and socially during the 20th century. In the United States, this was a continuation of a Puritan desire to combat idleness. Organizations such as the Boy Scouts of America and the Camp Fire Girls (both established in 1910) fostered an interest in doing crafts in response to concern about increased industrialization in everyday life. These organizations encouraged children and adolescents to experience making things by hand. Law enforcement organizations dealing with disruptions caused by adolescents during the 1920s promoted acquiring hobbies as a useful employment in a time when teenagers could acquire knowledge and meet people with similar interests.

Psychologist Werner Muensterberger argued that modern collecting is an "unruly passion," in which individuals compensate for some past disappointment or fear an uncertain future. Muensterberger suggested that the need to amass collections was a compensatory activity. Gardening evolved into a popular hobby after World War I, when women established Victory Gardens. Having a hobby was seen as a particular kind of solitary and productive pastime that could keep an individual properly busy and out of trouble. Industrial arts teachers lamented that rigorous technical skills had degenerated into recreational activities even though crafts and utilitarian or artistic objects made by hand had experienced resurgences as tangible links between the past and present.

The Unemployed

During the Great Depression, the unemployed and underemployed needed to fill time that was once devoted to work. Those who were employed did not necessarily have leisure time, but they needed inexpensive alternatives to commercial entertainment. This effectively turned leisure time into another form of work. A century after William S. Tower employed his artisan skills to make toys. The National Homeworkshop Guild was established in Rockford, Illinois during the Depression so unemployed men could make toys in home workshops for charities. By 1935, the guild had over 150 clubs located throughout the United States.

Hobbies Made Popular

Otto C. Lightner established *Hobbies* magazine in 1931. During the 1930s, hobbies became a craze in the United States as a result of maximum work hour codes that were enacted by the National Recovery Act of 1933 that codified leisure time by creating a five-day workweek. James S. Stanley established the Leisure League of America in New York City in 1934. Earnest Elmo Calkins argued that individuals should select hobbies that provided dramatically different experiences from their daily occupations in order to be well rounded. Calkins categorized hobbies into four groups: making things, acquiring things, learning things, and doing things. Calkins asserted that making things as a hobby provides an outlet for achieving personal satisfaction with hand-craftsmanship. Making things may have been the first hobby to emerge, since hobbies often include activities that were once considered to be occupations.

Cultivating hobbies became popular in the United State after World War I, when work schedules became more regulated so adults had more leisure time. During the Great Depression, unemployed individuals developed hobbies—"do-it-yourself" activities to fill time and economize. Men took on gardening as a practical hobby that produced home-produced fruit and vegetables to supplement the family economy. Although most people sought activities that provided physical pleasure and relaxation rather than the mental stimulation from hobbies, for some the psychological benefits of mastering a hobby reflected the satisfaction previously gained for excelling in a career. Companies manufactured craft supplies or kits for hobbyists that were made of molded plastics and could be assembled with glue and finished with paint. In *Hobbies for Everybody* (1934), author Ruth Lampland asserted that hobbies created a vital outlet for self-expression. The demand for hobby supplies resulted in the manufacturing and sales of hobby products. Models and kits were produced so that hobbyists could assemble something attractive and useful in a short amount of time. Adult education classes were offered to support and foster interest in pursuing hobbies.

During the 1950s, cultivating hobbies became a part of American material culture when homeowners began to integrate hobby-oriented spaces into houses. Sewing rooms, workshops, photographic darkrooms, and recreation/family rooms were added to houses. The baby boom generation, those born between 1946 and 1964, seemed to become a generation of collectors. Since the 1950s, collecting has become a popular hobby for many Americans. Local, regional, and national amateur clubs promoted and created awareness for various kinds of collecting. Individual collectors indulged their interests by attending organized shows, conventions, and swap meets. Increased wealth and leisure has given more people opportunities to take up mass-produced crafts or to pursue enthusiasms in collecting, scrapbook compiling, and quilting. Hobbyists can trade and sell items on eBay and other online venues for pleasure and profit. Manufacturers targeted baby boomers because of their tendencies to accumulate and display things including records, coins, toys, and ceramic figurines in home museums.

During the second half of the 20th century, hobbies became a marketable industry. However, specific hobbies were also fostered by grassroots movements during the 1960s, when crafts, such as making ceramics, textiles, and jewelry, that were cultivated by the anti-materialist counterculture groups began to be offered as courses in art schools. By the end of the century, the terms *handicraft* and *artisan-made* became synonymous with "one-of-a-kind" items with consumers, regardless of their method of production. An example of emerging grassroots hobby organizing is amateur astronomer John L. Dobson, who designed an affordable and portable Dobsonian telescope. He then launched a movement to understand the universe when he cofounded the San Francisco Sidewalk Astronomers in 1967. This group popularized sidewalk astronomy by engaging ordinary people in cities, national parks, and forests in astronomy as a hobby. The San Francisco Sidewalk Astronomers set up telescopes on sidewalks on clear evenings and taught interested passers-by about the stars and planets in the night sky.

See Also: Hobby Horses; United States, 1783 to 1860; United States, Colonial Period.

Bibliography. Donna R. Braden, *Leisure and Entertainment in America* (Henry Ford Museum & Greenfield Village, 1988); Earnest Elmo Calkins, *Care and Feeding of Hobby-Horses* (Leisure League of America, 1934); Lydia Maria Child, *The Mother's Book* (Carter and Hendee, 1832); Steven M. Gerber, *Hobbies: Leisure and the Culture of Work in America* (Columbia University Press, 1999); Joseph M. Hawes and N. Ray Hiner, *American Childhood: A Research Guide and Historical Handbook* (Greenwood Press, 1985); Werner Muensterberger, *Collecting, An Unruly Passion: Psychological Perspectives* (Harcourt Brace & Company, 1994); W.J. Rorabough, *The Craft Apprentice: From Franklin to the Machine Age in America* (Oxford University Press, 1986).

Meredith Eliassen
San Francisco State University

Hobby Horses

A hobby horse is a child's toy composed of a stick with a horse's head at one end. The child straddles the stick horse and "rides." The hobby horse has links to ancient spring and harvest festivals across Europe.

The word *hobi* in Middle English was a diminuitive of Robin, or Hobbe, and it was used to describe a small horse. It may have been derived from an actual horse called Dobbin or Robin. Hobby was in use as the name of a small falcon at this time, and in 1298 the phrase *hobby horse* first came into use to describe a small horse. The term was later used to describe the horse-shaped frame used in Morris Dances at May festivals. Eventually it came to describe a wooden stick horse or rocking horse in the 17th century. A hobby horse could not carry its rider anywhere; hence the word *hobby* came to describe a pastime without a valued outcome. Two types of child's toy have been described as hobby horses: the

More elaborate versions of hobby horses included wheels, rocking devices, and seats, as in this 1908 photograph.

stationary rocking horse, a finely crafted and ornate toy on curved rockers, or more commonly the stick horse. The stick horse had a painted wooden or fabric horse's head at one end, and some versions had a seat and wheels. The head was raised by reins or handles, and as the child straddled the stick and trotted, the horse's head rose and fell.

After World War II, and before commercial manufacture of toys, the hobby horse remained a popular toy with children, its head being easily constructed from a stuffed sock tied onto a shortened broom handle, or carved from wood. Reins were made of ribbon or leather, buttons and glove fingers were sewn on as eyes and ears and wool was used for the mane.

The hobby horse has links to ancient corn festivals. Demeter, the corn goddess, was depicted in ancient Greek carvings with a dark horse's head. Until the mid-20th century the last sheaf of corn in a harvest was described as the "mare" or "the maiden." It was carried through the fields and stored above the hearth in the great hall until May Day, when the corn was formed into a loaf in the shape of a man or woman to be shared by villagers at the Spring Festival. In Roman times, a horse was sacrificed in the cornfield, its tail was placed above the hearth of the ruling family, and its head on a stick became a prize for competing villagers.

Visual aspects of those rituals remain in the 'Obby 'Oss festival in Padstow, England, where a man hidden under a heavy, fabric-covered wooden frame swings a mast bearing a horse's skull or emblem head above festival goers, as captured on film by Peter Kennedy in 1953. Today, festival horses are fabric covered wicker frames into which a man steps, hoisted by shoulder straps. Fake legs give the impression that the man sits astride the horse as he prances, waving the horse's head on a stick. In 2000, the town of Banbury in England revived its ancient Hobby Horse Festival, banned by the Puritans 400 years previously and reflected in the child's rhyme (traditional):

Ride a Cock-horse
To Banbury Cross
To see a fine lady ride on a white horse
With rings on her fingers
And bells on her toes
She shall have music wherever she goes.

The hobby horse, therefore, is a child's toy with a connection to ancient festivals in which the horse is an aspect of the corn goddess and the seasonal cycle of planting and harvest.

See Also: Ancient Greece; Europe, 1200 to 1600; Europe, 1600 to 1800; Playing Alone; Pretending; United Kingdom.

Bibliography. Banbury Town Hobby Horse, www.kickback.btinternet.co.uk/Town.Horse/Town.Horse.html (cited August 2008); E.O. Harbin, *Games of Many Nations* (Abingdon Press, 1954); Glenn Kirchner, *Children's Games Around the World* (Benjamin Cummings, 2000).

Janice Kathleen Jones
University of Southern Queensland

Hockey (Amateur)

In most parts of the world where it is played, "hockey" means ice hockey unless otherwise indicated. Like baseball, hockey is a sport whose origins are difficult to pinpoint precisely: Rather than appearing all of a sudden as an individual's invention, it developed over time out of a tradition of field sports brought by Europeans to North America. Field hockey, hockey-like games, and mounted hockey-like games like polo have been played throughout the Western world since the ancient era, probably because of the ease of creating the equipment in an age when most adults had a knife and at least rudimentary woodcarving skills.

If the essence of baseball-like games is the use of a bat to strike a pitched ball in the air, the essence of hockey is the use of a curved stick to move a contested ball on the ground; two very different families of games, the ancestors of the very different hockey and baseball, developed from virtually identical playing conditions and resources. In the case of ice hockey, the "ball" is a flat-bottomed puck that slides across the ice instead of rolling on it. In other respects, the mechanics of the modern sport are highly similar regardless of the playing surface.

Field Hockey

The modern sport of field hockey is more a sibling or cousin of ice hockey than its predecessor, but hockey-like games played on grass surfaces are the oldest in the family. Modern field hockey was developed by 1870s English cricket clubs as a game to play in cold weather; key changes they made to the informal rules of the sports that came before were a ban on raising the stick above shoulder level and the introduction of the striking circle, an area in front of the goal from which shots must be made.

Through the British Army, field hockey spread through the British Empire—which in that era comprised one quarter of the globe. Today, especially at the amateur or scholastic level, field hockey is often a women's sport. Women have played it since only a few years after the cricketers developed the mens' game; the first organized club, the Molesey Ladies Hockey Club in England, was founded in 1887.

Since the 1970s, artificial turf has been used for most professional field hockey playing surfaces, but amateur field hockey is ultimately an opportunistic sport that can be played in any empty field with a reasonably flat surface and a place to put two goals.

Ice Hockey

Just as opportunistic, ice hockey has much in common with the evolution of street games: it originated as a way to take a sport for which the equipment is already available, and to place it in a new playing environment. More physical, aggressive, and injury-prone than field

Today, especially at the amateur or scholastic level, field hockey is often a women's sport. Women have played it since only a few years after the cricketers developed the mens' game throughout the British empire.

hockey—which had intentionally shied away from rugby-like aspects in the development of its rules and practices—ice hockey may have been influenced by lacrosse, a Native American sport played throughout Canada and the northern United States.

Some early "ice" hockey games may actually have been played on packed snow, using the same fields that were used for field hockey in the warm months; eventually the sport developed its own identity, not as an alternative to or surrogate for field hockey but a game all its own, and with that identity came the preference for the slick smooth surface of well-planed ice and the flat puck in place of a ball.

The rules of ice hockey were established in the same decade as those of modern field hockey, in Montreal, and its popularity spread quickly across Canada, the United States, and the colder countries of Europe.

As with many sports, the adoption of formal rules at the organized professional level had an impact on amateur play by providing an authoritative text to appeal to; a sense of "how to play the game" is instilled by such organization, even among the players who are not bound by those rules. Much more recent innovations are hockey played with skates indoors or on street surfaces. Roller hockey, on rollerskates, has been played since at least the 1940s; inline hockey is a more recent development. School gym classes sometimes play a form of indoor hockey using a tennis ball or other rubber ball, generally without skates. Floorball, similarly, uses a Whiffle ball with shorter sticks to play hockey in gymnasiums.

There are also hockey variants incorporating brooms, unicycles, special shoes to grip the ice that have come from various cultures, and air hockey, a popular feature of arcades especially in the northeastern United States. Air hockey uses tables slightly smaller than billiards tables, with air blowing upwards as a plastic disc skids across the surface, knocked back and forth by players trying to hit it into the opponent's goal.

See Also: Baseball (Amateur); Curling (Scottish); Street Games.

Bibliography. M.R. Carroll, *Concise Encyclopedia of Hockey* (Greystone Books, 2003); Michael McKinley, *Hockey: A People's History* (McClelland and Stewart, 2006).

Bill Kte'pi
Independent Scholar

Homo Ludens (Huizinga)

In 1938 Johan Huizinga (1872–1945) wrote *Homo Ludens: A Study of the Play Element in Culture*. This was the last book written by this Dutch comparative linguist and cultural historian. It remains one of the most influential books about play. A later critic of it, Roger Caillois, stated that though most of its premises are debatable, it opens up many ideas for research about play. The title of this book comes from *homo*, meaning man, and *ludens,* meaning play. Huizinga writes that play is interwoven with culture, and the essence of play is that it is fun. He further writes that play cannot be reduced to anything else. Play cannot be viewed as a function of something else; you play because you want to play. He argued that while play is a part of culture, since animals play, play exists before culture. The fact that animals play also proves to him that play is not founded on rationality; play is irrational. Usually play is not serious, but there are exceptions, as in the case of ritual.

He presented his ideas for *Homo Ludens* first in lectures he gave as Rector of Leyden University in 1933, and in later lectures in Zurich, Vienna, and London. He wrote in the foreword to *Homo Ludens* that while he titled these lectures: "The Play Element of Culture," many wanted him to call it "The Play Element in Culture," and in the latest translation into English, the unidentified translator continues to use "in" because the translator writes that it sounds better. However, Huizinga found the use of "in" rather than "of" important for two reasons. First, Huizinga considered play cultural rather than biological; he said calling play instinctual is wrong and reductionist. Because it was cultural, he called his study historical rather than biological. Second, he said that all aspects of culture derived from play. He wrote that all elements of culture have a play element.

He described play as, first, a voluntary activity that is enjoyable and is not imposed by physical necessity or moral duty (unless it is a rite or ceremony). He described play as, second, disinterested, and in that it is not utilitarian (linked to the biological needs of nutrition, reproduction, or self-preservation). Play is its own reward. He described play as, third, something outside of ordinary life both in terms of space and time in what he refers to as a "magic circle." This resembles ideas of rites of passage developed by Arnold Van Gennep, who described parts of rites of passages as being set apart from ordinary life; it is even more similar since Huizinga alludes to the magic circle in terms of initiations. Finally, he described play as something that transported a group of people to a different world from the ordinary world. The ideas of the magic circle combined with the idea of transporting people to a new world resembles ideas of liminality developed by Victor Turner in many of his works.

Outline of the Work

Homo Ludens outlines how play exists in all human activities. For example, Huizinga describes one way play is involved in language is as a metaphor, which he calls a play on words. Languages, religion, drama, all elements of life, have play in them. However, Huizinga did not describe all forms of play since he wanted to talk about how play relates to culture, thus, he describes what he called the "higher" forms of play in the chapters of the book, which he describes as language, contest, law, war, knowing, poetry, mythopoesis, philosophy, and civilization. In chapter two of the book he focuses on how play, as expressed in language, refers to play as a contest, so that battle is play, and play is battle in Anglo Saxon.

In chapter three he says that culture comes from play, and he talks about practices like the potlatch of the Kwakiutl, which he says is essentially a contest. In chapter four, he shows how law is play, since legal procedures are games, and since lawsuits resemble contests with a passion for argument and counterargument and a desire to win. He says that while ideas of right and wrong dominate Western law, the desire to win remains more important than right and wrong in other cultures.

In chapter five he says that war contains elements of play including rules for acceptable and unacceptable conduct during warfare. In chapter six he writes about games of knowing more than others. He says archaic man believed knowledge gave them magical power over the cosmos; ritual contests of knowledge directly influence the cosmos. In chapter seven he writes about how poetry is a type of play, and that much of the poetry of the past shows elements of a contest.

In chapter eight he says that myths originate in play. Myths personify the objective world, and this process of personification is play. In chapter nine he talks about how philosophy originated with play, as it has the element of contests. For example, he writes about how the sophists used rhetoric in a playful manner to defeat their opponents, and he says Nietzsche's use of competition was a return to this type of competition. In chapter 10, he talks about how art originates with play since it has a competitive element. He states that all true ritual is sung, danced, and played. He sees the play element most clearly in song and dance, and less clearly in the plastic arts. In chapter 11, he asserts that all past civilization has play elements. He states that civilization: "does not come *from* play like a babe detaching itself from the womb; it arises *in* and *as* play and never leaves it." In chapter 12, he states that contemporary civilization also has play, but that the play element has decreased in present-day civilization because people do not want to follow the rules. Despite this, he said play never leaves civilization.

Reaction to Huizinga

People who have modified and criticized *Homo Ludens* include Mechthild Nagel, Roger Caillois, and Jacques Ehrman. Many have stated that Huizinga's ideas were influenced by his religious views. His talk about play as spiritual was an attack on materialism and on man being a rational being. Nagel states that the method of *Homo Ludens* resembles the phenomenological method of Heidegger that premises leads to a bad ideological mapping of play.

He especially criticizes Huizinga's idea that play is always benevolent, stating that we no longer can afford this naïve notion. Caillois states that while Huizinga emphasized play as competition, which he called *agon*, play can take three other forms which he called *alea* (chance), *mimesis* (role playing), and *vertigo* (being out of control). By combining these elements, Caillois describes human behavior in general. He also says we can find no clear division between play with its rules and structure, and *paidia*, which is spontaneous and unstructured. And he notes that play goes back and forth between being sacred and profane. Ehrman and others argue that while Huizinga saw leisure as an element of play, leisure developed only recently in human history. They also criticized his idea that play was a civilizing force, but current civilization was losing the play element.

See Also: Caillois: *Man, Play and Games*; Play as Competition, Sociology of; Play as Mock War, Sociology of; Sociological Benefits of Play; Speech Play.

Bibliography. Roger Caillois, *Man, Play and Games* (University of Illinois Press, 2001): Jacques Ehrmann, Cathy Lewis, and Phil Lewis, "Homo Ludens Revisited," *French Studies* (Yale University Press, 1968); Johan Huizinga, *Homo Ludens: a Study of the Play-Element in Culture* (Routledge, 1998 [1938]); Mechthild Nagel, "Play in Culture and the Jargon of Primordiality: A Critique of Homo Ludens," *Play & Culture Studies* (Ablex Publishing Corporation, 1998).

Bruce Josephson
Baekseok Cultural College

Hornby

Hornby is a British company that is a market leader in the manufacture of scale railway models. In 1920 Hornby, then known as Meccano Ltd. and based in Liverpool, released its first train, a clockwork "0" gauge (1:48 scale) model, and electric trains quickly followed. Since then, Hornby has produced a huge number of model trains and accessories that have been largely aimed at children, but have also won considerable popularity among adults.

The company's founder, Frank Hornby, was an English inventor and businessman. In 1899 he began developing interchangeable metal strips that could be used to build toy bridges, trucks, and cranes. He patented the invention in January 1901 and marketed his first construction sets in 1902. In 1907, Hornby registered the "Meccano" trademark as the name for his products, which enjoyed significant commercial success. Hornby also developed and manufactured a number of other toys and model kits, including trains. During the 1920s Hornby's "0" gauge train sets sold well and many engines and accessories were released.

In 1938 Hornby introduced a new "00" gauge of model trains under the name "Hornby Dublo." Approximately half the size of the "0" gauge trains, the locomotives were diecast, while the carriages and wagons were generally made of tinplate. Both clockwork and electric sets were available, and the range expanded quickly. With the outbreak of World War II, however, production was curtailed and was completely suspended in 1942. Production resumed in peacetime, but did not reach full capacity again until 1948.

Hornby Dublo thrived during the early 1950s, but began to struggle toward the end of the decade. The company was slow to realize the potential of plastic and lost ground to competitors, especially Tri-ang Railways, who quickly developed plastic-bodied trains. The rivalry continued until 1964 when Tri-ang's parent company,

Lines Brothers, purchased Meccano Ltd. The two firms were subsequently merged to form Tri-ang Hornby and the former Hornby Dublo products were discontinued in favor of Tri-ang's less costly plastic designs.

In 1971 Meccano Ltd.'s owner, Lines Brothers, filed for bankruptcy and Tri-ang Hornby was sold to the Dunbee-Combex-Marx business conglomerate. Relaunched as Hornby Railways in 1972, the range was also upgraded to make it more attractive to adult enthusiasts, with improvements such as finer detailing and better paint finish. Throughout the 1970s a steady flow of new locomotives, rolling stock, and other accessories was released. Other new products included a steam-powered model of Stephenson's Rocket and a multiple train control system called Zero 1. The market, however, was extremely tough, and in 1980 Dunbee-Combex-Marx went into liquidation. Nevertheless, a management buyout put Hornby back on a sound footing as an independent firm named Hornby Hobbies, which was floated as a public company in 1986.

The early 1990s saw Hornby again facing competition from newcomers such as the Welsh firm Dapol, and established foreign manufacturers such as Lima, an Italian company, and the Chinese-owned Bachmann Industries. But Hornby fought back. To cut production costs, the company began moving its manufacturing to China in 1995, while a variety of new products were also released. Especially successful were Hornby's range of model engines and accessories based on the television series *Thomas the Tank Engine and Friends*, and another range based on the locomotives featured in the film adventures of Harry Potter. Hornby also expanded through the acquisition of Lima in 2004, Airfix (a plastic model kit manufacturer) in 2006, and Corgi (one of the world's oldest makers of diecast toy cars) in 2008. Into the 21st century, therefore, Hornby retained its position as Britain's leading model railway manufacturer.

See Also: Airfix; Hobbies; Meccano; Models.

Bibliography. Chris Ellis, *The Hornby Book of Model Railways* (Navigator, 2005); Michael Foster, *Hornby Dublo Trains: 1938–1964: The Story of the Perfect Table Railway* (Cavendish, 1980); Anthony McReady, *The Toy Story: The Life and Times of Inventor Frank Hornby* (Ebury Press, 2002).

Bill Osgerby
London Metropolitan University

Horse Racing (Amateur)

While the term *amateur horse racing* can be applied to any horse race that is not governed by professional organizations, it is applied specifically to a certain type of horse racing generally conducted in Britain, Ireland, and France. In that sense it is most commonly referred to as point-to-point, or steeplechase, racing. Currently there are approximately 120 of these races that are run in Britain, with others run in Ireland, where amateur horse racing and hunting are both very popular. The races are strictly regulated, as are the jockeys, through organizations such as the British Amateur Jockey's Association.

The first time this kind of race was mentioned in print was in 1793. There are, however, references to exactly this type of racing dating back to the early 1750s in Ireland, when two horses were raced on a 4.5-mile course. This course had fences, water, and other obstacles that the horses and riders had to clear. Of course, in practice, this type of racing may go back earlier than that, and the kind of course was very similar to the terrain over which fox hunts were conducted. To this day, there is a very strong tie between amateur racing and hunting, especially in how their respective seasons occur at different times of the year.

The early races were run cross country over a course from one town to another—a practice that still exists. Church steeples were the targets (they were easy to spot) for the racers to go after and were the "points" referred to in the term *point-to-point*. As the riders were racing from one steeple to another, the term *steeplechasing* came into use. The terms *steeplechase* and *point-to-point* were often used interchangeably but have now come to mean two different things. Steeplechasing (which is the older of the terms) is now a race on a circular course that contains water, ditches, and fences over which the horses must jump. The idea, which started to become popular in the early 19th century, is to replicate a cross country course with streams or other bodies of water and the necessity to jump over fences. The most famous of the steeplechases in Britain is the Grand National, which has been in existence since 1836. Point-to-point is still used to describe a race run on a cross country course.

The horses in steeplechasing and point-to-point were, and are, the same as those used for fox hunting. Steeplechase and point-to-point racing were considered to be an excellent way to keep horses in shape in winter, when fox hunting was not in season. The course was set on the same type of terrain that fox hunting was conducted. Amateur horse racing increased in popularity through the early to late 19th century and into the early 20th century in the years before World War I. Siegfried Sassoon's partially autobiographical novel *Memoirs of a Fox Hunting Man*, part of the *George Sherston* novels, describes in a personal way the lives of the country set in those years as well as details about fox hunts and point-to-point competition.

Horses that compete in point-to-point racing today are thoroughbred hunting horses, although some exceptions are allowed. The most critical criterion is that the horse must be an active hunting horse. No horse can be allowed to run in a point-to-point unless it has been certified as having been on a requisite number of hunts in the previous year.

A typical point-to-point race as run in either Britain or Ireland is conducted over a course of at least three miles. Sometimes the course is longer, and some races, for younger horses, are shorter. Point-to-point racing is still most frequently run over normal farm terrain. There are some prepared courses, but these represent a minority of cases. In either case there must be at least 18 fences and two of these must have ditches. The race is run twice over the same course. Horses that race in point-to-point are eligible for what are known as the hunt races, such as the Grand National.

Amateur horse racing is pursued with a great deal of competitiveness and intensity. It is not a sport without serious injuries. A recent report in the United Kingdom concluded that amateur horse racing in Great Britain and Ireland, compared with professional jump horse racing in Great Britain, Ireland, and France, is actually the more dangerous of the two forms. The authors of the report concluded that although amateur horse racing had not been studied in depth, it appeared as though it presented a serious risk, as amateurs have more falls and are subjected to a greater number of injuries. The recommendation for more study was based on the objective of determining means of preventing the higher incidence of accidents and injury.

See Also: Europe, 1600 to 1800; France; Ireland; United Kingdom.

Bibliography. Amateur Jockeys Association of Great Britain, www.amateurjockeys.org.uk (cited September 2008); Ganesh Balendra et al., "Injuries in Amateur Horse Racing (Point to Point Racing) in Great Britain and Ireland During 1993–2006," *British Journal of Sports Medicine* (v.41, 2007); R. Green, *The History of the Grand National: A Race Apart* (Hodder & Stoughton, 1993); Dido Harding, *Cool Dawn: My National Velvet* (Mainstream, 1999); Nancy Mitford, "At A Point-to-Point," *A Talent to Annoy: Essays, Journalism, and Reviews, 1929–1968* (Sceptre, 1996); Stewart Peters, *Irish Grand National: The History of Ireland's Premier Steeplechase* (Stadia, 2007).

Robert Stacy
Independent Scholar

Human Relationships in Play

Play is, by its very nature, social. When we think of play, we often visualize interacting with others, but even when we play alone, such as in the card game of Solitaire, we are playing by rules that others have created. It is through the different types of playful interactions that we learn how to get along with others and we develop a sense of who we are as individuals. This process of development, facilitated by play, begins with birth and continues throughout one's lifetime.

Infancy

Since many cognitive and physical abilities are in the process of developing, the play of infants is relatively limited. Research on infants tells us that they are aware of others around them, including other infants, but little direct interaction exits. Most play of infants can be categorized as three types: (1) solitary play, when the infant finds enjoyment entertaining him/herself, such as playing with their toes; (2) onlooker play, where the infant watches the play actions of others; and (3) one-on-one play, such as peek-a-boo, where the play is initiated by the parent or caregiver and the infant is the recipient of these actions. This last type of play, parent-child play, is the most prevalent.

Parent-child play during infancy and toddlerhood is the foundation for later play in childhood. Parents and caregivers model ways to enter social activities, how to take turns, how to follow the rules, ways to encourage and motivate others, and how to be a good winner and loser. Interestingly enough, mothers and fathers may play differently with their infant. While both parents are

When a parent plays with a child during infancy and toddlerhood, it is the foundation for later play in childhood, as well as being a useful tool in bonding with their child and teaching them skills.

likely to incorporate play with daily responsibilities (e.g., bath time), fathers are more likely to have simple playful interactions with the infant. The gender of the child may also affect parent-child interaction. For example, fathers of male children are more likely to engage the infant in physical or active play than fathers of female children.

Siblings offer another prime example of play in infant relationships. If the siblings are close in age, for example 4 years and younger, the older child often interacts with the infant in more playful way. It is not uncommon that in these interactions the older child takes on the dominant role, often scaffolding and teaching the infant various ways to respond and participate. As children grow, play among same-gender siblings becomes more competitive and can result in sibling rivalry. As to the difference between sibling-infant play and parent-infant play, some debate remains. Some experts believe that sibling-infant pairs engage in more pretend play than parent-infant pairs, while others believe the opposite.

Playful interaction with an infant takes on new meaning sometime between 4 to 6 weeks of age, with the emergence of what is referred to as the "social smile." The social smile is a big, happy smile that the infant gives when they recognize or respond to their caregiver's behavior. This voluntary emotional response signals that play is now truly reciprocal in nature. For example, when the father covers his face with his hands and then opens them while saying "peek-a-boo," the baby's smile tells the dad that "I like what you are doing." The father enjoys seeing his child happy and will then be more likely to repeat the action. And so the game and playful interaction goes on. Early-life playful social interactions such as Peek-a-Boo and Where's Your Tummy? lay the foundation of many later social competencies including turn-taking, establishing trust, and forming attachment.

During infancy, forming an attachment to one's caregivers is important for lifelong psychological and emotional well-being. Attachment, that give-and-take emotional relationship between two individuals, is often enhanced through play activities, such as those discussed above. Healthy attachment to parents or caregivers can facilitate the development of language, the interpretation of facial expressions and body language, the ability to take another's perspective, and the development of empathy and concern for another. As the child begins to better understand others as well as him/herself, the child's ability to cooperate, compromise, and use self-control improves. Down the road, these skills contribute to better peer interaction, greater peer acceptance, and deeper friendship. In other words, an infant's healthy attachment to his or her caregiver lies at the heart of a child's social competence. If an infant fails to develop trust in a caregiver, he or she may not develop trust later on with friends. Thus, playful behavior between caregiver and infant becomes essential for laying the groundwork of future relationships in the child's life.

Toddlerhood

The emergence of toddlerhood brings about some new forms of play along with those seen in infancy. Toddlers will still engage in solitary play, as in a child who sits with a pile of crayons and paper, coloring a picture and remaining unconcerned with what others are playing or doing. However, we also see the appearance of parallel play during this age. In parallel play, two children may be sitting near one another and playing the same activity, but not interacting or collaborating on any part of their activity. A prime example is two children each building separate towers out of a common set of blocks. Also found in toddlerhood is symbolic play, where children utilize more of their language skills, use toys as play props, and incorporate both of these into pretend play.

Starting around 2 to 3 years of age, play begins to shift more to interacting with peers than with parents and family members. As children develop the ability to walk and talk, they begin to gain a sense of independence and autonomy. Children at this age are also likely to be more involved with nursery school, daycare, or playgroups, which provide more opportunities to interact with peers. As a result, the toddler's social circle begins to widen and include more nonfamily members.

These new forms of play that we see in toddlerhood have a direct effect on children's proficiency in forming relationships. When a child enters the realm of pretend play, people, objects, behaviors, the room, and language all come together to form the play environment. Language is particularly important. When a child says to her friend, "Let's pretend that..." the language determines what social role or identity the children will take on, as well as how they will interact with objects and with each other. Furthermore, language will continue the same pretend play scenario or change it when a participant says, "I don't want to do this anymore." By asserting autonomy, the child is learning about self limits and his or her right to not participate in certain activities.

Preschool

Once a child reaches preschool, around the age of 4, whom the child plays with determines who their friends are. Children at this age will begin referring to someone as their "friend" if they play together often or like to play the same games or activities. "Sienna is my friend because she and I like to play dress-up." Children at this age are also more likely to be friends with other children of the same gender. In fact, even when children are engaging in gender-neutral activities, which make up a large portion of preschool play, children of this age still prefer same-gender peers. There is still debate about whether this preference is the result of socialization or inborn preferences. However, we do know that one of the reasons that boy-girl friendships are difficult to maintain at this age is that boys engage in more play fighting or rough-and-tumble play, which are particularly elusive to their female peers.

As mentioned above, rough-and-tumble play becomes more popular, mostly with boys, during preschool. Recognized by its similarity to real fighting, rough-and-tumble play differs in the important aspect that, while it can appear violent, it truly is friendly in nature—all who are engaged are laughing and smiling. This type of play is typified by games of chase that often involve elements of "right and wrong," such as in the game Cops and Robbers. In addition to being popular with males, it is also found in females growing up in a male-heavy environment.

Though play tends to happen within gender at this age, play is a great way to get a group of children with mixed abilities to interact with one another. Sociodramatic play, or play that involves taking on different social roles and using play props, such as costumes, dolls, and plastic toy tools, is especially useful in this arena. For example, going to the grocery store is something that most, if not all, children are familiar with. Playing "grocery store" allows each child to have an active role.

Through these interactions, children can learn about each other while further developing their social skills.

Rough-and-tumble play incorporates several social competencies. It allows for turn taking in the sense that children will take turns being dominant and being submissive; this is not the case in true fighting. Rough-and-tumble play also promotes the development of empathy. Only friends engage in rough-and-tumble play. And in cases where one friend gets a bit too rough and accidentally hurts his or her buddy, offerings of care and forgiveness follow. In a society that tends to view caring and nurturing as feminine characteristics, these instances of helping a friend get up, making sure he is O.K., and apologizing, are extremely important for young boys. Therefore, it is through bouts of rough-and-tumble play that young boys get the opportunity to express their compassion to a friend. Along with trust, compassion is another positive social skill that is important in social problem solving, peer affiliation, and social competency. Do not assume, however, that only rough-and-tumble play contributes to the development of empathy; there is a plethora of other types of play (e.g., sociodramatic play) found at this age that also contributes to the same competencies.

School Age

During the preschool years, we saw the beginnings of friendship. As children reach school age, their play becomes primarily peer-influenced. Play with friends becomes more focused with less variety of games and activities, as well as fewer play partners. Play and play partners reflect more of one's own interests. And, as school, organized team sports, and other extracurricular activities take up a considerable portion of the school-age child's time, self-initiated and free play decline. It should be noted, though, that if given the opportunity, school-age children will engage in self-initiated play.

Given that play is less solitary at this age, cooperative play becomes a central focus. Cooperative play involves more than one person, the establishment of rules, and an understanding of and participation in teamwork. Concepts of fairness and justice also enter into this realm of group play. Participants need to be able to agree upon the interpretation of the rules, follow the rules, and give sanctions when rules are broken. In this sense, teams and playgroups must learn the skills behind cooperation and collaboration and be self-governing.

Rough-and-tumble play continues to be prevalent, especially for boys. In fact, this type of play is more popular for school-age children than any other age. Within the category of boys' rough-and-tumble play, it is important to note that both boys who are and boys who are not accepted socially participate in this type of play; however, the socially rejected boys are more likely to turn aggressive as they play and often do not express their concern or compassion when they have gotten too rough and hurt another. While this type of play generally decreases as children move from school age to adolescence, individuals who continue to play in a rough manner run the risk of becoming a bully.

Interactive play involves not only cooperation, but also other social competencies such as perception of others and perception of the self. In addition to being a useful competency in future relationships, playful or not, perception of others, or the ability to interpret signals from other people, is integral in play relationships at this age. For example, if a child does not possess the ability to properly decipher social signals and cues, playful actions may be viewed as being aggressive, resulting in the child responding in an antagonistic way. Perception of the self is equally as important. As the child makes a greater shift to the world of peers, group play takes a critical role. The child's developing sense of self is influenced by their ability to relate to and interact with friends and classmates. During this time, groups of children will engage in different forms of play on the playground during recess. With the child's improved physical skills and more advanced agility, their adeptness at playing and succeeding in these games and group activities facilitates approval of their peers.

As a result of an increase of playful relationships being focused on friendships, peer culture becomes central to development at this age. Peer culture refers to an unwritten, yet understood, set of values, rules, and behaviors of a group of youths. These accepted ways to behave then determine one's social acceptance and status within that particular group. Adherence to these set standards determines group membership and provides a social identity to other peers. Play actions and play language can be a way to get other children to conform or to be excluded by creating and maintaining group members—those who are part of the in-groups and those who do not belong. For example, "Last one there is a rotten egg" specifies a loser or nonmember. Other elements of peer culture include common activities and rituals (e.g., "step on a crack, break your mother's back").

Adolescence

As individuals age, the term *play* becomes less readily used to describe free time. During adolescence, there seems to be a linguistic switch, and play becomes "leisure." The purpose of leisure at this age is primarily to socialize and to relieve stress and can be divided into two categories, active leisure and media leisure. Active leisure includes what may be thought of as more traditional play, athletics and sports, and talking, which was rated the number one teen leisure activity according to one study. Media leisure refers to activities involving computers or electronics, television, and reading.

As technology continues to advance, this type of leisure activity, particularly surrounding computers and computer games, is gaining popularity with this age group. When thinking about social interactions of individuals who participate in online gaming and those who do not, both groups spend the same amount of time with parents, friends, and in sport and active leisure. Gamers spend less time, however, on homework and reading than nongamers and gamers who spend most of their time gaming alone spend less time with friends. Gamers who game with friends also spend leisure time with friends and family. Thus, though there is still skepticism about the social benefits of this type of play, research is showing that it may not be completely negative.

Leisure, like play, can be solitary or interactive and takes both forms during the teenage years. The type of play in which they engage can depend on family composition (authoritative, authoritarian, indulgent, or neglectful). Youth from controlling or authoritarian families spend more time than in any other type of family composition in solitary leisure. Youth from neglectful families engage in the least amount of solitary leisure. Youth from permissive or indulgent families depend on their families to satisfy their leisure needs. Finally, youth from nurturing, authoritative families receive the greatest satisfaction from their leisure activities, both with family and with friends.

Talking with friends, a form of active leisure, is a great way for adolescents to test different ideas about life and themselves. When a teen considers ideas regarding what careers might be interesting, they are engaged in learning more about their own values. When a friend confides in another about concerns they have pertaining to their current boyfriend or girlfriend, both use trust and gain skills in compassion. It should be noted, though, that the extent to which gain in these advanced social skills is attained is based on the setting for the conversations (e.g., being in a park versus being at a concert), with whom the youth is talking (e.g., to friends versus acquaintances), culture, and same- versus mixed-gender groups. Participation in athletics/sports carries several benefits, assuming the team environment involves a prosocial peer group. In that case, identity formation and sense of self come from challenging oneself in an athletic setting. This can result in positive self-esteem, school achievement, positive view of one's adult life, and civic/community involvement.

Media leisure can also affect relationships. We have already seen that gaming can affect time spent with friends and family. Watching television can also affect relationships in that while engaging in this activity, one learns social roles through the programming they choose to watch. Furthermore, given that teens tend to have more control over what media they use and how they use it, this media can provide opportunities for initiation and self-regulation. These effects of media socialization are particularly strong for nonindustrial societies. Teens in many of these societies tend to pick up on Western cultural ideas, especially when they differ from traditional values. These new values come into play when the teen interacts with parents, teachers, and their peers. For example, a teen's concept of dating may be changed by being influenced by what they have seen in movies and television programs.

Adulthood

Much of the information about leisure in adulthood focuses on the social activities of older adults. It is likely that once the individual enters adulthood, life becomes too demanding, with careers and starting families, and these individuals just do not have the spare time to participate in research studies. It is also likely that during the time of early and middle adulthood, these individuals are playing with their children in the manners described in previous sections.

Much of the leisure time of older adults is social in nature, though reasons for one's involvement in various activities differ. Some adults play games (e.g., card games) or participate in certain physical activities (e.g., bowling) for mental or physical fitness. In this case, even though they compete against another person or a team (e.g., in tennis or bowling), the competition is really about improving one's own skill level and not necessarily beating the opponent(s). Therefore, the motivation behind the competition is more about self-challenge and experiencing a sense of accomplishment than the win/

lose outcome of the game. Other older adults maintain participation in a specific activity for a sense of continuity; it is something they have done throughout their lives. Still others schedule time for play and recreation as a way to provide structure to their days. For example, an individual may know that on Wednesday afternoon she plays bridge and Friday mornings is the golf league. Pre-scheduled leisure activities also help to pass time and avoid boredom, basically taking the place of a job once held. Finally, adults may engage in leisure activities for a sense of belongingness and camaraderie.

As we near the end of life, the connections we have made with others often involve coming to terms with the loss of those relationships. This can be because of several factors, such as diseases like Alzheimer's, moving into retirement communities, or death. Spending time participating in leisure activities with others helps one through these final life transitions. Playing games for physical and/or mental fitness can help ward off the negative effects of aging. Playing for a sense of belongingness and camaraderie can help promote one of our basic needs in life—to be loved and accepted—particularly during a time when friendships and other relationships may be decreasing.

See Also: Fantasy Play; Play as Learning, Anthropology of; Play as Learning, Psychology of; Play as Learning, Sociology of; Psychological Benefits of Play; Social Psychology of Play; Sociological Benefits of Play; Team Play.

Bibliography. David Cohen, *The Development of Play* (Routledge, 2006); David Elkind, *The Power of Play* (Da Capo Press, 2007); Anthony Pelligrini, "Boys' Rough-and-Tumble Play and Social Competence: Contemporaneous and Longitudinal Relations," in Anthony Pelligrini, ed., *The Future of Play Theory* (State University of New York Press, 1995).

Joyce Hemphill
Laura Scheinholtz
University of Wisconsin, Madison

Hungary

Hungarian play and leisure life reveal several themes. Hungarian tribes migrated west into the Carpathian Basin from the east, creating a conceptual orientation of being located somewhere between the east and the west. This orientation has been applied to the geographic, political, and economic situations of Hungary at various points throughout history, and evidence supports this notion when considering Hungarian play culture as well. Richly documented village traditions reveal a range of children's games and activities that engender children and instruct them in their appropriate social roles. Many folk forms still exist through a significant urban folk revival movement in the 1970s. Finally, the complex history of Hungary is revealed through manifestations of play, including those that reveal a pre-Christian basis, forms that were contributed by various historical ethnic groups, and uses of play for a catharsis of dramatic political realities.

The Christianization of Hungary in 1000 C.E., coincidental with its statehood, linked Hungary to the West in many ways. Games of chance popular among the merchant classes and banned by the Church in Europe, like gambling and dice playing, were likewise banned by the Hungarian Church. Chess, also banned until the pieces began to resemble the Western feudal order, was known to be in Hungary by 1429, after which a significant Hungarian Chess culture developed. Games that were likely of more Eastern origin include the games of Nine Men's Morris (*Kettös Malom*), a game whose playing grid was easily marked into the ground by nomadic people; Tip-cat (*Bigézés*), a hitting stick game that likely came along Eastern trading routes to the West; and Knucklebones (*Astragalos*), thought to have been reintroduced by the Ottoman Turks during their occupation of Hungary in the 16th and 17th centuries.

Certain traditions also reflect the pre-Christian identity of nomadic Hungarian tribes. Eggs, for example, a symbol of fertility also used in Eastern shamanistic practices and rituals, can be found in Hungarian traditional games. One popular custom that remains is the Easter game of "sprinkling," where males in the village would go around to the girls' houses to collect painted eggs and spray the females with water, sometimes reciting a poem as well. Children's folksongs and singing games also contain lyrics that reference shamanistic practices, such as the beating of a drum for healing purposes.

To prepare children for their adult lives, folk singing and dance games engender them into their proper social roles. Girls' dance forms tend to be in circles or chains, generally regarded as a remnant from older cultural practices from the East. In terms of physical movement, the emphasis is on unity of simple movement, not individualism. Lyrics often refer to proper ways of grooming, taking care of a baby, or preparing for marriage. A popular folk wedding game includes hiding the identity of several girls, entrusting the groom-to-be to go around the circle and try to figure out which is his bride-to-be.

Traditionally, dancing was one of the few ways for older unmarried boys and girls to interact. Evidence that paired dancing—generally regarded as a cultural influence from the West—is a way for young lads to attract women is demonstrated in highly active male dancing, often requiring physical prowess with kicks, stamps, and quick leg movements. Women, much more limited in movement, are at the mercy of their male dance partners and must be able to follow their lead at any given moment. Regional variants of the czárdás, a paired dance considered to be the national dance, differ according to local culture and ethnic makeup. This dance, as well as several other folk dances from villages in neighboring countries that contain significant Hungarian ethnic populations, are popular today in dancehouses, urban centers of folk revival that flourished from the 1970s on.

Toy culture in Hungary includes peasant toys that reflected the environment around them, such as toys made out of wood, corn cobs, almonds, chestnuts, and straw, formed into simple animal or doll structures. A popular contemporary Hungarian toy is the Rubik's Cube, a three-dimensional movable puzzle designed by a Hungarian design professor, Ernö Rubik, in 1974. While the conceptual mechanics of the toy resemble simpler wooden puzzles of logic found in traditional society, the story of the mismanagement of the cube for mass production under Soviet Socialist rule was so legendary that it was even made into a dramatic play.

The frustration felt by many Hungarians under various complex political realities was sometimes manifested in sport. This was the case at the 1956 Summer Olympics in Melbourne. The Soviets had violently quelled the Hungarian uprising of October 1956, while the Hungarian water polo team was en route to the games. Hungarians had dominated the sport of water polo, a European import, for much of the century. When the team learned the news of the crushed rebellion upon arrival in Melbourne, they took their revenge at the semifinal match that paired them against the Soviets. The game became infamous, known as the "Blood in the Water" match, when officials stopped the game because of violence that was said to have turned the pool water bloody red. The Hungarians eventually won the gold that year, a moment of pride for a distraught nation that took on exaggerated significance in the face of the political situation.

Rubik's Cube variants from 2 × 2 × 2 to 7 × 7 × 7. The popular toy was invented in 1974 by a Hungarian design professor.

See Also: Central Asia, Ancient; Europe, 1200 to 1600; Europe, 1600 to 1800; Folk Dancing; Jacks; Rubik's Cube.

Bibliography. Glenn Kirchner, *Children's Games Around the World* (Benjamin Cummings, 2000); András Lukácsy, *Játszd Újra: A Világ Alapjátéka* (Kner Press, Hungary, 1988); Frederic V. Grunfeld, ed., *Games of the World* (Holt, Rinehart and Winston, 1975); Sándor Petényi, *Games and Toys in Medieval and Early Modern Hungary* (Medium Aevum Quotidianum, 1994); Katalin Peter, *Beloved Children: History of Aristocratic Childhood in Hungary in the Early Modern Age* (Central European University Press, 2001).

Lisa M. Overholser
Indiana University

I

Iceland

Tracing its origins to the Viking settlements in the early Middle Ages, Iceland's pastimes included traditional methods of proving prowess or skill in battle such as wrestling, archery, and walking along oars on the outside of boats. Building models and dioramas connected with Iceland's Viking heritage is popular with many people, as are Wargames. Reading remains popular—Iceland has more bookstores per capita than any other country in the world.

Hiking and camping remain popular among both Icelanders and tourists to the country, and many ride Icelandic horses. Because of the climate, many children are involved in snowboarding and tobogganing. Skiing down slopes can be challenging, and more people are involved in cross-country skiing. Because of some fast-flowing rivers, kayaking and whitewater rafting have attracted many tourists. The intense wind makes ballooning dangerous, as it is easy to be carried out to sea. As there is little flat land in the country, there are not many golf courses.

The Arctic Open held each year takes advantage of the summer sun, and play starts at midnight. Recreational badminton, fishing, hunting, and ping pong have their adherents, and Icelandic wrestling first started as a regular competition in 1907. Unlike the United States, where most students take part in school-based recreational sports, in Iceland, local voluntary amateur sporting clubs are the focus for most adolescents.

Many children learn how to play Chess at school, and the Skaksamband Islands did much to promote the game. In the 19th century, Daniel Willard Fiske (1831–1904), a U.S. book collector and scholar of old Iceland who lived in Florence, Italy, from 1881, donated 11 marble Chess sets to the people on the island of Grimsey, located within the Arctic Circle. Fiske Day is commemorated each year on November 11. His donation resulted in many people on the island developing Chess skills and the building of outdoor Chess sets, and has also led to many tournaments in Iceland. The country has produced six grandmasters.

In 1972 the world championship match between Bobby Fischer of the United States and Boris Spassky from Russia was held at Reykjavik, resulting in victory for Fischer and much publicity for Iceland. Fischer later moved to Iceland after being critical of the U.S. bombing of Belgrade in 1999. In the bitter winter, indoor games have flourished. Card games are popular amusements, with the Icelandic team winning the World Bridge Championship in Japan in 1991. Fiske's history of Chess and other "table games" included details of some of the more popular ones in Iceland, many similar to those played in other countries in the world. An Icelandic version of the board game Monopoly is called *Matador*, using important streets in Reykjavik.

See Also: Chess and Variations of; Denmark; Norway; Snowboarding.

Bibliography. D. Willard Fiske, *Chess in Iceland and in Icelandic Literature, with Historical Notes on Other Table Games* (Florentine Typographical Society, 1905); Illugi Jökulsson, "The Old Game Gets a Grip on the Young," *Iceland Review* (1986); Jóhannes Jósefsson, *Icelandic Wrestling* (Porh Bjarnason, 1908); Emilie U. Lepthien, *Iceland* (Childrens Press, 1987); Jonathan Wilcox, *Iceland* (Marshall Cavendish, 1996).

Justin Corfield
Geelong Grammar School

Idealization of Play

Attempts to define play are many and varied, and have proved largely fruitless, because of the complexity of the subject. Indeed, Johan Huizinga concluded that play was "not susceptible of exact definition either logically, biologically, or aesthetically." The folly of trying to reach a definition was emphasized by Brian Sutton-Smith, who made the point that no definition would be worthy of the name unless it covered all aspects of play, no matter how unattractive they might be. In an earlier piece with D. Kelly-Byrne he highlighted an unfortunate tendency among most commentators to focus solely on the positive aspects of play. For example, C. Garvey identifies five commonly accepted characteristics of play in most leading theories: positive effect, intrinsic motivation, free choice, active engagement, and non-literality. Garvey's summary will be familiar to many in today's playwork profession, because of its similarity to the definition developed by B. Hughes, and subsequently appearing in the second Playwork Principle, which defines play thus: "Play is a process that is freely chosen, personally directed and intrinsically motivated. That is, children and young people determine and control the content and intent of their play, by following their own instincts, ideas and interests, in their own way for their own reasons."

In the last 30 years this approach to the definition of play has become increasingly common. However, such an idealized view does not really stand up to scrutiny. Much of the following critique of that approach is taken from a chapter in the playwork textbook *Foundations of Playwork*.

First, is it always true to say that play is freely chosen, personally directed, and intrinsically motivated? In reality play takes many forms, not all of which manifest themselves in that way. Such a description is not just idealizing play, it actually understates the value of play—something we should never do. Time spent in a school playground during break-time immediately confronts us with the complexity of play, and the fact that many forms of play are: "chosen," but not "freely"; "directed," but not "personally"; "motivated," but not "intrinsically."

The crucial point that is missed by such a restrictive definition is that play has developmental value, even when it is not freely chosen, personally directed, and intrinsically motivated. For example, children who join in with the large game of football that often dominates school playgrounds are clearly playing, but some are only playing because they have been bullied into it. Obviously the quality of their play is substantially different from those children who have freely chosen to join in, but they still gain all sorts of developmental benefit from the experience. For example, being confronted with the stark realities of social interaction probably helps children develop their understanding of how to cope with differing levels of social status.

Lots of children take part in group activities that they are not personally directing—some children freely choose to be part of the crowd, even if that means being directed by someone else. In role play, the child who is directed to act the part of the baby when they would rather be the mom or dad is clearly not personally directing their play, but they may be gaining enormous social benefits as a result of their compliant behavior, in terms of group membership and possibly even negotiation skills.

The play behavior of teasing, which is often quite cruel, has clear developmental benefits for both parties involved. However the person on the receiving end cannot be said to be intrinsically motivated to take part. One of the most important benefits of play is the way in which it teaches us about hierarchies, and helps us find ways of coping with the injustices of everyday life. These are often harsh lessons, but nonetheless valuable.

In fact, we are seriously underselling the value of play in terms of both individual and species development, if we continue to espouse such definitions. The idealistic view of play provided by the "freely chosen, personally directed, intrinsically motivated" approach is not really tenable as a definition. Nevertheless, when working with children it is not necessary to abandon the idea altogether.

For example, the most valuable form of playwork is that which seeks to encourage the sort of play that is 'freely chosen, personally directed and intrinsically motivated'.

The second major way in which play has come to be idealized is in the idea that children determine and control the content and intent of their play. It is probably true that play is the only experience in a child's life where they may be in control of events. However, rather like the "freely chosen ... " definition, this is too often stated as if it were an all encompassing fact. Clearly, it is often true, but in reality there are many instances where children do not determine the content of their play, and yet still gain great benefit from the experience. As for children controlling the "intent" of their play, in many cases there is no "intent," except in the broadest emotional sense.

From the adult point of view some characteristics of play may appear to be somewhat negative. Play behaviors such as teasing, hazing and profanity do not sit comfortably with concepts of free choice and personal direction, especially for those on the receiving end. However, excluding such behaviors from our definitions of play is neither accurate nor helpful. In fact there may be benefits to be gained from even the most negative forms of play. Sutton-Smith suggests that "play has to do with the mammal need for protection and for stimulation". If so, then behaviors such as teasing and hazing probably have the function of preparing us to cope with social hierarchies, and the complexity of social status later in life. Whatever the function (and there may even be none at all), it is not helpful to exclude such behaviors from our understanding of the subject.

See Also: "Bad" Play; Bullying; Fantasy Play; Games of Deception; Human Relationships in Play; Play and Power, Psychology of; Play and Power, Sociology of; Role-Playing; Teasing.

Bibliography. F. Brown and C. Taylor, eds., *Foundations of Playwork* (Open University Press, 2008); C. Garvey, *Play* (Fontana, 1977); B. Hughes, *Play Environments: A Question of Quality* (PLAYLINK, 1996); J. Huizinga, *Homo Ludens: A Study of the Play Element in Culture* (Routledge and Kegan Paul, 1949); B. Sutton-Smith, *The Ambiguity of Play* (Harvard University Press, 1997); B. Sutton-Smith and D. Kelly-Byrne, "The Idealization of Play," in P.K. Smith, ed., *Play in Animals and Humans* (Blackwell, 1984).

Fraser Brown
Leeds Metropolitan University

Imperial Toy

Founded in 1969, Los Angeles-based Imperial Toy LLC is best known for its Bubbles and Novelties and also distributes or manufactures girls' role-play toys and steel trucks. Imperial is also responsible for water pistols, rubber snakes, paddle balls, and roll caps, and manufactures low-priced yo-yos and marbles. Its yo-yos have a crown design on them. The yo-yos produced include: Candy Club, Champion, Giany Teeny, Hi-Tech, Hot Wheels, Imperial, Superstock, Super Sonic Space, and Teeny.

It manufactures SuperMiracle, Miracle, Buddy "L," Livin' Large, Runway Pink, and Legends of the Wild West. Other copyrighted licenses include Nickelodeon; SpongeBob SquarePants; Dora the Explorer; Go, Diego, Go!; Backyardigans; Little Tikes; Thomas the Tank Engine; Bob the Builder; Batman; Ford; Dodge; Jeep; GM; and Universal Monsters. Imperial has offices in Moderna, Italy, and Hong Kong, as well as in Los Angeles. It distributes from Hong Kong, Memphis, Tennessee, and San Diego, California, to over 50 countries worldwide.

The company was founded by Fred Kort, a Holocaust survivor who came to Massachusetts in 1947 to work for General Electric. Transferred to Los Angeles, he worked for Martin Feder in the bubble business, then in 1969 he introduced the Hi-Bounce or Teeny Bouncer ball and launched his family business. Kort became a leading member of the Los Angeles Jewish community, noted for his philanthropy. He died in 2003 and the Kort family sold the company to Peter Tiger and Art Hirsch in 2006.

In 1997 an explosion triggered by roll caps killed four employees. Imperial Toy also manufactured a toy feeding set that was subject to recall by the U.S. Consumer Product Safety Commission after revelations that the nipple on the toy baby bottle posed a potential choking hazard. The company recalled 100,000 Cuddles Feeding Sets and Cuddles Meal Time sets sold at discount stores for $2.00 each between 1995 and 2001. An earlier recall in 1995 involved 100,000 Tammy the Turtle, Peppy the Penguin, and Sally the Seal toys as well as feeding sets and toy trucks that posed a fire hazard because they created sparks. Discount stores such as Ben Franklin and Revco sold the Chinese imports for $2.00 to $4.00 from 1993 to 1995.

Imperial continues to expand. Buddy "L" joined its product line in 2002. Nickelodeon and Viacom chose Imperial as their outlet in 2006. In 2007 its Little Tikes sprinkler won a design award. In March 2008 Imperial purchased One Stop Toy, a company that since 1994 has provided prize-redemption toys for amusement centers. The same year it announced licensing agreements for Barney, Little Kitty, and Marvel products including sand and bubble toys. Imperial advertises its environmental friendliness on its home site. It notes recycling, reduction in packaging, and the first ever 100-percent recyclable bubble bottle, produced in 2007. Imperial also complies with appropriate safety testing standards—ASTM (formerly American society for Testing of Manufactures), EN-71 (flammability and migration of certain elements), and RoHS (restriction of hazardous substances).

See also: United States, 1960 to Present; Water Play; Yo-Yos.

Bibliography. Michael Aushenker, "Fred Kort, Philanthropist and Holocaust Survivor, Dies at 80," *The Jewish Journal*, www.jewishjournal.com (cited July 2008); Imperial Toy, www.imperialtoy.com (cited August 2008); KidSource.com, "CPSC, Imperial Toy Corp., Announce Recall of Toy Feeding Sets," www.kidsource.com (cited July 2008).

John Barnhill
Independent Scholar

India

The second-largest country by population with over one billion people, India is heir to vast empires with deep history, and birthed four of the world's major religions. Its position at the nexus of ancient trade routes and long association with the British Empire have influenced its cosmopolitan, multiethnic, and multilingual culture.

The official national sport is field hockey, and older generations still follow the national teams with deep emotional investment. Soccer is increasingly popular in some regions, and tennis is a popular sport to play in the cities where there is less room for a cricket pitch.

Squash and bowling are urban sports among those who can afford to join the clubs that own the indoor courts or pay the fees for the lanes—space in India's cities is at a premium. Table tennis, which can be played in many homes, is both popular and egalitarian. Indoor volleyball is very popular as a recreational sport in all regions of the country and at all ages; basketball, on the other hand, has not yet attracted the attention of the urban Indians who could turn to it for recreation as so many other urban-dwellers do, and remains a sport taught in children's gym classes.

But far and away, the most popular sport in India either to watch or to play is cricket, and it is followed and pursued with the same sort of passion as soccer in Europe. Among young people, especially in rural areas throughout the subcontinent, a local cricket variant called *gilli-danda* is widely popular. The name of the sport comes from the gilli (a stick about three to six inches long) and danda (12 to 18 inches long) used in place of a cricket bail and bat. Variants are common.

In northern India and in the Indian Army, the "game of kings"—polo—continues to be popular. India introduced polo to the Western world during the time of British rule, after the sport's lengthy history in Persia and Central Asia. Badminton is a popular youth and adult recreational sport throughout India. The game originated on the subcontinent, a British adaptation of the native sport called *poona*.

A recent recreational sport is throwball, which is played mainly in India and South Asia. Played at school and in informal clubs, throwball pits two teams of seven players (and five substitutes waiting on the sidelines) each on either side of a net within a rectangular playing space. The game is much like volleyball—the ball is passed back and forth without touching the net, in the hopes that the receiving team fails to catch it—but instead of being volleyed, the ball must be caught with two hands and immediately returned with one hand. Since it depends so much on reflexes more than strength, the game is easy to play with mixed groups of men and women, children of different ages, or adults and teenagers.

A team tag game native to the subcontinent is *kabaddi*, which has spread throughout south Asia and to the British Army. Two seven-member teams (five members in reserve) play on a court half the size of a basketball court. Each team takes turns sending players to the other side to try to tag opponents, who defend by linking hands. Formal matches are segregated by age and weight; informal play is less scrupulous about fair matches or follows the age-old convention of team captains alternating turns picking players from the assembled group, in order to form balanced teams.

A similar game is *Kho Kho*, with 12-member teams. The essentials—tag and avoid being tagged—are the same, but in *Kho Kho*, one team kneels in the middle of the court with alternate players facing in opposite directions while the other team sends two or three members onto the court, who the kneeling team has to try to tag. A more complicated game than *Kabaddi*, *Kho Kho* has specific rules about who can tag, who can move in which direction, and so on; the objective is to tag players on the opposing team as quickly as possible.

A game just for girls, played in the southern part of the country, is *Koozhangal*, a basic game that will be familiar to people around the world. A stone is thrown in the air, and before it lands, another stone has to be picked up. Then two stones are thrown and two stones have to be picked up—and so on.

Chess

Chess may or may not have originated in India; its origins are unclear in the historical record. Certainly, several early sources attribute the game to India, but because of the country's involvement in cross-continental trade routes, it was responsible for introducing and popularizing many things it did not originally create. A precursor to Chess is certainly Indian: *Chaturanga*, a 6th-century game that differentiated its pieces the way Chess does and in which the endgame depended on a single piece, as with Chess's king. Whether Chess itself began in India, we could say that at least its narrative did.

Children's Games

Magic tag is a tag-and-chase game, in which a particular substance such as wood, stone, or metal is declared "magic." Any player touching something made of that substance is safe from tags, but it's considered against the spirit of the game to simply remain touching said substance—the idea is rather to run and be chased, using such safe touches to claim temporary amnesty. (It is also poor sportsmanship for "it" to linger near a safe player waiting for them to disengage from the magic substance.)

Sota-pani is played with at least 10 players, one of whom is designated "it." The others sit in a circle staring straight ahead, while It runs around the exterior of the circle, carrying a handkerchief. Players must pay attention and try to determine whether or not the handkerchief has been dropped behind them (generally easy in games with small children, since they will give it away with their reactions). The player behind whom the handkerchief has been dropped should grab it and then chase It, attempting to play-hit them with the knotted end of the kerchief before It rounds the circle and comes back to the player's spot.

Vultures and Crows is a two-player game using six different colored markers, pens, crayons, and so on, and a board or piece of paper on which to draw. The vulture player alternates with the crows player, attempting to eat them (by jumping them and removing them from play) before the crows push the vulture into the corner, where he has no available moves.

See Also: Ancient India; Central Asia, Ancient; Chess and Variations of; Cricket (Amateur).

Bibliography. Arnold Arnold, *World Book of Children's Games* (Fawcett, 1972); Jesse Hubbell Bancroft, *Games* (MacMillan, 1937); Marilynn G. Barr, *India: Exploring Ancient Civilizations* (Teaching & Learning Company, 2003); Robbie Bell and Michael Cornelius, *Board Games Round the World: A Resource Book for Mathematical Investigations* (Cambridge University Press, 1988); Roger Caillois, *Man, Play and Games* (University of Illinois Press, 2001); Sarah Ethridge Hunt, *Games and Sports the World Around* (Ronald Press Company, 1964); Glenn Kirchner, *Children's Games Around the World* (Benjamin Cummings, 2000); Nina Millen, *Children's Games From Many Lands* (Friendship Press, 1943).

Bill Kte'pi
Independent Scholar

Indonesia

The Republic of Indonesia covers some 13,667 islands, and has a population of 235 million (2007), nearly 60 percent of which live on the island of Java. Some 45 percent of the entire population of the country are ethnic Javanese either living on the island of Java, or on other islands in the archipelago. There are written chronicles of parts of Indonesia, especially Java, going back to before the arrival of the Dutch in 1603, with the Dutch gradually taking over the entire archipelago.

Javanese traditional entertainment revolved around puppet shows with the *wayang kulit*, the shadow puppets, operating behind a screen, and the *wayang golek*, stick (or "rod") puppets operated from below. Javanese folklore, history, and indeed politics are full of allusions to puppeteers, puppet masters, and puppets, and there is a Wayang Museum in Jakarta. Music in Java, and also in some other parts of Indonesia, revolves around the *gamelan*, a band that plays symbolic music. Each village in Java has at least one *gamelan* band, and the lore of the village can be expressed in music.

Dances are also common, many focusing on Hindu mythological themes—even though most of Indonesia is now Muslim—with large numbers of them drawing from the *Ramayana*, as well as local festivals and dances set around the agricultural cycle. On the island of Bali, the only majority Hindu part of Indonesia, Hindu pageant plays were more pronounced, with the *Kecak* explaining parts of the Ramayana, although some dances such as the *Barong* dance have been adapted for the large number of tourists who visit the island. Kite-flying, swimming, and sailing, often in boats with outriggers, have been used by many locals, with many also offered for use by tourists.

There has always been a large Chinese population in the country, especially in cities, and Mahjong remains popular, as does Chinese Chess. The Dutch brought with them many European games including the European/Indian version of Chess, although most Indonesian Chess sets have elephants rather than rooks or castles; and the bishops are generally royal "advisers."

Chess is now taught in many schools, and tournaments in the country, as well as promotion of the game, is undertaken by the Persatuan Catur Seluruh Indonesia. Some games such as Backgammon, and a number of card games, have been popular locally, with imported board games remaining the preserve of the middle class and the elite. The board game Monopoly was so popular in the country that a Jakarta version was produced called *Monopoli*, with various streets in the Indonesian capital marked. Some schools also teach the piano and other Western instruments, although the guitar is more popular with young Indonesians.

The growth in the local education system in the country from the 1930s led to a rise in recreational sports, with many boys and young men throughout Indonesia being heavily involved in playing soccer, which has rapidly spread around almost every inhabited island in the country. Some teams are supported by companies and local communities. Badminton, basketball, and netball have become popular, especially after the Indonesian badminton team brought back four medals from the Atlanta Olympic Games. Golf remains the sport enjoyed by the wealthy. Indeed, in the late 1990s, during the last period of the Suharto government, political commentators wrote about "golf diplomacy" and "golf politics," following the appointment of a few of Suharto's golfing partners to senior government positions.

See Also: Chess and Variations of; Golf (Amateur); Malaysia; Netball; Soccer (Amateur) Worldwide.

Bibliography. Miguel Covarrubias, *Island of Bali* (Alfred A. Knopf, 1937); Victoria Clara van Groenendael, *The Dalang Behind the Wayang* (Foris, 1985); Edward Horton, *Indonesia* (Raintree, 2004); Sarah Ethridge Hunt, *Games and Sports the World Around* (Ronald Press Company, 1964); Charles R. Joy, *Young People of East Asia* (Oldbourne, 1962); Ward Keeler, *Javanese Shadow Puppets* (Oxford University Press, 1992); R.L. Mellema, *Wayang Puppets* (Royal Tropical Institute, Amsterdam, 1988).

Justin Corfield
Geelong Grammar School

Inter-Gender Play

The topic of gender and play is covered extensively in literature on play. This research frequently looks at how boys' and girls' play activities differ, explanations of why these differences occur, and how gender impacts playmate preference and gender separation. The importance of differences in play and gender is in identifying whether biology or culture has more of an impact in the difference, and looking at whether attempting to change play patterns is useful. Finally, explanations for the commonly found result that children self segregate by gender when forming playgroups are explored. Although differences in play based on gender have been found across many play contexts, it is important to note that these differences are for groups and do not take into account individual variation.

Similarities Between Girls and Boys

Boys and girls engage in many of the same activities. They both enjoy dramatic play, playing with objects, and playing socially with others. When selecting roles to play, both boys and girls tend to select roles of the same gender; for example, girls prefer to play moms and boys tend to play brothers or fathers. Boys and girls tend to develop at similar rates and follow similar patterns of play development from infancy to early childhood to adolescence.

Although differences in play based on gender have been found across many play contexts, gender separation is less common among smaller groups of children and in more intimate settings, such as with siblings.

Differences in Play Based on Gender

Gender differences in play activity have been found in a number of areas. Boys' and girls' play differs physically, socially, and in their preference for play objects and play activities. Boys and girls also differ in the types of play themes they prefer.

Physically, boys' play tends to be more vigorous and involves using more space. Boys are also more likely to engage in rough-and-tumble play, which involves play fighting and wrestling. These differences in motor play begin to appear around 4 years of age. Another physical difference is in play space preference—boys tend to prefer to play outdoors when given the choice, while girls tend to prefer to play indoors. As boys' play is more active, they are also more likely to take physical risks during play such as jumping from playground equipment or accessing higher points. Their increased risk taking also leads to more physical injuries for boys during play.

Boys' and girls' social groups differ as well. Boys' play tends to be more argumentative especially in playing games; their play also more likely involves competition. Boys are more likely to be involved in organized sports and team play especially, as they get older. They tend to prefer more competitive sports and activities. Boy groups tend to be larger and more open, while girl groups tend to be smaller and more intimate. Girls tend to prefer more cooperative play and are more likely to use polite language in play. They are also more likely to be more conciliatory during play. Although they are seen as conciliatory, there is as much conflict in girls' play as in boys' play; however, this conflict is focused on social relations rather than the activity. According to Brian Sutton-Smith, girls' play is about inclusion in that girls use inclusion and exclusion as power tactics for play, while boys use physicality and aggression.

Boys and girls demonstrate differences in activity preferences. These results are generally based on Western school settings. Girls are more likely to engage in more sedentary play activities like painting, looking at books, and playing with dolls. Girls are more likely to prefer tabletop activities, while boys are more likely to engage in building, playing on the floor, and riding on play vehicles. Girls also are more likely to play with puzzles and color pictures. In outdoor play, boys are more likely to engage in games with rules. Boys and girls both engage in chase games. When engaging in chase, boys are more likely to finish chasing by engaging in rough-and-tumble play like tackling and play fighting. Girls' chase games are more likely to have a base or a safe area.

The themes for play also differ based on gender. Girls' play is more likely to include home-based themes and domestic roles. They also tend to play out everyday activities like shopping or family routines. Boys' play is more likely to involve superheroes and have play based on more adventurous activities and fantasy themes. They also prefer stories of gore and phantasmagoria. Boys are less likely to base their play on the props that are available to them. Boys also spend more time enacting their play routines, while girls spend more time planning their play.

Although girls' play is seen as more nurturing, and their play language is more conciliatory, they do engage in activities such as destroying and torturing their dolls. Barbie dolls in particular have been the focus of destruction by girls. Many girls resist the idea that they must be sweet and nurturing by expressly engaging in this type of destructive activity.

Adult attitudes also differ in the types of play children engage in. Destruction of dolls, for example, would be an activity that adults discourage. In schools, stereotypical girls' play is more likely to be encouraged than stereotypical boys' play. Teachers are more likely to have mandates against rough play and gun play, which are stereotypically boy activities, than they are to discourage typical girl activities like table games. In general teachers ban such rough activities based on the belief that the rougher boys are bullying and taking advantage of the girls.

Overall, there is robust evidence for differences between boys' and girls' play behaviors and activities. However, there are many more similarities than differences between the play of boys and girls. Focusing on the differences masks these similarities.

Explanations for Gender Differences

Explanations of gender differences in play run from the biological to social learning theories. According to biological theories, play differences are attributed to biological differences between boys and girls, in that girls have a genetic predisposition to engage in play activities that are seen as feminine. Boys would have a genetic predisposition to prefer masculine activities. Evidence of some brain differences between girls and boys and the importance of hormones in shaping behavior are often given as evidence for why boys and girls play differently. In addition, gender differences in play preferences are seen for nonhuman primates, suggesting some biological basis for play preference.

Social learning theories suggest that these differences are because of social influences, in that children are given differential treatment from birth based on their gender. Boy infants, for example, are more likely than girls to have their parents play with them roughly. Boys and girls are given different play objects and are encouraged to act in stereotypical ways overtly through praise and encouragement for these behaviors. They also are encouraged to engage in stereotypical activities as they view media images and through commercial culture.

Social learning theory explains that boys and girls who do not engage in stereotypical play are discouraged from engaging in play that is not stereotypical. Boys and girls are often teased by peers if they engage in play that is seen as not gender appropriate. They are also discouraged by adults, who express concern if boys show too much interest in doll play or if girls are seen to be tomboys. Consensus suggests that girls have more latitude to explore across gender roles and activities than boys.

Constructivist play theories see children constructing identity through play as they attempt to come to an understanding about their roles and how to interact. Differences in play between boys and girls are seen to be a reflection of the society that the children are experiencing.

Gender-based play activities differ across cultures. It has been suggested that this is because of the importance of play for practicing adult roles and preparing for adult life. Gender play reflects the differences in gender roles found in adult society. Societies with greater division in labor between men and women are more likely to see more defined differences between boys' and girls' play.

Efforts have been made to change stereotypical play patterns in children. Some have led to efforts to end war play, while others have encouraged giving gender stereotypical toys to children of the opposite gender. The idea behind challenging gender roles is that the toys that children play with can impact their social and cognitive skills. If boys have more opportunities to play with dolls, they will develop more nurturing abilities, and if girls are given building toys, they will develop greater spatial relations. Not having the opportunity to play with these toys may limit their future abilities. In addition, changing play patterns is seen as a way of challenging dominant power structures between boys and girls.

According to some feminist theory, encouraging more competitive play structures for girls can help better prepare them for administrative roles normally held by males. In addition, decreasing boys' violent play should lead to a decrease in violence in society at large. There has been some debate about the effectiveness of this effort. The effort to change children's play behaviors continues with a focus on allowing more cross-gender play activities, purchasing toys that encourage cross-gender play, and in decreasing the amount of rough play.

So far an explanation for the differences in boys' and girls' play has not been completely explained. Generally, most researchers come down to a nature and nurture combination to explain these differences in behaviors.

Playmate Preference and Gender

Boys and girls tend to prefer to play with same gender peers. Same gender preference also occurs among nonhuman primates. Preference for playing with same-gender peers begins in early childhood and becomes more pronounced in the elementary school years. This continues through adolescence, when play rituals begin to turn to more cross-gender contact through courtship games and dating. Best friends are generally of the same gender. Imaginary playmates are also more likely to be of the same gender.

Several factors have been attributed to this development of groups based on gender. First, there is the idea that children choose same-gender playmates because they have similar play patterns. Others have suggested that dominance in play may be the significant factor in creating same-gender groups. Girls have difficulty influencing boys during play, so in order to avoid being dominated by boys, they avoid them. Social structures may also have an impact on separation of play groups by gender. Barrie Thorne found that schools and school personnel acted in ways to encourage gender separation by having segregated classes and by encouraging competition between girls and boys during games. She also found that gender was a more significant segregating factor than race or ethnicity.

Boys and girls maintain this separation through teasing and taunting. Boys and girls are excluded from each others' activities with taunts of, "only girls can play," or "boys only." Boys or girls will also tease members of their own gender for engaging in cross-gender play, thus serving as a policing force for gender separation.

Play in Group Settings

Although there is a general separation of groups, there still remains a large amount of contact and conflict across groups. For example, a common issue on many school playgrounds is "rituals of pollution," which Catherine Garvey describes as when one gender will be contaminated if they are touched by the other gender. These rituals such as threats of kissing or germs provide an ongoing source of both contact and conflict. Cross-gender chasing is also common as a way of enforcing separation of groups by gender. Cross-gender chasing also often involves taboos like kissing and giving cooties. Boys and girls also will invade each others' space to disrupt the play activities of the opposite gender.

Outside of schools there was less emphasis on same gender groups. Homes, churches, and neighborhoods did not offer as many options for creating same-gender groups so there was more likelihood of cross-gender play groups. In addition, as neighborhoods, churches, and homes are under less observation, there is less likelihood that they will be sanctioned for engaging in cross-gender play groups.

Girls are more likely to enter cross-gender groups, with boys more likely to be sanctioned for trying to enter into girl groups. Girls tend to try to enter cross-gender groups based on the activity. Differences exist for boys who attempt to enter cross-gender groups. In some cases, during outdoor play, boys who have less physical coordination are left out of play groups for more physically fit boys. These boys often engage in the more sedentary play groups of girls. On the other hand, boys who have higher status have the ability to cross gender borders, as they have the cultural capital to avoid being teased for crossing gender boundaries.

The separation of genders during play results in what is described as the development of different cultures for boys and girls. The different styles of play—rough and tumble, large groups for boys, quiet and intimate groups for girls—makes interaction across groups difficult. On the other hand, there are more contacts across groups than generally recognized. Boys and girls engage in cross-gender chase and teasing. They also engage with each other when smaller groups allow for more interaction like in homes, churches, and neighborhoods. In addition, depending on the activity, there is some regular crossing of the gender lines based on the activity or the social status of the crosser and their willingness to tolerate teasing for crossing gender lines. Working across gender lines can be difficult, as both adults and children encourage gender separation. School personnel often compound the competition across groups by engaging in competitive games based on gender.

Overall, there are general differences between boys' and girls' play patterns. Gender separation is also a common occurrence, especially in schools. Explanations for the separation include the influences of peers and adults who encourage separation. Gender separation may also be a result of play preference, in that children prefer to play with peers who have like interests. Gender separation is less common among smaller groups of children and in more intimate settings.

See Also: "Bad Play"; Boys' Play; Girls' Play; Play as Learning, Anthropology of; Rhetorics of Play (Sutton-Smith); Wargames.

Bibliography. Joan Baxter, *The Archeology of Childhood: Children, Gender and Material Culture* (AltaMira Press, 2005); Joe Frost, Sue Wortham, and Stuart Reifel, *Play and Child Development* (Merrill-Prentice Hall, 2006); Catherine Garvey, *Play* (Harvard University Press, 1990); James Johnson, James Christie, and Thomas Yawkey, *Play and Early Childhood Development* (Longman, 1999); Gerard Jones, *Killing Monsters: Why Children Need Fantasy, Superheroes, and Make-Believe Violence* (Basic Books, 2002); Nancy Carlsson Paige and Diane Levin, *The War Play Dilemma* (Teachers College Press, 1987); Vivian Paley, *Boys and Girls: Superheroes in the Doll Corner* (University of Chicago Press, 1986); Brian Sutton-Smith, *The Ambiguity of Play* (Harvard University Press, 1997); Barrie Thorne, *Gender Play: Girls and Boys in School* (Rutgers University Press, 1995).

John A. Sutterby
University of Texas, Brownsville

International Play Association

The International Play Association's (IPA's) *raison d'être* is "to protect, preserve and promote the child's right to play as a fundamental human right," enshrined in the United Nations Convention on the Rights of the Child (UNCRC). Founded in 1961, IPA has developed into a dynamic international network organization with members in around 50 countries and many active groups.

The roots of IPA are in Scandinavia, where emerging barriers to children's play were first identified in the 1930s. Spreading urbanization and increases in road traffic led to the designation of specific areas for children's play. By 1937, Stockholm/Sweden sported nine parks with trained play leaders, and in Denmark, adventure playgrounds in which children were allowed to build their own habitats emerged in 1945. Interest in quality play opportunities for children grew. In 1958, 10 European country representatives met to discuss playgrounds and leadership, and three years later in Denmark, IPA was born.

The United Nations (UN) International Year of the Child in 1979 injected IPA with great vigor and represents a defining moment in its development. From its first triennial conference outside Europe in Ottawa, Canada, IPA blossomed into a truly international movement with an impressive membership base. Global triennial conferences have been held in England, France, Italy, Canada, Netherlands, Yugoslavia, Sweden, Japan, Australia, Finland, Portugal, Brazil, Germany, and Hong Kong—with its 50th anniversary conference held in Wales in the United Kingdom in 2011.

IPA played a significant role in the 1980s in ensuring that the child's right to play was included in the UNCRC. Through Article 31, play became part of this treaty, which is a benchmark against which a nation's treatment of its children can be measured. It provides an important tool for play advocates around the world. Crucially, it marks a shift from seeing play as a need to accepting it as a child's universal human right.

IPA provides a forum, which embraces a wide range of disciplines and sectors, is a vehicle for interdisciplinary exchange and action, and contributes a child perspective to policy developments throughout the world. Throughout its history, IPA has uniquely kept its focus on children's play and, after half a century of existence, it continues to operate solely through the dedicated efforts of volunteers. They often work in close association with national, and a growing number of international, organizations.

Promoting the child's right to play is arguably becoming more important, compared to the context of IPA's inception in the mid-20th century. IPA understands play to be children's natural behavior. A child's healthy development—physical, social, cognitive, creative, and emotional—depends on it. Play is spontaneous, self-motivated, controlled, and initiated by children themselves, not something created by adults for children. The adult role—exemplified by trained playworkers or "animateurs" rather than "supervisors"—is about facilitating play, that is, supporting rather than directing it.

The modern world has created many barriers—physical and social—to children's free, unstructured play and has severely reduced their independent movement. In industrialized nations, play opportunities and easy access to natural surroundings cherished by older generations when they were children are greatly diminished, both in urban and rural environments. Here, children's time is becoming increasingly programmed, and directed by adults. Competition for land and the dangers of road traffic combine to restrict the outdoor informal places where children used to play. Fear of litigation has reduced many playgrounds to sterile, boring places shunned by children.

Play space design often acts to exclude children with disabilities. Adult fears about child abduction, harm by strangers, pedophiles, risk, and bullying often keep children indoors, creating an overprotective "cotton wool culture." While at school, recess times are sometimes reduced to cram in more formal learning, or children are punished by taking away their playtime. In developing countries, barriers include toxic and polluted environments and lack of time to play because of child labor; in institutionalized settings such as refugee camps, orphanages, and homeless shelters, opportunities to play can be severely curtailed through institutional bureaucracy. Here, therapeutic play has a role in helping children recovering from violence and the trauma of displacement.

Play is the essence of childhood. IPA is fundamentally about protecting children's right to be free to explore and discover the physical and social world around them and continues to work for a world fit for children, where all children can play.

See Also: Adventure Playgrounds; Denmark; Playground Movement, U.S.; Risk in Play; Sweden; Unstructured Play.

Bibliography. Rhonda L. Clements and Leah Fiorentino, eds., *The Child's Right to Play: A Global Approach* (Praeger Publishers, 2004); International Association for the Child's Right to Play, *Play and Creativity: Report of the 10th International Conference of the International Association for the Child's Right to Play (IPA), Stockholm, 1987* (International Association for the Child's Right to Play, 1988); International Play Association—Resources Section, www.ipaworld.org (cited August 2008).

Ute Navidi
International Play Association

Iran

Iranian children and adults tend to play with items manufactured predominantly in China and in the Middle East. Still, a large pirated toy market exists for Western products, and all classes of people have access to these. Since the 1990s, Iran's increasing interest in pro-Islamic values has affected its toy market, as has the economic downturn of the Middle East in current political turmoil.

Iranian men gather for coffee and Dominoes, as well as traditional games such as Chess or tabletop sports involving skills like flicking counters at opponents' pieces to eliminate them. Iranian women enjoy segregated sports such as basketball, tennis, and swimming. Daughters in families without discretionary income to pay fees for pool or court admittance will miss out on sporting activities, but gather with friends to share electronic games. Sons in urban and rural families enjoy pick-up ball games and all manner of electronic games. Younger children are likely playing with cuddly toys or simple mechanical pieces manufactured in China; some of these will include pirated copies of toys popular in Canada or the United States. An example often brought to the fore in political wrangling is Barbie.

Dara and Sara are Iran's answer to Ken and Barbie, developed and marketed by the Institute for the Intellectual Development of Children and Young Adults, a government agency affiliated with the Ministry of Education. The siblings were born as characters in school books; since becoming dolls, their lives have developed new stories sold on cassette along with the dolls. Dara is about eight years old, young enough under Islamic law for Sara to appear in public without a headscarf, although the four Sara models each come with head scarves.

As one might expect, Dara and Sara help each other solve problems and turn to their loving parents for guidance. And as one might expect, they are not nearly so popular with Iranian children as with the adults, who purchase them for nieces or granddaughters. The dolls sell for about half the cost of an American Barbie doll, but four times the price of a pirated Barbie.

Aside from Dara and Sara, toys that quote Quranic verses or prayers have increased in popularity since the inception of the Institute for the Intellectual Development of Children and Young Adults (abbreviated as Kanoon). Islamic booksellers mourn the heyday of children's publishing, which enjoys a rich history dating back to the Persian Empire. Although the 1960s were a golden time for children's books, the Islamic Fundamentalist movement of 1979 halted many publishers, and despite Kanoon's working with its older relative the Children's Book Council (founded in 1962) reading is not considered as popular a pastime as sports or gathering with friends. Kanoon and the Children's Book Council continue to organize regular storytelling festivals and traditional literature events throughout urban areas, and to encourage play based on traditional mythology and legend through the development of toys and games related to these tales.

Despite these efforts to increase awareness of heritage and community values, one is as likely to find LEGOs and Disney logos as Kanoon labels in most households, and illegal satellite dishes offer children Western television, creating the desire for entertainment-related toys, easily available in urban and rural areas.

See Also: Boys' Play; Dolls, Barbie and Others; Girls' Play; Saudi Arabia.

Bibliography. Children's Literature in Iran, www.macondo.nu (cited July 2008); Database for Children's Culture & Literature of Iran, www.iranak.info (cited July 2008); Mark Edward Harris, *Inside Iran* (Chronicle Books, 2008); Glenn Kirchner, *Children's Games Around the World* (Benjamin Cummings, 2000).

Wendy Welch
University of Virginia, Wise

Iraq

In the early 1930s the British archaeologist Sir Leonard Woolley, digging at the site of the ancient city of Ur, uncovered what became known as the "Game of Ur," then the oldest surviving board game in the world, dating from 2600 B.C.E., although a game recently found in Iran is believed to 500 years older.

It consisted of a board inlaid with lapis lazuli, shell, bone, and red limestone; had 38 squares; and was found with two sets of seven pieces. Many scholars and games enthusiasts have tried to work out the possible rules, and although a commercial version of it was made out of cardboard in the 1970s, the exact rules have not been ascertained.

Stringed instruments were used in medieval Baghdad, which was a great center of culture for the region. In the north of the country, the long-necked lute is played by the Kurds and the Turkmens. During the 1930s, Iraqi orchestras included both Jewish and Muslim musicians. Drama in medieval and early modern times was largely along the lines of Koranic stories and morality tales, used to educate children and adults alike. During Ottoman rule, Turkish games such as *Tavla*, similar to Backgammon, became common, with some card games appearing from the 18th century. Chess also gained many adherents and is now run under the aegis of the Iraqi Chess Federation. In the 1970s there was a revival of interest in Iraqi classical music, largely through the creation of the National School of Music and Dance. Western-style music was also encouraged with the Iraqi National Symphony Orchestra. Some Iraqis also play the bagpipes for important festivities such as marriages.

It was the reorganization of the country's education system in the 1920s that transformed sport in the country. Soccer quickly became the sport of choice for most boys and young men in the country, and Iraq become a member of the Asian Football Confederation, which was established in 1954. However, it was not until 1986 that the Iraqi soccer team was invited to participate in the World Cup. For most occasions since then, for political reasons, the team has not been allowed to participate—being under the control of Saddam Hussein's son Uday—although it competed well in the games played in 2008 in the run-up to the 2010 World Cup.

Swimming has long been an important part of Iraqi national identity, with the Tigris and Euphrates Rivers providing much of the water for the country. During the 1980s, Iraqi President Saddam Hussein swam in the Tigris near the Tikrit each year to commemorate his escape following the failed assassination attempt on the Iraqi Prime Minister Qassim in 1959. Boating, boxing, volleyball, and basketball have also been popular, with the Baathist government of Saddam Hussein building many sporting facilities and encouraging participation by women. Falconry was also popular among the Bedouin tribesmen. Board games such as Monopoly were played by family members of the elite, and with the upsurge in violence following the invasion of Iraq in 2003, many people have stayed at home, resulting in an increase in indoor games, especially computer games.

See Also: Assyrian/Babylonian Backgammon; Chess and Variations of; Culture; Soccer (Amateur) Worldwide.

Bibliography. Dynise Balcavage, *Iraq* (Times Editions, 2003); Simon Freeman, *Baghdad FC: Iraq's Football Story* (John Murray, 2005); Dora Jane Hamblin, *The First Cities* (Time-Life Books, 1973); Susan M. Hassig, *Iraq* (Marshall Cavendish, 1993); Arnold Zable, "Harmonies in Old Iraq," *The Age,* Melbourne, Australia (September 22, 2007).

Justin Corfield
Geelong Grammar School

Ireland

Until recent times, research on children's play, or *súgradh,* in Ireland was limited. However, there are exceptions—the Irish Folklore Association and the Gaelic Athletic Association (GAA) are both a rich resource on the history of play and sports of Irish children during the last century. Recently the issue of play in Ireland was addressed by the Irish government to meet commitments made in the United Nations Convention on the Rights of the Child (1989) and the National Children's Strategy (2000); during the consultation process with children, the lack of play opportunities was the most frequently cited concern of children throughout the country. This led to the first Irish National Play Policy in 2004.

The Gaelic Athletic Association (GAA) was established in 1884 to revive and nurture traditional, indigenous pastimes, especially hurling and Gaelic football. Hurling is a game similar to hockey, in that it is played with a small ball and a curved wooden stick. The stick, or "hurley" *camán* is curved outwards at the end, to provide the striking surface. The ball or *sliothar* is similar in size to a hockey ball but has raised ridges. Hurling is thought to be Europe's oldest field game and was introduced to Ireland by the Celts. Hurling features in Irish folklore to illustrate the deeds of heroic mystical figures, and it is chronicled as a distinct Irish pastime for at least 2,000 years. Gaelic football can be described as a mixture of soccer and rugby, although it predates both of those games. It is a field game that has developed as a distinct game similar to the progression of Australian Rules. The GAA is the largest sports organization within the primary education system in Ireland for children aged 4 to 12 years, and both games remain extremely popular with children.

A road sign seen in Ireland attests to the committment to protecting the rights of children at play.

Folklorists in Ireland conducted "The Schools' Scheme" as it is popularly known, which represents the largest folklore collection ever carried out with children in Ireland back in 1937–38. Over a period of 18 months almost 100,000 children aged between 11 and 14 years of age in 5,000 primary schools were involved in researching and recording material dealing with a wide range of Irish folk traditions. Among other topics, the collection includes material on folktales and folk legends, riddles and proverbs, songs, play activities, games, and traditional pastimes. The children collected this material mainly from parents and grandparents, and from older members of the local community. The result of the scheme was the Schools' Manuscript Collection, which extends to more than half a million manuscript pages. This rich resource remains in constant use today by a wide variety of academic disciplines.

In more recent times, the publication of the first National Play Policy in 2004 was an acknowledgement that in the past, children's play has been seriously neglected at policy level. There was a serious deficit of public play spaces; in 2004 Ireland had 405 golf courses but only 168 public playgrounds for a population of 840,955 children under the age of 14. Previously, there had never been any ring-fenced government funding for play, and there was a poorly developed societal awareness of the value of play. While the objective of the National Play Policy is to provide children with more play opportunities in a variety of settings, there has been a strong focus on increasing the number of public playgrounds throughout the country, in which they have been very successful. More recently still, the government launched the National Recreational Policy for Children (2007) which focuses on the play and recreational needs of adolescents.

Currently ongoing is a government-led national longitudinal study of children titled "Growing up in Ireland." It is following the progress of 18,000 children over seven years. The main aim of the study is to examine the life of Irish children and how they are developing in the current social, economic, and cultural environment. One of the objectives of the longitudinal study is to examine the play activities and sports that children enjoy. All of these recent developments have led to an increase in academic publications dealing with play from a variety of disciplines such as sport, education, anthropology, sociology and folklore.

See Also: International Play Association; Rugby (Amateur); Soccer (Amateur) Worldwide; United Kingdom.

Bibliography. Gaelic Athletic Association, www.gaa.ie (cited July 2008); National Children's Office, *National Recreational Policy for Young People* (National Children's Office, 2007); National Children's Office, *Ready, Steady Play–A National Play Policy* (National Children's Office, 2004); National Folklore Collection, www.ucd.ie/folklore/english_html/english_home.htm (cited July 2008); United Nations, *Convention on the Rights of the Child*, www.unicef.org/crc/crc/.html (cited July 2008).

Carol M. Barron
Dublin City University

I Spy

I Spy is a guessing game, frequently played as a car game, and especially associated with family trips. Play begins—sometimes spontaneously—when someone says, "I spy with my little eye something beginning with the letter {letter}" or "I spy with my little eye something {color}." Other players then have to try to guess the object. When played in the car, the object may not remain in view; the identifier is usually expected to point out when the object has disappeared, and this may render the round null or may act as a clue (especially when playing with younger children). The correct guesser traditionally initiates the next round.

Phrases can be used instead of single words, for instance, "I spy with my little eye something beginning with SLS," for speed limit sign, but this can complicate matters, especially if a guesser has identified the right object but the wrong phrase.

The game is played in many countries, but the game phrase varies. German speakers ask, "*Ich sehe was, was du nicht siehst, und das ist* [color]" (I see something that you don't see, and that is...). Spanish colors begin play by saying, "*Veo, veo*" (I see, I see), and are interrogated by sing-song rote: What do you see? (A thing.) What thing? (A wonderful thing!) What color? ([color], [color]).

See Also: Car and Travel Games; Play as Entertainment, Psychology of; Play as Entertainment, Sociology of.

Bibliography. Arnold Arnold, *World Book of Children's Games* (Fawcett, 1972); Patricia Evans, *Rimbles: A Book of Children's Classic Games, Rhymes, Songs, and Sayings* (Doubleday, 1961); Glenn Kirchner, *Children's Games Around the World* (Benjamin Cummings, 1991).

Bill Kte'pi
Independent Scholar

Israel

Play and games associated with a particular society are often said to reflect the ethos of that society. What games are played, how they are played, and the content of the games themselves exemplify a group's fundamental ideology, spirit, and nature. When play and games embody the ethos of a society, they can become analytical material for interpreting the identity and character of that society. Play theorist Brian Sutton-Smith talks not only of how play and games can reflect and interpret a society's identity and character, but also how play and games are a form of "bonding a community" or creating what anthropologist Victor Turner referred to as *communitas*, an intense community spirit based on social equality, solidarity, and togetherness.

In Israel, Zionist ideology, which believes in a national homeland for the Jewish people in the "Land of Israel," was, and to a large extent still is, the underlying force behind Israeli communitas. The role of games in both reflecting and reinforcing this Zionist ideology is best illustrated in the card and board games produced and played during the 1940s, 1950s, and early 1960s, the period before and after the establishment of the State of Israel.

Benjamin Barlevy is recognized as the pioneer of the Israeli game industry. Over a 50-year period, he manufactured and produced well over 100 original Hebrew games. As was true of other Hebrew game manufacturers at the time, Barlevy based his games on Zionist themes that familiarized children with the "Land of Israel." Through these games, children became acquainted with Israel's plants and animals, national institutions, Hebrew literature, the military structure, and the map of the country. The main purpose of his games was to instill national ideals and values into the minds of Israeli children. Through his games, Barlevy promoted a sense of communitas and a love for Israel among much of the Jewish population.

Zionist Influence

Until the 1960s many of the card and board games played throughout Israel reflected the strong Zionist spirit prominent at the time. The 1967 war, in which Israel conquered Arab territories on almost all of her borders, is identified as the turning point in Israel's ethos and sense of communitas. Although the war of 1967 was a clear victory for Israel, the conquering of Arab lands caused an ideological split between those who wanted to keep and expand the territories and those who wanted to return them.

According to Haim Grossman, who has done extensive research on the militaristic elements in card and board games in Israel before 1967, the Six Day War games were the culmination of the Wargames that were so popular in the 1940s and 1950s and was the "beginning of the end of the war games wave." The Zionist spirit no longer dominated Israeli society. According to sociologist and historian Oz Almog, the changes in the type of games played "reflect[s] the passage from a national-conformist-educational orientation to a scientific-pluralistic-critical one."

The rapid economic prosperity that Israel experienced after 1967, along with a doubling of the population, mainly because of Jewish immigration, contributed to major changes in the feeling of communitas that was prominent before the war. As cities and settlements grew the feeling of a national community spirit weakened.

Not only were people more politically divided, but they were socially, economically, and culturally divided as well. As many Israelis became wealthier *Chutz La'aretz* (which literally means "outside of Israel") became much more attractive, especially to the young members of society. Israelis took more of an interest in games imported from abroad, which had general themes not necessarily related to Israel and nationalism. Games such as Monopoly, Risk, Scrabble, and the like, became more fashionable than the old games. Other games, such as Rummikub, invented by Ephraim Hertzano in the 1950s, and Master Mind, created in 1970 by Mordecai Meirowitz, were developed in Israel, although they did not become popular in Israel until after they had become internationally known. Most Israelis today are not even aware that these games originated in Israel.

The high-tech revolution, which took place in Israel in the 1990s, changed the way that games are played. Although many of the board games have been transformed onto the computer screen, the manner in which they are played has changed considerably. Online games are often played alone, opposite anonymous playmates not only from Israel but, more significantly, from all over the world.

If play and games reflect the ethos of a society, it is evident that the ideology, spirit, and nature of Israeli society have adjusted to a new reality. Until 1967 Israel saw itself as a small, united country, fighting for its existence. After 1967, Israeli society became more concerned with finding a place in the wider world and has taken on many of the values and ambitions of Western society. Games of the past reinforced the Zionist ethos and reflected the communitas that shaped Israel's character in its early years. This has given way to new games based on an ideology that focuses on Israel's desire to establish her place in the world community by both playing and producing games with more universal themes. One of the aims of early Zionism was to make Israel "a nation like any other nation"—the adoption of games from abroad symbolizes the success and coming of age of the Zionist program.

See Also: Monopoly and Variations of; Rhetorics of Play (Sutton-Smith); Risk, the Game; Rummy and Variations of; Scrabble.

Bibliography. Oz Almog, "It's Not Just a Game—A Glimpse at the Zionist Propaganda Workshop," in *A Trip Across the Country: Games From Mr. Barlevy's Store* (Eretz Israel Museum, 1999); Haim Grossman, "War as Child's Play: Patriotic Games in the British Mandate and Israel," *Israel Studies* (v.1/9, Spring 2004); Brian Sutton-Smith, *The Ambiguity of Play* (Harvard University Press, 1997); David Tartakover, *A Trip Across the Country: Games from Mr. Barlevy's Store* (Eretz Israel Museum, 1999).

Avigail Morris
Ben Gurion University

Italy

Play in Italy has a long and rich historical tradition. Some games were introduced as early as 2,000 years ago by the Romans, who had in turn often learned them from Greeks or Etruscans. The late political unification of the country (1861) has, then, contributed to the large number and variety of traditional Italian games, whose regional and at times municipal roots can still be recognized. Another factor that has contributed to such a variety has been the significant foreign influences and dominations that have shaped almost 2,000 years of the peninsula's history.

A historical account of such a complex variety must be integrated into a sound theoretical framework. With this objective, it seems pertinent to refer to the framework proposed by the French philosopher and sociologist Roger Caillois (1961). His classification of games into four categories, according to the dominant roles respectively played by competition, chance, simulation, and vertigo, offers a solid background against which to assess relevant sociohistorical questions. One could, for instance, wonder why chance games have played an important role for several centuries in some Italian regions, especially in Naples and the south. In this sense, the argument that will be put forward maintains that different games reflect different socioeconomic constellations and patterns, and that there are no such "clear-cut" phenomena as "northern" or "southern" Italian games. It seems more appropriate, in contrast, to underline the commonalities of most Italian games with their "foreign" counterparts and the cross-civilizational origins of their main characteristics and evolution.

Ancient Games

To begin with, most Roman games had Greek roots. Before the Roman conquest, large areas of Southern Italy were flourishing Hellenic colonies where trade was the core activity and both agonistic and chance games were widely played. The peninsula's new rulers borrowed more ancient traditions, to which they added a degree of codification and grandiosity. The Latin word for play, *ludus*, involved a certain level of learning, self-discipline, and codified rules. The Roman *ludi* and the well-known gladiatorial fighting (that were not *ludi*, but *munera*) were mainly performed by professionals and thus cannot be understood as proper games.

In another respect, nevertheless, they are relevant as they contributed to the popularity of games linked to them: first of all, of course, gambling. Such games, mainly played with bone dice, despite being illegal, were popular with all social classes, laborers as well as aristocrats and emperors. The historian Suetonius even devoted a booklet to dice playing, and the emperors Augustus and Claudius were apparently enthusiast players. Other writers, such as Cato and Horace, associated it with an alleged decay of public ethics and urged youngsters to find less immoral pastimes, like, for instance, playing with tops. Besides its application to gambling, dicing was a rather sophisticated recreation, sometimes taken very seriously. The game *Latrunculi* (Robbers or Soldiers) dealt with protecting and attacking and, while comparable to Chess in terms of complexity, testifies to the persistence of the cultural legacy of early Roman shepherds and soldiers. While we have sound archaeological evidence of dice games and other board games, it is known that the Romans also entertained themselves with agonistic play. *Harpastum*, for instance, was an amateurish ball game that preceded modern football and rugby, although with a much higher degree of violence.

Increasing Game Variety

Most ancient games survived during the Middle Ages, despite the subsequent waves of invasions and the negative attitude of the Roman Catholic Church. In the latter's view, play was a source of evil, especially as long as it allowed the waste of time, waste of money, and rise of enmities and vain, mundane passions. Such an attitude did not, however, prevent Italian people from welcoming new games from distant countries. Chess entered Italy from the south in the wake of the Arabic conquest of Sicily, starting in 827. A pair of players was represented by the Arabic authors of the splendid mosaics of Palermo's Cappella Palatina, whose building had begun in 1143.

Other representations of Chess players are to be found in the coeval mosaics of the Basilique of San Savino, in the northern city of Piacenza. In the very same decades, Dominoes arrived from China, thanks to the trade of the Republic of Venice. The general improvement in the economy after the beginning of the 11th century and the rise of republics and free cities in many regions brought about new traditions, customs, and social attitudes toward play. While large parts of Europe welcomed the diffusion of tournaments and other recreations linked to feudalism and knighthood, Italy was evolving toward an early urban civilization.

Cities such as Venice, Florence, Genoa, Milan, and many smaller ones became centers of trade both within Europe and between Europe and the East. Despite the considerable accumulation of wealth on the part of several traders, businessmen, and bankers, such an emerging mercantile bourgeoisie stuck to rather moderate customs. Money and profit were the principal aims, and their pursuit did not allow for luxurious or time-demanding recreations. As argued by the great historian of the Renaissance Jacob Burckhardt, the Italian city was a rather compact social environment, without the clear class divisions between nobility and peasants that characterized feudal societies in other European regions.

At least until the rise of principalities in the 15th century, merchants, mediators, and salesmen enjoyed simple and popular games, for example, dice games in various forms, both for leisure and as a way to make further profits. According to Burckhardt, a certain Buonaccorso Pitti from Florence, a merchant who used to play with ordinary people as well as with European princes, was possibly the first professional gambler in modern history. Since most Italian cities were ruled by republican institutions, a sense of commonality often prevailed and manifested itself in a

Children in a Roman park play "the national Italian sport"—football, or American soccer. Football betting pools have become a principal pastime for millions of Italians from all regions and social classes.

number of public festivals, which in turn contributed to enhancing such a "common" civic identity.

Mysteries drew on religious feelings and Triumphs celebrated military victories, while processions and carnivals, through curious blends of sacred and worldly elements, strengthened the sense of belonging to the municipal community. As regards games, cards, dice games, and gambling were popular across all social strata. Gamblers and cheaters of any kind were active on the public square (the *piazza*), especially on market days. Despite their moral condemnation by the Church and famous intellectuals such as Dante and Petrarch, they were often tolerated, and in a sense their business was functional to the urban economy. Several cities instituted a *Potestas baratariorum*, that is, a local authority in charge of supervising and regulating the activity of the *barattieri*, the gamblers. Their incomes were in fact an important source of public revenue—no matter how immoral such deals might have been judged to be.

The rise of principalities in many cities (e.g., Milan, Florence, and Naples) in the 15th century brought about a redrawing of social hierarchies and stronger differentiations in culture, habits, and games. The civic dimension of festivals and celebrations lost its central role, and occasions such as festivals and Triumphs became mainly sources of legitimization for the ruling families or the prince. On the other hand, the new nobility, centred on the court of the *Signore*, often a former military leader, developed new and more sophisticated tastes. In the courts of the 15th century, strictly aristocratic games made their appearance.

Tarot Cards

One of the best known, and still remarkably mysterious, was the card game of Tarots. While cards had already been in use in Italy in the late 14th century, tarot cards were introduced in the first half of the 15th century, notably in Milan and Ferrara. The earliest decks were commissioned from famous painters by Filippo Maria Visconti, Duke of Milan, and Leonello d'Este, marquis of Ferrara. Their enigmatic depiction of human virtues and vices, their allegories, and their elegant mythological motives answered to political as well as to cultural demands.

On the one hand, tarot figures drew a symbolic thread between ancient heroes and modern patrons, that is, the princes who had commissioned them; on the other, they somehow expressed the inquisitive spirit of an age, the Renaissance, where men and their rulers were searching for more secular solutions to the questions of government, scientific investigation, and life in general. Tarots remained mainly games of the upper classes, like the new princely aristocracy.

Games for the Masses

In the meantime, the inhabitants of the countryside, the peasantry and the sharecroppers, enjoyed different games, although as has been previously noted, until the age of the Renaissance differences between city and country, rich and poor, had not been remarkably striking. A key difference was, of course, in time management. Peasants were first of all concerned with work and had much less spare time. Furthermore, they had less money, and gambling, although practised, was less common.

Among "rural" games, those played with a ball were particularly popular. *Pallamaglio* (Pall Mall), an ancestor of contemporary croquet, has been spreading from southern Italy since the 14th century. *Pallone con bracciale* (a *bracciale* is a rather heavy cylinder worn over the forearm) was regulated for the first time in the 16th century and has since become one of the most popular team games in Italy. Played in *spheristeria*, it rapidly evolved into a fully fledged professional sport that is still popular in some regions, namely Piedmont and Tuscany. Youngsters and older people have carried on playing an amateur version in public squares in small villages. Such a game relied on muscular strength, especially in the forearms, and agility. In general terms, ball games were harsher than their subsequent evolutions. Their Roman origins are evidenced by their diffusion in Latin countries: Basque *Pelota*, Valencian *Pilota* and French *Jeu de Paume* share several characteristics and rules.

Apart from ball games, villages and rural areas welcomed other simple, although often challenging, forms of game and leisure. The range of objects to be thrown varied from tops (*trottole*), to cheeses, to small discs (*ruzzole* or bigger *ruzzoloni*). Such entertainment was mainly popular in the hills of central Italy and, while offering an occasion for recreation, reproduced the ancient bond between man and nature.

Despite her early urbanization, Italy moved rather slowly toward industrial modernity, partly as a result of her late unification (1861) and lack of raw materials and energy sources. The decades following the birth of the national state witnessed a widening economic, social, and cultural gap between an increasingly poor south and some northern regions. Such a gap was partly reflected in the evolution of play.

The Lottery

The large Southern city of Naples became homeland to any kind of lottery. *Lotto* (lottery) had made its appearance in the 17th century in Genoa, where people used to bet on political appointments. In Naples, the largest Italian city in the 19th century, the game found fertile ground, especially in the wake of the economic decline that had followed the unification with northern Italy. Playing *lotto*'s numbers became a widespread activity and a source of social and political concerns.

Matilde Serao (1856–1927), a proudly Neapolitan journalist and novelist, described in her *Paese di Cuccagna* (The Land of Plenty), the weekly dream of a decent life that *lotto* represented among the poor of Naples. She vividly depicted the hopes, the frustrations, and the attachment to a game that she labeled "Naples brandy," or "opium." As has been sometimes colorfully represented in comedies, Neapolitan *lotto* was, and in part still is, enmeshed with magical elements, superstitions, and especially the interpretation of dreams, which are supposed to provide the right numbers to be played when the night is over, and a new difficult day begins. Benedetto Croce (1866–1952) and Antonio Gramsci (1901–37) are probably the most insightful scholars who have attempted to locate the origins and characteristics of *lotto*. Croce, a Neapolitan himself, agreed with Serao and the French writer Honoré de Balzac, who had defined lotteries as the "opium of the poor."

While it is true that lotteries enjoyed popularity among the poor, they have often attracted rich people as well, as the whole history of gambling in Italy shows. Gramsci, a leading Marxist thinker, concentrated on the vicious circles triggered by continuous lottery playing. In his view, exaggerated expectations of "good luck" contributed to the passivity and lack of entrepreneurship of peoples who were already trapped in an oppressive and stagnating society. Furthermore, chance games provided a strong obstacle to the cause of emancipation to which Gramsci himself was committed. One must, however, recognize that lottery games have been widely popular across other Italian and European regions, where they did not prevent subsequent rapid economic development.

Industrialization and globalization have contributed to the reshaping of several popular games, rather than causing them to be swept away. *Lotto* has been modernized and adapted to the needs of the electronic era. Its sole concessionaire, *Lottomatica*, has recently acquired the American group GTECH and is currently one of the largest world lottery operators, with an immense online network across more than 50 countries. The rise of football (American soccer) as the "national Italian sport" has, then, provided ground for new football betting pools. Their main example, the *Schedina*, a weekly list of 13 matches whose outcome has to be predicted by gamblers, was introduced in 1946 and has since become one of the principal pastimes of millions of Italians from all regions and social backgrounds. At the same time, the dark side of modern gambling has made its appearance under the clothes of illegal betting, large-scale smuggling, trafficking, and organized criminality.

Modern Gaming

As regards video games, Italy is currently home to eight million consumers. In the last decades, however, the winds of globalization have been balanced by a gradual rediscovery of the local dimension, with its traditional games and pastimes. Old ball games, medieval representations, and historical board games have made their reappearance, together with a longing for slower community life. At the beginning of the 21st century, Italy's ancient traditions are thus resurfacing in the context of an ever more postmodern society. Maintaining a balance between old and new, "communitarian" and "individualistic" elements, is one of the challenges play is facing in contemporary Italy.

A famous Sicilian writer and Nobel Prize winner, Luigi Pirandello, had ironically depicted the effects of alienation on games and creativity in his 1916 tale "La Carriola" (The Wheelbarrow). In Pirandello's short story, a serious and successful lawyer and professor had finally found his authentic self in playing "the wheelbarrow" every day with his puzzled dog, for just a few seconds. His subtle irony might have something to say to those numbers of Italians who increasingly see games as just a moment of relief and not of creativity, as their rich and varied history would seem to suggest.

See Also: Ancient Rome; Caillois: *Man, Play and Games*; Dice; Gambling; History of Playing Cards.

Bibliography. Lesley Adkins and Roy A. Adkins, *Handbook to Life in Ancient Rome* (Facts on File, 2004); J.P.V.D. Balsdon,

Life and Leisure in Ancient Rome (Phoenix Press, 2002); Jacob Burckhardt, *The Civilization of the Renaissance in Italy* (Echo Library, 2006, first pub. 1868 as *Die Kultur der Renaissance in Italien)*; Roger Caillois, *Man, Play and Games* (University of Illinois Press, 2001); David Stone Potter and D. Mattingly, eds., *Life, Death, and Entertainment in the Roman Empire* (University of Michigan Press, 1999); Paola De Sanctis Ricciardone, *Il Tipografo Celeste: Il Gioco del Lotto tra Letteratura e Demologia nell'Italia dell'Ottocento e Oltre* [The Heavenly Printer: *Lotto* in Italian Literature and Demology From the 19th Century on] (Dedalo, 1986).

Ernesto Gallo
University of Turin/University of Birmingham

J

Jacks

Jacks (or Knucklebones) is one of the oldest games in the world. Bones, thought to be playthings, have been found in prehistoric sites in Kiev, Ukraine, and in ancient Greece and Rome, depictions of gods and mortals playing the game were placed on vases and coins, sculptures and paintings.

Under the guise of different names, the game is found in almost every country. The playing pieces are simple and easily found, so the game readily adapts to a diverse range of locations. It can be played alone or with others, and the way it is played depends on the materials used, which reflect the culture and environment of the players.

Nobody knows how the game was played in prehistoric times, but in classical times, *Pentalitha* (Fivestones), as it was known, was played with five pebbles or knucklebones. They were thrown into the air and caught on the back of the hand, a movement familiar to anyone who has played the game. While there is no record of all the variations in play, it is highly probable that the game was played in much the same way as children play today.

Later, a small pottery ball was added, which made the game a little easier to play, as the bounce of the ball allowed more time to snatch the pieces up from the floor. The use of a ball or marble was recorded as early as the mid-16th century. In 1560, Netherlands artist Pieter Breughel completed his painting titled *Children's Games,* a lively visual catalogue of more than 80 games played by children at that time, including two girls playing Knucklebones.

From earliest times, sheep's knucklebones have been replicated in a wide range of materials, including precious stones and metals, ivory, wood, and plastic. Before colored plastic pieces were readily available, children in Australia colored sheep's knucklebones by painting them, soaking them in ink, or boiling them on the stove in a tin filled with water and flower petals.

The knucklebones were precious, saved carefully and patiently from the traditional Sunday roast dinner until there was a set of five. Sometimes, if having patience was too difficult, they were gathered from the carcasses of sheep that had died in the paddocks. They were boiled and scraped clean, or, if there was no hurry, left outside under a weighted, upturned tin for the ants to clean. When the knucklebones were ready, a game could begin.

Jacks, as the game is commonly known in English-speaking countries, is one of the most accommodating of games—almost anything can be used as a playing-piece, provided it is small enough, has enough weight, and does not roll away. Pick up a few stones from the

All jacks games share the same strategy: toss an object in the air and scoop up pieces before the object bounces.

ground and you can start playing immediately. The materials used are often those most readily available.

Throughout the world, the game is played with bones, stones, ceramic cubes, spiked metal jacks, and little hand-sewn bags filled with beans, rice, or sand. One very skilful version, played in Asian countries, uses chopsticks or lengths of bamboo as playing pieces, and a lime or lemon in place of a ball.

The steps in the game are based on the traditional work of women in the home and include "grinding the rice," "sweeping the floor," "carrying water," and "weaving." The game may have as many names and versions as there are countries. Knucklebones, Fivestones, Jacks, Dibs, Snobs, Bestas, Diketo, Terrespil, Pacheta, La Payanita, O-Tedama—the list is endless, and so are the opportunities for play.

See Also: Ancient Greece; Ancient Rome; Australia; Boys' Play; Girls' Play.

Bibliography. Arnold Arnold, *World Book of Children's Games* (Fawcett, 1973); Joan Baxter, *The Archeology of Childhood: Children, Gender and Material Culture* (AltaMira Press, 2005); Joe Frost, Sue Wortham, and Stuart Reifel, *Play and Child Development* (Merrill-Prentice Hall, 2006); Glenn Kirchner, *Children's Games Around the World* (Benjamin Cummings, 2000); Nina Millen, *Children's Games from Many Lands* (Friendship Press, 1943); Iona Opie and Peter Opie, *Children's Games with Things* (Oxford University Press, London, 1997).

Judy McKinty
Independent Scholar

JAKKS Pacific Toys

Founded in 1995, the toy company JAKKS Pacific has acquired some of the best-known toy licenses in the United States, including Cabbage Patch Kids, Neopets, and the Care Bears.

JAKKS was the third toy company started by Queens native Jack Friedman, who had gotten his start in sales 30 years earlier at the Norman J. Lewis Associates toy company (NJL). In 1970, he left NJL to form his own company, reversing the initials of his former employer to LJN. The new company capitalized on the increasing commercialism of television and movies by acquiring the toy licenses for various media, from Magnum P.I. and the Thundercats to E.T. and Gremlins. As the company became more successful, it attracted the attention of Universal and was acquired in 1986. Though Friedman was given a new contract, he was unhappy running LJN from its new California offices and struck out on his own again, starting THQ Inc. as a video game company that specialized in licensing games based on the movies produced in nearby Hollywood studios. THQ flourished for the first few years until the video game industry grew more sophisticated, to the point that its emphasis on cutting-edge technology and graphics exceeded Friedman's grasp of the market; as a man from the toy industry, not the computer industry, he was by his own admission operating in a frame of reference that the industry outgrew.

JAKKS Pacific was his next venture, cofounded with friend Stephen Berman, who had headed a fitness products company before joining THQ. Perhaps learning from LJN's acquisition, Friedman founded JAKKS with the express goal of acquiring other toy companies. The field, especially outside of the game industry, was led by the Big Two of Hasbro and Mattel, and outside of those two the remaining pie was divided into many tiny slices that Friedman felt could and should be consolidated. Funds for such consolidation were first generated by a 10-year deal with Titan Sports, the parent company of the World Wrestling Federation (now the WWE), for a line of action figures based on wrestling personalities.

The wrestling toys were meant to be for the 1990s and 2000s what the smaller, cartoon- and comic-book-driven G.I. Joe toys had been for the 1980s. In 1997, two years after the company's founding, JAKKS acquired two manufacturers of die-cast cars: Remco and Road Champs (acquired in emulation of Mattel, owner of the Hot Wheels brand). The toddler toy line Child Guidance was soon acquired as well, to compete with Mattel's Fisher-Price toys and Hasbro's Playskool.

JAKKS operated with a small corporate staff and only a dozen American warehouse personnel, conducting its manufacturing and most of its warehouse activities in labor-cheap Asia. The WWF action figures rose in popularity, and by the end of the decade the company had acquired Berk, an educational toy company with licenses from Disney, Nickelodeon, and Sesame Street. More licensed products followed, with the acquisition of Flying Colors, maker of Looney Toons lunchboxes and Harry Potter art supplies. *Fortune* magazine named JAKKS one of the 100 fastest-growing companies in its 1999 overview.

In the 21st century, JAKKS has continued to expand, acquiring various licenses and smaller companies and reorganizing them in line with Friedman and Berman's goals of competing on the Mattel/Hasbro level.

See Also: Hasbro; LJN; Parker Brothers; TSR.

Bibliography. Deborah Jaffe, *The History of Toys* (The History Press, 2006); Don Wuffson, *Toys* (Henry Holt, 2000).

Bill Kte'pi
Independent Scholar

Japan

Despite Japan's leading role in computer-based play over the last two decades, as signaled by the arrival of Nintendo's "Family Computer," play has traditionally had a significant role in Japanese history by establishing and reinforcing strict social norms, especially in terms of family values and gender roles. Despite the stereotypical image of the Japanese as workaholics, which was popularized during the 1980s when the nation's economy was booming, play in Japan is not only for children. Both adults and children are often engaged in different types of play. Play for children, particularly in a traditional cultural context, was a means through which they learned social values from their elders. Respecting elders, acquiring social skills, learning manners, and other pragmatic objectives have been major purposes of play, in addition to simply having a good time. Analyzing how children play therefore reveals many of the fundamental values that have characterized Japanese society.

Play for adults also reflects Japan's emphasis on work-related human relationships, even on weekends and vacations. Bars, golf courses, and other locations where adults play are also places where business relationships are established and strengthened. The separation between work and play therefore is not as clear as in many Western societies. The modernization of play, particularly the arrival of Nintendo Wii, however, initiated a shift in the way in which the Japanese consider play.

While computer games individualized the style of play, Nintendo's new console successfully reversed the trend by creating a public space in a house around which family members gathered to play together. Classic literature reflects the significant role that play has played in Japanese history.

In *Ryojinhishou*, a compilation of *tanka* verses from the Heian Period (794–1185), one of the verses reads, "Was I born to play? When I hear small children play, I get excited although I am no longer a child." Play in Japan has been not simply entertainment, but also opportunities for education and self-reflection.

Cross-Generational Play

When children and adults play together or make handmade toys together, play becomes a means of passing down knowledge and wisdom. Cat's cradle (*Ayatori*), and Marbles (*Ohajiki*), for example, are kinds of play that many small girls engage in together, as well as with their mothers, and frequently with their grandmothers. Similarly, flying kites requires boys to work with their father or grandfather to learn how to make a good kite.

Through play, children and adults have a chance to discuss not only play or toys, but also school, friends, and life. While grandmothers and mothers would know tricks that small girls had not learned yet, and grandfathers and fathers would be able to fly a kite higher and longer because of their knowledge of how to balance the weight, they also provided their children and grandchildren with advice for their future. In this process of cross-generational interactions, it was not only practical knowledge about the play or the toy that was passed down to a younger generation, but also knowledge of life and values. Play is an occasion for personal growth for many children.

Cross-generational interaction through play is particularly important and meaningful in Japan, where the teaching of Confucianism is strong. One of the most fundamental Confucianist messages for its students is to respect their elders. When adults show how to make a toy or how to make a kite fly higher, children are exposed to the depth of knowledge that the adult possesses. Through this experience, they learn to be humble in front of their elders and those with more experience. Additionally, they learn the importance of learning through imitation. Instead of being given a lecture, they observe what adults do and emulate their behavior. Doing so while making a toy naturally encourages children to emulate adults, even when they are not involved in play. Through this interaction they learn what to do and what not to do in their daily lives through imitation. This craftsman-like style of interaction has been a key component of the Japanese style of cross-generational play.

When children played with friends of the same age group, they would alter toys that they had made with their parents or adjust the way of playing that they had learned from their elders. While play on the one hand established a cross-generational tie and a Confuciunist path of passing down knowledge and values, on the other hand it offered children a locus where they could apply their lessons to form their own style of play, and eventually their own perspective on life.

Japanese Traditional Play

In some cross-generational play, such as with beanbags, known as *otedama*, girls would play primarily with their grandmothers rather than with their mother. In this act of play, children learned fundamental and traditional values in Japanese society. For example, through *otedama*, girls learn to sew, a basic skill for females in a traditional Japanese society; how to sit on their knees, an appropriate way of sitting for females; and other social norms and manners. With its roots in the Heian Period, *otedama* is a way to pass down traditions from generation to generation. Many forms of play have contributed to the survival of traditional lifestyles and values against the wave of modernization.

As *otedama* taught small girls how to sew or to sit on their knees, many games reflected and reinforced gender roles. Playing house, or *mamagoto*, which became popular in the Edo Period (1603–1867), for example, was developed as play, reflecting the historical fact that small girls often served as cooks for various communal events such as festivals. Children learn not only appropriate manners at the table, but also how fathers, mothers, sons, and daughters should act in various family occasions such as inviting guests, visiting acquaintances, sending and receiving gifts, et cetera. *Origami*, or the art of folding paper into figures, is a prototypical example of a game being training for acquiring manners. In Japan, when one offers a gift, it is always expected to be wrapped with a cloth or paper. Depending on the shape of the object, wrapping can be cumbersome. Learning how to make figures, therefore, is a playful way to learn how to fold paper neatly for good presentation.

Now that modern forms of play have become more popular than traditional games among children, games such as *otedama* or *Ayatori* have become seasonal. Children rarely play these games except during New Year's vacation in early January and summer vacation in August. Since these cross-generational games have survived in modern Japanese society and elders are able to play with their grandchildren without learning modern games, such as computer games or playing with trading cards, traditional play is shared by children and their grandparents. As a result, playing traditional games is one of the major events of vacations for many children. An increasing number of nuclear and younger families moving to urban areas help these traditional plays to become seasonal, since many children only have a chance to see their grandparents a few times a year, during summer and New Year's vacations. Only in early January do Japanese children fly kites, for example. When asked what they are most looking forward to about their vacation, many children respond by saying they most look forward to playing board games or another type of traditional games with their grandparents.

Adult Play

As the Chinese character for play used in the modern Japanese language suggests, the idea of play is strongly associated with children. The character is an ideograph,

The original Pachinko *machines were built as toys for children and had simple mechanisms; however, today's machines, such as in this Tokyo* Pachinko *parlor, are a cross between pinball machines and video slot machines.*

which represents a child floating on water and another wandering around. Play, however, has also been important for adults in Japanese society. In the past, play has been connected to religious events. Play referred to dances and songs during religious ceremonies. *Kemari*, a game that is over 1,400 years old, is often considered one of the earliest forms of soccer and was a part of prayer for world peace, fertility, good health, and family happiness. The yard in which people played *kemari* was considered sacred and was surrounded by a special set of trees: a willow, a cherry, a pine, and a maple, one each on all four corners.

Some of the games popular among children nowadays used to be for adult gambling. *Sugoroku*, or a Japanese variety of Parchisi, for example, had been repeatedly banned by the government after it was first banned in 689 C.E. Emperor Shirakawa from the 11th century named the game of *Sugoroku* as one of the three vexations that troubled his nation. In many period adventure dramas on television today portraying the Edo Period, a *Sugoroku* playhouse is shown as a place where lower-class citizens gather to indulge themselves with gambling while many crimes and briberies among higher-ranking officials also take place. Even in a contemporary context, the word "play" sometimes carries negative connotations when associated with adults. The word is often a euphemism for gambling on such sports as horseracing, bicycle racing, and speedboat racing, as well as referring to various sex-related businesses, from the consumption of pornography to visiting a red-light district. In a more contemporary context, many adults frequent *Pachinko* parlors. From comic books to soap operas, images of a father spending his time and money on *Pachinko* often symbolize a father who cares little about his family.

Work and Play

Regardless of the type of play, Japanese adults tend to play with their coworkers, even for business reasons. In this respect, the separation between work and play is not very distinct. Going to a bar after work for drinks with coworkers is a typical way of spending weekday nights for many business people. While their conversation topics are not limited to work, the hierarchy from the office often remains during after-work playtime. Superiors at work tend to dominate the conversation, have more say regarding which food to order, and determine when to leave. Similarly, on weekends, many go to play golf with their coworkers or bosses. In some cases, weekend golfing is where business deals are made. In this respect, play is used as a means to successful business.

Younger generations, however, do not always agree with such a bridge between work and play. Many no longer go for drinks with their bosses or coworkers on weekdays and for excursions on weekends. In the past, many corporations organized sectional or departmental trips for its employees. The number of such trips has decreased because of a lack of interest among the younger employees in spending vacation time with those from work and in following the hierarchical relationship at the office. Their clear separation between work and play frequently concerns middle managers, for whom after-work play with their subordinates has been the norm. The idea of play as a means for learning and teaching as manifested in many of the traditional plays fails to attract much support in a modern context. The clear separation between work and play that younger generations make excludes coworkers from their private time.

Despite the separation between work and play, family has had little to do with adult play in Japan. Instead of going home directly from work and going out with the family or spending time with the family on weekends, play frequently involves personal friends and acquaintances rather than family members. Family plans may even be compromised for the sake of friendship. It is therefore very common to see family members having different plans on almost every weekend, a father with his coworkers, a mother with her coworkers or local community friends, and children with their friends.

Computer Games

In addition to an increase in the number of nuclear families, the arrival of computer games also strengthened the trend toward individualization and the fragmentation of the family during play. Since the early 1980s, many Japanese people, regardless of their age, have avidly played computer games at home. Most consoles and computers existed in a private area in a house, particularly in bedrooms. Children, for example, invited their friends home to play games in their bedroom. Similarly, adults stayed in their bedroom or study to play a game on a computer. The handheld computer game device, such as the Game Boy, further individualized contemporary play in Japan.

The trend was reversed, however, by the arrival of the Nintendo Wii in late 2006. Unlike previous models of computer game consoles, Nintendo envisioned that its customers would use Wii as a means of interactions among family members. Not only does a Wii allow family members to play together, but the console can serve as a bulletin board for the family. With a Wii console, a child playing a game can send a message to his or her parent at the office. As a result, Wii became a console that shifted play to a means of cross-generational family interactions rather than a more individualized environment. This is the reason why one of the developers of Wii called the console "a public space in the house." To attest to this change, many of the consoles are in living rooms rather than in bedrooms.

The idea of play in Japan has had four fundamental bases. The first two deal with the demography. The example of a classical Japanese verse shows that play has been an important concept to help one understand the Japanese adult lifestyle as well as that of youths. The latter two deal with participation: individual and collective. The rapid move from collective playing to individual playing characterized the recent trend of play in Japan. Nintendo's Wii is at the forefront in striving to reverse this shift. Although the Japanese emphasis on friends and coworkers as partners for play remains strong, the new game console also allowed play to be found in a family environment.

See Also: Boys' Play; Girls' Play; Marbles; Play as Learning, Anthropology of; Play as Learning, Sociology of.

Bibliography. Charles J. Dunn and Laurence Broderick, *Everyday Life in Traditional Japan* (Tuttle Publishing, 2005); Patricia Evans, *Rimbles: A Book of Children's Classic Games, Rhymes, Songs, and Sayings* (Doubleday, 1961); Glenn Kirchner, *Children's Games Around the World* (Benjamin Cummings, 2000); R.H.P. Mason and J.G. Caiger, *A History of Japan: Revised Edition* (Tuttle Publishing, 1997); Nina Millen, *Children's Games from Many Lands* (Friendship Press, 1943); Hazel Richardson, *Life In Ancient Japan (Peoples of the Ancient World)* (Crabtree Publishing Company, 2005).

Yuya Kiuchi
Michigan State University

Jigsaws

To create a jigsaw puzzle, a picture is attached to a wood or cardboard backing and is then cut into smaller pieces. When the puzzle reaches the consumer, he or she pieces it together again so that the original picture is visible. Originally educational in purpose, the jigsaw has been used to entertain and advertise since the 1800s. Besides teaching, the jigsaw puzzle allows its assembler to improve and demonstrate memory, concentration, and peripheral vision. These skills have been tested since 1760, with a variety of changes offering ever-greater challenges.

The Advent and Growth of Puzzles

The exact origins of jigsaw puzzles remain unknown, although the British mapmaker John Spilsbury began producing puzzles in 1760. His "dissected maps," intended to instruct schoolchildren in geography, are widely believed to be among the first jigsaws. To produce them, Spilsbury mounted maps on hardwood and cut around the countries' borders with a marquetry saw.

Later versions of puzzles continued to be educational. Publishers of children's books created jigsaws to teach the alphabet, arithmetic, government, natural history, science, and religion. Puzzles for amusement soon followed. After 1800, nursery rhymes, fairy tales, books, and memorable events found their way to jigsaws, which became a means of family entertainment. Eventually, puzzles became a promotional strategy, with retail stores offering puzzles with certain purchases and companies printing advertisements on jigsaws.

By the dawn of the 20th century, jigsaws were a booming business, with sales and rentals available through circulating libraries and drugstores. The craze for jigsaws grew even stronger during the Great Depression, when puzzles seemed to lift the spirits of Americans by offering a relatively inexpensive means of escaping reality. Ten million jigsaws a week were sold at the height of the puzzle's popularity in 1933. Those numbers would decline after World War II, though jigsaws continue to be popular educational tools, entertaining games, and promotional offerings.

Modern Transformations

Puzzles themselves have undergone a major transformation. When jigsaws first appeared, they featured engraved and printed maps, carefully tinted with watercolors, pasted on thin mahogany boards; these were then cut with a handheld fretsaw and packaged in wooden boxes with plain printed labels, which included an uncolored guide map to assist children. Even the cheapest versions of these earliest puzzles were too expensive for most working families: prices ranged from seven shillings and sixpence to 21 shillings at a time when the average worker earned only one or two shillings a day.

By the mid-19th century, the manufacturers of jigsaws moved to more attractive packaging, generally with guide pictures pasted on the lid. These changes came at a time when the cost of making the puzzles decreased because less-costly lithographs, cheaper softwoods, and power scroll saws replaced earlier materials and methods. Further changes in materials occurred throughout the 1800s, with the invention of the jigsaw (1880) and the use of plywood backings. Jigsaws continued to be too expensive for the majority of families: a 500-piece jigsaw puzzle cost about $5 at a time when the average monthly salary was $50.

Cardboard, first used for children's puzzles, was introduced as the standard backing material for jigsaws late in the 19th century. These more affordable cardboard puzzles could be produced through a die-cutting process, which used thin strips of metal with sharpened edges attached to a plate to form a die that could then be placed in a press that would cut the cardboard into

A globe puzzle is often made of cardboard or styrofoam, and the curved pieces fit together to form a globe.

shapes. Used as early as 1890 for simple puzzles, die cutting technology advanced to allow increasingly difficult lightweight cardboard puzzles with interlocking and figure pieces. Now a 300-piece cardboard puzzle could be purchased for 25 cents or less, and advertisers could afford to give jigsaws away in promotional campaigns.

New types of puzzles followed this wave of popularity. During the Great Depression, this included weekly puzzles sold by more than 200 manufacturers. Patriotic puzzles emerged during World War II, some of them even using war-related shapes. The 1950s produced jigsaws showcasing the general contentment of Americans, while the 1960s introduced a rapidly changing life by highlighting social issues and introducing circular jigsaws and works of art commissioned for use in puzzles. By the 1970s, licensed characters and merchandise became a mainstay of jigsaws, which eventually included mystery puzzles, three-dimensional puzzles, and specialty puzzles in the 1980s and 1990s.

See Also: Academic Learning and Play; Crosswords; Play as Catharsis; United States, 1900 to 1930; United States, 1930 to 1960.

Bibliography. Elliott Avedon, *The Study of Games* (Krieger Pub., 1979); Marcel Daresi, *Puzzle Instinct: The Meaning of Puzzles in Human Life* (Indiana University Press, 2002); Anne D. Williams, *The Jigsaw Puzzle: Piecing Together a History* (Berkley Books, 2004).

Anastasia L. Pratt
State University of New York

Jordan

The Hashemite Kingdom of Jordan was created after World War I but has a history going back to ancient times, with modern-day Jordan occupying the land on the east bank of the River Jordan. A part of the Seleucid Empire, it was controlled by the Romans and was later a part of the Byzantine Empire, having been taken over by the Arabs, the Seljuk Turks, the Crusaders, the Seljuk Turks again, and the Ottoman Turks.

Historically, many of Jordan's games have involved shows or ability, prowess, strength, or guile, such as horseriding and racing, camel riding, archery, wrestling, and the like. The making of saddles, bridlewear and brightly colored horse blankets has been important. There is also a history of rug weaving. Under the long period of Turkish rule, many of the traditional pursuits of the Turks were followed by the locals, with Backgammon and playing cards being common with many men. As Jordan has a very high rate of literacy, reading has also been popular.

There are a number of musical instruments specific to Jordan, such as the *gasabah*, a type of recorder; a *ganum*, similar to a harp; the *durbakkah*, an earthenware drum; the *duff*, similar to a tambourine; and the *ud*, a stringed instrument. Often when Arab music is played in public, it is accompanied by people pounding their feet, clapping hands, or forming a chorus using small drums, as well as dancing. The most famous local dance, the *debkah*, is the origin of the Spanish flamenco, which people from the Jordan area took with them to Spain in the 9th century. There is also the *sahjeh* dance, which is popular with the Bedouin, which tells of heroic actions in history. This usually involved a sword dance. Music now also plays an important part of life at home, with recorded music or music heard on a transistor radio becoming common from the 1960s. There are also many bands, the most famous being the Royal Jordanian Armed Forces, which plays European military instruments, especially drums, and also bagpipes. Some of the most attended concerts are those held in the Roman theater in Amman.

Much of the celebrations that form a regular part of Jordanian life are connected with Muslim or Christian festivals. In August, the Jerash Festival for Culture and Arts brings together many craftsmen and others who take part in performances or show their work. The Jordanian National Handicraft Project has also done much to preserve many aspects of Jordanian culture. In mid-November, the Aquaba Sports Festival involves aquatic sports including waterskiing. Hot air ballooning at Wadi Run has also attracted many people. The increase in education from the second half of the 20th century led to many sports being introduced as recreational activities, with soccer rapidly attracting a large following. Mention should also be made of the Scout and Girl Guide movements, established respectively in 1954 and 1938, and now merged to form the Jordanian Association for Boy Scouts and Girl Guides. It has promoted hiking, camping, and activities that have helped many underprivileged people in the country.

See Also: Backgammon; Boys' Play; Spain; Syria; Turkey; Water Play.

Bibliography. Ann Dearden, *Jordan* (Robert Hale, 1958); Leila Merrell Foster, *Jordan* (Childrens Press, 1991); Sarah Ethridge Hunt, *Games and Sports the World Around* (Ronald Press Company, 1964); Glenn Kirchner, *Children's Games Around the World* (Benjamin Cummings, 2000); Ministry of Information of the Hashemite Kingdom of The Jordan, *Jordan* (Hutchinson Benham, 1978); Coleman South, *Jordan* (Marshall Cavendish, 1997).

Justin Corfield
Geelong Grammar School

Jump Rope

Jump Rope, also known as Skipping Rope, is an ancient game that has been enjoyed by children for thousands of years. At various points in its history, it has been considered a suitable game only for boys or for girls, but in the last 50 years it has become a socially acceptable pastime for children of both sexes.

Jump Rope's longevity as a game can be attributed to its minimal equipment needs and to the many ways in which the game can be played, both individually and in groups, as well as to its entertainment value. Jump Rope is also credited with providing physical, social, and psychological outlets for children because not only does the game engage them in exercise, it also frequently involves them in group play and in the sharing of jump rope rhymes, which are often antiauthoritarian and antiadult.

Scholars speculate that cave dwellers jumped rope, and preserved records and images show that jumping rope was an important activity for ancient Egyptians, Greeks, Romans, and Chinese. In these civilizations, boys learned to jump rope in order to gain strength and agility that they could use in athletic competitions, in hunting, and in battle.

In the early 1940s, many children used jumping rope as a form of play. It only required a rope, and anyone could play.

Jumping Rope and Gender

Boys' participation in Jump Rope never died out in the following centuries, but in Victorian England and America, Jump Rope experienced a resurgence in popularity as industrialization relocated more children to the crowded cities where play spaces were small and few. Even then, Jump Rope was still generally considered to be a boys' game that stressed athletic ability and individual competition, and which was far too strenuous for girls.

Yet by the end of the 1800s, girls too began to Jump Rope, particularly in urban areas, as the changing cultural mores permitted them to take part in more physical activities, and their clothing styles were altered to make allowances for their new, more active, lifestyles. As girls took to the city streets with their ropes, however, they changed the rules of the game, making Jump Rope into a more collaborative and social practice. Girls often jumped rope in groups with two girls (called enders) turning the rope for the others, and they started to recite chants and rhymes to help them keep in step with the rhythm of the rope and to alternate jumpers and enders. Jump Rope quickly became the domain of girls, and most boys soon turned to more outwardly competitive pursuits.

As boys abandoned jump roping, psychologists and folklorists became interested in the Jump Rope rhymes that the girls were using. The earliest of the girls' chants were written down in the 1880s, and many Jump Rope rhymes were studied and recorded throughout the first half of the 20th century as important works of folk literature. The Jump Rope rhymes have their roots in singing games, counting-out rhymes, and nursery rhymes, and they vary regionally and generationally, as works of folklore often do. Their obvious function is to help the jumpers maintain a sense of rhythm and improve their Jump Rope skills, but the rhymes, with their nonsense, humor, and observations about school, families, and common problems, also help children, historically girls, to negotiate the world around them.

Modern Rope Jumping

Since the 1960s and 1970s, however, Jump Rope has become a more gender-neutral game in which both boys and girls can freely participate. It has retained its competitive heritage through the many Jump Rope competitions that are held each year all over the world, and its collaborative side can also be seen on many playgrounds and sidewalks, as well as in team competitions. Additionally, Jump Rope has emerged as an important exercise for cardiovascular health, prompting many adults, as well as children and teenagers, to jump rope on a regular basis. Jump Rope For Heart, a physical fitness program started in 1978, has helped to increase Jump Rope's popularity and visibility, and with the health benefits, pleasure, and participation options that it offers, Jump Rope is likely to have a future that is as long as its past.

See Also: Boys' Play; Girls' Play; Play and Sports Education; Spontaneous Group Play.

Bibliography. Roger D. Abrahams, ed., *Jump Rope Rhymes: A Dictionary* (University of Texas Press, 1969); Jump Rope For Heart and Hoops For Heart, "Jump Into the Fun!," www.aahperd.org/jump (cited July 2008); Elizabeth Loredo, *The Jump Rope Book* (Workman Publishing Company, 1996); Peter Skolnik, *Jump Rope!* (Workman Publishing Company, 1974).

Ramona Anne Caponegro
University of Florida

K

Kayaking and Canoeing

Both canoes and kayaks have long histories as modes of transportation, but also as pleasure and sport craft. The canoe, a simple, open, keelless boat able to accommodate one or more people and propelled by a single-blade paddle, is a design of the indigenous cultures of the Americas. The kayak, on the other hand, is an innovation of circumpolar indigenous groups, such as the Inuit, and has a covered deck and generally one or two "cockpits" for paddlers who employ a double-bladed paddle to propel their craft.

Primarily used by Aboriginal people for trade, subsistence, and travel, canoes and kayaks also served recreational purposes in indigenous cultures. British author Anna Jameson, for example, described an 1837 race involving 30 canoes of Aboriginal women. While the canoe as a working vessel is credited with opening up the interior of Canada to Europeans during the era of the fur trade, it also played an important role as a recreational vessel for the French and Métis men who worked the trade. In the midst of the hardships and danger that characterized their lives, the Voyageurs also used their crafts for racing and testing their skills.

Widespread recreational use of canoes and kayaks, however, did not occur until the late 19th century. Scot John MacGregor is commonly credited with popularizing canoeing in the English-speaking world, as he was responsible for the creation of the first canoe club, in Richmond, England, in 1866. The club hosted the first canoeing regatta, a social event centered on boat races. Most scholars would argue, however, that despite MacGregor's influence, the popularity of canoeing in Europe never rivaled that in the North America continent. In Canada, in particular, the canoe has been seen as an important symbol of both national heritage and culture.

Canoe and kayak clubs, in the tradition of MacGregor's 1866 experiment, have enabled both crafts to have relevance in historical and contemporary urban environments. The infrastructure that developed from such clubs resulted in the creation of an international paddling body, the Internationalen Representation for Kanusport (IRK), in 1924, as well as the establishment of canoeing and kayaking as demonstration sports at the Paris Olympics in the same year. They became official Olympic sports in 1936 and 1948, respectively. These developments, in turn, have created a system for recreational training and competitive development for urban youth.

Most people's experiences with canoeing and kayaking in North America, however, are associated with wilderness travel. Through the camping system, children have been exposed to paddling in instructional settings, as well as on canoe trips. Wilderness travel outside of the sphere of camping has made use of the canoe in the con-

Kayaks, with their covered decks, have roots in the indigenous cultures of Arctic regions.

tinental interior, and the kayak moreso in coastal areas. Both boat types are also used by whitewater enthusiasts, recreationally and competitively. The reasons for embarking in either craft are as diverse as the uses of the boats themselves. For some, the desire to paddle can be explained by a love of the landscape and nature and a need to "get away from it all." For others, it is about reliving a heritage, refining skills, or tasting adventure. Whatever the appeal, paddling remains an important recreational pursuit in a number of geographical contexts for people of all ages.

See Also: Canada; Europe, 1800 to 1900; Play as Mastery of Nature; Sailing.

Bibliography. Roger Caillois, *Man, Play and Games* (University of Illinois Press, 2001); Jamie Benidickson, *Idleness, Water, and a Canoe: Reflections on Paddling for Pleasure* (University of Toronto Press, 1997); John Jennings, Bruce W. Hodgins, and Doreen Small, *The Canoe in Canadian Cultures* (Natural Heritage Books, 1999).

Jessica Dunkin
Carleton University

Kazakhstan

Kazakhstan is the largest of the Central Asian Republics, and the wealthiest of the five that were part of the Russian Empire and then the Soviet Union, until its independence in 1991. It shares borders with the Russian Federation, China, Kyrgyzstan, and Uzbekistan. The country is wealthy, with extensive oil holdings, but little of this wealth has reached people in the countryside.

Many cultural pursuits in Kazakhstan came from its geographical position on the Silk Road, introducing Turkish games such as Backgammon, Dominoes, and cards, and Chinese games such as Chinese Chess and Mahjong. Horseriding skills and wrestling tested many adolescents and young men.

While Kazakhstan was part of Russia, education became compulsory for all children, and as a result, many took up European sports such as soccer and volleyball, as well as swimming. The Arasan Baths in Almaty, the capital of Kazakhstan, provided steam baths, which have been a form of relaxation for many people. Although Chess has been played by Kazakhs since at least the late Middle Ages—two carvings believed to be Chess pieces were found in neighboring Uzbekistan in 1972 and dated from about 200 C.E.—it was during the Russian period that Chess was taught in many schools in the country and became popular. Important Kazakh Chess players such as Boris Ayrukh, Darmen Sadvakasov, Vladislav Tkachiev, Anatoly Vaisser, and Evgeny Vladmiro, have done much to encourage playing among the young. The Young Pioneer Movement was heavily promoted in Russia, and it led to many children becoming involved in hiking, camping, and participating in many group activities including model-making and designing mechanical toys.

Ice skating became popular during the Communist period, spurred on by success in Olympic sporting events by Russian athletes. The biggest skating rink in the whole of Central Asia is located at Medeu, on the outskirts of Almaty, and smaller ones, the Olympic Skating Rink and the Dinamo Stadium, in the capital. There is a cable car in Almaty that takes people from near the Palace of the Republic to the foothills of Zailiysky, Alatau, where the television transmitter center is located. Since the dissolution of the Soviet Union, independence has led to increased foreign investment. There is an Aqua Park in Almaty that is enclosed so that it can be used over the long winters, and a Fantasy Land Amusement Park. There is also a large bowling alley in central Almaty and smaller ones in the suburbs and other towns.

See Also: Amusement Parks; Chess and Variations of; Mahjong; Russia; Uzbekistan.

Bibliography. Bradley Mayhew, Paul Clammer, and Michael Kohn, *Central Asia* (Lonely Planet, 2004); Martha Brill Olcott, *Kazakhstan: Unfulfilled Promise* (Carnegie Endowment for International Peace, 2002); Giles Whittell, *Central Asia* (Cadogan Guides, 1996).

Justin Corfield
Geelong Grammar School

Kenner

Kenner was a U.S. toy company from the 1940s into the 1990s. Major products include Play-Doh, the Easy-Bake Oven, Nerf, and G.I. Joe. Hasbro absorbed Kenner in 2000. In 1947 Albert, Phillip, and Joseph L. Steiner of Cincinnati, Ohio, established Kenner Products, a toy company, named after Kenner Street, where their offices were located. Kenner was a pioneer in national television advertising, beginning in 1958 with the sponsorship of the popular children's show *Captain Kangaroo.* Kenner introduced the Kenner Gooney Bird as a corporate mascot in the early 1960s.

The bird was integrated into the company logo "It's Kenner! It's fun!" and in puppet and animated television advertisements, including one commercial produced by Jim Henson, better known as the creator of the Muppets. Kenner phased out the bird by 1974. Kenner opened a year-round New York showroom in 1963. In 1967 the brothers sold to General Mills.

Kenner's first product was the Bubble-matic gun of 1947, and its Bubble-rocket of 1949 sold a million units. Its major success was the Girder and Panel construction sets introduced in 1957. They followed with the Give-a-Show projector in 1959, the Easy-Bake Oven in 1963, the "gun that shoots around the corner" in 1964, and the Spirograph in 1966. Give-a-Show was a good seller for over 20 years.

Kenner also produced a phonograph for toddlers and a "jukebox" with songs recorded by employees. Baby Alive was the top-selling doll in 1973, before being discontinued for a time and then reappearing in the 1990s. Over nine million dolls were sold by 2008.

General Mills merged Rainbow Crafts, which it acquired in 1965, and four-color Play-Doh into Kenner in 1970. Play-Doh dates from 1954, when the original toy, produced only in the color white, hit the market. Kenner produced action figures and playsets for Star Wars between 1977 and 1985, the Six Million Dollar Man action figures in the 1970s, and the Starting Lineup sports action figures beginning in 1988. Kenner obtained the Star Wars contract after Mego Corporation refused it in 1976, and the Kenner 3.75-inch action figure became the industry standard, persisting to this date. The SuperPowers collection of DC Comics superheroes of 1984–86 and M.A.S.K. and Ghostbusters figures in 1985 and 1986 gave way in 1990 to the Dark Knight and subsequent Batman characters. The 1970s Stretch Armstrong was 13 inches tall and could stretch to four feet.

In 1981 Kenner ventured into die cast toy cars with its Fast 111s, but backed out after a short time. Other 1980s products were Strawberry Shortcake mini dolls, and Care Bears plush toys. That decade saw Play-Doh expand to eight colors. In the 1990s Kenner revitalized Batman, had a smash with Jurassic Park toys and introduced the wildly successful Littlest Petshop toys for girls. Nerf toy choices expanded as well, and Kenner introduced radio-controlled toys. G.I. Joe, the 1960s hit, reemerged with much greater articulation in his body and authentic uniforms and gear from Australian, British, and American forces. G.I. Jane dates from 1997.

In 1975 Kenner topped $100 million in sales. In 1978 it topped $200 million, primarily because of the success of *Star Wars.* In 1983 Kenner opened a plant in Tijuana, Mexico. In 1996 it launched its first Web site.

General Mills spun off Kenner and Parker toys to form Kenner Parker Toys in 1985 (the fourth largest toy business in the United States) and sold the company to

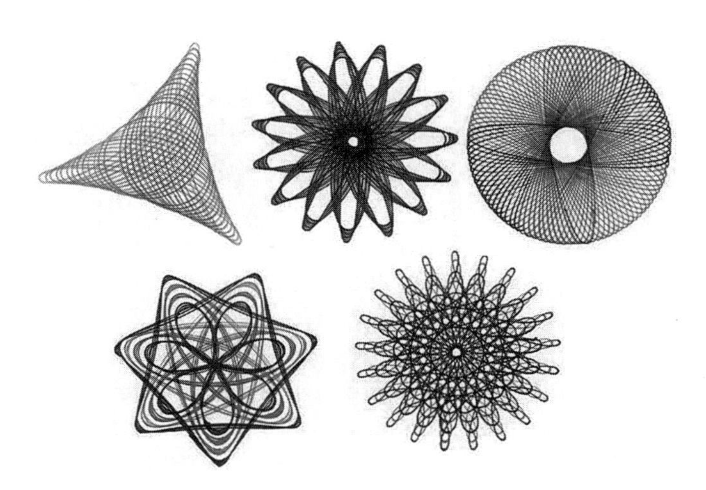

Spirograph was introduced into the U.S. market in 1966, using plastic gears and pens to create intricate designs.

Tonka in 1987. In 1987 Tonka sales topped $300 million. Tonka (and Kenner) became part of Hasbro by 1991. Hasbro closed the Cincinnati office and absorbed Kenner's product lines in 2000.

After the demise of Kenner, some former employees in Cincinnati began benefitting financially from the prototypes they had acquired during their time with the company. A prototype Boba Fett from the Star Wars series sold for $10,000 on eBay. The prototype fired a rocket from its back, while the commercial product could not. And an entrepreneur organized a company that specialized in acquiring and selling the items that former Kenner employees had received as mementos or retrieved from the trash over the 50-year history of the company. Hasbro was not amused, citing its absolute ownership of Kenner intellectual property.

See Also: Action Figures; G.I. Joe; Hasbro; Parker Brothers; United States, 1960 to Present.

Bibliography. Gary Cross, *Kids' Stuff: Toys and the Changing World of American Childhood* (Harvard University Press, 1999); Kenner Toys.com. The History of Kenner, web.archive.org/web/20050309200733/www.kennertoys.com/history/history4.html (cited August 2008); Wikipedia, "Kenner," en.wikipedia.org/wiki/Kenner (cited July 2008); Williams, Lance, "Toybox to Cashbox: Kenner Toys Pay Off," *Business Courier of Cincinnati* (February 27, 2004).

John Barnhill
Independent Scholar

Kenya

Kenya, located in east-central Africa, has a population of 37 million (2007) and was occupied by the British in stages from 1888, gaining its independence in 1963. It still has a sizeable British and European population, numbering up to about 34,000, and some 90,000 people in the country are ethnic Indians.

Traditionally, for the African population of the country, life revolved around villages, where most men worked as farmers or herders, and women remained in the village looking after the children or making handicrafts. As a result, from an early age, boys were involved in activities that helped them in hunting or demonstrated prowess. Using a slingshot and having an ability to hunt were both important. Some boys were also involved in fashioning models or tools, with girls involved in weaving. Traditional dances were taught by parents and village elders. Play involved Hide-and-Seek, ball games, some role-playing games, skipping, and using *ol Trzebinski*, a Kenya hula-hoop, Frisbees, and the like. There are games similar to Jacks, played with stones. Checkers is far more popular than Chess, and men enjoy games of *Kigogo* or *Mancala*, which involves moving counters (often colored stones, seeds, or shells) around a board to capture the pieces of an opponent. There are many regional variations of Mancala, and the boards can range from elaborately decorated wooden ones to markings in the sand.

With the introduction of schools to the country, children began to participate in team events such as soccer—which is now very popular as a recreational sport throughout the country, although the very poor use a bundle of rags when they cannot afford a ball—and also, because of British influence, rugby and netball. Many children learn to swim, and athletics has become very popular, as many children were inspired by Kenyan runners, who have won many Olympic medals. Gradually, other sports such as volleyball, boxing, golf, and hockey have been introduced, and cross-country running, orienteering, and hiking also remain popular.

The British community in Kenya enjoyed a very high standard of living, and much of their social life revolved around the clubs that were found in cities and most towns in the country. There, social sports gatherings would take place, including cricket and indoor games such as billiards, playing card games, and darts. Some of these clubs have survived, but many have been forced to close, and none now have the "Color Bar" to exclude nonwhites. Robert Baden Powell, the founder of the Boy Scout Movement, retired to Kenya, where he died. He did much to encourage boys (along with his wife, who encouraged girls) to live active and healthy lives.

Many children have become regular users of the Youth Clubs in Nairobi, Mombasa, and towns throughout the country, where young people gather to play on billiards tables or listen to music, exchange stories and socialize, or play on pinball machines. There is a range of toy shops in Nairobi, most located in shopping centers. The development of computer games has also attracted much of the youth of the country, although only the wealthier ones can afford to play many of the games or own their own computer.

See Also: Africa, Traditional Play in; Boys' Play; Cricket (Amateur); Frisbee; Girls' Play; Hide & Seek; Rugby; Soccer (Amateur) Worldwide.

Bibliography. Dane Kennedy, *Islands of White: Settler Society and Culture in Kenya and Southern Rhodesia* (Duke University Press, 1987); Glenn Kirchner, *Children's Games Around the World* (Benjamin Cummings, 2000); E.O. Harbin, *Games of Many Nations* (Abingdon Press, 1954); Robert Pateman, *Kenya* (Marshall Cavendish, 1993); Errol Trzebinski, *The Kenya Pioneers* (Heinemann, 1985).

Justin Corfield
Geelong Grammar School

Kick the Can

Playing group games outdoors has been around for centuries, perhaps as long as humans have interfaced. These games are unending in type, as rules for the games change dependent on the players themselves. Kick the Can is a game that combines parts of other popular children's games, such as Tag and Hide & Seek. Most often this game has been played by groups of children of varying ages. The essence of Kick the Can is in the connections and feelings of belonging that games provide.

Perhaps Kick the Can was born of using rules from known games. When given the time and freedom to play with rules, new variations emerge. Kick the Can has the hiding and finding elements of Hide-and-Seek and the chasing and "it" elements of Tag. Kick the Can is played in various ways.

The basic rules of this game are easy to learn and allow multiple age groupings to play together. One child is "it," and all the others hide, trying not to be seen by the person who is "it." If a child is found by the child who is "it," that child goes to "jail," a spot chosen at the beginning of the game. The child who is "it" actively seeks the hiding players while also keeping guard of the can. An actual can is generally used, often an old coffee can. The can has the power to release anyone in jail if kicked by one of the non-"it" players. The player who kicks the can shouts "alli, alli, oxen free," and all those jailed run back out to hide. And the game continues on.

Any number of children (at least three) can play this game. This allows entire neighborhoods of children to play together. It is often a game that is played until dusk or until parents call children back to their homes.

As outdoor and unstructured play of children continues to dwindle, the game of Kick the Can is becoming less and less known to each generation. In the last 50 years, the time children spend outside in unstructured activities has decreased each decade. At one point in time, teenagers played Kick the Can with younger children, and the game and its variations were passed on from child to child. Past generations remember this game fondly, and it was enough of a cultural phenomenon that it was the central player in a 1962 episode of the television show *The Twilight Zone* and was incorporated later in the 1983 film of the same name.

In the "Kick the Can" episode of *The Twilight Zone*, Charlie, a retirement home resident, is longing for his youth, when he comes upon some children playing Kick the Can near his home. He ponders the idea that playing games like Kick the Can are in children's blood and that possibly the reason people grow old is that they stop playing. His wistfulness encapsulates all that this game represents. It is about youth, but also freedom, control, fear, cleverness, quickness, connectedness, belonging, and a whole world of trust, where the players know the rules will be followed for the sake of the game.

See Also: Hide & Seek; Spontaneous Group Play; Tag.

Bibliography. Henry Bett, *Games of Children: Their Origin and History* (Gale Group, 2000); Howard Chudacoff, *Children at Play: An American History* (NYU Press, 2008); Patricia Evans, *Rimbles: A Book of Children's Classic Games, Rhymes, Songs, and Sayings* (Doubleday, 1961); Glenn Kirchner, *Children's Games Around the World* (Benjamin Cummings, 2000).

Joanna J. Cemore
Missouri State University

Kite Flying

Kites have been an enchanting motif of history and play throughout the tenure of human life in the world. Whether featured as the subject of an ancient art exhibition, the diary entry of a Japanese Buddhist monk, or a vivid and perhaps embellished schoolchild's account of his or her outdoor exploits, kites have been there.

Kites are popular worldwide, and often emulate flying insects, birds, and other real and mythical creatures.

Whether a science exhibit on the history of flight or documentaries relating the details of extreme sports, religious ceremonies around the world, or unusual military tactics, none would be complete without reference to kites. In forms as simple as sticks, paper, and twine as complex as the calculations required to build a bridge, and as diverse as the many forms taken by nature herself, kites have been a source of joy, discovery, and inspiration for centuries.

Typically, kites, like other aircraft, consist of a frame made of lightweight material such as plastic or wood, covered by a thin layer of paper, plastic, or fabric in order to catch the wind. The most common kite shapes are diamond, delta/triangle, box, or sled. These simple shapes are combined in endless variation around the world to create colorful representations of birds, butterflies, mythical creatures, and ships, bound only by the scientific principal that the kite generate enough lift to overcome its weight. A long line, often on a spool, is attached, which is used to control the kite's movement while taking off, maintaining altitude, or maneuvering in the air, and coming down.

The earliest known evidence of kites in history is credited to the Chinese in 400–500 B.C.E. Kites were also mentioned throughout the B.C.E. period in both Italian and Roman culture as well. Following the travels of Marco Polo in China in the late 1200s, kites and flying spread through Europe. By 1600 they had become commonplace, in part because of the increasing use of Dutch trading routes between the East Indies and Europe. The earliest kites were used for a variety of religious and cultural purposes, such as influencing the weather or harvests or to celebrate significant events, like the birth of a child.

In addition to religious and recreational purposes, kites were employed to explore flight principles by Leonardo Da Vinci and the Wright Bothers. After the San Francisco earthquake of 1906, a camera hoisted on a kite provided a bird's eye view of the earthquake damage, a technique later duplicated in efforts to gain aerial information for private, scientific, or military purposes. A schoolboy flying a kite in the town of Niagara, Ontario, provided the initial inspiration for engineers trying to establish a line across the gorges of Niagara Falls, inspiring future suspension bridges.

The contemporary recreational use of kites is defined by the categories of sport kite flying, kite fighting, and power kiting. In sport kite competitions, kites, often with additional lines to allow complex maneuvers, are judged according to qualities of artistic and technical merit, in a form of aerial choreography. Kite fighting makes use of smaller, more maneuverable kites on a single line, coated with abrasives for the purpose of bringing opponents' kites to the ground by slashing the line or initiating contact with the competitors' kites in a way that will force them out of the wind and to the ground. Kite fighting is especially popular in India, Pakistan, Thailand, Japan, Korea, and Afghanistan (where a Taliban prohibition on kite flying was recently lifted). Power kiting adapts technology and the energy potential of kites to augment snowboarding, surfboarding, or skateboarding; lightweight "buggy" vehicles; or in actual flight, like hang gliding.

See Also: Afghanistan; Ancient China; Ancient India; Ancient Rome; Central Asia, Ancient; India; Japan; Korea, North and South; Pakistan; Skiing; Snowboarding; Surfing.

Bibliography. Henry Bett, *Games of Children: Their Origin and History* (Gale Group, 2000); Rosanne Cobb, *Kites: Flying*

Skills and Techniques, from Basic Toys to Sport Kites (Firefly Books, 2007); The Drachen Foundation, www.drachen.org (cited July 2008); Maxwell Eden, *The Magnificent Book of Kites: Explorations in Design, Construction, Enjoyment & Flight* (Black Dog & Leventhal Publishers, 1998); J. Katz, "Sky's the Limit," *The Wave Magazine* (v.8, 2008).

Melissa Gemeinhardt
New Orleans University

Korea, North and South

Korea is located on the Korean Peninsula in East Asia. Although the peninsula has been divided into two separate nations—North Korea and South Korea—since 1948, before this division Korean people lived as a single nation since the 7th century, and both North and South Koreans share traditional forms of plays.

Koreans have enjoyed playing a plethora of traditional games and sports, especially on traditional holidays or folk festivals such as *Sollal* (Lunar New Year's Day; the first day of the first month on the lunar calendar), *Dano* (Midsummer Celebration; the fifth day of the fifth lunar month), and *Chusok* (Autumn Evening; the 15th day of the eighth lunar month).

Yutnori is a Korean board game involving four players or teams. The game is played by a player throwing *yut* (or four wooden sticks with markings ranging from one to four) on the ground. According to the way these sticks land, the player then moves his or her *mal* (game piece) around the board. The player who brings all *mal* home first wins. *Yutnori*, traditionally enjoyed on the Lunar New Year, is often played on a straw mat in the courtyard and is accompanied by loud voices and wild excitement.

Outdoor Games

Men and boys of all ages fly *yeon* (or kites), typically from the first to the 15th day of the first lunar month. A game is often played where people try to cut the string of each others' kites by exercising a swinging motion until one of the two strings of another player's kite is severed. Also, at the end of the season, *yeon* with well wishes, such as "away with evil, welcome good luck," written on them would be flown and cut loose to take away the year's bad luck.

Jegichagi, mostly played by boys, is a game similar to hackysack, in which a *jegi* (or shuttlecock), made of a coin wrapped in feathers and paper or cloth, must be kept in the air using nothing but one's feet. When the *jegi* hits the ground, the player loses his turn to another.

Neolttwigi, enjoyed mainly by girls and women on the Lunar New Year's day, is similar to seesaw, except that *Neolttwigi* participants stand on each end of a *neol* (or board) and then jump in the air, propelling the person opposite into the air. It is believed that women of the noble class used *Neolttwigi* to help them see over the wall that surrounded their house, as women in old times were rarely allowed out of the living compound, except at night.

Kune, Korean swings, are hung very high, often seven yards or more, in trees or on a tall framework for a single swing. Standing on a board, girls and women swing as high as they can, sometimes alone, and sometimes in pairs. This long rope swinging was enjoyed on Dano and Chusuk (May 5 and August 15 on the lunar calendar).

Korean Sports

Ssireum, Korean-style wrestling, is the oldest Korean traditional sport. It is somewhat similar to Japanese *Sumo*. To play *Ssireum*, two wrestlers face each other in a sand-covered ring in the grappling position. They each grab their opponent's *Satba* (a long sash wrapped around the players' waist and the right thigh). They then rise to a standing position and attempt to force their opponent to touch the ground. Competitions were traditionally held on Dano (May 5 on the lunar calendar) and during the summer and autumn months.

Taekwondo is a Korean martial art that is popular around the world. Taekwondo can be loosely translated as "the way of the hand and foot," or "the art of kicking and punching." It has some similarity to Karate in Japan and Kungfu in China. Under the tutelage of a master, the martial artist goes through stages of training and practice—physical, mental, and spiritual. The student masters the discipline of each stage leading up to earning a black belt, which symbolizes the highest skill.

South Korean Sports and Games

While both South and North Koreans continue to enjoy traditional games, they also have developed distinct contemporary forms of play. With the rapid growth of the economy since the Korean War, people in South Korea enjoy an improved quality of life, with increased leisure time and a greater variety of sports and games. Various Western sports, such as soccer, baseball, table tennis, billiards, tennis, golfing, and rollerblading, have gained great popularity as recreational sports. Soccer, the number one team sport in Korea, is played by almost every child and man on the dirt fields at local schools. The 2002 World Cup, which Korea and Japan cohosted, fueled this enthusiasm. South Koreans cheered as their team placed fourth in the finals.

South Koreans enjoy playing cards, especially the Japanese flower cards, *Hanafuda* (or *Hwatoo* in Korean). The most common game is Go Stop, in which the leading player announces either "go" or "stop" to continue or finish the game.

With widespread access to computers and high speed internet, young Koreans are very fond of online games including an American game called Starcraft, and a Korean game called Lineage. In urban areas, there is a PC bang (or Internet room) on almost every street.

North Korean Games

The North Korean government heavily controls and protects North Korean culture. Group games that have goals and purposes are promoted.

Children who are yet too young to be recruited into the military experience military-like training in a form of various playful games, such as "stealing flags," "targeting tanks," and "defending a position."

Japanese Hanafuda (flower cards) playing cards are popular in Korea and are used to play a number of games.

The government organizes mass games on national holidays, such as the birthday of their late Communist leader, Kim Il-sung. In these mass games, large numbers of participants take part in highly regimented routines that demonstrate group dynamics rather than individual ability. In card stunt, for example, thousands of well-trained school children hold up colored cards to create single huge mosaic pictures. This type of performance is one of few events that North Korea has allowed foreigners to view.

See Also: Central Asia, Ancient; Kite Flying; Soccer (Amateur) Worldwide; Wargames.

Bibliography. Arnold Arnold, *World Book of Children's Games* (Fawcett, 1972); Henry Bett, *Games of Children: Their Origin and History* (Gale Group, 2000); E.O. Harbin, *Games of Many Nations* (Abingdon Press, 1954); Sarah Ethridge Hunt, *Games and Sports the World Around* (Ronald Press Company, 1964; Glenn Kirchner, *Children's Games Around the World* (Benjamin Cummings, 2000).

Joon Sun Lee
City University of New York

Kyrgyzstan

A landlocked republic in Central Asia, Kyrgyzstan was a part of the Russian Federation and then the Soviet Union until it gained its independence in 1991. Sharing borders with Kazakhstan, Uzbekistan, Tajikistan, and China, some 65 percent of the population are ethnic Kyrgyz, with about 14 percent being ethnic Uzbeks and 12.5 percent being ethnic Russians.

The country has a large population of sheep, and from an early age, children are involved in rounding up sheep and training dogs. Boys also practice with a slingshot, and young men test their skills and prowess in wrestling in a version of the Afghan game *Pahlwani.* Keen horsemen, many Kyrgyz men are involved in hunting, using falcons and hawks that are trained over long periods of time. Many boys and young men are also involved in the rearing of the hawks. Men are also involved in playing horseback competitions such as *Buzkashi*, when teams fight over the carcass of a goat or sheep. Marco Polo went through the region in 1271–72, and he described some of the customs but did not mention the pastimes and games played in modern-day Kyrgyzstan. One game that probably dates from that period is known as *Kiss-Ku* or *Kesh-kumai* ("kiss-chase") played on horseback by Kyrgyz and Uighur people.

While Kyrgyzstan was a part of the Soviet Union, compulsory schooling led to a great emphasis on European games, such as soccer, which was introduced into schools and youth clubs around the country and remains popular. Younger children have been involved in playing with building blocks and LEGOS, as well as playing with jigsaw puzzles and playing games outdoors like Hide and Seek. Dolls are also popular with girls, many made from cloth with knitted or stitched faces, although increased access to Russian goods from the 1960s led to the introduction of many plastic dolls. The Young Pioneer Movement encouraged children to take part in hiking and camping. Teenage boys enjoyed board games and Wargames, with Soviet battles during the Great Patriotic War (World War II) being the most popular. Since the nation's independence, there has been a greater emphasis on medieval history and Kyrgyz nationalism in schools, which, in turn, has led to a change in Wargaming habits, although the ethnic Ukrainian and Russian communities still follow much the same lifestyle as they did when it was part of the Soviet Union.

See Also: Afghanistan; Boys' Play; Girls' Play; Soccer (Amateur) Worldwide; Russia; Ukraine; Wargames.

Bibliography. Joan Baxter, *The Archeology of Childhood: Children, Gender and Material Culture* (AltaMira Press, 2005); Glenn Kirchner, *Children's Games Around the World* (Benjamin Cummings, 2000); Bradley Mayhew, Paul Clammer, and Michael Kohn, *Central Asia* (Lonely Planet, 2004); Nina Millen, *Children's Games from Many Lands* (Friendship Press, 1943) Giles Whittell, *Central Asia* (Cadogan Guides, 1996).

Justin Corfield
Geelong Grammar School

L

Laos

A land-locked country in southeast Asia with a small population, Laos has received heavy cultural influences from Thailand and China, and less so from its other neighbors, Cambodia and Vietnam. The elite in precolonial Laos were dominated by the royal families and the ethnic Chinese, most of whom maintained their power after France made Laos a protectorate in 1907. As a result, many of the games played among the elite tended to include Chinese Chess, Mahjong, and other traditional Chinese pursuits. In villages, and also in the towns—there were no real cities until the 20th century—children played Hide-and-Seek, and played with kites and marbles, while the adults often played musical instruments or took part in forms of gambling involving cockfights or dice. The community would participate in dancing to mark phases in the agricultural year. There are also games involving popping seeds from fruits, and a game called *Ga To* involving a ball made from tightly-woven rattan that must be kept in the air for as long as possible. This game has developed, with Thai influence, into *Takraw,* which is a sport recognized by the Southeast Asia Games. Canoe racing on the Mekong also has attracted many people to participate and to watch.

The arrival of the French brought soccer, Chess, and *boules* to Vientiane, which became the administrative capital for Laos, and soccer quickly spread around the country. There were never many French in the country, but with the Laotian elite often going to schools in Vietnam, where they were taught in French, there was a ready market among the wealthier people for such games. Soccer quickly became popular with teenagers and young men. Playing with dolls, balls, toy boats, and cars has also been common for many years, as has the card game *Phuy-tong.* Katay Don Sasorith, prime minister of Laos from 1954 to 1955, wrote about the game in 1931.

Independence in 1953 led to an increase in the school population, and it was not long before new games were taught to children. However, in the late 1950s, Laos was involved in a war that essentially only ended in 1975. This conflict saw the destruction of much of the countryside, many of the rural people heading to the towns, and in this new urban society, greater cultural influence from the United States, leading to the importation of U.S.-made games and toys to compete with French dolls and toys. Toys were also fashioned from war wreckage, such as shell casings. Water pistols, both simple and sophisticated, are sold during the water festival each year in April.

The Communist takeover in 1975 led to an influx of some Russian advisers and technicians, as well as additional Vietnamese influence. These advisers brought with them European-style Chess, which had previously only been played by the elite. Greater prosperity from the mid-1990s led to an influx of tourism and a more open lifestyle that led to the building of bowling alleys, and the onset of elaborate Wargames, which took place in the Americas and Western Europe, with complicated rules. With many Laotian exiles returning to their country from the United States, France, Australia, and elsewhere, together with more foreign expatriates working or settling in the country, it is likely that Western-style games will become even more popular in Laos.

See Also: Boys' Play; China; Girls' Play; Soccer (Amateur) Worldwide; Thailand; Wargames.

Bibliography. Judith Diamond, *Laos* (Childrens Press, 1989); Stephen Mansfield, *Laos* (Marshall Cavendish, 1998); Katay Don Sasorith, "The Game of Phuy-tong," in René de Berval, ed., *Kingdom of Laos* (France Asie, 1959).

Justin Corfield
Geelong Grammar School

Latvia

Latvia, located in the Baltic in northeastern Europe, was controlled by the Teutonic knights in Medieval times, and then by Sweden. It was a part of the Russian Empire for about 200 years. Gaining its independence in 1918, it was occupied by Russia in 1940, the Germans in 1941, and then Russia from 1944 until 1991, when it again became independent. During that time, with most people in the country speaking Latvian, it has managed to keep its cultural identity, and some of this is reflected through its games.

In Medieval times, most of the pastimes involved military prowess, and the Teutonic knights were passionate about jousting, swordplay, and other combat sports, as well as archery. This continues to be seen through interest in fencing, and also adventure playgrounds around the country.

In 1886 the first bicycle club was established in Riga, later the capital of independent Latvia. Initially it operated purely for recreational cycling, but later it became a sports club. Because of the climate, skating, ice hockey, skiing, snowboarding, and tobogganing have also been popular, and walking and hiking also have long histories within the country, especially after native Janis Dalins won a number of international walking competitions, transforming the pastime into a sport.

The Riga Chess Society was established in 1890, followed by the Riga Chess Club in 1898. Aron Nimzowitsch (1886–1935), born in Riga, was one of the great Chess players of the 1920s but failed to win any world championship, although he remains famous for his book *My System* (1925), which led to a new vocabulary of Chess. However, the best-known Latvian chess grandmaster was Mikhail Nekhemyevich Tal (1936–92), who was born in Latvia and became the Latvian champion at the age of 16, winning five Soviet titles and writing what are regarded as some of the wittiest books on Chess. Mention should also be made of Andreas Ascharin (1843–96), born in Estonia but a school teacher in Riga from 1879; and Lucius Endzelins (1909–81), who competed at the Chess Olympiad at Buenos Aires in 1939, and later settled in Australia. The Latvijas Saha Savieniba is the current parent body for Chess in the country. Backgammon and card games, especially Bridge, are also played by many people in Latvia, particularly in cities and towns. The Americans introduced recreational basketball into the country after World War I.

Because of the Russian occupation of the country, many Latvians fled overseas, especially to the United States, Canada, and Australia, and many were able to maintain their cultural identity. With Latvian independence in 1991, large numbers of exiles returned to Latvia, and this led to a resurgence of Latvian nationalism, including the Latvian National Song Festival of 1873, which was an important event in the country's history.

Wargaming was very popular during Russian occupation, but most of it was restricted to historic battles, such as the defeat of the Teutonic knights by Alexander Nevski at Lake Peipus, the Russo-Swedish Wars, or Napoleon's invasion of Russia in 1812. Since independence, scenarios include the fighting in 1918 and also in 1940–45. There has also been greater interest among teenagers and young men in fantasy Wargames. *Dungeons & Dragons* books and Warhammer figures are sold in Riga and other cities in Latvia and are also purchased from overseas through the internet. *Monopols*, the Latvian version of the board game Monopoly, features important streets and train stations in Riga.

See Also: Chess and Variations of; *Dungeons & Dragons*; Estonia; Lithuania; Monopoly and Variations of; Wargames; Warhammer.

Bibliography. Peter J. Babris, *Baltic Youth Under Communism* (Research Publishers, 1967); E.O. Harbin, *Games of Many Nations* (Abingdon Press, 1954); Raymond Keene, *Aron Nimzowitsch: A Reappraisal* (Batsford, 1974); J. Rutkis, *Latvia: Country and People* (Latvian National Foundation, 1967).

Justin Corfield
Geelong Grammar School

Lead Soldiers

Fifty-four-mm soldiers representing the British in the Crimean War era were made by Imperial Productions in New Zealand.

The term *lead soldiers* is often applied to a variety of types of figurine, not all of which are wholly made of lead. The word *soldier* here commonly refers to all sorts of military figures, including such things as knights and cowboys. Lead soldiers are used for a variety of purposes: as toys, for use in various types of games with formal rules, and as decorative pieces. In the last few decades, the phrase *lead soldier* has given way to *lead figure*.

In 1893 British toy maker William Britain invented a method of hollow casting lead figures and went on to found Britains, Ltd. This highly successful company dominated the industry for the better part of a century, producing high-quality miniatures. Hollow casting is a method whereby metal is poured into a mold, hardens as it touches the edges of the mold, and then the excess metal is poured out again before it has a chance to solidify. This results in hollow figures, usually with a hole in the base that the metal has been poured out through. At the time of its invention, the process meant that three-dimensional figures could be made fairly cheaply, as less metal needed to be used. Prior to the invention of this process, figures had been made mostly in Germany, using an alloy of lead and tin. These figures were almost two-dimensional, and as a result are known as "flats."

Lead has always been expensive, and in the latter half of the 20th century, was recognized as poisonous. In the 1960s, increased safety regulations in the United Kingdom meant that Britains, Ltd. had to shift their production to plastic. Other companies copied them, notably John Hill and Company (known as Johillco) and Hank Bros.

Lead soldiers were initially produced as either collectibles or childrens' toys. Commonly, contemporary military figures were made. This started to change in 1913 when H.G. Wells published *Little Wars*, a simple codification of rules for battles between lead soldiers, using Britains' figures. Prior to this, Wargames of this nature had really only been used in Prussia to train military officers; called *Kriegsspiel* (a German word for Wargame), they used wooden blocks to represent troops rather than miniatures. Wells's rules codified the movement of the figures and utilized a spring-loaded cannon. The games were designed to be played on a large flat surface, with a living room floor given as the example.

Modern Soldiers

Modern lead soldiers are made from an alloy of lead, tin, and antimony. The antimony allows the metal to take very fine detail when sculpted. These figures tend to be made for use in role-playing games, such as in *Dungeons & Dragons*, or for Wargames of the sort produced by Games Workshop.

Scale is important when dealing with lead soldiers, as they come in a variety of sizes. There are two main ways of expressing scale, either as a ratio or the measurement from toe to head. For example, the scale of Britain's military miniatures is generally 1:32, making a human figure 2 1/4 inches or 54-mm high. There is obviously considerable variation in this. Other common scales are 15 mm (used by wargamers looking to depict large battles), 25 mm (used in role-playing games such as *Dungeons & Dragons*) and 54 mm (collectible figures).

See Also: *Dungeons & Dragons*; Germany; Minifigs; Play as Mock War, Psychology of; Play as Mock War, Sociology of; United Kingdom; Wargames.

Bibliography. John Bobek, *The Games of War: A Treasury of Rules for Battles with Toy Soldiers, Ships and Planes* (AuthorHouse, 2007); Norman Joplin and John T. Waterworth, *Britain's New Toy Soldiers, 1973 to the Present: Traditional Gloss-painted Metal Models* (Schiffer Publishing, 2008); Dominique Pascal, *Collectible Toy Soldiers* (Flammarion, 2003); H.G. Wells, *Little Wars* (Frank Palmer, 1913).

Justin Parsler
Brunel University

Leapfrog

From a historic and cultural standpoint, Leapfrog continues to be a playful physical challenge with slight variations found throughout the world. In the United States, it is most often played at the end of the school's calendar year, when elementary school children are organized into groups and participate in a variety of field day events. The first player rests both hands on his or her knees and bends over while tucking his or her chin to the chest. The terms *giving a back* or *making a back* are used to explain the body stance formed as a player rests their head on the thighs and hunches the body forward. On a leader's signal, another player runs up and places his or her hands on the shoulder of the stooping child and straddles their legs to vault over the player's body. The distance between players is commonly between eight and 10 feet, which allows all players a running start to make the vault.

Early Accounts

Still played in Egypt today, ancient Egyptian players called the game *Khuzza Lawizz.* Its popularity continued throughout the Middle Ages, and it was vividly included in Pieter Breughel's oil painting on oak panel titled *Children's Games*. This Dutch painting (1560) featured peasant children playing a large variety of children's activities, including a group of six boys playing Leapfrog. Bruegel's painting also identified a variation of the game called Buck. In this early variation, one player began the game by stooping down with their head touching the side of a building or an available schoolyard wall. The second player would run and spring onto the back of the first, while holding up as many fingers as desired. This player chanted, "Buck, Buck, how many horns do I hold up?" The Buck had to guess the correct answer, or the player jumped down and repeated the action. If the Buck guessed correctly, the roles were reversed.

The game also began with a series of players forming a two- or three-person Buck, in which other children jump upon their backs.

Team Leapfrog races became very popular in the late 1800s. Early games author Josephine Pollard described Leapfrog as being a capital exercise and a good recreation on a winter's day when kept going until halted by the school bell. She found the game very satisfying since all players had equal turns. Advanced modifications included Foot and Half and Fly-the-Garter, which challenged the player to jump from greater distances, as identified by scratching a line into the dirt, sometimes called the garter, and in which players vaulted over the side of the player instead of the player's back.

Many early 1900 descriptions of Leapfrog had strict rules to follow. Any child suddenly raising their body while a player leaped over the body would be penalized or ridiculed by other playmates. There were also strict penalties against a player who knuckled down with their fists into the shoulders or back of the player he or she was jumping over. The misconduct was termed *spurring,* and teachers punished players unless both hands were placed flat on the shoulders or back.

In early France, Leapfrog was called *Le Saut de Mouton* (the Sheep's Leap), and the player placed an object such as a handkerchief on the back of the crouching player to be snatched while leaping over the stooped player. The Japanese adaptation is called *Senakawatari.* The primary difference is that the player jumps on the backs of the other players, who are situated close enough in the stooping position to create a continuous row of human backs.

From a children's literary standpoint, characteristics of the game were described in chapter three of Lewis Carroll's *Alice's Adventures in Wonderland* (1865), in which a continuous race-like game was played in order to dry the clothing of Alice and the other characters in the story, after the group had narrowly escaped drowning in a pool of water caused by Alice's tears.

See Also: Egypt; Europe, 1200 to 1600; France; Spontaneous Group Play.

Bibliography. Lewis Carroll, *Alice's Adventures in Wonderland* (Macmillan and Co., 1865); John Champlin and Arthur E. Bostwick, *Young Folks' Cyclopedia of Games and Sports* (Henry Holt & Company, 1890); Josephine Pollard, *Sports of All Sorts* (McLoughlin Bro's, 1889); H.D. Richardson, *Holiday Sports and Pastimes for Boys* (William S. Orr & Company, 1848); Samuel Williams, *The Boy's Treasury of Sports, Pastimes, and Recreations* (Lea and Blanchard, 1847).

Rhonda Clements
Manhattanville College

Lebanon

Lebanon is a country in the Middle East, on the eastern shore of the Mediterranean, and thus proximate to Cyprus, Israel, and Syria. The homeland of the ancient Phoenicians, Lebanon was controlled by a succession of empires over the centuries, each leaving a mark. The modern government is an artifact of French rule, and in the early 20th century the country was predominantly Christian, with large Muslim and Druze populations. Today, Muslims make up the majority of the country, though the Christian presence is still significant at about 40 percent. Different government positions are filled, by law, by members of different religions, to preserve a balance of power.

Soccer is by far the most popular sport in Lebanon, at both the professional and amateur levels. Rugby, golf, and tennis all have their adherents as well. One of the faster-growing sports in Lebanon, as it is in many parts of the world, is basketball. Long an obscure sport outside of the United States, with little amateur participation, basketball has been expanding rapidly.

In Lebanon, basketball has been played since the 1930s, but the 21st century has seen it achieve true popularity. Several of the basketball teams in the Lebanese Basketball League are associated with soccer clubs, but newer teams like Bluestars are basketball-only, reflecting the shift away from basketball as a second-class sport. More Lebanese youth are playing the game, both in and out of school.

Because of Lebanon's geography, the small country is able to enjoy both winter and summer sports: the mountainous regions allow for skiing and snowboarding, while the temperate Mediterranean beaches are perfect for swimming and sailing, both of which are quite popular. Skiing was introduced in 1913, when the country was still part of the Ottoman Empire, and became popular in the 1930s, when amateur ski clubs and resorts opened up around the country; the sport has remained prominent since.

A popular children's game in Lebanon is a tag game called Do You Have Fire? The player who is "it" approaches each of four players (usually) while they are at their respective corners of the playing area, or designated objects like trees, stairs, doorways, and so on. "It" asks the player, "Do you have fire?" and the player responds "No, my neighbor has fire." "It" cannot leave the corner until the player has finished answering.

Corners (or their designated objects) are "safe," and while "It" is occupied with asking one player if he or she has fire, two of the other players try to switch places. Their job is to get from one safe corner to another; "It" must try to tag one of them first. The tagged player is "It" next.

See Also: Ancient Greece; Sailing.

Bibliography. Arnold Arnold, *World Book of Children's Games* (Fawcett, 1972); Jesse Hubbell Bancroft, *Games* (MacMillan, 1937); Robbie Bell and Michael Cornelius, *Board Games Round the World: A Resource Book for Mathematical Investigations* (Cambridge University Press, 1988); Roger Caillois, *Man, Play and Games* (University of Illinois Press, 2001); Sarah Ethridge Hunt, *Games and Sports the World Around* (Ronald Press Company, 1964); Glenn Kirchner, *Children's Games Around the World* (Benjamin Cummings, 2000); Nina Millen, *Children's Games From Many Lands* (Friendship Press, 1943).

Bill Kte'pi
Independent Scholar

Legend of Zelda

Legend of Zelda is a mythic quest action-adventure game that set the Guinness world record for the longest-running action-adventure series of all time, spanning 1986 to 2007, and was the first Famicom Disk game released in Japan. For American players, the game was released in 1987 on the Nintendo Entertainment System (NES) and was revolutionary to gaming. Gamers could save their games and continue at a later time, exploring the expansive, detailed world map without an exact linear progression.

In all Zelda games, Link is the main playable character, with Zelda serving the role as the fairytale princess waiting to be rescued. This may sound familiar to Mario fans, and in fact, Mario's designer and creator, Shigeru Miyamoto, is also responsible for Zelda.

The game has gone through several iterations on many platforms, with 14 games total in the main series. The Legend of Zelda set the standard for the series with Link on a quest, gathering Triforce in order to save Zelda from Ganon/Ganondorf. The Legend of Zelda II: The Adventure of Link has Link collect Magic Crystal pieces to wake Zelda from an enchanted sleep. The first and second games in the series had an animated television series based loosely on them that ran as part of *The Super Mario Bros. Super Show!*

Next, the game Legend of Zelda: A Link to the Past was one of the front-running titles for the Super NES and was re-released as A Link to the Past & Four Swords for the Game Boy Advance (GBA). A Link to the Past also spawned a running comic miniseries in Nintendo Power. Four Swords was the first multiplayer game in the series.

The video game series went handheld with the release of Link's Awakening for the Game Boy, and moved Link from the kingdom of Hyrule to the high seas. Returning to a wasted Hyrule, the critically acclaimed Ocarina of Time was produced in three dimensions for the Nintendo64 system, and gamers played Link as both a child and an adult. Majora's Mask, the direct sequal to Ocarina, transports Link to Termina, where he has 72 hours before the moon crashes into the planet.

Back to handheld, Oracle of Ages and Oracle of Seasons were released together for the Game Boy Color and can be played alone or can exchange saved data to unlock features.

Then, The Wind Waker was released for the GameCube and had Link back onboard a ship, controlling the wind. Also for the GameCube, Four Swords Adventure could be played alone but continues the multiplayer mode started in Four Swords if all four players link their GBA up to the GameCube, as Link splits himself into four with the power of the four swords. Also for the GBA is The Minish Cap, where Link can shrink in size.

Twilight Princess was the launch game for the Wii and took advantage of the innovative Wiimote. It also transformed Link into a wolf, for an interesting twist on the playable protagonist. In addition to the Wiimote, the Wii Zapper is one way to play the shooting game Link's Crossbow Training.

Finally, the Phantom Hourglass continues where the Wind Waker left off, as Link sails the uncharted seas. But the series is not over yet. There will be more Legend of Zelda games in the near future.

See Also: Mario; Mortal Kombat; Sonic the Hedgehog; Tomb Raider.

Bibliography. *Guinness World Records: Gamer's Edition 2008* (Guinness World Records Limited, 2008); Steven L. Kent. *The Ultimate History of Video Games: The Story Behind the Craze That Touched Our Lives and Changed the World* (Three Rivers Press, 2001); J. Patrick Williams et al., eds., *Gaming As Culture: Essays on Reality, Identity and Experience in Fantasy Games* (McFarland, 2006).

Cathlena Martin
University of Florida

LEGOs

LEGOs are small, plastic, colorful interlocking blocks manufactured as toys for children. The LEGO company began in 1932, when Ole Kirk Christiansen, a Dutch carpenter, began selling wooden toys to the children of Billund, Denmark. Two years later the company adopted the now famous LEGO name, which is a contraction of the Danish phrase *leg godt*, or "play well." The interlocking brick—LEGO's most famous and popular line of toys—did not appear until 1949; until then, the company focused on the production of traditional wooden toys. In its 75-year history, LEGO has grown from a fledgling toy workshop to a vibrant multinational corporation that produces nearly 19 billion LEGO pieces a year. Today's children, the company estimates, spend five billion hours a year playing with LEGOs, and a philosophy of play drives the company's mission. According to a corporate profile, "It is the LEGO philosophy that 'good play' enriches a child's life—and its subsequent adulthood. With this in mind, the LEGO Group has developed and marketed a wide range of products, all founded on the same basic philosophy of learning and developing—through play."

The Growth of Plastic LEGOs

After World War II Christiansen purchased a plastic injection-molding machine to produce toys; beginning in 1949 the company made its toys from cellulose acetate, but switched to a more durable material (acrylonitrile butadiene styrene) in 1963. Although LEGO continued to produce wooden toys until 1960, the new plastic interlocking bricks would quickly become the company's trademark item, and by the early 1950s the majority of LEGO toys were made with plastics. The concept did not originate with LEGO, however, and the true inventor of the interlocking plastic block was Hilary Harry Fisher Page, a British child psychologist. Page founded Kiddicraft in 1932 and began producing a line of plastic "sensible" toys in 1937; in 1939 he introduced Kiddicraft Self-Locking Building Bricks, the forerunner to the LEGO. LEGO began producing its own line of "Automatic Binding Bricks" in 1949; by 1953 they were renamed "LEGO Bricks."

In 1958 Godtfred Kirk Christensen took over the lead management position at LEGO, when his father and founder of the company, Ole Kirk Christiansen, passed away. Godtfred had worked for the company since its inception and was instrumental in developing the revolutionary LEGO System of Play in 1955. The LEGO System consisted of 28 building sets and eight toy vehicles, and was considered innovative in that players had the freedom to build and expand as they pleased, without having to stick to a precise set of directions. Shortly thereafter, LEGO patented its now famous "stud-and-tube" coupling system, which made models far more stable.

In 1963 Godtfred Kirk Christensen redefined the mission of LEGO and stated that the company's products would be characterized by the following: unlimited play potential; made for both boys and girls; fun for every age; year-round play; healthy, quiet play; long hours of play; development, imagination, creativity; the more LEGO, the greater the value; extra sets available; and quality in every detail. By 1968 there were 218 different LEGO pieces (not including color variations) and the company was producing 57 different sets and 25 vehicles. It was also during this period that LEGO launched DUPLO bricks, which were about twice the size of the traditional LEGO brick, and were marketed for younger children, who would find the larger sizes more suited to their developing motor abilities.

The Third Era of LEGO

LEGO considers the 1970s to be its "third era," a period that is marked in the company's history by the introduction of LEGO minifigures, toy characters that could populate LEGO environments. With six distinct parts—head, torso, hips, arms, hands, and legs—the figures could be easily manipulated, and with the C-grips on the figures'

LEGOs are innovative in that they can be used to build and expand at will without having to follow directions, prompting individual creativity and unstructured play.

hands, they could hold LEGO accessories. It was an important development and signaled that role-play and personal interaction with the toys would become a hallmark of product development. The 1970s also witnessed the increasing role played by LEGO's third-generation Christensen, Godtfred's son Kjeld Kirk Christensen, who would become the company's CEO in 1979, a position he held until 2004. Kjeld led the company to focus more on child development and saw to it that LEGO's "different product ranges were to take account of the child's needs and abilities at each stage in its life—continuously aiming for optimum stimulation of the child's creativity and imagination," according to the LEGO group. Under Kjeld, LEGO produced more theme-based sets, such as 1979's space series. Increasingly, stories, role-play, and themes were becoming part of the LEGO brand, which was marketed as a product line that would enhance a child's imagination and development.

Development Through Play

LEGO established its Educational Products Department in 1980 (renamed LEGO Dacta in 1989), which extended Kjeld's development-through-play philosophy more deeply into the company's core mission. This change allowed LEGO to reposition itself in the marketplace; more that "just bricks," LEGO sought to offer exciting and innovative learning experiences. This would eventually merge the LEGO brand with schools, enabling "educators to cover a wide range of curriculum targets within science, technology, engineering and maths in a fun, hands-on and engaging way," according to the LEGO Group. Today the company produces such learning sets as the Renewable Energy Set, which provides students with the opportunity to experiment with alternative energy sources, and Early Simple Machines Set, which introduces young children to basic mechanical principles.

LEGO Mindstorms

The most important development of the 1990s, and one that continued on the previous decade's focus on educational play, was the creation of LEGO Mindstorms. These were sets that merged the traditional LEGO brick of the 1950s with the computer technology of the 1990s. Equipped with electric motors, touch and light sensors, and a computerized brick, Mindstorms sets could be used to build moving LEGO models. The product line was updated in 2006 as Lego Mindstorms NXT, a full-fledged robotics kit. The NXT brick has input ports for sensors that give robots the ability to react to touch, sound, light, and ultrasonics. The NXT also has three servo motors, which give robots the ability to move. Alpha Rex, a humanoid robot, walks on two legs and can be programmed to perform a variety of tasks. Through Dacta, LEGO has incorporated its educational missions into the Mindstorm product line and is currently in partnership with several universities to advance the technology.

Licensing and Theme Parks

In recent years LEGO has lent its name to a variety of media-related tie-ins, creating sets that merge with popular entertainment brands, such as Star Wars, Batman, SpongeBob SquarePants, Harry Potter, Indiana Jones, and Speed Racer. LEGO also holds a 30 percent share in the LEGOLAND amusement parks, which operate in Billund, Denmark; Windsor, England; Günzburg, Germany; and Carlsbad, California. LEGO remains a privately-held corporation, owned and operated by the Christiansen family. Kjeld Kirk Christensen is currently the richest man in Denmark and has a fortune that is estimated to exceed $3 billion.

See Also: Blocks; Casual Games; Denmark; Erector Sets; Toys and Child Development.

Bibliography. Joan Baxter, *The Archeology of Childhood: Children, Gender and Material Culture* (AltaMira Press, 2005); Maaike Lauwaert, "Playing Outside the Box—On LEGO Toys and the Changing World of Construction Play," *History and Technology* (v.24, September 2008); LEGO Group, "LEGO Timeline," www.lego.com (cited July 2008).

Joshua Garrison
University of Wisconsin, Oshkosh

Liberia

Liberia's creation dates back to 1847, when freed slaves and their supporters from the United States established the Republic of Liberia in West Africa to help former slaves return to Africa. The country's flag, and the capital, Monrovia, demonstrate the connection to the United States, with the mainstay of the economy originally being rubber plantations for the Firestone Company. Many of the people in the country are desperately poor, and during the fighting in the 1990s, there were thousands of child soldiers participating in the war.

Traditionally, children in Liberia have played similar games to elsewhere in West Africa, with spinning tops, the use of hoops, ball games, marbles, and the like, as well as Hide-and-Seek, all being popular. Quite a number of the schools in Monrovia and the major towns in the country were run by missionaries, and this meant that some European and North American games have been introduced. Soccer is commonly played, being popular with many of the street children, as well as the wealthier people, as is volleyball. Children from wealthier families have also been involved in baseball, which was introduced because of Liberia's connections with the United States. Because of its location, swimming is popular in the country.

Handicrafts in Liberia included the fashioning of masks and the making of drums, and women and girls were involved in embroidery, sewing, spinning, and weaving. Much of this continued through until 1980, when the Tolbert government was overthrown and the country gradually began a civil war. The Liberian Jungle, in Bushrod Island, was the major club in the country for dancing and cultural shows. During the troubles since 1980, most of the social clubs in the country were destroyed, as were a large number of church halls and the large Masonic Temple in Monrovia. The disruption in schooling made matters worse, with the vast majority of schools closing down for most of the period from 1989 until 1996.

As peace has returned to the country, some missionary groups, such as the Roman Catholic Salesian Fathers, have tried to help street children and others traumatized by the war and social dislocation to readjust. The Don Bosco Programs of the Salesian Brothers has introduced many children to simple European toys and pastimes, with other groups encouraged to take part in woodworking and crafts. There has also been a reemergence of the music industry, influenced when local soccer star George Oppong Weah turned to music as a way of getting the country back on its feet. The Liberian Girl Guides Association was founded in 1920, and the Boy Scouts of Liberia was founded two years later, the latter having about 2,400 members.

See Also: Africa, Traditional Play in; Boys' Play; Girls' Play; Hide & Seek; Soccer (Amateur) Worldwide.

Bibliography. Esther Warner Dendel, *The Crossing Fee: A Story of Life in Liberia* (Victor Gollancz, 1968); Glenn Kirchner, *Children's Games Around the World* (Benjamin Cummings, 2000); Bram Posthumus, "Liberia," in Simon Broughton, Mark Ellingham, and Jon Lusk, eds., *The Rough Guide to World Music: Africa & Middle East* (Rough Guide, 2006); Thomas D. Roberts, *Area Handbook for Liberia* (U.S. Government Printing Office, 1972).

Justin Corfield
Geelong Grammar School

Life

There are two significant games bearing the name "The Game of Life," one of which is not really a game at all, but an experiment in cellular automation, while the second is a popular family board game.

Conway's The Game of Life is named for its inventor, mathematician John Horton Conway, and was presented in the October 1970 issue of *Scientific American*. It was based on the work of game theorist and mathematician John von Neumann. This "game" is not really a game at all in the common sense of the word, but rather a mathematical simulation of cellular genetics—an intellectual puzzle.

A checkerboard is used and each square is deemed to be a cell that is either "alive" or "dead." As turns progress, cells either die or come to life, depending on the number of living neighbors they have; a cell with two live neighbors dies, one with more than three dies, one with three stays stable. A dead cell with three live neighbors comes to life.

The Game of Life is fascinating for several reasons. First, it has the characteristics of a Universal Turing Machine, as modeled by Alan Turing, in that it can process any set of well-formed instructions. Second, the complex patterns that emerge from simple rules and an initial set-up has profound implications across a range of sciences. It is important to the study of games because it helps show how simple rules can produce very complex results.

It can be debated whether The Game of Life is, in fact, a game at all: Once the board has been initially set up, there is no player intervention. This has—with some justification—led it to be called a zero-player game, but

The Game of Life is an ideal game for family members of all ages, as winning is slanted more toward luck than skill.

it would be easy to argue that the initial setup of the game board constitutes "playing" the game, even though there are no set goals, nor any winner.

Life, also known as The Game of Life, is also a popular board game. It was first created in 1860 by Milton Bradley under the name The Checkered Game of Life, and as a result of its success, Bradley was able to form the Milton Bradley Games Company; MB Games, which is now a subsidiary of Hasbro. In 1960 the game was resurrected and redesigned for MB Games's centenary. Now called The Game of Life, it is still published today, though there have been design tweaks since the 1960 version.

Players progress along a track, spinning a wheel numbered one to 10, rather than rolling a dice. A choice can be made between paths: career (business in the 1960 version) or college. College places one in debt, but means a higher salary later on. The playing pieces are cars, to which pegs are affixed to represent extra family members when a player has children or gets married. The board features mountains, giving a pleasing three-dimensional feel. Other features include such things as insurance policies, "major life feats" (like climbing Mount Everest), promissory notes, and stock options. Many of the details vary, depending on the version of the game. The 1992 version adds rewards for such things as recycling and learning CPR.

Although players are given many options within the game, it is essentially one of luck, which means that, though essentially competitive, it lets adults and younger children play together without the outcome being preordained, thus making it an ideal family game. This accessibility, combined with the very tactile nature of the board and playing pieces, as well as the fundamental elegance of its design, has made it a family favorite for more than 40 years.

See Also: Game Theory; Hasbro; Human Relationships in Play; Toys and Child Development.

Bibliography. Arnold Arnold, *World Book of Children's Games* (Fawcett, 1972); J.H. Conway, "Game of Life," *Scientific American* (October 1970); Margaret Hofer, *The Games We Played: The Golden Age of Board & Table Games* (Princeton Architectural Press, 2003); Deborah Jaffe, *The History of Toys: From Spinning Tops to Robots* (The History Press, 2006); Robert McConville, *The History of Board Games* (Creative Publications, 1974); Raymond H. Miller, *Inventors and Creators—Milton Bradley* (KidHaven Press, 2004).

Justin Parsler
Brunel University

Lincoln Logs

Lincoln Logs are a set of notched building logs less than an inch in diameter and cut into various lengths; the set also includes windows, doors, and blocks shaped to create roofs and chimneys. Originally crafted of redwood, Lincoln Logs are now made of stained pine. This toy, an enduring commercial success, also reflects significant values of its era and serves as an early example of mass marketing of toys.

Their inventor, John Lloyd Wright, acknowledges the influence of his father, architect Frank Lloyd Wright, in their design. Wright specifically cites as his inspiration a system of floating beams interlocked to opposing piers that his father used while building the Imperial Hotel in

Tokyo. However, some scholars also note Lincoln Logs' similarity to Joel Ellis's 1866 Log Cabin Playhouse and speculate that Wright may have played with this toy as a child. Created between 1916 and 1917, Lincoln Logs emerged just after two other popular construction toys, Tinker Toys and the Erector Set, appeared.

In 1918, Wright began marketing Lincoln Logs through his company, Red Square Toy Company. His original marketing slogan, "Interesting playthings typifying the spirit of America," suggests in several ways the rich mix of cultural influences surrounding Lincoln Logs. First, this toy illustrates how Friedrich Froebel's kindergarten philosophy had spread through Europe and North America by the early 1900s. Catherine and Frank Lloyd Wright used Froebel's theories in educating their children. John Lloyd Wright and his siblings played in a large playroom deliberately filled with every variety of blocks—educational toys inspired by Froebel's "Gifts" for young children.

Lincoln Logs also represent a response to the anxiety many Americans of the Progressive Era felt about urbanization and the resulting changes in American society. This concern triggered an interest in rural pastimes, evinced by the founding of organizations such as the Boy Scouts of America and the Camp Fire Girls, the success of sports marketers such as L.L. Bean, and nostalgia for log cabins. Wright's use of Lincoln's name for his toy evoked an earlier, more simply rural, and in his mind, more egalitarian time, when any boy could grow up to be president. Moreover, the name Lincoln Logs responds to a patriotic urge to "buy American" emerging around World War I.

The popularity of Lincoln Logs continued throughout the 20th century. Made of wood, they were unaffected by the restrictions on materials that curtailed the production of metal toys during World War II. An instant success in 1918, Lincoln Logs reached their peak of popularity in the 1950s, coinciding with the childhood of the baby boom generation and providing an early example of mass marketing for toys. Among the first toys advertised on television, Lincoln Logs were promoted in 1953 on *Pioneer Playhouse*, specifically targeting educated and affluent parents. Since their commercial introduction, over 100 million sets of Lincoln Logs have been sold worldwide.

See Also: Boys' Play; Erector Sets; Froebel, Friedrich; Tinker Toys; United States, 1900 to 1930.

Bibliography. Joan Baxter, *The Archeology of Childhood: Children, Gender and Material Culture* (AltaMira Press, 2005); E. Cho, "Lincoln Logs: Toying With the Frontier Myth," *History Today* (1993); Friedrich Froebel, *Friedrich Froebel's Pedagogics of the Kindergarten: Or, His Ideas Concerning the Play and Playthings of the Child,* Josephine Jarvis, tr. (University Press of the Pacific, 2003); Deborah Jaffe, *The History of Toys: From Spinning Tops to Robots* (The History Press, 2006); Andrew McClary, *Toys With Nine Lives: A Social History of American Toys* (Linnet Books, 1997).

Mary Ruth Moore
University of the Incarnate Word

Lionel

For half a century, Lionel was the leading American manufacturer of electric trains, among the most popular toys for boys during that time. By the 1960s, the era of trains, and the era of Lionel, had passed.

Joshua Lionel Cowen (1877–1965) built his first electric train, the battery-operated Electric Express of 1900, as a store window display. When customers asked to buy not the product but the train advertising it, Cowen founded the Lionel Manufacturing Company. By 1906 Lionel train sets featured authentic detail, three-rail tracks for smooth operation, a wide variety of rolling stock, and transformers that allowed kids (and adults) to control the speed of the trains.

Cowen introduced "0" gauge in 1915, and it came to dominate by the 1930s. In the 1920s, he opened a precision tooling operation in Italy and added gates, lights, stations, and many more accessories. The depression saw the company's first deficit year, 1931, and Lionel went into receivership in 1934 to avoid bankruptcy. During World War II and the 1950s, Lionel prospered.

Lionel became a boy's Christmas wish, and in 1950, Joe DiMaggio hosted the *Lionel Clubhouse* on television. But Americans moved to the suburbs after World War II and later began flying commercial planes across the continent. The Twentieth Century Limited, Pennsylvania Station, and Joshua Lionel Cowen all passed in the 1960s. The Lionel Corporation went bankrupt and sold out to General Mills in 1969.

General Mills licensed the Lionel name and products and put the trainmaker under Model Products

Corporation (MPC). MPC changed the axles and trucks to reduce friction and allow longer trains and in the 1980s it produced "O" gauge trains, scaled 1:48. Lionel LLC produced about $70 million worth of "O" gauge trains a year, 60 percent of the market.

In 1979 General Mills reintroduced the American Flyer, which Lionel bought from bankrupt A.C. Gilbert in 1967 shortly before its own failure. American Flyer produces collectors' items—"S" gauge (1:64) with a two-rail track rather than the three rails used by Lionel.

Shifting of production to Mexico in 1982 alienated fans, who objected to the quality of Mexican trains or to the loss of an 80-year history of American manufacture. Production returned to the United States in 1984.

Collector Richard P. Kughn bought Lionel in 1986. New products and reproductions of prewar trains rekindled Lionel's appeal. Lionel also made its toys more realistic, with more accurate scale and details. A 1989 locomotive electronically produced realistic locomotive sounds.

Out of the train business, Lionel Corporation became a holding company for ventures including Lionel Leisure World, a chain of toy stores. When Lionel Corporation went bankrupt in 1993, Kughn bought the original trademark and no longer operated as a licensee.

Kughn sold out to Lionel, LLC, which continued producing reproductions and developing new lines that were ever more detailed and expensive. Remote control and built-in electronics and speakers added realism. Lionel, LLC owns the Lionel brand and products but has no direct link to the original Lionel Corporation. Since 1995 various licensees have used the Lionel name on their products. In 2001 Lionel ended U.S. production, outsourcing to China and Korea. The backlash was less than that of the Mexican venture.

In 2004 shortages of the popular Polar Express set jacked the $229 price to $449 on eBay. In 2006 the Lionel electric train became the first electric toy inducted into the National Toy Hall of Fame. Also in 2006 Lionel began selling sets through Macy's, Target, FAO Schwarz, and outlets other than the hobby shops where it had been selling them. Sales that year were $62 million.

In 2000 MTH electric trains accused Lionel of misappropriation of trade secrets, and in 2004 the Union Pacific Railroad sued for inappropriate use of the names and logos of Union Pacific and defunct lines it had acquired. Union Pacific received $640,000 and royalties in 2006; MTH received $40.77 million, which was overturned on appeal. Lionel filed for bankruptcy, fired its CEO and 17 other high-level employees, and reemerged from bankruptcy in March 2008. MTH received a reported $12 million.

During its peak in the 1950s, Lionel sold two-thirds of the model trains sold in the United States.

See Also: Boys' Play; United States, 1900 to 1930; United States, 1930 to 1960; United States, 1960 to Present.

Bibliography. Deborah Jaffe, *The History of Toys: From Spinning Tops to Robots* (The History Press, 2006); Andrew McClary, *Toys With Nine Lives: A Social History of American Toys* (Linnet Books, 1997) Lionel Central Stations, www.lionel.com/centralstation/findex.cfm (cited August 2008) Strong Museum; Lionel Trains, Toy Hall of Fame, www.strongmuseum.org (cited August 2008).

John Barnhill
Independent Scholar

Lithuania

Located in northeastern Europe, Lithuania shares borders with the Russian Federation, Poland, Belarus, and Latvia. In medieval times it was a large and powerful kingdom, often joined with Poland, and then became a part of the Russian Empire. In 1918 it gained its independence, but Russia invaded in 1940, the Germans in the following year, and Russia soon afterwards, with Lithuania only becoming independent again in 1990—the first state of Russia to break away, although its independence was not recognized by the world community until 1991.

Since medieval times, and possibly before, the fashioning of clay whistles has been popular in Lithuania. Many are made in the shapes of horses or soldiers for use by boys, or birds or flowers for girls. Kite-flying has also been a pastime for centuries, as has model-making, marbles, Hide-and-Seek, and other almost universal games.

Traditional Lithuanian village pursuits have involved folk dancing and singing. However, with the rise in nationalist awareness in the late 19th century, a writer, Matas Grigonis, started collecting details on games that were intrinsically and culturally Lithuanian, and the result was a book he published in 1911, which contained details on 200 Lithuanian games. There was also a rich Jewish culture in the country that, prior to the Holocaust, had a large and vibrant Jewish population, accounting for as many as 30 percent of the population in some parts of the country. This led to involvement in the Zionist youth group *Hapoel*. One Lithuanian custom has been making birdhouses, which includes using old wagon wheels on the roofs of houses to encourage storks and other birds.

During the Russian Occupation, the Young Pioneer Movement involved many children in hiking and camping in the same manner that the Boy Scout and Girl Guide movements had done before 1939. Wargaming also became popular, and many teenage boys and young men (and also older men) were involved in recreating battles from Lithuania's medieval history, from the Napoleonic Wars or other conflicts. With a large amount of Wargaming literature published in Poland, this has helped Lithuanian Wargamers, as the countries share so much history and heritage. It was not until after independence in 1991 that Wargaming including the 1918–20 and 1940–45 engagements became politically acceptable. As well as Wargaming, many boys and men were also involved in making Wargame dioramas, or designing and making model railways.

Most schoolchildren in Lithuania learn how to play Chess, and among the prominent Lithuanian Chess players have been Markas Luckis (1905–73) and Vladas Mikenas (1910–92), who both competed at the Chess Olympiad at Buenos Aires in 1939. The Lietuvos Sachmatu Federacija continues to oversee Chess in Lithuania. Other indoor games such as card games, Backgammon, and Dominoes also have a following in the country.

See Also: Backgammon; Chess and Variations of; Dominoes and Variations of; Estonia; Kite Flying; Latvia; Poland; Wargames.

Bibliography. Peter J. Babris, *Baltic Youth Under Communism* (Research Publishers, 1967); United States Holocaust Memorial Museum, "Hidden History of the Kovno Ghetto" (United States Holocaust Memorial Museum, 1997); Sarah Ethridge Hunt, *Games and Sports the World Around* (Ronald Press Company, 1964); Sakina Kagda, *Lithuania* (Marshall Cavendish, 1997).

Justin Corfield
Geelong Grammar School

LJN

American toy company LJN operated from 1970 to 1994, when it was folded into parent company Acclaim Entertainment. (The brand was revived in name only in 2000 to publish the Dreamcast video game Spirit of Speed 1937.) Toy executive Jack Friedman left Norman J. Lewis Associates in 1970 to form his own company: LJN are the initials of his former employer, reversed. Though it made its own original toys as well, LJN was best-known as the manufacturer of tie-in toys. They held the license to toys based on the movie *E.T.*, for instance, and the *Thundercats* cartoon—as well as an American license for Voltron toys, *Dune*, *Magnum P.I.*, and *Gremlins*.

They produced the best-selling and still-collectible Wrestling Superstars toys from 1984 to 1989, based on the license from the World Wrestling Federation (now called the WWE). The action figures were known for their accurate representations of the wrestlers, rather than the somewhat cartoonish and simplified facial renderings used in most media tie-in action figures. Different lines of figures (the most popular of which was the eight-inch size) included popular wrestlers like Andre the Giant, Hulk Hogan, Roddy Piper, Big John Studd, the Iron Sheik, Superfly Snuka, King Kong Bundy, Captain Lou Albano, Bobby "the Brain" Heenan, Classy Freddie Blassie, Jimmy Hart, and future governor Jesse "the Body" Ventura.

In 1986, LJN was acquired by Universal and began its entrance into the video game market, producing titles for the then-new Nintendo Entertainment System. When Acclaim Entertainment purchased LJN from Universal at the end of 1988, it decided to focus solely on video games and closed the toy division in the following year. As a video game publisher, LJN focused on media tie-ins, much as it had with its action figures. Licenses included *A Nightmare on Elm Street*, *Back to the Future*, *Beetlejuice*, *Friday the 13th*, the "incredible crash dummies" from safety PSAs, *Jaws*, the *Karate Kid*, Pictionary, the *Punisher*, *Spider-Man*, *Who Framed Roger Rabbit*, the WWF (continuing LJN's association with them, even while the toy license was picked up by Hasbro), and the *X-Men*.

Nintendo limited the number of games a given company could issue at a time as a form of hands-free quality control. Acclaim's ownership of LJN was a way for them to double their output. Unfortunately for LJN, because they were given so many media licenses, they were soon associated with subpar games; because of the limited communication between licenser and licensee during production process, and the rushed nature of media tie-in work, media tie-in games tend as a group to be some of the poorest.

See Also: Action Figures; Boys' Play; Fantasy Play; United States, 1960 to Present.

Bibliography. Elliott Avedon, *The Study of Games* (Krieger Pub., 1979); Sally Ann Berk, *Tomart's Encyclopedia of Action Figures: The 1001 Most Popular Collectibles of All Time* (Black Dog & Leventhal Publishers, 2000); Gerard Jones, *Killing Monsters: Why Children Need Fantasy, Superheroes, and Make-Believe Violence* (Basic Books, 2002); Andy Slaven, *Video Game Bible, 1985–2002* (Trafford Publishing, 2002).

Bill Kte'pi
Independent Scholar

London Bridge

"London Bridge is falling down" or "broken down" is one of the most recognizable children's phrases across the English-speaking world. Generations have known this song both as a game and a nursery rhyme in England and across the world.

The earliest known English text dates from the 18th century (Tommy Thumb's *Pretty Song Book*, 1744). There are some indications that the game dates back further, to the 16th century. It has also been suggested that the origin of the rhyme relates to King Olaf of Norway destroying London Bridge in 1008; there is some debate over the exact date, as it has also been noted as 1014. The rhyme is said to symbolize the many London Bridges that have been built and destroyed in history. Is it also been suggested that the refrain "My fair lady" refers to a tradition and myth that burying a virgin in the foundations of a bridge would ensure its strength.

As a singing game, it is most commonly associated with two children forming an arch by raising and joining their hands to form the bridge. Other children file through the arch in a single file, holding the waist or clothes of the person in front. They all sing the rhyme, and at a certain point, the arch is lowered and a child is caught. The child is asked to choose a side, and they stand behind one of the arches. Children play the game until all children are behind the arches. The game is usually ended by a tug of war to decide which arch wins the game.

Other game variations: When a child is caught the bridge sways the child back and forth until they choose an arch to stand behind. Children captured by the bridge are held in a marked area known as the "Tower of London," and after all children are caught, a game of Tag ensues. The first two children caught by the bridge makers form the arch for the next game. When a child is captured by the bridge they choose which arch maker to replace, the former arch rejoins the other children in the line.

There are a number of verses and variations of the rhyme London Bridge. The most common first verse known in England is:

London Bridge is falling down;
Falling down, falling down,
London Bridge is falling down,
My fair lady.

The first English printed version of London Bridge had five verses. However, the game has been played singing 10 different verses. There also are over 20 other verse variations in English alone.

London Bridge is also known as Broken Bridge (Scotland), *Le Pont Levis* (France), *Die Messner Brucke, Zieh Durch* or *Die Goldene Brucke* (Germany), Charleston Bridge (United States), and *Podul de Piatra* (Romania). Other European countries known to play and have variations of London Bridge include Spain, Holland, Denmark, Italy, and Hungary.

See Also: Cooperative Play; Singing Games; Spontaneous Group Play; Tag.

Bibliography. M. Cooper, *Tommy Thumb's Pretty Song Book* (1744); L. Daiken, *Children's Games Throughout the Year* (Batsford, 1949); Patricia Evans, *Rimbles: A Book of Children's Classic Games, Rhymes, Songs, and Sayings* (Doubleday, 1961); Joe Frost, Sue Wortham, and Stuart Reifel, *Play and Child Development* (Merrill-Prentice Hall, 2006); Glenn Kirchner, *Children's Games Around the World* (Benjamin Cummings, 2000); Nina Millen, *Children's Games From Many Lands* (Friendship Press, 1943).

Anna-Marie Millbank
Independent Scholar

Loo

Loo is a card game played with a standard 52-card deck. It was introduced to England in two forms from France around 1660 and was probably relatively new to France at the time. The name appears in so many different spellings in its early attestations that it is impossible to identify one as a standard, but all were derived from the French *lenterlu*, a nonsense word used in lullabies.

Loo is a trick-taking game for at least five players (and up to 17), and lends itself to sizable gatherings; it has been favored both by gamblers and as a household game (in which form it shows up in the writings of Jane Austen). In both forms of the game—which differ mainly in the number of cards dealt to each player, being three-card Loo and five-card Loo—players try to win tricks from the pool and are "looed" if they fail to do so, forcing them to contribute money (or points) to the pool. Some house rules place a fixed amount on the cost of being looed; gambling establishments often followed the original rule, which called for a looed player to double the amount of the pool, contributing to the game's poor reputation because of the spectacular losses an unlucky player could experience.

In Loo, the jack—a card whose name changes in many card games—is called Pamphilus, a character from Medieval erotic comedies, from whose name the word "pamphlet" (originally a short printed story about his adventures) is derived.

See Also: France; Gambling; History of Playing Cards.

Bibliography. Elliott Avedon, *The Study of Games* (Krieger Pub., 1979); Roger Caillois, *Man, Play and Games* (University of Illinois Press, 2001); David Parlett, *The Oxford Guide to Card Games* (Oxford University Press, USA, 1990).

Bill Kte'pi
Independent Scholar

Luck and Skill in Play

At the most basic level, it seems easy to distinguish between the concepts of luck and skill. Luck can easily be conceptualized by a roll of the dice, with a goal of obtaining some particular result. Skill enters this scenario only in that the roller needs to be able to physically handle the dice and give them a roll. Similarly, skill can easily be conceptualized when thinking of a seasoned bowler lining up to prepare to release the bowling ball, or when thinking of an able gymnast preparing to dismount from the balance beam.

Significant training and attention to the important elements of performing each of these activities will determine the outcome of the performance. Luck may enter either of these scenarios with unexpected and untimely events during performance. For example, at the instant just before the bowler prepares to release the ball or the gymnast dismounts, a loud distraction occurs, causing a shift in focus. But what at first seems easy to distinguish is not so with more thought. The concepts of luck and skill will be explored through this entry, with a particular focus on definitions, types of games available, the impact of luck and skill on performance (with consideration given to differing ability levels), the role in luck and skill as reasons provided for success and failure, and finally, a look at superstitions as a way to attempt to control luck.

Definitions

Before examining these specific constructs and their relationship to games, it is useful to first define them. Luck is defined as "a force that brings good fortune or adversity." Luck is random; its occurrence is unpredictable and random. Conversely, skill is defined as the ability to use one's knowledge effectively and readily in execution or performance, or to exhibit the dexterity or coordination needed to execute learned physical tasks. Experiences via practice and playing are needed to develop skill, although it is true that some are inherently more skilled at certain types of activities than others.

It is important to note that luck can be either positive or negative. That is, someone may experience luck that works in their favor (i.e., good luck), or they may experience luck that works against them (i.e., bad luck). Rather than experiencing skill as either good or bad, one develops some degree of skill in some particular activity. That is, a person can be unskilled, low skilled, moderately skilled, or highly skilled. In terms of conceptualizing these constructs, this distinction points to a fundamental difference: luck tends to be unstable and uncontrollable, while skill is developed over time via concentrated attention and practice and is more stable and controllable.

Types of Games

Whether discussing board games, card games, or physical games, all games can be considered based on the level of skill required and the amount of good luck required to succeed (or the influence of bad luck and its impact on failure). Some games are exclusively games of luck; these include games that do not require any thinking or trained physical ability to perform. Examples of these games would include dice and other games of chance. Some games require both good luck and skill to succeed. In these games, often a chance-based event happens, and then the player applies some strategy or physical skill based on that event. Examples of these games include Poker and Backgammon. Finally, some games are almost exclusively skill-based. To be successful in skill-based games, significant practice of physical skills and/or in-depth knowledge of strategy is needed. Examples of these games include most athletic sports. But, even in games that are strongly skill-based, luck can affect the outcome of the event.

The consideration of luck and skill can also be examined based on the degree of interaction that occurs within a particular activity. Some activities require little interaction with others, whether they are teammates or opponents. These activities are classified as coacting activities, and include such activities as golf, bowling, and single rowing. On the other end of the spectrum are interacting activities; these activities require a high degree of interaction and coordination of team members or opponents, and include activities such as basketball, soccer, and volleyball. Activities in the middle of this continuum are those that require both interaction and coaction, and include sports like baseball and tennis.

Obviously all of these activities require high skill levels for better performances, and luck can play a role in success or failure, as well. However, it can be argued that luck can play a greater role in activities along the interactive end of the continuum. Since luck is uncontrollable and occurs in more dynamic situations, interactive activities are more conducive to the occurrence of luck (either good or bad). That is not to say that luck plays no part in success and failure within coacting activities; certainly luck may come into play in these types of events, as well.

Impact of Luck and Skill

It is believed that there is a certain reliance on skill in the performance of tasks. That is, first and foremost, when explaining someone's performance, their skill level is used as the most important factor. This is especially true among the most highly skilled, even though at that level, luck is still considered to play a role. Tiger Woods has frequently said that an element of luck is involved in any tournament win. With new or novel activities, however, skill is not necessarily used as the main element explaining performance. Indeed, when performing some new activity, successes are often explained with a larger degree or emphasis on luck, compared to explaining success of an activity that is not new or novel. For example, consider the father-daughter duo that hears about the ancient sport of Irish road bowling and heads out to the course to give it a try. They end up in third place at the end of the event, placing above some teams that have more experience. When explaining this outcome, many will believe that luck played some role in their outcome. Some may also say that they have a knack, or an inherent natural ability for the sport. For more definitive explanations of skill, more experience will be needed.

When these two constructs are examined closely, it becomes clear that where skill and luck differ can be difficult to determine. Good luck can certainly help a performer have a successful outcome, even over a more skilled opponent. Indeed, most would agree that skill deficiencies can sometimes be overcome with other elements of performance, including luck. But, it is believed that given multiple occurrences or competitions, the more skilled opponent will prevail most often, as instances of luck will be unpredictable and sporadic.

Luck and Skill Preferences

When examining preferences for activities that tend to be more luck or skill based, males, when compared to females, prefer activities that are more skill based, rather than luck based. That is, when given choices about what activities to engage in, males more often than females will choose games that require skill for success. In these skill activities, males also tend to have a greater expectancy of success than females. This increased expectancy is important, as it is believed to also contribute to levels of persistence when encountering difficulty in completing activities. With luck-based activities, generally no gender preferences are evident. That is, both males and females tend to choose luck-based activities at the same rate.

Attributions

The concepts of luck and skill are major players in a theory of motivation developed by Bernard Weiner called

Some games are exclusively games of luck and do not require any thinking or physical ability to perform. Winning on a slot machine is purely a matter of luck, as they are programmed to pay out a certain percentage of the money wagered.

attribution theory. In this theory, future activity involvement and performance are predicted based on the reasons individuals give for the results of past performances. And, regardless of the specific reasons, it is believed that these explanations can be classified along internal or external dimensions. Luck is an external dimension; it is very difficult to control luck or cause luck. Ability is an internal dimension; in most cases, through effort, practice, and good instruction, people can improve their ability to perform.

For an illustration of these attributional categories, imagine a situation where a tennis player loses a tennis match on a very windy day against an opponent she typically defeats handily. This player might attribute the loss to external circumstances (i.e., the wind), rather than her ability, which is internal. She might consider having to play on such a windy day as an unlucky occurrence, and thus since such windy days are rare, she would expect a win the next time she plays this opponent. Indeed, with the attribution of the loss to luck, which is considered uncontrollable and unstable, this player will probably have future expectancies of success against this opponent, regardless of condition. On the other hand, this player may attribute the loss to her ability (or more appropriately, her inability) to play in the wind. She may believe that she has not practiced enough under windy circumstances, acknowledging that on the rare windy days, she often has cancelled her practice sessions. In this case, the loss is explained internally, and this player will probably take advantage of opportunities to practice and develop her ability to play in windy conditions in the future.

Attempting to Control Luck

While it is generally accepted that luck is uncontrollable and unpredictable, there are some, particularly athletes, who may try to control the occurrence of luck through the use of superstitions. Superstitions are held when someone believes some unrelated action has an impact on performance. A fairly common superstition in sport consists of wearing certain clothing during competitions. A rather well-known example is that of Michael Jordan wearing University of North Carolina shorts under his NBA shorts during games. The purpose of superstitions can be tied to the invocation of good luck, as the user is attempting to increase the likelihood of a good performance or win as a result of the superstitious behavior.

Summary

Thus, while at first it seems easy to distinguish between luck and skill in play activities, when taking closer look, it is apparent that these concepts are not easily delineated. At many levels of play, both luck and skill have a role in determining outcomes. The extent of those roles may be debated, and participants may disagree as to how much of a particular result was because of luck and/or skill. The intriguing conclusion is that, when everything is said and done, it may never be known how much of a result was because of skill, and how much was because of luck. This sentiment is reflected in the well-known quote from Samuel Goldwyn, "The harder I work, the luckier I get."

See Also: Backgammon; Bowling; Boys' Play; Gambling; Girls' Play; Original Play; Piaget and Play.

Bibliography. Paul Davis, "A Consideration of the Normative Status of Skill in the Purposive Sports," *Sport, Ethics, and Philosophy* (v.1/1, April 2007); Kay Deaux, Leonard White, and Elizabeth Farris, "Skill Versus Luck: Field and Laboratory Studies of Male and Female Preferences," *Journal of Personality and Social Psychology* (v.32, 1975); Robert Simon, "Deserving to be Lucky: Reflections on the Role of Luck and Desert in Sports," *Journal of Philosophy in Sport* (v.34, 2007); Robert Weinberg and Dan Gould, *Foundations of Sport and Exercise Psychology* (Human Kinetics, 2007).

Jessie Daw
Northern State University

M

Mahjong

Mahjong (alternately spelled Mah-jongg) is a Chinese tile game with mysterious beginnings—experts suggest alternate dates for the conception of the game—but has a promising future with worldwide competitions and leagues. Mahjong has transcended cultures, finding popularity from Argentina to South Africa, and bringing people together from all walks of life to enjoy this game on the internet, in tournaments, in parks, and in Mahjong parlors.

Historians agree that Mahjong evolved from older Chinese card games that were played for money; however, there is a debate about when and how the game was developed, because there is no early documentation on the game. Mahjong resembles many other ancient Chinese games, particularly card games such as *Ya Pai* or gambling games, because the symbols on the Mahjong tiles represent the currency that was once used in place of cards.

Erwei Dong claims that the game was developed by Confucius around 500 B.C.E., whereas Jelte Rep writes that Mahjong was formally developed in 1846. He asserts that Chen Yu-men, an imperial servant and diplomat from Ningbo, combined different card games and introduced tiles in place of cards. During the Cultural Revolution in China beginning in 1966, Mahjong was targeted as a tradition that led to corruption because of the gambling involved; the ban was lifted in 1998. As a result of the ban, traditional rules were abandoned, and the Chinese adopted the newer rules of Hong Kong, where Mahjong had become a game for young people. In 1998 Mahjong was officially recognized as a sport and international tournament rules were created.

Mahjong may have been reintroduced to Europe instead of making a first appearance in the 1920s. According to Stewart Cullin, Mahjong was introduced to Europe in 1895 with the name of Kahnhoo by W.H. Wilkinson. However, Kahnhoo did not succeed as Mahjong did, which may have been because of its similarity to the currently popular game of Dominoes. In the 1920s, Mahjong reached its height of popularity worldwide when expatriates returned home to introduce the game, with spectacular results.

American Joseph Park Babcock introduced Mahjong to the United States in the 1920s, where it became an instant hit after he Americanized the rules and tile markings. L.L. Harr, an Englishman, returned to Great Britain to introduce the game he knew as *Pe-Ling*. It became immediately popular with the royal court and Mahjong clubs sprang up everywhere. Harr and Babcock were at odds over the rules of the game and a rivalry was formed: Harr went so far as to campaign

Although it uses tiles instead of cards, Mahjong is similar to Western-style card games such as Rummy.

against Babcock's interpretation of the rules. Today, there are a variety of rules that exist for playing Mahjong, though in tournaments an agreed-upon standard is always used.

In 1923, a man from Amsterdam known by the initials J.P. wrote a letter to the editor of a Dutch paper in order to find out more about the game of Mahjong. When no one knew of it, the firm Perry & Co. of Amsterdam contacted the Dutch branch of their American company and immediately began selling the game in Amsterdam. Soon the Netherlands Mah-Jongg League was founded and the game extended to the Dutch colonies.

In Japan, a soldier named Saburo Hirayama, who had learned the game in China, opened a Mahjong school in 1924, which led to the formation of the Japanese Mahjong League. This league decided on uniform rules for the country. In 1931 Mahjong was forbidden in Japan during their war with China, but people still played. In the 1980s, Japanese gangs in the United States were involved in running games such as Mahjong in Californian Poker rooms.

At the end of the 1920s, America's love for Mahjong faltered as new games were developed. Recently there has been a resurgence with the American Mah-Jongg Association formed in 1999. The first World Championship in Mahjong was held in 2002, and in 2005 the European Mahjong Association formed and held the first Open European Mahjong Tournament in the Netherlands. Countries that belong to the European Mahjong Association include Austria, Denmark, Finland, France, Germany, Hungary, Italy, the Netherlands, Russia, Slovakia, Spain, and Sweden. The Mahjong World Series Tournament started in 2007, to be held annually, with cash prizes offered to winners.

The worldwide love affair with Mahjong began in the early 1920s and the game has become popular again across the globe with the advent of online game-playing. Web sites offer free play of Mahjong where a user can play alone or enter a tournament online with other players. These Web sites offer socialization through chat rooms, similar to the socialization available in a Mahjong parlor or a group of friends playing together on a rainy day. Mahjong continues to bring people from different backgrounds together, whether online or at world tournaments.

See Also: Ancient China; Dominoes and Variations of; Japan; Gambling; United States, 1900 to 1930.

Bibliography. American Mah-Jongg Association, www.amja.net (cited June 2008); Stewart Culin, "The Game of Ma-Jong," *The Brooklyn Museum Quarterly* (October 1924); Erwei Dong, "Games, Toys, and Pastimes," *The Greenwood Encyclopedia of World Popular Culture* (Greenwood Press, 2003); European Mahjong Association, mahjong-europe.org (cited June 2008); European Mahjong Association, "Member Organizations," mahjong-europe.org/nations (cited July 2008); Jelte Rep, *The Great Mahjong Book: History, Lore and Play* (Tuttle Publishing, 2007); Takeshobo Co., Ltd., *Competition Mahjong Official International Rule Book* (Mahjong Museum 1998); William N. Thompson, "President's Commission on Organized Crime," *Gambling in America: An Encyclopedia of History, Issues, and Society* (ABC-CLIO, 2001); World Mahjong Limited, www.world-series-mahjong.com (cited June 2008).

Michelle Martinez
Sam Houston State University

Malaysia

In Malaysia, the majority Malay community, the Chinese, the Indians, and the Europeans have all contributed in different ways to the wide and diverse number of pastimes available in the country. The nation consisted of a number of kingdoms until the arrival of the British, who established colonial rule over the region in a myriad of guises, resulting in the establishment of the Straits Settlements (which included Singapore), the state of Johor, the Federated Malay States, the Unfederated Malay States, North Borneo (ruled by the North Borneo Company), and Sarawak (technically independent, but with a British rajah). The first four, with the exception of Singapore, came together to form Malaya in 1957, and they all came together as the Federation of Malaysia in 1963; Singapore left the area in 1965.

The games played by the Malay community have included bull-fighting and other tests of strength. However, many traditional pursuits persist, including dancing, playing music, and *Main Wau*, the making and flying kites. Kites tends to be more popular in the northern states of West Malaysia, especially in Kelantan, although they can be found throughout the country. Their shape is unique to Malaysia, with a central support holding together a large sideways oval piece of stretched cloth, and a curved tail in the shape of a bow. Shadow puppets (*wayang kulit*) are also common, and many children make their own puppets from cardboard. There are also board games such as the game *Main Rimau* (Tiger Game), which is especially popular in Kelantan. Another game which dates back to at least the 17th century—it is mentioned in the *Sejarah Melayu* by Tun Sri Lanang—is *Sepak Raga*, played with a ball made from woven rattan that has to be kept in the air for as long as possible. The version now often played by schools and community groups is *Sepak Tackraw*, with two opposing teams rather than a number of individual players. Other Malay games include *Belaga Buah Keras*, played by two people and mainly in Pahang, and *Tebar Jala* (Throwing the Casting Net), particularly good for small children.

In the Chinese community, Chinese games are mainly played, especially Mahjong, with sessions lasting many hours, often from the afternoon to early the following morning. Chinese Chess is also still very popular, in spite of the easy availability of Indian/European Chess. Most Chinese games are played indoors, although children—Chinese, Malay, Indian and European—can be seen in the streets role-playing, playing Hide-and-Seek, playing Hopscotch, or more commonly now, playing soccer. Badminton and, to a lesser extent, volleyball, have also become extremely popular, as has Ping Pong, especially among Chinese teenagers.

The British brought large numbers of recreational sports with them to Malaya, and there are amateur cricket clubs and places for playing rugby, golf, and polo. The former British clubs such as the Selangor Club and the Malacca Club provide a venue for many games. There are now also many youth clubs around the country being used for billiards, darts, and access to jukeboxes and pinball machines. There are also amusement arcades in some cities, especially Kuala Lumpur, and a number of bowling alleys.

Because of the great demand for gambling games, and the desire of the police to regulate them, Assistant Police Commissioner C.T. Dobree wrote a detailed study of these gambling games—those involving lotteries, cards, dominoes, dice and others, which was published in 1955 to help magistrates differentiate between contested gambling cases they were hearing.

Although the London version of Monopoly was heavily played in Malaysia in the 1960s, a Malaysian version, with Kuala Lumpur and Putrajaya, was produced. The success of the three films of *The Lord of the Rings* (2001–03) briefly led to great interest in *Dungeons & Dragons*, but this has largely given way to the proliferation of Western computer games in Malaysia, which, because of the affluence of the country, have come to dominate the lives of many children, especially those in Kuala Lumpur and other big cities such as Georgetown and Johor Bahru. Most of these focus on Western simulations, although there has recently been an increase in the number made incorporating Chinese themes, which have proved popular, especially with Chinese boys.

See Also: China; *Dungeons & Dragons*; Indonesia; Kite Flying; Mahjong; Monopoly and Variations of; Rugby; Soccer (Amateur) Worldwide.

Bibliography. C. Bazell, "The Rules for Some Common Malay Games," *Journal of the Malayan Branch of the Royal Asiatic Society* (November, 1928); C.T. Dobree, *Gambling Games of Malaya* (Caxton Press, 1955); A.H. Hill, "Some Kelantan Games and Entertainments," *Journal of the Malayan Branch of the Royal Asiatic Society* (August 1952); N.J. Ryan, *The Cultural Heritage of Malaya* (Longman, 1971); Mubin Sheppard, *Living Crafts of Malaysia* (Times Books International, 1978).

Justin Corfield
Geelong Grammar School

Maple Story

Maple Story is considered the classic success story of the free MMORPG (Massively Multiplayer Online Roleplaying Game) cluster, only bowing to Runescape in terms of popularity in Europe and America. It has over 50 million users worldwide and servers in 14 different locations, making it one of the most broadly disseminated games online. Maple Story is available as a free-to-play, Internet browser-based game, although a small download is initially required for the game to function. Unusually for an MMORPG, the game is two-dimensional in appearance and runs on a side-scrolling platform. This is allows for the low graphical complexity of the game to function on many machines; like Runescape, one of Maple Story's great strengths is that many low-performing computers can cope with the game engine, and thus it is disseminated in a far wider context than many other MMORPGs which require top-end processors and graphics cards to run.

Maple Story follows the conventions of most role-playing games. The player takes control of an avatar and completes quests or kills monsters in order to gain experience points, equipment, and treasure. At level eight or 10, players are able to choose a class—warrior, bowman, mage, or thief (pirate is also available in some versions), and are allowed to assign points gained through levelling in order to specialize within each class. As with most MMORPGs, these classes teach a series of specific abilities that players use to create characters with diverse skills. These allow players to form a character that is specialized in one area, rather than a master of all talents, in a direct echo of the class system created by the progenitor of all MMORPGs, *Dungeons & Dragons*. Interestingly, the ability to become a healing class, one of the staple abilities for many MMORPGs, is not available until level 30. Joining groups or forming more long-term relationships by forming guilds with other players is possible, but the game does not place as much emphasis on group play; this is a result both of the age bracket targeted and the capabilities of the game itself.

Maple Story has been criticized for the fact that despite advertising itself as "free-to-play," users buy in-game currency (Mesos) with real money in order to buy themselves more powerful equipment, to change their appearance, and to purchase vanity objects such as pets. The act of charging players for secondary services either within or to improve the game's performance is, in fact, a relatively common action in nonsubscription games; Runescape and Silkroad Online provide premier servers to paying members, and Second Life (although not technically a game) functions almost wholly through the trade of Linden for real money (and vice versa). As with many free-to-play MMORPGs, the game tends to attract younger players who are not able to sustain the cost of playing subscription MMORPGs such as World of Warcraft. The content, narrative, and actions undertaken within the game tend to reflect this, including the formation of less complex social structures.

The game is represented through anime-style graphics as well as expressing visual, narratological, and ludic conventions familiar to both the anime and role-playing game genres. However, the play style is often criticized for the excessive amount of "grinding" (repeated activity of the same task to gain experience or coin) needed to progress; a strategy used by many free-to-play MMORPGs to retain players and, sometimes, to cover a lack of narrative complexity. Overall, however, the game's popularity suggests that despite these aspects, it provides a satisfying ludic experience that is supported by the huge amount of players around the world.

See Also: *Dungeons & Dragons*; Role-Playing; Runescape; Silkroad Online; World of Warcraft.

Bibliography. Steven L. Kent, *The Ultimate History of Video Games: The Story Behind the Craze That Touched Our Lives and Changed the World* (Three Rivers Press, 2001); Daniel Mackay, *The Fantasy Role-Playing Game: A New Performing Art* (McFarland & Company, 2001); Maple Story, www.maplestory.com (cited July 2008); Lawrence Schick, *Heroic Worlds: A History and Guide to Role Playing Games* (Prometheus Books, 1991); J. Patrick Williams et al., eds., *Gaming As Culture: Essays on Reality, Identity and Experience in Fantasy Games* (McFarland, 2006).

Esther MacCallum-Stewart
University of East London

Marbles

People have been playing with marbles since ancient times. These small, solid spheres are among the oldest playthings discovered. The first "marbles" may have been round seeds and nuts, gathered from the ground and rolled or thrown. Marbles is a game rich in tradition and lore. The game has been played in much the same way throughout history, and its traditions have been passed down through countless generations to the present day, when it is played in schoolyards, streets, parks and wherever there is space to play freely and to scratch a ring in the ground.

No one knows when marbles were first used in play, but archaeological evidence suggests they have been around for at least 5,000 years. The oldest marbles discovered, a set of small stone balls and rectangular blocks dating from 4000 B.C.E, were found in the grave of a child in Nagada, Egypt. The blocks may have been used to form an arch through which the marbles were rolled. Marbles-type games played with nuts and knucklebones are mentioned in Ancient Greek and Roman literature, and Roman soldiers, playing games for recreation, carried marbles with them throughout the empire.

Marbles was a popular pastime with European children in the 16th to 18th centuries. Pieter Breughel's painting, *Children's Games* (1560) includes two groups of children playing different marbles games, and the game Cherry Pit is mentioned in Shakespeare's *Twelfth Night*. Children's games were popular motifs with Dutch tile makers of the 17th and 18th centuries. Several marbles games have been identified among the hand-painted illustrations on Dutch wall tiles.

The invention of marbles "scissors" in the mid-1800s generated the first German glass marbles, and in 1884 the invention of the first automatic marble-making machine by Samuel C. Dyke in Akron, Ohio, led to the mass production of clay marbles, and finally to the production of the glass marbles children play with today.

Anyone who has played Marbles as a child will remember it as a "seasonal" game, suddenly appearing in the playground and disappearing just as mysteriously. The game is as popular, noisy, and lively today as it was in years gone by, although the passion some children feel as competitive players and avid marble collectors can sometimes lead to disagreements, resulting in the game being banned from the playground. Strict rules govern Marbles tournaments, the competitions for adults and children held annually in several parts of the world. The oldest of these is the British and World Marble Championship, which began in the 16th century and is held every Easter at Tinsley Green in Sussex, England.

The lore of the game has been adapted to new ways of playing. Terms common in the 1950s like *dub up, fudging, spans, knuckle down,* and even *taw,* are not so familiar to children now. Instead, there are new terms, like *gutters, bombs, takeovers,* and *shooter*. Of course, the lore varies from place to place, and according to the game being played.

The movements of people across the globe have enriched the game and added to the lore. The Chinese Flick, where a marble is catapulted by bending the middle finger back and letting it go, is used in some playgrounds while in others flicking has entirely disappeared, with players simply bowling marbles along the ground. The decrease in flicking can be seen as a "de-skilling" of the game. In years gone by, anyone who could not flick a marble was at a real disadvantage.

The richest lore is to be found in playgrounds that foster a very strong Marbles culture. Children have names for different types of marbles, based on color and patterning—names like Froggies, Cat's Eyes, Spaghettis, and Ice Cream Jellies. Each marble has a swapping value in relation to the others, and the children also identify marbles by size.

Walk into any toy shop today, and chances are you will find marbles for sale, especially "in season." However, the encroachment of buildings, sealed surfaces, and landscaped gardens onto children's playing areas makes

Marbles can be played "for fair" (all marbles returned to owner) or "for keeps" (winner keeps, loser weeps).

it difficult to find places to dig holes, play "tracks," and draw rings in the dirt for a game of Marbles. Children have to adapt as best they can or give up and find something else to play.

See Also: Ancient Egypt; Ancient Greece; Ancient Rome; Europe, 1600 to 1800.

Bibliography. Iona Opie and Peter Opie, *Children's Games with Things* (Oxford University Press, London, 1997); Marble Museum: Origin of the Game: www.marblemuseum.org/originofgame.html (cited August 2008); American Toy Marble Museum, "A Brief History of the Birth of the Modern American Toy Industry in Akron, Ohio," www.americantoymarbles.com/akronhist.htm (cited August 2008).

Judy McKinty
Independent Scholar

Marco Polo

Marco Polo is the name of a popular game played by children in a swimming pool. The reason why this popular form of Hide-and-Seek has been named after Marco Polo—the famous Italian traveller who went to the court of the Great Khan of China together with his father and uncle in 1271 C.E.—are not known. Whether the name alludes to the exploratory character of the game and of Polo's travels or not, there are several variants of this game in the Americas, Australia, and the United Kingdom, and some have alternate names, such as Mermaid on Rocks, or Alligator. The game may also be played on dry ground by slightly adapting its rules.

Marco Polo seems to be an easily modifiable game, which can be defined as a game of verbal call-and-response. One of the three or more players in Marco Polo is "it" and must locate the other players by using their voice and their hearing. "It" shouts "Marco," and the other players must respond by shouting "Polo." Once "it" manages to find one of the other players, that player becomes "it." In more complex variants, the other players can get out of the swimming pool (Mermaid on Rocks).

Marco Polo is also a location-based game, not just because "it" is confined to a specific space, but also because "it" must locate the other players by using auditory clues. In this game, there is bipolarity in the reversal of roles; in other words, players take turn in being "it," there are repeated actions, a routine to be repeated, rules to be observed, and verbal signals to be used. What is more, since, as Vygotsky has pointed out, by playing we experiment, or learn to play out different social roles, through Marco Polo, children may be able to learn what it means to be a social outcast (as "it" in the game, isolated, confined to a specific space, and unable to "see" the others).

Marco Polo is such a well-known game in the United States that characters playing Marco Polo often feature in American cartoons, television series, films, and commercials. Characters are usually shown cheating, misunderstanding, changing, or ignoring the rules of Marco Polo, which has the effect of producing hilarity in the audience. For example, Bart Simpson of *The Simpsons* has been shown cheating at the game, or in an ironic sequence, revolutionary leaders (most of whom) turned dictators play Marco Polo in the *Family Guy*. In some cases the terms used are not *Marco* and *Polo* but, to comic effect, a show catchphrase, as in *South Park*.

Indeed, games online are sometimes defined as "marco polo" games, when players make call-and-response exchanges.

See Also: Hide & Seek; Play as Learning, Anthropology of; Spontaneous Group Play; Water Play.

Bibliography. J.S. Bruner, A. Jolly, and K. Sylva, eds., "Nature and Uses of Immaturity," *Play, Its Role in Development and Evolution* (Basic Books, 1976); Joe Frost, Sue Wortham, and Stuart Reifel, *Play and Child Development* (Merrill-Prentice Hall, 2006); Catherine Garvey, *Play* (Harvard University Press, 1990); L.S. Vygotsky, *Mind in Society* (Harvard University Press, 1978).

Maria Beatrice Bittarello
Independent Scholar

Mario

Mario, Nintendo's leading man, is arguably the most recognizable playable character in video game history and has been inducted into the Guinness Book of World Records as the most prolific video game character by starring in over 116 distinct video game titles, not including remakes or rereleases. Though he started in 1981 as a nondescript barrel jumper in Donkey Kong, he quickly received his own game, teaming with brother Luigi in the 1983 Mario Bros. arcade game. Here, he debuted his occupation as an Italian plumber to set the stage for eradicating pests from pipes. Though he still usually incorporates pipes, Mario has moved out of the sewer and into the Mushroom Kingdom to save princesses, particularly Princess Toadstool/Princess Peach, since the 1985 release of Super Mario Bros. for the Nintendo Entertainment System (NES).

Super Mario Bros. was placed in the Guinness Book of World Records as the best-selling video game of all-time. The Super Mario Bros. series is also in the Guinness Book of World Records as the best-selling video game series of all time, with over 155.4 million copies sold worldwide. The series has been re-released for every Nintendo platform, with the latest being the Wii.

Typically, Mario collects coins as he navigates various worlds, including on land, in the sea, and in the air, in order to save a princess. Mario has battled various characters, but his arch nemeses remain Bowser/King Koopa, and Wario, who premiered in Super Mario Land 2: Six Golden Coins, but has gone on to star in his own games including the Wario Land series and the WarioWare series.

However, Mario isn't linked to only side-scrolling platform games like Super Mario Bros. He stars in an ensemble Nintendo cast in diverse games like Super Smash Bros., a fighting game; Mario Kart, a racing game; Super Mario Strikers, a soccer game; Paper Mario, a role-playing game (RPG); and Mario Party, an electronic board game that includes minigames. These game series have been released and re-released on a variety of Nintendo consoles and handhelds from the NES to the Wii, from the Game Boy to the DS.

In addition to video games, Mario has branched out into comics with Super Mario Adventures (an anthology of comics from Nintendo Power) and television with series like The Super Mario Bros. Super Show! He also stars in the 1993 film *Super Mario Bros*. This was the first movie to be based on a video game and stars Bob Hoskins as Mario. Super Mario Bros. also made a significant appearance in the *Wizard* (1989), which unveiled Super Mario Bros. 3 and the Power Glove.

For 10 years, Mario's marketing rival was Sega's Sonic the Hedgehog, who first appeared in 1991. But this ended with Sega losing the console market and creating games for Nintendo's platform, starting with the 2001 Sonic Adventure 2: Battle. Mario and Sonic can now be seen competing side by side in Mario & Sonic at the Olympic Games.

As the main man of the Nintendo powerhouse, Mario has a long life ahead of him. At 18 years old and having conquered over 10 gaming platforms, Mario is still going strong.

See Also: Arcades; Legend of Zelda; Mortal Kombat; Sonic the Hedgehog; Tomb Raider.

Bibliography. *Guinness World Records: Gamer's Edition 2008* (Guinness World Records Limited, 2008); Steven L. Kent, *The Ultimate History of Video Games: The Story Behind the Craze that Touched Our Lives and Changed the World* (Three Rivers Press, 2001); David Sheff, *Game Over: Press Start to Continue: The Maturing of Mario* (Cyberactive Media Group, 1999).

Cathlena Martin
University of Florida

Matchbox

Matchbox cars are die-cast toys produced by Mattel. The name comes from the toy's original packaging—a small box like a matchbox—when the toys were first produced in 1953 by British toy company Lesney Products. The packaging led to another distinctive feature of the toys: because each was produced to fit the same size package, the scale varied by vehicle, an unusual choice at a time when so many model toys were produced at precise scales like 1:87 or 1:43.

But Matchbox toys were toys, meant to be played with—they just happened to be far more detailed, and made as replicas of specific makes and models of cars rather than just generic vehicles. The low price and attention to detail made Matchbox both a value-added brand name and a household name, a toy available to and owned by every child. The brand had no serious competition in either the United Kingdom or the United States until 1968, when Mattel (not yet the owner of the Matchbox brand) introduced Hot Wheels. Other companies had tried to out-Matchbox Matchbox. Hot Wheels matched the competing brand in level of detail but focused on cus-

Matchbox cars grew in popularity because they were detailed and made to replicate specific makes and models.

tom versions of real-life car models, and show cars—as well as the distinctive feature of low-friction wheels that made the cars ideal for racing on toy tracks.

The brand was an extraordinary success, and Matchbox adopted low-friction wheels in 1970, followed by a number of special lines—the Super Kings and Speed Kings were built larger than traditional Matchbox cars, and with wider (more raceable) wheels, while the Scorpions were rechargeable electric cars (out Hot Wheeling Hot Wheels). The brand lost ground only for a few years, and by the mid-1970s, Matchbox was the leading toy car again. Aircraft, ships, and science fiction lines followed, but Lesney Products fell on hard times when the British economy receded in the late 1970s. The company went into receivership, and the Matchbox brand was sold to a group that eventually became reorganized as Matchbox International, going public on the New York Stock Exchange in 1986. The company was sold to Tyco Toys in 1992, which was then acquired by Mattel in 1997.

Both Hot Wheels and Matchbox cars continue to be sold, and Matchbox continues to be a die-cast product and a popular collectible.

See Also: Airfix; Boys' Play; Meccano; Models.

Bibliography. Roger Caillois, *Man, Play and Games* (University of Illinois Press, 2001); Joe Frost, Sue Wortham, and Stuart Reifel, *Play and Child Development* (Merrill-Prentice Hall, 2006); Deborah Jaffe, *The History of Toys: From Spinning Tops to Robots* (The History Press, 2006); Andrew McClary, *Toys With Nine Lives: A Social History of American Toys* (Linnet Books, 1997); Brian Sutton-Smith, *The Ambiguity of Play* (Harvard University Press, 2001).

Bill Kte'pi
Independent Scholar

Maypole Dancing

The maypole dance, which is among the oldest fertility dances, is a circular dance steeped with mystical symbolism, where individuals of one sex take possession of individuals of another sex by circling and enclosing them. Dancers perform a circular dance, holding colored ribbons attached to a pole decorated with flowers and greenery representing a tree. Ribbons become intertwined onto the pole or into a web around the pole in the circular course, and players then retrace their steps in reversed order to unravel the ribbons. The maypole folk dance traditionally as a fertility dance is associated with May Day (May 1) and the Swedish Midsummer Day (the Saturday closest to June 24).

May Day is a cross-quarter day marking the midpoint of the Sun's progress between the vernal equinox and the summer solstice that celebrates the return of spring and verdure. Midsummer Day, celebrating the summer solstice, is an ancient pagan festival, transformed by Christian traditions into St. John the Baptist's Day. However, when cultures did not permit dancing between unmarried men and women during the season between the sowing and the harvest, maypole dancing provided an acceptable alternative to dancing forbidden by religious creed.

In England, maypole dances date back to the May Day revels of Plantagenet kings, who ruled from 1154 to 1485. Maypoles were erected on village greens, using public funds, and were decorated with garlands, flowers, and colored ribbons. Milkmaids, instead of carrying pails on their heads, wore garlands of flowers and ribbons, and danced to bagpipe or fiddle music. Feasting, games, and sporting contests occurred after the maypole dance when men and women competed for kisses. During the Renaissance, dramatic characters participated in spectacular performances of popular stories including "Robin Hood and his Merry Company," and "Jack in the Green." Morris dancers performed English folk dances based upon rhythmic stepping and choreographed figures that frequently concluded with a maypole circular dance to the tune of "Sellinger's Round" (1670).

During the early 20th century, some all-women's colleges in the United States adopted maypole dances as part of elaborate May Day celebrations. In the southern United States, a superstition related to May Day celebrations dictated that if you were to go out at sunrise and look into a pond or pool of water, you would see the reflection of your love, or if you made a wish, it would come true. In the United States, "May Morning" festivities for children celebrated the coming of spring in the ancient Roman tradition when flowers are in bloom.

During the *ballo della cordella* in Italy, a pole is placed into the ground to symbolize the living tree that is sanctified as a fertility center to be danced around. This variation of the maypole dance has been attributed to the erotic festival *Ludi Florales* held in ancient Rome from April 28 to May 2 as part of the annual Flora cult. In Scandinavian celebrations, the Maypole has cross-arms that are decorated with wreaths and occasionally wooden figures. Dancers perform circle dances around a tall pole decorated with garlands, painted stripes, flowers, flags, and emblems. This tradition dates back to the 18th century, and was derived from French and Italian "art" dance forms that were transplanted into England. A ceremonial queen was chosen to preside over the celebration and maypole dance in the Germanic tradition practiced in France, Austria, and Germany. Basque sword dancers often conclude performances with *cinta dantza*—a fast-paced ribbon wind around a maypole.

See Also: Ancient Rome; Europe, 1200 to 1600; Folk Dancing; Morris Dancing.

Bibliography. Jamake Highwater, *Dance: Rituals of Experience* (Oxford University Press, USA, 1996); Sarah Ethridge Hunt, *Games and Sports the World Around* (Ronald Press Company, 1964); Essaka Joshua, *The Romantics and the May Day Tradition (The Nineteenth Century Series)* (Ashgate, 2007); Michael Prestwich, *Plantagenet England 1225–1360 (New Oxford History of England)* (Oxford University Press, USA, 2007); Curt Sachs, *World History of the Dance*, (W.W. Norton & Co., 1937).

Meredith Eliassen
San Francisco State University

Mazes

A maze consists of a series of lines that create a pattern involving a path or series of paths. A maze pattern can be adapted to any geometric shape and be constructed with straight or curved lines, or even a combination of both. The design of a maze may be unicursal, where the path does not offer any choices, or it could be in a branching design, which provides a series of alternate pathways. Both designs have been used for centuries in architecture, art, literature, toys, games, and even as tests of intelligence. Mazes can be one-dimensional and carved or drawn on a flat surface, or they may be three-dimensional and built using stone, wood, or even a cornfield. The patterns in mazes can be aesthetically pleasing, or they may present a puzzle that challenges players to find their way through the maze, which is as mentally stimulating as it is entertaining. Since mazes may be any size and shape and can be constructed from virtually any material, the applications for mazes are almost limitless.

Historical Examples

Archeologists have found examples of mazes of all shapes and sizes throughout the ancient world. Maze designs have been uncovered in such countries as Greece, Italy, Switzerland, England, France, Egypt, the United States, Mexico, Norway, Iceland, and Finland. There are also examples on the African continent. These ancient mazes range from designs on coins and in various types of artwork to maze patterns created by using turf, pebbles, and even larger stones. The applications of these mazes were highly varied, and the purposes of some are still being debated today. Mazes have been found in mosaic pavements, carved into hillsides, on religious and other artifacts, and in many temples, churches, and cathedrals; evidence of maze structures has been found both inland and along many coastlines, fueling speculation that these were used for navigational purposes.

Mazes are also present in literature from different countries and different genres; probably the most famous example is the myth of Theseus and the Minotaur, where Theseus's life depends upon his ability to master the complex pathways of the labyrinth (a word often used interchangeably with maze), defeat the Minotaur, and escape Crete. Mazes appear in works of fiction and nonfiction, and have been studied by archeologists, sociologists, and psychologists.

Mazes have been found in mosaic pavements, carved into hillsides, on artifacts, in many temples, churches, and cathedrals, and are often part of a garden design, using hedges to create a life-size maze.

Maze Applications

The psychological applications of mazes include using them to test the intelligence of the subject, which can be human or an animal such as a mouse. Psychologists analyze such data as the length of time it takes the subject to complete the maze, how many times the subject came to a dead end and had to backtrack, and whether the subject was able to use memory and learning to complete the maze faster on subsequent trials.

Perhaps the most well-known use of mazes is for entertainment, and there are many types of puzzles, games, and toys that incorporate mazes or maze patterns. A circular maze game that players held in their hands, tilting it back and forth to roll marbles through the maze pattern and into holes on the toy, was patented in the late 19th century, and various forms of this maze game are still available today. Some of these can be larger and more complex, where players tilt the playing field by turning a knob as they try to guide the marble through the maze, avoiding holes cut into the bottom, until they reach the end.

Mazes of all shapes and sizes are also available in puzzle books and from many Web sites, some of which enable players to construct their own mazes. Printing multiple copies of such mazes enables players to compete against each other to see who can complete the maze the in the shortest time, and this type of challenge can appeal to children as well as adults. Many video games also incorporate different types of mazes; these include mazes that players must navigate from beginning to end while avoiding nasty creatures, and ones in which players travel the same maze, gathering different objects to score points as they are chased by various creatures trying to stop them.

Another popular form of maze entertainment is in the form of corn mazes, where entire corn fields are turned into gigantic mazes that guests must find their way through. The mazes may be in a traditional geometric shape, or they may be in the shape of people, landmarks, or patriotic symbols. Corn mazes are usually created in the fall, and in October there are haunted corn mazes in which children and adults can have a frighteningly good time as they wander through and are greeted by all sorts of scary creatures.

Mazes of all sizes and shapes have captivated the human mind for centuries, offering a path to follow or a puzzle to solve. Mazes are a good source of entertainment that provide enjoyment and mental stimulation as players race against the clock to find their way to the end, and completing one quickly provides a good psychological boost as well as a feeling of satisfaction and accomplishment. Mazes have fascinated people for centuries, and their popularity continues today as new mazes are created to challenge the imaginations and problem-solving skills of players around the world.

See Also: Play as Entertainment, Psychology of; Psychological Benefits of Play; Puzzles.

Bibliography. Elliott Avedon, *The Study of Games* (Krieger Pub. Co., 1979); Jo Edkins, "Introduction to Mazes and Labyrinths," gwydir.demon.co.uk/jo/maze/intro/index.htm (cited July 2008); W.H. Matthews, "Mazes and Labyrinths," www.sacred-texts.com/etc/ml/ (cited July 2008); Jeff Saward, *Magical Paths: Labyrinths & Mazes in the 21st Century* (MITCH, 2008); Craig Wright, *The Maze and the Warrior: Symbols in Architecture, Theology, and Music* (Harvard University Press, 2004).

A. A. Hutira
Youngstown State University

McFarlane Toys

McFarlane Toys (formerly Todd Toys) is the fifth largest action figure manufacturer in the United States. The company is not only commercially successful, but has also had a significant stylistic impact on other manufacturers of action figures, raising the bar for the entire industry in terms of sculpting and painting detail. McFarlane Toys also gained a reputation for including props or comic books in their releases.

The company was founded in 1994 by Canadian comic book illustrator, writer, and entrepreneur Todd McFarlane. McFarlane had gained a reputation as a comic book artist in the 1990s, after giving the character Spiderman a complete makeover while working for Marvel Comics. McFarlane Toys was originally founded to produce models for McFarlane's vastly successful independent comic book series *Spawn*, which revolves around the eponymous character's struggle against the forces of hell. The comic book world of *Spawn* and its characters have remained a cornerstone of McFarlane Toys' line of production (the 35th *Spawn* series having been released in June 2008), but the company's horizon has since broadened, and it now produces figures from numerous other fields. These reflect the company's target audience, which ranges from the age of 15 to 30, as McFarlane has stated on several occasions. The figures include a military set, a series called "Movie Maniacs," which features characters like *Halloween*'s Michael Myers or the Terminator; figures of famous musicians, like members of KISS or Elvis Presley; and sport lines: baseball, basketball, football, hockey, and a now discontinued series of NASCAR figures. Characters from popular culture like Maurice Sendak's *Wild Things*, or characters from television shows like *The Simpsons*, and characters from movies also continue to be produced.

In addition to licensed figures of both fictional characters and celebrities, McFarlane Toys regularly produces figures of its own invention, such as a series called "Dragons" and their own variations of characters based in fantasy, horror, fairytales, or science fiction. The latter include a controversial set of figures based on L. Frank Baum's children's book *The Wonderful Wizard of Oz*, which portrays a partially dressed Dorothy bound and tortured by the Munchkins and has strong sadomasochistic overtones.

As a result of the company's products often being on the border of mass-market taste (according to the unofficial philosophy that many adolescents like those things best that shock their parents), a number of the figures have been labeled adult only, and big retailers like Toys "R" Us have on several occasions refused to display or sell a number of the company's products. This has not, however, hindered the company's success. It sold over 10 million toys in 2003 and has a cult following, the McFarlane Toys Collector's Club, a club devoted to the collection of the company's action figures with more than 100,000 members worldwide. This is because of both the artistry of the company's products and its founder, who, despite considerable commercial success in various fields, enjoys a reputation of anticorporate independence.

Recently the company has been criticized by fans for moving too strongly into what is perceived as a mainstream direction, focusing on less original and more commercially "safe" figures, such as their "McFarlane's Sports Picks" line, as well as for creating new lines and then discontinuing them. In addition, there have been complaints about the declining build quality of their figures, as well as of a lack of movability, as many of the figures resemble statues more than action figures.

See Also: Action Figures; Dolls, Barbie and Others; Hobbies; Lead Soldiers; Models.

Bibliography. John Fried. "Things I Can't Live Without: Todd McFarlane," *Inc.* (January 2005); Gerard Jones, *Killing Monsters: Why Children Need Fantasy, Superheroes, and Make-Believe Violence* (Basic Books, 2002); Steve Kiwus, *Babes, Beasts, and Brawn: Sculpture of the Fantastic* (Dark Horse, 2006); Wes Orshoski, "Music and McFarlane: A Lucrative Marriage," *Billboard* (May 2002).

Johannes Fehrle
Albert-Ludwigs-Universität

Meccano

Meccano is a model construction kit made by Meccano Ltd. It was first produced in 1901 by Frank Hornby (1863–1936), who was at that stage a clerk living in Liverpool, England. The kit was advertised as "Mechanics Made Easy," and it included a number of perforated metal strips, plates and girders, wheels, gears, and axles, as well as nuts and bolts to connect and hold the pieces together. All of the perforations were spaced at half an inch apart, and the nuts and bolts were of a standard size. The only two tools needed were a screwdriver and a wrench. The machines that could be made were only limited to the imagination of the person who purchased the kit.

Initially, Hornby was able to buy parts from other manufacturers, but soon the kits became so popular that he had to start making his own parts. Establishing a factory at Duke Street, Liverpool, the new parts were friendlier to children, with rounded corners, and created from thicker and stronger steel. In September 1907 Hornby finally registered Meccano as a trademark, and in May of the following year, he formed the company Meccano Ltd. The kits became so popular, especially with boys as Christmas presents, that in 1914 Hornby had to build a new factory at Binns Road, Liverpool, and the company operated from there for the next 66 years. Factories were also opened in France, Spain, and Argentina to cope with the demand.

A motorcycle built with the Meccano motion system 50 kit, sold in 2005 and manufactured in France and China.

Hornby sold the Meccano in sets numbered 1–6, each one containing more pieces and allowing a greater scope for building something, and were also progressively more expensive. Gradually further numbers were introduced, and in 1937 the sets were renamed with letters of the alphabet. By that time Meccano sets were selling well around the world, with great demand all over the British empire, especially from Australia and New Zealand, and from the British, and other, communities in South America. Frank Hornby became a member of the British Parliament for Liverpool.

The Meccano Guild was established in 1919 to encourage the use of the toy. From the 1920s there were regular school competitions between schoolboys over who could build the most elaborate machine, with working trains and airplanes created along with buildings and bridges. For adults, there were also clubs and regional competitions. *Meccano Magazine* was published from 1916 until 1981, suggesting new designs and highlighting changes in what was available.

With the onset of World War II, the war effort resulted in the factory producing military supplies, and even after the war, demand for supplies for the Korean War meant that production did not come back to its prewar level until 1953. Sets continued to sell well, but there was a downturn in sales in the early 1960s.

This was as much because there was so much Meccano still around—it was very hard to break, and fathers passed it to their sons—as because other interests were arising. In 1964 Lines Bros. Ltd. bought the company, and they changed the color scheme and added zinc strips. In 1970 they started introducing electronic parts. After Lines Bros. went into liquidation in 1971, Airfix Industries bought Meccano and continued making a range of sets. However, they also found themselves having difficulties, and in 1980, they sold the factory on Binns Road, with most production coming from the factory in France. General Mills bought the British company Meccano Ltd. in 1981, but four years later it was sold to Marc Rebibo, a French businessman. He ran it for four years and then sold it to François Duvachelle, another Frenchman, who tried to restructure the company. Eventually, in 2000, 49 percent of the company was bought by Nikko—a Japanese toy manufacturer—but this was sold back in 2007. Meccano is still manufactured in France and China. The demand is now not just among teenage boys, but also from many Meccano enthusiasts—the International Society of Meccanomen was established in 1989, with 600 members in 30 countries.

See Also: Airfix; Boys' Play; LEGOs; Models; Play as Learning, Sociology of.

Bibliography. Joan Baxter, *The Archeology of Childhood: Children, Gender and Material Culture* (AltaMira Press, 2005); Allen Levy, ed., *The Meccano Magazine Anthology* (PEI International, 1995); Brian Sutton-Smith, *The Ambiguity of Play* (Harvard University Press, 2001); Geoff Wright, *The Meccano Super Models* (New Cavendish, 1980).

Justin Corfield
Geelong Grammar School

Memory and Play

As an activity that requires cognitive engagement, play has the capacity to impact memory, both the formation of individual memories and the capacity for improved memory function. Children engaged in play are more adept at memory for several reasons—one reason is that memory is an emotionally charged experience, and emotionally charged experiences are often more readily recalled. As well, because play is a fun and intrinsically motivated experience, learning experiences that involve play increase a child's motivation for learning.

Play in learning experiences increase attention to the task, and attention is a critical component in using the working memory and storing information in long-term memory. Finally, because play increases executive function, specifically self-regulation, through processes such as private speech, children engaged in play become more able to focus their attention—which increases their capacity to regulate learning and memorize necessary information. Play may also be a useful strategy for helping children with Attention Deficit–Hyperactivity Disorder (ADHD) increase executive function to improve attentional capacity, and therefore increase memory and improve learning. Play is an effective learning tool that has even been shown to enhance memory in babies as young as 12 months.

Memory

Memory is most easily divided into working memory (or short-term memory) and long-term memory. Working memory receives input quickly, has a limited capacity (in general, 7 ± 2 units), and is brief in duration (five to 20 seconds). In contrast, long-term memory has both practically unlimited capacity and duration, but input can be relatively slow, and the speed of retrieval depends upon the representational and organizational strategies used in the process of memorizing. Some psychologists perceive working memory more as a process than a storage place, and working memory is best understood as the processing space for whatever we are currently thinking. Repeated use of new information helps us to store that information in long-term memory, and repeated recall of previously learned information makes us more able to retrieve that information from long-term memory for use in working memory.

Long-term memory can be further categorized into explicit and implicit memory. Explicit memory is knowledge stored in our long-term memory that we can recall and use. For instance, facts and theories learned in school are explicit memories. Implicit memory is memory that we cannot consciously recall, but that influences our thoughts and behaviors. Emotional experiences and prejudices are often implicit memories. Procedural memories—the memory used in executing familiar skill sets—can also be implicit. For instance, you may not remember the exact particulars of how to ride a bike, but you can easily execute the required movements.

Construction of Knowledge and Meaning

The basic premise of constructivism is that the learner constructs meaning through experience with the environment. This theory holds that children do not receive knowledge as a complete package from their teachers and parents but, rather, that they build knowledge from scratch to build an understanding and interpretation of the experience.

Chess and Meaningful Memory

An understanding of Chess is useful in better understanding how play can impact memory development and function. In classic cognitive psychology research with Chess players, researchers identified the phenomenon that Chess masters could look at a Chess board only for a few seconds and reconstruct the board from memory, whereas novice Chess players could not do this. However, when Chess masters viewed a board with randomly placed pieces for the same amount of time, they were no more adept at reconstructing the board from memory than were the novices. Researchers came to understand that Chess masters were still operating within the 7 ± 2 constraints of working memory, but that their understanding of Chess configurations allowed them to place a meaningful structure on the pieces and engage in chunking. Instead of remembering 7 ± 2 pieces (as the novices did, and as the Chess masters did when viewing the random board) they remembered 7 ± 2 meaningful chunks.

Increased knowledge in an area leads to the capacity to chunk information. As an individual learns to identify patterns and structure in environment, he/she is able to cluster related information together, thus expanding the capacity of working memory. Chess research has noted that children who play Chess regularly may be able to function at a high capacity in Chess play, even if their other learning capacity is still normal for their age. This may be because children who play Chess regularly have increased familiarity with Chess patterns and therefore are more adept at chunking this information into meaningful units.

General play may serve a similar purpose. When a child plays, he or she is exposed to a variety of new situations, circumstances, and experiences. Exposure creates familiarity, which helps the child to construct new cognitive structures. These structures enable the child to better chunk related information for increased memory in these areas, particularly since these areas are fun and related to the child's interest. For instance, a child who struggles at math or spelling may be able to name dinosaurs by era, recall all of a particular athlete's statistics, or cite from memory the lines of a favorite book.

The Role of Attention in Memory

A basic premise of memory theory is that whatever we pay attention to moves into working memory. There are many stimuli in the environment, and only those to which we pay attention will actually register in our short-term/working memory. Things to which we repeatedly pay attention and think about in our working memory will move into long-term memory. So attention is key in the process of learning and forming memories.

Many strategies can be used in learning environments to increase the learner's attention to the task at hand, but central to the issue is making the learner want to pay attention. When the learner is intrinsically motivated to learn, he/she will choose to pay attention, which therefore increases the likelihood of moving the information into long-term memory.

Play and the Development of Executive Function

Related to the concept of attention is executive function. Executive function involves several components, including working memory, cognitive flexibility, and self-regulation. Children with higher levels of executive function are better able to control their focus and therefore to purposefully choose the direction of their attention. Executive function therefore impacts learning, memory, and behavior. And play has been shown to increase executive function. When children participate in play environments, particularly when they are provided with a safe context in which they are free to make their own choices and decisions, they increase their capacity for executive function. This increased executive function strengthens their ability to focus on specific learning tasks and remember better. So, children who play more when they are young may actually be better able to learn when they are older, precisely because of their well developed capacities for executive function.

Some researchers suggest that executive function, particularly self-regulation, is a core issue in ADHD. Some theorists suggest that those children diagnosed with ADHD just have poorly developed self-regulation skills. In fact, although it has not been studied in children, research with rats indicates that the drive to play may be related to ADHD. The right frontal cortex is the region of the brain responsible for paying attention, planning, and sensitivity to social cues. In a research study in which rats' right frontal cortexes were surgically altered, experimental rats had increased levels of both higher overall activity (indicative of ADHD) and also of play-fighting with their peers. When the rats had an extra hour of play activity per day, their general hyperactivity was controlled. Jaak Panksepp, the behavioral neuroscientist who conducted the research, has speculated that play therapy might also be useful for children with ADHD, as a way to control the urges that lead to hyperactivity. Though this has not been empirically studied in ADHD children, the theory suggests that play could be an energetic outlet that would allow children with ADHD to better focus during nonplay times—which could support both learning and memory. Further, if play does strengthen executive function, then children with ADHD would also improve because of this play-induced benefit.

Self-Talk

Self-talk, or private speech, is one strategy that children can be taught to use in play environments, and that is useful for helping children develop self-regulation. Adults may naturally use silent self-talk, thinking through the steps of a task to accomplish or repeating affirmations in a difficult situation. Children have not developed the capacity for silent self-talk to be effective, so they should be encouraged to use self-talk. For instance, if a child is learning his or her telephone number, it is useful for him or her to repeat the number out loud.

Not only does this help the child to learn his or her telephone number, but it teaches him or her something about the deliberation nature of memorization—a skill that can be applied to other learning circumstances. In this same way, when children use self-talk in play, they develop self-regulatory skills that will be useful in other situations and contexts. One example would be that a child playing a new sport can use self-talk to strengthen key skills during practice and games. A child learning a dance routine or song can use self-talk to improve his or her memory of the steps or music. A child playing a card or board game can use self-talk during his or her turn to make sure he or she is following the directions appropriately.

In preschoolers, private speech occurs most often during make-believe play. When children are playing out roles in fantasy or make-believe play, they often talk themselves through what they believe are the appropriate activities or actions. This strengthens their understanding and memory of those actions and also strengthens their capacity for self-regulation. However, structure and private speech are inversely related—the more structured playtime is, the less children engage in private speech in the activity; the less structured the activity, the more private speech children will use. Therefore, child-directed play is most appropriate for helping children to utilize private speech and develop self-regulation and other components of executive function, which are key for increasing a child's capacity for learning and memory.

Baby Memory and Play

Even babies can learn and remember through play. In one study, 12-month-old babies were shown five toys, and a unique way to play with each toy, for 20 seconds each. Parents were not allowed to observe, to make sure that parents did not coach their child on how to use the toy. The babies were given the toys again after three minutes, one week, and four weeks, to see if the babies remembered how to use the toys. After three minutes, babies remembered and replicated 3.5 of 5 ways shown (about 70 percent). After one week and four weeks, they remembered 2.5 (50 percent) of the activities shown. Babies who had been shown the toys but not the activities spontaneously replicated about 1.5 (30 percent) of the target activities. Even for very small babies, the fun of play—even just the fun of watching someone else play for a brief period—can lead to increased memory retention.

Memory Games

Memory games are a common childhood learning activity. In the classic game, a deck of cards with pictures, numbers, or words is used. The cards are arranged randomly on a table. In each turn, the child flips over two cards. If he or she makes a match, he or she earns a point and removes the cards from the table. If he or she does not make a match, he or she returns the cards to face-down position. The goal is to remember the location of as many cards as he or she can, so that if a card is flipped whose partner previously was revealed, he or she can remember the appropriate location and make a purposeful match. For younger children, a deck with pictures will be more appropriate. For older children, words or even mathematical card decks (e.g., matching a card with an equation to another card with the correct solution) will be useful and challenging. The point of the game is to challenge working memory in a fun context. Allowing children to compete against each other for points or prizes can increase motivation and fun in the activity.

Play as a Learning Tool

Because play is, by definition, a fun experience, the participant is intrinsically motivated to participate. When play is incorporated into the learning experience, it therefore increases both intrinsic motivation for the learning activity and attention to the task at hand—and that increased attention means the learning activity is processed in working memory and potentially moved into long-term memory. Further, because play is an emotionally charged activity (i.e., fun and exciting, as opposed to neutral) and because emotional events are more easily remembered and recalled, learning experiences that occur in a play context may be more easily remembered. Play also increases a child's capacity for self-regulation, which improves attentional abilities. Finally, play expands the child's knowledge set, leading to a greater capacity to chunk knowledge into meaningful pieces and therefore remember larger amounts of information within the constraints of working memory.

See Also: Academic Learning and Play; Piaget and Play; Play and Learning Theory; Play and Literacy; Play as Learning, Psychology of; Play as Learning, Sociology of; Play in the Classroom; Psychological Benefits of Play; Psychology of Play (Vygotsky); Teacher-Child Co-Play.

Bibliography. Robin Henig, "Taking Play Seriously," *New York Times* (February 17, 2008); Pamela Klein and Andrew Meltzoff, "Long-Term Memory, Forgetting, and Deferred Imitation in 12-Month-Old Infants," *Developmental Science* (v.2, 1999); Jeanne Ormrod, *Educational Psychology: Developing Learners* (Merrill/Prentice Hall, 2003); Alix Spiegel, "Creative Play Makes for Kids in Control," *NPR* (February 21, 2008); Alix Spiegel, "Old-Fashioned Play Builds Serious Skills," *NPR* (February 27, 2008); Vikki Valentine, "Q&A: The Best Kind of Play for Kids," *NPR* (February 27, 2008); Anita Woolfolk, *Educational Psychology* (Allyn & Bacon, 2005).

Kimberlee Bonura
Walden University

Mesoamerican Cultures

The term *Mesoamerican cultures* indicates the pre-Columbian civilizations that flourished in Central America in the territories of contemporary Mexico, Guatemala, Belize, El Salvador, and Honduras. Among the most important Mesoamerican cultures are the Olmechs (the "rubber people" of the La Venta region, who flourished around 1200–400 B.C.E.), the Toltechs of Teotihuacan (600–1500 B.C.E.), the Maya (extending from Guatemala to Mexico), and the Aztec Tenocha (a name given to the Mexica or Chicimeca, the Nahuatl-speaking people of the Valley of Mexico). There were several differences in the way play activities such as ball-games, ritual and ceremonial dances, and ritual clowning were organized in different geographical areas and in different time periods; nonetheless, religion, exercise of power, and play were closely intertwined in all the cultures of Mesoamerica.

Some forms of the pre-Columbian Mesoamerican ball game, which was already practiced in 1400 B.C.E., have survived until today, such as the *Mixtec* ballgame. Mesomerican cultures practiced several kinds of ball games, as illustrated by representations of stick-and-ball games on murals in the sacred city of Teotihuacan, or by figurines portraying ball players found all over Mesoamerica. The size of the rubber ball varied—from the dimension of a grapefruit to a weight of up to eight or nine pounds—as well as the specific equipment required, the parts of the body used to project the ball, and the (ritual) contest of the ball game.

The masonry ball courts had roughly the form of an horizontal capitalized letter "I," a structure apparently connected to the four cardinal directions as well as to the movement of astral bodies. The players scored points by hitting the ball toward markers in the end or lateral zones. Spectators watched the game on platforms located at each end zone; betting on favorite teams or players was a widespread practice.

The main difference between contemporary ball games and the Mesoamerican ball game is that players rarely used their hands and feet. Ball games required remarkable skill; since the ball was heavy and made of solid rubber, and the players used helmets with facial grids, gloves, padded clothing, thick belts, and hip and knee pads.

Scholars have long tried to answer the elusive question: What was the meaning of the ball game? Ball games are mentioned in myth; for example, in the Quiché Maya epic the *Popul Vuh*, in which the Hero Twins played life and death ball games with the Lords of the Underworld in myth time, or in the Aztec myth in which the sun god Huitzilopochtli oppposed his sister Coyolxauhqui (the moon goddess). The rubber ball most probably symbolized the sun, and as Anthony A. Shelton and others have argued, the ball game played out opposing dualisms. The Aztec ball game *Ullamalitzli* was connected to the creation of the cosmos through its founding myth, and gave expression to a series of oppositions between death and regeneration, the sun and the moon, the earth and the nether world, and the universal cycle of dry and wet season. As in the

Aztec game, Mayan ball games also put into relation decapitation, death, fertility, and regeneration; but they may also have had divinatory purpose.

In the monarchic city-states of the Maya and in the Aztec empire formed by a confederation of city-states, ball games were early on linked to political authority, and served to strengthen the power of the dominant elites. In particular, the Aztec framed the *Ullamalitzli* in a complex religious and ritual construction, which included human sacrifice on large scale, and transformed games into public spectacles, supportive of the hegemony of Tenochtitlan, the city centre of the Aztec empire.

The French structuralist Christian Duverger, author of a study on play in the Aztec culture, argues that the Aztec feared play because they thought that it could lead to chaos and disintegration of the social structure upon which their state was built on, and thus of the state itself. In his view, Aztec play is reduced to "representation"; one of his many examples is that of the captive prisoners who were forced to play "mock" games with "fake" weapons, which precluded the human sacrifice of the "losers." The play enacted on such occasions was mere representation, because the outcome had already been decided.

Some scholars also consider as play the much discussed "flowery wars" of the Aztec state. These were ritualized fights comparable, according to Shelton, to medieval tournaments, which aimed at the capture of sacrificial victims. Those who died in such conflicts were thought to be admitted to the sun's paradise.

Board games were also known and practiced in Mesoamerica. For example, the Aztecs played *Patolli*, a game played with red beans on a board that could be cross-shaped (and sometimes have a center). This board game is comparable to the European game of Checkers.

In Mesoamerica dance, play, ritual, and ceremony were closely interconnected, though private dance was also practiced. Royal Maya dance seems to have been composed and full of dignity; the movements of ritual clowns impersonating animals and demonic supernatural beings by wearing masks were, instead, very animated. Ritual clowns used to parody with dances, mottoes, and jokes the misdeeds of leaders. The communal ceremonial dances of the Aztec were linked to calendar festivals; they had telling names such as the Dance of the Fire Serpent, or the Dance of the Flowers, and were performed in honor of the gods and goddesses of the pantheon.

Dance and dramatic representations often had warfare as their theme, as well as the deeds of emperors and ancestors. Nonetheless, the most famous Mesoamerican dance, still performed today, remains the *Danza de los Voladores* (Dance of the Fliers): four dancers are represented in manuscripts as wearing feathers and rich costumes, while they fling themselves from ropes twisted around a tall pole. The dance was probably performed in honor of the sun, or for the gods of the four cardinal points.

See Also: Checkers and Variations of; Mexico; Play as Mock War, Sociology of; South Americans, Traditional Cultures.

Bibliography. David Carrasco, ed., *The Oxford Encyclopedia of Mesoamerican Cultures: The Civilizations of Mexico and Central America* (OUP 2001); Christian Duverger, *L'esprit du Jeu Chez les Aztèques* (Mouton 1978); Anthony A. Shelton, "The Aztec Theatre State and the Dramatization of War," in Tim Cornell and Thomas B. Allen, eds., *War and Games* (Boydell Press 2003); Michael Werner, *Concise Encyclopedia of Mexico* (Fitzroy Dearborn Publishers, 2001); E. Michael Whittington, ed., *The Sport of Life and Death: The Mesoamerican Ballgame* (Thames & Hudson, 2001).

Maria Beatrice Bittarello
Independent Scholar

Mexico

Mexico has always been proud of its traditional toys. Despite the lack of "research" on the developmental benefits of playing, there has been a longstanding production of marvelous toys throughout the last century, showing the importance of play as a social activity for children, and helping them acquire motor and cognitive skills.

Effective learning aids have been used as toys in the sense that they have been useful to help acquire specific skills. Effective learning aids are toys because they provide meanings to manipulate them over and over to master the learning itself. Martine Mauriras from the United Nations Educational, Scientific and Cultural Organization (UNESCO) said that there are any number of games across cultures that are excellent learning aids, even though the learning they provide has nothing to do with a regular school curriculum. Traditional play and games are instructive because most of the time they were designed to teach something valued by the culture, like a social skill, or a dexterity needed to learn something else (i.e., to count, to wait, to listen, to share).

Mexico has a great deal of traditional play and games, most inherited from Spain (from which it won its independence in 1810), and some from their pre-Hispanic ancestors. It has been known that many Latin American countries share a great deal of traditional games, but all of them have been transformed and innovated. These games are characterized by having been shaped by social, historical, and economic purposes, and by doing so, games and play acquired forms of particular cultural expression in different regions within Mexico.

Despite the fact that play is considered a low-priority activity in comparison with education and work, the great variety of traditional play and games that Mexico has are considered productive, especially for small children. Until recently, there have not been studies or professional research in Mexico about the importance of play in the development of children, but there are many elementary teachers and motor-education therapists using traditional games or nursery rhymes in their work. The latter tends to complete two aspects: (1) the benefits of play, and (2) the transmission of cultural identity to young children.

Traditional Mexican Toys

As for traditional Mexican toys, museums and private collectors all over the country have been collecting them since the 1970s. There are skilled artisans that devote their life work only to creating toys. These artisans create the toy through all of its processes, and their families even participate as a family tradition. Many traditional toys in Mexico were related to Catholic rituals and festivities during Spanish rule, and later to independence.

The majority of traditional toys in Mexico are the legacy of historic and economical processes that were intertwined with pre-Hispanic and European traditions. Missionaries from Spain used puppets to evangelize Mexicans after the fall of the Aztec empire. One can find toys made with different materials: rubber, tin, metal, wood, fabrics, corn leaves, and clay. Also, there is a very reputable tradition of miniature toys—mostly made in metal—that are prized for their perfection in details.

Modern Play

In respect to traditional play in modern Mexico, it has been a paramount ingredient in children's lives. Not just social and cultural symbols are being taught through play, but motor and cognitive abilities. Traditional games in Mexico are mostly for infants, toddlers, and preschoolers, and could be divided into specific skills that little children need to learn. There are a lot of games to learn: sharing, hiding, jumping, singing, counting, learning rules, and learning motor coordination.

Games meant to sort out (*Sorteo*) are the basic games that Mexican children need to learn first. Sorting is used to help decide players in a game of teams or to learn to resolve differences in opinions, and they are also used to introduce learning of rules. There are various kinds of games based on sorting, and in many of them the children circle a child who points out somebody within the circle, while everyone recites a verse or a song. When the last word is said, the pointed-out child is chosen.

Another popular way to play a sort-out game is called *Gallo, Gallina* (Cock, Hen), which is about choosing one of two players. The children stand facing each other within a short distance. One of them starts by saying: "*Gallo,*" and they advance, one foot in front of the other, in a straight line. The other player says "*Gallina,*" advancing the same as the first player. They advance against each other until one of them places his or her foot on the other player and wins. Rhymes are another kind of play taught to preschoolers. Rhymes in Mexico are played where every child holds hands and walks while they sing, forming a circle. There are rhymes that involve jumping, clapping, or kneeling in addition to singing. Group games are for preschoolers. Group games could be with children in a circle, or in a line, and most of them involve running or copying an animal.

There are many games involving Hide-and-Seek, having to stay still, and games with more complex jumping. Also, there are many games that are played with a traditional toy: marbles, balls, kites, spinning tops, and stick horses. There is a game called *Acitrón de un Fandango* that involves passing little objects—such as pebbles or marbles—from child to child, while everybody sings a song with nonsense lyrics. The game requires a lot of hand coordination, because every time the pebble arrives at its original holder, the song is sung faster and faster. The child who holds two pebbles at the end of the song loses.

Games of the Ancients

Nowadays we claim that games, play, and toys are for children, but ancient Mexicans reserved games for ceremonial purposes. Even though there were feline figurines made of clay with wheels that we can appreciate in anthropological museums in Mexico, toys were not made for children to play with. Historians like Miguel León Portilla have noted that games like *Patolli* and the ball game *Juego de pelota*, were played by Aztecs, Mayans, and Toltecas, as one the many methods that these cultures used to express a relationship between themselves and their gods and the universe. *Patolli* was a table game played by four players and is similar to modern Parcheesi.

As it was related to cosmogonic ideas, *Patolli* had 52 cells, which represented the time cycle for the Aztecs, and four players, representing the four sacred elements. *Juego de pelota* is a game played since 1200 B.C.E. with a rubber ball in big fields next to pyramids; the fields often formed a gigantic letter "I." The players kicked the ball with their shoulders, thighs, and upper arms into a ring located in the side of the pyramid. It has been said that both the ball and the ring represented the sun and the Earth, and the game was played to help sustain balance between the forces of the universe.

See Also: Kite Flying; Mesoamerican Cultures; Native Americans; Play as Learning, Anthropology of; Spontaneous Group Play.

Bibliography. Martine Mauriras Bousquet, "What Makes us Play? What Makes us Learn?," *Prospects* (v.13/4, 1986); Luz María Chapela, *Play at School* (*El Juego en la Escuela* (Paidós, 2002); Ivan Ivic, "An International Project on Traditional Children's Games," *Prospects* (v.13/4, 1986); Glenn Kirchner, *Children's Games Around the World* (Benjamin Cummings, 2000); Nina Millen, *Children's Games from Many Lands* (Friendship Press, 1943).

Yma N. Ríos Orlandi
Independent Scholar
Ana Luisa Baca Lobera
University of Puerto Rico

Mille Bornes

Mille Bornes ("a thousand milestones") is a French card game that simulates a road race, combining strategy and luck. This family-friendly game serves socializing and skill-building purposes for younger players, while offering strategy challenges and nostalgia for older ones.

Although three independent players can enjoy a match, Mille Bornes is ideally played in two teams of two. Before computer versions gained popularity, it was marketed as a family activity, and parents and children have ample opportunity to display interactive dynamics.

The game fosters competition. Players slow or stop opponents through road hazard cards showing, among other things, flat tires and stoplights. Mille Bornes requires concentration, since participants must remember which cards have been played by teammates and opponents. It encourages strategic thinking; teammates must decide how fast to "drive" their car, whether to focus on moving themselves forward or delaying opponents, and choosing which cards to discard at critical moments. Players must also cope with the element of chance as they draw cards, and the psychological guesswork of staving off harmful intentions from the other team.

The recommended age being 8 through adult, Mille Bornes offers early exposure to the grown-up concept of driving. In the days before computer simulations, youngsters could race at 125 miles per hour toward a finish line in their imaginary car. Undoubtedly, the strategic elements of the game appeals to adults long after the mystery of driving has lost its allure.

Mille Bornes also exposes children to the French language. Except in the Netherlands, where the Dutch-language version of the game is known as *Rijwielspel* (and simulates a bicycle tour) the game's cards are marketed worldwide in French. Some decks include another language—English and Spanish among the most popular—alongside the French.

Created in 1954 by Frenchman Edmond Dujardin, Mille Bornes is widely considered a derivative of the American game Touring, first produced in 1906. Touring went out of circulation in 1975, when Mille Bornes was enjoying popularity.

Online versions of Mille Bornes are available, as well as regular and deluxe boxed sets. Collector's editions now include tins shaped like racecars. Mille Bornes does not use a board, only the deck and a plastic holder for cards as they are drawn and discarded. While the number of computer tournaments suggests it may not be among the top 100 online games, the card version was inducted into the *Games* Magazine Hall of Fame. That publication describes inductees as meeting or exceeding "the highest standards of quality and play value." Cursory examinations of online communities suggests the game is more popular with males than females and is often enjoyed by players over the age of 35, who in some cases mention remembering the card game from their childhood.

Culturally, the game's name references the charming European custom of posting mileage between towns on small stone markers alongside the road. The name has also been used for a French film depicting a coming-of-age road journey following a funeral. And of course Mille Bornes also nods in the direction of the cross-cultural adage "The journey of a thousand miles begins with a single step."

The game is valued in certain editions for its artistically delicate cards, the number varying slightly by version. Cards depict the speed of travel using animals (snail for the slowest speed, birds for the swiftest) and also illustrate road hazards in eloquent detail. For players who speak no French, the cheerful pictures tell more than the words.

See Also: Cooperative Play; Europe, 1940 to 1960; France; Luck and Skill in Play; Play as Competition, Sociology of; Play as Learning, Sociology of; Pretending.

Bibliography. About.com, "Touring," boardgames.about.com/od/gamehistories/p/touring.htm (cited June 2008); Gilles Brougère "Some Elements Relating to Children's Play and Adult Simulation/Gaming," *Simulation & Gaming* (v.30/2, 1999); Margaret Hofer, *The Games We Played: The Golden Age of Board and Table Games* (Princeton Architectural Press, 2003).

Wendy Welch
University of Virginia, Wise

Minesweeper

Minesweeper is a single-player computer game that has been bundled with versions of Microsoft Windows since 1992, making it one of the most widespread computer games in the world. The game is used in educational contexts and has also attracted the attention of researchers in mathematics and artificial intelligence.

The aim of the game is to clear a rectangular field of mines, using guesswork and probability analysis. While Minesweeper is available for a large number of platforms, and can also be played online, the most widespread versions are the ones bundled with Microsoft Windows operating systems. Minesweeper was first included with

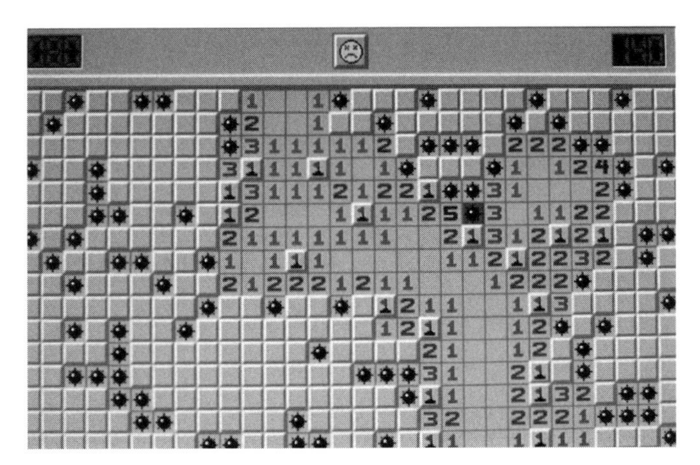

Minesweeper is included in every version of Microsoft Windows, making it an extremely widespread game.

Windows 3.1 (1992) and has been included in every version since. However, the game has its origins in mainframe computing, and similar game mechanics were employed in games such as Depth Charge (1976), Hurkle (1978), and Mugwump (1978).

The original Windows version was developed by Microsoft employees Robert Donner and Curt Johnson in 1990. Because of the large number of copies of the Windows operating systems, Minesweeper is probably one of the most widespread computer games in the world. Because of its simple gameplay and short duration, it is probably also one of the most widely played computer games. In conjunction with the fact that Minesweeper is installed on many office PCs by default, this has led to moral panics about the loss of productivity caused by the playing of casual games in work environments, for which the game has often been used as a poster child.

However, the game has also been hailed as a productivity booster, in that it allows office workers to take breaks without leaving their desks. One study conducted in the Netherlands in 2003 found that playing games at work like Minesweeper can increase productivity and job satisfaction. The game has also been used in educational settings, particularly in mathematics and computer science. For example, it has been successfully employed to teach students the basics of formal logic at Michigan Technical University since 1995.

In mathematics, Minesweeper has been a subject of study since the 1990s. Most importantly, mathematician Richard Kaye was able to prove that Minesweeper is NP-complete, thus connecting the game to one of the $1 Million Prizes of Mathematics. Kaye has demonstrated that algorithms can be implemented directly in the game, and that solving the Minesweeper consistency problem would be paramount to solving the Traveling Salesman Problem.

Minesweeper has been played competitively for a number of years, and top players are able to clear a 16 x 16 board in 10 seconds. However, the competitive Minesweeper community has been plagued by claims that the standard Windows version enables players to cheat. In popular culture, Minesweeper has also left its mark. The game was featured on an episode of the television show *Numb3rs,* and J.K. Rowling, the author of the *Harry Potter* series of children's books, played the game while she was trying to give up smoking. It has been featured in a number of political cartoons, such as a depiction of the map of Afghanistan in the style of the game.

See Also: Game Theory; Luck and Skill in Play; Mazes; Play as Entertainment, Psychology of; Psychological Benefits of Play; United States, 1960 to Present.

Bibliography. Tony Delgado, "Beyond Tetris—Minesweeper," www.gamesetwatch.com/2007/02/column_beyond_tetris_minesweep.php; Paul Hyman, "On-the-Job Gaming," *Computer User* (v.22/2, 2004); Richard Kaye, "Minesweeper is NP-complete," *American Intelligencer* (v.22/2, 2000); Patti Frazer Lock and Allan Struthers, "Using the Game Minesweeper to Introduce Students to Proofs," *Abstracts of Papers Presented to the American Mathematical Society* (v.20/1, 1999); Dana Mackenzie, "Addicted to Logic," *American Scientist* (May–June, 1999); Elizabeth Renzetti, "The Games People Play," *The Globe and Mail* (August 23, 1997).

Julian Kücklich
University of the Arts, London

Minifigs

The term *minifig* is a contraction of the words *miniature* and *figurine.* It is a generic term used to refer to such figures and the name of a company that makes them. Miniature figurines come in a variety of scales and are made from an assortment of materials. Lead soldiers are a type of miniature figurine, but alloys of lead or plastic are commonly used in modern construction. "Scale" refers to the size of the figure, and is usually expressed as the height of a male human figure in millimeters, though sometimes also as a fraction, or in inches. It is one of the more important factors used when defining such figures. A dizzying array of different scales and special terms for these scales has been used over the years.

Some of the more common modern scales are: 15 mm, which is generally used for mass Wargaming battles; 20 mm, which is also called HO or OO, and is the scale common to most model railways; 25 mm, which is mostly used for small-engagement Wargaming and for use in role-playing games; and 54 mm, which is generally a scale used for collectible, decorative figures. However, while these are the most common sizes, there are many other scales, and many individual terms to designate those scales used by particular companies or in particular hobbies.

Miniature figurines are used in a number of different pastimes. Wargamers use them to represent troops in battles. In general, a small-scale figure is used in a large battle. For large battles featuring tanks, 6.2mm is often used; 15 mm is most popular for those eras that feature massive troop deployment, from ancient through medieval, pike and musket, and Napoleonic; and 25 mm and 30mm are used for smaller-scale skirmishes. In games where large numbers of troops are being represented, one figure will often be representative of many men.

The painting of such figures is a hobby in itself, with collectors and gamers alike often taking great pride in how well-painted their figure collections are. Figures are often used in role-playing games, such as *Dungeons & Dragons,* to help moderate combat. Not all role-playing games use figures, and they are far from mandatory in any such game.

LEGO produces a range of miniature figures, which sometimes are called Minifigs. These are intended to be used in conjunction with environments created using LEGO bricks.

Minifigs is also the name of a company that started life as Alberken Miniatures in the United Kingdom in 1964 and is still in production. Alberken Miniatures became Minifigs in 1968, and specialized in producing figures to be used in Wargames. They produced a very wide range of cheap figures, initially in 20 mm scale and later in 25 mm, which was also known as their S range, and debatably the first true 25-mm figures ever professionally made. Minifigs were, and still are, a supplier of vast numbers of figures to the Wargames market, and played no small part in pioneering the hobby in the United Kingdom in the 1970s. Although early figures were often criticized as being poorly sculpted, the range of figures they produced was marketed at the low price that Wargamers needed.

In 1986 Minifigs secured the rights to the Ral Partha fantasy range, including some of the earliest figures designed for fantasy role-playing games—specifically tailored for *Dungeons & Dragons*—and were hugely successful. The company is still active: they produce 12 mm, 15 mm and 25 mm Wargames figures, as well as a fantasy range.

See Also: Action Figures; Boys' Play; *Dungeons & Dragons*; Lead Soldiers; LEGOs; Wargames.

Bibliography. Peter P. Perla, *The Art of Wargaming: A Guide for Professionals and Hobbyists* (U.S. Naval Institute Press, 1990); Neil Thomas, *Ancient & Medieval Wargaming* (The History Press, 2008); Neil Thomas, *Wargaming: An Introduction* (The History Press, 2005); J.D. Williams, *The Compleat Strategyst: Being a Primer on the Theory of Games of Strategy* (Dover Publications, 1986).

Justin Parsler
Brunel University

Models

Modeling has been traditionally viewed as the creation of scale representations of objects for hobbyists and entertainment for games, play, and expression. Examples of this include toys like cars, trucks, animals, and human-like dolls. It can also be considered a scale representation with time compression or exaggeration to emphasize a behavior or phenomenon.

Models represent the most basic act that informs play—visualization, imagination, and comprehension. The basis of knowing may come from our experience in the world through our sensory perceptions and how we represent the world and our experience in our mind. This process is called mental modeling, and this very basic process of awareness and comprehension can become more elaborate through replication and production of objects, as well as elaboration through comparison, combination, and reduction, or what we know, experience, and imagine. What is important to consider in modeling are some of the actions associated with it: pretense, imitation, replication, and scale—all of which are key elements of play and playful activities; play in this sense is more than a special case of learning. Play seems to be an embodiment of learning that allows for skill and knowledge development without the consequences of performing for survival, or in the case of deep play, for status. Models can include objects, including mental constructs that can be used for imaginative and symbolic play, as well as games that imitate systems, like Chess imitates medieval war and and a toy stethoscope can allow for the playful imitation of being a doctor—both in the natural world and as representation. Modeling can also be viewed as pretense in the form of behaviors for the theater and dramatic purposes, where the son of a farmer in Ethiopia can become the king of Denmark for a school production of Hamlet—literally, a play.

The process of modeling allows the individual to create an understanding through gathering observable aspects of an object or phenomenon, and through attempts to imitate and elaborate, express and communicate: to create understanding. Modeling can also be considered a form of expression, where artifacts may be created to communicate and instruct. This process of understanding and meaning making often takes place through deconstructing the object, reassembling or replicating it, and then attempting to use it to understand or create understanding in others—this can be considered modeling.

The toy industry is adept at finding the latest tools, uniforms, activities, objects, and language for the entertainment and instruction of young people. Many of these toys are models of objects that have important cultural capital, whether they are vehicles, weapons, animals, buildings, or fantasy items.

The Process of Modeling

Modeling is a deeper process than some of these physical manifestations. As a mental process, modeling can include behavior, objects, ideas, and qualities; models as objects can also include values, communication, and replicas of other objects as representation. In many ways, modeling is a very serious form of play, where scientific habits of mind, language, and cultural values are shared and refined, and through this, our understanding of the world is developed.

Regarding science, Lord Kelvin, one of the early pioneers in the field of physics once said, "I am never content until I have constructed a mechanical model of the subject I am studying. If I succeed in making one, I understand; otherwise I do not."

The process of model creation is the basis for much of the way we conduct modern science, and many of our cultural and civil advances come from imitation and replication of things found in nature through comparison, combination, and reduction. This process for learning is dependent upon our logical systems of language and representation; i.e., the role of calculus and mathematics became an annotation system for modeling systems and phenomena from the natural world and, presently, in the subatomic and the yet unknown; images and words become a means for communicating complex experiences from the past, in the present, and for the future.

If play is an evolutionary adaptation for cultural transfer, then models are one of the ways that humans learn to play and transfer culture, thus deepening and extending knowledge of the tools, rules, language, roles, and actions that represent the epistemic frameworks of what are the values, conventions, and purposes of social groups and society. If we transfer our sociocultural and cognitive frameworks to objects that offer affordances and efficacy, these models become our tools and become powerful learning tools in and of themselves.

This process of representation can be considered modeling, which in psychological literature is a cognitive feature that comes from our perceptions and memory and intent to recognize and symbolically represent objects and phenomena—modern psychology and cognitive neuroscience work toward understanding this process by which we recall objects, qualities, process, and context. The dynamic and complex systems of representation we use to communicate, as well as to prepare and to act in the world, are the result of these biochemical interactions between mind, body, and world, and the act of making meaning. This mental process of representation has been called mental modeling and comprehension.

The mental models approach makes the case that the processes we use to draw conclusions are the same processes we use to comprehend and produce language. With language, we may tune our perceptions though the creation of words to denote concepts, qualities, and objects, and through this, we draw boundaries of what is a specific thing in itself, as opposed to that which is other, or not the thing in itself. This process of mental modeling distinguishes comprehension from reasoning in that with language comprehension, we construct an object that represents the essential information, or nature of the object, and makes sense, whereas reasoning requires the willingness to try and construct alternative models that represent all of the possibilities. With this in mind, mental models may be a very productive form of academic play—logical, fantastic, social, cultural, and scientific.

Modeling Practices

Modeling can range in practice from imitation in the form of drama, the construction and replication of objects like cars, homes, battles, and natural and fictional settings of all types and possibilities. These can all be done through symbol systems, in the case of mathematics and science, or through roles and dialog in the humanities in the form of narratives as text, cave painting, and interpretive dance. Academic play, play in a formal instructional setting, can include very purposeful well-defined problems, or flights of fancy.

Along with these approaches, there is also the modeling of the hobbyist. The creation of folk productions of animals and natural features, as well as objects and ideas from the realms of the spiritual, often comes about through personal interest and affinity for an object or subject, where the individual creates a model to understand.

Often models can also be considered toys. Toys are cultural objects that may be proportionally scaled representations and may be of very high fidelity to

A young boy admires the model Mini Cooper miniature car that he and his father had just constructed.

the original or very low fidelity. An example of a low-fidelity toy might be a doll made of straw, or it could be much more elaborate in the case of dolls made to simulate humans and other living creatures with uses for saving lives and studying crash safety. In addition, there are many individuals who form collectives and clubs that collect and create scaled replicas of very large objects like trains, cars, ships, spacecraft, castles, and natural phenomena like ecosystems such as coral reefs. Modeling in this sense takes on the role of craftsmanship and entertainment.

Modeling seems to have come from early approximations of humans imitating what animals did successfully. Through imitation and the creation of tools and systems of planned, or choreographed, behavior, humanity may have began hunting and gathering through the use of blunt objects and sharpened tools, as well as observing behaviors they may have seen as being successful; i.e. a group of wolves hunting may be imitated by a group of humans.

This leads to the idea that drama and acting can be considered a form of modeling. Mimesis is thought of as mirroring or representing the perceived in the world, and to some extent it represents the process of assimilation, where the individual imitates another until they eventually become that person or thing. The applicability of this can be shared from theater to spiritual festivals and religious rites, in the sense that we may enact, or model, an event in history, a great or tragic battle or hunting trip, or even the struggles of a family in an urban setting.

Modeling also extends to the creation of replicas of other objects and might just be the factory of our memory and representation from the production line of our senses and experience.

See Also: Adaptive Play; Airfix; Dolls, Barbie and Others; Hobbies; Lincoln Logs; Meccano; Play and Learning Theory; Play as Mastery of Nature.

Bibliography. E. Auerbach, *Mimesis: The Representation of Reality in Western Literature* (Princeton University Press, 2003); V. Colella, E. Klopfer, and M. Resnick, *Adventures in Modeling: Exploring Complex, Dynamic Systems with StarLogo* (Teachers College Press, 2001); S. Heaser, *Making Doll's House Miniatures with Polymer Clay* (Cassel, 2000); P. Johnson-Laird, *How We Reason* (Oxford University Press, 2006); K. Orton, *Model Making For the Stage: A Practical Guide* (Crowood Press, 2004); S. Paine, *How to Build Dioramas* (Kalmbach Publishing Company, 1999); Brian Sutton-Smith, *The Ambiguity of Play* (Harvard University Press, 2001); Y. Bar Yam, *Dynamics of Complex Systems* (Westview Press, 2003).

Brock Dubbels
University of Minnesota

Monopoly and Variations of

The shrewd, cunning, or just plain lucky player gets filthy rich within a few hours, but then again, they are as likely to go to jail or declare bankruptcy. In the game of Monopoly, players start on equal footing, but the roll of the dice and the luck of the draw soon tip the balance of wealth into a few players' favor. Monopoly is a competitive real estate acquisition game in which players travel around the board, seeking to procure colorful deeds and avoid paying rent to others. This cutthroat game rose to popularity at the height of the Great Depression and continues to be the best-selling game of all time—more than 250 million sold. Since its advent, the thrill of wealth accumulation and economic domination has attracted roughly 480 million players around the world. Indeed, the phrase, "Do not pass Go, do not collect $200!" indicates immediacy in the American vernacular.

Charles B. Darrow is often credited with Monopoly's creation, but a number of forerunners inspired Darrow's hit game. Educator and single-tax enthusiast Elizabeth J. Magie created the Landlord's Game in 1904. Many of Monopoly's features originated with this game, including the concept of property ownership, free parking, Go to Jail, and utilities spaces. Magie's game interested business and economic students at universities across the country and many professors used it as a teaching tool. However, when Magie submitted the idea to the Parker Brothers toy company, they rejected it because of its complexity, educational nature, and overtly political agenda. In 1932, Dan Layman, a former college Landlord's Game fan, created a similar version complete with official rules (something Magie's game lacked) and renamed it Finance. Again, Parker Brothers turned it down citing its complexity and length of play as critical flaws.

Then, in 1933, unemployed repairman Charles B. Darrow's college friend introduced him to the Land-

Monopoly has versions for 103 countries and 37 languages. Most foreign editions use local currency and property names. The thrill of wealth accumulation and economic domination has attracted roughly 480 million players around the world.

lord's Game. Enthralled with the game, and with plenty of time on his hands, Darrow continued to play on his own, adapting elements of the game. He redesigned the board, added color, renamed the properties with Atlantic City street names, and started playing his Monopoly game with friends and neighbors. Soon, Darrow was inundated with special orders for the game.

He approached both Milton Bradley and Parker Brothers with it, but both companies turned him down saying the game was too long, complex, and unfamiliar to game players. Undaunted, Darrow produced more sets and sold them through New York's FAO Schwartz toy store and Wanamaker's and Gimbels department stores. Monopoly's incredible success during the 1934 Christmas season caught Parker Brothers president Robert Barton's attention, and he quickly negotiated a deal with Darrow. Within 18 months, Parker Brothers sold more than two million games. To ensure the Monopoly windfall, Parker Brothers bought out or shut out the competition. They purchased the patents on both Layman's Finance and Magie's Landlord's Game, trademarked virtually every aspect of the game, and sued other toy companies that tried to capitalize on Monopoly's success with games like Inflation, New York, Big Business, Carnival, and Easy Money.

In spite of their initial wariness, Parker Brothers profited handsomely from Monopoly fever. It appears that in the midst of their financial woes, Americans embraced opportunities for wealth, if only in fantasy. As America emerged from the Depression, Monopoly became a symbol of American life. Sales slumped slightly in the late 1930s but rose again during World War II, as the game was a popular morale booster among soldiers. Further, Waddington, Inc., the British firm licensed to manufacture the game in Europe, produced special

Monopoly sets with hidden maps, tiny compasses, and real money hidden inside. Red Cross workers delivered the specially made Monopoly games to Allied soldiers inside German prisoner-of-war camps, who then used them to escape. Cold War era sales continued to climb as the game combined elements of capitalism with the concept of nuclear family togetherness. The game was banned, however, in Communist countries.

Today, there are many variations on the original Monopoly game. Hasbro, Inc. (which acquired Parker Brothers in 1991) publishes official tournament rules for marathons, fundraisers, and even underwater tournaments. Manufactured in 26 different languages for more than 80 countries, enthusiasts play Monopoly virtually everywhere, and world records are set for locations and length of play (99 hours in a bathtub, 286 hours in a tree house, etc.). Variations include Braille, electronic, internet, and the children's editions Monopoly Jr., Don't Go To Jail, and Advance to Boardwalk. In 1994, California company USAopoly obtained licensing rights to manufacture theme-specific Monopoly games based on a number of themes including notable locations, sports teams, corporations, popular films, cartoons, and television programs. Some have become collector's items.

See Also: Hasbro; Parker Brothers; Play as Competition, Psychology of; Play as Competition, Sociology of.

Bibliography. Marvin Kaye, *The Story of Monopoly, Silly Putty, Bingo, Twister, Frisbee, Scrabble, Et Cetera* (Stein and Day, 1973); Rod Kennedy, Jr., *Monopoly: The Story Behind The World's Best-Selling Game* (Gibbs Smith, 2004); Philip E. Orbanes, *Monopoly: The World's Most Famous Game and How It Got That Way* (Da Capo Press, 2006); James Poniewozik, "ARTS-Monopoly: The Board Game Retools for the Age of Starbucks," *TIME* (September 25, 2006).

Jennifer Terry
California State University, Sacramento

Monte Bank

Monte Bank, also called Mountebank, Monte, or Spanish Monte, is a gambling card game played with a "Spanish deck"—a standard 52-card deck with the eights, nines, and 10s removed (making 40 cards). Less frequently played at home, it is usually played in gambling establishments, where a house dealer takes the role of the banker, dealing a top and bottom layout of two cards each face-up on the table. Players then wager on the top or bottom, and the deck is flipped over to reveal the bottom card, or Gate. If the Gate is the same suit as the top or bottom, the banker pays out those bets, while collecting on the others.

As a gambling establishment game, the odds work out well. No player is taking a significant risk, and most of the money passes back and forth between players, with the banker as a middleman. Frequently enough, both top and bottom will lose, providing a big collection for the banker, to make the game profitable for the house. There is no particular strategy to the game, which is little more than chance. Its popularity in the United States began with the prospectors during the Gold Rush of 1849, who had significant capital and few assets or expenses.

See Also: Gambling; History of Playing Cards; Spain; United States, 1783 to 1860.

Bibliography. Elliott Avedon, *The Study of Games* (Krieger Pub., 1979); Roger Caillois, *Man, Play and Games* (University of Illinois Press, 2001); T. Denning, *Spanish Playing Cards* (The International Playing-Card Society, 1980); David Parlett, *The Oxford Guide to Card Games* (Oxford University Press, USA, 1990).

Bill Kte'pi
Independent Scholar

Montessori

Maria Montessori was an Italian humanitarian, physician, and educator. She is best known for the development of the Montessori Method during the early 1900s. She proposed a way of educating young children by addressing the strengths and needs of the whole person and teaching life skills and independence. This approach was vastly different than the educational approach of the time—the Lancasterian method, in which large groups of children were taught to recite and regurgitate facts taught by the teacher. Montessori was also opposed to the traditional concept of play as necessary for children's learning and development. This caused great opposition to her approach in the United States for many years. Despite much critique, the Montessori method has significantly influenced early childhood education around the world. Today, thousands of Montessori schools exist around the world.

Maria Montessori's Background

Maria Montessori was born in Chiariville, Italy, in 1870. Her father was a government official and her mother came from a well-educated, affluent family. When Maria was 5 years old, her family moved to Rome, and as a result she had many more educational opportunities than in her birth town. Throughout her life, she was encouraged and well-supported by her family, and was the first woman to graduate from medical school at the University of Rome in 1896. Women were not admitted to medical school in those days, and it was reported that she appealed to the Pope in order to gain admission. Maria was very successful during her tenure at medical school and passed her test with a score of 105 (a score of 100 was considered exceptional). Early on in her medical career she worked at a children's hospital, had a private practice, and represented Italy at several international conferences.

Based on some of her early medical experiences with children with cognitive impairments, she became convinced that these children would benefit most in an educational setting rather than a hospital. Beginning in 1897, she began developing a program of education for those children considered impossible to educate. In 1898, she gave a lecture at the Educational Congress in Torino about the training of the disabled and was subsequently appointed by the Italian Minister of Education to the Scuola Ortofrenica, an institution devoted to the care of those with mental retardation. In this setting, she further developed and tested her theories, which combined the ideas of educational scholar Froebel with her own interdisciplinary training in medicine, education, and anthropology. As a result of her program, several of her students passed the state examinations in reading and writing with above-average scores.

Also in 1898, Maria Montessori gave birth to her first and only child, Mario. She had a romantic relationship with a man whom she did not marry. Both had agreed to remain single, but later he married someone else. Mario was sent away to a wet nurse and then to boarding school while Maria continued her efforts in the education of children.

Growing Success

Because of her success with children otherwise considered uneducable, Montessori was asked to start a school for children in a housing project in Rome. It opened in January 1907, and she called it *Casa dei Bambini* (Children's House). The Children's House was essentially a childcare center in an apartment building in a poor neighborhood of Rome. Montessori was focused on teaching the students ways to develop independence and skills at their own pace. Through careful observation of these children and their development, she created the Montessori Method—educational principles designed to provide children with the skills to live successfully in their world and to contribute to society at large. She developed specific materials that facilitated children's independence, as well as their cognitive and visual motor development. While many of the activities were independent in nature, she made sure that the curriculum also included opportunities for children to collaborate with one another and to care for their environment. Her educational method was unique at the time, since it was based on her understanding of the child's cognitive, physical, and emotional development.

Her success in Rome did not go unnoticed. In 1913, Alexander Graham Bell and his wife Mabel invited her to the United States. Both were interested in her teaching methods and founded the Montessori Educational Association in their Washington, D.C., home. Interest in the Montessori Method increased when Maria was invited to set up an exhibit at the Panama International Exhibit in San Francisco. This exhibit featured an authentic Montessori classroom from which onlookers could view the method through a glass wall. While many were lauding the Montessori Method around the world and considered Montessori to have completely revolutionized education, interest in America began to quickly dwindle after a scathing review by William Heard Kilpatrick, a professor at Columbia University's Teachers College. His primary critique of her method was that it was too restrictive and did not aim to develop the young child's imagination. Only a few Montessori schools remained in the United States until 1950 when Nancy Rambush, an American educator, revived interest in the method.

In 1922, Montessori was appointed as Inspector of Schools in Italy. Shortly after, she was exiled from Italy for opposing Mussolini's fascist regime. A devout pacifist, she did not believe in training children to be soldiers and advocated for world peace. Montessori fled to Spain, but left for Larden, Netherlands, in 1934. It was there she opened the Montessori Training Center. Her work continued to spread worldwide and training centers were founded in London and India. Throughout her life she advocated for peace and in 1949, 1950, and 1951 she was nominated for the Nobel Peace Prize. Maria Montessori died in 1952 in Holland.

Montessori Method—View of Children

There are several different principles and beliefs that set Montessori education apart from the traditional methods of education. The Montessori philosophy is built upon a deep and profound respect for children and their abilities. Montessori believed that children enter the world ready to learn, with an innate sense of curiosity and purpose. According to her, "the secret of childhood" was that children would spontaneously engage in tasks that helped to further their development as long as they were not restricted by adult demands. In this view, she believed that children strive for purpose and order in their activities and exploration of the environment.

Montessori advocated for children working to develop themselves into productive adults, yet understood that children are not "adults in small bodies." She advocated for the development of an internal sense of accomplishment rather than engaging in learning tasks for an external reward. As a result, prizes, grades, and tests were discouraged in the traditional Montessori school. Montessori believed that children needed to live in freedom. According to her writings, freedom is the development of self-discipline—the ability to choose what to do, rather than to be subject to one's emotional desires. Montessori teachers are critical in facilitating this development by allowing choice in the classroom, while simultaneously maintaining high expectations for behavior and performance.

Montessori Stages of Development

Montessori believed that children transition through four distinct phases that prepare them for learning, which was termed "the constructive rhythm of life." Each phase is represented as a plane of development spanning a six-year time termed a "sensitive period." During a given sensitive period, the child is biologically primed to master specific skills and concepts. According to Montessori, two phases, birth to 6 years, and 12 to 18 years, are considered volatile periods with significant changes in learning and development, whereas the periods from 6 to 12 years and 18 to 24 years are considered stable periods in which strengthening and integration of skills developed in the earlier phases occurs.

Within each plane, specific stages are delineated. The first plane, birth to 6 years, is broken down into two stages. Montessori termed the first stage the "unconscious absorbent mind," which runs from birth to age 3. During this time, infants and toddlers absorb cues and information from the environment and model and imitate them. This period lays the foundation for future development and learning as the infant's brain development is undergoing tremendous physiological changes and meeting many different milestones in language and learning. According to Montessori, most problems during the infant–toddler period stemmed from adult views of children as helpless and dependent. These feelings and subsequent actions deterred children from their innate drive to act on and make sense of the world.

The period from 3 to 6 years of age is termed the "conscious absorbent mind." During these preschool years, children make order out of the environment by becoming a factual and sensory explorer of their world. In doing so, the child brings to his "consciousness" those earlier ideas and impressions formed during the unconscious stage.

During the second plane, ages 6 to 12 years, children shift their focus from development as an individual to that of a social being. According to Montessori, children in this phase move beyond the "absorbent mind" to the "intellectual mind." Their physical and mental growth allows them to explore their world with increased concentration, attention, and intellectual fortitude. Children in this phase seek to understand the "how, when, and where" of questions, using their powers of logical thought and reasoning. This period of development is also marked by an interest in the world beyond the home and classroom.

The plane representing the ages 12 to 18 years is characterized by children's reconstruction of themselves as social beings within a community including peers, family, and society. Children become most interested in work and academic studies that are most directly related to the real world.

The final plane of development between the years of 18 and 24 is characterized by self-motivation in learning and an ability to apply knowledge to the real world.

Children are now young adults who are able to use their knowledge and skills in conjunction with the resources of the outside world to continue to develop their knowledge base and positively impact their communities.

Montessori Method—Curriculum

Montessori's view of children as competent, curious learners is reflected in the curriculum and materials across all planes of development. Montessori classrooms are characterized by allowing for long periods of time for uninterrupted work and activity (some as long as three-hour work cycles), mixed age groups in two- to three-year spans, beautifully crafted and aesthetically pleasing surroundings for learning, and freedom to select materials and activities that are innately interesting to the child.

Most Montessori programs are geared toward the preschool years from the ages of 3 to 6; however, there is a growing popularity of programs that serve infants and toddlers, as well as elementary and high school–aged children and youth.

Montessori Primary Curriculum

The primary classroom (preschool classroom) includes children from 3 to 6 years of age, and the curriculum focuses on six key areas/experiences: practical life, sensorial, language, mathematics, music and art, and cultural subjects and peace education.

Practical Life—The practical life areas provide materials and activities geared toward helping children develop competence in the skills of everyday living, as well as providing a foundation for those skills that will support learning in other areas of the classroom. The practical life area often contains materials for activities such as sewing, buttoning, pouring, cutting, and preparing a snack for the class, and gardening or cutting flowers for the school. A single activity such as cutting a carrot provides an opportunity for children to focus their attention and energies on preparing the task, working on the task, and then finishing it. This process teaches children the importance of following a sequence of smaller tasks to complete a larger task, and also can enhance other skills such as eye-hand coordination, independence, order, concentration, self-esteem, and working as part of a community.

Sensorial—Beginning from the third year of life, children are introduced to the sensorial area of the classroom, which includes activities and tasks that aid in understanding the process of classifying and categorizing knowledge. Montessori believed that sharpening the senses was necessary for future intellectual development by increasing perceptual and sensory skills and helping the child move from concrete understanding to abstract awareness. For example, a sensory activity might require a child to order a series of shades of the color blue from darkest to lightest. Doing so is believed to help refine judgment and perceptual skills.

Language—Language in the Montessori classroom is supported through numerous interactions among children, their peers, and the teachers. A child's ability to act on the environment with freedom provides a rich social context for oral language development, especially given the mixed-age structure of the classroom. Montessori also created specific materials that would aid in the development of written language. The most widely used material is the sandpaper letters. Each letter of the alphabet is represented as a three-dimensional object. This design allows children to employ multiple learning modalities, including the visual and kinesthetic exploration of letters, and allows children to form a mental representation of the letter in their mind. The letters may also be used to form words during a learning activity. A unique and related feature of Montessori programs is that many children learn how to write in the cursive form first. Montessori believed that this type of writing was easier for the child, as its form is more like the looping and scribbling of a toddler or young preschool child.

Mathematics—Montessori believed that the foundational skills needed for logical mathematical thinking were developed in the sensorial and practical life areas. Mathematic materials consist of counting beads, geometric shapes, and concrete materials that introduce children to abstract concepts such as fractions.

Music and Art—Montessori classrooms provide opportunities for education in both art and music. Montessori believed in the importance of creating a beautiful, aesthetically pleasing classroom environment for children to encourage children to act upon the materials. In the early 1900s, aesthetic education was developed indirectly through interaction with beautifully crafted materials and a wide array of sensory experiences. Today, most Montessori programs understand the need for activities that further self-expression, such as drawing, painting, and sculpting. Music awareness training is developed through the use of Montessori bells, which help in the development of pitch. In contemporary Montessori programs, implementation of musical games, rhyming, and instrumentation are often used.

Cultural Subjects and Peace Education—Montessori viewed the needs of humans as universal and advocated for the need to study the diversity of our world to understand the complexities of human interaction. After having lived through the destruction of two World Wars, she became adamant that the role of educators was to work to establish peace. She believed that if the educational environment could help children develop the skills of respect, tolerance, and compassion, they would transmit these characteristics to their larger world—in her view, children are the hope of peace for the world. A peace curriculum is a component in most Montessori schools. This aspect of the curriculum exposes children to the needs of humanity, respect, tolerance for diversity, and the importance of bettering the conditions for all humanity.

Montessori Elementary Curriculum

The elementary curriculum is constructed to rouse the curiosity and imagination in children ages 6 to 12 and to present material in such a way that each unit was connected to the other. To do this, Montessori developed a thematic study of Cosmic Education. This program includes the "Great Lessons," stories of the universe that provide a foundational knowledge of the universe and earth, but with "holes" that facilitate children's interest in searching for answers. After reading a story, teachers invite children to develop questions about the story and then search for answers using classroom tools and outside research. Accordingly, manipulative materials are still used in the elementary classroom, and students are encouraged to conduct research beyond the school walls. Within this framework, children exercise the freedom to study questions of interest; however, as they seek the answers to one set of questions, they are invariably led to study a related content area, thus leading to understanding of the interrelatedness of all life and knowledge.

Montessori Adolescent Education

Shortly before her death, Montessori had begun to develop plans for the education of older children and teenagers, but this work was not completed. Her plans for these age groups included many of the same components, such as independence building, understanding the self in community, and peace education. Again, using a developmental framework, she envisioned a curriculum that would address the adolescent's vulnerability, combined with powerful intellectual skills and a sense of justice. For this age group, she recommended work on a farm or in a store. She believed that adolescents needed to demonstrate self-sufficiency and that working on a farm would help teach them about the social and economic exchange, as well as teaching them to value physical, as well as intellectual, work.

The Role of the Teacher

The role of the teacher in the Montessori program is very different than in traditional schools. Montessori teachers begin educating children with an understanding that children are individuals and have unique capabilities. The role of the teacher is to carefully prepare the environment and learning materials for children, demonstrate lessons with materials when needed (most often when new material is introduced), and observe children's interactions as they work in the classroom. The teacher does not interfere with a child's work, except when requested or in order to help redirect children when needed. By doing so, the teacher comes to understand individual developmental patterns and can provide more challenging work in a controlled way as each child masters their work.

Montessori Materials

In order to develop self-discipline, the Montessori Method is characterized by an emphasis on self-directed activity on the part of the child, and clinical observation on the part of the teacher. Montessori believed in the concept of a "prepared environment," one designed to meet the needs of the children and optimize independent learning and exploration. According to Montessori, play is not viewed as the vehicle for children's learning, although play is considered an important part of most early childhood programs,

Montessori believed that play, toys, and games were not as entertaining or satisfying to children as more practical activities. She believed that toys could only hold children's attention and interest for a limited time, whereas purposeful engagement with tasks that facilitated development could be sustained for great lengths of time and lead to more internal satisfaction. Accordingly, games, dramatic play, and other types of toys are not found in most Montessori schools. Instead, Montessori designed specific learning materials that aided children's independent learning and exploration and understanding of specific content. However, she cautioned against reliance solely on these materials, as she believed that they were secondary to the interaction between teacher and child.

Traditional Montessori materials may consist of maps, puzzles, colored beads, as well as geometric shapes, all of which are located within reach of the children. Materials are also characterized by the use of autodidactic (self-correcting) equipment to introduce various concepts. A self-correcting material allows children to see their mistake with a task and correct it themselves, rather than being corrected by the teacher. Montessori materials are typically displayed on low shelves and categorized by use (see learning areas detailed previously). Teachers suggest materials after a period of observing children to determine developmental strengths and challenges.

Controversies over the Montessori Approach

Although the educational field has been highly influenced by the work of Maria Montessori, there are many critics of her approach, particularly with regard to the education of young children. Some educational experts are concerned with the lack of dramatic play experiences, the lack of highly structured group time, the lack of emphasis on the performing and creative arts, and the rigid nature of the use of Montessori materials, which have not been updated since the early 1900s.

Research on the Effectiveness of Montessori Education

Research studies on children who attend Montessori programs suggest favorable learning outcomes, particularly in reading, math, and science. A study published in 2006 that compared inner-city students attending a Montessori program by lottery and those attending a neighborhood public school found higher test scores and learning outcomes in those attending Montessori schools. Research on Montessori programs tends to be limited by many methodological issues such as sample size, lack of longitudinal data, and issues surrounding other factors, such as parental school choice.

Montessori Accrediting Agencies

Today, there are approximately 5,000 Montessori schools in the United States and approximately 7,000 worldwide. The majority of Montessori schools are independent private schools; however, there are several public Montessori programs organized under state charters. Of these schools, only a fraction are affiliated with one of the two major accrediting organizations—the American Montessori Society (AMS) and the Association Montessori Internationale (AMI).

A school does not need to be accredited in order to call itself "Montessori," which has led to confusion and inconsistency in application of the approach. Those individuals desiring to teach in Montessori schools are generally encouraged to seek training and certification in an AMI- or AMS-accredited program. Most training centers require the candidate to hold a bachelors degree and undergo study in the Montessori Method, as well as having several hundred contact hours in an accredited Montessori school. Dr. Maria Montessori significantly influenced educational practice in the 20th century. Her influence continues and is seen in some form in almost all school settings today.

See Also: Europe, 1900 to 1940; Italy; Play as Learning, Anthropology of; Play as Learning, Psychology of; Play as Learning, Sociology of; Play as Rehearsal of Reality; Play in the Classroom; Toys and Child Development.

Bibliography. Joe Frost, Sue Wortham and Stuart Reifel, *Play and Child Development* (Merrill-Prentice Hall, 2006); Angeline Stoll Lillard, *Montessori: The Science Behind the Genius* (Oxford University Press, 2007); Paula Polk Lillard, *Montessori Today: A Comprehensive Approach to Education from Birth through Adulthood* (Shocken, 1996) Maria Montessori, *The Montessori Method* (Dover, 2002); Maria Montessori, *The Secret of Childhood* (Random House, 1982); E. M. Standing, *Maria Montessori: Her Life and Work* (Plume, 1998).

Elizabeth Matthews
Abigail M. Jewkes
Hunter College, City University of New York

Morris Dancing

Although it is known that Morris dancing existed in England in late medieval times, with mentions of it in the 15th century—possibly as early as 1448, but certainly by 1483—the exact origin of the world "Morris" is debated by historians, and many concur that the name might have originally been "Moorish Dance"—as the Moors occupied parts of southern Spain until 1492. It has been claimed that the pageant known as the *Moresca* was devised to celebrate the capture of Granada in

1492 by the armies of Ferdinand of Aragon and Isabella of Castile, and this pageant is still performed at Ainsa-Aragon, in the northeast of Spain. With Katherine of Aragon, the daughter of Ferdinand and Isabella, coming to England and marrying Prince Arthur, and later Prince Henry (Henry VIII), it is possible that the tradition might have been brought with her, or alternatively, with other English people connected with Spain. Certainly, Henry VIII's court enjoyed masque dances, offering another possible origin of the name.

In 1599 Shakespearean actor William Kempe is recorded as having been the "head master of Morrice dancers," and William Shakespeare himself mentions a "Whitsun morris-dance" and "a morris for May-day." King James I specifically mentioned in his *Declaration to His Subjects Concerning Lawful Sports to Bee Used,* that Maypole Dancing was legal. However, when Oliver Cromwell took control of England in 1649, all such dancing was banned by his Puritan government. With the Restoration of the Monarchy in 1660, Morris Dancing not only had a revival, but became popular as an outward representation of the end of Puritan Britain. This was particularly celebrated on Whitsunday, which coincided with the birthday of King Charles II.

Gradually Morris Dancing came to villages and towns around England, each using a slightly different manner. It took place on holidays, such as May Day, and also during fairs and fêtes. In the late 19th century, a number of folklorists tried to record what they could about the custom, and as a result there are detailed accounts by Cecil Sharp, Maud Karpeles, and Mary Neal.

A Revival of Morris Dancing

There was a considerable revival of Morris dancing in the late 1890s and through to the 1930s, and Morris dancing once again became common during village fairs. After World War II, with the permanent population of villages falling, many women started to take part in Morris dancing, although some purists were against the idea. During the late 1970s, when there was a rebirth of interest in local history in England, Morris dancing had another revival, and there are many dancing groups around the country. English people overseas took up Morris dancing as a symbol of "Englishness," and there are Morris dancing groups in Australia, Canada, and New Zealand, as well as in Hong Kong and wherever there are expatriate communities, such as Utrecht, in the Netherlands, and Alsace in France.

See Also: Europe, 1200 to 1600; Europe, 1600 to 1800; Europe, 1800 to 1900; Europe, 1900 to 1940; Folk Dancing; United Kingdom.

Bibliography. Lionel Bacon, *A Handbook of Morris Dances* (The Morris Ring, 1974); E.C. Cawte, "The Morris Dance in Hereford, Shropshire and Worcestershire," *Journal of the English Folk Dance and Song Society* (v.9/4, 1963); John Forrest, *The History of Morris Dancing 1483–1750* (James Clarke & Co. Ltd., 1999); P. Lucas, "Bibliography of the Morris Dance," *Journal of the English Folk Dance and Song Society* (v.1/1, 1914); J. Needham and A.L. Peck, "Molly [or Morris] Dancing in East Anglia," *Journal of the English Folk Dance and Song Society* (v.1/1, 1932).

Justin Corfield
Geelong Grammar School

Mortal Kombat

In the early 1990s, fighting simulation video games, or "versus fighters," enjoyed a surge in popularity. The most prominent of these games were Street Fighter II: The World Warrior (Capcom, 1991) and Mortal Kombat (Midway, 1992). Like many games before and after, Mortal Kombat found itself at the crux of technological innovation and public controversy. While Street Figther II trades in a cartoon aesthetic, the more realistic graphics and over-the-top violence of Mortal Kombat made the game a target for criticism. As the controversy ballooned into a broader cultural debate about violent video games, profits from Mortal Kombat soared. Its console release was a massive success, and the game spawned a continuing series of sequels and spinoffs.

The popularity of Street Fighter II in 1991 inspired Midway to make its own foray into the fighting simulation market. While mimicking the basic gameplay mechanics of that game, Mortal Kombat emphasizes visual realism through its use of digitized images of real martial artists, while simultaneously pushing its violent content into the unreal: In the game's "finishing moves," characters eviscerate one another with their bare hands, beheading their opponents and ripping out their internal organs.

The game's combination of visual realism and extreme brutality was an unwelcome development in the eyes of many who were already wary of violence in video games. The late 1980s had seen arcade games such as NARC (Midway, 1988) and Splatterhouse (Namco, 1988), which featured graphic depictions of gore and invited players to engage in what some took to be gratuitously violent acts. While those earlier games sparked controversy, Mortal Kombat's extreme popularity made it an opportune target for groups interested in censoring video game content.

Game Violence Leads to a Rating System

Violence in popular culture had long been an issue of concern for parents and others who intuited a connection between the content of a society's fictions and the course taken by the society itself. The violent horror and action films of the 1970s and 1980s had created wariness about media content. Precursors to video games such as pinball machines had long been criticized for their supposed morally corrupting character; when the video arcade emerged in the 1970s, it was quickly seized upon as a place of potential danger for impressionable youths. The combination of violence and gameplay was alarming to some critics, who noted that a child could only watch a movie, but could—and indeed was required to—participate actively in the violence of a video game. The release and popularity of Mortal Kombat in arcades, and the game's home-console release the following year, brought the debate to a fever pitch.

On September 13, 1993, the game was simultaneously released on every major home console, a release dubbed "Mortal Monday" in the game's massive marketing campaign. The success of the home console versions brought the violence of Mortal Kombat into the home; by December of the same year, the U.S. Senate was holding hearings on video game content. The games industry made a move of appeasement, offering to self-police by applying ratings to their products. Even with violent or other potentially objectionable content labeled on video game packaging, concern about games' possible influence on players persisted; 10 years after Mortal Kombat was released, a similar furor erupted around Grand Theft Auto III (Rockstar, 2001).

An Expanding Brand

A number of sequels to and spinoffs of Mortal Kombat have been released over the years, from Mortal Kombat II (Midway, 1993) to Mortal Kombat: Armageddon (Midway, 2006), with more installments planned for the future. The games have also spawned, among other entertainments, theatrical films, a touring live show, and an animated television series. The later installments in the series are no tamer than the original, but they have not drawn the critical fire that the early games did. The controversy has moved on; Mortal Kombat is now less a political watchword than it is a long-lived brand name.

See Also: Arcades; "Bad" Play; Boys' Play; Grand Theft Auto; Street Fighter I and II.

Bibliography. Edmund L. Andrews, "Industry Set to Issue Video Game Ratings as Complaints Rise," *New York Times* (December 9, 1993); Justine Cassell and Henry Jenkins, *From Barbie to Mortal Kombat* (MIT Press, 1998); Andreas Jahn-Sudmann and Ralf Stockmann, eds., *Computer Games as a Sociocultural Phenomenon: Games Without Frontiers, Wars Without Tears* (Palgrave Macmillan, 2008); J. Patrick Williams, et al., eds., *Gaming As Culture: Essays on Reality, Identity And Experience in Fantasy Games* (McFarland, 2006).

Daniel Reynolds
University of California, Santa Barbara

Mother-Child Play

Mother-child play is an enjoyable activity shared by a mother and her child that facilitates the child's opportunity to choose, lead, and/or initiate play, while the mother responds accordingly or initiates play. Through this activity, children may express and process their emotional, physical, and cognitive needs while using objects or toys in a variety of ways, according to their ability. Therefore, mother-child play is important to the child's development in a large range of areas. It changes according to a child's developmental stage and according to the environment or culture in which it occurs. This shared play is also important in enhancing the mother-child relationship and is influenced by it. In order to better understand mother-child play, it is important to understand what mother-child interaction encompasses.

Mother-Child Interaction

Mother-child interaction can be defined as the initial relationship between a mother and child that provides the social basis on which child development in all areas occurs. Mother-child interaction is dynamic and complex and is characterized by a mutual influence of the mother and the child. Much importance is placed on aspects of a mother's behavior that influence this interaction. These include: maternal sensitivity and maternal responsivity, defined as sensitive and accepting behaviors of the mothers toward their child (for example, "I understand that it is difficult for you, and appreciate your effort"); maternal involvement, i.e., qualitative and adaptive maternal behaviors while interacting with her child (for example, the mother is involved in the child's play, rather than sitting on the side, as an observer); and maternal control style, namely, the mother's tendency to support or control the child's autonomy (for example, "You need help," "I will show you how to build a tower"). These behaviors are seen in mother-child play.

Factors That Influence Mother-Child Play

The mother's own experiences as a child, as well as her cultural and educational background, influence her perception of play in general, and specifically of the goals of shared play. Some mothers view shared play as an opportunity for enjoyable experiences with their child. Others view play as a means for learning and acquiring values, such as helping others (for example, feeding a doll or listening to adults), habits (for example, singing to a doll before putting it to sleep); and/or new skills such as linguistic, social, cognitive, and independent learning (for example, via puzzle or computer games).

The mothers' perceptions of the goal and value of shared play also affect the frequency of shared play throughout the day. In addition, the previously mentioned factors may have an effect on the mother's responses to the child during shared play.

This may display itself in the following behaviors: affirmations, where the mother affirms the child's choice of toy or object and play behaviors through words or gestures, thus encouraging the child to repeat behaviors, such as, "You're working well," or "You did the puzzle just right!"; structuring and parental scaffolding, namely, the mother encourages play through use of verbal or nonverbal messages she provides the child, e.g., "First we place the big block, and then we place the small one on it"; modeling and guidance—providing a physical or verbal example (modeling) or sign how to use the toy or object or giving new ideas for play, e.g., the mother puts her hand over the child's hand to help him or her thread beads on a string, or says, "Maybe the doll is hungry?"

Other mother-child behaviors include mutual compliance—the balance between the mother complying with the child's initiatives, and the child complying with hers, e.g., the child chooses a game in which the mother joins, and then she incorporates ideas that the child has added into their new activities; mediation, where the mother provides graded cues according to the needs and abilities of the child; and the adaptation of the environment according to the needs of the child with regard to the number and types of toys available for play so that the child will not feel emotionally or cognitively overwhelmed, or become bored because of a lack of stimulation as well as adjusting the noise levels, lighting, temperature, and size of the play area.

As children develop, shared play extends to games with more extensive rules, sport games, creative art, or hobbies.

The Play Environment

Mother-child play is a daily experience occurring in a variety of settings such as at home, outdoors, or in the car. Further, shared play may occur throughout the day: during feeding, bathing, waking up, going to sleep, or as part of a child's leisure time. Within all of these environmental and temporal contexts, the involvement of a mother in her child's play can vary according to the situation. She may be actively involved or observe from the side.

Types of shared play may include: use of toys for investigating or practice, most commonly used among babies and young children; shared creativity (drawing, pasting, sculpting); reading a book; games with rules (Monopoly, cards); symbolic play (taking care of a doll, driving a train); dramatic play (functional games with a plot or story); rough-housing or physical play (tickling,

Catch, Hide-and-Seek, water games); and integrating activities that are not necessarily play (counting cards to learn math).

Developmental Stages

From infancy to adolescence, the style of mother-child play undergoes changes. These changes are dependent on a child's motor, cognitive, linguistic, social, and emotional development. At each stage, a mother uses a variety of activities, behaviors, and responses, such as those previously noted, including mediation, modeling, and environmental adaptations, in her interactions with her child.

Infancy: birth to 6 months—The infant is involved in behaviors of investigation and self-stimulation (the pleasant sensations of moving arms and legs, looking at faces, putting objects in the mouth). The mother is the one who provides the stimulations with the purpose of receiving a response from the baby.

6 to 12 months—The baby becomes mobile in a small area, moves on its stomach, rolls over, and crawls. It is able to move itself to different objects and uses a variety of in-hand manipulations. Likewise, the baby's motor abilities to imitate familiar gestures and activities increase. In shared play the baby begins to initiate play. For example, the baby may give a ball to the mother so that she will play with him. The mother may roll the ball to the baby and request that he or she roll it back to her.

12 to 24 months—The toddler's mobility increases. Play occurs in open spaces, and includes movement and manipulation of items. In addition, language skills are more developed and toddlers understand much of what is said to them and are able to express themselves through a number of words. Shared play may also include songs with movements and simple symbolic play experience (holding a doll, imitating telephone conversations, feeding himself with a spoon).

24 to 36 months—Motor coordination and control are improved, allowing the child greater movement in the near environment. Play may include climbing on objects, ball games, and manipulation of more complex toys (threading beads, building blocks). Imitation skills improve, and symbolic play becomes more complex, for example, undressing or feeding a doll, or driving a toy car through an area. These improved abilities may manifest themselves in shared play through reciprocal interaction, including games with rules such as Hide-and-Seek games.

36 to 48 months—Children at this stage have greater language skills that enable them to express their wants and needs during the play experience. They still enjoy the process of playing, but not necessarily the outcome product. For example, they enjoy drawing or building with blocks, but do not relate to the outcome product or take pride in it. During mother-child play, children use language as a form of communication, and also as a means to make the mother laugh. They enjoy reciprocal games, taking turns, creative play, and symbolic and dramatic play, in which they are able to dramatize parts of a story or plot that the mother joins in.

48 to 60 months—The child begins to show interest in the outcome products of play. In addition, the child is able to imitate reality in a more sophisticated manner. The child understands turn taking and is able to partake in an activity, working toward a common goal. Dramatic play becomes rich in detail, and the child enjoys reenacting imaginary scenes, and integrating language through play by using rhymes and telling funny stories.

60 to 72 months—The child becomes interested mostly in games that emulate reality. Reproducing reality may express itself in creative activities (drawing a house) or in make-believe play. The child focuses on outcomes, including winning and losing, as seen in games with rules such as Monopoly, card games, Catch, and building houses or models of cars. Children initiate and want to control the games, and they often negotiate the rules of the interactive game with their peers and with adults. As they develop, shared play extends to games with more extensive rules, sport games, art, or hobbies.

Cultural Perspectives

The definitions of mother-child interaction and of concepts related to mother-child play described above are based on theories developed within Western culture. However, according to modern theories, such as Piaget's theory, content, structure, and function of play development for a child are not universal but, rather, are influenced by the specific culture of the children and their families. It is therefore understandable that mother-child play would be different across groups and cultures.

In modern societies, mother-child play occurs throughout the day, and so in these societies, mothers view play as an integral and meaningful aspect of their parenting role, thus placing much emphasis on being involved in their children's play activities. In addition, these parents believe that through play, they are preparing their children for coping with different conditions including social, educational, and financial situations. Therefore, the mother-child interaction is directed toward preparing the child for developing social and academic skills. An example of this is seen in the United States, where mothers tend to use two central strategies to integrate their children's play into daily life: strategies of segregation and strategies of inclusion. In strategies of segregation, the mothers share their time between housework activities and playing with their child. For example, the mother is cooking, stops to play with the child, and then returns to cook. In strategies of inclusion, the mother integrates play with housework activities. For example, the mother plays Hide-and-Seek games with her child while cooking or includes the child in cooking activities, while pretending he is a real cook.

Cultural differences, though, do exist among modern societies. For example, there are differences between the play-form of mothers in the United States and that of Taiwanese mothers. In the United States, much is centered around the child. This is evident in the number and variety of games and toys used during mother-child play (e.g., imaginary play, functional shared play, and use of fantasy are legitimate aspects of shared play). In contrast, play in Taiwanese culture is often based on teaching obedience, in particular to the adult. Shared play may occur through use of stories to educate the child or instill values, or imaginary games where the emphasis is on developing appropriate social behaviors.

Mother-Child Play in Developing Cultures

In developing societies, such as the Mayan culture, mother-child play differs from modern societies for a number of reasons: (a) in these societies, the death rate among children is higher. A mother may limit her relationship and play with her child as a means to protect herself from depression and emotional distress if a child should die; (b) children are brought up in an extended family, and therefore have relationships with many adults at the same time; (c) often, older children are involved in caring for and playing with younger children, and (d) parents expect their children to grow up to be disciplined and motivated members of the community; parents prepare their children to work and fight and place little emphasis on play interactions; (e) in these societies, it is a common belief that children until the age of 5 or 6 years do not understand enough, and therefore it is not necessary to play and speak with them; (f) it is a common belief that babies need to sleep, and parents mainly act to put their child to sleep, and reduce arousing stimulation, including the stimulation of play; and (g) to a large extent, the children have independence and autonomy to decide how they wish to use their time. Consequently, researchers have found that the most common types of play in the Maya tribe, for example, are among children or by themselves. It is very rare that mother-child play takes place.

Populations With Special Needs

Children with special needs (SN) often are limited in their ability to play in general, and specifically with children of the same age. Therefore, mother-child play has great importance for these children. Experts in the field of child development recommend that parents choose suitable equipment and toys according to the abilities and needs of their child and adapt the environment so that the child can play in a safe and enjoyable manner. The involvement of the mother in the play of children with SN is essential, because often, without her help, the child may not be able to experience enjoyable play times.

Therefore, it is important that mothers of children with SN have the necessary knowledge about the child's ability to play and other skills in order to assist their child in play activities, for example, to provide objects with a variety of textures or options for outdoor and movement play for children with sensory deficits, to choose games with large pieces for children with motor difficulties, to provide appropriate seating according to physical needs, and to reduce the number of toys in the play area to enable the child with attention or regulation deficits to choose activities they desire. In addition, it is recommended to find strategies to improve the mother-child interaction during shared play, for example, by providing simplified instruction with use of modeling, to allow the child time to respond to cues from the parent and to encourage channels for communication.

See Also: Cooperative Play; Finger Games; Human Relationships in Play; Piaget and Play; Psychological Benefits of Play; Toys and Child Development.

Bibliography. Susan Bazyk et al., "Play in Mayan Children," *The American Journal of Occupational Therapy* (v.57/3, 2003); Reuven Feuerstein, Pnina S. Klein, and Abraham J. Tannenbaum, *Mediated Learning Experience. Theoretical, Psychosocial and Learning Implications* (Freund Publishing House,

Ltd., 1991); Wendy, L. Haight et. al., "Universal, Developmental, and Variable Aspects of Young Children's Play: A Cross-Cultural Comparison of Pretending at Home," *Child Development* (v.70/6, 1999); David F. Lancy, "Accounting for Variability in Mother-Child Play," *American Anthropologist* (v.109/2, 2007); Eric W. Lindsey and Judith Mize, "Parent-Child Physical and Pretense Play: Links to Children's Social Competence," *Merrill-Palmer Quarterly* (v.46/4, 2000); Margaret M. McGarth, Mary C. Sullivan, and Ronald Seifer, "Maternal Interaction Patterns and Preschool Competence in High-Risk Children," *Nursing Research* (v.47/6, 1998); Lisa M. Noll and Carol Gibb-Harding, "The Relationship of Mother-Child Interaction and the Child's Development of Symbolic Play," *Infant Mental Health Journal* (v.24/6, 2003); L. Diane Parham and Linda S. Fazio, eds., *Play in Occupational Therapy for Children* (Mosby, Inc., 1997); Loree A. Primeau, "Orchestration of Work and Play Within Families," *The American Journal of Occupational Therapy* (v.52/3, 1998).

Amiya Waldman Levi
Naomi Weintraub
Hebrew University, Jerusalem

Music, Playing

Piano ivories and guitar strings resound with questions of who, what, when, where, why, and how. Who plays, for what purpose, by what means, and to what ends matters as much as when and where we listen. An outdoor festival performance of "I Wanna Be Sedated" means something entirely different to radio listeners at a dental office.

Infants and adults have played music throughout the ages and across cultures. Arnhem Land storytellers have spent multiple centuries relating information through music to attentive listeners in Australia. Across the globe, modern Mexican balladeers have integrated news commentary on political crises and natural catastrophes within folk lyrics since the 19th century.

We conflate play with performance in what modern rationalists once identified as mindless pleasure. Yet Plato and Aristotle placed high value on musical training long before Descartes' separation of will from understanding. Provided we do not taint a performance with tasteless interpretation, Aristotle thought we could improve our minds by learning how to play music correctly, while avoiding vulgar games or senseless banging.

Playing music well requires coordination and cooperation among composers, performers, listeners, industry workers, and the works of art. According to Christopher Small, "musicking" calls for an interrelated number of tasks: performing, listening, rehearsing, practicing, composing, lighting, and serving. We all contribute to the musical event by performing this work at this time in that place with those participants.

Musical performance connotes a social act that plays on and off a patterned score of bars and notes (what). Performers and listeners practice or hear music in parts, 15 minutes today or an hour tomorrow (who and how). We discover that delight resides more in the means of actuation than in the ends of perfection (why). And we contemplate the authenticity of a "one-night only" performance in and between recorded copies then and there (when and where).

The "When" and "Where"

Sound performance has more than a 40,000-year history. Aristoxenus and Ptolemy thought about music in the 4th century B.C.E. and 2nd century C.E., respectively, and an association between play and music flourished in ancient Greece. As Carol Gould and Kenneth Keaton write, musicians of the Middle Ages and early Renaissance rarely worked from scores, but instead improvised and memorized most of their pieces. Singers also added embellishment during the Baroque period to compositions by Corelli and Handel. Later composers quickly grew impatient with such "disfigurations" and "distortions" of their work. The original and its copy began to receive different interpretive weights.

Modern-day forms of technology reconfigure times and spaces of musical play. Contemporary recordings simulate new imaginative worlds where performers seem present precisely because of their absence. We envision our favorite band member or singer in a remote studio when we listen to a recording. We also move and dance in response to a recording's inherent demand for an embodied reaction by gestures encoded in its disembodied sound, as Philip Auslander observes. Our perceptions of original performances change with the introduction of new technologies and their copies.

Material apparatuses such as computers collapse space and time, bringing musicians from rural areas into closer contact with urban collaborators. Mechanical tools also modify the physical and mental skills essential to the organization of labor, as Jon Frederickson reminds us. A performer may "lay down" a single track today for a producer who cuts and pastes everything together tomorrow. Historically, musicians made "on the spot" changes in response to conductors or colleagues gathering at the same place and time, yet click track tempos have imposed an inorganic and isolating clock on the recording process.

A machine determines how to measure time and revolutionizes our interaction with sound. Interestingly, vibrato (the combination of periodic changes in amplitude, frequency, and timbre) remains unaffected by technology, while vocals occasionally sound too personal and overproduced.

The "when" of playing music directly relates to "where" performance occurs. Music moves as packets of sound waves released by instrumental vibrations and voices through the ether. Waves change into nerve impulses and rush through our neural networks, leaving a psychophysical impression. We usually respond instantly to the sonic sensation: "I love that song," or "Please, no more!"

Liminal performers migrate from one public or private space to another. A location like the local baseball park may or may not regularly host musical performances, yet players creatively convert these transitory places into suitable spaces for their instruments or voices. As Michael Bywater notes, space acquires a transitional status as the performance progresses and the performer adapts. Much work remains for theories of space and time as recording technologies quickly and unpredictably change.

The "What"

A ritual account of who performs what to whom illuminates the interrogatives. We express communion with others through performances of praise or pardon. As actors or spectators, we follow rules of bowing or clapping to express gratitude and preserve the performative character of a musical ceremony. Émile Durkheim thought of this ceremonial spirit in "collective we" terms. As we play an instrument or digital track, the ritual question of what this means requires an answer based in serious practice, disinterested observation, imagination, and pleasure.

We can appreciate the uniqueness of serious play when we distinguish it from game play. Following Abraham Schwadron, the former directs our attention toward its means rather than its ends. Serious play does not focus on defeating the competition or winning the award. It instead finds pleasure in the educative process of discovering new arrangements or unanticipated sounds. Game play does not fret over philosophical or psychological matters but instead looks to concrete categories based in gratification such as gold, silver, or bronze statues. Performance locates a place for play in the serious study of music.

A sensitive perception of this difference fulfills the prerequisite for disinterested observation. Although mistaken for lack of interest, this idea points to a selfless and impartial motive behind what music playing means for its observers. We play to share our skill, knowledge, or appreciation with others. A disinterested demeanor grounds what we play in a sensory world packed with competing demands for rewards.

Imaginary symbols allow us to rehearse music in our heads against a standard rendition, similar to Schwadron's "inner hearing." Diverse symbols shore up thought processes in the mind. The treble or bass clefs create images of octaves dancing in our heads. We play with a new idea of how to arrange a piece and bring it to fruition by visualizing what it might sound like. We also imagine particular sounds in order to release potential energy or maintain emotional distance from a bothersome memory. What we play can reduce stress and place us in a world of make-believe.

Images produce multiple kinds and degrees of pleasure. We take a different kind of pleasure in playing instruments or mixing music for a loved one than for a group of strangers. Degrees of pleasure vary according to our attitudes toward social events. We may derive more pleasure from attending Austin City Limits than the Newport Folk Festival because of our preference for hearing a greater number of bands. An accurate assessment of intensity depends on a conscious interaction between our minds and the outer world. We bring a serious, disinterested, imaginative, and pleasurable perspective to bear on the meaning of what we play.

The "Who" and "How"

A composer plays with sound and seeks the right performer to realize his or her vision. As performers we have a general idea of what to do with a composition. Through trial runs, we sort out fingering errors and refine expression. We may choose to break a particular piece into fragments and practice them in reverse or random order, spending more time on the difficult parts.

A conductor guides an orchestra toward unity, while the audience applauds at appropriate intervals. The amount of public participation clearly varies between genres, from low to high in classical and rock, respectively.

Artificial categories of "musicians" and "listeners" collapse with mash-up computer technologies that encourage consumers to become producers. "Musicking" grants everyone from computer engineers to stage managers the symbolic rights to participate. How we play together requires cohesive skills, coherent expression, and corporeal communication.

Think of eye-hand coordination, memorization, and the mental agility to quickly anticipate and correct mistakes. Watch a pianist practice at speeds of a dozen notes per second with various hand contortions and finger arrangements. These skills say nothing of the enormous investment he or she makes in time and physiological or psychological stress management, as Mary Reichling writes.

Expression offers us a conscious choice as performers: should we improvise or adhere to a standard representation of the score? The former option calls for a premeditated or spontaneous deviation from notation, such as an increase or decrease in ornamentation. Eric Clarke writes that Stravinsky and Ravel considered any one such departure a distortion of their work. The latter choice suggests that real aesthetic meaning resides in a strict representation of the script.

Nonverbal expression signifies rich communicative possibilities. Examples of mannerisms, gaze directions, hand and arm lifts, or neck and head bends draw awareness to spontaneous signals. For instance, a wink shared between an audience member and a performer may have started as a mere twitch. Simon Frith identifies these collective behaviors as a "rhetoric of gestures" that contrast with and complement verbal communication. The twitch or wink might indicate a gap in what is read from the outside of an audience member's body (a flirtatious wink) and what is meant from the inside of a performer's body (a nervous twitch).

Communicative exchanges between those on and off stage create an intricate system of automatic adjustments based on feedback. A frown or smile says a lot in a short span of time about the quality of the performance. Effective conductors regularly use body language to communicate intentions. A slight upward or downward glance at one member of the orchestra might signal him or her to make a volume adjustment. The "who" and "how" imply that composers, performers, listeners, and everyone else involved in the musicking event care equally about nonverbal expression.

The "Why"

Aristotle found dignity in the doing. Reasons for playing originate in our individual affinities and group affiliations. We may have come from a musical family, or perhaps we spend a lot of time around connoisseurs at the local music shop. Appreciation and education contribute their own motives for playing. Intellectual curiosity may occur naturally within us, accentuated by those with whom we socialize.

We may also play to show off our good taste. An exotic instrument or an underground recording deserve "collective we" auditions in Durkheim's ritual sense. Some of us restructure our life rituals around doing just that: We devote an hour a day to our favorite tunes, or several days a week to searching for the latest singer-songwriters on the internet in anticipation of sharing our discoveries with others.

Public performances often bring creative minds together. By spending time with our violin on the street corner, we might attract new fans and forge interesting collaborations. Playing our songs in public spaces creates great potential to reach like-minded individuals. We might also teach willing learners how to pick up an instrument through an exchange of money or free time.

Playing music yields positive psychological and physiological benefits, as Antoine Hennion points out. The act of playing places us in a positive frame of mind. We resolve stress and tension through sound and silence as welcomed distractions. Noise distinguishes itself from music by our positive or negative responses. We automatically dismiss a noisy radio station whose distant transmitter emits static.

We play music to understand the place of authenticity and fabrication in our lives. When musicians perform "live" in front of the camera's eye, concert audiences choose between the unmediated body at stage center or the mediated flat-panel screens at stage left and right. We learn how to make sense of the spectacle.

Musicians negotiate felt tensions between authentic practice and fabricated performance in front of "live" audiences. The very term "live" only became part of our modern lexicon after the advent of the gramophone and radio, as most concerts were originally performed by musicians "in actuality." The degree of authenticity attributed to any single performance depends on an audience's active acceptance or rejection as it plays out at a particular time and place.

Music playing reminds us of why we think, feel, speak and act the way we do. We look for confirmation of behavior based on ideal images of our favorite performers that reinforce bonds of age, gender, class, race, ethnicity, and sexual orientation. Music playing helps us understand ourselves in relation to others. It is an act of interpretive empathy steeped in expression, exchange, and influence. As Evan Eisenberg suggests, when we play a recording, it is as though someone else were expressing our feelings. When we play an instrument, it is as if we express someone else's feelings. We base these responses in symbolic value, patterned participation, and a seriously playful life. The good life depends on imaginative pleasure as much as it does on serious work. Playing music is one way to realize all of these activities at once.

See Also: Folk Dancing; Musical Chairs; Play as Entertainment, Psychology of; Play as Entertainment, Sociology of; Singing Games.

Bibliography. Philip Auslander, "Performance Analysis and Popular Music," *Contemporary Theatre Review* (v.14, 2004); Michael Bywater, "Performing Spaces: Street Music and Public Territory," *Twentieth-Century Music* (v.3, 2007); Eric Clarke, "Understanding the Psychology of Performance," in *Musical Performance: A Guide to Understanding*, John Rink, ed. (Cambridge University Press, 2002); Émile Durkheim, *The Elementary Forms of Religious Life* (Free Press, 1995); Evan Eisenberg, *The Recording Angel* (Yale University Press, 2005); Jon Frederickson, "Technology and Music Performance in the Age of Mechanical Reproduction," *International Review of the Aesthetics and Sociology of Music* (v.20, 1989); Simon Frith, *Performing Rites* (Harvard University Press, 1996); David J. Hargreaves and Adrian C. North, eds., *The Social Psychology of Music* (Oxford University Press, 1997).

Christopher Joseph Westgate
Texas A&M University

Musical Chairs

Musical chairs is a popular game often played at birthday parties. It is known under similar names in different languages (for example, "chair dance," "chair game," or "going to Jerusalem") and practiced in many countries in Europe, Asia, and America. This game has ancient origins: a similar game (*Khambada Gadane*) has been played in southern India since the 14th century. Musical chairs is usually played by children, but there are also variants for teens and adults. The game's popularity derives from the fact that it can be played indoors and outdoors by a fairly large group of players, and from its easy requirements. In the simplest version of the game, the players are counted and a number of chairs one fewer than the number of players is arranged, usually in a circle or in a line back to back. Other closed shapes can also be chosen, provided the players are able to walk without difficulty around the group of chairs.

According to Howard Gardner's "multiple intelligences theory," from an educational and psychological point of view, these preliminary steps are related to mathematical and visual-spatial skills and abilities.

At the start of the game, the players stand in a circle outside the chairs. A nonplaying person, usually an adult, plays recorded music or a musical instrument. While the music is playing, the players in the circle walk, march, or dance around the chairs. The music suddenly stops, and each player must rush to one of the chairs and try to sit down as quickly as possible. Of course, there is one less chair than there are people, and one player is always left standing. This person is eliminated and play continues until one player remains.

Game Requirements

These steps of the game develop attention, perception, and coordination of gross motor skills. Indeed, in order to perform adequately, a subject must be able to comprehend and organize incoming visual, auditory, and kinaesthetic data and to form judgements with regard to them. Further, an individual must be able to respond quickly to the requirements of the context, exploring the space and moving his or her body with appropriate and accurate gestures and movements. In addition, a person must be able to recall the movements he or she used in the past in order to accomplish the next successful performance. In fact, when complex activities such as walking, marching, or dancing are performed, a subject must properly engage his or her muscles and muscle groups in the right sequence. Moreover, when a fast movement is required, the individual must also quickly choose the most effective trajectory. Not all children can perform these tasks easily and instinctively: approximately 15 percent of students attending primary school experience motor difficulties. For these children, training will be required, and performing games like musical chairs can improve their gross motor skills.

Alternate Versions

In another version of this game, which is played in the swimming pool, floating balloons are attached to the side of the pool by short strings. Participants hold hands and move in a circle while the music plays. When the music stops each player must grab a balloon. The player who has no balloon, or whose balloon bursts, is eliminated. In this version, gross and fine motor skills are required and enhanced. In fact, the players increase their gross motor skills by performing wider movements of arms, legs, feet, or the entire body, and fine motor skills when carrying out smaller muscle movements, which occur in the hands and fingers. In practice, in hand-eye coordination the eyes direct attention and the hands and fingers execute given tasks. Examples of this kind of actions can be grasping others' hands and getting hold of inflated balloons.

Competitive versions of musical chairs are considered able to motivate children in increasing their efforts, fostering self-awareness and goal-awareness. Yet these goals can be achieved also in cooperative learning situations. In a cooperative version of musical chairs, at the beginning of the game there are as many chairs as players. Then a chair is removed and the adult asks the children how, in spite of this, each participant can find a place to sit. Possible answers are chair sharing or sitting on another player's lap. In another cooperative version, the principle rule is that, when the music stops, the players' feet must not touch the floor. Since it is not a player, but a chair, that is eliminated in each round, participants must try to find a place to sit or stand on the chairs that are left, helping one another to squeeze up into an area that gets smaller and smaller. The educational and psychological goals of the noncompetitive versions are those of enhancing in little children their ability to interact effectively in society, solving social problems and cooperating with others.

See Also: Cooperative Play; Play as Competition, Psychology of; Play as Entertainment, Psychology of.

Bibliography. Jyotsna Kamat, "Education in Karnataka Through the Ages," www.kamat.com (cited July 2008); Sarah Ethridge Hunt, *Games and Sports the World Around* (Ronald Press Company, 1964); Barrie Thorne, *Gender Play: Girls and Boys in School* (Rutgers University Press, 1995).

Alessandra Padula
Università degli Studi di L'Aquila

Myanmar

Many serious "games" are played by the Burmese—actual games and metaphorical ones. There is a "name-game" over what to call the troubled nation (Burma or Myanmar), or it may refer to the daily "survival game" for nearly half of the Burmese population who live under the poverty line. Historically, Myanmar has been playing a tense "waiting game" for most of the past 42 years of international isolation, waiting to be noticed, and waiting for international help. The military junta, which has ruled the country since the 1962 coup d'etat, officially changed the country's name from Burma to Myanmar in 1990, but until today many opposition groups do not recognize this change and continue to use the name Burma intentionally. The "name-game" and ensuing confusion in the media is indicative of the Orwellian state that prevails: torture has been institutionalized as political instrument, and campaigns of forced relocations, forced labor, slavery, and the persecution of ethnic minorities are commonplace—thus the different forms of play found there are somewhat different from Western notions of play.

For many Burmese children, playing has become a last escape from the devastating reality, but the opportunities to take part in such amusement are rare. Many children love to play and put *thanaka* on each other—the powder from a local tree that people use on their faces and bodies as a natural protection from the sun. Also, the Myanmar puppetry and marionette performances depicting the stories of Lord Buddha are a famous form of art and play in Myanmar, despite the rise of popularity of modern entertainment. The Moustache Brothers are a famous group of comedians who perform rare political satire for tourists in a country where satire is a serious crime. The Moustache Brothers' show brings together a courageous mix of traditional Burmese dance theatre laced with social satire aimed at the military junta.

Overall, the Burmese people have shown their resilience and their serene nature, which is also reflected in their toys, most of which are made of colorful papier-mache. The *Pyit Taing Haung* toy, for instance, is translated into "that which always rights itself when thrown down": in Myanmar, a person who rises up again in the face of downfall in life is often likened to this toy. In times of crises, the power of play to overcome such dreadful memories is important, and the significance of soccer as a leisure activity needs to be emphasized here. A colonial legacy brought by the British to Burma in the 18th century has resulted in a soccer-frenzied nation, where live broadcasts of European soccer are widely watched and celebrated.

Notably, however, there are two extreme play-sides in Myanmar: those children who have the financial backing of their parents to enjoy the latest computer games in the increasingly popular game centers of the capital Yangon, and those who do not. The majority of Burmese children are subject to a lack of protection, low educational standards, and the difficult health prospects of living in Myanmar, a desolate situation that worsened considerably with the landfall of Cyclone Nargis in 2008, leaving nearly 700,000 children under the age of 17 in need of long-term assistance. Months after the cyclone, teachers in makeshift schools and newly created "play-spaces" report that children are severely traumatized by the disaster and that they find it difficult to concentrate, as even a gust of wind or increasing rainfall throws them off track. Thousands of children are emotionally vulnerable and are at risk of long-term psychological trauma, while wealthier children are exposed to the latest computer and video game trends. It seems that on and off the computer screen, winning or losing is a matter of life or death in Myanmar.

See Also: Play as Catharsis; Play as Rehearsal of Reality; Soccer (Amateur) Worldwide; War.

Bibliography. Andrew Marshall, *The Trouser People* (Viking, 2002); David Steinberg, *Burma—The State of Myanmar* (Georgetown University Press, 2001); The United Nations Children's Fund (UNICEF), "The State of the World's Children 2008," www.unicef.org/sowc08/docs/sowc08.pdf (cited July 2008).

Andrea Valentin
University of Otago

N

Napoleon

There are several games named for Napoleon or based around Napoleonic themes or battles. The original board game, Napoleon, now in its third edition, was published by Gamma Two Games in 1974, as part of a series of games all concerning major battles or battle game scenarios. Subsequent variations have included strategy games, simulations, and educational computer games. Overall, the usage of Napoleon as a generic title for strategy or war games centring on the battle of Waterloo demonstrates its usefulness as a trope, rather than its genuine success in any particular title.

Napoleon is a block Wargame. This means that the units displayed on the board are represented by small wooden or plastic cubes. The cubes are marked on at least one side with a unit designation, and are initially placed on the board facing the player, so that their opponent cannot see which block represents which unit. Some block games have an additional mark on the block showing if the unit is incapacitated or "dead"—this is initially placed face down. Obscuring the nature of the units is one of the many tactics used in Wargames to express the "fog of war," whereby the nature of the unit is initially invisible to the enemy player. Block Wargames initiated from L'Attaque (1908), which was itself an early version of Stratego. Napoleon was one of the first block Wargames.

Napoleon is turn based, with players taking part in the Waterloo campaign, beginning on June 15, 1815. Each turn lasts a third of a day, with the French moving first on the morning of the 15th, the English and Prussians in the middle of the day, and the French again in the evening. The next day, this order is reversed, and so forth. The game can be played with two or three players (French, English, and Prussian sides). If three players are used, there are caveats for the Allied (English and Prussian) side. The board shows a map of the area around Waterloo, with lines denoting transport routes connecting various points. Markers can be grouped together or separately across the board and must move along these points.

Napoleon's second incarnation is as a card game of trickery and tricks, in which each player is dealt a hand of five and must win each trick in order to succeed. Each player bids in order to win each trick, and on the amount of tricks they will win, with each subsequent bid becoming higher, or else the player must pass. "Nap" or "Napoleon," "Wellington" and "Blücher" (the names of the three major generals at Waterloo) are used to describe various bids within the game. The highest bidder chooses trumps, and his or her companions must try to beat his or her card by progressing around the table. The winner of each trick begins the next trick, and so on. The game is won when all possible cards are played and all tricks are won; the player who has won the most tricks wins. The game can also be played for money, where it is usually referred to as "Penny Nap."

Napoleon as a computer game has also undergone several iterations, including a Gameboy Advance title in which this author suspects a great deal of *liberté* was taken with history (or else Napoleon really did fight abominable snowmen and ogres at Waterloo). Most often, like the board games, this takes the form of strategy gaming in the RTS (real-time strategy) format or "God"-style management game. The game of Napoleon for the Public Broadcasting Service (PBS) in the United States is a turn-based educational game that presents the player with simple strategy decisions and a variety of outcomes. It is a typical example of low-grade educative gaming.

See Also: History of Playing Cards; Play as Mock War, Sociology of; Stratego; Wargames.

Bibliography. Elliott Avedon, *The Study of Games* (Krieger Pub. Co., 1979); Robbie Bell and Michael Cornelius, *Board Games Round the World: A Resource Book for Mathematical Investigations* (Cambridge University Press, 1988); Melvin Dresher, *The Mathematics of Games of Strategy* (Dover Publications, 1981); Neil Thomas, *Wargaming: An Introduction* (The History Press, 2004).

Esther MacCallum-Stewart
University of East London

Native Americans

Play served a variety of purposes and was ubiquitous in the lives of Native American men, women, and children prior to and after European contact. While the activities and implements of play varied among different tribes and geographic locations, play as a process of socialization, physical and mental development, and relaxation held a central place for Native American peoples from the deserts of the American Southwest to the frozen landscapes of the Arctic.

The process of play took many forms for Native Americans. From an anthropological and archeological perspective, the two most documented forms of play among Native Americans were games and toys, since material evidence provides a way of recording and analyzing the functions and types of play among the indigenous peoples of North America.

Odds and Probability

In general, Native American games included those that involved the odds of probability and guessing and those that employed the physical strength, dexterity, and endurance of the participants. As a form of play limited to adults, games of chance primarily included throwing dice-like objects with various markings and colors on one or two sides and using counting instruments for keeping score. Common dice-like objects included narrow strips of wood and cane, animal teeth, shells, shaped bone, fruit pits, colored beans and grains, and pottery disks. Common counting devices included stones and sticks placed onto a hide or cloth and wooden pegs placed into a board. Native American men and women played dice-like games for amusement and gambling, but these games often had religious and ceremonial importance and thus, in such instances, were limited to men.

Guessing games made up another form of play and such games of chance were widespread among Native American tribes. Guessing games involved participants selecting in which hand, bundle, or particular object a small item was hidden. Often played in large groups opposite one another, these games were social in nature and often accompanied by drumming and singing. They were also based on the amusement of deceiving an opposing group about the whereabouts of the item through diverting the group's attention and moving the item from one place to another. Such games were usually associated with betting and were meant for adult play.

Physical Development

Play for Native American children and young adults commonly involved games that developed their physical development and the skills necessary for them to function with efficacy in their environments. Archery games, for example, provided boys and young men with the opportunity to practice developing both accuracy and strength conditioning. Archery games consisted of shooting arrows through stationary or moving hoops, shooting an arrow at the ground in an attempt to cross an opponent's arrow, and shooting arrows at targets such as cacti, trees, and bundles of grass. Other archery games focused purely on strength, as young men and boys would see who could shoot an

A Native American tribe playing the Bone Game, an ancient and complex ritual used as a method of conflict resolution and an alternative to aggression. The game is played between two teams of equal size with a minimum of five players per team.

arrow the farthest or over a bluff of trees. Such games, however, were not limited to bows and arrows. Other games utilized the throwing of javelins and darts. Like archery games, these competitive activities functioned both as forms of amusement and as preparation for hunting and warfare.

Native American games that involved sticks and balls were widespread across North America, and these contests furthered the physical development of children and young adults. Furthermore, these games oftentimes developed a necessary competitive and aggressive spirit among boys and young men essential for their future role as warriors. Perhaps the most documented history of a Native America game is that of lacrosse, named by early French Canadians because the lacrosse stick resembled a bishop's crosier.

The violent nature of lacrosse, called "little brother of war" by southeastern tribes, is well documented and viewed as a game closely associated with battle. Played in regions ranging from the Great Lakes to the Northeast, lacrosse consisted of opposing teams each carrying, passing, and throwing a ball past or through the opposing team's goal, oftentimes an object such as a rock or tree or two vertical poles. Players used wooden sticks with closed or unenclosed triangular pockets on one end and a ball made of wood or a ball that was hide-covered and packed with animal fur. Native Americans played lacrosse on fields from more than a mile long to fields approximately 100 yards long. The number of players on a team depended greatly on the region and cultural purpose of the event. Lacrosse games with 1,000 players on each side have been documented.

Games of this magnitude, however, primarily served as exhibitions to impress important figures such as tribal and government dignitaries. Games, even between competing tribes, seldom had more than 100 players and oftentimes had as few as 20 players on each side. Regardless of the size of the game, fierce competition remained a constant attribute of play. In this way, lacrosse became a cathartic means of settling disputes between individuals, families, and tribes. Moreover, the frequently violent nature of play in such a competitive activity mirrored the aggression needed in times of combat and functioned as a form of training through a surrogate of warfare.

Games for Women

Shinny and Double-Ball were two popular stick-and-ball games for Native American girls and young women. Both of these games, in their various styles of play, were common across North America. Unlike lacrosse, Shinny and Double-Ball focused more on the amusement and socialization of play rather than a form of competitive play closely associated with battle. The game of Shinny usually consisted of a single stick curved at the end for striking a wood or buckskin ball. Teams of young women and girls competed against one another by hitting, passing, and shooting a ball through an opposing goal of two posts, stakes, or blankets.

Some historians have linked Shinny with the game of field hockey, but it should be noted, similar games were also played around the world. Double-Ball, as most anthropologists have labeled the game, was a throwing game of dexterity. Using sticks, sometimes straight and sometimes with a slightly curved end, participants played catch with two balls, sacks, or billets tied together with a cord of animal skin. In addition to just being a throwing game, Double-Ball also included competition. In such competitions, participants passed, caught, and hurled the double-ball with their sticks in an attempt to eventually place it near an opposing team's goal. Double-Ball, as a form of play, provided young women and girls with a fun method of physical exertion and social engagement. Some early ethnographers connected the game of Double-Ball to the European and American game of Graces popular in the 19th century, but little evidence supports that the purpose of the game was to develop elegant movements among girls and young women.

Doll Playing

Similar to the universal importance placed on games, the ubiquity of children's playthings gives evidence of the high value Native American communities put on implements that engaged the young in an imaginative, mimetic, and kinesthetic process of learning and enjoyment. Toys for children varied among Native Americans, but common playthings included dolls, miniatures, tops, and string. Dolls were a favorite toy among Native American children, both boys and girls. The material for dolls depended greatly on geographic location. Inuit fathers carved dolls for their children from bone, walrus ivory, stone, sealskin, and driftwood. In the West and Great Plains, wood, cloth, and various hides became suitable materials for doll making. Where corn was plentiful, such as in the northeast, Native Americans made dolls from cornhusks.

Regardless of the materials used, Native American children took great pleasure in playing with dolls, whether elaborate or simple in design, because such play essentially reproduced life through an imitative and imaginative process. For example, girls wrapped their dolls in blankets or placed their dolls on cradleboards and, in their own way, became mothers by caring for their dolls with much love. Additionally, learning to make clothes and other items for dolls provided girls with the skills that would become vital for their roles as mothers. For parents, encouraging doll play began a method of preparing their daughters to eventually take care of children of their own.

In fact, in some Native American cultures, doll playing ended for a girl once she had her first menstruation, for she was now ready for motherhood. Similar to archery games and lacrosse for boys, doll playing functioned as a form of enculturation for girls, whereby they learned the skills and knowledge necessary to fulfill their roles as women in a given societal framework. While boys played with dolls as well, their play often reenacted hunting and warfare. Miniature bows and arrows made from plant stalks and thorns, miniature canoes made from birch bark, and miniature horses carved out of wood often accompanied boys' dolls as they imitated the roles of their fathers, uncles, and other men of the tribe. Doll playing provided children with identity formation and provided many of the necessary skills for them to prepare for adult roles in their communities.

Additional Children's Playthings

Two of the most widely used playthings for Native American children, in addition to dolls, were spinning tops and string for the activity commonly known as Cat's Cradle. Top spinning, as archeological evidence shows, dates back over several thousand years in North America and was perhaps the most common implement of play since tops have been found throughout what is now Canada and the United States. Top design varied from finger tops to string tops. Made primarily from wood and bone and, among the Inuit, walrus ivory, tops offered children much enjoyment, as the toys often were used in games. Keeping the top within a marked circle or square, attempting to knock down an opponent's spinning top with a stone, and seeing whose top could spin the longest were a few of the games children were fond of playing with each other. Another favorite pastime for children involved creating an intricate arrangement of loops around their fingers with string or sinew in order to form imaginative designs and figures. Anthropologist Franz Boas documented the sophistication of Native American designs in the string game he knew as Cat's Cradle and considered the intricacy of Native American string figures to be much greater than those of other cultures. Figures of deer, wolves, beaver, stars, lightning, and spider webs are just a few of the designs recorded by anthropologists and ethnographers, and the creation of such figures and designs illustrates play as a process of creative expression.

Play for Native Americans was an essential part of life, for it offered enjoyment and good fellowship. It also functioned as a process of socialization and physical and mental development for children and young adults. Native Americans considered play an integral component of living. Play—in all its forms—had a variety of purposes and was not a trivial pastime for America's indigenous peoples.

See Also: Arctic Play (First Nations); Boys' Play; Dolls, Barbie and Others; Girls' Play; Play as Learning, Anthropology of; Play as Mastery of Nature; Play as Mock War, Psychology of; Play as Mock War, Sociology of; Spinning Tops.

Bibliography. Stewart Culin, *Games of the North American Indians* (University of Nebraska Press, 1992); Mary Jane Lenz, *Small Spirits: Native American Dolls from the National Museum of the American Indian* (National Museum of the American Indian, 2004); Helen B. Schwartzman, "The Anthropological Study of Children's Play," *Annual Review of Anthropology* (v.5, 1976); Thomas Vennum, Jr., *American Indian Lacrosse: Little Brother of War* (Smithsonian Institution, 1994).

John J. Laukaitis
Loyola University Chicago

Netball

Netball is a skillful, fast-moving, noncontact team sport mainly played by girls and women. Its origins are in the game of basketball, which was invented by James Naismith for boys at the School for Christian Workers (later the Young Men's Christian Association or YMCA), in Springfield, Massachusetts, in 1891. A women's variant of basketball was immediately established and was later introduced to England in 1895. In 1895, Clara Baer asked Naismith for a copy of the rules. The subsequent rule package contained a drawing of the courts with lines penciled across it, simply to show the area various players could best patrol. Baer misinterpreted the lines on the court and thought players could not leave these areas.

Restrictions on player movement on the court remain a feature of the game. The outfits worn at the time hindered movement such as running and dribbling and also contributed to the restrictive modifications. By 1897, the Baer version of the game, which featured baskets, divided courts, and larger balls, was also played in England. The game became very popular. However, without standardized rules, different versions of the game, including variations in the number of players, existed.

Standardizing Netball

In 1901, the first rule book was printed and the game was renamed netball, as baskets were replaced by rings with nets. The rule book spread to English-settled countries such as Australia, New Zealand, South Africa, and the West Indies. Despite the existence of a rule book there were still variations in the rules until 1960, when key Commonwealth countries met to standardize the rules and establish what is now known as the International Federation of Netball Associations (IFNA). World championship events played every four years were also established. In 1995 netball was recognized as an Olympic sport and included in the Commonwealth Games program from 1998. Australia has since dominated the international competition.

The aim in netball is to score more goals than the opponents while stopping them from scoring. It involves seven players from each team playing on a rectangular hard indoor or outdoor court (100 x 50 feet) and uses a round ball, similar to a soccer ball. Each player has a specific position, with restricted movement allowed on the court. The game involves quick and accurate passing between team members, with the rules preserving netball's status as a noncontact and fast-paced sport. In many countries modified versions have been designed for junior players as young as

5 years old to provide a positive learning experience as they gain confidence and build up skills they need to play netball. These modifications vary and may include shorter playing periods, more flexibility on court positions, smaller balls, and lower goals.

Netball is a female-centered sport and is unparalleled in providing women with opportunities to be involved locally and internationally in all aspects of the game including playing, umpiring, and administering. As women's role in society developed through the World War II years and beyond, so did the game, with many more countries and participants now involved.

The game has spread to Asia and Africa and is the most popular sport for women in both Australia and New Zealand. Most netball is played in schools or in club teams affiliated with regional and national associations. While traditionally netball has been played only by girls and women, boys (in mixed teams) and men (in separate competitions) now also play. At elite levels, there is increasing professionalization of the game, with televised coverage of matches and players being paid.

See Also: Australia; Basketball (Amateur); Boy's Play; Girl's Play; United States, 1900 to 1930.

Bibliography. Thomas Hanlon and Human Kinetics, *The Sports Rule Book* (Human Kinetics, 2004); Julia Hickey and Anita Navin, *Understanding Netball* (Coachwise Ltd., 2006); International Federation of Netball Associations, www.netball.org (cited July 2008); Jane Woodlands, *The Netball Handbook* (Human Kinetics Publishers, 2006).

Jeffery Adams
Massey University
Lynette Adams
Sport Waitakere

Netherlands

The Netherlands is located in northwestern Europe, with a coastline on the North Sea. It is sometimes erroneously referred to as Holland, after one of its larger regions; its residents are known as the Dutch. At only 41,500 square miles, it is the largest of the "Low Countries," the low-laying countries along Europe's northern river deltas. More than half of the country sits at or below sea level, with water levels controlled by an elaborate system of dikes, canals, and seawalls. Over 90 percent of the country's 16 million residents live in cities. A center of international trade and commerce since at least the 17th century, it has a long history as a industrious and cosmopolitan country.

Games and Pastimes

With an economy focused on trade and commerce, the Dutch were able to enjoy games and pastime that came from all over the world on the ships that made their way up and down the Rhine, the Meuse, and the Schelde rivers. Over time, they developed their own practices and preferences, some of them still popular today.

Sjoelbak, for example, is a "shovelboard" game that developed in the 19th century from a 15th-century British game called "Shove Ha'penny." In *Sjoelbak,* two players slide 30 wooden discs down a six-foot-long table, trying to navigate through any of four arches at the far end of the table. The game is scored by the number of discs that land in each slot. It remains a popular game in youth centers, in sjoelbak clubs and tournaments, and in families, particularly in the winter months.

Cards are another favored pastime, played not just in the home but in cafés and social clubs as well. Most Dutch card games fall into the *Jass* category, also known as "trick-taking" games, where players follow a series of finite rounds known as "tricks." The national game is *Klaverjas*, where four players form two teams to try to outscore the other.

Demand for traditional puzzles and games remains high in the Netherlands, although most national toy producers have moved their operations to China and the number of privately owned toy stores has begun to dwindle in the face of competition from chain stores. Video and computer gaming is becoming more prevalent and is expected to override the popularity of older games over the next decade.

Outdoor Play and Sports

The Dutch enjoy a variety of outdoor play, including soccer, sailing, rowing, and swimming, but two pastimes really stand out: cycling and skating.

The bicycle was invented in France and perfected in the United States, but it was adopted wholeheartedly by the Netherlands in the late 19th century. Within a year after the first cycle arrived in 1868, a Amsterdam importer had opened the world's first bike-rental service. In 1871, the first biking club was formed. Today, there are an estimated 12 million bikes in a country of 16 million people, and more than half the population bikes regularly—often for transportation, but also for enjoyment. It is probably the most bike-friendly nation in the world, with dedicated bike lanes along most roads in the cities and thousands of miles of bike paths all over the country.

With the entire country rich in rivers, canals, and ponds, and a long stretch of coastline on the North Sea, there are plenty of opportunities to play in the water. But the Dutch also like to play on the water, especially in the winter. Skating came to the Netherlands many centuries ago, and by the 17th century it had become an important part of the Dutch identity.

For generations, skating was an egalitarian pastime. Rich and poor, young and old, male and female, none of it mattered on the the ice. During the coldest winters, "ice-fairs" sprung up along the rivers and canals, offering refreshments, entertainments, and games for the masses. In races, skaters and sledders vied for prizes ranging from fattened geese to gold and silver trophies.

The mass popularity of skating began to fade in the 19th century. The upper and middle classes, in particular, began to favor indoor ice rinks to rivers and ponds. Ironically, this was the point at which speed-skating really began to develop as a formal sport, with new skates propelling speed-skaters at greater and greater velocities. The tradition of long-distance speed-skating lives on in a competition known as the *Elfstedentocht*.

Elfstedentocht literally means "the 11-city race." It originated in Friesland sometime in the 19th century and was formalized as an event in 1890. Competitors try to make the 125-mile trip along a network of canals, rivers, and ponds around 11 cities in Friesland in a single day. The event routinely draws up to 300 serious racers, who are then joined by an average of 16,000 people who just want to enjoy the experience. The *Elfstedentocht* can only be held in years when the ice is six inches thick—hardly an annual occurrence. In fact, the *Elfstedentocht* has only been held 15 times since 1890. The last race was held in 1997. A longtime member of the committee that decides if the ice is sufficiently thick for a race recently told the World Wildlife Fund that he was concerned that climate change was leading to such dramatically warmer winters that the *Elfstedentocht* might become a relic of the past.

See Also: Boys' Play; Girls' Play; History of Playing Cards; Skating; Soccer (Amateur) Worldwide.

Bibliography. J.C.H. Blom, *History of the Low Countries* (Berghahn Books, 2006); Roger Caillois, *Man, Play and Games* (University of Illinois Press, 2001); Glenn Kirchner, *Children's Games Around the World* (Benjamin Cummings, 2000); Peter Jan Margry and Herman Roodenburg, eds., *Reframing Dutch Culture (Progress in European Ethnology)* (Ashgate Publishing, 2007); Nina Millen, *Children's Games From Many Lands* (Friendship Press, 1943); Simon Schama, *The Embarrassment of Riches: An Interpretation of Dutch Culture in the Golden Age* (Vintage, 1997); Colin White and Laurie Boucke, *The Undutchables: An Observation of the Netherlands, Its Culture And Its Inhabitants* (White-Boucke Publishing, 2005).

Heather K. Michon
Independent Scholar

New Zealand

Despite its geographical remoteness, New Zealand has made a significant contribution to the scholarly understanding of play as the context for Brian Sutton-Smith's research. In his 1981 book *A History of Children's Play*, Sutton-Smith surveys not only the variety of children's play manifested between 1840 and 1950 but also the manner in which it reflected the changing political economy and social ideology of New Zealand society. In its focus on mainly Scottish- and English-influenced games played by *pakeha* (New Zealand Europeans), the work also constituted one of the first major comparable research projects to Elsdon Best's (1925) *Games and Pastimes of the Maori*.

Sutton-Smith's book charts the transformation of play from pioneer children's unorganized and unsupervised activities, through to the impact of greater levels of adult interest and regulation of children's recreational activities at the turn of the 20th century. Play in an agrarian frontier existence revealed little parental intrusion, which on the one hand stimulated children's self-reliance in crafting their own play activities, but on the other hand revealed less-romanticized accounts of physically violent and raucous forms of play. Girls, inhibited by social constraints and heavy restrictive garments (the latter presumably dictated by the former), feature much less in written accounts of the diversions offered by the outdoors.

Popular Games

A commonly cited and popular outdoor game for gangs of boys was Cowboys and Indians. Many historical accounts of New Zealand childhood cite the relevance of this game for its seeming preference over other potential Maori and *pakeha* variations. Although a stalking game called "Maori" is recorded as having been played in the 19th century, a more common interpretation of Cowboys and Indians is found in Alan Mulgan's (1944) comments that: "Generation after generation of New Zealand boys have fed with shining eyes on the stories of European and Indian scouts and have scarcely realized that these men have prototypes in their own land." Variants of the game are also noted in the form of "French and English" and eventually the Hollywood-influenced Cops and Robbers.

As an archipelago with the two main islands, Te Ika a Maui (North Island) and Te Wai Pounamu (South Island), New Zealand also possesses regional dialects that are evident in children's games. Some researchers argue that chasing and tagging games divide New Zealand into the south, comprising of Southland and Otago, where children play "Tig," a central area to the north and south of the Cook Strait where "Tag" is played and the north where "Tiggy" is played. While Tig appears to have been brought to New Zealand by early British settlers and Tag is the standard term used in North America and Australia, researchers suggest that Tiggy appears to be a "New Zealand innovation."

With the shift toward the greater influence of commercially produced resources for, and adult management of, children's play, like many other countries, New Zealand experienced an influx of overseas products from a wider range of cultures. While New Zealand imported toys from Europe and America as early as the 1840s, a hundred years later one locally produced toy became so popular that it went on to become a major Kiwi icon—the pull-along toy Buzzy Bee. Furthermore, children's participation in organized sports eventually came to define the popular meaning of the term *play*. However, it might be argued that games such as King of the Castle, Stacks on the Mill, and No Man Standing were probable training grounds for the game of rugby and its required skills of defense, scrummaging, and tackling.

See Also: Boy's Play; Girls' Play; New Zealand Maori; Tag; United Kingdom.

Bibliography. Arnold Arnold, *World Book of Children's Games* (Fawcett, 1972); E. Best, *Games and Pastimes of the Maori* (Government Printer, 1925); Brian Sutton-Smith, *A History of Children's Play: New Zealand, 1840–1950*, (University of Pennsylvania Press, 1981); Brian Sutton-Smith, *The Ambiguity of Play* (Harvard University Press, 2001) M. Trewby, *The Best Years of Your Life: A History of New Zealand Childhood* (Auckland: Viking, 1995).

Gareth Schott
University of Waikato, New Zealand

New Zealand Maori

Maori are the *tangata whenua* (indigenous people) of Aotearoa, which is a group of islands in the South Pacific, now known as New Zealand. Their ancestors were Polynesian seafarers who traveled from the fabled homeland of Hawaiki to New Zealand, on well-planned migrations, in large ocean-going *waka* (canoes) over 1,000 years ago. Maori became numerous and developed into an energetic, healthy, and mobile population with stable social structures and a love for game playing. Each autonomous tribal community developed their own distinctive dialects, *nga mahi a te rehia* (entertainments), *kawa* (ways of doing things), and *tikanga* (customs) based on the values of *mana* (personal prestige), *tapu* (inherent sacredness), and *utu* (reciprocity).

Maori Games

A multitude of games were invented, developed, and hybridized in the centuries after Polynesians first settled New Zealand. Their volume can be appreciated from the renowned research of early anthropologist Elsdon Best, who recorded over 80 distinct pastimes from within the *Tuhoe* tribe alone. Best highlights popular pastimes as *papa takaro* (board games such as *Mu Torere*), *kopapa* (surfing), *Mahi Ringaringa* (hand games), *Whai* (string games), *Poi* (ball games), *Pirori* (hula hoops), *Potaka* (spinning tops), *Haka* (dance), and *Teka* (spear throwing).

Additionally Harko Brown lists ancient games that were played without gender bias such as wrestling (*nonoke mamau*), athletics (including *kaipara* and *wera-te-patu*), canoe racing (*waka hoehoe*), stick play (*mau rakau, poi rakau, korari, karo*) ball play (involving *poi, poi toa,* and *ki* implements), stone stacking (*toka-toka*), problem-solving (*tupea*) and kite flying (*manu tukutuku*). The two Maori games best known internationally are *ki-o-rahi*, a ball game, which was introduced into 31,000 schools by U.S. curriculum directors in 2005, and the board game *Mu Torere,* which is utilized in education worldwide, for example in the Ph.D. mathematics program at St. Joseph's University in Philadelphia, Pennsylvania.

Games were practiced in *paka whakawai* (schools of arms) to transfer skills and techniques from playgrounds to battlefields, to promote learning in *whare wananga* (education centers), to problem-solve everyday situations, and to pass on values and intellect from one generation to the next. According to Burns, games were taught to *tamariki* (children) from an early age to develop their individuality and to implant in them desirable qualities. Game playing was encouraged as a freedom of expression and was never restricted to a time or place. Best supports the idea that game playing was openly fostered at all times, even during the most sacred of rituals, such as *tangihanga* (funerals). Annually, during Te Tau Hou (The Maori New Year), the independent tribes all over New Zealand would congregate for important large-scale festivals. These celebrations, called *Matariki*, were exciting times for ancient tribespeople to display their competitive skills and abilities over several fervent weeks of feasting, dancing, and game playing. It was a time of *rangi marie* (peace), when intertribal warfare ceased.

The Maori populations increased steadily to some 200,000 by the time Captain James Cook first visited New Zealand shores in 1769. Early settlers regarded Maori as an advanced civilization. Their high intellect and physical prowess were associated with the way they utilized cultural games. After 1800, European numbers increased markedly, and the mounting impacts of colonization resulted in the decimation of Maori populations. These high death rates combined with suppressive social policies effectively blunted traditional game-playing adherences. By 1890, Ian Pool claims the Maori population had plummeted to just 36,000, and traditional games were highly stigmatized and rarely played, surviving only tenuously in their *marae* (traditional homeland) enclaves.

A Maori girl is shown holding an elaborately decorated canoe paddle in a 1920 photograph.

Today's Maori

Today, New Zealand has a more inclusive social agenda, the Maori population has increased to over 500,000, and many health and education initiatives are utilizing *mahi takaro.* The games attract far less mainstream resistance and are now openly popularized in many competitions and *Matariki* festivals. Some of the pragmatists who are acknowledged as having led Maori games revivals are Thomas Ellison, Sir Apirana Ngata, Te Puea Herangi, Val Irwin, Ihirangi Heke, Paora Johanson, Hoturoa Kerr, Te Ngaeha Wanikau, Gloria Reihana, and Kipa Munro. Several authors, including Elsdon Best, Alan Armstrong, Jeff Evans, and Bob Maysmor have also disseminated important information on games.

See Also: Australian Aborigines; Kite Flying; Spinning Tops; Surfing.

Bibliography. J. Belich, *Making Peoples: A History of the New Zealanders from Polynesian Settlement to the End of the Nineteenth Century* (Penguin, 1996); E. Best, *Games and Pastimes of the Maori* (Te Papa Press, 2005); H. Brown, *Nga Taonga Takaro: Maori Sports and Games* (Raupo, 2008); P. Burns, *Te*

Rauparaha: A New Perspective (Reed, 1980); P. Finney, "The Development and Diffusion of Modern Hawaiian Surfing," *Journal of the Polynesian Society* (1960); L. Hakaraia, *Matariki: The Maori New Year* (Reed, 2004); C. Orange, *The Story of a Treaty* (Bridget Williams, 1989); F. Palmer, "State of Maori Sport," in M. Mulholland, ed., *State of the Maori Nation* (Reed, 2006); R. Pere, *Ako: Concepts and Learning in the Maori Tradition* (Te Kohanga Reo National Trust Board, 1982); I. Pool, *The Maori Population of New Zealand 1769–1971* (Auckland University Press, 1977).

Clive C. Pope
University of Waikato
Harko Brown
Kerikeri High School

Nigeria

Play in Nigeria challenges our conventional view of play as separate from work, usually requiring commercial toys and games, and rarely involving music. On the contrary, Nigerian children often combine their household chores, including child care, with play. They use natural objects instead of toys, play together in groups, and music, rhymes, dancing, and singing are important parts of their play activities.

The combination of chores and play can be seen in an example from southeastern Nigeria where eight children, ages 6 to 9, after returning from school, set out for the nearest stream, where they gather fresh water for their mothers. They carry large empty plastic containers and clay pots balanced on their heads. One of the older children becomes a "singer" and calls out "*Akwukwo e-e*" (leaf) many times, and each time the children respond with an exclamation "*Eyeewoo*." Once the singer names the type of leaf the others should find, they run into the bush to find it. Any child who does not find that type of leaf is "punished" by being made to sing the running song. They pass a small group of girls who build miniature houses with the local clay-like sand while carrying their younger siblings tied on their backs or in their laps.

Few families can afford imported toys found in local markets, but there are unlimited possibilities for the creation of playthings from local natural and manmade materials. A piece of wood is tied on a girl's back as a doll, a type of leaf pushed on a stick twirls like an airplane propeller as the child runs, and games in the sand can be created with pebbles and seeds. Toys are built out of household objects such small milk cans, sugar cube boxes, pen caps, and bicycle rims. Children also imitate adult activities in play. Boys like to imitate masquerades at special times of the year. They dress up and create costumes and masks from wood, straw, and paper and may go from door-to-door to collect small rewards or coins. Girls perform their own dance routines and have songs with content relevant to children's lives.

Nigeria is a vast country and is the largest and most populated country in the sub-Saharan region of Africa, with over 140 million people who speak over 400 languages. It extends from arid areas of the north to the rainforests of the south. Children who live near water may enjoy play that involves jumping and splashing in water. Children who live in the rainforest may enjoy mudsliding during the rainy season, and during the dry season they may engage in moonlit games and storytelling by adults in the evenings.

In such a warm climate, outdoor play is frequent, and two of the most popular activities in Nigeria are soccer for boys and step-dance play for girls. Other physical games include many kinds of Hopscotch, Chase, and Hide-and-Seek, which are variations of those seen in Western countries. This is a country where a rich tradition of play and games has been passed down through families and generations, and even with the continued impact of modernization through radio, television, and imported playthings, children will continue to play with whatever is available around them.

See Also: Africa, Traditional Play in; Role-Playing; Soccer (Amateur) Worldwide.

Bibliography. Eva Nwokah and Clara Ikekeonwu, "A Sociocultural Comparison of Nigerian and American Children's Games," in Margaret Duncan et al., eds., *Diversions and Divergences in Fields of Play* (Ablex, 1998); Eva Nwokah and Clara Ikekeonwu, "Games, Pastimes and Toys in Sub-Sahara Africa," in G. Hoppenstand, ed., *The Greenwood Encyclopedia of World Popular Culture* (Greenwood, 2007); Anne Rosenberg, *Nigeria—The Culture (Lands, Peoples, and Cultures)* (Rabtree Publishing Company, 2000).

Eva E. Nwokah
University of North Carolina, Greensboro

Norway

The country of Norway is home to many unique games. Winter sports are the country's most popular, but with nearly half of the population registered as members of the Norwegian Sports Federation and roughly three out every four children regularly taking part in sporting activities, Norway is broadening the scope of their leisure activities. Some of the newer games that have become more popular, especially with the youth of the country, are aerobics, handball, jazz ballet dancing, and swimming. The majority of the games played in Norway take place in the outdoors, where the natives take on the rough terrain in sports such as dog sledding, cross-country skiing, downhill skiing, ski jumping, snowboarding, ice skating, ice golf, curling, and football. In addition to these better-known sporting activities, the citizens of Norway take great pride in playing various distinctive card games. Some of the more famous card games played in Norway include *Mattis*, *Spar Dame*, *Amerikaner*, *Vri atter*, *Gabong*, *Gris*, and *Gnav*.

Mattis is the Norwegian equivalent of Sweden's *Skitgubbe* and is a beating game in which there is no limit to the number of players. *Spar Dame*, or *Spardam*, is the Norwegian version of Hearts. *Amerikaner* is a trick-taking game in which four players are each dealt 12 cards, discard four, choose trumps and then call a card in which the holder will become the bidder's partner. *Vri atter* is the country's version of Crazy Eights. *Gabong* is a game that is of the eights group. This version calls for the game to be played with three full decks shuffled together. *Gris*, the Norwegian version of Pig, calls for the player, when they have obtained four of a kind, to place their thumb on the edge of the table. Finally, *Gnav* is a game of the Cuckoo family in which a special set of cards is played with. People can also play the game with a set of pieces similar to Chess pawns in which the identity of the piece is on the base.

Although card games are highly popular in the country, most of the natives prefer to play outdoor sports. Norway has had a long history of athletic prowess on the international stage. In fact, only Russia has won more medals in the Winter Olympic Games than Norway. In particular, the country has dominated in the Nordic combined events. The event, which began in 1924, involves cross-country skiing, as well as ski jumping. Since the event began, Norway has received a total of 26 medals, with the next closest country tallying 14.

By far, cross-country skiing is the country's most popular outdoor activity. In recent years, though, alpine skiing has become more common, with more than 400 lifts and over 250 smaller tows serving the slopes across the country. While ski jumping has decreased in popularity over the years, there are still some 600 ski jumps in Norway. The top draw each year is the annual Holmenkollen Ski Festival, which takes place just north of the capital of Oslo. The festival, which is over 100 years old, has become a national attraction and a top tourist attraction, with well over a million visitors each year.

Norway is definitely a sporting country. A recent survey showed that regular physical activity is engaged in by over 40 percent of the adult population. Fifteen percent take part in regular competitions, and 3 percent are considered top-flight competitors. With its vast outdoor terrain, the natives of Norway have a long history

A Norwegian performing a snowboarding trick called a wallride—riding the board up a wall—in Hafjäll, Norway.

of braving the elements and engaging in various outdoor activities.

See Also: Curling (Scottish); History of Playing Cards; Skating; Skiing; Snowboarding.

Bibliography. Hjalmar Hjorth Boyesen, *A History Of Norway: From the Earliest Times* (Kessinger Publishing, 2007); Anthony Ham, *Norway (Country Guide)* (Lonely Planet Publications, 2008); Sakina Kagda and Barbara Cooke, *Norway (Cultures of the World)* (Benchmark Books, 2006); Deborah L. Kopka, *A Ticket to Norway* (Carolrhoda Books, 2000); E.O. Harbin, *Games of Many Nations* (Abingdon Press, 1954); Elisabeth Holte and Solvi Dos Santos, *Living in Norway* (Flammarion, 1999); Norway—The Official Site in the U.K., "Winter Sports in Norway," www.norway.org.uk/culture/sports/winter/winter.html (cited July 2008); Norweigan Scenery, "Sports in Norway," www.reisenett.no/norway/facts/nature_outdoors/sports.html (cited July 2008).

Patrick Trotti
Independent Scholar

O

Odd Man Out

Odd Man Out is a simple decision ritual, one of many used among children and street athletes. While devices like Rock Paper Scissors are competitive, Odd Man Out is one of several used not to determine a winner but simply to pick members from a group—for instance, it could be used to decide who rotates out of a team when an odd number of players have formed two teams for a pick-up game of basketball, forcing the remainder player to stay off-court and wait his or her turn.

In Odd Man Out, everyone in the group, on the count of "one, two, three, shoot," throws fingers. If any one player has thrown a number no other player has thrown, he's the odd man out. This is repeated until that result occurs. If in a group of five, the first round's results are 11222, players shoot again. If the results are 12333, players shoot again, until a result like 22331, in which case the player who shot "one" leaves the group.

A similar method for picking between two people—which could be used to settle the second round in our previous example—is odds and evens. One person calls or is assigned odds. On the call of "one, two, three, shoot," both players throw fingers, and if the sum is an odd number, odds is selected. (It needs to be determined in advance whether being selected means being the winner or loser.)

See Also: Play Community; Playground as Politics; Spontaneous Group Play.

Bibliography. Arnold Arnold, *World Book of Children's Games* (Fawcett, 1972); Elliott Avedon, *The Study of Games* (Krieger Pub. Co., 1979); E.O. Harbin, *Games of Many Nations* (Abingdon Press, 1954); Glenn Kirchner, *Children's Games Around the World* (Benjamin Cummings, 2000); Nina Millen, *Children's Games from Many Lands* (Friendship Press, 1943).

Bill Kte'pi
Independent Scholar

Old Maid

Old Maid is traditionally a matching game for two to eight players that is played with a deck of 51 pictorial paper or plastic playing cards. The intent of the game is to match pairs of cards. Old Maid is a game dictated by chance and luck, rather than skill. All cards are dealt, and each player takes a turn drawing a card from the prior player's hand, discarding pairs as they are collected. There is no winner in Old Maid; however, there is a clear loser—the person left holding the unmatched card, or the old maid.

Sets of cards are sold specifically for playing Old Maid, but the game can just as easily be played with a regular deck.

This matching game was originally played using the traditional playing card set with the removal of a queen. As color printing became more available, specialized card sets of matching characters were developed for children. In the United States, this matching game was gendered and became known as a girl's game. Many specialized sets have 33 cards, often with 16 pairs of men in occupations such as butcher, postman, and policeman, and one old maid. The characters on the cards are often taken from daily life, enforcing ideals of work and family, but may vary to include other subjects such as cartoon characters. The gendered nature of this game is particularly enforced with the odd remaining card being that of a spinster, or an old maid. In 1994 a gender-reversed version of the game, "Old Bachelor: The '90s Version of Old Maid," was produced by University Games, featuring women in modern jobs such as Consuelo Cardiologist, Mayor Meyer, Fannie Firefighter, Edna Editor, and an Old Bachelor.

Similar matching games are found in various countries. In France, a similar game, *Le Vieux Garçon* or The Old Boy, is played with the removal of the jacks of hearts, diamonds, and clubs. A German version of this game, Black Peter, also uses a specialized pack of cards, with the lone card being that of a fierce black cat wearing boots and a hat, or a chimney sweeper. The Italian version of the game is known as *Uomo Nero*, or black or bogie man.

While card games have fallen out of favor to a degree, the cultural presence of Old Maid continues. The HBO series *Sex and the City* had an episode built around the idea of Old Maid, "Luck Be an Old Lady." While this episode predominately sought to address the cultural iconography of single, aging women and the negative ideology of the old maid, the card game was clearly evident in one scene when a female character receives a set of Old Maid cards for her 35th birthday as a gag gift; the cards then reappear later during a bus trip and are actually used to play a game.

The popularity of this nostalgic game continues in the United States. In recent years, Kikkerland Design Inc. redesigned and released a set of Old Maid cards on clear plastic cards, including modern references such as Dot Com Darius and Unibrow Unis. Despite changing gender ideologies, traditional concepts of gender, work, and family persist in this card game. The less-than-subtle message enforcing the ideal of marriage upon girls continues to be present.

See Also: Girls' Play; History of Playing Cards; Poker and Variations of; United States, 1960 to Present.

Bibliography. John Gough, "Card Games," *Australian Primary Mathematics Classroom* (August, 2001); International Playing Card Society, www.i-p-c-s.org (cited July 2008); Catherine Perry Hargrave, *A History of Playing Cards and a Bibliography of Cards and Gaming* (Dover Publications, 2001); David Parlett, *A History of Card Games* (Oxford University Press, USA, 1991).

Daniel Farr
Randolph College

Organized and Sanctioned Play

Play is, in most places in the world, considered every child's right. Play serves many useful purposes in child development, including impacting cognitive, emotional, and social development. This view of play was not always the case, however. As recently as the mid-1800s, play was seen as meaningless and a waste of time. It was also thought to be ungodly and immoral, as religion was the main focus for many individuals. Many societal issues of the time, including political, social, and economic issues, played a role in the changing perspectives of play, particularly organized play. Throughout the last 125 years, organized and sanctioned play has seen tremendous growth, and it is now commonplace in American society. Many of our nation's youth have a plethora of options to choose from when it comes to spending time away from school in organized activities. This growth has been influenced by many factors, and several of these, including history of organized play, sponsoring agencies, the prevalence of organized play (including ethnicity and gender trends), and differing purposes, are examined here.

History

The foundation for organized play was initiated in the last part of the 1800s and was strengthened in the early 1900s. Prior to the mid-1890s, organized play was virtually nonexistent. Prevailing ideas at the time focused attention on religion and living a pure and clean life. Slowly, perspectives began to change.

Early on, sports were seen as opportunities to take a break from everyday life. While those located in larger urban areas had neither the time nor the space for organized activity (unless they were very wealthy), those who lived in farmlands and in other rural communities had opportunities to engage in organized activity, often in conjunction with local festivals and holidays. But, particularly as they relate to youth, sports became more important, as they were viewed as a tool for reaching important goals in life, including the development of positive character attributes such as loyalty, teamwork, self-confidence, persistence, sportsmanship, and handling adversity.

While a number of individuals played a role in the changing perspectives on organized play, particularly influential in changing societal views about the role of organized play were Theodore Roosevelt and Luther Gulick. Roosevelt held a firm personal view of the importance of physical activity throughout his adult life. This conviction resulted from experiences he had as a youth, including being both sickly and a victim of bullying. His father built a gymnasium at their house for him, and he worked out vigorously to increase his strength and stamina. Because of his personal experiences, when he ascended to the office of President of the United States, emphasizing the development of "strenuous life" was one of his mainstay perspectives, particularly as it related to adolescent males. He believed in part that the future of the nation rested in the physical capabilities of its youth, and that to develop as an economic power, the United States needed youth with strength and the psychological traits he believed accompanied a trained physical body. Thus, he was a strong advocate of organized youth sport programs, especially for boys.

Sporting Organizations

Around this same time, Gulick was working at the Young Men's Christian Association (YMCA) Training School to try to shift the curriculum of the YMCA from calisthenics to team-oriented activities and sports. A strong focus of Gulick's was the importance of organized activities for youth; indeed, he thought that chaos and negative behaviors would result when kids played without supervision and organization.

In 1903, Gulick introduced the Public Schools Athletic League (PSAL), the first interscholastic sports program, to New York City's school system. In PSAL, boys had the opportunity to participate in the team sports of basketball, baseball, and soccer against other schools within New York City. Girls also participated in the PSAL program, but their activities were less strenuous and typically consisted of walking, with high school girls being able to participate in some track and field events. By 1910, at least 17 other cities across the United States had formed similar interscholastic sports leagues for students.

School-supported sports opportunities continued to grow through the 1930s. At this point, school-supported sport experienced criticism, driven primarily by the current educational philosophy. More specifically, those who had been involved in the continued growth of organized school-based sport programs (i.e., physical educators, coaches, recreation professionals) believed that these opportunities had become too competitive and were actually detrimental to the development of preadolescent and adolescent boys. As a result of the cutbacks in school-based activities, a number of nonschool agencies developed out of school-organized sport opportunities for youth. These agencies were both locally as well as nationally based and included such entities as the YMCAs, Little League Baseball, and Boys and Girls Clubs, among others.

By the 1960s, the various types of sponsoring agencies had been solidified: kids participated through either a nationally available program such as Little League or an organization like the YMCA. Around this time, many national governing bodies for specific sports also began focusing efforts on youth. Examples include the United States Tennis Association, U.S.A. Volleyball, and U.S.A. Gymnastics; most sports have a national governing body that is involved in structuring organized activities for youth interested in their sports, as well as serving the interests of the sport at all levels. Other organizations provided organized play for youth; some were developed specifically for that purpose, while others included organized sport offerings in conjunction with other activities. Many of these organizations, in addition to offering organized opportunities to those who wished to participate, also provided rules and regulations for play, in effect providing sanctioned opportunities. As the 20th century progressed, so did the rise of organized and sanctioned play opportunities for youth.

Sponsoring Agencies

A variety of options exist for the sponsorship of organized youth play activities. One way these opportunities have been classified is through a school or nonschool designation. The offering of organized youth sport activities through the schools is fairly unique to the United States, while most other countries offer sports programming through private clubs. In U.S. schools, two types of sports programs can be found: intramural and interscholastic offerings. Interscholastic sports opportunities typically begin in late grade school (grades four through six) and continue on into middle or junior high school. Organized interscholastic opportunities continue to be offered through high schools and into the collegiate ranks. Intramural programs are not as readily available as interscholastic programs, and when found, they are more typically offered through larger urban schools that can readily support increased numbers of participants through facilities and staffing.

Nonschool opportunities in the United States continue to grow, with activities being offered through community agencies, private sport clubs, national youth service agencies, and park and recreation departments. Community agencies (e.g., YMCA/YWCA; Boy's and Girl's Clubs of America), national youth service agencies (e.g., Boy Scouts of America; Police Athletic League), and park and recreation departments tend to provide a variety of organized play opportunities for youth and adults. Offerings vary from agency to agency and from park department to park department, but most offer a wide variety of activities and levels of involvement and competition to meet the needs of the local population. Private sport clubs are typically narrower in their offerings. Most private clubs are organized around one sport (e.g., soccer), and they tend to provide training and team participation opportunities based on age groups. While community agencies, service agencies, and park and recreation departments are largely nonprofit, some private sport clubs are for profit.

Prevalence of Organized/Sanctioned Play

Although it is difficult to determine the prevalence of youth involvement in organized play prior to the mid-20th century, rates have been estimated since the early 1970s. During that time, it was estimated that approximately 20 million youth between the ages of 6 and 16 participated in organized sport. In the mid- to late 1980s, participation rates for youth were estimated at 35 million each year, with 80 percent of those participating in nonschool programs. In addition, recent figures from the National Council on Youth Sports estimate that 52 million American youth, or 65 percent, participate in at least one organized sport, with 40 percent of those participants being female. While it is true that the overall population continues to increase, it is also true that the rate of participation in both school and non-chool activities continues to increase.

Community agency–sponsored activities are estimated to have the largest share of sport participants, with approximately 45 percent of youth participating through these agencies. Park and recreation programs are believed to have the second-largest share, with approximately 30 percent of youth participating in community recreation programs. Interscholastic opportunities are typically limited by team size restrictions. That is, given that each school fields one team in each level of competition (e.g., varsity, junior varsity, junior high), the number of participants is limited by practicality and desired squad size. Depending on the size of the school, team size restrictions can eliminate a large number of possible participants. Accordingly, trends in participation rates indicate that peak participation occurs around the age of 11 to 12, and drop out rates for youth sport participants involved in organized activities increase from 12 to 18 years old.

While a steady increase exists in the number of organized participants, youth are getting involved for the first time at younger and younger ages. As we move toward the end of the first decade of the 21st century, programs providing organized sport experiences to tod-

Little League Baseball is a nonprofit organization in the United States. It was founded in 1939 and organizes children's leagues of baseball and softball, having grown tremendously from a league of three teams in Pennsylvania.

dlers have emerged. Gymnastics, swimming, and golf programs enroll and hold competitions for 3-year-olds, while other sports are offering organized opportunities for 4- through 6-year-olds. These opportunities span a wide variety of activities, including traditional activities such as soccer, tennis, bowling, and baseball, as well as nontraditional and controversial activities, such as mixed martial art combat fighting.

Ethnicity and Gender

When Gulick and other like-minded colleagues, such as Joseph Lee, Jane Addams, and Clark Hetheringon, worked to promote organized youth activities in the early 1900s, their efforts were directed primarily at boys. They were inclusive when it came to ethnicity, however, and worked to provide opportunities to children of all backgrounds. Indeed, by the latter part of the 20th century, youth of various backgrounds participated in organized activities at varying rates. Sports such as basketball, baseball, and football experience similar participation rates by a variety of races. Other sports, however, tend not to have as much diversity; these include activities such as golf, swimming, tennis, and skiing. A variety of factors, including social and economical, can impact levels of involvement, as well. Generally, however, organized opportunities have been available to youth of all ethnic backgrounds.

The same cannot be said for gender, however. Since one of the primary goals of organizing activity opportunities was to help develop a strong workforce to promote the United States as an economic power, as well as to enhance moral development, the focus at the time was primarily on boys. Indeed, girls were seen as more passive, and sports were deemed not appropriate for the sensitive nature of girls. Although Gulick's PSAL program sought to be progressive and included girls, most other opportunities for organized sport activities were focused on boys through the 1960s. Excepting some extreme instances (e.g., the All-American Girls Baseball League of the 1940s), opportunities for girls were generally limited to school play days that focused on broad participation by all girls, rather than competition. However, in the early 1970s, with the passage of Title IX, an educational amendment requiring equal opportunities for males and females, the opportunities for girls to participate in school-based sport programs increased significantly.

Community-based programs followed suit and began providing a variety of participation opportunities for girls. In the early 21st century, males still have higher rates for participation than females, but females have significantly more opportunities than in the past few decades. These opportunities continue to increase in both number as well as activity. Indeed, girls are participating in traditional activities such as basketball, soccer, tennis, softball, and volleyball, but opportunities also exist for girls to break barriers in what have been viewed as traditional male activities, such as wrestling, football, and ice hockey.

Differing Purposes

Historically, the purpose of organized play has been to help make our nation stronger and develop positive character traits, at least from an administrator perspective. In recent decades, however, we have seen a change in the purposes and ideals being held by the parents and other adults involved in youth activities. That said, most adults involved with youth sport will verbalize the positive character traits as the important goals of involvement. But in some cases adult behavior seems to reflect other goals.

When contrasting youth unstructured play with organized youth play, many differences emerge. Unstructured play tends to be governed by flexible rules that kids will bend to make their games fair. For example, when choosing teams, kids will make sure the two best athletes are on different teams, and they will also handicap skilled players if they are dominating the game. Kids can also be the ones making the decisions about playing position, length of game, strategy, and so on; indeed, their goals are to have fun and to keep the game close. In organized youth play, most, if not all, of the team- and game-related decisions are made by adults, with the primary goals being physical skill development and winning. And rather than striving to have a fair and even competition, wins by larger margins equate to greater domination, as emphasized by the adults involved.

Other differences exist that highlight the importance of well-structured youth involvement. For example, in organized youth sport, safer opportunities tend to exist, as playing fields and equipment are regularly examined. Whereas in unstructured play, kids may be put into situations where injuries may result, they typically do not consider safety issues as adults would. Additionally, adult coaches tend to have received at least a minimal level of sport-specific coaching training, as this is often required by the sponsoring agency (whether school or nonschool based). When youth engage in unstructured play, they most often do not have sport-specific training to be shared with the other youth involved.

A history of support and continued growth has brought numerous opportunities for organized play to our youth. Through both school and nonschool options, it appears that organized activities will continue to grow for the youth of our society. The potential benefits of developing good character, achieving fitness, creating good citizens, developing a sense of sportsmanship, providing an opportunity for developing leadership, and learning how to be a good team member will continue to guide the development and administration of these activities, and support for these activities, both school based and nonschool based appears to be strong.

See Also: Anti-Competition Play; Athletics (Amateur); Boys' Play; Cooperative Play; Girls' Play; Playground Movement, U.S.; Unstructured Play.

Bibliography. Jack Berryman, "The Rise of Boys' Sports in the United States, 1900 to 1970," in Frank L. Smoll and Ronald E. Smith, *Children and Youth in Sport: A Biopsychosocial Perspective* (Brown and Benchmark, 1996); Bob Bigelow, *Just Let The Kids Play: How to Stop Other Adults from Ruining Your Child's Fun and Success in Youth Sports* (HCI, 2001); Darrell J. Burnett, *It's Just a Game! Youth, Sports & Self Esteem: A Guide for Parents* (AuthorHouse, 2001); Jay Coakley, *Sports in Society: Issues and Controversies* (McGraw-Hill, 2001); Tom Farrey, *Game On: The All-American Race to Make Champions of our Children* (ESPN Books, 2008); James Humphrey, *Child Development Through Sports* (Routledge, 2003); Jim Thompson, *Positive Coaching: Building Character and Self-Esteem Through Sports* (Warde Publishers, 1995).

Jessie Daw
Northern State University

Original Play

Play that comprises activities and behaviors that allow the individual to explore new, creative, or novel outcomes may be described as original play. The links to boundary testing and creativity are particularly strong in original play, as are the notions of experiment, exploration, and unexpected or unintended outcomes from play.

Original play is often located in play behaviors that fall into the category of boundary testing and stretching. These actions are not just limited to physical actions, but may include the testing of social and emotional boundaries. Through play, children are engaging with the boundaries of their physical, emotional, and social worlds, stretching those boundaries and developing a true sense of their place and role in relation to the whole environment.

Play provides a medium through which these experiences of original play can be embraced in the play mode, where risk-taking is encouraged and failure provides an opportunity to learn and develop. This holistic engagement with the wider environment is a hallmark of a true play experience that both informs and supports the development of the individual.

Testing physical boundaries can be observed in play behavior that stretches the child's personal physical attributes or the properties of the physical world. It may be observed in the child jumping over puddles or small streams, swinging from ropes or on the best furniture, testing their own physical strengths and weaknesses.

Children use physical play to calibrate themselves against both other children and their own previous best. Throwing sticks across a field, testing how far different people can throw, or checking today's throw against previous personal markers, provides evidence against which each child locates themselves in the physical world. Children encourage each other to undertake physical challenges such as climbing, walking along walls, skateboarding, or riding bikes. These are all kinds of play that test physical boundaries and skills.

In addition, children may take their physical boundary testing into the testing to destruction of the physical world. Playing with toys until they break or bending a stick until it snaps provides information through play about the physical properties of the environment. Building dams at the seaside and finding novel ways to manage the water is not only great fun, but also offers the opportunity to manage and control parts of the physical environment.

Such boundary testing in the physical world can also lead to physical injury as children develop their understanding of their own limitations and follow the lead of other players. Scrapes and knocks are an essential element of original play in the physical environment, allowing children to encounter and manage danger and risk. This physical experience of the real world contributes to an ability to calculate risk and to take appropriate action in a range of novel or new settings, which will ensure that the child develops strategies to manage their own safety.

Social boundary testing through play enables the child to engage with the accepted norms of society and to develop personal self esteem. Taking social risks through play offers children many opportunities to experiment with alternative personae and to explore the cultural context of their social world. These novel forms of play allow children to test the boundaries of suitable behavior in social settings, from showing off to performing and trying out adult roles.

Play allows the child to confront the boundaries of their social setting. In many cultures, children are afforded a special status within the family or social group. Children play at being cheeky or testing the knowledge and patience of their elders, often being indulged and encouraged when very young, then guided into the accepted behaviors as they get older.

Emotional Boundaries

Perhaps the most trying set of boundary-testing behaviors for adults are the emotional ones. Children play at interactions in relation to their emotions. They engage with scary stories and frightening situations, experiencing fear, anger, euphoria, revulsion, and extreme well-being in the course of their playfulness. At times children will go to any extreme to provide an emotional element to their play. They will create complex rituals for others to follow and thoroughly relish the opportunity to provide different accounts leading to emotional outbursts.

Teasing and testing the limits of others' emotions bring different insights into the emotional landscape of the players. The range and complexity of these forms of play can be very difficult to untangle for the observer, as much of it is specific to the players. For example, the use of name-calling, such as "Jenny the penny," may seem innocuous at first, but for the teased and the teaser, it may have a deeper meaning brought into sharp focus by repetition over time and even recalling an embarrassing situation.

Play activities based on testing the limits of adult tempers are common in many households and schools. Children often manage their interactions with adults to explore these emotional boundaries, setting up situations that involve adults and lead to the limits of emotional interaction. These forms of boundary testing play can be very complex, involving many people, but the playing child will be testing their own and others' emotional boundaries throughout and seeking their own original responses through play. In spite of the strong emotions experienced in these forms of play, the child seeks feelings of well-being associated with emotional play, which are achieved through a sense of control and capability in their emotional landscapes. Novel situational play that is used by the child to experience revulsion, for example, tests the boundaries of their own sensibilities and may include rituals of burying potions or other organic items in the garden, or even in the bottom of a refrigerator, to be dug up and examined at a later date.

In all of this, the child is in control of their play, and even when a game of Wolf or Hide-and-Seek involves being chased and possibly caught by another player, the key to the novel elements of these forms of play is in changing and emerging different forms in the overall game. Groups of children innovate and reinvent traditional forms of play and bring their own particular spin on the tried and tested play patterns that they may learn from other children.

A Range of Insights

Original play allows children a range of insights into the complexities of the world while allowing the individual a means to control the amount and level of stimulation received. Children using boundary testing in their play are active agents in managing and gauging the levels of stimulation received through their play.

Creativity is closely linked to the notions of boundary testing. Children develop a sense of wider opportunity in their play, and this can lead to novel and different creative uses of the raw and not-so-raw materials in their environment. Developing an understanding of the nature of materials allows children to solve problems using these very materials.

There are many stories of children playing long and hard with the box that contained the carefully chosen present: The play potential of a simple cardboard box can be greater than that of a specific toy. The box allows the child to explore its properties and can be anything required to support play, making the possibility of new and different play ideas more appealing to the child.

On the other hand, many toys are designed to be played with in one or two fairly prescribed ways, and the toy may not fit the child's current play ambitions; the toy thus may be rejected at the time for being too rigid in the way it can be manipulated. Alternatively, the child may attempt to use the toy in an unusual way, which could break either the toy or the child; for example, how many dolls have met their end by being parachuted from a second-story window as part of a game of fairgrounds or as a member of an assault course?

Everyday Objects

Finding creative uses for everyday objects is an aspect of play that many may recognize. The child will first of all test the object to understand its properties, from taste and smell through to bend ability and breaking points or fixing points. Through these forms of play, the child is better able to bring novel uses for the object. A sheet becomes a tented home, sticks are transformed into people, and a toy train develops a personality when put next to a washing-up bowl.

Watching children creating these worlds for their own imaginative play provides a wealth of understanding about how creativity can be nurtured. Many creative adults will argue that the best way to seek creative responses to a situation is to enter a play mode and work forward to unfold their ideas and creativity.

In these modes of creative play, new suggestions for everyday experiences in the physical, emotional, and social world may come to the fore, and the player, as child or adult, finds expression of their inner and outer experiences. Creative play allows for flexibility in response to play experiences. Some experts suggest that an enriched environment encourages the playing child to more flexibility, which, in itself, contributes to the flexible nature of the environment, which is described as compound flexibility. Other experts suggest that play enables the development of a combination of flexibilities referred to as combinatorial flexibility. This interest in the flexibility brought about through the engagement of a player in a rich and flexible environment suggests that there are benefits to the player in seeking out new and flexible responses through play.

Setting forward in play mode allows the player to engage with no preconceptions as to outcome or end product. In play there is no correct way to undertake an activity. This freedom to experiment leads to an unbounded experience of the world. Children and other players meet each new occasion for play with an interest in finding out what the potential for the situation can offer. They bring new eyes, hands, and feet to the situation, along with a fresh view on what can be possible.

Through this approach, play allows for a whole range of possibilities and unexpected outcomes from any situation. Children become adept in their play at seeking novel uses for items in their world, and these nontraditional approaches lead toward ideas for the next generation of players. Children playing together create stories and a rich cultural life for their engagements. This builds and is passed on to new players, who enter Vygotsky's "zone of proximal development" through the play process. Social networks and situations are the sharing ground for all sorts of playing and playfulness, as each new group of children builds their own version of a play culture that engages and supports their new forms of play.

Innovation and creative leaps are made possible through original play. For most situations, play builds neatly upon previous behaviors. Children use their play to consolidate previous experiences and playfulness through repetition. However, there are times when the child at play may make a creative or innovative leap in their play. This allows them to extend their repertoire and experiences beyond their current stage of development.

Play allows for exploration of situations, people, and things and of the possibilities of finding novel interactions between them. Children identify and invent new roles and try out the experiences from other viewpoints in their play. Excitement and engagement through play take the child into new situations and different elements of the play environment, which provide opportunities to try out different ways to do things and to play with their physical, social, and emotional environment.

Original and novel play makes it possible for the individual to make the most of his or her environment and to respond to the changing values and complexity of the world.

See Also: Anti-Competition Play; Athletics (Amateur); Boys' Play; Cooperative Play; Girls' Play; Unstructured Play.

Bibliography. F. Brown, ed., *Playwork: Theory and Practice* (Open University Press, 2002); J.S. Bruner, ed., *Play: Its Role in Development and Evolution* (Basic Books, 1976).

Sue Palmer
Leeds Metropolitan University

Ouija Board

The Ouija board is a Parker Brothers product that has been sold since 1901 (Parker Brothers bought the product and all associated intellectual property in 1966 from the estate of inventor William Fuld). The name is meant to be pronounced "wee-jah" but is more commonly pronounced "wee-gee." The Ouija is the most famous example of a spirit board, an instrument that has been around for thousands of years, repopularized in the late 19th century with the spiritualism fad.

A basic divination device, the Ouija board consists of a board and a planchette. The board has YES and NO written in the corners, with the alphabet and numbers aligned in the middle. The planchette is a wedge-shaped piece that can be moved along the board to point at the letters or YES and NO. The user or users place their fingers on the wedge and move the planchette to spell out answers to questions asked. In theory, the users do not move the planchette themselves but, rather, allow it—and the unseen, spiritual, or magical forces guiding it—to move. The questions are assumed to be asked of the dead, or of "the spirit realm" (which may or may not be inhabited by the spirits of the deceased).

Ouija boards are thus part of a larger class of divination devices that consist of the user moving an instrument that is intended to be guided by spiritual forces or—from the 20th century on—by unconscious impulses. Such devices are as old as civilization, as old as religion. Dowsing rods and magnets are among the oldest devices of the class. Ouija boards are also closely related to automatic writing, the practice of allowing one's writing hand to inscribe a message one is not conscious of—whether because of a trance state, supernatural forces, or other means. In particular, Ouija boards and automatic writing are kin in that they can be practiced and explained both by parties who subscribe to supernatural explanations and by parties who see them as instruments of psychological discovery; and both

It is not known when the Ouija board was invented; however, a similar board was found in China dating to 1200 B.C.E. The Ouija is the most famous example of a spirit board, repopularized in the late 19th century with the spiritualism fad.

are abhorred by some religious groups as gateways to demonic possession, as the abandonment of will and invitation to external forces represents for them an act much like presenting an open wound to a germ-filled environment.

Automatic writing and Ouija boards were especially popular among adherents of spiritualism, a Second Great Awakening religious movement that began in the United States, spread to Europe, and was particularly popular from the 19th century through the end of World War I.

The Great Awakenings are cycles of American religious history during which a great many new movements are created and existing denominations are tested, modernized, or returned to basics; they are often characterized by both religious revivals and social reform movements. The growth of spiritualism transpired at a time when many American denominations were dividing over the slavery issue or reforming to adapt to modern needs; at the same time, many new sects came about, from the Church of Latter-Day Saints to Christian fundamentalism to Unitarianism.

Though the general tendency of mainstream Christianity at the time, especially among the Protestant denominations that formed the bulk of American Christianity, was to de-emphasize the supernatural aspects of their framework of belief, spiritualism focused especially on the supernatural. The spiritualist churches that developed accepted belief in a benevolent, omnipotent, monotheistic God but were otherwise characterized by their belief in the persistence of existence of the spirits of the deceased, and the communication with same, via mediums or devices like the Ouija board.

Spiritualism developed alongside such occult movements as the Hermetic Order of the Golden Dawn and the Theosophists, and much like the New Age movement of the later 20th century, it included not only devoted spiritualist churches but more general trends that were adopted by people who continued to identify as members of some other denomination. Practitioners of automatic writing, Ouija boards, and other mystical practices popular at the turn of the century could include Methodists, Presbyterians, Jews, atheists—no conflict was necessarily perceived between the use of such devices and the mainstream beliefs taught in one's place of worship. This divide between mainstream religious belief and lay magical practice, common and ancient in much of the world, was a novelty for the United States, and the success of spiritualism undoubtedly paved the way for later interest among Americans in Buddhism, Carlos Castaneda, reincarnation, out-of-body experiences, and perhaps even UFOs and aliens.

As early as 1852, even before Sigmund Freud proposed his model of the subconscious mind, English scientist William Benjamin Carpenter suggested that Ouija boards were guided not by spiritual forces but by what he called the "ideomotor effect." Carpenter's articulation of the idea would likely have been affected by Freud's work had it been available, but the notion is perfectly understandable on its own: The body can move in response to impulses beyond the conscious mind, without those impulses needing to originate from outside the person entirely. Carpenter's argument was that there was a rational explanation behind devices like the Ouija board, without needing to accuse its users of lying or cheating.

When Fuld developed his version of the board, Ouija boards had been in use for decades—in fact, the original patent on his model had actually been taken out by his employer, Charles Kennard, before Fuld took over the business. The novelty of the Kennard-Fuld model was largely that the board and planchette were sold together, and with a particular design; previously, planchettes had often been sold by themselves, with the "board" drawn on a piece of paper by the user at home. Fuld was an aggressive businessman, and used the patent of the Ouija board to prevent other companies from using that name, regardless of the similarity of their product to his; though other spirit boards remained on the market, the Ouija board remained the most successful of them, and was eventually purchased by Parker Brothers. Though "Ouija board" is no longer a registered trademark, the company does own the trademark on "Ouija."

See Also: Games of Deception; Parker Brothers.

Bibliography. Nicola Brown, Carolyn Burdett, and Pamela Thurschwell, eds., *The Victorian Supernatural* (Cambridge University Press, 2004); John B. Buescher, *The Other Side of Salvation: Spiritualism and the Nineteenth-Century Religious Experience* (Skinner House Press, 2004); David Clifford, Elisabeth Wadge, and Alex Warwick, eds., *Repositioning Victorian Sciences* (Anthem Press, 2006); Robert S. Cox, *A Sympathetic History of American Spiritualism* (University of Virginia Press, 2003).

Bill Kte'pi
Independent Scholar

Glossary

A

absorbent mind Developed by Maria Montessori, a theory that divides childhood into two phases. The first, known as the period of unconscious creation or unconscious absorbent mind occurs from birth to age 3 and involves the unconscious acquisition of basic skills; the second, known as the period of conscious work or the conscious absorbent mind, occurs after age 3 and involves developing a mathematical mind and seeking freedom.

accoutrements Accessories for clothing that include cartridge box, bayonet belt, and scabbard for toy soldiers.

Acitrón de un fandango Mexican game that involves passing small objects from person to peson while singing a nonsense rhyme.

acrobatics Human feats of balance, agility, coordination, strength, and flexibility.

acrylonitrile butadiene styrene (ABS) Common thermoplastic used to make rigid, molded products.

action-adventure games Video games that require a player to overcome obstacles.

action figure Posable plastic toy, usually a character from a movie, television show, or video game.

action role-playing game Role-playing video game that uses elements of many action and action-adventure games.

addiction Compulsive psychological or bodily dependence on a substance or practice (e.g., video game addiction).

Addison, Joseph (1672–1719) Essayist and poet who wrote about daydreaming, among other themes.

Adler, Alfred (1870–1937) Austrian medical doctor and psychologist who founded the School of Individual Psychology with Sigmund Freud and others, sparking the psychoanalytic movement.

advantage First point scored after deuce in tennis.

adventure One of five traditional genres of children's literature, according to the Strong National Museum of Play.

adventure games Earliest type of video game; play focused on solving puzzles by interacting with characters, usually in a nonconfrontational manner.

adventure playground Playgrounds with child-oriented perspective in play. Developed from C. Th. Sørensen's 1931 plans to reuse wastelands, bomb sites, and building sites as places where children can create, shape, dream, and imagine reality.

advergames Online games based on and linked to advertisements.

affect Conscious, subjective aspect of feeling or emotion; the external display of an emotion or mood.

affective attunement Interpersonal contact necessary to human relationships, involves resonance of one person's affect to another's. Often, affective attunement refers specifically to the bonding between parent and child.

affirmation Act of asserting the existence of truth of something or of stating something.

age-appropriate At the correct level for chronological (actual) age.

Agon Abstract strategy game with no random or unknown elements; perhaps the oldest board game.

agôn Greek word for conflict; refers to all competitive play in Caillois's model of play.

alea Refers to all games of chance in Caillois's model of play.

All-American Girls Baseball League (AAGBBL) Women's baseball league developed with the financial support of Phillip Wrigley in 1943 to offer an alternative form of baseball when men were being drafted for World War II.

Allen, Margery; Lady Allen of Hurtwood (1897–1976) English landscape architect who actively promoted child welfare and who wrote a series of works about playgrounds.

All England Croquet Club Organization founded in 1868 to sponsor tennis and croquet competitions in England; became the All England Lawn Tennis and Croquet Club.

Alligator Eyes also known as **Submarine** Variation of the water game Marco Polo. When the person who is "it" calls "alligator eyes," she or he can swim under water with eyes open for one breath.

alpine skiing Downhill skiing.

amateur Athlete who does not play for payment (is not professional), but who pursues a sport as a leisure pastime.

American Bowling Congress (ABC) An organization founded in 1895; developed the rules and equipment standards of bowling.

American Coaster Enthusiasts Club (ACE) Organization of roller coaster enthusiasts. Since its inception in 1978, the group organizes events, publishes magazines and guidebooks, and works to preserve roller coasters.

American Gladiators American competition television show (1989–1996) that pitted amateur athletes against the show's gladiators (paid employees) in contests of strength and ability.

Americans with Disabilities Act (ADA) American civil rights law (1990) that prohibits discrimination on the basis of disability and calls on public accommodations including recreation facilities to be accessible.

America's Cup Premier yachting race.

Amerikaner Norwegian trick-taking game.

amusement park Commercially operated collection of rides, games, and shows for family amusement and entertainment.

anagrams Word created by rearranging the letters of another word.

angling Sport fishing with hook, line, and usually rod.

Animal Chess Also known as Jungle Chess or *Dou Shou Qi*. This traditional Chinese abstract strategy game for two players is a forerunner of Stratego.

aquathlon Continuous two-stage race where swimming precedes running.

arbitrage (v.) To place a combination of bets so that if one loses, the other wins. To arbitrage implies having an edge with no or little risk.

arcade Public gaming facility with video games.

arcade console Upright apparatus on which games are played.

archery Sport that involves shooting bows with arrows.

articulated Segments attached by movable joints.

Asian Football Confederation (AFC) An organization founded in 1954 to govern football (soccer) in Asia, which includes Australia but excludes Israel and Cyprus.

Âs Nàs A popular 17th-century game played in Persia (now Iran).

aspiration Will to succeed; ambition.

assistive devices Equipment used to increase, maintain, or improve functional capabilities of individuals with disabilities.

Association for Children's Play and Recreation (Playboard) Organization that coordinated work in child's play in the United Kingdom from 1982 until it was dismantled in 1987 and basically subsumed by the Sports Council (as the Children's Play and Recreation Unit) in 1988.

Association for Play Therapy (APT) Organization founded 1982 to promote play, play therapy, and credentialed play therapists.

Association for the Study of Play (TASP) A major international organization of scholars founded in 1974 that continues to meet annually and to publish an annual volume, *Play & Culture Studies.*

Association of Adventure Playworkers Organization of professional playworkers founded in the United Kingdom in the 1970s.

associative play Play in which children participate in separate activities but interact through the exchange of toys and discussion.

athletics Active diversions that require physical exertion and competition.

attention Component process underlying observational learning.

Australian Open Tennis tournament started in 1905 and held yearly as one-quarter of the Grand Slam tennis tournaments.

autism Brain development disorder that impairs social interaction and communication.

available metabolic energy According to Surplus Resource Theory, the combination of the amount of energy available in reserve and the physiological capacity for sustained vigorous activity.

Avalanche Rock paper scissors sequence of rock, rock, rock.

avatar Digital or graphical representation of a person or computer used in a virtual reality site or chatroom.

axe-throwing Traditional Estonian activity involving measuring the distances that axes have been thrown.

Ayatori Japanese version of the string game Cat's Cradle.

B

baby foot Also known as table soccer, foosball, and table football; tabletop game based on soccer, or association football.

backgammon Two-player board game, where pieces are moved according to throws of the dice.

backpacking Also known as trekking, tramping, and bushwalking; activity combining hiking and camping.

badminton Racquet sport where two players or two teams of two players hit or volley a shuttlecock over a net.

Baffle Gab Word game in which players are given five words that they must use in either a sentence or story.

bagatelle Table game where balls are knocked into holes guarded by wooden pegs. A short cue is used.

Balderdash A word game like the parlor game Dictionary. Players attempt to define unknown words and guess when others have supplied an accurate definition.

ball and paddle game Predecessor of console games.

balloon Tough, nonrigid bag filled with gas or heated air. Earlier versions were made of dried animal bladders.

Banco Imobiliário Brazilian version of Monopoly; literally "Real Estate Bank."

Bandura, Albert (b. 1925) Canadian psychologist specializing in social cognitive theory and self-efficacy.

Bandura's Social Learning Theory Expansion of Julian Rotter's ideas where the four requirements for people to learn are attention, retention, reproduction, and motivation.

Ba Quan Vietnamese game; literally means "three ligature."

Ba Que Vietnamese game; literally means "three pegs."

base Place a runner must touch before scoring in baseball, softball, and kickball.

baseball Ball, usually 9 to 9.25 inches in circumference and 5 ounces in weight, composed of leather covering layers of wool and polyester or cotton yarn around a core of rubber, cork, or a mix of the two.

baseball bat Smooth wooden or metal club used to hit the ball thrown by the pitcher in baseball. The bat is at most 2.75 inches in diameter at its thickest part, no more than 41 inches long, and usually no more than 36 ounces in weight.

baseball glove Protective handgear used to help catch the ball in baseball.

baseball mitt Protective handgear used to help catch the ball in baseball.

basketball Round ball of rubber, leather, or synthetic leather used to play basketball. The ball comes in three sizes.

basketball hoop Horizontal, circular metal hoop supporting the net through which the basketball must be placed in order to score.

Bateson, Gregory (1904–80) British anthropologist, social scientist, linguist, semiotician, and cyberneticist.

batter Offensive player trying to hit the ball thrown by the pitcher in baseball.

batter's box Area in which batter is positioned while at bat in baseball.

battledore Badminton racket.

battledore and shuttlecock Earlier version of badminton played with small rackets (called battledores) and shuttlecocks, which are passed back and forth over a net.

bear baiting Sport forbidden by Charles I when he reissued the Book of Sports in 1633; involves baiting and killing bears in an arena.

beat 'em up Games also known as hack and slash games; video games that focus on close-quarters combat.

beautiful play In a game, a well-played moment in which every player seems extraordinary.

bébé French word for baby; refers to a class of dolls that look like babies or young children.

behavioral theory Theory supporting the idea that behavior is conditioned through positive and negative reinforcement.

bell-ringing Ringing of handbells and church bells for entertainment.

Belmont Stakes Horse race that happens on the Saturday on or after June 5; part of horseracing's Triple Crown.

best-ball Players proceed as normal in the game of golf, but the lowest score of all the players on the team counts as the team's score.

bibeloterie ("knick-knackery") Miniature toys and baubles that both adults and children collected in Europe from 1600 to 1800.

Bid Whist Partnership trick-taking card game that uses the standard 52-card deck as well as two jokers.

Big Business Version of Monopoly.

Bigézés Hungarian hitting stick game that likely came along Eastern trading routes to the West.

Bingo Lottery-style game in which numbered balls are drawn at random and players cover the corresponding numbers on their cards.

biological simulation Simulation video game that allows the player to experiment with genetics, survival, or ecosystems. This type of video game is often educational in nature.

bisque Unglazed clay used to create figurines and dolls.

Black Lady Version of Hearts.

Black Man Also known as *Uomo Nero* and Bogie Man; Italian version of Old Maid.

Black Maria Version of Hearts.

Black Peter German version of Old Maid.

blind average Score of a higher handicap golfer on a particular course.

BMX Also known as bicycle motocross; specific form of racing and performing tricks on specially designed bikes.

boardgame Game played on a specially designed board; alternative spelling is board game.

Boggle Word game that requires players to find words by linking letters on adjacent dice.

bomba Also known as the kill; a play in the sport volleyball where the volleyball is spiked over the net in such a fashion that the other team cannot respond the volley.

bombs Colloquial term used to describe a move in marbles.

bone Domino.

boobla Also known as bubble hockey and Super Chexx; tabletop arcade hockey game covered by a special bubble dome.

Bordieu, Pierre (1930–2002) French sociologist whose work tends to focus on aspects of the dynamics of power in social internactions.

Boston Schoolyard Initiative Partners Policy aimed at rebuilding schoolyards throughout Boston through a public-private partnership.

Boticelli Dramatic parlor game similar to a *tableaux vivante* but using words.

boules Version of the game *pétanque*, similar to lawn bowling.

bowls Also known as lawn bowls; balls are rolled toward a specific target, with the ball coming closest determining the winner of the game.

box One of the most basic kite shapes.

Box Ball Popular playground and street game that involves drawing a four-box grid on which various players will compete.

Boys and Girls Clubs of America (BGCA) National club designed to help promote responsible citizenship, competence, usefulness, and belonging.

Boy Scouts of America (BSA) Youth organization founded in 1910. The BSA emphasizes responsible citizenship, character development, and self-reliance.

British and World Marble Championship Marble festival held yearly at Easter; began in 16th century.

British Association of Play Therapists Professional body that governs therapy, training, research, and membership of Play Therapists in Britain.

Broken Bridge Scottish version of children's song *London Bridge*.

bubble hockey Also known as boobla and Super Chexx; tabletop arcade hockey game covered by a special bubble dome.

Buck Variation of leapfrog.

buckle-pit Ordinary material also used for play in early Europe.

bullfighting Popular sport in Spain and Mexico where a matador taunts and kills a bull at close range.

bureaucratization A characteristic of contemporary organized play that manifests itself in overt rules and regulations.

business simulation games In a business simulation game, the player controls the economics of the game, which is generally centered around a business or economy.

Buzkashi Central Asian team sport where players on horseback attempt to place an animal carcass into a goal.

C

caber toss Traditional Scottish event in which a large wooden pole is tossed; part of the Scottish Highland Games.

Cache-Cache French version of Hide and Seek.

Caillois, Roger (1913–78) French philosopher and sociologist who studied the relationship between play, games, and culture.

Callao Club British club.

camogie Celtic team sport; women's variant of hurling.

Camp Fire Girls American youth organization founded in 1910; became coed in 1975.

Canadian Scrabble Championship Invitation-only English-language Scrabble tournament played by the top 50 Canadian players; held every two to three years.

Canasta Card game similar to Rummy that uses two decks of cards and four jokers.

Canfield Common name for Solitaire games that include gambling.

canoe Small, light boat that is pointed at both ends and propelled with a paddle.

Caps Also known as Skelly, Skelsy, Skellzies, Scully, Tops, and Skully; children's game played in New York City and other urban areas.

Capture the Flag Traditional game played by teams that attempt to capture their opponents' flags.

carambole Also known as carom billiards and carambole billiards; version of billiards in which the cue ball must strike two object balls.

card Domino.

card shark Expert card player; sometimes used to refer to a dishonest player or cheater.

Carnival Version of Monopoly.

Carolina Cyclone Roller coaster.

cartes blanches Situation in *Piquet* that arises when, after the deal, one player has a weak hand (no cards above 10), and points are scored as a result.

cartomancy Form of divination, specifically forecasting or foretelling, by reading cards like Tarot cards.

cartoon Caricature or humorous drawing; during the 20th century these drawings were serialized and published in many newspapers, magazines, and comic books.

Casa dei Bambini Literally "Children's House"; Maria Montessori's school for children, opened in 1907.

casino Public building used for gambling.

Castles Also known as Pyramids; game played in ancient Rome using nuts and clay marbles.

catcher In baseball the position behind home plate; the catcher receives the ball from the pitcher.

catchy Variation of the chasing game known as tag.

Cat's Eyes Name for a marble with a particular color and pattern.

Chair Dance Alternative name for Musical Chairs.

Chair Game Alternative name for Musical Chairs.

Chameleon Top Variety of spinning top.

chance luck Unknown and unpredictable phenomenon that causes a particular result.

Charleston Bridge American version of children's song *London Bridge*.

Chasers Variation of the chasing game known as tag.

Chasing and Hiding Australian version of Hide-and-Seek.

Cherry Pit Name for a marble with a particular color and pattern.

cherrystones Ordinary material used for play in early Europe.

Chess Olympiad International biennial Chess tournament organized by FIDE.

Children's Happy Evenings Association (CHEA) Voluntary organization developed in 1888 with the mission of providing play opportunities for the youth of the United Kingdom.

china Ceramic material created by heating raw materials in a kiln.

Chinese Checkers Board game for two to six players; variation of game Halma.

Chinese Flick Version of playing marbles that uses an Asian method of projecting the marble.

Chinese River Game Also known as Chinese Chess.

Chuncara Inca board game using dice and colored beans played in Bolivia, Equador, and Peru.

Chutes and Ladders Children's board game that is a variation of Snakes and Ladders.

city-building games Simulation video games that put the player in the role of city planner or leader, allowing the player to develop structures for food, shelter, health, economic growth, spiritual care, etc.

club houses Structure designed as a meeting place (secret or otherwise) for all of the members of a group.

clubs Suit of cards that represent the peasant class in France.

Cluedo Also known as Clue; mystery crime fiction board game.

cobnut Game played in Europe before 1600, wherein the cobnuts were moved and also used as currency to measure gains and losses.

Cock-stele European throwing game (prior to 1600) where a chicken was buried up to its neck in the ground and young men threw sticks or arrows (cock-steles) at its head.

cognitive skills Mental abilities that allow people to process external stimuli; include thinking, reasoning, and intellectual ability.

coin-operated arcade game Video game or pinball machine that operates when a certain amount of money has been placed into it.

Colossus Roller coaster.

comic opera Light-hearted opera with happy ending and some spoken text.

comics Stories told in graphic form through the presentation of sequential images.

competition Contest for which a winner can be determined.

compulsive readers Also known as ludic readers; readers who become immersed in the world of the story, letting the external world slide away.

computer game Game played on a computer or computerized platform.

computer role-playing game (CRPG) Role-playing video game of the Western tradition; the player creates a character, who moves along a nonlinear storyline by making choices.

computer simulation games Video games that mix skill, chance, and strategy to simulate some aspect of reality.

conscious absorbent mind Second stage of Montessori's formulation of the absorbent mind. In this stage, children aged 3 and above develop a mathematical mind and seek freedom.

console Cabinet to house electronic devices.

console role-playing game (CRPG) Role-playing video game of the Eastern tradition; the player controls a party of predefined characters through a linear storyline that has been dramatically scripted.

construction and management simulation games (CMS) Video games in which players manage, build, and expand fictional projects or communities.

construction toys Toys that encourage building and engineering.

constructive play Play that involves creative problem solving, including the building of objects and structures.

constructive rhythm of life Maria Montessori's term for children's four distinct phases that prepare them for learning.

contest Occasion on which a winner can be declared from among the contestants, or players.

Convention on the Rights of the Child (CRC, UNCRC) International convention adopted in 1989 to define the civil, economic, political, social, and cultural rights of children.

cooperation Process of working or acting together.

cooperative play Social interaction that involves a combination of the sense of group identity and organized activity.

coordination Effective interaction of movements.

Corkscrew Roller coaster.

Cosmic Education Thematic study developed by Maria Montessori to rouse curiosity and imagination in students while also connecting information from one unit to the next.

course rating Evaluation of a golf course's level of difficulty for a scratch golfer, as determined by the USPGA.

Cowboys and Indians Wargame based on the American West before full settlement.

crèche doll Figure representing someone who was present at the birth of Jesus Christ, as indicated by the Bible story. Jesus, Mary, Joseph, wise men, kings, shepherds, or any number of animals are often formed as crèche dolls.

crescendo Rock Paper Scissors sequence of paper, scissors, rock.

Crorepati Baopaar Pakistani version of the board game Monopoly.

cross-country running Sport in which teams of runners complete a course over either smooth or rough terrain with the main intention of reaching the finish line first.

cubaholics Players addicted to using the Rubik's Cube.

Cubist's thumb Ailment related to excessive use of the Rubik's Cube.

cue Tapering rod used to strike balls in pool or billiards.

cue sports Games of skill that use a cue to strike a ball.

cultural subjects and peace education One of the six key areas in Maria Montessori's schools.

cup and ball Game played in colonial America; requires tossing a ball and trying to catch it in a cup when both the ball and cup are attached to a string.

curling Game in which heavy stones are slid on ice toward a target.

D

D&D *Dungeons & Dragons.*

Dance Dance Revolution (DDR) Also known as Dancing Stage.

Dancing Stage Also known as Dance Dance Revolution; music video game that asks players to compete particular dance moves by following the visual and audio cues; music video game that asks players to compete particular dance moves by following the visual and audio cues.

Dara Iranian doll developed in response to Barbie.

deal Distribute cards to the players in a card game.

Debebekosh Ethiopian version of Hide-and-Seek.

decathlon Athletic contest that consists of 10 events.

deck Also known as pack; set of 52 playing cards.

deck Set of dominos, traditionally 28.

defenseman Player whose role is to defend against the other team and prevent the opponent from scoring.

definite probability Actual chance that a particular outcome will occur in a given situation.

delta/triangle One of the most basic kite shapes.

demonstration sports Events at the Olympics from 1912–92. Participants received medals that were not counted among the country's official medals.

Depth Charge A 1976 video computer game similar to Minesweeper.

Detective Physical parlor game that requires the "thief" to find the "detective."

deuce In tennis, a tie that requires two successive points to win the game.

developmental delay Failure to meet certain developmental milestones by the expected time period.

dexterity Adroitness with hands; ability to perform tasks with the hands.

Diabolo Game of skill for which a spool was tossed using a string suspended by two sticks; played in colonial America.

diamond One of the most basic kite shapes.

diamonds Suit of cards that represent the bourgeoisie in France.

Dibeke South African running ball game.

diecast Process of creating toys and other objects by injecting a molten metal alloy into a steel mold (the inverse of the object's intended shape) under high pressure.

die cutting Method of cutting various shapes by using sharp-steel ruled stamps or rollers.

differential reinforcement Method of reinforcement, in operant conditioning, that targets an incompatible or different behavior than that for which change is required.

Dipanonit Variation of the chasing game known as Tag.

discard In card games, the act of throwing out a useless card or failing to follow suit.

discovery Term for a toy that fosters learning and creativity through play, according to the Strong National Museum of Play.

dissected map Early version of a jigsaw puzzle which involved attaching a map to some kind of backing and then cutting it along borders.

dominant strategy Action that is a player's best move, regardless of any other player's move.

dominant strategy Equilibrium situation in which both players maximize their outcomes.

Dominos Several games played using small rectangular blocks or tiles; also the tiles used to play those games.

double-ball Native American game in which players used sticks to catch two billets, balls, or sacks tied together with animal skin.

double-bladed paddle Paddle with blades at both ends of the cross bar; used for kayaking.

double-down In Blackjack, the process of doubling a bet after receiving the first two cards.

Double Dutch Variety of jumping rope in which two people turn two ropes and one or more people jump within those ropes.

downhill skiing Also known as alpine skiing; sport and recreational activity involving sliding down snow-covered hills with ski boots bound to long skis.

dramatic parlor games Parlor games that require some sort of acting.

Draughts Checkers.

draw game Any version of Poker in which the players are dealt a full complement of cards that they may later exchange.

duathlon Athletic contest that involves running and cycling events.

dub up Colloquial term used to describe a move in marbles.

dumb show Also known as mime; performance using gestures and body movements but no words

Dungeon Master (DM) Selected participant in *Dungeons & Dragons* who describes the game to other players.

E

Early Learning Centre (ELC) International toy retailer created in 1970 that creates toys for children up to the age of 6. More than 51 ELC retail stores are found in Saudi Arabia, the United Arab Emirates, Qatar, and Oman.

Easy Money Version of Monopoly.

efficient outcome Also known as a pareto optimal outcome; in this situation, one player's success causes another player's loss.

ego In psychoanalytic theory, the conscious mind.

ego orientation Also known as outcome orientation; occurs when a player measures success based on whether an opponent was defeated.

Eisstock Swiss variation of curling played during the winter, often compared to *pétanque* on ice.

Elastics Version of playing Marbles that uses elastic to project the marble.

El Banquero Version of Monopoly played in Urugay.

electronic toy Toy that requires an external energy source in order to function.

electronic video game Video game that requires an external energy source in order to function.

Elias, Norbert (1897–1990) German sociologist who helped to shape process or figurational sociology.

emotional equilibrium Playworkers have to take emotional equilibrium into account when considering how to create the best play environment.

empathy One of the human attributes developed during play.

enders Those holding and twirling the rope in jump roping.

equality Characteristic of contemporary organized play that manifests in open access to players, regardless of birthright, social class, sex, or religious belief.

Erikson, Erik (1902–94) Developmental psychologist and psychoanalyst who formulated a theory on social development of human beings. Erikson's theory of development begins with infancy and continues through adulthood.

escape the room Type of online graphic adventure game for which the object is to escape a mysterious room.

ethical stance Playworkers have to take ethical stance into account when considering how to create the best play environment.

exergame Video game that requires the player to exercise.

extreme fighting Form of fighting that involves mixed martial arts.

F

face cards Playing cards with the jack, queen, and king.

fair Carnival or traveling show with rides, games of skill, and sideshows.

fairy tale Fictional story, often involving traditional characters, told to amuse or teach a moral.

fairy tales One of five traditional genres of children's literature, according to the Strong National Museum of Play.

falconry Hunting with birds of prey.

Fan-Tan Vietnamese game involving heavy gambling.

fantasy One of five traditional genres of children's literature, according to the Strong National Museum of Play.

fashion doll Dolls designed to feature appearance and clothing style.

Fastaval in Århus Role-playing conference held every spring in Denmark.

Feast of Fools Medieval festival celebrated throughout Europe. Mocking the church officials and practices was a common occurrence; so, too, were masks and disguises.

Fédération Internationale de Basketball Amateur (FIBA) Association that governs international competitions of basketball.

Fédération Internationale de Domino (FIDO) Group that organizes international dominos competitions.

Fédération Internationale des Échecs (FIDE) Association created in 1924 to govern chess competition.

Federation Internationale De Volley-Ball (FIVB) International governing body for volleyball, founded in Paris in 1947.

fell running Also known as mountain running and hill running; sport of running and racing off-road.

fencing Art or sport of swordfighting.

festival Time reserved for celebrating and feasting.

field events Throwing and jumping events in track and field competitions.

field hockey Game played like ice hockey, but on a grass field and with a ball instead of a puck.

fighting simulation video games Also known as "versus fighters"; an action video game that literally simulates one-on-one combat.

figure Model of a bodily form.

figurine Small sculpted or molded model of a human, animal, or religious form.

Finance Version of Monopoly.

finger-throwing game Earlier version of Rock Paper Scissors played as early as 2000 B.C.E. in Egypt.

first-person shooter game (FPS) Video game which is seen through the perspective of the character controlled by the player.

first toy Toy, usually a stuffed animal or a blanket, that plays an important role in an infant's life and development. Donald Woods Winnicott studied the role and significance of the first toy during and after infancy.

Fitter Britain Movement 1930s movement in the United Kingdom to promote increased physical activity among children.

Fivestones Pentalitha Game played in ancient Rome as a divination (by women) or to gamble (by men).

Flashlight Tag Variation of the chasing game known as Tag that involves shining a flashlight on opponents instead of tagging them.

flexibility Playworkers have to take into account when considering how best to create such an environment.

floorball Indoor team sport developed in Sweden during the 1970s. The game involves team members using sticks to move a ball with 26 holes in an attempt to score.

flush Poker hand consisting of all five cards in the same suit.

fly fishing Method of angling that uses a fly rod, fly line, and artificial bait to catch fish.

Flying Top Variety of spinning top.

Fly the Garter Version of Leapfrog.

folklore Stories, proverbs, riddles, and songs of a culture, usually part of that culture's oral tradition.

follow the leader Group activity that involves following and often mimicking one person (the leader).

foosball Also known as baby foot, table soccer, and table football; tabletop game based on soccer, or association football.

Foot and Half Version of Leapfrog.

football Name of several sports, all of which involve kicking a ball with the intent of scoring a goal.

formal games Games played by a game community, who follow established rules and focus on winning the game.

Fort-Da Also known as gone/here and played by young children; similar to Hide-and-seek.

forward Player whose role is to attempt to score.

four-ball Golf played between two teams of two players. Each player plays his/her own ball, but the lowest score counts for the team.

foursomes Golf played by two teams of two people, where each team has only one ball and players alternate playing it.

Fox and Geese Scandinavian board game in which geese try to surround the fox so he could not move and the fox tries to catch the geese.

Fox and Hounds Version of Hares and Hounds in which the hounds try to catch the fox and the fox tries to evade capture.

fox hunting Also known as horse and hound; activity that involves using dogs to hunt a fox.

freedom Playworkers have to take freedom into account when considering how to create the best play environment.

freestyle cross-country skiing Technique that involves pushing off with both legs and resembles skating.

freestyle Frisbee includes Frisbee played for fun between friends and more specialized routines designed with the Frisbee.

free time In Surplus Resource Theory, time not required for work or other serious survival activities.

French Deck Standard deck of 52 cards.

French Top Variety of spinning top.

friendly games Games played by a play community, who collectively decide the rules of the game.

Frisbee golf Game in which players try to throw a Frisbee through openings, much in the same way that golfers try to hit balls into openings.

Froebel, Friedrich (1782–1852) Theorist who proposed that children have unique needs and capacities and, in formulating that theory, laid the groundwork for modern education.

Froggies Name for a marble with a particular color and pattern.

fudging Colloquial term used to describe a move in marbles.

Fulla Alternative to Barbie created in Saudi Arabia.

Full Sequence Pairs Also known as the Pairs Sequence; any game of Whist in which two people are partnered for the duration of the game.

Funeral Game played in Lebanon wherein children mimic the ceremony of a funeral.

G

Gabata Game similar to the Egyptian and Inca game *Mancala* and the Japanese game *Shogi*. *Gabata* is played in the Congo and in Ethiopia and asks players to capture the colored seeds held by other players.

Gaelic Athletic Association (GAA) Amateur sporting organization that promotes Gaelic games like hurling, camogie, Gaelic football, handball, and rounders.

Gallo, Gallina Literally "Cock, Hen"; Mexican game.

gamble (noun) Risky act or money risked for possible gain; (verb) play games for money or take a chance.

game Amusement or pastime; contest with rules to determine a winner.

game community Group of people who join together to play a particular game and who focus on winning that game.

Game of 20 Squares Egyptian board game.

Game of Ferses Earlier version of Draughts.

gamer Also known as gamester; person who plays games.

gamesmanship Learned behavior developed during play; refers to the level of respect one has for competitors, for the rules of the game, and for the results of the game.

gaming Playing games; gambling.

gaming platform Operating system on which a video game or computer game is played.

garter Line in the dirt used when playing Leapfrog.

Gato Name for Tic-Tac-Toe in Chile, Mexico, and Costa Rica.

Geertz, Clifford (1926–2006) American anthropologist who advocated trying to interpet the symbols of another culture. "Deep Play: Notes on the Balinese Cockfight" is one of his most well-known essays.

Giant Slalom Alpine ski race in which skiers must race between poles ("gates") spaced at greater distances from each other than in the traditional slalom.

Girl Guides Association Name for Girl Scouts outside of the United States; original movement parallel to Boy Scouts but intended for girls.

Girl Scouts of America American version of Girl Guides Association; movement parallel to Boy Scouts but intended for girls.

giving a back Body stance formed in Leapfrog as a player rests his or her head on the thighs and hunches the body forward.

gliding Recreational activity and competitive sport that involves flying unpowered aircraft known as gliders and sailplanes.

Globe Top Variety of spinning top.

glove Protective handgear used to help catch the ball in baseball.

Gnav Game of the Cuckoo family that uses a special set of cards.

Go A board game for two players, played with black and white game pieces on a 19 x 19 grid, which originated in China, and then spread to Korea and Japan.

goalie Player whose job is to protect the net and keep the opponent from scoring.

goal line Line where the scoring goal stands.

God games Video games, often without a set goal, that allow a player control over the lives of people within the game.

Goff Early version of hockey, played with a curved club.

Goffman, Erving (1922–82) Canadian sociologist who studied social interaction in the form of dramaturgical perspective.

Going to Jerusalem Alternative name for Musical Chairs.

goofing around Fooling around; playing around.

Goose Board game developed in Italy during the 15th century. The object of the game was to be the first person to reach the end of the journey.

government simulation Simulation video games that focus on the politics, government, and policies of a country but rarely on warfare.

graphic adventure games Video games that require players to make choices in order to guide the course of the game, which is seen in graphic form on the screen.

grass skiing Started in France in 1966; uses short skis on wheels to ski on grass slopes in order to train for winter skiing events.

gratification Positive emotional response to the fulfilment of a desire.

Great American Revolution Roller coaster.

gridiron football American football.

Gris Card game, version of Pig.

group games Games that by definition cannot be played by only one person.

Guild of Poor Brave Things Group established in 1894 in the United Kingdom to help disabled boys to create a productive place for themselves within society.

gutters Colloquial term used to describe a move in marbles.

gymnastics Sport that displays strength, agility, and balance through a series of exercises.

H

hack and slash games Also known as beat 'em up games; video games that focus on close-quarters combat.

haka Dance among the Maori of New Zealand.

halatafl Viking game similar to Chess; predecessor of Hounds and Hares.

half balls Version of stickball played with balls cut in half.

Half-Iron Triathlon with race distances of 1.2 miles (1.9 km), which is half the distance of the races in a full triathlon.

hanafuda Japanese playing cards.

handball Gaelic game similar to squash or racquetball; played by two, three, or four players using a gloved hand instead of a raquet.

handball Team sport in which two teams of seven players each (including goalies) pass and bounce a ball in order to try to score by getting it into the goal.

handicap Measure of an amateur golfer's ability to play over 18 holes. This number represents the number of strokes over par the golfer is likely to perform on an above-average day.

handicraft Work or craft produced by hand.

Hand-In-and-Hand-Out Indoor game.

Handy-dandy Guessing game, played with a small object hidden in the palm of a hand hidden behind the player's back.

Hangman Word game where one player chooses a word and indicates the number of letters in the word. Other players must find the word by choosing one letter at a time. Each incorrect letter results in the drawing of a body part on a stick figure. The goal is to guess the word before the character is hanged.

Harpastum Amateurish ball game played in Italy; earlier version of modern football and rugby, although with a much higher degree of violence.

Heads-or-Ships Ancient Roman game involving tossing coins, like Heads-or-Tails.

Head Start School readiness progress founded in 1965 in the United States that continues to help children throughout the country.

Heads Up Another name for the classroom game called Seven Up.

hearts Suit of cards that represent the clergy in France.

height jumps Track and field events that measure the vertical distance of a jump.

heptathlon Athletic endeavor, usually track and field, consisting of seven different events.

high jump Track and field event for which a competitor runs toward and leaps over a horizontal crossbar. The runner's goal is to jump ever-increasing heights without knocking the bar over.

hiking long walk for exercise or pleasure.

hill running Also known as mountain running and fell running; sport of running and racing off-road.

hit In Blackjack, the way to ask for another card.

Hit Me, Hit Me Schoolyard game played in poor towns of South Africa that reenacts the brute force to which the children are subjected.

hnefatalf Viking game similar to Chess.

hobby Enjoyable activity undertaken during one's free time.

hockey puck Vulcanized rubber disc three inches in diameter used in ice hockey.

hockey rink Ice rink designed specifically for the game of hockey.

hockey stick Used in hockey to handle the puck.

hole Card dealt face-down in poker.

homely objects Toys related to tools used in the home.

home plate Base over which the batter, as an offensive player, stands and over which a runner must pass in order to score.

Honors Ace, king, queen, and jack of the trump suit in games of Whist.

hook Portion of fishing rod at the end of the line; used to hold bait.

Hopscotch Children's skipping game that requires a grid to be drawn in the dirt or on the sidewalk.

Hornussen Swiss sport that is a mix of golf and baseball.

Hounds and Hares Version of Hares and Hounds in which the hounds try to catch the hares and the hares try to evade capture.

Hounds and Jackals Egyptian board game.

housie-housie Bantu version of playing marriage or house.

Huizinga, Johan (1872–1945) Dutch historian whose 1938 work *Homo Ludens* discusses the influence of play on European culture.

hula hoops Toy hoops twirled around the body for entertainment.

Hunts Version of Hares and Hounds in which the hunter tries to catch the prey and the hunted tries to evade capture.

hurdle (noun) Light movable barrier over which runners must jump in certain track and field events; (verb) to jump over an obstacle.

Hurkle 1978 computer game similar to Minesweeper.

hurling Outdoor team sport played with *hurleys* (sticks) and *sliotars* (balls); ancient Gaelic in origin.

Hurling Irish game similar to hockey, played with a small ball and a curved wooden stick.

hustler Player who takes advantage of less-skilled competitors in money games.

Hwatoo Korean gambling game.

I

Ice-cream Jellies Name for a marble with a particular color and pattern.

ice hockey Game played by two teams of six skaters who try to maneuver a puck into their opponent's goal.

iconic status Status assigned by the Strong National Museum of Play to toys that are well-remembered and respected.

id In psychoanalytic theory, the primitive instincts and energies that exist beneath all psychic activity.

If You Love Me, Dearest, Smile Physical parlor game.

ilinx (vertigo) Category of play that addresses or deals with the ecstatic states, according to Roger Caillois's theory of play.

ilinx (vertigo) Refers to all forms of play that create a sense of disorder or an alteration of perception according to Caillois's model of play.

imitation Act of copying another person's actions.

Indigenous Games Project South African organization devoted to reinforcing community values and promote interactions between communities through traditional games.

Individual Psychology Differential psychology or the psychology of individual differences.

infield Diamond-shaped portion of a baseball field.

Inflation Version of Monopoly.

informal games Games played by a play community that collectively decides the rules of the game.

injection molding Process of creating toys and other objects by injecting a molten plastic into a mold (the inverse of the object's intended shape) under high pressure.

innovation Category used by the Strong National Museum of Play when the toy significantly changed how subsequent toys are played with or designed.

Innovative Playground Research Project Organization that presents case studies from around the world and suggests that partnerships between the private and public sector can build and maintain playground spaces.

Institute of Park and Recreation Administration (IPRA) Created in 1926, IPRA brought together parks and garden managers to provide outdoor recreational facilities to establish supervised games sessions.

Institute of Playleaders Organization of professional playworkers founded in the United Kingdom in the 1970s.

intellectual games Games that require or develop intelligence.

intellectual mind Phase of a child's development that follows the absorbent mind in Maria Montessori's theory. In this phase, children explore their world with increased concentration, attention, and intellectual fortitude.

intellectual stimulation Playworkers have to take intellectual stimulation into account when considering how to create the best play environment.

interactive fiction Also known as text adventure games; video games that require players to make choices in order to guide the course of the game, which the computer would then describe.

interactive movies Video games that emerged with the technology of the laserdisc. They allow a player to control some actions within prefilmed full-motion cartoons or live-action sequences.

intercollegiate athletic system System that develops and controls sports competition between colleges and universities.

International Bubble Hockey Federation (IBHF) International governing body for bubble hockey competitions and rules.

International Cricket Council (ICC) International governing body of cricket founded in 1909, when it was known as the Imperial Cricket Conference.

International Federation of Dominos Group that organizes international dominos competitions.

International Federation of Netball Association (IFNA) Association that governs international competitions and rules of netball.

International Golf Federation (IGF) Organization that arranges international amateur golf competitions.

International Olympic Committee (IOC) Group that organizes and regulates the modern Olympic games.

International Play Association (IPA) International, nongovernmental organization founded in Denmark in 1961 to protect, preserve, and promote the child's right to play as a fundamental human right; members come from any profession that works for or with children.

International Rugby Board (IRB) International governing and rule-making body for rugby union.

International Table Hockey Federation (ITHF) International governing body for table hockey; organizes the world championship every two years.

International Table Soccer Federation (ITSF) International governing body for competitions of table soccer.

International Top Spinners Association (ITSA Spin Top) International organization that shares information and stories about spinning tops while also encouraging participation in the art and sport of top spinning.

International Water Ski Federation (IWSF) International organization that governs water-skiing events, sets official international rules, and coordinates the work of national federations.

Ironman Annual triathlon race famous because of its television coverage, race conditions, and extremely difficult conditions.

J

Jacks Game that involves throwing and picking up various jackstones between bounces of a small rubber ball.

Jai alai Cuban game developed from the Basque game *pelotari*. The game involves tossing a ball and catching it in a basket attached to one player's hand.

Jan-Ken-Pon Alternative name for Rock Paper Scissors.

javelin spear thrown as a weapon in competitive track and field events; also the event in which the spear is thrown.

Jegichagi Traditional Korean game.

jester A jokester or the ordinary material used for play in early Europe.

Jeu de Paume French game that shares several characteristics and rules of *Pallone con Bracciale*.

jointed bodies Doll or figurine bodies composed of several parts attached at moveable joints.

Joint National Committee for Training in Playleadership Organization of professional playworkers founded in the United Kingdom in the 1970s.

jokes Humorous anecdote or jest; often part of classroom play.

jousting Activity in which two people spar with each other; traditionally a medieval European sport in which two mounted knights charge each other with lances.

judo Japanese martial art.

Juego de pelota Ballgame using a rubber ball played by Aztecs, Mayans, and Toltecas.

juggling Throwing and catching several items at the same time.

jumble Word game that requires players to unscramble letters in order to form words; often used as a classroom teaching aide.

jumping events Track and field events that involve jumping.

jump rope Also known as skipping rope; length of rope, usually with handles at both ends, swung around while a person jumps over it.

Jungle Traditional Chinese board game that prefigured the game Stratego.

junk playground Also known as adventure playground; playgrounds with child-oriented perspective in play. Developed from C. Th. Sørensen's 1931 plans to reuse wastelands, bomb sites, and building sites as places where children can play and create.

K

Kabadi Where two teams try to invade each other's territory.

Kabal Meaning "secret knowledge," this version of solitaire is played in Poland, Denmark, and Norway.

kaipara Type of athletic pursuit undertaken by the Maori of New Zealand.

Kalq Australian Aboriginal game of throwing spears and deflecting them with wooden shields.

karate Style of martial arts that involves sharp blows and kicks to an opponent's pressure-sensitive points; based on traditional Japanese system of unarmed combat.

***Karo* Stick** Game played by the Maori of New Zealand.

Karpetalakhi In the game, two teams of men use their belts to lash at each other, with one group guarding children hidden under a carpet and the other trying to release them; when the children are finally released, they appear to be magically revived.

kayak Small canoe propelled with a double-bladed paddle.

Kemari Ancient Japanese game considered one of the earliest forms of soccer and part of prayer for world peace, fertility, good health, and family happiness.

Khuzza Lawizz Ancient Egyptian version of Leapfrog.

ki a New Zealand Maori practice of carrying delicate eggs in woven flaxen basets at the end of a braided rope. Ki has become a form of martial arts.

Kigogo Kenyan game of moving counters (often different colored stones, seeds or shells) around a board to capture an opponent's pieces.

kill Also known as the bomb; play in volleyball where the volleyball is spiked over the net in such a fashion that the other team cannot respond to the volley.

kindgergarten Preschool for children aged 4 to 6 that prepares them for elementary school.

Ki-o-rahi Ball game played by the New Zealand Maori.

Kip Variation of the children's chasing game known as Tag.

kite Object created by a light-weight frame and covering attached to string and flown in the wind.

Klondike Variety of Solitaire.

knickknack Also known as a novelty; an inexpensive and mass-produced object purchased or collected for amusement.

knock-knock jokes Humorous anecdotes that follow a particular pattern of interaction between the joke teller and the audience; often part of classroom play.

knucklebone, or astragulus The anklebone of cloven-hoofed animal served as a naturally good item to play like dice.

Knucklebones More commonly known as Jacks; descended from an ancient Roman game.

knuckle down Colloquial term used to describe a move in marbles.

Kunettwigi Common Korean folk game.

kung fu Generic word for Chinese martial arts.

Kvatrutafl Viking board game.

Kyodai Computer brands of Mahjong Solitaire; may be a modernized version of the old Chinese game known as The Turtle.

L

La Bataille French version of War, played by children and adults.

La Belle Lucie Variety of Solitaire.

labelling game Game in which someone, usually an adult, points to an object and then names it with the intention of increasing a child's vocabulary and comprehension.

lacrosse Competitive team game created by Native Americans; two teams use long-handled rackets to transport, throw, and carry a ball toward a net to score.

Ladies' Game Early European version of Draughts.

La Française des Jeux French governmental organization responsible for regulating all games involving money.

La Marelle French version of Hopscotch.

Landlord's Game Version of Monopoly.

language One of the six key areas in Maria Montessori's schools.

language games Games designed to develop or expose language skills.

La Nivernaise Version of Solitaire.

lapta Game like baseball, where players use a bat to hit a small, heavy stick, in Belarus.

Last Word Board Game Timed word game that asks players to list words that fit into a specific category and begin with a specific letter.

L'attaque Original version of Stratego that appeared just before World War I in France.

lawn bowls Also known as bowls; balls are rolled toward a specific target with the ball coming closest determining the winner of the game.

Leap, Frog, Leap Singing game for children dating back to ancient Rome.

Le Cadran Variety of Solitaire.

left bower Jack of clubs in Euchre.

leisure Time for recreation and amusement.

Le Jeu de Quilles French version of land bowling.

Le Jeu des 7 Familles (family game) French game played by both adults and children.

Le Loi Salique Variety of Solitaire.

length jumps Track and field events that measure the horizontal distance of a jump.

Le Pont Levis French version of children's song *London Bridge*.

Le Saut de Mouton Game like Leapfrog; literally means "the sheep's leap."

Les Billes French version of marbles.

Les Patiences French game like solitaire.

Le Vieux Garçon French version of Old Maid; literally means "the old boy."

life simulation Also known as Artificial Life Games; simulation video games that involve living or controlling at least one artificial life.

life styles In Alfred Adler's theory, these are interpersonal approaches to living based on feelings, behaviors, and past experiences.

light gun shooters Shooter video game that uses a pointing device for work with computers or a control device for use with home consoles and in arcades.

line cord made for fishing; attached to the fishing rod.

literary word games Games that use a player's knowledge of words and literature.

lithograph Printed image made from a flat surface; type of printmaking.

little brother of war Lacrosse in southern Native American tribes.

Little League Usually children's variation of formal games, as in Little League Baseball.

logic or word-play games Parlor games involving mental exercises.

logic puzzle Puzzle that derives from the field of deduction; includes matrixes and mazes.

London Bridge Singing game that dates back to the thirteenth century.

longevity Classification used by the Strong National Museum of Play if the toy has appealed to children across multiple generations.

long jump Track and field event in which the athlete attempts to jump as far as possible after having run to and jumped from a given mark.

lottery Game of chance that awards prizes to the player whose purchased lot is drawn.

Lotto Game of chance like Bingo; can also refer to the lottery.

Lotto ("Lottery") Made its appearance in the 17th century in Genoa, where people used to bet on political appointments.

Lottomatica Italian company that acquired the American group GTECH and is currently one of the largest world lottery operators, with an immense online network across more than 50 countries.

love Signifies "zero" in tennis.

luck Unknown, unpredictable phenomenon that causes an event to end in a particular fashion.

ludic readers Also known as compulsive readers; readers who become immersed in the world of the story, letting the external world slide away.

Ludo Board game in which two to four players race around a board, moving according to rolls of a die.

ludus In Callois's model of play, *ludus* is all play that is structured and institutionalized; opposite of *paidia*.

M

Mahjong A game for four players that originated in China; involves skill, strategy, and calculation, as well as a certain degree of chance.

Mah-jongg Variation on the spelling of Mahjong.

Main Rimau Literally "Tiger Game"; played in Malaysia.

make-believe Pretend or imaginary play.

making a back Body stance formed in Leapfrog as a player rests his or her head on the thighs and hunches the body forward.

Malibu surfboard Surfboard with a longboard shape on which most surfers learn to surf.

Mancala Egyptian board game.

Mancala Kenyan game of moving counters (often different colored stones, seeds, or shells) around a board to capture the pieces of an opponent.

Mankata Traditional Congolese game that involves making an hollow in the ground and then placing stones around those of one's opponent in order to capture their pieces.

marathon Foot race of 26 miles 385 yards (42.195 km).

marble Small ball of glass used for various games.

Marco Polo Water game where one person tries to find the others playing by yelling "Marco," to which the other players must respond "Polo." This game is very similar to Alligator Eyes and Submarine.

Marelle French version of Hopscotch.

Marn Grook Traditional game called "Game Ball"; played by the Djab Wurrung people in western Victoria, Australia.

marrowbone Ordinary material also used for play in early Europe.

martial arts tournaments Organized displays of the codified practices of training for combat.
Massively Mini Media Player Game ipod-style video game.
massively multiplayer online first-person shooter game (MMOFPS) Virtual world in which many players, each controlling a character and seeing the game through the perspective of that character, interact and engage in virtual combat.
massively multiplayer online role-playing game (MMORPG) Role-playing game played online with hundreds of players interacting in real time.
Master Mind Simple code-breaking board game played by two players; invented in 1970 in Israel.
mastery orientation Situation in which a player measures success based on self-set standards. Winning does not matter if the player does not play well.
Matador Icelandic version of Monopoly.
match play Game of golf in which the player with the highest points score wins.
mathematics One of the six key areas in Maria Montessori's schools.
Mattis Norwegian card game.
maximum benefit payoff The best reward possible in a given situation.
maze games Video games that require a player to navigate a maze, which constitutes the entire playing field.
medley Musical composition that uses pieces of many other songs.
Mehen Egyptian board game.
memory games Games that require using one's memory skills and that develop memory skills in turn.
Merelles Also known as "The Mill"; early European version of Draughts.
Mermaid on Rocks Version of Marco Polo.
Metropolitan Public Gardens Association (MPGA) Organization created in 1882 to campaign for the creation of small play areas for children in London.
microgenetic perspectives Changes that occur over very brief periods of time (i.e., seconds and minutes) in Vygotsky's evaluation of human development.
Mik Cambodian version of Hopscotch.
Military Variation of Whist in which several teams, each led by a captain, play visiting opposing teams.
military strategy board game Board game that requires players to make decisions about military matters.
military strategy game Game that requires players to make decisions about military matters.
Mill Also known as "Merelles"; early European version of Draughts.
mimesis Act of copying or imitating.
mimicry (simulation) All games of simulation, wherein one assumes a role, wears a disguise, or identifies with a person, according to Caillois's model of play.
miming Type of acting where facial expressions, gestures, and movements replace speech.
Minister's Cat Logic parlor game.
Mintonette Original name of volleyball.
mitt Protective handgear used to help catch the ball in baseball.
mixed strategy Also known as a randomized strategy; probability distribution over a player's entire set of strategies.
modeling Method of teaching through representing the desired behavior so that the student will learn through imitation.
Moksha-Patamu Morality game where the snakes corresponded to vices and the ladders to virtues.
Mölkky Finnish game of Skittles.
monkey-bars Playground equipment on which children travel from one side to the other by swinging from their arms.
Montessori, Maria (1870–1952) Italian physician and educator who designed a method for educating children in which children are encouraged to make maximal decisions and to learn through observing and correcting themselves.
Montessori Method Educational method that emphasizes self-directed activity by the child and clinical observation by the teacher. Developed by Maria Montessori.
Morabaraba South African game boards created in the dirt.
Moraff's Computer brand of Mahjong Solitaire; may be a modernized version of the old Chinese game known as The Turtle.
Morgenstern, Oskar (1902–77) Austrian economist who cofounded game theory.
Morpion French version of Tic-Tac-Toe.
Morra Finger game of chance played by two people in Ancient Rome.
Morris Dance English folk dancing based on rhythmic stepping and choreographed figures by groups of dancers.
motivation component Process underlying observational learning.

motor reproduction component Process underlying observational learning.

motor skills Skills based on the ability to use the body's muscles.

mountain biking Sport of riding bikes off-road, over rough terrain.

mountaineering Mountain climbing.

mountain running Also known as fell running and hill running; sport of running and racing off-road.

Mugwump Early 1978 computer video game similar to Minesweeper.

Multiple Intelligences Theory developed by Howard Gardner that argues people have a variety of different and measurable intelligences. Gardner's categories are bodily-kinesthetic, interpersonal, verbal-linguistic, logical-mathematical, naturalistic, intrapersonal, visual-spatial, and musical.

music and arts One of the six key areas in Maria Montessori's schools.

music box Decorative box that, when opened or wound, plays music.

music games Video games that require a player to follow sequences of movement or to develop specific rhythms.

mystery One of five traditional genres of children's literature, according to the Strong National Museum of Play.

N

Naismith, Dr. James (1861–1939) Inventor or creator of basketball.

Nanpure Japanese name for Sudoku; abbreviation of the English and Japanese words for "number place."

Napoleon at St. Helena Variety of Solitaire.

Napoleon's Square Variety of Solitaire.

Nash Equilibrium Situation in which each player's response to another player's strategy is the best possible or tied for the best possible in that pairing.

National Basketball Association (NBA) North American professional basketball league.

National Children's Strategy 10-year Irish strategy developed in 2000 to respect, cherish, and encourage children.

National Collegiate Athletic Association (NCAA) Association that organizes the athletic programs of colleges and universities; current membership consists of about 1,200 institutions, conferences, organizations, and individuals in the United States

National Hockey League (NHL) Professional hockey league established in 1917.

National Institute for Play (U.S.) American nonprofit public-benefit corporation focused on bringing the unrealized knowledge, practices, and benefits of play into public life.

National Invitation Tournament (NIT) Men's college basketball tournament sponsored by the NCAA.

National Playing Fields Association (NPFA) Founded in 1925, this was the first national body to make the case for increased outdoor play for children and increased provision for that play.

National Recreational Policy for Children Irish policy adopted in 2007 to provide a strategic framework for the development of recreational opportunities aimed primarily at young people.

National Recreation and Parks Association Organization whose goal is "to advance parks, recreation and environmental conservation efforts that enhance the quality of life for all people."

National Scrabble Championship American Scrabble tournament held every one to two years.

Ncuva South African board game created in the dirt.

negative reinforcement Way to encourage behavior by taking away an aversive condition (e.g., not losing playtime when all work is completed).

Neolttwigi Marbles, as played by Korean girls.

Nerf Balls Balls made of a foam-like material that makes indoor play safe.

nesting doll Doll inside of which are several smaller dolls.

New York Version of Monopoly.

Nguni South African version of Stick Tag.

Nine Men's Morris Strategy board game for two players that was first created in ancient Rome.

Nintendo Entertainment System (NES) Original 8-bit video game console.

nonplayer characters (NPC) Main characters, guest stars, walk-ons, and bit parts in role-playing games.

nonsense One of five traditional genres of children's literature, according to the Strong National Museum of Play.

non-strictly-competitive game Also known as a non-zero-sum game; in this situation, cooperation can help players because one player's interests are not entirely contradictory to the interests of other players.

non-zero-sum game Game that usually involves cooperative play.

Nordic skiing Also known as cross-country skiing; sport and recreational activity that involves sliding along snow-covered land with ski boots attached to skis at the toes but unbound at the heels.

novelty Also known as knickknack; inexpensive and mass-produced object purchased for amusement.

Number Place Translation of Nanpure and Sudoku.

numeracy Skill with numbers and mathematics.

nursery rhyme Traditional poem or song taught to young children.

Nzango Congolese game.

O

odds on Display amounts a bookmaker will pay out on winning bets.

odds Probability of a particular outcome.

Ohajiki Japanese marbles.

Old Roger Dramatic singing game where a ring of children act out the parts of the chorus in order to relate incidents from a play about a funeral for Old Roger.

Olympics International multisport event for winter and summer sports. The Olympics occur every four years.

one-on-one play Competitive play, especially in an active athletic pursuit, between two people.

online persona Virtual presence a person assumes in an online game, chat room, or other virtual reality setting.

onlooker play Type of play in which a child observes those playing but does not participate. In onlooker play, the child learns new behaviors and skills through observation.

on-rails shooter Shoot 'em up videogame in which the player has a predetermined path, in contrast to the free movement of a first-person shooter game.

ontogenetic perspectives Development over a lifetime according to Vygotsky's evaluation of human development.

operant conditioning Process wherein behavior is shaped by reinforcement or punishment.

origami Art of paper folding.

outcome orientation Also known as ego orientation; occurs when a player measures success based on whether an opponent was defeated.

outfield Section of a baseball field beyond the infield, contained by the extensions of the first and third baselines.

outguessing regress Unavailability of accurate predictions or confident expectations.

P

pack Also known as deck; set of 52 playing cards.

pack Set of dominos, traditionally 28.

Padiddle Car game that involves looking for and identifying oncoming cars with only one functioning headlight.

paideia Greek word for education; refers to the cultural heritage passed from one generation to the next.

Paidia Extreme of Caillois's model for play that involves unstructured and anarchic play; opposite of *ludus*.

Pairs Sequence Also known as the Full Sequence Pairs; any game of Whist in which two people are partnered for the duration of the game.

Paley, Vivian (b. 1929) Child psychologist, kindergarten teacher, and early childhood education researcher.

Pall Mall Rural Italian ancestor of Croquet.

pantomime Performance using gestures and expressions but not words.

Paper Chase Version of Hares and Hounds in which the hunter tries to catch the prey and the hunted tries to evade capture.

paper doll Flat doll, made out of paper and able to be clothed with paper outfits.

Paper Scissors Stone Club Organization devoted to playing and strategizing about Rock Paper Scissors; created in London in 1842.

papier-mâché Technique in which forms (including doll's heads) can be formed by mixing wet paper pulp with glue or paste.

paragliding Recreational activity that consists of gliding in a parasail.

parallel play Concept within developmental psychology that explains the manner in which children play side-by-side without interacting.

Paralympics International sporting tournament for people who are physically disabled.

pareto optimal outcome Also known as an efficient outcome; in this situation, one player's success causes another player's loss.

pari-mutuel Form of betting used in horseracing, greyhound racing, jai alai, and other sports events that occur in a relatively short period of time. In pari-mutuel betting, all bets are held in a single pool and payoff odds are calculated according to the number of winning bets within that pool.

Parten, Mildred (b. 1933) Psychologist who studies the development of young children's play.

party games Multiplayer video games that generally consist of a variety of minigames.

Password Word game in which one player must guess a word based on his or her partner's one-word clue.

pastime Leisure activity; diversion.

Patience British name for Solitaire.

Patolli Game played by Aztecs, Mayans, and Toltecas.

pattern-based puzzles Puzzles that are solved by recognizing and ordering a pattern (e.g., jigsaw puzzles, Rubik's Cube, etc.)

Paume 12th-century French game that prefigures tennis.

payoff Maximum benefit; the best reward possible in a given situation.

payoff matrix Possible strategies available to a player and the payoff possible for making that choice depending on other players' actions.

Peek-a-Boo Game played with babies. The adult hides his or her face, then reveals it, saying "boo."

Pe-Ling Version of Mahjong.

Pelota Basque game that shares several characteristics and rules of *Pallone con Braccialed*; played in Belgium, Italy, Paraguay, and Uruguay.

Pelotari Earlier version of Jai Alai; Cuban.

Penny-Pricks Indoor game.

Pentalitha Fivestones Game played in ancient Rome as a divination (by women) or to gamble (by men).

pentathlon Athletic contest with five events.

perceptual set Mental predisposition to perceive one thing in favor of another.

Pétanque Also known as *boules*; French lawn bowling game.

pet-raising simulation Digital pets; video games focused on how a player interacts with one or few life forms.

Petrushka Russian version of Punch and Judy.

phantasmagoria Optical illusion; used for projected ghost shows before the cinema was fully developed.

phantasmagorical play Play involving fantasy and a juxtaposition of unlikely things; part of Brian Sutton-Smith's theories of play.

phylogenetic perspectives Development over evolutionary time according to Vygotsky's evaluation of human development.

physical activity Playworkers have to take physical activity into account when considering how to create the best play environment.

physical games Parlor games blending movement and intuition.

physical play Play that involves actual physical activity, as opposed to mental activity or virtual presence.

Piaget, Jean (1896–1980) Swiss philosopher and developmental theorist who studied children and famously formed a theory of cognitive development.

Picha Inca game involving dice; played in Ecuador and Peru.

Pickle Variation of the chasing game known as Tag.

pick-up games Variation of informal or friendly games.

piggyback Ride on another person's shoulders or back.

Piggy in the Ring Indoor game played in early Europe.

Pirori Version of Hula Hoops played by the Maori of New Zealand.

pitcher In baseball, the player who throws the ball to the catcher, trying to keep the batter from hitting it and scoring.

pitcher's mound Slight elevation in the center of the baseball diamond where the pitcher stands.

Planchette Triangular or heart-shaped device that moves to spell out messages in Ouija.

platform games Video games that involve traveling between different levels, each of which is known as a platform.

play community Group of people who join together to play a game, deciding upon the rules together.

player entities Virtual characters created to operate within a videogame or an online game.

Player versus Player (PvP) Video game or online competition between more than one live player. PvP stands in contrast to games that require a human player to compete against computer-generated characters.

Play Ethos Peter K. Smith's formulation of the belief that play is an essential part of development.

playground Outdoor area designed for children's play.

Playground Association of America (PAA) American group founded in 1906 to promote parks as recreational facilities; later became the National Recreation Association.

Playground for All Children Playground built in 1984 in Flushing Meadows–Corona Park, Queens, New York City. This was the first playground designed for regular use by both disabled and able-bodied children.

playground games Variation of informal or friendly games.

playhouse Structure, however impermanent, in which children play games related to traditional home life.

play supervisors Adults employed to help children with their play activities and to create a safe environment during the New Deal era in America.

Pochen German version of Poker.

Pochspiel German version of Poker.

pocket billiards Also known as pool; game played on a pool table with six pockets.

Podul de Piatra Romanian version of the children's song *London Bridge*.

Poi Form of juggling with balls on ropes, held in hands, or swinging in various circle patterns practiced among the New Zealand Maori.

pole vault Track and field event that involves jumping over a high horizontal crossbar with the aid of a long vertical pole.

Polichinelle French version of Punch and Judy.

polyurethane Clear, durable finish applied to diverse materials including wood as a wear layer.

pool Also known as pocket billiards; any game played on a pool table with six pockets.

poppet Doll or puppet.

Poque French card game similar to Poker brought to the port city of New Orleans during the early 19th century by itinerant traders and seamen.

porcelain Ceramic material created by heating raw materials in a kiln.

positional segregation Phenomenon in coed softball games where men take the skilled positions (pitcher, short stop, third base, and center field) and force women to take the less-skilled positions (catcher, first base, second base, and rover).

positive reinforcement Addition of a positive stimulus as a response to a desired behavior (e.g., giving stickers to a child who has just picked up his or her toys).

practical life One of the six key areas in Maria Montessori's schools.

practice play Play that involves repeating specific motions necessary for mastery of a specific skill required for a sport or game.

predicted probability Probability of winning, according to the casino, dealer, or sponsor of the game.

pretend play play that involves imagining a situation, relationship, etc.

pretense play Also known as symbolic play; involves transforming the physical world into a symbol (e.g., using a couch's cushions to create a fort).

Primero English card game similar to Poker.

private logic In contrast to common sense, private logic is an individual's reasoning to stimulate and justify a self-serving style of life. Private logic plays a large part in Alfred Adler's theories.

probability Odds or chances of a particular outcome.

professional Athlete who plays in return for payment.

programming game Computer game that allows the player no direct influence over the course of the game and is written in a domain-specific programming language that controls the characters.

Progressive Version of Whist.

protective frame Part of the paratelic state in reversal theory; in this state, the protective frame allows people to see themselves as immune from the consequences of failure and error.

prototype Standard or experimental example.

Public Schools Athletic League (PSAL) First interscholastic sports program introduced by Luther Gulic in the New York City school system in 1903.

puck Hard disc used in ice hockey (where it is made of hard, vulcanized rubber), floor hockey (where it is made of plastic), and shuffleboard (where it is made of metal and plastic).

puck control Ability of a hockey player to control the movement of a puck with a hockey stick.

Pulcinella Characters and puppet play from the 16th-century Italian *Commedia dell'arte*; became Punch and Judy.

Punch Buggy Car game in which players attempt to locate and name any Volkswagen Beetles in sight.

puppet Representational figure of person or animal controlled by an operator using strings held from above or supports from within (for example, using the hand or fingers).

puzzle game Video games that ask the player to navigate a complex location like a maze or to solve a logic puzzle.

Pyramids Also known as Castles; game played in ancient Rome using nuts and clay marbles.

Q

quantification Characteristic of contemporary organized play that manifests in measurements of and statistics on performance and competition.

Questions and Answers Word-play parlor game.

quoiting Ordinary material also used for play in early Europe.

R

race walking Long-distance athletic event in which one of the participant's feet must be in contact with the ground at all times.

radio-controlled cars Powered model vehicles controlled from a distance by an operator holding a transmitter.

rag doll Doll created entirely from fabric.

Rainbow Whist Variation of Whist in which players choose to play a color instead of a lady or gent.

randomized strategy Also known as a mixed strategy; probability distribution over a player's entire set of strategies.

Rape Me, Rape Me Schoolyard game played in poor towns of South Africa that reenacts the sexual violence to which the children are subjected.

rationalization Characteristic of contemporary organized play that manifests in strategies designed to gain a competitive advantage.

real-time strategy game (RTS) Strategic video game in which players operate as if in real time, without stopping to let another player (live or computer-generated) take a turn.

recapitulation Theory of play proposed by Hall in 1906, theory stating that in play people relive their evolutionary past.

records Characteristic of contemporary organized play that manifests in the organization of quantifiable information historically to provide incentives for competitors to match or outperform record holders.

Recreation Ground Act Law passed in 1859 in the United Kingdom to protect common land and to provide open spaces in urban areas for leisure activities.

referee Official expected to maintain fair play in a sports competition.

Relaxation and Recreation Theory Theory of play proposed by Lazarus (1883) and Patrick (1916) in which play activities to relax and release pressure are recommended as a follow-up to physically and mentally exhausting work.

relay Race in which successive members of a team run a specified portion; the team's combined time is compared to other teams in order to determine a winner.

relic doll Doll with a spiritual or ritual significance; rarely used as a plaything.

retention Component process underlying observational learning.

Réussites French game like Solitaire.

Reversal Theory General psychological theory of personality, motivation and emotion formulated by British psychologist Michael J. Apter in 1970s.

riddles Statements or questions with veiled meanings put forth as puzzles to be solved; often part of classroom play.

right bower Jack of spades in Euchre.

Rijwielspel Version of the card game *Milles Bornes*.

ritual Playworkers have to take ritual into account when considering how to create the best play environment

ritual play Play related to and used in social and/or religious rites.

rod Also known as a pole, used to catch fish.

roguelike Subgenre of video games involving a two-dimensional dungeon crawl. The game is random and emphasizes statistical character development.

role-playing Form of mimicry in which a person pretends to be another person or pretends to be in a particular situation.

role-playing games (RPG or CRPG) Video games based on traditional role-playing games. They generally cast the player as an adventurer who needs to travel through a predetermined storyline.

rollerblade Inline skate with one row of wheels under the sole of the supporting shoe; similar in appearance to ice skates.

Roshambo Alternative name for Rock Paper Scissors.

Rounders Sport played by two teams who alternate between batting and fielding; based on the game of stool ball.

Round the Corner Version of the game Play or Pay.

rover Extra infielder who plays in slow pitch softball.

rowing Sport in which teams race on rivers, lakes, or oceans on boats propelled by the use of oars.

Royal Game of Ur Egyptian board game.

Royal Lottery Created in 1776 by Louis XVI to unify drawing games and to make all monetary gains created by those games state funds.

rubber Elastic material, obtained from the latex tree, that can be vulcanized and finished into various products.

Rubicon Piquet Variation of Piquet in which play is concluded in six hands.

Rubik's Cube Mechanical puzzle invented in 1974 by Hungarian sculptor and professor of architecture Erno Rubik.

Rubik's wrist Ailment developed by people who play with a Rubik's Cube continuously for hours on end.

Ruff Version of Whist.

Ruff and Honors Version of Whist.

Rugby Football League (RFL) Governing body for rugby league in the United Kingdom.

Rugby League One main code of rugby football, involving outdoor, full-contact play between two teams of 13 players on a rectangular field with a prolate spheroid-shaped ball.

Rugby Union One main code of rugby football, involving outdoor, contact play between two teams of 15 players with an oval ball.

rule benders People who follow the rules but who innovatively change the rules for better play or who know the rules but modify them in order to give themselves an advantage.

rule changers People who evaluate the rules and change them to enhance play or to create a new game.

rule ignorers People who understand that rules exist but choose not to follow them.

rule manipulators People who know the rules but alter them in order to give themselves an advantage.

rules Prescribed guides for actions; in games and sports, these are the agreed-upon conventions that govern play.

Rummikub Tiled-based game for two, three, or four players.

running events In track and field competitions, running events are those that occur on the track and that involve running to try to win a race.

S

sandbagging Inflating one's handicap index in order to try to win a game of golf.

Sapo Literally "toad"; game played in Peru.

Sara Iranian doll developed in response to Barbie.

Scattergories Timed word game in which players must try to name an item for each of 12 characters. Each name must begin with the letter chosen by rolling a 20-sided dice.

Scattles Version of Skittles where all the pins are numbered.

Schema Established patterns of organization in which learning occurs, according to Piaget.

Scissor Sandwich Rock Paper Scissors sequence of paper, scissors, paper.

score Gain points in a game; number of points gained in a game.

scratch Golfer with a handicap of zero or less.

scrimmage Practice playing a sport.

Scully Also known as Skelly or Caps, among other names; children's game played in New York City and other urban areas.

secularism Characteristic of contemporary organized play that manifests in play for the benefit of the players, without attachment to religious observance or ritual.

see-saw Also known as teeter-totter; board (relatively long and narrow) suspended in the middle so that, as one end goes up, the other goes down.

SEGA Genesis 16-bit video game console sold starting in 1988.

self-discovery Playworkers have to take this aspect into account when considering how to create the best play environment.

self-efficacy Learned expectations about the probability of success in a given situation, as explained in Bandura's theory.

Senet Egyptian board game.

Sensation Seeking Scale Section of the Zuckerman-Kuhlman Personality Questionnaire devoted to determining the level of comfort a test taker has with taking risks or seeking sensation.

sensitive period Period of six years representing a plane of development within Maria Montessori's theory.

sensorial One of the six key areas in Maria Montessori's schools.

sensorimotor play Play, especially play on the part of infants, that involves using newly developed sensorimotor skills (i.e., all aspects of movement, sensation, and the interaction of the two).

sensory feedback In physical activities, the information provided from peripheral muscle contractions contributing to the awareness of muscle position.

set Practice of setting a volleyball in a high trajectory, to be followed by a spike.

shadow-puppet theater Ancient form of storytelling where the illusion of moving images is created through the use of opaque (and often articulated) figures in front of an illuminated backdrop.

Shanghai Computer brand of Mahjongg Solitaire; may be a modernized version of the old Chinese game known as The Turtle.

Shinny Simple version of hockey using a ball or can as the puck.

shoot 'em up games Video game genre where the player controls a character's vehicle and shoots many enemies.

shooter Colloquial term used to describe a move in marbles.

shooter game Video game that focuses on combat using projectile weapons like guns and missiles; may be either third-person or first-person.

Shove-Groat Original name for the game of Shuffleboard, often played by elderly people.

Shuffle Early European game played on a table or board with a number of parallel lines positioned about an inch apart.

Shuffleboard Game in which players shove wooden disks onto the scoring area marked on a smooth surface by using long sticks.

Shuffleboard puck Combination metal and plastic disc used to play shuffleboard.

shuttlecock High-drag projectile used in badminton. The shuttlecock is a cone formed by 16 overlapping feathers that meet in a ball of cork or rubber.

Shuttlecock and Battledore Earlier version of badminton played with small rackets (called battledores) and shuttlecocks, which are passed back and forth over a net.

Sickles Hand-eye coordination game played in colonial America; a ball with a hole in it is connected by string to a cup attached to a stick. The purpose of the game is to toss and catch the ball in the cup.

simulation game Game that simulates a real situation (e.g., stock market, community planning board, etc.) by a mixture of skill, chance, and strategy.

Skakalochka Games of skill including rope-skipping played by girls in Belarus.

skateboard Board with wheels on which a rider stands or crouches and propels forward with one foot.

Skibbie Variation of the chasing game known as Tag.

ski jumping Sport that involves skiing down an "inrun" with a take-off ramp and jumping for distance and style.

skill Learned ability.

skipping rope Alternative name for jumping rope.

Skitgubbe Swedish equivalent of Mattis, a beating game.

Slalom Alpine ski race in which skiers must race between poles ("gates").

sled One of the most basic kite shapes.

slide Plaything whose sloping chute allows children to descend.

slingshot Y-shaped stick with elastic between the arms that allows children to propel small things.

Sliothar Irish game in which the ball is similar in size to a hockey ball but has raised ridges.

slope rating Rating of a golf course's relative degree of difficulty for an average golfer.

Snakes and Ladders Board game for two to four players that involves rewarding virtues and punishing vices.

Snooker Form of pool played with 21 object balls and one cue ball.

Snowboarding Inspired by surfing and skateboarding; involves descending a snow-covered hill with both feet attached to a single snowboard.

soccer ball Inflated ball designed for use in the game of soccer.

Soccerex International business organization that centers on non-American football.

Social Cognitive Theory Explains individual's knowledge acquisition as directly related to the observation of others within the context of social interactions and experiences outside of media influences.

socialization and social interaction Playworkers have to take this aspect into account when considering how to create the best play environment.

Social-Learning Theory Bandura's theory of learning, which emphasizes the role of observation as a means of learning.

social play Involves interaction between peers.

sociodramatic play Type of free play that allows children to creatively and imaginatively engage in social interactions.

sociohistorical perspectives In Vygotsky's evaluation of human development, the changes that occur in a culture and the values, norms, and technologies that history as created.

Solitaire Mahjong May be a modernized version of the old Chinese game known as The Turtle.

solitary play Independent play.

Son of Beast Roller coaster.

Soul Surfers Online platform for international surfboard development projects.

Spades Suit of cards that represent the nobility in France.

Spaghettis Name for a marble with a particular color and pattern.

Spaldeens Small pink rubber ball. The product's name is the Spalding High-Bounce Ball.

Spanish Top Variety of spinning top.

spans Colloquial term used to describe a move in Marbles.

Spar Dame Norwegian equivalent to Hearts.

spatial intelligence Ability to visualize and judge physical spaces.

spatial skill Ability to understand the three-dimensional reality of a plan drawn or described.

specialization Characteristic of contemporary organized play that manifests in individuals who choose particular sports activities and particular roles or positions within that sport in order to achieve a competitive edge.

Speed skiing Sport in which competitors ski down a straight path as quickly as they can.

spike Practice of following a set with a rapid downward motion of the ball onto the other side of the net in volleyball.

spinner Domino.

spooning Swinging the croquet mallet in an arc.

spoon puppet plays Plays in which puppets made out of spoons (generally wooden spoons) serve as characters; popular in Armenia.

sports game Video game that simulates a sports event.

Spot Hearts Variation of Hearts in which every heart card is worth face value.

Sprinkling Hungarian game played at Easter. This game involves young men visiting young women, sprinkling them with water, and other traditional events.

Spud Variation of the chasing game known as Tag.

spurn Ordinary material also used for play in early Europe.

spurring Misconduct in Leapfrog where a player knuckles down with fists into the shoulders or back of the player being jumped over.

squidger Larger disc with which one plays the winks in Tiddlywinks.

SRO Silkroad Online.

stadium Sports arena with seating for spectators.

Stag Hunting Variation of Hares and Hounds.

stake Money risked in a bet.

stand In Blackjack, the term indicating that a player does not want another card.

standard deck Deck of 52 playing cards.

stealth games Video games that require subterfuge and specific, planned kills instead of overt mass killings.

steeplechase Foot or horse race with obstacles.

Steinstossen Heavy rock-throwing competition held in Sweden.

Stick ball Urban game similar to baseball but played with a broomstick and rubber ball.

stone Domino.

stone Piece moved around the board in Checkers.

stoolball Game played by women in Europe and colonial America. The game called for three stones to be bowled at a three-legged milking stool; later evolved into cricket.

Stoop ball Game played by throwing a ball against the stoop of a building; usually an urban game.

Straight Poker Hand consisting of five consecutive cards, regardless of suit.

Stratacoaster Roller coaster.

strategy game Game that requires a player to make decisions in order to play.

Street Playground Act of 1938 United Kingdom law establishing play streets; lasted until the 1990s.

Streets and Alleys Variation of the chasing game known as Tag.

strictly competitive game Also known as a zero-sum game; game in which one player's interests are strictly contradictory to another player's.

strictly dominant Always yields the best outcome regardless of what the other players do.

string games Game played by manipulating string (e.g., Cat's Cradle).

stroke play Game of golf in which the player with the lowest number of strokes wins.

structured play Play with specific rules and objectives; usually designed by an adult.

Stud Game Any version of Poker in which the players are dealt a mixture of face-down and face-up cards.

Submarine Also known as Alligator Eyes; variation of the water game Marco Polo. When the person who is "it" calls "submarine," she or he can swim underwater with eyes open for one breath.

Success French version of Solitaire.

Super Chexx Also known as Bubble Hockey and Boobla; tabletop arcade hockey game covered by a special bubble dome.

superego In psychoanalytic theory, the part of the psyche that has internalized society's values and standards.

SuperG Also known as Supergiant Slalom; alpine ski race in which skiers must race between poles ("gates") spaced at distances of 14 to 16 percent of the total vertical drop.

superhero Fictional crime-fighting character with supernatural powers or equipment; popular in children's comics and fantasy literature.

surrender In Blackjack, the term indicating that a player forfeits half of the bet and gives up the hand.

survivor horror games Video games that include traditional elements from horror movies, including characters considered "undead."

Sutton-Smith, Brian (b. 1924) Play theorist.

swing Play thing that allows movement back and forth in an arc.

symbolic play Also known as pretense play; involves transforming the physical world into a symbol (e.g., using a couch's cushions to create a fort).

sympathy One of the human attributes developed during play.

T

Tableaux Vivante Dramatic parlor game in which a famous painting is reenacted.

table football Tabletop game based on soccer, or association football.

table soccer Also known as baby foot, foosball, and table football; tabletop game based on soccer, or association football.

table tennis Also known as Ping Pong; game resembling tennis played on a table with paddles and a hollow ball.

Taboo Word game where teams compete to see who can guess the most words without using the phrases listed on the cards.

Tacanaco Incan board game that moves colored beans or seeds around the board using dice; played in Bolivia, Equador, and Peru.

tackraw Ball made from woven rattan and used in Thailand.

tactical role-playing game (TRPG) Sub-genre of video games that incorporate features of strategy games.

tactical shooters Variation of first-person shooter games and, less frequently, of third-person shooter games in which the player must carefully consider planning and teamwork.

tafl Viking word for board; means game played on board.

Tagati'a Traditional Samoan show of prowess and skill for men who are training for battle. The competition involves about a hundred people who are involved in javelin throwing and relies on distance and accuracy.

Taipei Computer brand of Mahjong Solitaire; may be a modernized version of the old Chinese game known as The Turtle.

takeovers Colloquial term used to describe a move in marbles.

Takraw A kick volleyball–type game played with a rattan ball; now recognized as a sport by the Southeast Asia Games.

tally Score.

target Sports equipment consisting of an object at which an archer or marksman aims.

Tarot Set of 78 divination cards.

Tauromachy Popular sport in Spain and Mexico where a matador taunts and kills a bull at close range.

Tavla Turkish version of Backgammon played in Bulgaria, Iraq, Pakistan, and Syria.

taw Term used to describe a move in Marbles.

Taw Egyptian version of marbles.

team cooperative Unit in sports or games.

Tebar Jala Literally "throwing the casting net"; played in Malaysia.

teeter-totter Also known as a see-saw; board (relatively long and narrow) suspended in the middle so that as one end goes up, the other goes down.

Teka Spear-throwing game practiced by the Maori of New Zealand.

Telemark Turn made in skiing when the outside ski is placed ahead and turned gradually inward.

Ten-Pin Bowling Sport or recreational activity that involves rolling a bowling ball down a wood or synthetic lane with the intention of knocking down as many of the 10 pins as possible; common version of bowling in the United States.

tesserae Playing dice with six sides developed in ancient Rome.

Texas Hold 'Em Variety of Poker in which players may use any combination of five community cards and their own two hole cards to make a hand.

text adventure Also known as interactive fiction games; video games that require players to make choices in order to guide the course of the game, which the computer would then describe.

third-person shooter game (TPS or 3PS) Video game in which the player-character is viewed from a distance so shooting and combat are seen from a camera perspective.

Thompson, E.P. (1924–93) English historian and socialist whose most famous work is *The Making of the English Working Class.*

Thumbs Up Another version of the classroom game called Seven Up.

ticket Domino.

Tic-Tac-Toe North American version of Noughts and Crosses.

Tig Version of Tag played in New Zealand.

Tiggy Variation of the chasing game known as Tag.

tile Domino.

Tipcat Hungarian hitting stick game that likely came along eastern trading routes to the West.

To Tom Vietnamese card game; literally "shrimp's nest."

Touring Version of the card game *Milles Bornes.*

tournament Sporting competition in which a series of games are played before a winner is determined.

Tower of Terror Roller coaster.

trading cards Collectible cards (e.g., baseball cards) that are not used for a particular game but that may be traded in order to add to a collection.

trail running Running on hiking trails.

transformation decks Playing cards where the traditional pips are replaced by an artist's drawings.

transitional object Object, like a blanket or stuffed animal, to which children become attached and use for comfort.

tree houses Structure built within the branches of a tree and used like a club house or a playhouse.

Tres en Raya Spanish version of Noughts and Crosses.

triathlon athletic competition involving swimming, cycling, and running.

trick In cards, the sequence of all the cards played in a single round.

trick avoidance games Like Hearts, Euchre, and Whist, where players attempt to evade taking tricks with cards containing penalties.

trickster Folktale character who tries to outsmart or outwit others but who does not always succeed. Often, the trickster's actions offer a lesson from which audience members may learn a valuable social lesson.

trick-taking card game Card games centered on a series of finite rounds known as tricks (e.g., Euchre, Bridge, Spades, Hearts, Pinochle, etc.).

Trip Him Up Game played in Belgium.

triple jump Field and track competition for which the competitor hops, skips, and then jumps into a sandpit, attempting to achieve the greatest horizontal distance.

Troco English lawn game played with balls, cues, and rings; the forerunner of Croquet.

trottole Italian tops that are often thrown as part of games.

trump In card games, the suit that has been declared to rank above all others for one hand.

TSR Tactical Studies Rules

Tugge Variation of the chasing game known as Tag.

Tug-of-War Sport or activity in which two teams hold opposite ends of a rope, each trying to pull the other side over a dividing line to win the contest.

turned doll Wood doll created through the turning of wood on a lathe.

Turtle Computer brand of Mahjongg Solitaire; may be a modernized version of the old Chinese game known as The Turtle.

TV Tag Variation of the chasing game known as Tag where safety can be achieved by stopping and naming a television show.

Twenty-One Also known as Blackjack; card game in which the player tries to get as close to 21 points as possible without going over.

U

ultimate Frisbee Noncontact team sport in which each team attempts to move the Frisbee to an end zone in order to score.

umpire Official responsible for mainting fair play and maintaining the rules in a sports competition.

unconscious absorbent mind First stage of Montessori's formulation of the absorbent mind. In this stage, children from birth to age three unconsciously acquire basic skills.

United Nations Convention on the Rights of the Child (UNCRC) International convention adopted in 1989 to define the civil, economic, political, social, and cultural rights of children.

United States Table Soccer Association (USTSA) American nonprofit organization associated with the International Table Soccer Federation (ITSF).

unoccupied play Not actively engaged in play.

Uomo Nero Also known as Black Man and Bogie Man; Italian version of Old Maid.

Upwords Word game like Scrabble, but where tiles can be piled on top of each other to create new words.

urban exploration Exploration of normally unseen areas (like rooftops, sewers, and underground utility tunnels) both in reality and in virtual reality game scenarios.

Urban Park and Recreation Recovery Program American program established in 1978 to provide direct federal assistance to urban localities for rehabilitation of critically needed recreation facilities and to encourage systematic local planning and commitment to continuing operation and maintenance of recreation programs, sites, and facilities.

USA Gymnastics (USAG) Governing body for gymnastics in the United States.

USA Rock Paper Scissors League Organization devoted to playing and strategizing about Rock Paper Scissors; founded in 2006 in the United States.

USA Volleyball Formerly known as the United States Volleyball Association (USVBA), the organization that governs volleyball competition and play throughout the United States.

U.S. Consumer Product Safety Commission American agency whose mission is to protect the public from unreasonable risks of injury or death. Special controls have been enacted in regard to toys and other products marketed for children.

V

Veblen, Thorstein (1857–1929) Norwegian-American sociologist and economist whose most famous work is *The Theory of the Leisure Class.*

vehicle simulation Video games that offer a realistic interpretation of driving a vehicle.

verbal dexterity Skill and ease with using words.

verbal dueling Games that require players to battle with words.

versus fighters Also known as fighting simulation video games; an action video game that literally simulates one-on-one combat.

vertical loop Basic roller coaster inversion that involves a continuously upward-sloping track that eventually completes a 360-degree loop.

vertigo Dizziness; illusion of movement; feeling of falling.

video game Game designed for play on a computer or computerized system.

video game system Computer platform that supports the play of video games.

Viking-Con Role-playing game conference held each fall in Copenhagen.

vinyl Shiny, tough, and flexible plastic.

virtual learning Learning that occurs through a variety of technological and at-a-distance techniques, but also through creating imaginary companions.

visual novel Video game with anime-style graphics that allows players to build plots as they proceed.

visual-spatial reasoning Ability to understand the three-dimensional reality of a drawing and to understand the two-dimensional reality of a space.

vocabulary game Any game designed to help improve vocabulary.

von Neumann, John (1903–57) Hungarian-American mathematician whose works contributed to many fields, including game theory.

Vri Atter Norwegian equivalent to the card game Crazy Eights.

Vygotsky, Lev (1896–1934) Russian developmental psychologist who founded cultural-historical psychology. Vygotsky's sociocultural theory focuses on child development and learning.

W

Wall Ball Group game that involves throwing a ball against a building; usually an urban game.

Wana Aboriginal Australian game played by girls, teaching them to defend their young by warding off attacks from other girls with large sticks.

Wargames Subgenre of video games that focus on strategic or tactical warfare on a map; game that simulates a military operation.

water skiing Sport or recreational activity that involves pulling a person on one or two skis behind a motor boat or cable-ski installation. The skier skims along the surface of the water.

Wayang Kulit Indonesian or Malaysian shadow puppets operated from behind a screen.

weakly dominant Strategy that yields an outcome at least as good and possibly better than an alternative strategy.

Wheel of Fortune American game show, board game, and video game modeled on Hangman. A word is indicated by blank spaces and players spin the wheel to determine how much money each letter will be worth and choose letters to fill in the blank puzzle. The goal is to win as much money as possible by correctly solving the puzzle.

whipping tops Type of spinning top moved by whipping.

Whist Trick-taking game with fixed partnerships and no bidding.

whittle Pare shavings from or cut little bits; like carving, can be used to create dolls and figurines.

wicket Small arch used in Croquet; three stumps topped by crosspieces in cricket.

Widow Version of Hearts.

Wii Home video game console released by Nintendo in 2005.

willing suspension of disbelief Aesthetic theory that refers to the willingness of a person to accept the premises of a work of fiction as true, even if they are fantastic or impossible.

winks Plastic discs used in Tiddlywinks.

word cross Early version of crossword puzzle.

word grids Games that require players to place words within a grid (e.g., crossword puzzles).

World Bridge Championship Competition organized every four years by the World Bridge Federation.

World Chess Federation (FIDE) Organization that oversees international chess competition.

World Cube Association Organization that organizes official international competitions of the Rubik's Cube and other Rubik's puzzles.

World Rock Paper Scissors Society Group devoted to playing and strategizing about Rock Paper Scissors; founded in 1918 as a successor to the Paper Scissors Stone Club.

World Scrabble Championship International English-language Scrabble tournament held every two years.

World Series of Poker (WSOP) Annual Poker competition held in Las Vegas; consists of 55 events.

Y

Ya Pai Version of Mahjong.

Yas Popular Swedish card game similar to Belote.

Ye Triumphe Version of Whist dating back to 1522, more popularly called Ruff and Honors.

Yo' Mama Urban verbal dueling game in which players compete to best each other with a derogatory "yo' mama" joke.

Young Men's Christian Association (YMCA) Organization dedicated to putting Christian practices into practice. Founded in 1844, the YMCA has offered housing, recreation, and bible study.

Young Pioneers Movement Communist youth organization; groups existed in virtually every Communist state, including China, Cuba, and Turkmenistan.

Young Women's Christian Association (YWCA) Counterpart of YMCA dedicated to women and women's causes; founded in 1855.

Yut Korean board game played especially during Korean New Year.

Z

zero-player game Computer game that uses artificial intelligence instead of players.

zero-sum game Game in which one player's interests are strictly contradictory to another player's; also known as a strictly competitive game.

Zieh Durch German version of children's song *London Bridge.*

zone of proximal development (ZPD) Second aspect of Vygotsky's theory; level of development attained when children engage in social behavior, with full development being dependent on full social interaction.

Anastasia L. Pratt
State University of New York